"Cavanaugh digs deep into boxing's colorful . . . past to rescue perhaps the most skilled (and learned) practitioner of the sweet science."

—Associated Press

"The golden age of boxing is brought back to life in *Tunney*. [It] shows how the boxer went against the grain of his sport with a lifelong interest in literature and the arts."   —*Connecticut Post*

"[The] buildup to the Tunney-Dempsey fights reads like a suspense novel. The prose is crisp and crackles with tension as he describes the fight; one does not have to watch the grainy newsreels to appreciate the drama. . . . Cavanaugh brings it to life in vivid detail."   —*The Tampa Tribune*

"[*Tunney*] will go far in reminding new generations that Gene Tunney wasn't simply a great fighter, he was one of the greatest any generation will ever see."   —*San Antonio Express-News*

"Thoughtfully researched . . . Cavanaugh's book on Tunney is unique in that he gives us the perspective on Tunney and his life in and out of the ring that many did not have. . . . Cavanaugh's book certainly gives justice to both Tunney's name and his record in the ring."

—*Las Cruces Sun-News*

"Cavanaugh leaves few cobwebs undisturbed. . . . The research reveals as much about the fight game of the first half of the twentieth century as it does about the social milieu in which it is set."   —Norwalk *Hour*

TUNNEY

BALLANTINE BOOKS
NEW YORK

TUNNEY

BOXING'S BRAINIEST

CHAMP AND

HIS UPSET OF

THE GREAT

JACK DEMPSEY

■

JACK CAVANAUGH

2007 Ballantine Books Trade Paperback Edition

Published in the United States by Ballantine Books,
an imprint of The Random House Publishing Group,
a division of Random House, Inc., New York.

BALLANTINE and colophon are registered trademarks of Random House, Inc.

Originally published in hardcover in the United States by Random House,
an imprint of The Random House Publishing Group,
a division of Random House, Inc., in 2006.

ISBN 978-0-8129-6783-8

LIBRARY OF CONGRESS CATALOGING-IN-PUBLICATION DATA
Cavanaugh, Jack.
Tunney: boxing's brainiest champ and his upset of the great
Jack Dempsey / Jack Cavanaugh.
p. cm.
Includes index.
ISBN 1-4000-6009-5
1. Tunney, Gene, 1898–   2. Boxers (Sports)—United States—Biography.
I. Tunney, Gene, 1898–   II. Title.

GV1132.T8C38 2006
796.83092—dc22
[B]   2006044858

Printed in the United States of America

www.ballantinebooks.com

2 4 6 8 9 7 5 3 1

Book design by Claire Vaccaro

To Marge, John, and Tara

■

They never called him "champ." He was unloved, underrated, shunned by his own people, rejected by history. Still, he was the best advertisement his sport has ever had.

—JIM MURRAY,
former sports columnist for
the *Los Angeles Times*.

■

CONTENTS

INTRODUCTION   xi

ONE *The Longshoreman's Son*   3

TWO *Kid Blackie*   20

THREE *The Reluctant Warrior*   36

FOUR *A Chance Meeting*   56

FIVE *Dempsey: Slacker or American Hero?*   69

SIX *The Great Bennah and Barney Lebrowitz*   92

SEVEN *Tunney Begins to Get Noticed—for a Price*   109

EIGHT *The Pittsburgh Windmill*   121

NINE *A Hornet's Nest*   134

TEN *The Faro Dealer from the Klondike*   143

ELEVEN *Tunney-Greb II and Sadness for Both*   165

TWELVE *The Sack of Shelby*   178

THIRTEEN *The Wild Bull of the Pampas*   203

FOURTEEN *A Dream Fight (for Women Fans)*   226

FIFTEEN *Tex Rickard's Worst Possible Nightmare*   237

CONTENTS

SIXTEEN *Dempsey Decides to Come Back* 246

SEVENTEEN *Gene Who? You Must Be Kidding* 256

EIGHTEEN *Rich Men, Poor Men, Beggar Men, and Thieves* 279

NINETEEN *The Manassa Mauler and the Manly Marine* 290

TWENTY *"Honey, I Forgot to Duck"* 304

TWENTY-ONE *The Prizefighter and the Heiress* 317

TWENTY-TWO *The Long Count* 335

TWENTY-THREE *Greenwich Village to Greenwich, Connecticut* 370

ACKNOWLEDGMENTS 407

PROFESSIONAL RECORDS OF JACK DEMPSEY AND GENE TUNNEY 417

SELECTED BIBLIOGRAPHY 423

NOTES 425

INDEX 453

Wearing a pinstripe gray suit, a white shirt, and a striped tie, the man sitting beside me on the New Haven Railroad train blended in perfectly with the other homeward-bound commuters on an early spring evening in the mid-1960s. Like most passengers in the car, he was immersed in one of New York's three afternoon newspapers of the time, the nightly ritual for daily riders to the Connecticut suburbs from Manhattan. On a rush-hour train like this, there is an unspoken rule not to bother a fellow rider. But suddenly breaking that commuters' rule, to my eternal gratification, my seatmate began to comment on the wretched condition of our car. "Isn't it ridiculous," he said, gesturing down the aisle. "Look at all the broken seats. You'd think they'd do something about it."

Turning toward him, I agreed, then realized who he was. And why not? After all, I had seen photos of him since I was a young boy, all the more so since I had grown up in Stamford, Connecticut, where he had lived ever since leaving the boxing ring and getting married in 1928. At first, I was reluctant to ask if he was indeed Gene Tunney, the enigmatic former heavyweight champion of the world, who had wrested the title from Jack Dempsey in 1926 before about 135,000 spectators in Philadelphia—then the largest crowd ever to witness a boxing bout. The same Gene Tunney who then met Dempsey a second time a year later in an even more famous fight at Soldier Field in Chicago before an even larger gathering of an estimated 145,000. Finally, I could resist no longer. "Pardon me for asking, but you are Gene Tunney, aren't you?"

"Yes, I am," answered Tunney, then in his late sixties and still handsome, with a ruddy complexion and tinges of gray in his brown hair. He then shook my hand warmly as I introduced myself.

Having met so many athletes as a sportswriter, and having been one myself, I have never been in awe of sports figures, with the exception of an elite handful including the enigmatic Joe DiMaggio; my boyhood idol, Stan Musial, the great St. Louis Cardinal slugger; the legendary sprinter Jesse Owens; the Negro Leagues baseball star Cool Papa Bell; and, yes, Jack Dempsey. I had met all of them, too, but never had I sat alongside any of them on a train, engaged in a memorable hour-long conversation, as I did with Gene Tunney. After growing up poor in Greenwich Village, Tunney had won the world heavyweight boxing championship but had largely been disparaged and even mocked because he had beaten the iconic Dempsey. Further, he had had the temerity, while still fighting, to become an intellectual and scholar, having lectured on Shakespeare at Yale and having discussed writing with friends and acquaintances like George Bernard Shaw, Ernest Hemingway, H. G. Wells, Thornton Wilder, John Marquand, and Somerset Maugham.

"Tunney, he reads books," was the dismissive and disparaging assessment of Tunney by one of Dempsey's bodyguards before the first Dempsey-Tunney fight, which Tunney was given virtually no chance of winning. That simplistic portrayal of Tunney was shared, as it were, by not only other boxing managers and trainers but also most sportswriters and fans, few of whom gave Tunney his due until well after he had retired. Not to say that Tunney himself did not offend sportswriters, including such journalistic paragons of the era as Grantland Rice, Damon Runyon, Ring Lardner, Paul Gallico, and Westbrook Pegler, with what they perceived to be intellectual pretensions and an aloof demeanor.

When I met Tunney, he was the chief executive officer of the McCandless Corporation, a conglomerate of rubber products companies based in New York, and a board member of a half-dozen or so corporations. Like the other commuters, he was headed home, in his case to his gentleman's farm in Stamford, where he had been living for more than thirty years with his wife, Polly Lauder Tunney, an heiress to the Andrew Carnegie fortune.

Since his retirement, Tunney had had practically no association with boxing. He rarely went to any fights and, indeed, said he had little interest in the sport that made him famous. "They're always asking me to come to the big fights and take a bow," he told me, "and of course they say they'll handle all the expenses. But I really have no desire to go. I have too many other interests. And they dislike me all the more for it." *They* was an allusion to the boxing establishment, which never much liked Tunney while he was fighting and carried that dislike into his retirement years.

If Tunney's boxing style—he was a masterful boxer in an era when topflight heavyweights were supposed to possess knockout power as Dempsey did—did not endear him to boxing fans, his aloofness from the sport following his retirement, coupled with his literacy, scholarly bent, and wealth, damn near made him a pariah. The boxing establishment expected former champions, especially great ones like Tunney, to make perfunctory appearances at major championship fights, and Tunney disdained the ritual. An avid reader of the classics since he was introduced to Shakespeare by a fellow marine during World War I, Tunney was far more comfortable talking about literature, politics, or even opera than boxing. Often assailed as a literary poseur or a phony highbrow while he was fighting, Tunney further alienated himself from the "fight mob," as it was often called, when, while still heavyweight champion, he lectured on Shakespeare at Yale. Yet to Tunney, that was far more uplifting and rewarding than being introduced as the man who beat the great Dempsey.

While Tunney distanced himself from the sport that made him rich and famous at a time when boxing, horse racing, and baseball were the preeminent sports in the United States, Dempsey, in his retirement, became more popular than ever. Strangely enough, he even seemed to rank higher than Tunney in the pantheon of great fighters. In his book *Boxing's Greatest Fighters,* published in 2006, the boxing historian and author Bert Randolph Sugar ranked Dempsey as the ninth best fighter of all time, while Tunney is listed at thirteenth, even though he had beaten Dempsey decisively twice and had a better overall record. Even more ironic—and a further testament to how Tunney, in retrospect, remains underrated—Sugar ranked Harry Greb, the great middleweight who once beat Tunney (and to a bloody pulp, at that) but then failed to defeat him in their next four fights, the fifth best boxer of all time behind Sugar Ray Robinson, Henry Armstrong, Willie Pep, and Joe Louis. But then Greb, like Dempsey, was a crowd-pleaser, albeit a dirty one, while Tunney was merely a wondrous boxer capable of knocking a man out—something he did forty-four times, only six fewer knockouts than Dempsey achieved.

Yet Tunney is one of the least remembered sports heroes of the Jazz Age. As the so-called Golden Era of Sport, the decade produced such sports legends as Dempsey, Babe Ruth, Ty Cobb, Red Grange, Bobby Jones, Bill Tilden, Helen Wills Moody, the great Thoroughbred racehorse Man o' War, and George Gipp—Notre Dame's "Gipper," later portrayed on the silver screen by Ronald Reagan—and yet Tunney's name is rarely mentioned along with these sports icons. And many sports historians feel that he was denied a niche because he beat—twice, no less—a public idol in Dempsey and refused to fulfill the popular perception of a fighter while becoming a dilettante. A case in point: long after he left the ring—indeed, right up until his death—everyone called Dempsey "Champ," although Tunney, who seldom, if ever, was addressed that way after he left the ring, had taken away Dempsey's heavyweight title. That could be, at least in part, because, as the veteran New York sports columnist Frank Graham said of Tunney in 1961, "No athlete ever succeeded in obscuring his own great skills so completely."

Though inextricably linked by their two fights, Dempsey and Tunney could not have been more different. Both grew up poor—Dempsey in dusty Colorado frontier towns, Tunney in Greenwich Village. Dempsey came to be known as "The Manassa Mauler" (after his hometown of Manassa in southern Colorado), a menacing, snarling, no-holds-barred stalker, while Tunney won a reputation as a masterful, almost mechanical, boxer who often held back when he had seriously hurt an opponent. Dempsey had loved to fight since he was a preteen, while Tunney learned to fight solely for self-preservation on the rough sidewalks of his New York City neighborhood.

As much a part of their story was the fascinating cast of characters around them in a time when you couldn't legally buy a drink, though there were more places to get one in New York, Chicago, and many other cities than there were before Prohibition. The dramatis personae of the Tunney-Dempsey saga reflected the boxing world, and the slick, wacky, and even weird characters who populated it or hovered around it during what Westbrook Pegler called "The era of wonderful nonsense." There was Tex Rickard, the onetime Texas sheriff, Klondike gambling house operator, and Argentine cattle rancher who became the most successful fight promoter of all time. There was the acerbic Jack "Doc" Kearns, Dempsey's manager during his championship reign and a former gambler, gold prospector, and semipro baseball player, whose most enduring legacy in boxing circles was having broken four banks in the aftermath of a financially plagued Dempsey title fight in Shelby, Montana. There was underworld kingpin Al Capone and Philadelphia mobster Max "Boo Boo" Hoff, both of whom may have tried to fix one or both of the Dempsey-Tunney fights. There was Jimmy Walker, perhaps the most flamboyant and controversial mayor ever in New York, whose bill, as a state senator, made professional boxing legal once again in New York state. There was Damon Runyon, a gifted writer who, like a number of other sportswriters, accepted money from fight promoters and managers and even owned part of some boxers; Abe Attell, a former featherweight-champion-turned-gambler-and-fixer who was said to have been involved with gangster Arnold Rothstein in the fixing of the 1919 World Series; Billy Gibson, a restaurateur and fight manager with close ties to underworld figures and high-ranking politicians, who served as Tunney's last and most influential manager; and assorted other "Guys and Dolls" (Runyon's phrase, of course) who were connected in some way with boxing in the Roaring Twenties.

Sweetening the Tunney story immeasurably was his secret romance with the beauteous socialite from Greenwich, Connecticut, Polly

Lauder—whom many thought was out of his reach—which became perhaps the most publicized and widely read love story of the 1920s. Even though she had inherited an estimated $50 million ($1.5 billion by today's standards), no one could say Tunney was wooing Polly Lauder for her money, since he had made $1 million for the second Dempsey fight—more money than any entertainer in history up to that point and the equivalent of more than $11 million today, a nice sum for one night's work in any era.

The magnitude of the heavyweight title in the 1920s is today difficult to comprehend, since the sport—hugely popular in the first seven decades of the twentieth century—has slipped so far both in terms of talent and popularity. Up until the 1920s, there were only eight weight divisions in boxing. Yet today there are seventeen at last count and four "governing bodies"—meaning that in an era when there are far fewer boxers than in the 1920s, 1930s, 1940s, and 1950s, you could conceivably have sixty-eight "world champions." Indeed, the sport had reached such a low point by 2006 that, in referring to the *four* heavyweight champions—there was only one in the Dempsey-Tunney era— Bert Randolph Sugar said, "You could put them in robes, trunks and wearing boxing gloves and their championship belts, and then put them in a police lineup, and not only would no one know who they are but no one would know what they do for a living." That was not the case in the 1920s, when everyone knew that either Jack Dempsey or Gene Tunney was the world heavyweight champion. It was sports' ultimate championship and would remain so into the 1980s, by which time Muhammad Ali had retired and the incorrigible, brutish, and almost universally disliked Mike Tyson briefly reigned as champion.

After retiring at thirty-one, Tunney reveled in a successful business career that owed more to his celebrity status than any particular business acumen while continuing to read voraciously, attend the opera, and, with his wife, socialize primarily with wealthy friends from New York City, Westchester County, Greenwich, and North Stamford. He also reared four children, one of whom, John, became a United States congressman and then a senator from California in 1970, when he was only thirty-six years old. Not surprisingly, new acquaintances often would bring up Tunney's two fights with Dempsey, and, somewhat reluctantly, he might talk about them. They were, after all, two of the most famous boxing bouts of all time. So much so that the day after both fights, the *New York Times* ran eight-column, three-line front-page headlines and more than a dozen stories about the epic encounters in its news and sports sections.

The adulation for Tunney turned out to be short-lived. As Tunney himself told me during that memorable train ride from Grand Central Terminal to Stamford, Dempsey, in losing his title, became more popular than ever. "Some of it may have been my fault because of how I reacted to what some newspapermen wrote about my reading habits and what they perceived to be my aloofness," Tunney recalled as the train rattled toward Stamford.

Little did Tunney realize after that first fight that Dempsey, who was considered the "villain" in their initial go-round, would become more popular than ever in defeat, and that Tunney, though a paladin of his sport, would be ridiculed for his literary tastes and his style of boxing. Not until years later did Tunney concede, somewhat sorrowfully, that Dempsey, the alleged wartime "slacker," epitomized a "people's champion," while he, Tunney, "The Fighting Marine" (whose fighting during the Great War was actually confined to the ring) never came close to endearing himself to the sporting public.

"I guess I could have handled it better," the all-but-forgotten champion said, nearly unrecognized on the Connecticut-bound commuter train, while, not more than forty miles away, Dempsey was still being hailed as "Champ" as he greeted adoring patrons for dinner at his Broadway restaurant. "I became the villain of the piece," Tunney wrote years later in alluding to his championship reign. "It gave me no satisfaction to know that I was an unpopular champion. I think I would have welcomed the chance to be spoiled by a bit of popularity."

Not that Tunney was complaining. He realized all too well that it was a stroke of good fortune that his father, a longshoreman who never could bring himself to watch any of Tunney's fights, gave his skinny, gangly son his first pair of boxing gloves when he was ten years old, more so that the boy would learn how to protect himself from neighborhood bullies than anything else. That gift launched an improbable boxing career that started in a tough New York neighborhood shortly after the beginning of the twentieth century. That pair of gloves also led to Tunney's meeting and marrying Polly Lauder, with whom he was to grieve over a devastating family tragedy involving a celebrated murder case. It also led to a long-lasting friendship with his old adversary, Jack Dempsey, whose title Tunney had won, but to whom he lost the hearts of boxing fans across the country. Tunney may have been the brightest boxing champion of all time, but, unfortunately for him, he twice beat the most popular champion the boxing ring ever knew.

TUNNEY

ONE

■

The Longshoreman's Son

Gene Tunney poses with the rest of the 1911 graduating class at St. Veronica's parochial school in Greenwich Village. Tunney is second from the left in the row second from the top.

<small>NEW YORK DISTRICT CHRISTIAN BROTHERS ARCHIVES</small>

John Tunney always liked a good fight—from afar. From the days of his boyhood in Ireland's County Mayo, where he grew up idolizing John L. Sullivan, the bare-knuckled and blustering heavyweight champion from Boston, to the years after he arrived in New York, where he came to worship another American-born Irish boxer, James J. Corbett, whose victory over Sullivan with padded gloves ushered in a new era in boxing, Tunney's favorite diversion was watching, reading about, or talking about boxing bouts. This was especially true if a bout involved Irish boxers, which in that era many, if indeed not most, did.

After emigrating to the United States around 1880 (although he claimed to have made a stopover years before as a boy sailor aboard a windjammer), Tunney reveled in observing two men go at it in the ring at "smokers," which abounded in New York from the 1880s until shortly after World War I. Usually staged in smoke-filled Knights of Columbus halls capable of seating several hundred patrons and in large basements of other fraternal organizations, smokers were designed to circumvent New York state laws against professional boxing, which at the time was held in disrepute in the United States and most of the world, except for England. Generally held on Friday and Saturday nights, smokers tended to attract a rowdy crowd of men, a large percentage of them Irish and Italian immigrants, most of whom placed bets with one another. Often raucous, the spectators at times produced fights as good as if not better than the ones in the ring. The police virtually never interfered and, indeed, promoters often hired off-duty officers to try to prevent the frequent disorders that erupted during bouts and that usually stemmed from excessive drinking.

As a stevedore on the Hudson River docks in the western part of Greenwich Village, known later as the West Village, Tunney also was accustomed to seeing but personally avoiding the fierce, bloody brawls between longshoremen competing for jobs at daily shape-ups, which determined who would load and unload freighters on a given day. Then there were the impromptu fights that broke out occasionally in the saloons that abounded in the neighborhood to which he and his family had moved in 1897. But even watching those fracases had little impact on Tunney, jaded at having seen so many of them, particularly on the docks, which were as mob-controlled around the turn of the twentieth century as they were a half century later. The same was true of the bloodletting that ensued from street fights involving Greenwich Village toughs, including members of the Hudson Dusters or Gophers, two of the more prominent of the notorious gangs of New York, which had maintained an intimidating influence on businessmen and residents on the lower West Side of Manhattan since the middle of the nineteenth century.

But Tunney abhorred violence when it involved any of his three sons, particularly James Joseph, the oldest, a spindly youngster who often returned home from school bloodied after having been accosted and beaten by one or more neighborhood bullies. In a poor neighborhood populated primarily by Irish immigrants of limited means, such as the one in which the Tunney family lived, flexing one's muscles, even in prepubescence, was, if not a way out, then possibly a way up.

James Joseph Tunney was no match for older and heavier youths who set upon him, either individually or in groups, if for no other reason than that he had refrained from gang activities and had attracted attention because of his athleticism, primarily in basketball, distance running, and swimming. That young Tunney was slight of build and usually loaded down with school and library books made him an even more vulnerable target for neighborhood toughs, as did his disinclination to fight back.

Aware of what was happening to his oldest son, whom he called "Skinny," John Tunney decided on James's tenth birthday to give him a pair of inexpensive boxing gloves he had spotted in a Greenwich Village department store. He did so not because he wanted James Joseph to follow in the footsteps of John Tunney's heroes of the past, but so that the boy could learn how to defend himself against neighborhood hoodlums. Much as he liked boxing, John Tunney, like his wife, Mary, wanted his eldest son to become a priest, a common desire on the part of immigrant Irish parents of the era.

The sight of the gloves entranced the boy, who had already become fascinated with boxing through the cartoons and columns on boxing by Robert Edgren in the *New York Evening World*. Infatuated with the gift, young Tunney, aided by his father, put on the twelve-ounce gloves (far heavier than the eight- and six-ounce gloves used by both amateur and professional boxers) and began sparring playfully with his younger brothers, John, seven, and Tom, six. By that time, James Joseph had become known as "Gene" to family members and friends—a name bestowed on him by his youngest of four sisters, Agnes, who, in struggling to say James, kept saying something that sounded much more like Gene.

John Tunney's own fascination with boxing was easy to understand. He had boxed, bare-fisted, as a teenager in Kiltimagh in County Mayo and, while weighing around 160 pounds, he had filled in occasionally and with no particular distinction as a substitute boxer at Knights of Columbus smokers in Manhattan. Also, Irish boxers, both those from the Old Country and those born in the United States, dominated the sport in the latter part of the nineteenth century and during the first two decades of the twentieth. With not much else to lift their spirits while toiling at what for the most part were menial, low-paying jobs, Irish immigrants like Tunney could take pride in Irish fighters like Sullivan—"The Boston Strong Boy," as he was called; Corbett, to a far lesser degree than Sullivan, from whom he had won the heavyweight title, to the chagrin of most Irish boxing fans; the freckle-faced, skinny-legged Bob Fitszimmons, who took away Corbett's title after having won the world middleweight title and later captured the light heavyweight championship; and the great middleweight champion Jack Dempsey from County Kildare. Reflecting the Irish dominance of boxing at the time, Irish-American boxers held five of the seven weight division championships in 1890.

Intrigued now by a sport to which he had previously given scant notice, young Gene Tunney soon began boxing with friends and older boys in the gymnasium at the Villagers Athletic Club, a hotbed of sports activity in the West Village. Remarkably quick for a boy in his early teens, Tunney even impressed Willie Green, a veteran professional lightweight fighter from Greenwich Village who often worked out at both places and eventually taught young Tunney the rudiments of boxing and occasionally sparred with him, to young Tunney's delight. With a newly instilled confidence in his ability not only to defend himself but also to retaliate, Tunney began to respond to older street-gang attackers with his fists, though only when his defensive tactics proved insufficient. Before long, the attacks on the scrawny Tunney began to abate as his reputation as a skilled boxer spread among the neighborhood's thugs. Whenever either of his brothers was threatened or set upon by young toughs older and bigger, Tunney approached the neighborhood hoodlums and warned them to leave his siblings alone or face the consequences. For his newfound boxing skills and the concomitant confidence they had instilled in him, Tunney would forever be indebted to Willie Green.

Though longshoremen historically have been better paid than other blue-collar workers, John Tunney brought home only fifteen dollars a week, the equivalent today of about three hundred dollars, hardly enough for a family of nine, even in the early 1900s. But despite the impecunious circumstances of almost all of its residents—most of whom usually shared a water closet with several other families—the neighborhood in which the Tunneys lived was hardly a slum. After living in an apartment on West 52nd Street, where Gene Tunney was born on May 25, 1897, the family moved to Perry Street in Greenwich Village five months later. Several years after that the Tunneys relocated to another tenement, two blocks north on Bank Street, close by the Hudson River docks where John Tunney worked and where the Tunneys' neighbors included John Dos Passos, who wrote much of his novel *Manhattan Transfer* there, and Willa Cather, whose novel *One of Ours* won the Pulitzer Prize in 1923.

New York was a city of just under two million when Tunney was born. It practically doubled in population a year later, though, in 1898, when all five boroughs, along with part of Westchester County, were consolidated into one city, with Brooklyn—up until 1898 the country's third largest city with a population of slightly more than a million—the major addition. If the city was growing geographically, it also was growing vertically. As the nineteenth century came to an end, the tallest structure was the thirty-story Park Row Building just to the east of City Hall in lower Manhattan, whose one thousand offices became available for occupancy when it opened in 1899.

Like most Irish immigrant parents in the West Village, John and Mary Tunney were both religious and strict. In the cramped quarters of the Tunney household, grace was said before all meals, and each of the six children was required to kneel at their bedsides and recite the Lord's Prayer and the Hail Mary before going to sleep. Sundays, the family went to church together at St. Veronica's, which—like many Catholic churches of the era—had been built through the largesse of its relatively poor parishioners and street fairs between 1890, when the lower church was built, and 1903, when the upper church opened its doors to what by then had become an astonishingly large congregation of about six thousand, mostly all of them Irish. The parochial school associated with St. Veronica's, like other parochial schools at the time, was both free and very strict. "I would estimate that at least three mornings a week the good brothers [at St. Veronica's School] would rap me on the knuckles for being late to school after my work at the butcher shop," Gene Tunney was to say years later. Such corporal punishment was not unusual in Catholic parochial schools right into the 1960s, but it was far worse in the early part of the twentieth century, when the behavior of some of the Christian Brothers and Sisters of Charity (who also taught at St. Veronica's) bordered on the sadistic.

"It was not uncommon for a Brother or a Sister to whack you across the hands or the back of your legs with a yardstick," Harold Blake, a graduate of St. Veronica's grammar school and a longtime parishioner and volunteer at the church school, recalled in 2004. "If you happened to tell your mother and father about getting whacked when you got home from school, they usually would say, 'You probably deserved it.' And sometimes the parents would then whack you, too, which discouraged a kid from telling them in the first place. You have to understand that the Irish parents years ago had a great deal of respect for the Brothers and Sisters who taught, and felt they could do no wrong, and so they never complained to school authorities. But that's how it was in the parochial schools."

During that era, the docks along the Hudson in the West Village thrived, and stevedores tended to live as close to the docks as they could, mainly because their primary mode of transportation at the turn of the century was their legs, since the opening of the New York subway system was still four years away. In all three tenement buildings in which the Tunneys had lived, John Tunney was never more than two blocks from the waterfront.

For a city boy growing up so close to the Hudson, there was much to do. From the nearby piers, Gene Tunney and his friends could look out on a seemingly endless parade of ocean liners, freighters, and tankers, along with trans-river ferries, side-wheel excursion steamers, lighters, railroad car floats in tow, barges, and occasionally a United States Navy squadron or even an entire fleet.

In the summer, though, the Hudson had a more adventurous allure for Tunney and his more daring friends. On hot nights, they would dive off the docks at the foot of West Tenth Street into the Hudson to swim. And when an ocean liner was berthed at a nearby pier, they were inclined to get even more daring. Aware of which steamship lines tended to be lax about security, the boys, almost all of them the sons of Irish immigrants, managed to get aboard some passenger ships and then find their way to the bridge. From there, about one hundred feet above the Hudson, one teenager after another would leap into the murky water below, often blessing themselves first, and then swim or dog-paddle back to the pier. Once, Tunney recalled some years later, he did what was known as a "soldier's dive," wherein one puts his hands at his sides and then dives into the water, headfirst. The dive could have killed or paralyzed young Tunney, he realized after, and he never tried the daredevil stunt again.

By the time he was eleven, Tunney, despite his frail-looking stature, had established himself as one of the best athletes at St. Veronica's School, excelling at basketball, baseball, swimming, and running, and good enough at the quintessentially New York City game of handball to hold his own with the Christian Brothers who taught at the school. Young Tunney's evident penchant for learning and the inordinate time he spent in the school library, much of it poring over books on Greek and Roman history, cast him as something of a prig to many of his classmates, who, like Tunney, were from poor families, and who, unlike Tunney, found school boring. "There was an inclination to poke fun at Gene's scholarly demeanor," Dr. Fred Van Vliet, a neighborhood physician, once recalled. "He was an inveterate reader as far back as I knew him, and my library had a sort of fascination for him as a boy, and I guess he must have browsed through every book in my possession."

Even some of young Tunney's closest friends tried to take advantage of his passive nature. "Some of us kids were pretty active and keen for boxing," Gene Boyle, a classmate at St. Veronica's School, later said, "and Gene was such a simple-looking chap at the time that we proceeded to go to work on him. But it wasn't long before we realized our mistake."

Indeed, Tunney's sports teammates, along with some of the budding toughs among the student body, found it hard to reconcile his passion for reading and his thespian activities at the school with his athleticism. Always eager to take part in theatrical productions, by the age of thirteen young Tunney was able to recite the soliloquies of such Shakespearean characters as Antonio, Portia, and Shylock and had played Antonio in *The Merchant of Venice* as an eighth-grader. This did not particularly impress most of his neighborhood friends, but it helped elevate his own self-esteem and delighted his teachers and his parents, whose education in County Mayo had been sparse, to say the least.

Despite his accomplishments, on graduating from St. Veronica's with the eighth-grade class of 1911, Tunney hardly looked as though he would make his mark in sports. At the age of fourteen, he was about 5′ 3″ and weighed around 115 pounds. In his class photograph, Tunney is dwarfed by most of the twenty-two other members of the all-male class, all of whom wore dark suits, white ties, and solemn looks, perhaps at the behest of the stern-looking Christian Brother sitting in their midst.

Few members of that class, as at many if not most parochial schools in New York, would ever pose for a graduation picture again. Like Tunney, most would never complete high school: he lasted only a year at De La Salle Academy in the East Village, while working before and after school for a neighborhood butcher. And having sprouted to 5′ 8″ in less than a year, he continued to show potential as a basketball player and distance runner. But Tunney had become more aware of his family's financial struggles and noticed, more and more, how his father, now fifty-two, would come home exhausted after twelve-hour workdays on the piers. He left school at fifteen to accept a job as an office boy that he had sought, unbeknownst to his parents, at the Ocean Steamship Company on the Hudson River waterfront, which primarily required him to run errands and make deliveries along lower Broadway. His labors earned him five dollars a week.

With friends, Tunney occasionally would make the half-hour walk to the second Madison Square Garden, between Fifth and Madison Avenues, and, for fifty cents, sit in the upper reaches of the arena to watch such champions as Benny Leonard, Johnny Dundee, Johnny Kilbane, Jeff Smith, and the crafty but often conniving Abe Attell, whom he would come to know years later. Since John Tunney was an avid fight fan, it would seem likely for him to have gone to Madison Square Garden with his teenage son, but he did not, perhaps to discourage Gene from becoming a fighter.

Within a year after going to work at the Ocean Steamship Company, young Tunney, after learning how to type on his own, was promoted to mail clerk at a salary of eleven dollars a week. Enthused by his new job, Tunney began looking ahead to even better positions within the steamship company, perhaps even eventually becoming a pier superintendent. That, he was sure, would make his father proud. Meanwhile, boxing had lost its appeal. For the still spindly Tunney, now 5′ 10″ and weighing about 125 pounds, basketball and long-distance running were now the dominant passions, to the extent that after work he would often run, with fellow runners, from the West Village northward on Fifth Avenue to the northern fringe of Central Park at 125th Street and then back, a distance of about ten miles. This was to prepare for track meets, in which he fared well but never well enough to ever win a race.

One night in the late spring of 1913, Tunney, sixteen years old, six feet tall and all of 135 pounds, encountered Willie Green, the fighter who had shown him some boxing basics at the Villagers Athletic Club, which was situated in a recreation center at Charles Street and Greenwich Avenue in the West Village. About to launch a comeback, Green was looking for someone to spar with at the club. It turned out to be Tunney, who, after watching Green work out, felt an urge to put on boxing gloves again. It would be a mismatch, to be sure, but it would be a challenge. And most certainly, it would be a learning experience.

About fifteen pounds heavier than Tunney, Green was no longer solicitous and gentle as he had been in his playful sparring with Tunney a few years before. All business now, Green peppered Tunney with a variety of punches while warding off virtually every blow the teenager threw.

During the week leading up to their second sparring session, Tun-

ney lay in bed at night going over the first confrontation, vividly recall-
ing Green's moves and the way he threw his punches while also remembering how he himself had failed to elude the veteran fighter's
blows and how he had shown slowness and uncertainty in throwing
his own punches. Certainly, he told himself, he could do much better.
And he did, but not much. Still thoroughly outclassed by Green, Tunney took another pounding. While walking home that night, Tunney
decided that he had been foolhardy to spar with Willie Green and that
he most assuredly had no future as a boxer. What he did have, though,
was a burgeoning career with the Ocean Steamship Company. It was
not only more promising but also entailed no physical punishment.

To Tunney's surprise, several men who had watched his second
sparring session with Green had been impressed enough by his performance to mention him to promoters of the smokers held on Friday
nights at a Knights of Columbus Hall on the Lower East Side. One of
the promoters approached Tunney at the Villagers Athletic Club and
asked if he would be willing to box Green at a smoker. Intermittently
legal in New York since the late 1890s, pro boxing was once again legitimate in the state. Two laws legalizing the sport had been passed: the
Horton Act of 1896, which legitimized boxing from 1896 until 1900,
when, because of a plethora of fixed fights, gangster influence, and
other unsavory matters, it was repealed. Then came the Frawley Act,
which relegitimized the sport in 1911 but in 1917 would be repealed
for essentially the same reasons as the Horton Act.

Catholic church halls and Knights of Columbus clubs were popular venues for the all-male smokers, whose crowds were usually an
eclectic blend of neighborhood politicians, businessmen, storekeepers,
factory workers, and longshoremen like John Tunney. While boxing
was banned, the public, theoretically, could not attend matches, since
they were held in private facilities. But when the sport was illegal, organizers of the smokers were eager to attract spectators and devised a
simple scheme to get around that prohibition: allowing spectators to
pay a dollar at the gate to "join" the Knights of Columbus or whatever
club was sponsoring the event and then "contribute" another dollar to
actually get in. In a milieu reeking of sweat, liniment, Vaseline, cigar
smoke, and at times blood, most spectators, seated on either folding

wooden chairs or bleachers, made wagers with one another on bouts involving fighters they had seen before; this way they had at least an inkling of whether their "boy" actually could fight, which many could not. Bouts usually ranged from three to eight rounds, and the ones that generated the most interest, betting, noise, and smoke were those involving neighborhood fighters and those from other parts of the city, all the more so when the neighborhood fighter was Irish—which was often the case in the West Village and many other parts of New York—and the outsider was either Italian, Jewish, or German.

Win or lose, for their efforts at places like the Knights of Columbus hall in Greenwich Village, fighters in the early part of the century usually received a sandwich and a soda and, sometimes, a portion of a betting payoff from a grateful spectator. After a bad performance, they might walk away amid a cascade of boos and catcalls, which usually amounted to a swan song. From the 1920s until the 1950s, when the smokers vanished from the boxing world, fighters at smokers were usually given used or broken pocket watches as prizes, which were actually subterfuges in lieu of cash. The fighters in turn "sold" the watches back to the smoker organizers for anywhere from five to fifty dollars, depending on the fighter's talent and, more important, his popularity. Sometimes, the watches—which fighters rarely, if ever, checked to see if they actually told time—were a prize that contained a prize, usually a five-dollar or ten-dollar bill tucked inside the watch casing. In this way, their amateur status remained intact.

To practically all of the several hundred spectators at the Knights of Columbus hall where Tunney had agreed to spar with Green, he was an unknown quantity—not an uncommon occurrence at smokers, since the bouts often featured fledlging boxers making their ring debuts. Green, by contrast, was well known, having started boxing at smokers a dozen years earlier; he was also popular since his perpetual-motion style guaranteed almost nonstop action. That was the case this night, but while the veteran threw a barrage of punches, few of them landed solidly, as Tunney, now accustomed to Green's offensive style, bobbed, weaved, and danced out of the way, while landing a good share of blows. After three rounds, it was clear that Green had outclassed Tunney, although the fight was classified as an exhibition and no winner was announced. But for Tunney the exhibition was an epiphany—both because he had acquitted himself well and because, for the first time, he had heard cheers. To Tunney, the sound was intoxicating and, as he walked toward the makeshift dressing room, he found that he could not wait to get back into the ring.

Tunney's euphoria over that performance was short-lived. A few weeks later, at a smoker in Manhattan, he found himself in a ring against Leonard Ross, an awkward and unorthodox young boxer who made Tunney look bad. More of a puncher than a boxer at the time, Tunney never landed a solid blow. He somehow managed to win the three-round fight, though not the plaudits of the several hundred fans; they booed both fighters at the end of the bout. Still, it was to provide yet another epiphany for Tunney.

"I know. I was terrible," Tunney, smarting from his lackluster performance, said later to Willie Ward, a young fighter from Greenwich Village who had been in Tunney's corner. The following day, Tunney learned from a friend that the promoter of the card had described Tunney as awkward and wild and had no interest in booking him again. Hearing that, Tunney was angered and stunned—angered over his poor showing and stunned at the promoter's description of him.

Tunney vowed never to be embarrassed in a boxing ring again, and, above all, never again to lose his composure. He also vowed never again to box an opponent without first learning everything he could about him—and, even better, first watching him fight. The secret of becoming a good fighter, Tunney was now convinced, was not only having good or even extraordinary skills, but knowing what to expect and being prepared to deal with it.

On the other hand, he thought, why continue to be frustrated, as he had been in his sparring with the far more experienced Willie Green and then with the clumsy and maladroit, albeit difficult to hit, Leonard Ross? At the age of sixteen, he had no aspirations whatsoever of becoming a professional fighter. And why should he? He already had been promoted at the Ocean Steamship Company in less than a year's time. And in an effort to get even further ahead in the company, Tunney was taking correspondence courses in mathematics and English, and if he continued to work and study hard, who knows? He might yet become a dock superintendent someday and earn as much as twenty-five thousand dollars a year.

If he wouldn't become a priest as his mother wanted, becoming a dock superintendent, he was sure, would make both her and his father happy. But word had begun to get around the West Village about his fighting ability, and, regardless of his bad showing against Leonard Ross, it was unlikely that anyone would try picking a fight with Gene Tunney, whether he ever stepped into a ring again or not. And that had been his father's intention when he gave him that pair of boxing gloves six years ago. So maybe now was a propitious time to forget about the sport that his father loved best.

About a month after his poor performance against Leonard Ross, Tunney once again ran into Willie Green, who had given up thoughts of a comeback. Green still liked to box recreationally and persuaded Tunney, still a gangling lightweight at 135 pounds, to spar with him occasionally at the Villagers Athletic Club and at the Greenwich Settlement House, also in the West Village. During most of their early sessions, Green clearly had the upper hand. But if Tunney was absorbing a multitude of blows from Green, he also was absorbing some valuable lessons. Above all, he had learned that a good defense was paramount in boxing. To hit and not be hit, he realized, was the key to success in the ring. Slugging it out at close quarters, and absorbing considerable punishment in the process, might work for some fighters, but to Tunney the most satisfying aspect of boxing was eluding punches, not landing them, and certainly not being hit.

He also had learned that Green, unlike many fighters, eschewed roundhouse punches; instead, his blows were short, crisp, and punishing. For another, he learned the art of feinting and how to slip or roll with punches—a technique wherein a fighter, while taking a punch, moves his head away as the blow lands, lessening the impact. The more Tunney sparred with Green, the more he improved, to the point where Green, with whom he was suddenly more than holding his own, suggested that he consider fighting at smokers again.

Taking Green's advice, Tunney, now a far better fighter, quickly established himself. By the time he was eighteen, he had gained a reputation as one of the best young boxers in Greenwich Village by winning a half-dozen amateur fights at the ubiquitous smokers in Manhattan and across the East River in Brooklyn. But in the end, despite his vast improvement and his success at the smokers, where his powerful right hand and skillful boxing had made him a crowd favorite, Tunney had no desire to become a professional fighter.

Sizable neighborhood followings, coupled with success in the ring, made a fighter a desirable commodity in New York, where, in the pre–World War I years, about a dozen professional fight clubs flourished along with scores of smokers. One of the best known of the arenas was the Sharkey Athletic Club, a drab arena that was situated in a top-floor loft of a pre–Civil War building just west of Columbus Circle on Manhattan's Upper West Side. Almost every New York fighter of note had fought at Sharkey's, as it was known, including Benny Leonard, before the incomparable lightweight champion became a headliner at the second Madison Square Garden. Having heard about Tunney and his growing Greenwich Village following, Billy Jacobs, the Sharkey A.C. matchmaker, set up a meeting at which he offered to feature Tunney in a ten-round bout.

"No fighter I have ever known has been given a star bout for his first professional fight," Jacobs said to Tunney, aware of Tunney's disinclination to fight professionally.

"Why should I box professionally?" Tunney replied. "I have two jobs, both of which are paying me fairly well."

Jacobs told him that, on the basis of what he had heard about his boxing talent, he could go far in the ring and earn more money than he was making at Ocean Steamship and as a part-time athletic director at a recreation center at Public School 41 in the Village. Tunney, though, resisted all of Jacobs's blandishments. Not about to give up, Jacobs called on Willie Green and Eddie O'Brien, a saloon-keeper and occasional boxing trainer from Greenwich Village, whose son had gone to St. Veronica's with Tunney and who knew Tunney. Jacobs asked them to convince the hot young prospect from the Village that it was in his interest to turn pro. Green and O'Brien not only convinced Tunney to accept Jacobs's offer but said that if he did they would work in his corner for as long as he liked.

"There isn't any fighter from this city that ever had such an offer, and you can lick anybody they throw into the ring with you," said O'Brien.

Tunney was convinced. He enjoyed fighting—or boxing, as he preferred to call it. And if he could make even twenty-five dollars for a professional fight, why that was ten dollars more than his father earned for a long week's work on the Hudson River piers and most certainly better than the sandwich and soda offered after fighting at a smoker. Further, he would be able to test himself against better fighters. And if he did not do well, he told himself, he would stop fighting entirely and focus on his job with Ocean Steamship and, at least for a while longer, his part-time position as an athletic director. Although only eighteen, Tunney had obtained that job several months earlier at P.S. 41, where he imparted boxing fundamentals he had learned from Willie Green to teenage boys. As to whatever happened to him as a boxer, he felt he had nothing to lose—except perhaps some confidence and self-esteem.

Tunney needn't have worried about his first bout at the Sharkey A.C., which was later the subject of a popular lithograph by the artist George Bellows, entitled *A Stag at Sharkey's*. Hundreds of friends and supporters from the Village had made the trek uptown to see Tunney make his professional debut on July 2, 1915, against a welterweight named Bobby Dawson. Looking at Tunney's pallid face and skinny frame at the weigh-in before the fight, Dawson gave a Panglossian smirk, as if to say, *This guy's a fighter?*

Tunney sensed Dawson's patronizing attitude toward him and knew that, from the opening bell, Dawson would come right at him. Dawson did and ran into a barrage of stiff left jabs, prompting him to change tactics and counterpunch. It did him little good, as Tunney, a far superior boxer, peppered Dawson repeatedly with left jabs and sporadic combination punches to the body. But Tunney's growing confidence was jarred by the veteran in the sixth round.

"He got me to lead with a left, and then stepped inside it and got me with a solid right to the solar plexus that shook me," Tunney said later. "After that, my arms got heavy as lead."

But not so heavy that Tunney was not able to catch Dawson with a left uppercut to the jaw that sent Dawson to the floor just before the bell ending the seventh round. Still dazed after the one-minute respite between rounds, Dawson did not come out for the eighth, giving Tunney his first professional victory—an eighth-round technical knockout before a crowd of about two thousand spectators. Cheered on wildly by his fans from the Village as he left the ring, Tunney, unscathed, smiled and waved. Dawson, Tunney realized, was hardly a good test, even though he had established a reputation as a durable and tough fighter who rarely was knocked down. And Tunney had not only put him down but would have knocked him out had Dawson not been saved by the bell. Maybe, just maybe, Tunney thought, he could really amount to something as a fighter. Still, he was nowhere near the point where he would even think about giving up his day job. For his first professional bout, and a main event at that, Tunney received eighteen dollars. Not much, but still better than a sandwich and a soda. Moreover, as he was to say sometime later, Tunney, for the first time since he had started boxing, felt the "ecstasy" of victory. Winning an unsanctioned boxing bout at an unregulated smoker was one thing; winning a professional fight, Tunney had just found out, was quite another.

Working two jobs and with little time to train, Tunney was to fight three more times in 1915. He won the first two bouts by knockouts, after which Willie Green, with whom he continued to spar, and O'Brien felt that Tunney was ready for stronger opponents and convinced him to fight Billy Rowe—like Tunney, a highly regarded prospect—at the Fairmont Athletic Club. Fight cards at the Fairmont were on a higher level than at the Sharkey Athletic Club, and in Billy Rowe he would be facing his toughest opponent yet. With an even bigger contingent of Greenwich Village supporters in attendance on December 1, Tunney showcased his defensive and boxing abilities, blocking virtually every one of Rowe's body punches. Meanwhile, he landed far more blows in the six-round no-decision fight.

Next to Madison Square Garden, in the second and third decades of the twentieth century, the Fairmont A.C. was the best-known boxing arena in New York. It had been established in an abandoned foundry by Billy Gibson, the proprietor of a popular restaurant in the East Bronx who would eventually figure prominently in Tunney's boxing career. Though he admittedly knew virtually nothing about boxing, Gibson heeded the advice of Tom McArdle, a former matchmaker at Madison Square Garden, to take advantage of the boxing boom in the early part of the century and open a fight club. It turned out to be a prescient move, which eventually led Gibson to become a successful boxing promoter and, later, an even more successful boxing manager, who was helped along to a considerable degree by friendships with influential New York politicians, judges, entertainment figures, and a number of upper-echelon mob figures in New York and Philadelphia.

In no rush to fight again, and certainly with no intention of making boxing a career, Tunney focused on his two jobs while sparring frequently with Willie Green at P.S. 41 before fighting again in July of 1916. Between then and December 8, Tunney fought five times, winning three of his bouts by knockouts and proving to be the decisive fighter in two nondecision bouts. That success began to get him a modicum of attention in some of the city's dozen daily newspapers and a larger following, especially in Greenwich Village. But proud as he was of his son's fistic accomplishments, John Tunney still would not go to see him fight. He had bought Gene a pair of boxing gloves so the boy could learn to defend himself against neighborhood bullies—not become a prizefighter. And John and his wife—whose lives, like those of most Irish immigrants in the West Village, centered on the resplendent neighborhood church—still clung to the hope that Gene would become a priest.

Jack Dempsey starting out in Colorado as "Kid Blackie." COURTESY OF TOBY SMITH

TWO

Kid
Blackie

I f Gene Tunney was beginning to attract some attention in the New York area, a slightly older middleweight was creating considerably more excitement among boxing fans in Colorado, Utah, and Nevada, thanks to a long string of knockouts. His name was William Harrison Dempsey—he had been named for the ninth president, William Henry Harrison, the first American president to die in office—but, at twenty, he had already gone through two name changes. After starting to fight professionally as Kid Blackie, he had taken the name of Jack Dempsey after the great Irish-born middleweight champion of the 1880s and 1890s, who had been nicknamed "The Nonpareil," as in unequaled, which he was as a fighter, having gone unbeaten in his first sixty-two fights. But like William Harrison Dempsey, the original Jack Dempsey also had changed his name, taking his father's surname after having been born John Kelly.

The ninth of eleven children of a onetime schoolteacher who became an itinerant miner, railroad worker, and farmworker after traveling west from West Virginia in a prairie wagon with his wife in the early 1880s, Dempsey grew up poor. The Dempseys first settled in Manassa at the southern tip of Colorado in the San Luis Valley, an agricultural area near the New Mexico border, 7,800 feet above sea level and surrounded by the Rocky Mountains. They had gone there to join a community, made up mostly of Mormon converts from the South, after hearing a missionary from the Church of Jesus Christ of Latter-day Saints espouse the virtues of the church. But the Dempseys did not stay in their one-room house in Manassa long, despite the hospitality of their new Mormon neighbors. Nor, for that matter, did they linger in any other town or city.

Asked about it years later, even Dempsey was uncertain about the family's peripatetic wanderings over the next decade or so. About eight years after William Harrison Dempsey was born on June 24, 1895, the family moved to Creede, about seventy-five miles north of Manassa, where Celia Dempsey ran a boardinghouse for a year and took in washing while Hyrum worked in a gold mine. A year later, the Dempseys headed even farther north, to the hardscrabble mining town of Leadville, which at ten thousand feet above sea level is the highest-altitude municipality in the United States. Other stopovers during the family's peregrinations included Uncompahgre, Montrose, and Telluride in western Colorado and Steamboat Springs in the northern part of the state, along with brief stayovers in such dusty Colorado frontier towns as Victor, Mount Harris, Rifle, Delta, and Meeker. All the while, Dempsey went to school intermittently, never getting beyond the eighth grade. But he made money washing dishes in a Montrose restaurant owned by his mother, probing underground mines for copper, gold, and silver, picking beets and potatoes, baling wheat, washing windows, cutting lawns, digging ditches, shining shoes, and selling newspapers at the corner of 16th and Market Streets in the section of Denver now known as LoDo, short for lower downtown.

In later years, Dempsey was to recall that his mother was the bedrock of the family, a tiny woman of Scottish, Irish, Cherokee, and Choctaw lineage who weighed about a hundred pounds. Both she and her husband, who was of Scottish and Irish descent, became Mormons as soon as they arrived in Manassa. Celia Dempsey remained a staunch

Mormon for the rest of her life. Hyrum Dempsey, though, was a "Jack Mormon," the name given to a Mormon who drinks, smokes, and in general violates the tenets of the Church of Latter-day Saints, as did William Harrison and most of his other six sons. "I know the church is right," Hyrum Dempsey was to say. "I'm just too weak to live up to their rules." Nor, as it turned out was he strong or determined enough to hold on to a job to provide sufficient subsistence for his growing family.

After leaving home in his mid-teens to earn money for his impoverished family, young Harry, as he was called by his family, lived a nomadic existence. For the next five years, he spent many of his nights in hobo jungles, where homeless men gathered to eat and sleep by campfires. In later years, Dempsey explained that hobos were itinerant, albeit unskilled, workers, while tramps may have been itinerant, but rarely, if ever, worked, and bums neither traveled nor worked. Thus, as Dempsey pointed out years later, he may have been a hobo, but never was a tramp or a bum.

Many other nights found the young Dempsey cloistered in mining camps while foraging for coal or silver for around five dollars a day, usually as a mucker, the lowest-paid and most undesirable job in a mine. Unlike most of the hobos he met, most of whom were considerably older, Dempsey felt that his stay in this netherworld was temporary. And if he was to get out, he was convinced, it would be with his fists. Through sparring with his two older brothers, both of whom were journeymen boxers, and through frequent street fights, he had become a good fighter. On the advice of his older brother Bernie, he had started at the age of twelve to soak his face and hands in beef brine to toughen his skin and to chew leather-hard resin—"pine gum," as it was called—from pine trees, which Bernie told him would strengthen his jaw, making it less vulnerable during a bout.

More than a half-century later, Dempsey would tell the New York *Daily News* cartoonist and sports columnist Bill Gallo, a longtime friend, that that long-ago beef brine soaking made his huge fists "hard as iron anvils." Considering how Dempsey was only knocked out once—if indeed it was a knockout—the pine gum may also have toughened his jaw, as brother Bernie said it would.

Hopping freight trains from town to town in Colorado, Utah, and Nevada, Dempsey would challenge local toughs, almost always bigger and older than he, to winner-take-all fistfights in mining town and railroad hub saloons. These fights were often sanctioned by bartenders with a vested interest; they allowed the no-holds-barred brawls held on sawdust-covered floors ringed by grizzled, and often gun-toting, customers. The emaciated-looking teenager hardly inspired fear when he strolled into a Western saloon frequented by rowdy, hard-drinking miners, cowboys, railroad workers, and other assorted roughnecks and in his high-pitched falsetto voice—which he had inherited from his father and which he found embarrassing—challenged anyone in the house to a fight. If anything, the challenge tended to elicit laughter. Three decades earlier, John L. Sullivan had issued similar challenges in bars in the Northeast. But when Sullivan threw down his gauntlet and bellowed, "I can lick any son of a bitch in the house," it was rare that anyone attempted to dispute the brawny, if not somewhat beefy, Boston Strong Boy, who carried about 200 pounds on a 5′ 10″ frame. Dempsey, by contrast, weighed around 130 when he in effect did the same thing.

With hunger as a motivating force, Dempsey rarely lost a barroom fight, usually disposing of an opponent with what would become his trademark punch: a left hook to the jaw or the abdominal area. With the barroom ruffian often still lying on the saloon floor, the bartender or an associate would then pass a hat around for financial contributions, half of which went to Dempsey and half of which went to the bartender. Indeed, bartenders often tended to be Dempsey's matchmakers.

At times, Dempsey would ask a bartender if there was a ruffian who had been giving him and perhaps customers any trouble and whom he would like to see beaten up. It was not always an easy sell. Maybe the bartender had a particular bully in mind who fit the bill, but then he could hardly be blamed for wondering how in the world this skinny teenager with the girlish voice could possibly get the best of the bar's major annoyance in a fistfight. In such cases of doubt, Dempsey would recite a list of nearby towns where he had rid saloons of churlish and unwanted patrons. You can check it out, Dempsey would tell the dubious barkeeps, after listing what in effect were his references. Sometimes, the bartenders did just that, but more often than not, they believed this hungry-looking kid, especially after Dempsey threw a few practice punches and showed some of his fighting moves.

While riding the rods, a dangerous mode of travel wherein hobos would grasp the slender steel beams beneath freight cars merely inches above track roadbeds and hold on for dear life—or tie themselves to the beams with rope or wire—as the train roared along at fifty or sixty miles an hour, Dempsey began to fight professionally as Kid Blackie in 1914 when he was nineteen years old. At least that's what most record books say. If they are to be believed, Dempsey made his pro debut on August 17 of that year when he fought an eight-round draw with a fighter named Young Herman in Ramona, Colorado. He then knocked out six of his next seven opponents before suffering his first defeat to one Jack Downey in April of 1915. But in fact, Dempsey was to say years later, he started fighting for money in 1911 when he was sixteen years old, and estimated that by 1916 he had had about a hundred fights, almost all of them in Colorado and Utah, and most of them for purses that rarely exceeded fifty dollars. That would be more than eighty bouts that Dempsey is listed to have fought by then in a number of record books, not unusual during the first two decades of the twentieth century.

Dempsey's manager in his early fighting days was his brother Bernie, himself a lightly regarded fighter. Indeed, Dempsey soon appropriated the name Jack Dempsey from his brother, who had taken the name of the great old Nonpareil. In a sense, the younger Dempsey's second name change came out of necessity. Bernie Dempsey, then close to forty, was booked to fight a middleweight named George Copelin in the tough Colorado mining town of Cripple Creek on November 19, 1915. But on the day of the fight, he told Harry, then twenty, that he could not go on.

"Harry, I feel terrible," Bernie told his kid brother, who had accompanied him to Cripple Creek. "It's the altitude, I think."

"Aw, come on, Bernie," brother Harry said, surprised that his older brother was suddenly being afflicted by the high altitude he had grown up in. "Anybody can flatten him."

"Then you flatten him," Bernie replied, while suggesting that his younger brother use Bernie's borrowed name to accommodate the promoter.

Dempsey, who by then had fifteen recorded professional fights as Kid Blackie under his belt, agreed to fight while brother Bernie served as his cornerman. But there was a problem. Most of the spectators had seen Bernie Dempsey fight, and he and his brother did not look alike. The promoter also was not keen on the idea. Nor was Copelin, though for a different reason. "I might kill that skinny guy," the 165-pound Copelin told the promoter on seeing the 150-pound Dempsey at the weigh-in.

Seeking to assuage the promoter's apprehensions, Harry Dempsey told him, "I'll flatten this big bum. You can go out and bet my end on it." Young Dempsey's confidence seemed to allay the promoter's fears and he agreed to have him introduced as Jack Dempsey. When the ring announcer did, there was a cascade of boos from the raucous crowd, many of whom knew they were looking at an impostor, something that was not uncommon in small-town fight clubs. As it turned out, though, they got to see an even better Jack Dempsey, who floored Copelin a half-dozen times in the first round and twice in the second. But then the new Jack Dempsey also became affected by the altitude. "I'm through. I quit," an out-of-breath Dempsey told brother Bernie in his corner after the fifth round.

"Go back out there," Bernie responded, sounding like an archetypal cornerman. "He's in worse shape than you are."

Determined to end the fight and avert what would be his first defeat, Dempsey sent Copelin to the canvas twice more in the seventh round. *If he gets up, I'm going to quit. Right in front of everybody. Even Bernie,* Dempsey said to himself. As it developed, to Dempsey's dismay, Copelin got up again. But this time the referee stopped the fight. It turned out Dempsey had fought for nothing since Bernie had spent almost all of the one-hundred-dollar purse that he had received in advance. The next day, Bernie went back to work in a silver mine and Harry, henceforth to be known as Jack Dempsey, clambered aboard a freight train boxcar in Cripple Creek and headed for Salt Lake City.

Following three straight knockout victories in Salt Lake City—the first one over Two-Round Gillian, who, not quite living up to his name, fell in one—Dempsey, by now a 160-pound middleweight, met Jack Price, a fringe boxing figure who had managed a few local fighters. Having seen Dempsey record those knockouts and aware of his earlier successes, Price told Dempsey he would like to manage him. He guaranteed better opponents, which meant bigger purses. Dempsey, weary of fighting third-raters for nominal purses, agreed. True to his word, Price arranged for a fight in Ogden, Utah, with a fighter who called himself the Boston Bearcat and claimed to have gone twenty rounds against the legendary Sam Langford. Maybe he had, but he lasted nineteen fewer against Dempsey, who, though outweighed by forty pounds, unloaded a left uppercut to the stomach that turned the Bearcat into a pussycat and sent him down for the count of ten in the opening round.

From the very beginning, boxing fans took to young Dempsey because of his aggressive style. Fighting out of a low crouch—which years later he attributed to working in low-ceilinged Colorado mines—and bobbing and weaving as he constantly stalked an opponent, the beetle-browed, blue-jowled young man seemed to carry into the ring a smoldering rage that did not abate even when a foe was badly hurt. Indeed, once he hurt a fighter, he pounced with a savage ferocity, raining blow after blow until the referee stopped the fight or Dempsey's opponent crumpled to the canvas. Conversely, when he was hurt, Dempsey never retreated, always standing his ground and, no matter how badly dazed, staying on the offensive, throwing lethal left hooks—a roundhouse blow with the left arm that became his signature punch—and powerful rights to the head and the body. If he was vulnerable it was on defense; he had little. But no matter. For Dempsey, defense was an afterthought if it was a thought at all. He could take a punch, almost with impunity, and not only withstand a hard blow, but respond with even more punishing punches. If anything, Dempsey was at his most dangerous when he was hurt, as opponents would soon find out. If young Gene Tunney was learning to become a polished boxer, and would eventually call himself a "pugilist," Dempsey was and always would be a fighter. Nobody would ever call Jack Dempsey a boxer, and certainly not a pugilist.

After six more victories in Utah under Price, four by knockout, Dempsey was convinced he was ready to move on to both a higher level and a grander boxing stage. "Let's go to New York and make some real money," Dempsey said to Price while they were having a drink at a bar in Salt Lake.

"New York? Are you crazy, Harry?" Price responded. "They got real fighters there."

"I'm a real fighter," Dempsey said.

"Okay, but I won't ride those damn rods with you," Price said.

The following day, Dempsey, who had taken scores of train rides, all of them free but none in a seat, bought his first train ticket. Price bought one, too. But even if they were not going to ride the rods, they were not exactly going to travel first-class. Their tickets called for them to share an upper berth during the three-day train trip. As Dempsey was to find out, it still beat riding under a freight car and trying to avoid a brutish, club-carrying railroad detective.

Ironically, his first two fights in New York would be at the Fairmont A.C., where the nineteen-year-old Tunney was finally catching the eye of some New York boxing writers. For Dempsey, who arrived in New York with just under thirty dollars in cash, it would be a bit more difficult. Without any connections in New York boxing circles and having been rebuffed by matchmakers, most of whom had never heard of Dempsey's victims, Price decided to make the rounds of newspaper sports departments in the city with a batch of clippings recounting Dempsey victories, most of them early-round knockouts.

The visits paid off. Nat Fleischer, then the sports editor of the *New York Press,* who five years later would start *The Ring* magazine and become the country's preeminent boxing editor and historian, agreed to write a story about Dempsey. So, too, did Damon Runyon of the *New York American,* a onetime sportswriter in Colorado, who already had been following Dempsey's burgeoning career. Runyon, who was to become one of the country's best-known sportswriters and a celebrated short-story chronicler of Broadway characters of the 1920s and 1930s, went even further, convincing Tom McArdle to book Dempsey to fight at the Fairmont Athletic Club, where McArdle had become the matchmaker for his good friend, Billy Gibson. A notorious grafter, Runyon may have been doing Dempsey a favor, but he also felt that before long promoters like Tex Rickard might very well be paying Runyon to write about this crude power hitter. Ever since his days as a sportswriter in Pueblo, Colorado, Runyon not only had had his hand out to promoters, he usually had both hands out. The more money he received from a promoter or manager, the more Runyon tended to like a fighter. If, as he often did, he also was given a piece—part-ownership of a fighter—he liked him even more. But even for a cynic like him, Dempsey was something special. For one, like Runyon, he was from Colorado, though Runyon had been born in Kansas—appropriately enough, Manhattan, Kansas. More important, Runyon, who had an eye for fistic talent, saw right away that Dempsey could actually fight.

Typical of many small fight clubs of the era, the Fairmont A.C. was a far cry from the elegant Madison Square Garden. For paying their "membership" fees at the Fairmont, spectators, almost always exclusively men, sat in wooden bleachers that surrounded the ring and rose almost to the ceiling. If an excited spectator sitting in the top row of the Fairmont A.C. suddenly jumped to his feet, he was more than likely to bang his head against the ceiling. But if the ceiling didn't get you, the heavy pall of cigar and cigarette smoke, which eventually rose to the upper tier of the bleachers, might.

Crowds at the Fairmont were notoriously raucous, even before bouts began, with spectators shouting at one another while making wagers on the next fight and with fights often breaking out in the crowd. If a fight went the distance, no decision was announced, so, theoretically, no one could win a bet unless the fight ended in a knockout. It did not take long for someone, most likely a promoter who knew that his customers wanted to wager on fights, to approach boxing writers and ask if they would provide their very unofficial "decisions"—usually for a price—after a fight. Ergo, the "newspaper decisions," on which the outcome of wagers depended in New York and in many other states during what might be described as boxing's probationary period. At a time when newspaper salaries, including those of sportswriters, were relatively low, managers sometimes found writers who would be voting on the outcome of bouts more than willing to lean over backward on behalf of some fighters.

For his New York debut in the Bronx, Dempsey was offered sixteen dollars. It may not have been much for a fighter who had knocked out eighteen of his first twenty-seven opponents while losing only one fight, but it was a bonanza for Dempsey and Price, who had been spending nights sleeping on benches in Central Park and feasting on the free lunches—usually a sandwich and a pickle—that were offered in many second- or third-rate Manhattan bars so long as you bought a five-cent beer or two. At 160 pounds, Dempsey was fifty-five pounds lighter than his opponent, Andre Anderson, a journeyman heavyweight and familiar figure at clubs like the Fairmont. Anderson took more than a few good shots to the head and body from the aggressive Dempsey, but never went down during the the the ten-round fight, which Dempsey won, at least in the eyes of the sportswriters: a classic newspaper decision.

Though he missed far more punches than he landed, Dempsey won over the crowd at the Fairmont A.C. with his stalking, freewheeling, and hard-punching style. Maybe he was a little green, but it was obvious that the swarthy dark-haired young man with the five o'clock shadow, misshapen nose, and baleful glare could punch, and he certainly was not dull. Dempsey, though, was disappointed. He had hoped to make a quick impression, particularly on the boxing writers who were present, by knocking out Anderson. Still, he did well enough for McArdle to book him for a second ten-round fight at the Fairmont A.C. two weeks later against another respected, though not particularly talented, journeyman named Wild Bert Kenny. Slightly more impressive than in his New York debut, Dempsey floored Kenny twice, but could not put him down for the count and had to be content with another newspaper decision. Mainly because of the larger crowd, many of whom had been curious to see the reputed knockout artist from out West, Dempsey's purse of forty-three dollars was almost three times more than he received for his first New York bout. That was a veritable windfall for Dempsey, who had been accustomed to fighting for anywhere from ten to twenty dollars, including what he later estimated at more than two hundred winner-take-all saloon fights.

But again, Dempsey was dissatisfied with his performance. The stories by Fleischer and Runyon had portrayed him, fairly enough, as a devastating knockout puncher, and here he was winning two ten-round decisions against a couple of run-of-the-mill pugs. Unfortunately, during the rest of his stay in New York, things would only get worse.

A few days after Dempsey's fight with Kenny, Jack Price, his manager, received a telegram saying that his mother was gravely ill in Salt Lake City. Price immediately left for home by train, leaving Dempsey without a manager and essentially alone in Manhattan. But within hours after Price had left for Salt Lake City, John Reisler, the owner of a Broadway barbershop, who, like many boxing managers of the era, had little if any experience in the sport, approached Dempsey at Grupp's Gymnasium, a well-known Harlem boxing gym. In a milieu rife with unethical characters, Reisler was among the worst—a piranha in the sinkhole of sports. Renown for matching, or mismatching, his fighters against far better opponents to ensure a bigger payday, Reisler realized that Dempsey was a legitimate prospect and was eager to take control of him. In an effort to do so, he had sent a phony telegram to Price saying that his mother was at death's door in Utah. The next day, Reisler told Dempsey that he had bought his contract from Price for fifty dollars and had also lent Price fifty dollars for his train fare home. Dempsey became furious. He knew Reisler was lying because no contract existed; from the time Dempsey and Price got together in the spring of 1916, it had been a handshake agreement, and Dempsey told Reisler so. Dempsey also came to doubt that Reisler had lent Price money to pay for his train fare home.

Nevertheless, Dempsey, who had already had to deal with a number of unsavory managers and promoters in the West, agreed to let Reisler manage him. He knew he had no one else to turn to and was eager to fight at least once more in New York, and although Reisler was obviously devious, at least he could probably get him another bout. After that, he thought, he would return to Salt Lake City and hook up with Price again. That seemed like a credible rationale, but, as Dempsey was soon to find out, it was not—not when you were dealing with someone like John the Barber, as Reisler was known within the New York boxing establishment

First, Reisler told Dempsey that he planned to match him against Sam Langford, perhaps the best fighter never to have been given a shot at a title.*

Dempsey had certainly heard of Langford, who, though he was thirty-six years old and losing his eyesight, was still one of the world's best fighters. What he didn't know was that Reisler also occasionally managed Langford and thus would collect a share of both purses in such a fight, not totally uncommon at the time.

"He'll kill me," Dempsey said to Reisler. "You're wasting your time. I won't fight him. He's too damned good for me." Reisler acquiesced regarding Langford, knowing there was no chance Dempsey would agree to fight him. Still, aware that matching Dempsey against a veteran quality opponent would ensure a sizable share of the purse, Reisler then suggested a fight with Ed "Gunboat" Smith, a leading heavyweight who during Jack Johnson's championship reign was billed as the "white heavyweight champion of the world," a meaningless title that fooled no one. Again Dempsey refused, convinced he was not ready for Gunboat Smith either. Reisler finally managed to convince Dempsey to fight John Lester Johnson, a veteran, and good, heavyweight, whom Dempsey had heard of and was at first reluctant to fight.

Making matters worse for Dempsey, the fight with Johnson was to be held at the Harlem Sporting Club, Johnson's home arena, where he was extremely popular. Out of money and with Reisler refusing to give

---

*Starting as a featherweight and working his way to the heavyweight division during a twenty-one-year career, Langford—outweighed by thirty pounds—had gone the fifteen-round distance with Jack Johnson in a fight for the "colored heavyweight title" before Johnson won the heavyweight championship and also had beaten such outstanding fighters as Philadelphia Jack O'Brien and Joe Gans, both of whom won world titles. Along the way, Langford, like most other leading black boxers, mainly fought other black fighters at a time when there was a pronounced color line in boxing. Nowhere was that more evident than in Langford's rivalry with another very good heavyweight, Harry Wills, whom he fought twenty-three times. Langford was so good that Bert Randolph Sugar rated Langford sixteenth, ahead of such boxing luminaries as Barney Ross, Archie Moore, Sugar Ray Leonard, Jake LaMotta, and Emile Griffith.

him an advance on the two hundred dollars he expected to get for the fight, Dempsey spent the night before the fight, Friday, July 14, 1916, sleeping on a wooden bench in Central Park. The following night, the Harlem Sporting Club was packed for the ten-round bout, which turned out to be a memorable one for Dempsey because of a body punch thrown by Johnson in the second round. It was a vicious left hook, which not only caused Dempsey to crumple forward as if he were to go down, but also broke three ribs.

"It was the hardest punch I ever took, and that includes everybody who ever hit me anytime, anywhere, and with anything," Dempsey was to say years later. "It busted three of my ribs like matchsticks."

Despite the pain, Dempsey fought on and lasted the ten rounds, though he was unable to hurt Johnson in the closely fought bout. The verdict among sportswriters rendering their newspaper decisions was split. Several thought Dempsey had won, which surprised him. "The rest were right: they said I had been beaten," Dempsey said, adding that the writers who voted for Johnson were actually half-right: "I wasn't beaten, I was massacred."

In its account of the fight, the *New York Tribune* said, "Jack Dempsey, a Michigan heavyweight, and John Lester Johnson fought an uninteresting ten-round bout to a draw at the Harlem Sporting Club last night. Johnson did most of the leading, but his punches had little effect on Dempsey, who was waiting to put over the big punch which he failed to deliver."

The story was wrong on two counts. Dempsey, of course, was not from Michigan. And John Lester Johnson's punches, especially the one that broke three of Dempsey's ribs, definitely did have an effect on Dempsey. "Every movement I made after that punch was just plain hell," Dempsey said. Somehow, the *Tribune* reporter did not seem to have noticed.

The reporter for the *New York World* who covered the fight was more perceptive when he wrote that Johnson had scored "an easy victory." He went on to say that Dempsey had "failed to live up to the reputation he earned in Salt Lake City and was an easy mark for the local boxer." Still in pain, Dempsey was having his three cracked ribs taped when Reisler came into his dressing room after the fight. "Nice fight, kid," Reisler said, well aware that Dempsey had not had a good night in the ring. "Our cut was only a hundred and seventy dollars. That's eighty-five each, less the fifty dollars I let your last manager have."

"But he sold me to you," Dempsey, who was expecting at least two hundred dollars, answered.

"Nope," John the Barber replied. "He borrowed fifty against your next fight."

Reisler then handed Dempsey thirty-five dollars.

"Thanks," said Dempsey, always gentlemanly out of a boxing ring or a saloon, even while being cheated out of money after having had three ribs broken in a fight he never should have taken.

With three broken ribs, Dempsey knew he wouldn't be able to fight for several months. There certainly was no reason to stay in New York, not when he only had a few dollars left. A few days after the Johnson fight, Dempsey ran into John the Barber in Grupp's Gymnasium. "I can't fight anybody for a while," Dempsey told Reisler. "I'm going home until my ribs heal."

Knowing that Reisler was aware of his dire financial straits and his three broken ribs, Dempsey thought that John the Barber just might be willing to pay for his train fare back to Salt Lake City. Dempsey seemed to have forgotten who he was dealing with. Reisler said, "Well, kid, let me know when you're ready to fight again."

At that, Dempsey left Grupp's, walked to the Hudson River docks and took a New York Central Railroad ferry across the Hudson to a pier near a New Jersey freight yard. Finding a freight that was headed west—experienced hobo travelers knew how to determine quickly which freights were headed in which direction, and even in some cases to which particular cities—Dempsey clambered under a freight car, positioned himself on several steel rods, and, with three broken ribs and some bitter memories of New York, readied himself for the long trip back to Salt Lake City.

If Dempsey still had to ride the rods and boxcars and sleep in parks in spite of all his knockout victories, Gene Tunney had no financial problems. He was making seventeen dollars a week classifying freight and doing other chores for the Ocean Steamship Company, and supplementing that with his job as the evening athletic director at P.S. 41 in Greenwich Village. And unlike Dempsey, Tunney, still in his late teens, always had a bed to sleep in at his parents' apartment. For six months he did not fight, but then he accepted an offer to meet another young prospect named K.O. Jaffe at the Polo Athletic Club in Harlem. Even though he hadn't fought in months, Tunney was developing a following in Greenwich Village, and also at the Ocean Steamship Company, and several hundred of his supporters turned out for the fight on July 21, 1916, exactly a week after Dempsey's last fight in New York. Jaffe wasn't a bad fighter, but Tunney had trained hard, feeling he might be rusty after a long layoff. Instead, he put on a superb display of defensive boxing. Jaffe only landed a few punches, none of them solid, as Tunney completely outclassed him.

Despite his broken ribs, Dempsey was back in the ring two months later in Salida, Colorado, where he had been working as a janitor in a brothel run by Laura Adams, one of Colorado's best-known madams. Though outweighed by about thirty pounds and without a manager, Dempsey, who now weighed about 170, flattened his opponent, a local boxer who fought as Young Hector, in the third round. While living in Salida, Dempsey briefly visited his family, now in Salt Lake City, and then resumed a relationship with Maxine Cates, a barroom piano player and prostitute in Salt Lake City, whom he had met the previous spring. Though she was fourteen years older than Dempsey and his parents strongly disapproved of the relationship, Dempsey was smitten by Cates, whom he called the sexiest woman he had ever known. At her suggestion, they got married by a justice of the peace on October 9, 1916, in Farmington, Utah, just outside Salt Lake City. He was twenty-one and she was thirty-five, and, as time would tell, there were more differences between them than that. At any rate, it most definitely was not a marriage made in heaven.

After having fought only once in 1916—on July 21—Tunney made up for it in December when he had four fights, all in New York, in three weeks. Tunney knocked out three of his four opponents and the fourth bout was a no-decision contest, which he clearly won, over George

Lahey, whom he had knocked out in his third professional fight sixteen months earlier. With some of the money he received for the fights, Tunney bought two pairs of boxing gloves to donate to the P.S. 41 recreation center. Short of funds, the center did not have the wherewithal to buy gloves for the young boxers Tunney tutored. Nine years before, John Tunney had bought his son a pair of boxing gloves so that he could learn how to defend himself against neighborhood toughs. Tunney, in buying the gloves, hoped they would both serve the same purpose for his young pupils at P.S. 41 and perhaps get them interested in the sport, which Tunney was getting to like better with each passing fight. After all, he had fought nine times and had clearly won every fight. But to Tunney it was just another way to compete, and James Joseph Tunney loved to compete, whatever the sport. As the momentous year of 1917 approached, he knew without a doubt that he would never make boxing a career.

Marine private James Joseph Tunney.
U.S. MARINE CORPS HISTORY DIVISION

THREE

The Reluctant Warrior

hen Congress, at the urging of President Woodrow Wilson, declared war on Germany on April 6, 1917, Gene Tunney, about to turn twenty, seemed the prototypical candidate coveted by the American armed forces. An all-around athlete, highly intelligent and personable, and a physical fitness buff long before it became a fad, Tunney seemed to be the personification of the man that a stern-looking and top-hatted Uncle Sam was pointing at in the famed World War I recruiting poster. As it was, Tunney did not have to be coaxed into enlisting for military service; he most certainly did not want to continue working as a rate clerk with the Ocean Steamship Company while other young American men were preparing to fight a war.

But in April of 1917 fighting in a ring was out of the question. About a month before the United States entered the war, Tunney injured his left elbow when he went crashing to the floor during a basketball game. Because of the persistent pain, Tunney eventually went to see a doctor, who put the elbow in a plaster cast for five weeks.

When the cast was removed, it became apparent that his left arm had atrophied and was shorter than his right. Though the pain was gone, Tunney was in no condition to fight or even train by the time the United States entered the war. That hardly mattered to Tunney, though, since boxing suddenly seemed trite in comparison with the war in Europe. Less than a month after Congress formally declared war, a Marine recruiting poster that read "Marines, Always First to Fight," caught Tunney's eye and convinced him that he wanted to be a marine. Without telling anyone, he went to a Marine recruiting station in Union Square in lower Manhattan on May 10 to enlist. But he was rejected on the ground that his left arm was partially paralyzed.

Determined to heal as soon as possible, Tunney went for several treatments at Bellevue Hospital in Manhattan. He also tried a number of home remedies that friends and relatives had suggested, and went to two doctors for heat treatments and massages. When the second doctor recommended that Tunney get an outdoor job that required some physical exercise, he reluctantly quit his job with the Ocean Steamship Company, where he'd been promoted to rate clerk and his weekly pay had soared from five to seventeen dollars in five years. At the advice of a friend, he became a lifeguard for the summer of 1917 at a beach in Keansburg, New Jersey, and worked nights as a bouncer at a local tavern. An excellent swimmer, Tunney had no trouble passing the lifeguard test and found that swimming about a mile before going on duty each morning after having done several miles of roadwork was a good way to stay fit.

By Labor Day weekend, when Tunney's tour as a lifeguard and bouncer ended, the arm was as sore as it had been when he went to Keansburg in June as a result of a friendly sparring session with another lifeguard. He became even more upset when he was unable to get his old job back at the Ocean Steamship Company, where business had slacked off dramatically. Not many people wanted to travel to Europe by ship with German submarines lurking in the North Atlantic. In need of money, but with his arm still bothering him, Tunney decided to fight again in the fall of 1917. It would be his first fight in eight months, and, in light of the condition of his left arm and a lack of adequate training, he didn't know what to expect. What he did know was that his father, now in his mid-fifties, was slowing down and making less money on the docks, and that his family needed financial help. Rarely using his left hand, Tunney won both fights easily.

Tunney, still fighting as a middleweight—maximum weight 160 pounds—started off 1918 with a second-round knockout on a left hook to the jaw demonstrating that his left arm seemed to be getting better. The fight earned Tunney his biggest purse yet, forty dollars, the equivalent of about two hundred dollars today. But it also made him feel guilty, knowing that his purse was more than what privates in the Army or the Marines made in an entire year while risking their lives in France. So he decided he would fight no more until his elbow was healed and he was able to enlist in the Marines and, he hoped, be able to serve overseas. Meanwhile, he could at least do something that was related to the war effort.

He did, getting a job on the Hudson River waterfront in Hoboken, New Jersey, which required him to check out aircraft parts that were being shipped to Army Air Corps bases in England and France. At twenty-five dollars a week the pay was relatively good, and far more than what the uniformed soldiers assigned to the pier earned in a month. Having to work among the soldiers while knowing they were earning far less exacerbated Tunney's sense of guilt at not being in the service, but in a small way he knew he was doing something to help the war effort. Despite the long hours he put in on the Hoboken pier, Tunney kept his night job as an athletic instructor at P.S. 41 in Greenwich Village, which meant that he was now the primary breadwinner in the Tunney household.

On a friend's recommendation, Tunney went to see a doctor on the Upper West Side of Manhattan who specialized in muscular ailments. It was an excellent recommendation, since the doctor, a German immigrant, diagnosed Tunney's arm problem as traumatic neuritis, and after five months of thrice-weekly treatments he cured the problem with an electrically operated therapeutic device that the doctor himself had invented. Assured by the doctor that he was now certain to pass the physical test given by the Marines, Tunney returned to the Union Square Marine recruiting station on July 17. This time, he passed the physical examination, was sworn in as a fifteen-dollars-a-month United States Marine, and was told to report for duty the next day.

No one at the Marine Corps base in Parris Island had ever heard of James Joseph "Gene" Tunney. He may have gone unbeaten in fourteen professional fights, but whatever coverage of those fights there had been was confined to New York and nearby New Jersey newspapers. That was just fine with Tunney. He felt that his boxing career, brief and successful as it may have been, was over. He certainly did not plan to do any boxing while in the Marines, and he had no intention of returning to the sport if he survived the war. At best, he might go back to work at the Ocean Steamship Company, where, someday, who knows? Maybe he'd still rise to dock superintendent.

But boxing soon intruded. During basic training, Tunney's drill sergeant at the Marine base in Parris Island dealt harshly with the recruits under his command, Tunney included, and repeatedly tried to provoke some of the young marines to challenge him with boxing gloves. After being hectored and humiliated in front of fellow recruits, some of the marines did challenge the sergeant, a powerfully built six-footer. In about a half-dozen of the bouts that Tunney saw, the sergeant, who obviously had had some boxing experience, easily outboxed the recruits. One day, the sergeant began to berate Tunney in front of the entire company of recruits. Tunney, aware that such behavior on the part of sergeants was common and that a response by a recruit could only make matters worse, remained silent through the taunts and insults. Finally, the sergeant went too far, calling him several names that Tunney felt cast aspersions on his family.

"Sergeant, nobody can call me that in fun or in earnest," Tunney said, bristling. "I'm ready to fight you anytime you say."

"Fine, Private," the sergeant replied with a smile. "I'll see you after the drill."

Later, with the entire company of recruits gathered in a circle, Tunney and the sergeant stripped to the waist, put on the boxing gloves that the sergeant always brought to his drills, and went at it. Having watched the sergeant box often, Tunney knew exactly what to expect—a wildly swinging opponent determined to end a fight as quickly as possible. That style had worked on recruits with no boxing experience. It would not on Tunney, who at 155 pounds was outweighed by about twenty-five. Ducking under several roundhouse punches that hit nothing but air, Tunney finally unloaded a left hook that caught the sergeant flush on the jaw, sending him reeling to the floor, unconscious, as the company of recruits serenaded Tunney with cheers.

"When he came to, we shook hands," Tunney said, "and we became friends. He was still the sergeant, old and experienced, and I was a rookie."

To Tunney, the fight did more than avenge the abuse that the sergeant had heaped upon him during a drill. It marked him as a boxer at Parris Island. Following basic training, Tunney's battalion of 1,512 enlisted men and forty-five officers boarded the troopship *De Kalb* on September 13 for the two-week-long voyage to the French seaport city of Brest. As it developed, the fourteen-day voyage was relatively uneventful. For Tunney, though, a chance meeting aboard the *De Kalb* with another marine would change his life forever.

Tunney had always liked to read. As a boy, he had devoured the Rover Boys series and several books by James Fenimore Cooper, and while reading Alexandre Dumas's *The Three Musketeers,* had flights of fancy where he envisioned himself as D'Artagnan. In his late teens, while already boxing, he had become enthralled by the works of Jack London, particularly a novel entitled *The Game,* about an idealistic young fighter who is killed during a bout—and which almost convinced him to quit the ring. In the Marines, Tunney soon learned, there would be ample time to read, although most marines, like most fighters at training camps, were far more inclined to fill their spare time by playing cards or shooting craps.

That was not the case with the clerk of Company D of the 11th Regiment at Quantico. While packing his kit the day before the 1st Battalion of the regiment left for Philadelphia to board the troopship, Tunney noticed that the clerk was jamming two books into an already packed kit, which he would be compelled to carry on his back wherever he went, whether it was on long training marches or into battle. Casting a close eye on the books, Tunney saw that they were leatherbound works by William Shakespeare. Tunney was amazed.

Having played the Prince in the court scene in *Romeo and Juliet* at the age of thirteen at St. Veronica's School, Tunney had at least a modicum of familiarity with Shakespeare. Curious, and looking for more reading material, he asked the clerk if he could read one of the Bard's books that he had brought along. Glad to accommodate an apparently literary-bent marine, the clerk gave Tunney *The Winter's Tale*, one of Shakespeare's most abstruse works.

Like most first-time readers, Tunney found reading *The Winter's Tale* rough-going. The company clerk, knowing Tunney was struggling, tutored him on the Bard, interpreting and clarifying some of the more difficult passages, and explaining Shakespeare's use of diction. Fortunately for Tunney, he and the clerk were in the same battalion and stayed together for several weeks after the *De Kalb* arrived in France, with the clerk continuing to tutor Tunney on the complex nuances of the Shakespearean style. Still, Tunney had to read *The Winter's Tale* about a dozen times to understand it. As he was to say years later, reading other Shakespeare works such as *Macbeth* and *The Merchant of Venice* would be easy by comparison.

While involved in bayonet training at a Marine camp near Brest, Tunney once again found himself involved in an unwanted fight. Because of overcrowded conditions, unrelenting rain, heat, mud, and demanding drill instructors, most of the marines were on edge—all of which may have accounted for the fight. "For some reason or other, one of the huskier members of the company picked a fight with me," Tunney was to recall some years later.

As with the sergeant in boot camp at Parris Island, it was a mistake that the marine would soon regret.

"What are you doing? Looking for trouble?" Tunney said, trying to avoid a physical confrontation with the belligerent marine. Without warning, the marine landed a punch that sent Tunney careening into a mud flat. Managing to avoid going down, Tunney spun around and hit the marine with a left hook to the jaw that sent him tumbling into a ditch just as a gunnery sergeant arrived on the scene. Hearing Tunney's side of the story, which was corroborated by several other marines, the sergeant took no action. Several bystanders told the sergeant they had never seen such a left hook. Neither, the sergeant replied, had he. And Tunney's left hook was not his best punch.

Several weeks later, Tunney's brigade of about 250 men left by troop train for Gièvres, a quaint French village in the center of France, about seventy-five miles southwest of Paris. There, the year before, a sprawling base had been built by Army engineers as a staging area, from where American forces went into battle, and where wounded soldiers and marines were brought for treatment. Adjacent to the base were an airfield, warehouses, and hangars that had been established at the same time for the nascent American Army Air Corps. With the actual fighting only a few miles away, Tunney's adrenaline began to flow, much as it did on the day of a fight. But Tunney, after months of preparing to fight the Germans, was in for a disappointment. So was the rest of Company D of the 5th Brigade of the 11th Marine Regiment. Instead of going into battle in what turned out to be the waning days of the war, Tunney and the rest of his company's leathernecks were assigned to guard the aircraft hangars and the hulking warehouses that contained observation balloons and other supplies at the Romorantin air base. As it was, the call to arms for Company D—nor for any other members of the 11th Regiment—never did come, since Germany surrendered and the war ended on November 11, 1918. As celebrations broke out on the base and in Gièvres and the nearby villages of Pruniers and Selles-sur-Cher, Tunney and most of his comrades in Company D were engulfed with mixed emotions—relief and elation that no more Americans would die or be wounded, but also an unspoken sense of disappointment that all the training they had received would never be tested on a battlefield. To Tunney, as he was to say in later years, the feeling was akin to that of a fighter who, after training for months for a big bout, suddenly is told that the fight has been called off. He knew that the comparison was frivolous in light of the enormity of the casualties sustained by American forces in France—126,000 killed in action or dead of wounds or disease and another 235,000 wounded. And those numbers paled to French and English losses of more than a million and a half dead and more than four million wounded.

When the war ended, Tunney had been in service for only five months, much too short a stretch for him to expect to be discharged soon. Shortly after he got to the base, Tunney was among about a thousand soldiers, marines, and airmen who turned out for a boxing program involving servicemen attached to Gièvres and the air base at Romorantin. On this particular night, base championships in various weight classes were being decided. When it came time for the middleweight bout, involving fighters weighing between 148 and 160 pounds, an Army captain serving as the ring announcer said that one of the fighters had failed to appear and that unless a volunteer would take his place, the boxer already in the ring would win the title by default. Seated nearby, the gunnery sergeant who had happened upon Tunney's impromptu one-punch knockout of the other marine a few weeks earlier outside Brest spotted Tunney.

"Go on, get in there," the sergeant said to Tunney. "You can lick him."

"No way," responded Tunney, suddenly realizing he had made a mistake in having told the sergeant that he had had several professional fights before joining the Marines.

"Go in and fight him, and I'll give you a day off from guard duty," the sergeant said, aware of how much Tunney and his fellow marines disliked the tedious and boring task of patrolling the balloon sheds.

Without any knowledge of how well, or how poorly, the soldier already in the ring could fight, Tunney found himself seduced by the sergeant's offer. His fellow marines, vastly outnumbered by the assembled soldiers, let out a collective roar as Tunney, wearing hobnailed boots, long pants, and a regulation khaki shirt headed for the corner of the ground-level canvas opposite the soldier clad in shorts and high-topped boxing shoes. The soldier, unaware of Tunney's boxing background—as was virtually everyone else in the cavernous YMCA hut in Gièvres—smiled confidently at the sight of this tall, gangly, and obviously unprepared marine.

The doughboy's smile did not last long. Nor did the laughter and taunts that Tunney's ring outfit elicited from the thousands of soldiers in the audience. Though the soldier had progressed to the base middleweight title fight, Tunney quickly determined that he was awkward and amateurish. Even while having to move about in heavy boots that gave him practically no traction on the loosely drawn canvas, and with his timing off from a lack of ring activity, Tunney knew he had nothing to worry about. With the Marine contingent getting louder with every punch Tunney landed, he eventually realized that he had become more than a last-minute substitute in an Army camp boxing bout: he was fighting for Marine Corps pride. Content to box and not try for a knockout against his overmatched opponent, although at that stage Tunney was more of a puncher than a boxer, he won the fight easily, his opponent declining to come out for the third round.

Overnight, Tunney became a celebrity among Company D's 250 marines, who were vastly outnumbered by the more than five thousand soldiers who were usually stationed at Gièvres and at the Romorantin air base, even in the months after the Armistice. For soldiers and marines restricted to the base on any particular night, boxing programs were the weekly highlights and, in a way, a respite for many troops. For a sport long held in disrepute by most adult Americans, boxing's exposure to many of the two million American servicemen who went abroad during World War I is believed to have helped popularize the sport after the war. Similarly, boxing programs at bases in the United States, which were often open to civilians, also created new fans and helped pave the way for the legalization of a sport that was illegal in most states during most of the nineteenth century and during much of the first two decades of the twentieth.

Because of their far greater numbers, champions in almost every one of the eight traditional boxing weight divisions at tournaments at bases in France or England during the war were soldiers and not marines. That Tunney was able to do so well after being conscripted from the crowd by a sergeant made him all the more popular among his fellow marines. He was to become even more popular in the weeks to come, knocking out a former professional fighter—who outweighed him by about forty pounds—to also win the base heavyweight title.

As a result of his victory, Tunney got assurance from his company commander that continued success in the ring would mean more time off for training and even less of the monotonous patrolling that Tunney had come to loathe. Amid the postwar boredom that Company D was experiencing at Gièvres, Tunney, the company commander knew all too well, was serving as a morale-booster. If the Marine company's members couldn't yet go home—and would not for months to come, since they had been in France for less than two months—they had a peacetime hero in their midst who seemed capable of licking any soldier-boxer from the middleweight to heavyweight classes. And now that he apparently was going to get more time to prepare for his fights, Tunney might just be unbeatable, the company commander felt, and, well now, wouldn't that be terrific for morale among a restless group of marines?

Within a matter of months, Tunney's reputation as a fighter had extended to U.S. military posts throughout Europe. Two weeks after his second victory, Tunney knocked out another former professional fighter, and then, a week later, another one. By now, to his Marine superiors, it seemed that Tunney, whose previous fights in France had all been held at Romorantin, was ready for a bigger stage: Paris. During that period Tunney was to see a good soldier-boxer execute a maneuver that he himself would adopt in the future, most notably in his most famous fight. The fighter's name was Jackie Clark and, whenever he found himself in trouble during a bout, Clark circled backward and away from his opponent, a novel move for a fighter at the time. Thereafter, Tunney did the same.

With the war over, it had become somewhat common to match the best U.S. military boxers against French professional fighters in front of audiences comprised of American and French doughboys and whatever civilians were interested in attending. Tunney's first fight in the French capital was against a leading French middleweight, Henri "K.O." Marchand, whom Tunney knocked out with a right uppercut to the stomach in the second round.

For all of his success in the ring, which had made him a celebrity of sorts at Romorantin—indeed, even many of the Army and Air Corps personnel had become his fans—Tunney still had to do guard duty. But he kept on winning in the ring, with his biggest victory coming in Paris when he beat Bob Martin, a U.S. Army military policeman who would eventually win the American Expeditionary Forces heavyweight championship and who outweighed Tunney by thirty-five pounds. And since Tunney's victory was reported in *Stars and Stripes,* the Army newspaper that circulated throughout Europe, all of a sudden almost every doughboy in France, Germany, and England knew about the marine giant killer from Gièvres.

In a further effort to bolster the morale of the million-plus American servicemen who were still in Europe months after the Armistice, the Army decided to stage an American Expeditionary Forces boxing tournament that would be held throughout France, with the semifinals and finals in Paris. One of the major incentives for a soldier, sailor, or marine to enter was the opportunity to avoid customary military duties and train for the upcoming tournament. Not to mention the opportunity to spend some time in Paris for those fortunate enough to go that far in the tournament, and, beyond that, to establish a reputation as a fighter.

Typifying the military, most of the participants had no choice as to whether they wanted to take part, but were entered by their commanding officers, who had a vested interest in the success of a fighter or fighters from a particular post, base, or ship. Not only would it be good for morale, but a soldier-fighter who won a title could reflect on the commanding officer who had sent him into battle, so to speak, in the first place. Thus, Tunney really had no choice when he was entered in the light heavyweight tournament, even though, at 165 pounds, he was ten pounds lighter than the maximum for that weight division. It did not matter, as Tunney won eighteen consecutive fights over a two-month period to qualify for the semifinals in Paris. In doing so, Tunney mainly relied on his punching power, especially a potent right hand that was capable of knocking out an opponent with one punch. That would turn out to be ironic since, in later years, Tunney would become renown for his boxing ability, while looked upon as a fighter who lacked a knockout punch.

"I was no Fancy Dan boxer in those days," Tunney was to say later. "I became one later because I could never see any percentage in exchanging punches on an even basis with somebody who can hit as well as you can." Bad hands also would be a factor.

Actually, Tunney was forced to rely more on boxing ability than his punching prowess very late in the AEF tournament, which proved beneficial, since it made him a much better boxer than he had been before joining the Marines and during his previous fights as a marine. In his eighteenth fight, in Tours, Tunney caught his opponent flush on the jaw with a right cross. The punch left his Army foe unconscious, but it also broke the knuckle above the middle finger of Tunney's right hand. The victory qualified Tunney for the semifinals in Paris two weeks later, but there was considerable doubt whether he would be able to compete. But even with a broken knuckle that would render virtually useless his "Sunday Punch"—his right cross to the head—in the AEF semifinals, Tunney knew that he had to fight on. Marines and soldiers fought on during the recent war with far worse injuries, he knew, and so some of his Romorantin comrades might not be inclined to be sympathetic to a boxer who had not seen action during the war dropping out of a boxing tournament because of a broken knuckle. Then, too, if he did drop out, he knew he would go back to guard duty.

In what was by far the biggest sports event held in Paris since before the war broke out, a capacity crowd of about 14,000 packed the Cirque de Paris sports arena for the semifinals. From the military came General John Pershing, the commander of American forces in France, and high-ranking members of his staff, along with top military brass from the American Navy, Marines, and Air Corps and from France and England, plus diplomats and leading political figures from about a dozen European countries.

Despite his injured, and still swollen, right hand, Tunney won all ten rounds of his semifinal fight against a veteran professional named K.O. Sullivan while relying almost entirely on his swift left jab and a punishing left uppercut.

Now Tunney had two more weeks to rest his injured right hand until the AEF light heavyweight championship fight against Ted Jamieson, a former amateur champion in the United States. For someone who had no intention of so much as sparring while in the Marines, here was Tunney, a reluctant warrior whose Marine boxing career was spawned by a bout with a sadistic drill sergeant in boot camp, on the verge of fighting for an AEF championship.

On the night of his championship fight with Jamieson, Tunney's right hand was better, but not much. Yet he knew that he would have to use it against Jamieson, who from the start had been favored to win the AEF light heavyweight title. He knew that he might break the knuckle again. But since this was his last fight in the Marines—or at least so he thought—he had nothing to lose, and to beat Jamieson he had to use the right. Nobody was going to beat Ted Jamieson with one hand.

Once again, the Cirque de Paris was jammed to its capacity for the AEF finals on April 26, 1919, with General Pershing and other high-ranking officers in a predominantly U.S. Army crowd, which also included several hundred marines, many of them members of Tunney's own Company D at Gièvres who had managed to get brief furloughs so that they could make the seventy-five-mile trip to Paris and root for Tunney.

As fast on his feet as Tunney, if not faster, Jamieson was heavily favored to win. During the early rounds, Tunney had trouble getting in his left jab, or indeed doing anything with his left, mainly because Jamieson knew he would be relying almost exclusively on that hand. By midway through the ten-round bout, Tunney realized it was time to throw the right, and throw it hard, hopefully when Jamieson least expected it. When he did, Jamieson, rather than try to block the blow, lowered his head and absorbed the punch on the crown. It was a brilliant tactical maneuver. Instantly, a flash of pain surged through Tunney's right hand and up his right arm. He knew immediately that he had again broken the damaged knuckle, but was able to conceal the pain.

Despite the break, Tunney continued to mix in right-hand blows with his left jabs, hooks, and uppercuts, but restricted them to Jamieson's body. Every one that landed—even to the body—hurt, but Tunney knew that without a two-handed attack he had no chance of winning. Fortunately for Tunney and his Marine supporters, he had saved his best. No way, he told himself, was he going to let down this small group of leathernecks so vastly outnumbered by Jamieson's Army supporters. In the tenth and final round, Tunney ducked under a right-hand punch and unloaded a vicious left hook that caught Jamieson on the jaw and dropped him to the canvas. Jamieson got up at eight, but the punch, along with some masterful boxing by Tunney, won him the round and the decision.

When the announcement was made, Tunney stood dazed and incredulous, finding it almost incomprehensible that he made it through the last three fights of the AEF tournament with a broken knuckle. Descending on his corner in a joyous frenzy, chanting "Tunney, Tunney, Tunney," the marines in the crowd engulfed the underdog AEF champion, slapping Tunney on the back as he smiled broadly. It was like no moment he had ever savored in his life.

Through the entire tournament, Tunney's mind-set was that boxing for him remained a diversion and that in no way could it be a stepping-stone to the resumption of a professional career that he felt had been ephemeral when he joined the Marines. But on this glorious April night in Paris, after receiving a bronze plaque emblematic of his victory, Tunney's thoughts drifted as he walked back to his dressing room amid lingering cheers. *Maybe all of this—winning a tournament I did not want to enter, and with only one good hand at that—was some sort of destiny,* Tunney thought. *Maybe it was meant to convince me that I was destined to be a fighter, after all, and that perhaps I actually could go somewhere in boxing once I get out of the Marines. If I was able to beat some pretty good fighters in the AEF tournament with a broken knuckle on one hand, maybe I could do even better as a professional with two good hands. Certainly I have nothing to lose by trying.*

A few weeks later, while in Paris for an Inter-Allied Games competition, Tunney received staggering news from home. His nineteen-year-old brother, John, who was three years younger, had been shot to death in a Manhattan nightclub on June 29. According to an assistant district attorney, a thirty-year-old man named James Fitzpatrick shot and killed Tunney after he accidentally dropped some cigarette ashes on the dress of a woman dancer at the Moon Club on West 13th Street, only a few blocks north of where the Tunney family lived. Fitzpatrick, who pleaded guilty to manslaughter, subsequently was sentenced to nine to twenty years in Sing Sing Prison.

Beside himself with grief, Tunney was particularly worried about the impact his brother's death would have on his parents and his brother Tom, a year younger than John, and his four sisters, Maude, and Rose, who were in their twenties; Margaret, who was fifteen; and Agnes, who was twelve. Tunney yearned to be at his family's side and to attend John's funeral, but it was not possible. He was thousands of miles from home and it was years before the advent of transatlantic air travel—indeed, Charles Lindbergh's epochal New York–to–Paris solo flight was still eight years away. Gene Tunney would have to mourn his brother's death alone in France. As the oldest son in a family of seven children, Tunney was extremely close to, and protective of, his brothers and sisters. Besides boxing with John and Tom at home, Tunney roughhoused with them and made sure to include them in pickup baseball and other games he played in the West Village streets or on the nearby docks. Though he did not play with them as much, he was equally protective of his sisters—to the point of often going to their girlfriends' homes when they went out at night as teenagers to escort them home through what was a very tough neighborhood.

Helping to assuage Tunney's grief somewhat was a chance meeting at the Inter-Allied Games with a remarkable young athlete named Eddie Eagan that would develop into a lifelong friendship. A student at Yale before he entered the Army as a lieutenant in the field artillery, Eagan had won the AEF middleweight championship and would also capture the title in the same weight category at the Inter-Allied Games. After the war, Eagan would return to Yale to captain a new boxing team, run track, and excel in the classroom. While at Yale, Eagan won a gold medal in the 1920 Summer Olympics in Antwerp, Belgium, in the light heavyweight class; captured the American amateur heavyweight championship in 1921, the year he graduated; and then earned a Rhodes scholarship. While studying at Oxford, Eagan also captured the British Empire heavyweight championship, becoming the first American to win a British amateur boxing title.

Twelve years after winning a gold medal in 1920, Eagan would be a member of the American bobsled team that captured the gold medal at the 1932 Olympics in Lake Placid, New York, making him the only athlete to win gold medals in both the Summer and Winter Games. After graduating from Yale and then Harvard Law School, Eagan became a federal prosecutor, attained the rank of lieutenant colonel in the Army Air Corps during World War II, served as chairman of the New

York State Athletic Commission, which oversees boxing in New York state, and became a law partner in a prominent Manhattan law firm.

Tunney took quickly to Eagan, attracted to him not only by his boxing ability but for his intelligence and broad range of interests beyond the realm of sports. Eagan had learned how to box while growing up on a cattle ranch in Colorado, and by the age of sixteen had won the amateur welterweight boxing championship of the West. He followed that up in 1918, while he was at Yale, by winning both the amateur middleweight and heavyweight championships of the West during tournaments in Denver and San Francisco. During that period, Eagan met and sparred with another Coloradan, Jack Dempsey, who on July 4, 1919, while both Eagan and Tunney were still in France, knocked out Jess Willard in the third round in Toledo, Ohio, to win the world heavyweight title. Intrigued by the Dempsey phenomenon and after learning that Eagan had sparred with Dempsey, Tunney peppered Eagan with questions about the new heavyweight champion—his style of fighting, his punching power, his ability to take a punch, and so on. Obviously impressed by Dempsey, Eagan marveled in particular at his punching ability and unrelenting aggressiveness, and, in Tunney, found a rapt listener. Before they parted in late July, Eagan suggested that Tunney join him at Yale after his discharge from the Marines.

"You'd make the football team. For sure," Eagan said to Tunney.

Eagan was to smile at Tunney's reply. "Eddie, I won't have any time for Yale," Tunney said, neglecting to mention that he had had only one year of high school. "I'm going to win the heavyweight championship of the world."

While stationed at Romorantin, Tunney had met a Marine corporal named Jack McReynolds who had been a sportswriter in Kansas City. McReynolds had covered several of Dempsey's fights in the West, and Tunney, like other American servicemen abroad, had begun to hear and read a lot about Dempsey. The young fighter's penchant for first-round knockouts and general ring savagery had made him a sensation and, moreover, earned him the shot at Willard's title.

If Dempsey were to lose eventually, McReynolds told Tunney, it would be to a boxer and not a puncher: his brawling style left him vulnerable, particularly to jabs and to a straight right. That, of course, presupposed that the boxer could avoid Dempsey's murderous left hook, which had knocked out more than two dozen opponents, or his damaging rapid-fire combinations. If the left hook could render an opponent senseless, so, too, could his powerful right cross or the combinations. And he most certainly could take a punch. Indeed, there was little margin for error by a Dempsey opponent.

"Is he really that good?" Tunney asked.

"He's very good," McReynolds replied. "He'll murder Jess Willard and take the championship when they meet."

"What's he like?" Tunney persisted.

"He's a big Jack Dillon," McReynolds responded.

Tunney was instantly struck by the analogy. He knew that Dillon was an outstanding fighter who had held the light heavyweight title from 1914 until 1916. He also knew that Dillon was a highly aggressive fighter who, fighting out of a crouch, constantly stalked opponents while throwing a barrage of punishing blows to both the head and body. But Tunney also knew that Dillon, known as "Jack the Giant Killer," had had trouble with skillful boxers like Mike Gibbons and Battling Levinsky who, in their tenth meeting in October of 1916, had taken away Dillon's title on a twelve-round decision.

McReynolds's assessment of Dempsey's style heartened Tunney, who although essentially a methodical boxer with extraordinary footwork and exceptional defensive skills, had demonstrated that he could knock out an opponent with one punch, usually his right.

"Then perhaps Dempsey can be beaten by clever boxing," Tunney said.

"Yes, Dempsey can be beaten by speed, defense, science, form," McReynolds replied. "When Jack Dempsey loses, it won't be because he's outfought, but because he's outboxed."

The more they talked about Dempsey, the more Tunney began to feel that perhaps he, with his vastly improving boxing skills, might be just the boxer to eventually beat the fighter that sportswriters were now calling "The Man Killer."

Aware of Tunney's limited experience and some obvious raw points, McReynolds smiled at the thought.

"Gene, you're young, you're fast, you're clever, you can take it," McReynolds said, obviously trying to encourage the young and still somewhat green AEF light heavyweight champion. "It ought to be possible for you to do that someday."

"I will," Tunney said. "I will."

On July 29, 1919, nine and a half months after arriving in France, Tunney and more than three thousand other members of the 11th Regiment left from Brest on the troopship *Orizaba* and arrived in Hampton Roads, Virginia, nine days later, on August 6. After almost two weeks at the Marine base in Quantico, Tunney was discharged on August 18 and several hours later boarded a train for the seventeen-hour ride to Pennsylvania Station in New York. Tunney may have won the AEF light heavyweight title, but there was no one to greet him when he arrived in Manhattan. Though he had told his parents in letters that he would be returning home soon, he decided to surprise them.

When Tunney left home for the Marines, he was six feet tall and weighed 158 pounds. Now, just a year later, he was 6' 1" and seventeen pounds heavier. But the country had changed significantly more than he had. Women could now vote—the Nineteenth Amendment had finally passed on June 4, 1919 and would be ratified August 18, 1920—but you could no longer buy a drink, at least legally, because the Eighteenth Amendment would take effect on January 16, 1920, of the same year, incredibly enough, just when tens of thousands of American servicemen were returning from France and looking forward to, among other things, having a beer or two with old friends at a downtown bar or at the neighborhood saloon. That hardly mattered to Tunney, who, like Dempsey, rarely took a drink. On the other hand, professional boxing, which had been outlawed again in 1917 in New York—it was also illegal in most other states—was still illegal, although a young state senator from Greenwich Village by the name of James J. Walker was working on a bill that would make it legal once more, at least in New York.

As his train got closer to New York, Tunney could hardly wait to get home to see his family. Certainly, with his brother John having died only two months earlier, it would be a bittersweet reunion with his parents, his brother, and his three sisters. There would be tears, Tunney knew, and there would be hugs and kisses. But he also could hardly wait to get into a boxing ring. He was on a roll, and did not want to delay now that he had decided to become a full-time professional fighter.

Both aboard the ship and the train carrying him home, Tunney felt a void. He had joined the Marines to fight the Germans, but never saw any action. Indisputably, though, there had been an upside. He had found out that he was a better boxer than he thought he was, and had been gratified by the support he got from his Marine comrades and the knowledge that his victories had, to a degree, bolstered their pride. And, he knew, he was lucky. Unlike many other American servicemen who had gone "over there," Tunney had come back alive.

Back in Greenwich Village, Tunney found that few of his old friends, and certainly hardly any other New Yorkers, knew he had won a boxing championship in France, and he was hardly anxious to talk about his boxing exploits in the service when he knew that several hundred doughboys from New York had died in the war. John Tunney, though, had bragged to just about everyone he knew—at church, on the docks, and in the neighborhood saloons—that his son had won the AEF light heavyweight title, and that it was through no fault of his own that he had not seen action.

As the days went on, the grief that had engulfed Tunney over his brother's death abated. It was time to help support his family. His father, now fifty-nine, was beginning to slow down in his work as a stevedore, and who knew how much longer he could continue loading and unloading cargo and luggage. Also, there was no GI Bill of Rights, as there would be after World War II, and apart from a small discharge bonus of fifty dollars, veterans of the Great War were left to shift for themselves. Tunney had served his country, but now it was time to go out and make a living. Maybe he could get back his old job as a rate clerk, or something else, at the Ocean Steamship Company. Certainly he wanted to box professionally again. But the big question on his mind was whether anyone in boxing had any interest in a Marine veteran from New York City who had won a championship in an American Expeditionary Forces tournament in a weight division no one paid much attention to.

*Dempsey awaits the opening bell in his
title fight against Jess Willard.*

FOUR

■

*A
Chance
Meeting*

B y 1920, Tunney was being billed as "The Fighting Marine,"
even though the only fighting he had done during World War I
was in a boxing ring. But no one on a Hudson River ferry
bound from Jersey City to Manhattan on a spring afternoon
seemed to recognize the handsome veteran although he did get more
than a few glances from some women passengers as he reclined on a
wooden bench in the cabin.

Conversely, just about everyone aboard who got so much as a
glimpse of another passenger—a swarthy man, also in his twenties, with
blue-black hair and a severe case of five o'clock shadow—instantly knew
who he was. Ever since his knockout of Jess Willard in Toledo, Ohio, on
the previous Fourth of July to win the world heavyweight title, Jack
Dempsey had been everywhere—in newspapers, magazines, movie
newsreels, even on advertising billboards. In less than a year's time, he
had become America's best-known athlete—bigger in stature than Babe

Ruth, baseball's "Sultan of Swat." Like Ruth, Dempsey also had a color-ful name that had been bestowed on him by sportswriter and fellow Coloradan Damon Runyon—"The Manassa Mauler," after the Col-orado town of Manassa where he was born and lived for about eight years—and already had become regarded as probably the most devastat-ing puncher in boxing history.

Dempsey looked relaxed, but inwardly he was worried. In a few months he would go on trial in San Francisco largely based on charges by his estranged wife that he lied to the government in seeking a draft de-ferment in 1917 during the recent war. Dempsey knew the trial would be marked by lurid and salacious testimony that would be highly embar-rassing for him and his family and could affect his career as a boxer. Eventually, Dempsey's presence caught the eye of the ex-marine, who was returning to his Greenwich Village home after signing a contract for his next fight in Jersey City and who had never seen Dempsey before. Turning to his manager, Billy Roche, Gene Tunney said, "I can't believe it's him. He's been on my mind ever since I won the AEF title. I've got to go over and meet him."

"Why don't you wait until you meet him in the ring," Roche said with a smile. "You've been saying right along that you're going to beat him someday."

Tunney returned the smile. He knew Roche was reminding him, good-naturedly, that he had told him and a number of others that he was already convinced he would beat Dempsey and take away his title, while conceding that he was not quite ready to try. Roche, a longtime manager, knew Tunney was a good prospect, but that at around 170 pounds he was more likely to win the light heavyweight title (as he had done in the AEF tournament) than the heavyweight crown held by Dempsey. And that even if that were to happen, Roche knew it was years away for the twenty-three-year-old Tunney; though he had not lost a fight, Tunney had only twenty-two professional bouts under his belt. Further, Tunney still had not fought a main event, not uncommon in an era when many fighters did not turn professional until they had more than a hundred amateur fights. (Tunney had had only a few be-fore turning professional at the age of eighteen in 1915.)

Hesitant, but exuding—perhaps *feigning*—confidence, Tunney

strode over to where Dempsey was reading a newspaper and quickly introduced himself. Though they had never met, Tunney felt reasonably certain that Dempsey had at least read about or been told of how Tunney had won the AEF light heavyweight title.

"Nice to meet you," Dempsey said in his incongruously high-pitched voice while shaking hands with Tunney. "How are things going?"

"All right, except that I'm having trouble with my right hand," Tunney replied. "I hurt the middle knuckle boxing in France more than a year ago, and it still hasn't healed."

Taking Tunney's right hand in his own huge hands—much bigger than Tunney's—Dempsey looked at it closely while gently feeling the sore knuckle. Tunney was touched, both by Dempsey's warmth, and his obvious interest in the injured knuckle. All the more so after Dempsey gave him some advice that would eventually help Tunney: to put black tape on the good knuckles on both sides of the injured one before putting on his boxing gloves. That way, Dempsey explained, when Tunney landed a punch with his right hand, the padding of tape on the good knuckles would absorb the shock from the injured knuckle.

The conversation lasted only a few minutes, but long enough for Tunney to sense Dempsey's friendliness, gentleness, and willingness to help a fellow fighter, even a relatively obscure one. After shaking Dempsey's hand again and thanking him profusely for his advice, Tunney returned to Billy Roche's side, anxious to tell him how gracious Dempsey had been to him. The Manassa Mauler may have projected an image of ferocity, but Tunney knew now that outside the ring he was a soft-spoken and friendly man who you could not help but like. For the rest of the ferry ride back to Manhattan, Tunney was fixated on Dempsey, plying Roche with questions about the new champion.

Did he really hit as hard as they were saying? Was his left hook actually far more dangerous than his right? Could he take a punch? Smiling again, while sensing Tunney's fascination with Dempsey, Roche answered every question that he could. He also told Tunney that anyone who could knock out Jess Willard had to be a very good fighter. After all, only one other fighter had done that, and that had happened in 1911 when the 6′ 6″ Willard was just starting out at the advanced boxing age of twenty-nine.

Debarking from the ferry, Tunney could hardly wait to get home to tell his parents, brother, and sisters how he had just met the great Jack Dempsey, and how nice he was. John Tunney already liked the new champion, both because he was part Irish and because he had taken the name of one of the best fighters ever born in Ireland, the original Jack Dempsey, the Nonpareil, for whom the elder Tunney had cheered wildly during a number of his fights on Coney Island and in Manhattan in the 1880s.

For all of his success as a Marine boxer, Tunney did not find himself in demand by fight managers or promoters when he returned home. Broke and unwilling to ask his financially strapped parents for any money, Tunney found himself unable to buy the boxing equipment he needed—shoes, trunks, punching bags, jump ropes, and so on—or to join a gymnasium where he could work out. Desperate for money and frustrated over his inability to attract interest, Tunney contacted the chief clerk at the Ocean Steamship Company to see if he could get his old clerk's job back, but found that the job had long since been filled. It was a fate similar to that of many other veterans who had expected, or at least had hoped, to get their old jobs back.

Reduced to running to and from Central Park and shadowboxing to keep in shape, Tunney eventually attracted the attention of Sammy Kelly, a former featherweight boxer from Greenwich Village who had become a boxing trainer and was interested in managing Tunney. During a subsequent meeting, it did not take Kelly long to become impressed with the former marine, whom he had heard about from several boxing associates, including Billy Roche. Asked by Kelly what he hoped to achieve as a professional fighter, Tunney said he planned to—and indeed was convinced that he would—take away Jack Dempsey's title. Kelly smiled, beguiled by the handsome young boxer's candor and confidence. He soon agreed to manage Tunney, advancing him a hundred dollars for the gear he needed and arranging for Tunney to train and spar at the City Athletic Club in Manhattan, where many of the city's best fighters worked out.

It was at the City Athletic Club that Tunney met Bernard Gimbel, a former football player and boxer at the University of Pennsylvania and son of one of the founders of the Gimbel Brothers department store chain. A good boxer who chose to go into business rather than professional boxing, Gimbel sparred occasionally with Tunney and they became good friends. Like Tunney, Gimbel approached boxing in an analytical fashion and, despite his relative inexperience in the sport, was able to point out what he thought were flaws in Tunney's technique. The friendship would be long-lasting, and Tunney, in the years to come, would credit Gimbel for having given him advice that made him a more polished fighter. At the City Athletic Club it soon became evident to Gimbel and virtually everyone else who got to spar with or just watch Tunney that he was an outstanding prospect. Now, Tunney felt, if only Sammy Kelly could get him in the ring. He was eager to fight, both because he needed the money and to convince managers and trainers that they had been mistaken in not seeking him out since his return from France.

Eventually, a business trip to Cuba by Kelly proved fortuitous for Tunney. To replace Kelly, Tunney chose Billy Roche. Tunney knew that Roche was a highly regarded and well-connected manager who was more likely than Sammy Kelly to get him fights. Roche, on the other hand, knew Tunney was a very talented boxer, already capable of beating many established light heavyweights and apt to do well financially both for himself and, of course, for Roche.

Successful managers of the era like Roche, Jack "Doc" Kearns, and Dumb Dan Morgan (who was called "Dumb" much like a three-hundred-pound man is called "Tiny") knew when they had a good prospect, and were smart enough to nurture their young tiger along. The trick was never to overmatch a talented young fighter, but at the same time not to restrict his opposition to pushovers (known in the trade as "tomato cans") who would merely serve as human punching bags. What they looked for as their prospects progressed were "worthy opponents," a boxing term that connoted fighters who had decent, but not particularly distinguished, records, and were capable of testing their fighters' resolve and skill. Tunney's first opponent since his discharge, Dan O'Dowd, fit that bill admirably.

Roche knew that O'Dowd could take a punch, but he also knew that he was unlikely to hurt Tunney. He also was aware that, a week before he was to fight Tunney, on December 16, 1919, O'Dowd had fought a close eight-round no-decision bout in Boston with Bill "K.O." Brennan, a leading heavyweight who had fought Dempsey the year before. Several hundred of Tunney's friends and fight fans from Greenwich Village made the short ferry trip across the Hudson River to Bayonne to see Tunney fight for the first time since he had returned from France. They were not disappointed as Tunney completely outclassed the far more experienced O'Dowd.

As the writer covering the fight for the New York *Daily News* reported, Tunney's style "befuddled O'Dowd" and that he hurt O'Dowd with "lightning-like jabs to the jaw and hard shots to the head and body." Despite the punishment O'Dowd absorbed, he never went down and lasted the eight rounds. Tunney's purse totaled two hundred dollars, of which Roche received fifty dollars. The next morning, an elated Tunney dumped all his cash earnings on the kitchen table as the family gathered for breakfast. Aghast at the amount of money her son had earned for a boxing match, Mary Tunney exclaimed, "God bless and spare the hands that can make so much money in one night."

Tunney smiled, surprised at his mother's words, since she and his father, proud as they were at him having won the AEF light heavyweight title, had steadfastly been opposed to him pursuing a boxing career. As it turned out, Mary Tunney had momentarily gotten carried away, and in the next few days reverted to remonstrating with her oldest son about his boxing. Why, she would repeatedly ask, wouldn't he consider becoming a priest? Or maybe a businessman. With his looks and intelligence, she would tell Gene, he would do just fine in either profession, preferably the priesthood. And she and her husband would no longer have to worry about him getting hurt. Through it all, Tunney would smile, touched by his mother's concern for his personal safety, but then would point out that, in the five years he had been boxing, no one had really hurt him. Then, in an effort to allay her concerns, he would tell her that he had no intention of making professional boxing a long career, and that, at most, he only planned to fight for a couple of years. Tunney also would point out that boxing could very likely open lucrative doors for him in the future, and that at a time when he had found it difficult getting work, he already had made $150 for one night's work, ten times more than his father was earning for a week's labor on the Hudson River docks.

Thirteen days after beating O'Dowd, Tunney was back in a New Jersey boxing ring, this time at the Jersey City Armory (armories were popular fight venues at the time), where he knocked out Bob Pierce, another experienced journeyman, in the second round. Again, several hundred friends and boxing fans from Greenwich Village, the vast majority of them Irish, traversed the Hudson by ferry to cheer for Tunney. Delighted at Tunney's following, promoter Charlie Doessererick asked Roche if Tunney could fight again, three days later, at the Bayonne Amusement Park on New Year's Day of 1920. Tunney, hardly spent after his second fight, agreed. Once again, he was matched against a veteran, Whitey Allen, a crude brawler from the Bronx whose talisman was a very potent right cross. As Roche had predicted, Allen threw a barrage of wild and errant right-hand punches at Tunney at the beginning of the fight. As he did, he left his body wide open, whereupon Tunney ripped several wicked uppercuts to Allen's midsection. The pattern continued in the second round before Tunney let loose with a short right-hand punch that caught Allen squarely on the jaw, sending him toppling to the canvas. The referee, who could have counted to twenty, stopped at ten and Tunney had his second straight second-round knockout. Nine more knockouts followed in 1920, giving Tunney eleven in a row, all of them in New Jersey, where Tunney continued to fight, since professional boxing was still outlawed in New York state.

Mainly because of Dempsey and Benny Leonard, the most popular fighters in the early 1920s, Tunney had attracted only scant attention during his first few fights since his discharge from the Marines. But interest began to pick up after his long string of knockouts. His most impressive victory during the stretch of victories leading up to his chance meeting with Dempsey was an eighth-round knockout of another journeyman, Al Roberts, on February 2 in Newark.

Though not a contender, Roberts was known to be a durable fighter. He demonstrated that trait clearly when he was knocked down and got up six times before the referee stopped the bout, which Tunney was to call one of the toughest of his career. The performance, before a crowd of about six thousand, earned Tunney his best coverage to date including an appraisal by the *New York Times* writer who covered the fight that Tunney's victory "stamped the former AEF pugilist as a promising candidate for heavyweight laurels."

Shortly after the Roberts fight, Roche bowed out as Tunney's manager, and Tunney turned to Frank "Doc" Bagley, who had managed him before he went into the Marines. For all of the managers like Billy Roche and Doc Bagley who brought talented young fighters along slowly, often for small purses and not necessarily without a long-range vested interest, there were also many like John "The Barber" Reisler who had both mishandled and cheated Jack Dempsey during Dempsey's less than successful first visit to New York in 1916. Venal, shortsighted, and totally uncaring about their fighters, no matter how talented, managers like Reisler would rush promising young fighters into fairly lucrative bouts against established boxers and then discard them after they had been beaten.

Bad as those managers were, there were others who were worse. In particular, they were the racketeers like Frankie Carbo and Blinky Palermo who, as nominal managers with no background whatsoever in boxing, guided some of their fighters to world titles in the 1940s and 1950s. Their modus operandi was simple, albeit nefarious. They made sure in advance that their fighters would not lose by arranging that opponents would, in the parlance of the ring, take a dive. In such an arrangement, a fighter would consent, to understate the case, not to do his best. Usually the boxer who was part of a fixed fight would go into a swoon and topple to the deck after being hit with either a phantom punch or a blow which in some instances did not have sufficient force behind it to kill a mosquito, let alone knock out a professional boxer.*

---

*Some close-eyed observers thought that was the case in the rematch of the fight between a very young Cassius Clay (later to become Muhammad Ali) and Sonny Liston in which Clay knocked out the former convict and union head-buster to win the heavyweight title. If the outcome of the first fight was suspect to many, the result of the rematch was well neigh scandalous. In the second fight, Liston, who had known links to mobsters, crashed to the floor and rested until he heard the referee intone ten after a right-hand blow by the now Muhammad Ali that seemed to have just grazed Liston's jaw.

Perhaps the classic case of ensuring that a fighter would not lose came a few years later and involved a 6′ 6″ 265-pound former circus strongman from Italy who was imported into the United States in 1930 by a group of New York mobsters at a time when, following the retirement of both Jack Dempsey and Gene Tunney, the heavyweight division had lost its luster. Primo Carnera had been discovered and turned into a fighter in Europe by Leon See, a Frenchman with limited experience as a boxing manager who was "persuaded," for a small portion of Carnera's future earnings, to turn over control of the awkward and light-punching Italian to a group of mobsters headed by Owney "the Killer" Madden, one of New York's most notorious gangsters. See could relate to the mob's machinations, since, it was widely believed, most of Carnera's fights in Europe had been fixed.

In Carnera, who had won sixteen of eighteen professional fights in Europe, eleven by dubious knockouts and all against second-rate fighters, the mobsters saw a potential heavyweight champion who just might excite the sporting world, so long as he had a lot of help along the way. Carnera, they realized, could only win the heavyweight title if they lined up opponents who would be rewarded financially so long as they agreed to fight not to win. Good-natured and naive almost beyond comprehension, Carnera proved easy to mold.

Through the connivance of the mobsters, a well-connected and dishonest manager in a former felon named Billy Duffy, along with a slew of other disreputable boxing managers of fighters willing to take dives, Carnera won his first twenty-four fights by knockouts, with most of them occurring in the first or second round. The short duration of such fights is easily explainable; fighters who had agreed to "go into the tank" felt that the sooner they went down and "took the count" the less their chances of being hurt.

As more and more of his "opponents" collapsed under less than withering assaults, Carnera became a folk hero of sorts, primarily to Italian-Americans, many of whom wondered how "The Ambling Alp," as he was dubbed by a sportswriter, had suddenly become such a good fighter. They, of course, did not know that most of his fights were better suited to the circus sideshows in which he once performed, and that foes who might have the temerity to try to beat Carnera might meet a far worse fate than merely feign being knocked out.

At least one opponent, Leon "Boom Boom" Chevalier, soon realized that Carnera was so awkward that he would have no trouble knocking him out and, in the process, making a name for himself. Chevalier's problem was that he had reportedly agreed not to do his best in the fight in Oakland, California, on April 14, 1930, but then changed his mind. Aware that such things might happen, the mobsters in control of Carnera made it a point to ensure that one of each of his opponent's cornermen was in on that particular night's charade. So when Chevalier returned to his corner between the fifth and sixth rounds, the mob's cornerman ran a sponge with either resin, red pepper, or some other visually impairing irritating substance across his eyes that served to temporarily blind him. Even while floundering around the ring and barely able to see in the sixth round, Chevalier still managed to land a number of punishing punches. But suddenly, following several light blows by Carnera, one of Chevalier's seconds, Bob Perry, threw a towel into the ring, the fistic symbol of surrender by a fighter's corner, whereupon the referee awarded the fight to Carnera on a technical knockout as the crowd—including hundreds of Carnera supporters—erupted with boos. Worse for Perry, he was attacked by a number of spectators as he left the ring and sustained an eye cut. Fortunately Chevalier—who had chosen to live dangerously, not in the face of Carnera's pitty-pat punches, but by defying the mob—lived to fight another day.

Through all of the fixed fights, Carnera—who had an extraordinarily long reach of eighty-five inches—thought he was winning his fights fair and square. Because so many of the "fights" were patently fraudulent, Carnera's entourage made it a point of leaving town in a hurry and rarely having him fight in the same city twice. During his first year under the mob's control, the twenty-four-year-old Carnera fought in no fewer than twenty-two cities, from New York to Los Angeles, with his last two bouts in Barcelona and London. He lost only one of his first thirty-two fights in the United States, a bout that the mob felt did not need fixing, before losing a second time, to eventual heavyweight champ Jack Sharkey in 1931, in a bout that also was on the level.

Carnera, and the mob behind him, had an even better year in 1932, winning twenty-four of twenty-six fights in twenty-one different cities, including London, Paris, Berlin, and Milan. Sixteen of his victories were by knockout as fistic tigers, one after the other, turned toothless in deference to the mob and better purses than they had ever received in the past. The Ambling Alp's only two losses were to journeymen American fighters Larry Gains and Stanley Poreda. But then both of those bouts, for whatever reason, were on the level. In each instance, Carnera often looked puzzled when, after he had landed halfway-decent punches, neither Gains nor Poreda went to the canvas.

Following his loss to Poreda, Carnera won fifteen fights in a row, twelve by knockout, all of them prearranged. The last of those victories, on February 10, 1933, was a thirteenth-round knockout of Ernie Schaaf, who died two months later following surgery to remove a blood clot from his brain. It was generally conceded by medical experts that Schaaf had suffered a serious head injury six months earlier in a fight with Max Baer. Though that was possible, Schaaf still had fought three times between the Baer and Carnera fights, winning twice and losing once without showing any ill effects.

Carnera was devastated by Schaaf's death, convinced that his punches had killed him. Of course the mobsters around him were reluctant to tell Carnera that his less than potent blows had only hastened Schaaf's death.

Nevertheless, the victory over Schaaf, along with the mob's connivance, set up a title fight with Jack Sharkey four months later on June 29, at Madison Square Garden Bowl, an outdoor arena in Long Island City, Queens. Sharkey, who had won the title from Max Schmeling a year earlier after beating Carnera in his previous fight, offered little resistance before being stopped in the sixth round by what appeared to ringsiders to be a very weak Carnera left uppercut. And Sharkey had demonstrated in the past against fighters such as Schmeling and Jack Dempsey that he could take a punch. He had also demonstrated, however, that, like most of Carnera's opponents, he was not always guaranteed to give his best on any given night.

To the delight of millions of Italians the world over, Primo Carnera had become the first Italian to win the heavyweight championship. That he was a raw and crude fighter with no punch didn't matter. Now, having pocketed most of Carnera's winnings and steering him to the heavyweight title, the mob stayed around long enough for Carnera to make two successful title defenses. But under constant fire from sports columnists and others who knew a boxing fraud when they saw one, the mob ended the charade by having Carnera defend his title against Max Baer on June 14, 1934. This time, the fix was not in and Carnera was on his own. Not surprisingly, the Ambling Alp took a beating from Baer, who, though outweighed by fifty-four pounds, knocked Carnera down twelve times before referee Arthur Donovan stopped the bout in the eleventh round. Devoid of the mob's protection in the fight, Carnera was exposed for what he truly was—a mediocre heavyweight who had been deluded into thinking he really could fight. But even though the fix was no longer in, the mobsters profited off the ponderous Carnera by betting on Baer, who they knew was a sure thing in a fight that was level.

As Budd Schulberg wrote in his book *Sparring with Hemingway*, Carnera "was the champion who sprang full and overgrown from the fertile mind of the mob. The mob giveth and there stood, in all his bogus glory, the innocent champion Carnera." Schulberg was so taken by the mob's buildup of Carnera into what he called "the most undeserving and unwelcome champion in modern ring history" that he wrote a novel about it entitled *The Harder They Fall,* which was made into a 1956 movie starring Humphrey Bogart, in his last movie role, and Rod Steiger. Max Baer, who preferred movie acting to fighting, in effect played himself in the roman à clef film.

Fighting largely unknowns after losing his title to Baer, Carnera won his next three fights but then was knocked out by Joe Louis on June 25, 1935, two years before Louis won the heavyweight championship. After losing three consecutive fights, two by knockouts, Carnera retired in 1937 at the age of thirty-one. Virtually broke after having had most of of his earnings looted by the mob that had controlled him, Carnera, desperate for cash, turned to wrestling, where, as had been the case when he performed in circuses in his native Italy and France, he was something of a freak show, although with the cachet of having been the heavyweight champion of the world.

As the veritable antithesis of Carnera, Tunney was perceptive enough to know whether any of his opponents were taking dives. Like Carnera en route to the heavyweight title, Tunney knocked out most of his opponents in 1920, his first full year as a professional. After what was regarded by some boxing writers as his breakthrough victory over Al Roberts, he knocked out his next six foes to raise his knockout streak to eleven, seven of which had occurred within the first two rounds. But in his next fight, on October 25, Tunney reinjured his right hand against a veteran journeyman named Paul Sampson-Korner and was forced to go the eight-round distance in a no-decision bout that many felt Tunney clearly won. Rather than bow out of two commitments and rest the hand, Tunney fought twice more in 1920, both times against Leo Houck, an experienced New Jersey heavyweight, whom he clearly outpointed both times in "no-decision" bouts while fighting almost exclusively with his left hand.

Discouraged by the recurring injuries to his obviously brittle hands, Tunney, in the aftermath of the Houck fight, began to wonder if the injuries were a bad omen. Despite his early success, both while in the service and as a professional, perhaps, he thought, he wasn't meant to be a fighter. Because of the injuries, he would have plenty of time to think about it.

In the meantime, he had noticed in the newspapers that Jack Dempsey was going to fight in Madison Square Garden for the first time on December 14 in his second title defense since he had won the heavyweight title seventeen months earlier. Dempsey's opponent was going to be Bill Brennan, a good but not outstanding heavyweight, whom Dempsey had knocked out two and a half years ago in Milwaukee.

Eight months had passed since Tunney had enjoyed that chance meeting with Dempsey during the ferry trip from New Jersey. Now, for the first time, he would finally get a chance to see the Manassa Mauler in the ring and find out, firsthand, whether he was really as ferocious a fighter as they were saying. Maybe Tunney himself wouldn't be able to fight again for some time, if indeed he decided to continue boxing at all. But he wouldn't miss the Dempsey-Brennan fight for anything in the world.

Dempsey: Slacker or American Hero?

Jack Dempsey "at work" (wearing patent leather shoes) in the Sun Shipyard in Philadelphia during World War I.
ANTIQUITIES OF THE PRIZE RING

I n 1920, Madison Square Garden was the most famous sports arena in the United States, if indeed not the entire world. It was the second of the first four buildings that would bear the name, and indisputably the most elegant.

Designed by one of the era's best-known architects, Stanford White, the second Madison Square Garden occupied almost five acres of what had been Madison Square Park between 23rd and 25th Streets and from Fifth to Madison Avenues. On the same site as the original Garden, the new structure was situated in an area of elegant hotels and fine restaurants and was close to Ladies Mile, the city's high-end shopping district, which stretched along Broadway from 14th to 23rd Streets and included such fashionable stores as A T Stewart's (the first department store in the United States), B. Altman, Lord & Taylor,

Brooks Brothers, and Tiffany's, most of which would later relocate as
the city's commercial district spread northward. Madison Square was
the epicenter of commercial life in New York in the second part of the
nineteenth century and was a logical place for a facility like Madison
Square Garden, which had first been called P. T. Barnum's Monster
Classical and Geographical Hippodrome (in keeping with Barnum's
propensity for hyperbole) and then Gilmore's Garden.

Built in 1889 and 1890 at a cost of $3 million, the second Garden
was one of the city's most ornate structures. To some New Yorkers, it
was also a monument to kitsch. On the outside of the yellow brick and
white terra-cotta building, its most distinguishing features were the
Roman colonnades along the main entrance on Madison Avenue and a
replica of the Giralda Tower of Seville in Spain that was topped by a
copper statue of the goddess Diana the Huntress. The statue towered
thirteen feet high, with Diana revolving on ball bearings so that her
bow and arrow would point into the wind. Spectacular though the
statue was, many New Yorkers found it too risqué, even at three hundred feet above street level, because the noted sculptor, Augustus
Saint-Gaudens, had fashioned her in the nude. Including Diana, the
second Garden was 323 feet high, surpassed in height in New York
only by the Pulitzer Building on Park Row.

A multipurpose structure, the second Madison Square Garden included an auditorium, which was designed to accommodate circuses,
horse shows, and rodeos, among other events. It also included a ball-
room, an opera house, a restaurant, and a rooftop cabaret for dining
and musical comedy productions. The second Garden, like the first,
stood on the site where P. T. Barnum had leased an abandoned railroad warehouse and train depot from the railroad tycoon William
Vanderbilt, who had moved his railroad operations twenty blocks
northward into an edifice that had been named Grand Central Terminal. Barnum had converted the warehouse and depot into an entertainment mecca for his circus and other events. The name was
changed to Gilmore's Garden after one of Barnum's bandmasters,
Patrick Gilmore, leased the building from Vanderbilt in 1875. When
Gilmore's lease expired three years later, Commodore Vanderbilt's
son, William, took over and began staging events that appealed to so-

ciety, such as horse and dog shows. Because of its location, he also named the building Madison Square Garden. But lacking any semblance of elegance, the old railroad depot was found wanting by its predominantly society gatherings and in 1889 Vanderbilt decided to tear down the drafty old shed.

With the help of such wealthy friends as John Pierpont Morgan, Vanderbilt put together a syndicate that raised the money needed to build a grandiose structure and paid Stanford White seventy-five thousand dollars for his services. The question on the minds of many people, though, was would the building's grandiloquence in itself be enough of a lure to attract spectators by the thousands. Almost assuredly, it was felt, it would not be.

It was Patrick Gilmore, the former bandmaster and second leasor of the first Garden, as all of the Madison Square Gardens would come to be known, who soon found out that boxing would be a strong attraction to complement the horse and dog shows, rodeos, circuses, and other events. Appearing on the first fight card ever held in the original Garden, on July 17, 1882—three years after the building opened—John L. Sullivan boxed a four-round exhibition with Joe "Tug" Wilson, described as a middleweight from England, but whom boxing records indicate was actually a featherweight (maximum weight 126 pounds) from Brooklyn, who in his five professional fights had been knocked out three times and fought two draws.

By then, the bare-knuckle era was on the wane, and both Sullivan—who had won the bare-knuckle heavyweight championship only five months before—and Wilson wore six-ounce gloves during the exhibition, which drew a standing-room-only crowd of about ten thousand to the auditorium, a huge gathering for a boxing bout at the time. The bout, like others before it in the Garden, had to be classified as an exhibition since boxing was still banned in the state, as much for the corruption endemic to the sport as for the fact that fighters fought with their fists, which only served to make boxing all the more disreputable.

Not surprisingly, much of the Garden crowd on that July night consisted of Irishmen from throughout the Northeast who were more than willing to condone Sullivan's loutish behavior and overindulgences so long as he kept on winning. When he strode into the Garden to a huge ovation, Sullivan had had eighteen professional fights and won all but two of them by knockouts, including the last fourteen. Only two fighters had avoided knockouts at the hands of "the mighty Sullivan," as he was called. In exhibitions, though, he tended to coast and seemed not to try for a knockout, as was the case against Wilson. Still, he pushed or knocked down the Englishman—whom he may have outweighed by up to sixty-five pounds—about twenty times and then hit him repeatedly before he had fully risen from the floor. But the ersatz Englishman survived the four rounds against the obviously ill-trained Sullivan, who, by midway through the bout, was huffing and puffing for breath. For lasting the distance, Wilson, under a prior agreement, received one thousand dollars of Sullivan's purse, reported to have been about five thousand dollars.

It may only have been an exhibition, but the *New York Times* ran a front-page story of almost two thousand words on the bout, whose capacity crowd, the story reported, included prominent politicians, brokers, "actors, burglars, confidence men, harlots, blacksmiths, keno men and jailbirds," along with "some of the heaviest villains of many cities." Whether anyone in the crowd knew, or even suspected or even cared, for that matter, that Wilson was indeed a Brooklyn featherweight and not an English middleweight was not mentioned in the *Times*'s story. But then such chicanery was common in boxing at the time and would remain so for many years.

Over the next three years, Sullivan would box at the Garden four more times, knocking out, in turn, Charlie Mitchell, the eventual, and actual, British heavyweight champion, who was outweighed by more than forty pounds; Herbert Slade, a "half-bred Maori" from Australia, as the *New York Times* described him; Alf Greenfield; and the fighter from whom he had won the title, Paddy Ryan. The last knockout was somewhat dubious since, less than a minute into the fight, police officers stormed the ring to stop the illegal bout. Since Sullivan had had the upper hand, the result was decreed to be a one-round knockout victory for Sullivan.

Ironically, the first widely known boxer to appear at the second Garden was Gentleman Jim Corbett, who boxed three opponents in exhibitions on February 16, 1892—seven months before Corbett would knock out Sullivan in the first "gloved" heavyweight title fight. Corbett returned to the Garden in December of 1896 when he fought a four-round exhibition as a benefit for Sullivan, by then more than one hundred pounds heavier than he was when he lost to Corbett and trying to extricate himself from bankruptcy by appearing in several stage productions and delivering temperance lectures around the country.

Twenty years would pass before another champion would appear in the second Garden. With boxing now legal under the Frawley Act, Jess Willard made his first title defense on March 25, 1916, nine months after he had knocked out Jack Johnson to capture the heavyweight championship in Havana. Without the roguish appeal of Sullivan or the all-around skills of Corbett, the ponderous and awkward Willard proved to be a poor drawing card in the first Garden fight to be staged by Tex Rickard, who in his own right would become a boxing legend. In a drab and unexciting fight before a crowd of about ten thousand, Willard retained his title by winning a ten-round decision over Frank Moran of Pittsburgh, but did not enhance his image in the process. It would be another four years before another heavyweight title fight would be held at the second Garden, and that one would prove to be much more interesting.

Illegal once again after the Frawley Act of 1911 was repealed by the New York State Legislature in 1917, professional boxing in New York had been moribund for three years. But then during the winter of 1920, Senator James J. Walker introduced a bill in the State Legislature that would, if passed, again legalize the sport in the state. Walker's bill mandated that virtually everyone connected with boxing—fighters, managers, trainers, cornermen, sparring partners, promoters, and almost everyone else—had to be licensed. Unlike the Frawley Act, which had banned decisions and limited bouts to ten rounds, the Walker bill permitted decisions and allowed fights to last a maximum of fifteen rounds. It also stipulated that the sport be governed by a three-member state boxing commission, whose commissioner would be unsalaried, and that fights be judged by a referee and two judges.

Aware that Walker was working on a bill that would again legalize boxing in New York, William Gavin, an English sportsman who was prominent in British boxing circles, contacted the state senator. Walker was interested in what Gavin had to say and invited him to meet with him in New York. Gavin had been instrumental in establishing England's revision of the Marquess of Queensberry boxing rules of the 1860s by which the referee and two judges—rather than just the referee—adjudicate a fight and had hoped to establish a similar sporting club in New York. Impressed by Gavin's proposal, Walker incorporated much of Gavin's ideas in his bill.

Walker, it could be said, had a vested interest in boxing. For one thing, he knew the sport was extremely popular in New York City and especially so in Greenwich Village, which he represented in the State Legislature, and that his name on the new law could only help his political aspirations. For another, he was a rabid fight fan and a fairly good judge of boxing talent. Having heard a lot about Tunney, his Greenwich Village neighbor, Walker got to see him during one of his fights in New Jersey and was impressed. Meeting Tunney for the first time, he was even more impressed by his good looks, articulation, and overall demeanor.

Forcing a Greenwich Village constituent like Tunney to travel across the Hudson River to fight, Walker realized, was ludicrous. Walker—"Jimmy" to just about everyone—decided to do something about seeing to it that Tunney, Dempsey, and Benny Leonard would no longer have to fight outside New York, from where many of the world's best boxers came. Walker was convinced that because of the sport's booming popularity in the aftermath of World War I, and the money it could generate for New York state, a bill legalizing boxing once again would pass in the State Assembly. He also knew, of course, that it would aid him politically, especially in New York City. But he knew that even though Governor Al Smith was from the Lower East Side of New York, where Leonard and many other outstanding boxers lived, there was no guarantee that he would sign such a bill.

While many downstate voters were Roman Catholic and Jewish—ethnic groups with large numbers of boxing fans—Protestant voters who predominated elsewhere in the state would most likely be against such a bill, and their representatives almost assuredly would reflect their opposition. Smith, with his eye on the White House, certainly did not want to alienate Protestant voters. He knew that if he ran for president that most Catholics would vote for him, but he had good reason to have doubts about Protestants, even though many had cast ballots for Smith, New York's first Roman Catholic governor, when he ran for the state's highest office. Thus, Walker knew that while his bill would probably be passed by the Assembly, Smith's signature on it was no guarantee.

As it was, the bill passed the State Assembly easily in late April of 1920 and went to Governor Smith to either sign or veto. Walker thereupon arranged to meet with Smith, with whom, though they were both Democrats from Manhattan, he had clashed in the past. At the meeting, Walker pulled out all the stops in beseeching Smith to sign the measure into law. Besides invoking the names of Benny Leonard, Jack Britton, Joe Lynch, Tunney, and other prominent New York fighters, Walker stressed that professional boxing, if it were run properly, also would, as it had in the past, serve as a vehicle to financial success for talented fighters from poor neighborhoods such as the one in which Smith and Leonard grew up on the Lower East Side of Manhattan.

Impressed with Walker's arguments, Smith told Walker that, all right, he would sign the bill, but only with a caveat. As a Catholic with an eye on the White House, Smith did not want to be put in the position of a Catholic governor signing a bill that would primarily benefit Catholics—most fighters at the time were Irish and Italian—that had been sponsored by a Catholic. He would sign it, though, if Walker could somehow get—by nine o'clock Monday morning—letters and telegrams of support from at least a hundred Protestant clergymen. He didn't want any messages of support from Catholic priests—and no rabbis, either. As with the Irish and Italian fighters and fans, there were too many Jewish fighters and Jewish fans, Smith reasoned, and it would be too easy to get their support, too.

Walker looked at Smith in disbelief. What Smith was asking, he instantly felt, was utterly impossible, especially in three days' time, and over a weekend, at that. He told the governor so, but Smith was adamant. Either Jimmy Walker was going to come up with at least a hundred letters of support from Protestant ministers or Smith would veto his boxing bill. After remonstrating with Smith and, in exasperation, complaining that Smith had virtually given him an unattainable goal, Walker left the governor's office, deeply disappointed. Within hours, though, Walker had a brainstorm that would guarantee both the hundred letters of support from Protestant ministers and thus the enactment of his bill into law. All it would take would be a phone call to an old friend.

The friend was Anthony J. Drexel Biddle, a socially prominent Philadelphian who had been an amateur heavyweight boxer, good enough to have sparred with John L. Sullivan, Philadelphia Jack O'Brien, and then Tunney when they were in the Marines together in 1919, and who became the Marines' foremost expert on jujitsu and bayonet and dagger fighting during two world wars. An avid fight fan who was a member of one of Philadelphia's oldest and most prominent families, Biddle also was the founder of a nationwide Bible society that included hundreds of ministers. Within an hour after leaving Al Smith's office, Walker was on the phone with Biddle, explaining his predicament.

"Don't worry about a thing," Biddle said soothingly to Walker. "Just leave everything to me."

"But what do you want me to do, Major?" Walker asked, using Biddle's Marine title.

"Do nothing at all, Jim," Biddle replied. "Just relax."

When Al Smith arrived at the governor's office in Albany the following Monday morning, he was astonished at what he found. Stacked on his desk were more than six hundred telegrams and letters from Protestant ministers expressing their support of the Walker bill. Summoned to Smith's office by the incredulous governor, Walker had a ready explanation. "It's very simple, Al," Walker said with a smile. "Protestants also like boxing."

After leaving Smith's office, Walker called Biddle, both to express his gratitude and to ask how in the world he had managed, in such short time, to have prevailed on hundreds of ministers to deluge Smith with their letters and telegrams. Biddle, gratified that he was able to help out his good friend, explained that he had recently given another sizable donation of around a half-million dollars to the Bible society. Immediately after receiving Walker's distress call on Friday afternoon, Biddle had in turn called the Bible society's New York office and asked that it notify all of the society's state chapters forthwith about the urgent need of members to express their support of Walker's bill by Monday morning.

"You see, we're a congenial organization, Jim," Biddle told a delighted Walker.

Keeping his end of the bargain, Governor Al Smith signed the Walker bill into law on May 20, 1920. Unlike the Horton and Frawley acts, which had previously legalized boxing only to be repealed, the much more comprehensive and pragmatic Walker Law lasted and has governed the sport in New York state ever since.

Passage of the bill into law—and the way Walker accomplished it—earned Walker a modicum of fame, at least on sports pages throughout the country. Along with another bill that Walker introduced that same year, which permitted professional baseball to be played on Sundays, it also endeared him to sports fans in the state. His work ethic and eloquence as a speaker also impressed his colleagues, and he eventually became the Democratic floor leader. Besides ending blue laws that affected boxing and baseball, Walker also was behind a law that outlawed the Ku Klux Klan in New York at a time when the organization was making inroads in some parts of the state, and sponsored several pieces of social welfare legislation that became law.

Because of those accomplishments, coupled with his oratorical skills and engaging personality, Tammany Hall leaders convinced Walker to run for mayor of New York in 1925. He agreed to do so, and although he had no administrative experience, Walker won the mayoral election by a resounding 402,123 votes over Frank Waterman, the head of the Waterman Fountain Pen Company.

For all of his effervescence and friendliness, Walker was something of a paradox. For one thing, he dreaded traveling faster than twenty miles per hour in a car, although he was constantly in a hurry because of his tendency to be late. For another, he actually hated crowds and did not like being touched, yet no New York City politician ever reveled in the adulation of its people or endeared himself as much as

Jimmy Walker. Whether strutting along Broadway or Fifth Avenue during a parade in a cutaway coat, striped pants, silk top hat, and a gleaming smile, or amusing neighborhood gatherings with off-the-cuff speeches brimming with optimism and wisecracks, "Our Jimmy," as practically all New Yorkers called James John Walker, was the personification of New York and its open rebelliousness toward social restraints during the Jazz Age. No politician in memory had ever brightened the city's spirits as Walker did, as he dashed about town to civic ceremonies, neighborhood festivals, and funerals of people he had never met, or broke from the ranks of the St. Patrick's Day Parade to sprint up the steps of St. Patrick's Cathedral on Fifth Avenue to kiss the archbishop of New York's ring with a flair that delighted the crowd.

If ever a politician was at the right place at the right time, it was the dapper, charming, and beguiling Jimmy Walker—as much at home with bishops and cops as he was with some of the city's most corrupt politicians and notorious gangsters. New York had had ninety-nine mayors before him, but the city had never had one before like Walker, and by the time he left office seven years after his first inauguration, many of her citizens hoped she would never, ever, elect another one like him again. He was a rogue, but a charming one, and in a city where most citizens went to a church or a synagogue on a fairly regular basis, he managed to carry on a very public affair with an actress named Betty Compton while he was married without getting pilloried for it either by the public or even his extremely forgiving wife.

More than a few people felt that Walker worked so hard to legalize boxing in his state because of his passion for the sport—a legacy of having gone to fights with his father, also a politician, then working as an usher at fight cards at the Avonia Athletic Club in Greenwich Village, and, later, occasionally filling in as a referee during bouts at Brotty's Liquor House across from Flannery's Saloon on Hudson Street, also in the Village. Another reason, they felt, was that one of his Greenwich Village constituents was Gene Tunney, a promising boxer who had been forced to cross the Hudson River to fight in New Jersey, where boxing was legal.

If he wasn't at a fight, a ball game, or a civic gathering, Walker was apt to be found at fashionable restaurants like the Casino in Central Park, Rector's, Delmonico's, or Tex Guinan's 300 Club rather than at City Hall, where he spent as little time as he could, usually showing up around noon and leaving before five. When his mayoral opponent in 1929, Fiorello La Guardia, criticized Walker for accepting a raise from $25,000 to $40,000 (the equivalent of more than $100,000), Walker responded, "That's cheap. Think of what it would cost if I worked full time." It was a cynical rejoinder, but it was typical Walker and most New Yorkers loved it.

Eventually, New York's love affair with Walker began to wane. In the face of growing editorial criticism of Walker's travels abroad, his affair with Betty Compton, and his alleged misconduct of city business, he was reelected in 1929 over La Guardia, a former congressman, despite La Guardia's charges of rampant graft and payoffs to judges and city officials by underworld bosses. But over the next two years, as the scandals widened, three separate investigations were begun. The most dramatic was one conducted by a committee headed by a retired and highly esteemed judge named Samuel Seabury, who had been picked by Governor Franklin Delano Roosevelt. In June of 1932—the year Roosevelt would be elected to his first of four terms as president—Seabury set forth an array of charges against Walker, accusing him of malfeasance, misfeasance, and nonfeasance. After testifying before the committee that August, Walker abruptly resigned as mayor on September 1, 1932, saying he was doing so to spare himself from "an un-American, unfair proceeding conducted by Governor Roosevelt against me."

Nine days after resigning, Walker left for Paris, both to avoid possible prosecution and to join Betty Compton, whom he would eventually marry. As he boarded the liner *Conte Grande,* a reporter said to him, "Everyone is for you, Jim. All the world loves a lover."

"You are mistaken," Walker, a master of the pithy quote, replied. "What the world loves is a winner."

Returning three years later to a hero's welcome by a crowd of several thousand on a Manhattan pier, Walker was to serve as an assistant legal counsel for the New York State Transit Commission and as the city's labor czar under his old political adversary, Fiorello La Guardia, before becoming president of a recording company. Walker died in 1946 at the age of sixty-five. An estimated twenty thousand people passed by his coffin at the Frank Campbell Funeral Home in Manhattan, and more than five thousand mourners, including Jack Dempsey, attended his funeral at St. Patrick's Cathedral, while another ten thousand amassed outside on Fifth Avenue.

Enactment of the Walker Law meant that Gene Tunney, Benny Leonard, Jack Dempsey, and other leading fighters could now legitimately fight in New York state. Leonard and Dempsey did shortly after Smith signed the bill into law, but Tunney fought five of his remaining six fights in 1920 in New Jersey and one in Philadelphia. The no-decision provision of the New Jersey boxing rules had no effect on Tunney's first three bouts after his chance meeting with Dempsey, since he knocked out all three opponents inside of three rounds after taping two good knuckles on his right hand as Dempsey had recommended. The last three of his bouts that year went the distance, meaning there were no outright winners. It was clear, though, in all three bouts that Tunney had thoroughly outclassed his opponents.

Meanwhile, Dempsey made his Madison Square Garden debut eleven days before Christmas against Bill Brennan, who in sixty-five professional fights had been knocked out only once, by Dempsey in the sixth round of their first fight in Milwaukee on February 25, 1918. Their rematch was to be Dempsey's first fight in New York since the summer of 1916 when he fought three relatively unimpressive no-decision bouts for very little money and then rode the rods back to Salt Lake City.

His first fight with Brennan was staged only eleven days after he settled a score with Fireman Jim Flynn, who had knocked Dempsey out for the first and only time in his professional career in a fight that had raised both eyebrows and suspicions on February 13, 1917. A professional fighter since 1900, the 5' 9" Flynn had fought such notable boxers as Jack Johnson and the man from whom Johnson won the heavyweight title, Tommy Burns, along with three men who won the light heavyweight championship—Philadelphia Jack O'Brien, Jack

Dillon, and Battling Levinsky—and such other leading fighters as Sam Langford and Billy Papke. But by 1917 Flynn—whose nickname, "The Pueblo Fireman," derived from his days as a fireman in the Pueblo Fire Department and a switchman on several Colorado freight train lines—had been fighting for seventeen years and was rarely beating anyone. He had lost his last five fights—three of them to Dillon and one each to Levinsky and Fred Fulton, another onetime Great White Hope—when he met Dempsey in Murray, Utah, a suburb of Salt Lake City. At that stage, Dempsey, twenty-one, had lost only one of thirty-four fights. Dempsey's fight with Flynn was only ten seconds old when Flynn caught Dempsey with a left to the jaw that sent him to the canvas on his knees. Dempsey not only was counted out, but stayed down for another twenty seconds.

The outcome stunned the crowd. It also gave rise to rumors that Dempsey had taken a dive. In a column more than a decade later, Joe Williams, a widely known sportswriter for the Newspaper Enterprise Association, wrote that Dempsey had "laid down, as the boys say," in the fight. "I understand he got three hundred for taking a synthetic belt on the whiskers and that he carried the money tucked away inside his trunks when he entered the ring."

According to Williams's account, Dempsey, in agreeing to dump the Flynn fight, "possessed more of an immediate urge for money than an ambition to rise to the top ranks in the fight game." Since Dempsey was still occasionally riding from town to town beneath freight cars and his purses rarely exceeded a hundred dollars, it was true that he was usually in need of money. By then, too, he was married to Maxine Cates, who, after their divorce, claimed that Dempsey had indeed thrown the Flynn fight because they needed money badly. Dempsey himself always insisted that the fight was on the square. But then, too, there were exigent circumstances that some people thought might have inspired Dempsey to do whatever he could to make as much money as possible at the time.

Even Flynn seemed surprised at the knockout. "Well, it was this way," he explained some years after his most notable victory. "I hit him with a one-two. But just put it down that I didn't exactly knock Dempsey out. He just forgot to duck."

Or maybe Dempsey hadn't intended to duck.

A few weeks after his loss to Flynn, Dempsey received a letter from Fred "Windy" Windsor, who had promoted the Flynn fight and, to Dempsey's surprise, offered to manage him. Not only that, but Windsor told Dempsey he could book him a number of lucrative fights in the San Francisco Bay area. Given his dismal, even dubious, showing against Flynn and Windsor's lack of managerial credentials, Dempsey was skeptical, but, after discussing the offer with Maxine, he decided to accept and they left for San Francisco in late February. Maybe Windsor knew that the Flynn fight was hardly a barometer of Dempsey's potential. Indeed, maybe he knew even more about the fight than he would ever say.

In three fights in the Bay Area—all of which were restricted to a maximum of four rounds under a state law governing boxing— Dempsey lost one, drew twice, and made less than two hundred dollars over a three-week span. That bad streak turned out to be insignificant in the overall scheme of things, though. In April, Dempsey got a telegram from his mother informing him that his youngest of four brothers, Bruce, had been stabbed to death during an apparent robbery attempt while he was selling newspapers in downtown Salt Lake City. Dempsey hurried home for the funeral but arrived too late. Importantly, though, he got to spend some time grieving with his father, who had become invalided with arthritis and an assortment of other maladies, his ailing mother, and two brothers and a sister who were also sick and unable to work. Although he never said so, it is quite possible that his family's collective medical problems, financial struggles, and tragedies gave Dempsey further impetus to succeed.

He certainly needed both inspiration and motivation. During the past year, Dempsey had failed to make an impression in either New York or the San Francisco Bay Area—which was the country's primary boxing mecca at the time—during his first appearances there, his marriage was falling apart; a brother had been murdered; everyone in his immediate family was ailing in one way or another; he had practically no money; and had found out after the funeral that he had lost his job in the Tacoma shipyard. Surely, things could not get any worse.

Depressed over it all, Dempsey was about to look for work in Salt

Lake City when he got a letter from Jack "Doc" Kearns, who was starting to establish himself as a fight manager whose claim to fame as a boxer, he often said, was having fought, and lost to, two welterweight champions—Mysterious Billy Smith and Honey Mellody.* Afterward, Kearns had been a gambling house dealer in Nevada, a gold prospector in the Klondike, a taxi driver, a bartender, and a semiprofessional baseball player. But it was as a fight manager that he was to make his mark.

A gaudy dresser, the 5′ 10″ Kearns wore suits with spats, checkered vests, shoes that practically glistened, gleaming silver and gold tie pins, garish ties, an outsized diamond ring, and snap-brim fedoras or straw hats, and he splashed himself with heavy doses of cologne that he was convinced attracted women to him. What did attract some women was his money—he always had an ample supply of ready cash—and his glibness and embroidered stories. Though he would not be considered handsome, Kearns fancied himself a ladies' man and he frequently boasted of conquests, real or imaginary. Vain about his appearance, he retained a reasonably slender physique through a managerial career that lasted into the 1950s when he managed Joey Maxim to the world light heavyweight title. Over that long stretch, Kearns never let ethics or morality affect his decisions. Perhaps the least of Kearns's vices was his drinking, which was plentiful and would be a factor in his eventual breakup with Dempsey many years later.

For Dempsey, the connection with Kearns would be the beginning of a long and fruitful association, but one that was to be marred by acrimonious clashes over money that would linger well past their partnership as fighter and manager. After receiving a one-way train ticket

---

*In *The Ring Record Book*'s listing of Smith's professional opponents from 1890 through 1911, there is no mention of a Jack Kearns or a John Leo McKernan, Kearns's real name, although, allowing for the sometimes haphazard record-keeping of the time, it is still possible that Kearns did indeed fight Smith, or, if not, made it an apocryphal part of his clouded résumé. However, a Jack Kearns is listed as Honey Mellody's first opponent on March 20, 1901, in Boston when Mellody registered a second-round knockout. Whether that Jack Kearns was actually the former John Leo McKernan remains problematical. More credible, it would seem, is the one-fight record of Jack Kearns—with his birth name of John L. McKernan appended to his nom de boxe—listed by Universum Box Promotion, a reputable Internet service, which claims to list the records of more than 250,000 boxers, past and present. This listing shows Kearns as a lightweight with only one professional fight, a three-round knockout suffered at the hands of one Maurice Thompson on November 29, 1906, at the Grand Opera House in Victor, Colorado, where Dempsey had had some of his early, and unrecorded, fights and worked in one of the city's thriving gold mines in 1913 and 1914 when he was eighteen and nineteen years old. Kearns would have been twenty-four years old at the time of the Thompson bout.

from Kearns for a trip from Salt Lake City to San Francisco, along with a five-dollar bill (which went a long way for an ex-hobo like Dempsey), Dempsey was on his way back to the Bay Area. For Dempsey, after three years of working under managers who were often as broke or even more broke than he was, he knew that he finally had one that he could count on.

Kearns, unlike many managers, knew boxing. Shrewd and gregarious, Kearns seemed to be acquainted with every promoter in the country along with hundreds of other people involved in the sport and scores of sportswriters. Kearns also knew how to guide a fighter along, making sure he was not in over his head, especially a potentially valuable fighter like Dempsey. For such guidance and connections, Kearns always felt that he was entitled to more of a fighter's share than the law permitted. As a rule, a manager was allowed to receive one-third of a boxer's purse, but Kearns generally took 50 percent on the grounds that he did far more for his fighters than other managers did, including getting them bigger purses than they would otherwise receive. Or at least so he told them. Because of his track record and his connections, very few of his fighters, it seems, refused to go along with Kearns's usurious terms.

The association between Dempsey and Kearns clicked from the start, with Dempsey going unbeaten in his first eight fights under Kearns, including victories over two highly ranked heavyweights, Ed "Gunboat" Smith and Carl Morris, in his last two fights in 1917. Even though Kearns held on to at least two-thirds of Dempsey's ring earnings, Dempsey still was making more money than he ever had, so there was no reason to complain, at least not yet. Still, Dempsey was hardly content. Maxine had gone back to work in a brothel and they rarely saw each other in 1917. Late in the year, she returned home to Yakima, Washington, before winding up in another brothel, this one in Cairo, Illinois. Dempsey continued sending money to her in care of her mother in Yakima, but he would not see her again until three years later in a San Francisco courtroom under extremely unpleasant circumstances.

After winning his last five fights in 1917, Dempsey began to attract national attention in 1918 when he won eighteen fights, seventeen of them by knockouts, with twelve of those ending in the first round. His only loss was to Willie Meehan, a short, stocky plodder with an un-orthodox style that seemed to flummox Dempsey. It was Dempsey's second loss to Meehan, who had also beaten him in Oakland in 1917, also in a four-rounder. In two other bouts that year—both "no deci-sion" contests—Dempsey appeared to have lost the first to Billy Miske and then won the second in a rematch six months later.

In his third fight of 1918, Dempsey evened matters with Fireman Jim Flynn, whose first-round knockout of Dempsey a year and a day earlier had some boxing people rolling their eyes. Vastly different from the virtually defenseless fighter that had shown up for their first fight, Dempsey went at Flynn in a fury in his now patented deep crouch. Be-fore Flynn could land a blow, Dempsey rocked him to sleep with a crushing right cross about a minute into the first round, leaving spec-tators to wonder if this could be the same Dempsey who had lost so ig-nominiously to the Pueblo Fireman a year ago. Of course it wasn't; this one was unshackled and trying to win.

Now that Dempsey had complemented his high-voltage offensive power with some semblance of a defense—Kearns had convinced him to bob and weave out of a low crouch, which made him harder to hit—he began to command more attention. And by fighting all over the country—in 1918 alone he would fight in sixteen states, from San Francisco to New York—Dempsey would get to show a lot of people that he was without a doubt the most exciting, and most devastating, young heavyweight around.

But 1918 was marred by a public relations blunder that hurt Dempsey's image. With the war still on and Dempsey the target of barbs about his draft deferment, Kearns acceded to a government re-quest to have photographs taken of Dempsey in a pair of striped work clothes and cap ostensibly at work in a South Philadelphia shipyard while they were in town for a fight in early November before the war ended. The photographs were then circulated to newspapers and wire services in the hope of encouraging more people to take war-related jobs on the homefront. Several of the photos showing Dempsey hold-ing a pneumatic drill got wide currency. Unfortunately for Dempsey, the full-length photos of him in striped workmen's clothes revealed that he was wearing patent leather shoes—hardly de rigueur in a shipyard. It became apparent to everyone that the photo op had been intended to show that Dempsey, in between fights, was doing his part for the war effort. Of course, the scheme boomeranged and succeeded only in further casting Dempsey as a draft-dodging slacker.

Following his breakthrough years of 1918 and 1919, matters other than boxing came to absorb Dempsey during most of the spring and summer of 1920. After winning the title from Willard on July 4, 1919, in a three-round knockout in a fight promoted by Tex Rickard, Dempsey did not fight again until September 6, 1920, apart from two exhibitions.

In early June of 1920 Dempsey had gone on trial in federal court in San Francisco on charges that he had defrauded the government by lying on an application for a draft deferment during the Great War. Dempsey had been indicted after his former wife, Maxine Cates Dempsey, who had been a prostitute when he married her in October of 1916 and remained one both during and after their divorce in February of 1919, wrote to Harry Smith, a sports columnist for the *San Francisco Chronicle,* alleging that Dempsey had not supported her financially as he had claimed in dependency papers that he had filed with his draft board and was indeed a draft dodger.

For seven days, Dempsey sat in court, listening to an array of witnesses that included Maxine, who at forty was fourteen years older than her ex-husband; his mother, Celia, a tiny white-haired woman in her sixties, and a naval officer named John F. Kennedy (no relation to the latter-day president), who testified that Dempsey had been in the process of enlisting at the Great Lakes Naval Training Station in Illinois just before the war ended. Without Dempsey, Celia Dempsey said, "We wouldn't have had anything." Her testimony seemed to make it clear that Dempsey had indeed been the sole support for the family, which included her husband, who was hobbled by arthritis, and two sons and a daughter, unable to work because of varying illnesses.

Celia Dempsey's testimony also refuted that of Maxine, who, testifying a day earlier, said she had received about nine hundred dollars from Dempsey in 1918 and 1919, half as much as Dempsey's lawyers contended. But then Dempsey's lawyer, Gavin McNab, a well-known

San Francisco attorney to whom the champion and Jack Kearns had been referred by a White House aide, produced three Western Union employees from Salt Lake City who testified that Maxine had received a large number of payments by wire from Dempsey. One of the Western Union men, a night manager in Salt Lake City, said Maxine had told him, "Jack always sends plenty of money when he has it."

Through it all, Dempsey appeared to be tense and nervous, often tapping on the defense table in front of him. The champion had good reason to be nervous. He knew that the outcome of the trial would have a profound bearing on his boxing career, along with his commercial endorsements and a serialized movie entitled *Daredevil Jack* that he had made the previous year in Hollywood but which had not yet been released. And he knew that if he were found guilty, he would be further reviled as a slacker, which to Dempsey would be worse than losing his title.

Taking the witness stand on the sixth day of the trial before a packed courtroom, a composed Dempsey said he had contributed to the support of his family since he was a teenager working in Colorado mines and at odd jobs and as a fledging professional boxer. He also insisted he had given financial support to Maxine throughout their marriage and that, contrary to her earlier testimony, had never struck her or any other woman. Dempsey also testified that he had contributed about $330,000 to various war relief charities during the war.

On June 15 the case went to the jury. Dempsey did not have to wait long to hear his fate. After only ten minutes of deliberations, the jury had reached a verdict: not guilty. The courtroom erupted with cheers.

Hearing the jury foreman read the verdict, Dempsey smiled for the first time in more than a week. "I'm the happiest boy in the world," Dempsey told reporters. "Now I can start square and not feel that people are thinking that I tried to get out of doing my duty." Despite his acquittal, Dempsey knew that many people would still perceive him as a slacker and draft dodger. It would hurt deeply, but at least he could go on with his life as the heavyweight champion of the world.

Further embittered and threatening to publish about thirty letters in which she claimed Dempsey had instructed her to say he was supporting her during the war, Maxine eventually resumed her life as a prostitute. Five years after the trial, she was killed when fire raced through a bordello where she was working in Juárez, Mexico.

Despite her allegations against him, Dempsey was devastated when he heard of Maxine's death. Close friends said that he had never gotten over his love for her and that Dempsey may still have loved Maxine when she died.

Neither before nor after the trial, no one ever dared call Dempsey a slacker to his face. Not that he would have hit whoever might have been so foolhardy; the Manassa Mauler could appear to be almost psychopathic in the ring, but outside of it he was always gentle. But some people felt free to call him just that in the anonymity that a crowd provides. So while Dempsey knew he was being called a slacker, he had never heard himself called one until the night he knocked out Bill Brennan in Milwaukee in 1918, nine months before the end of the war.

"I started down the aisle to go to Bill's dressing room," Dempsey recalled. "And then from both sides of the aisle I heard a word that I was to know for years after that. 'Slacker,' a guy in the middle of a row yelled at me. When I turned that way, somebody on the other side of the aisle said, 'Slacker, you were lucky to win.' I had been called everything, but not this."

The glow from his victory over Brennan, one of his most impressive performances yet, had lasted only a matter of minutes. Now, in his dressing room, he sank into a chair, devastated by what he had just heard. "I wanted to die," Dempsey said, "and for some years after that, I wished I had died."

Prepared to fight again after a month's rest following the trial, Dempsey still worried about public reaction when he climbed into a ring once more. Then, too, who would he fight? Even Kearns knew that there were no viable challengers out there. The problem was solved when Billy Miske, who had twice gone the distance with Dempsey in 1918 and had served as a sparring partner before Dempsey's fight with Willard, wrote to Dempsey and asked that he make his first title defense against him. Ailing with Bright's disease—a kidney ailment named for a British doctor—Miske told Dempsey that medical bills had left him broke and that he needed a good payday so that he could take care of his wife and children. Determined to help an old friend whom had never been knocked down in fifty-eight fights, Dempsey convinced Kearns that he should give the thirty-five-year-old Miske the first shot at his title. Though he felt Miske had no chance of beating Dempsey—but then, who did?—Kearns agreed, realizing that in promoting the fight, he could capitalize on Miske having gone the distance with Dempsey twice, sixteen rounds in all without being floored.

The fight was held at a minor league baseball stadium in the resort town of Benton Harbor, Michigan, on Labor Day afternoon, September 6, 1920. In light of Miske's illness, Dempsey was convinced that he would offer little in the way of opposition. But despite his failing health, Miske withstood considerable punishment during the first two rounds and managed to nail Dempsey with a number of good punches to the head. But in the third round Dempsey put his friend down for good with two powerful blows to the jaw.

"I knocked him out because I loved the guy," Dempsey said later. Some people might think that was a strange way to show his affection for Miske, but Dempsey felt that the quicker he ended the fight, the better it would be for Miske, whose purse of twenty-five thousand dollars was his largest ever.

With enough money now to pay for his medical bills, Miske regained his health. He then won his last twenty fights, some involving credible opponents like Willie Meehan, Tommy Gibbons, and Bill Brennan. But then the Bright's disease recurred, ending his career in 1923. Less than a year later, on New Year's Day of 1924, he died at the age of thirty-nine. As he lay dying, Miske was reported to have turned to his wife and, in an obvious reference to Dempsey having given him first crack at his title as a favor, told her, "Tell Jack thanks from Billy."

The rematch with Brennan at Madison Square Garden three months after the Miske fight would be Dempsey's third since he won the title from Willard a year and a half before. Some war veterans did not take kindly to Dempsey doing some of his training for the Brennan fight aboard a decommissioned United States Navy destroyer berthed on the Hudson River waterfront. He also did roadwork in Central Park, where he had often slept when he first came to New York in 1916 in search of both fights and money at a time when his customary mode of long-distance transportation was hopping on a freight that was bound for a railroad yard in the vicinity of wherever his next fight was scheduled.

Sure enough, the slacker charges surfaced again in the New York papers, enough to unnerve and upset Dempsey. And on the night of the fight in the second Madison Square Garden, before a standing-room-only crowd of more than fifteen thousand, Dempsey heard far more boos than cheers.

From the opening bell, it was evident that Brennan was vastly improved since his first fight with Dempsey. In the second round, Brennan brought most of the crowd to its feet when he landed a right uppercut that jarred Dempsey and buckled his knees. Imbued with confidence after his impressive start, Brennan proceeded to hold his own with Dempsey over the next nine rounds with neither fighter giving any quarter in a surprisingly close bout. Finally, in the twelfth round of the scheduled fifteen-round fight, Dempsey, who had missed wildly with dozens of rights to the head through most of the fight and had appeared uncharacteristically tentative, dug a vicious right uppercut just under Brennan's heart. As Brennan doubled over in pain, Dempsey unloaded a left hook—his best punch—to Brennan's right side that sent the challenger down on his hands and knees. Brennan struggled to his feet a split second after referee Ed Haukop had counted him out.

The victory had not come easy for Dempsey, who seemed to win over the crowd by his ability to absorb a number of powerful punches to the head that probably would have knocked out most fighters. Still, most of the cheers were for Brennan, who had lasted longer than any other fighter Dempsey had faced in his seven-year professional career.

When ring announcer Joe Humphreys raised Dempsey's hand and announced that he had retained his title, the crowd cheered, as much for Brennan's gallant stand, it seemed, as for Dempsey. While Dempsey appreciated any cheering that was intended for him, he was all the more grateful that no one booed him. At least for a while, apparently, the slacker charges had been muted.

Leaving Madison Square Garden unnoticed and unrecognized, Gene Tunney, who like most of the spectators had just seen Dempsey fight for the first time, found himself impressed with the body assault that had put Brennan down for the count of ten. But he also was surprised at how often Dempsey missed badly with his right hand, and how, in missing, he had left himself wide open. At times, Brennan had taken advantage of those openings, but often he had been slow to react to them. If Bill Brennan could hurt Dempsey on several occasions, well then, a really good fighter could certainly do even better; a really good fighter could beat Dempsey.

As he walked out of the Garden and into a light snowfall that enhanced the glowing Christmas lights on Madison Avenue, Tunney, with only twenty-nine fights under his belt, compared with Dempsey's seventy-five—and probably a score more that had never been recorded during Dempsey's early days as a fighter—felt convinced that eventually he might be just the fighter to do so. And if he did, it would be with his right knuckles taped exactly as Dempsey had suggested. Now, mused Tunney, wouldn't that be ironic?

SIX

The Great Bennah and Barney Lebrowitz

The indefatigable Battling Levinsky.
THE STANLEY WESTON COLLECTION

B arney Lebrowitz could be forgiven for not always knowing where he was when he awoke on the morn of a new day. After all, he thought nothing of fighting in as many as four different cities in a week, and as often as ten times in one month—more than most fighters do nowadays in a year. There were also times, early in his career, when Lebrowitz had to pause before remembering *who* he was. Was he still Barney Lebrowitz? Or had he already morphed into Barney Williams? Or maybe, by now, he had become transformed into Battling Levinsky.

When he outpointed Jack Dillon on October 24, 1916, his victory was a triumph of perseverance since it followed ten previous bouts between the two, which had resulted in two victories by Dillon, one by Levinsky, one draw, and six no-decision fights. Beyond that, the eleventh fight was particularly significant for Levinsky since it enabled him to become the first Jewish light heavyweight champion and the second Jew at the time to hold a title; the other was Al McCoy, real name Al Rudolph, the son of a kosher butcher in Brooklyn, who had captured the middleweight championship two years earlier.

Few fighters ever entered a boxing ring as often as Levinsky, even at a time when it was not uncommon for a boxer to fight at least once a week, if not more. According to *The Ring Record Book and Encyclopedia,* Levinsky had 274 fights between 1910 and 1929, when he retired. But that does not include the more than a hundred bouts that boxing's "Iron Man" had from 1906, when he started fighting professionally at the age of fifteen, to 1910 when *The Ring* began counting his fights, or at least trying to keep up with him. Indeed, from 1912 through 1916, Levinsky averaged twenty-seven fights a year, with a high, in 1914, of thirty-five bouts (although some sources claim that he may have had as many as fifty that year). Even if the total was only thirty-five, that was as many as Jess Willard had ever fought and more than some latter-day heavyweight champions such as Ingemar Johansson, John Tate, Michael Dokes, Gerrie Coetzee, Tim Witherspoon, and Greg Page had had during their professional careers.

According to *The Ring Record Book and Boxing Encyclopedia,* Levinsky outdid even himself on New Year's Day of 1915 when he had three fights, all of which the record book said went the distance for a grand total of thirty-two rounds. Fighting at the Broadway Social Club in Brooklyn at 11:00 A.M., an unheard of time for a boxing bout in later years, Levinsky supposedly went ten rounds with a well-respected heavyweight, Bartley Madden. Less than four hours after that bout ended, according to an account in *The Ring* magazine, Levinsky went another ten rounds against Soldier Kearns at Brown's Athletic Club in Manhattan. Then that night, seventy-five miles away in Waterbury, Connecticut, Levinsky supposedly climbed into a ring at the Waterbury Auditorium at ten o'clock and, appearing none the worse for twenty previous rounds of fighting—assuming he had fought twenty previous rounds that day—battled another leading heavyweight, Ed "Gunboat" Smith, to a twelve-round draw.

No decisions were rendered in the two New York bouts, according to *The Ring Record Book* in keeping with the rules of the Frawley Act, which prohibited winners from being declared. However, Nat Fleischer claimed that in both of Levinsky's purported fights in New York on that New Year's Day he had the edge.

Over the years questions arose as to whether Levinsky actually did engage in three bouts in one day in three different places. For one thing, there do not seem to have been any newspaper accounts of Levinsky having fought in New York on New Year's Day of 1915. Then, too, the records of both Madden and Kearns do not list them as having fought Levinsky on that date. Admittedly, many fights went unrecorded in the era, including many of Levinsky's, but the documentary evidence—a story in the sports section of the *Waterbury Republican* on January 2, 1915—seems to indicate that while Levinsky did fight on New Year's Day of 1915, he fought only once—in Waterbury—and not twice or even three times. If he had already fought twice before, seemingly the *Waterbury Republican* story would have mentioned it.

Levinsky, though, always insisted that he did indeed have three fights that day, and his obituaries thirty-four years later mentioned his claimed, but unsubstantiated, boxing trilogy, which came to symbolize the Battler's indefatigable work ethic. Also, Nat Fleischer lent at least a modicum of credence to Levinsky's claim when, in an article in his magazine in 1969, he wrote, "Levinsky set a record which will stand for as long as we have boxing when he appeared in three bouts, all of which went the limit, for a total of 32 rounds." Regardless of how many fights the Battler had on that New Year's Day, he was back in the ring five days later, fighting another ten-rounder in New York.

Successful as Levinsky became, he could not compare in skill or popularity to Benny Leonard, who held the lightweight title (maximum weight: 135 pounds) from 1917 to 1925 and is generally acknowledged as the best lightweight of all time. During that span, Leonard lost only one fight, and that defeat was suspect. Left virtually destitute by the 1929 stock market crash in which he lost more than $1 million, Leonard returned to the ring six years later, in 1931, at the age of thirty-five. Paunchy, balding, and slower both afoot and with his once rapid-fire punches, Leonard still won eighteen straight fights in the span of a year, albeit against handpicked opponents not likely to disrupt his comeback, but then was knocked out on October 7, 1932, by Jimmy McLarnin, who five months later was to win the world welterweight title. That defeat ended a remarkable twenty-one-year career during which Leonard, indisputably the greatest Jewish fighter ever, endeared himself to immigrant Jews when many of them, if indeed not most, were living in cramped ghettos, struggling to make a living, and finding it difficult to assimilate in American society.

To many of them, "The Great Bennah," as he was called, was demonstrating, like Levinsky and other outstanding Jewish fighters, in the early part of the twentieth century, that contrary to a widely held view that Jews were both physically weak and lacking in courage, they could indeed be as tough as the Irish, Italian, and German boxers who had long dominated the sport. More than that, Jewish fighters, many of whom proudly wore the six-pointed Star of David on their trunks, also instilled a sense of pride in Jews, as much as songwriters like Irving Berlin and George Gershwin and entertainers like Eddie Cantor, Al Jolson, and George Burns.

Articulate, personable, and good-looking, Leonard, like Tunney and many other fighters, had learned to fight for sheer preservation. Also like Tunney, Leonard was not eager to battle it out when outnumbered or outsized; thus, at first, he merely tried to dodge the punches of the Irish toughs who preyed upon Jewish boys on the Lower East Side of New York where Leonard lived. Before long, the small and frail-looking Leonard, actually Benjamin Leiner, was fighting with a skill and ferocity that soon earned him a reputation among the young Irish hoodlums as a Jew not to be picked on en route to the neighborhood baths. That reputation was further enhanced when Leonard began boxing at one of the neighborhood settlement houses as a teenager.

Soon after, Buck Areton, a former fighter who worked with young boxers at the settlement house and had an eye for boxing talent, convinced Leonard to become a professional fighter, even though he was only fifteen years old. His first fight, in 1911, was hardly auspicious. Matched against a much older and experienced bantamweight (118-pound limit) fighter named Mickey Finnegan, Leonard, pale and nervous as he entered the ring, was knocked down twice and thoroughly outclassed in a scheduled four-round bout that was stopped in the third. Undaunted by the loss, Leonard proceeded to knock out three of his next four opponents and finish the year with six victories and only one defeat. Leonard displayed early on the inestimable ability of hitting without getting hit in return, the elusive objective of all prize-fighters. "He who hits and runs away lives to box another day," he once said in describing what was to become his boxing mantra.

As his victories mounted, his popularity grew, particularly in his Lower East Side neighborhood, where he became a hero to many Jews—though not to his parents, once they found out, somewhat belatedly, that young Bennah had become a fighter. Most Jewish immigrants, in their struggle to make ends meet and ensure a better life for their children, had little interest in sports. Most of them hoped their children would get a good education and then perhaps become a doctor, lawyer, or businessman. Sports, they felt, were a waste of time and diverted them from family values and traditional beliefs. And of all the popular sports in the New World, they saw boxing as the most degrading and most dangerous even though most of the first generation of Jewish parents had never seen a prizefight. A boxing ring, surely, was no place for a Jewish boy, especially in a country where excellent opportunities abounded. That several Jews already had won world boxing titles was, to the few who were aware of it, meaningless, and, worse, potentially harmful since early-day Jewish champions like Abe Attell, Harry Harris, Al McCoy, and Ted "Kid" Lewis might inspire young Jewish boys to get into boxing.

In fact there had been a Jewish champion as far back as 1791, when Daniel Mendoza, a native of London's poor Whitechapel neighborhood and only 5′ 7″ and 160 pounds, won the world heavyweight championship, which he held for four years. Mendoza, a Sephardic Jew, was a ring revolutionary in that during an era of roughhouse brawling, he introduced a scientific style of boxing, predicated on jabbing, counterpunching, and strong defense, qualities that were virtually unknown during the early days of the bare-knuckle era. After losing his title in 1795 when he was thirty-one, Mendoza became London's most renowned boxing instructor.

By the second decade of the twentieth century, six Jews had won world titles and, in total numbers, Jews were third behind Irish and Italian professional boxers. That number continued to grow in the 1930s when seven Jews held world titles. The high point was in 1933 when Maxie Rosenbloom (light heavyweight), Ben Jeby (middleweight), Jackie Fields (welterweight), and Barney Ross (lightweight) held half of the eight world titles then recognized.*

In all, during the first four decades of the twentieth century, nineteen Jewish boxers won world championships, a number surpassed, and only slightly, by Irish and Italian fighters. For many young Jews, Italians, and Irish-Americans, boxing, for all of its inherent risks, was seen as a way out of poverty. Also, Jews who grew up in crowded ghettos such as in New York's Lower East Side or the Maxwell Street neighborhood in Chicago were disinclined to take up baseball or football because playing fields were virtually nonexistent. Boxing, by contrast, required little space, and settlement houses, where the sport was taught, abounded in Jewish ghettos.

"You did it for money, no other reason," said Danny Kapilow, a good welterweight of the 1940s who once held Rocky Graziano to a draw in a fight that many observers thought Kapilow had won. "It was very hard to get jobs before the war, and if you did, you were lucky to make six dollars a week. You could make a lot more fighting, especially if you were any good."

Some Jewish fighters of the era conceded that the street fights they got into after being attacked by Irish and Italian teenagers helped them develop into boxers.

"As a kid growing up in an Italian and Irish neighborhood in West New York, New Jersey, right across the Hudson River from Manhattan, I got into a lot of fights after being called a Jew bastard and worse," said Charley Gellman, who won sixty of sixty-five professional fights while fighting as a middleweight under the name of Chuck Halper in the late 1930s. "It definitely was one of the things that eventually got me into boxing."

Both Gellman—who graduated from Columbia and went on to be-

---

*Today, by contrast, there are seventeen weight classes, most of which carry prefixes of "junior" and "super" so that television networks can publicize more fights as title bouts.

come a union official and, later, executive director of three New York City hospitals—and Kapilow—who also became a union official—agreed that in the 1920s, 1930s, and 1940s an awful lot, if indeed not most, of the upper-echelon Jewish fighters tended to be smart fighters. Johnny Ray, not the popular singer of the 1950s and 1960s but the manager of former light heavyweight champion Billy Conn, said he was convinced that Jewish fighters tended to be smarter. As a classic case, Ray recalled Conn's first fight against Joe Louis, on June 18, 1941, in which Conn, a skillful boxer who was ahead on points, got headstrong and tried to knock Louis out in the thirteenth round, but then paid for his fistic tomfoolery when he himself was knocked out in the round. "If Billy had a Jewish head instead of an Irish one, he'd be the champ," Ray said.

Like Leonard and Levinsky, many Jewish fighters took on assumed names in the ring, mainly to keep their parents from knowing that they had become professional boxers. Most were furious when they found out, but some, though angry at first, changed their opinions about their sons new calling once they found out how relatively lucrative boxing could be. Abe Attell delighted in telling about his mother's reaction when she found out from a neighbor—the most customary way that a Jewish fighter's venture into pugilism was unveiled—that he, the thirteenth of sixteen children born to Mark and Annie Attell—had become a boxer in 1900, when he was sixteen years old. Remonstrating with young Abe when he returned home from a fight one night, Annie Attell suddenly calmed down when Attell handed his mother the fifteen dollars he had received for his bout that night. "You mean the fight is over, and you got fifteen dollars?" she said to her son. "And you don't have no cuts on you at all." Smiling, Attell nodded his head affirmatively, whereupon his mother said, "Abe, when are you going to fight again?"

Benny Leonard related a somewhat similar experience. Coming home from a bout with a severe bruise under one eye, Leonard found himself undergoing a verbal beating from his parents who suspected he had taken up boxing. "My mother looked at my black eye and wept," recalled Leonard, who proceeded to admit he had become a fighter and handed over the twenty dollars he had made that night. Leonard's father, Gershon, a sweatshop tailor who had to work all week to make that much money, had a different reaction. "All right, Benny, keep on fighting. It's worth getting a black eye for twenty dollars. I am getting verschwartzt [blackened] for twenty dollars a week."

Because of their misgivings over his fighting, Leonard promised his parents that once he made a substantial amount of money, he would retire from the ring. And he did, at the age of twenty-eight in 1925, as the undefeated lightweight champion after having moved his mother and father to a better neighborhood in East Harlem, which was then predominantly Jewish and Italian, shortly before he won the lightweight title in 1916. But then six years later, in 1931, twenty years after his first professional fight, Leonard returned to the ring to try to recoup some of the more than $1 million he had lost during the stock market crash.

All the while, Leonard was lionized among Jewish sports fans, both for his wondrous boxing skills—he lost only twenty of 211 professional fights—and his impeccable behavior, both in and out of the ring. Into his nineties, Budd Schulberg, the novelist and longtime fight buff and occasional boxing writer, still spoke of Leonard in awe. "For most kids of my boyhood, the biggest heroes were the cowboy movie star Tom Mix and the great actor Douglas Fairbanks, Jr.," said Schulberg. "But my hero, and many of my friends', was Benny Leonard. In our household, he was always referred to as 'The Great Benny Leonard' just as my parents would refer to 'The Great Houdini' and 'The Great Caruso.' I think that Leonard was to many young Jews what Ali became to young blacks many years later."

Not everyone felt that way about the Great Bennah, who took unabashed pride in finishing a fight with every strand of his slickeddown, pompadoured dark hair still in place. During his early days as a fighter, Leonard, like other Jewish boxers, was the object of anti-Semitic taunts. Fighting in a small town in western Pennsylvania against a fighter known as Irish Eddie Finnegan, Leonard could not help but hear shouts exhorting Finnegan to "kill the kike" and "murder the yid." Enraged by the epithets, Leonard, who was winning the fight easily and thus had began to coast, began to unleash a withering assortment of blows that opened up cuts over Finnegan's eyes and ripped a gash in his lip. Bleeding profusely, Finnegan finally grabbed Leonard and in the ensuing clinch blurted out in Yiddish that his real name was not Finnegan, but Seymour Rosenbaum, and that since he was also a Jew, could Benny please take it easy?

Leonard, convinced that Finnegan was telling the truth, mainly because of his obvious fluency in Yiddish, proceeded to let up over the last few rounds. Despite the beating he endured, Finnegan retained his assumed name, and not only did not request a rematch with Leonard but made sure to stay away from talented Jewish fighters for the rest of his nondescript career.

After four successful title defenses and only one loss in seventy-two fights, Leonard decided to try to win the welterweight title while still holding on to his lightweight crown, which no one had ever done. To do so, Leonard would have to beat Jack Britton, the reigning welterweight titleholder, and that seemed entirely possible, since Britton, at thirty-seven, was eleven years Leonard's senior and, in the eyes of many observers, beginning to slip. Moreover, Leonard already had clearly beaten Britton in two newspaper decision fights in 1917 and 1918. Thus it was no surprise that Leonard was made a 3-to-1 favorite to beat Britton in their fifteen-round fight on November 26, 1922, at the Velodrome, an arena in the Coney Island section of Brooklyn that had been designed for bicycle races.

Before a pro-Leonard capacity crowd of about 25,000, Leonard appeared lethargic and tentative during most of the bout. That Leonard would be so cautious against Britton seemed odd, considering how Britton, like Leonard, was primarily a boxer and not renowned as a knockout puncher. Indeed, Britton had not knocked out any of his last thirty-four opponents. The fight was close and marked with some good exchanges, but Leonard appeared to be far off form, missing repeatedly with his hardest-thrown punches, often by wide margins. Through twelve rounds, Britton appeared to have had the upper hand. But in the thirteenth, Leonard drove a powerful left uppercut to Britton's midsection, close to the beltline, which sent Britton to the floor on one knee. Grimacing in apparent pain and propping himself up with his right glove, Britton appealed to referee Patsy Haley to call a foul.

Instead, Haley waved Leonard toward a neutral corner and began a count.

As Haley counted, Leonard, who never did reach the neutral corner, lurched forward and unleashed a left hook to the head of Britton, who was still leaning on one knee. The blow sent Britton to the floor on his back and stunned the pro-Leonard crowd. Britton arose quickly, but Haley ordered both fighters to their corners and notified ring announcer Joe Humphreys to tell the crowd that he had declared Britton the winner on a foul. Ringside spectators, confused by the outcome, screamed at Haley, demanding an explanation for his decision. Leaning across the ropes, Haley then told both fans at ringside and sportswriters that he had disallowed Britton's claim that he had been fouled by a low blow and was about to start a count when Leonard hit Britton while he was down.

Much as the New York crowd adored their beloved Bennah, even his most ardent fans could not excuse him for what is regarded as the most unethical breach of conduct a fighter can commit—hitting a man when he is down. That Leonard could do something as audaciously unsportsmanlike was extremely unlike him, fans felt, and surely he must have known that to punch a fighter who was already on the canvas would cost him the fight. As it was, a crowd that had never seen Leonard lose filed out of the Velodrome, both incredulously and numbed. Why had the Great Bennah, always a model of decorum in and out of the ring, resorted to such egregious behavior? Worse, given his relatively poor performance, could Benny have thrown the fight, albeit in a most unconventional manner?

But if so, why had he taken so long and absorbed so much punishment along the way? Why, too, if Leonard had agreed to lose the fight, had he come so close to flooring, and perhaps even knocking out, Britton in the eleventh round?

Strangely, the New York State Athletic Commission, which oversees professional boxing in New York state, did not take action against Leonard for hitting Britton while he was down. Perhaps even stranger, there was no uproar in the press or elsewhere over his flagrant foul and the suspicions it had aroused. In the opinion of the commission, which met the day after the fight, the fight was satisfactory, as the *New York*

Times reported, "and did not merit investigation." Leonard himself conceded he had done wrong, but it hardly sounded like an act of contrition. What made the State Athletic Commission's disinclination to order an investigation all the more puzzling was the common knowledge that Leonard was friendly with some of New York's most notorious gangsters, including Waxey Gordon and Arnold Rothstein.

"In those days it was almost impossible for famous fighters like Leonard not to get to know well-known gangsters," Budd Schulberg said. "And there definitely was a shadow over Benny's fight with Britton."

More than a quarter-century later, and a year after Leonard had died of a heart attack while refereeing a bout in New York, his trainer, Manny Seamon, said that the fight had been fixed. According to Seamon, Leonard's manager, Billy Gibson, who later also was to manage Gene Tunney and who was known to be friendly with some high-level mobsters, had told Leonard at the weigh-in on the morning of the Britton fight that he couldn't win the bout—meaning, of course, that Leonard was to lose deliberately.

All that revelation (if it was one) did was earn Seamon the enmity of Leonard fans, who by then had elevated the late Benny to iconic status. If anyone was to be forgiven for an abominable breach of boxing behavior, Leonard fans felt, it was the Great Bennah.

While most Jewish fighters who changed their names took Jewish-sounding pseudonyms, some did not. Mainly because most boxing fans during the early part of the twentieth century were Irish, more than a few Jewish boxers at the time adopted Irish names, feeling that would not only get them more fights but more fans. In addition to Al McCoy, there were fighters like Vincent Morris Scheer, who held the world junior welterweight title from 1926 until 1930, while fighting under the name of Mushy Callahan. A native New Yorker whose family moved to Los Angeles when he was two years old and who did most of his fighting on the West Coast, Callahan took his name change to an extreme when he converted to Catholicism, married an Irish girl in 1934, and had a son who became a priest. After retiring, Callahan, a favorite of Hollywood boxing fans, was a technical director on a number of boxing films during which he taught the rudiments of prize-fighting to such actors as Errol Flynn (for *Gentleman Jim*), Elvis Presley (for *Kid Galahad*), and James Earl Jones (for *The Great White Hope,* a movie about the career of Jack Johnson).

Then there were the rare instances when gentile fighters, whose fighting base was heavily populated by Jewish boxing fans, took Jewish names. The best-known fighter to do so was Sammy Mandella, an Italian from Rockford, Illinois, who, aware that many fight fans in the Chicago area in the 1920s were Jewish, dropped the second *a* from his surname so that boxing fans, and especially Jewish ones, would think he was Jewish. While reigning as the world lightweight champion from 1926 until 1930, Mandell beat two future champions and Hall of Famers, Jimmy McLarnin and Tony Canzoneri. When he defended his title for the third time, in 1930, against Al Singer at Madison Square Garden in New York, most Jews in the audience favored Singer, since he was a New Yorker, or had mixed emotions in watching what they thought was a fight between two top-of-the-line Jewish boxers. As it developed, the only real Jew in the bout, Singer, won the title with a first-round knockout.

By far the most prominent fighter to profess to be Jewish, without first changing his surname, was Max Baer, who on June 14, 1934, won the heavyweight championship by knocking out Primo Carnera. At the suggestion of his manager, Ancil Hoffman, Baer wore a Star of David on his boxing trunks, which made him hugely popular among Jewish fans. Because Baer came to prominence about the same time as Adolf Hitler, his perceived Jewishness resonated. Publications such as the *California Jewish Voice* and the *Detroit Jewish Chronicle* acknowledged Baer as a symbol of Jewish toughness at a time when Hitler and his Nazi party were depicting Jews as weak.

Baer became a hero to many Jews when he knocked out former heavyweight champion Max Schmeling, a symbol of Nazi pride, in New York in 1933, the year Hitler came to power. Baer himself agreed that his claim of being a Jew was somewhat tenuous, since his only Jewish blood connection had been his father's mother, who, Baer maintained, was Jewish. "That made my father 25 percent Jewish, since, in the Jewish faith, you are what your mother is, and my grandfather's mother was Jewish, which made him Jewish, and, I guess, my dad at least part Jewish," said Max Baer, Jr., who became an actor, best known for his role as Jethro Bodine in *The Beverly Hillbillies* television series. "But my dad wasn't brought up as a Jew, and certainly wasn't a practicing Jew." Maybe the most convincing argument against Baer's popular perception as a Jew came from the great trainer Ray Arcel, who said he had often shared shower rooms with Baer and that, after seeing Baer up close, he could see that he lacked a defining symbol of male Judaism.

By contrast, Battling Levinsky inexplicably anglicized his name in a city with a heavy Jewish population when he began to fight professionally in the first decade of the twentieth century. Born Bernard Lebrowitz in a lower-middle-class section of North Philadelphia, he took the name of Barney Williams, lest—like other Jewish fighters—his parents found out he had become a boxer. As it was, his entry into boxing was unusual. While working as an apprentice for a downtown jeweler in Philadelphia, the owner of the store suggested that Lebrowitz, then sixteen, join a boxing club and learn the rudiments of the sport so that he might be a valuable asset in defending the store's stock in the event of a holdup or while delivering jewelry to a customer.

Slender, with blond wavy hair and blue eyes, the handsome and personable Lebrowitz was a good fit in the store, looking like anything but a boxer. After store hours, Lebrowitz took quickly to boxing, priding himself on his defense. No matter how hard they hit, opponents found Lebrowitz almost impossible to knock out. Remarkably, Levinsky had more than 125 fights before he was technically knocked out—meaning the referee had stopped the bout without starting a count. Lebrowitz fought often, since his purses tended to be small, ranging from as little as twenty-five to a hundred dollars. But despite his success, he rarely found himself booked in big arenas until he hooked up with Dumb Dan Morgan. It was Morgan who got him booked in scores of main events in New York and other major boxing cities, which meant much larger purses and, eventually, the light heavyweight title.

One of boxing's most colorful characters, Morgan had managed Abe Attell late in his career and was managing future champions Al

McCoy and Jack Britton and a number of other highly rated fighters when Lebrowitz, still fighting as Barney Williams, walked into Morgan's Broadway office on July 20, 1913, and asked if Morgan would become his manager. Morgan, who had heard about Lebrowitz, agreed and immediately told him that his first move as his manager was to change his name from Barney Williams to Battling Levinsky. That was something of a surprise since, among boxing insiders, a "Levinsky" was a term used for a mediocre Jewish fighter.*

Over the next four years, Battling Levinsky would have the astonishing total of 115 fights, including thirty-five in 1914, his first full year under Morgan. By the end of that stretch, Levinsky, with well over two hundred professional fights in all, had two cauliflower ears, a boxing term for ears disfigured in the ring, and his eyes were surrounded by scar tissue. Yet he was only twenty-seven years old and still handsome, and, with his blond hair, still very much a Golden Boy of the prize ring. Most of his fights during that period were no-decision affairs, and Levinsky lost only three outright while appearing to win most of the others. Flushed by Levinsky's success, Dumb Dan Morgan made one of the dumbest decisions of his managerial career, persuading Levinsky to meet Jack Dempsey, then a twenty-three-year-old rising heavyweight star who had knocked out ten of his last sixteen opponents in the first round.

Crafty and beguiling, but a shrewd negotiator, Dan Morgan was one of a handful of managers who dealt solely with fighters they felt were prospective champions. Others included Jack Kearns, who man-

---

*In the early 1930s Harry Krakow, a fighter from Chicago's Maxwell Street area, decided to metathesize into "Kingfish Levinsky," a pseudonym that combined the names of a character in the *Amos 'n' Andy* radio show and his boxing hero, Battling Levinsky. A heavyweight without a punch and, at best, a feeble jab, Levinsky achieved his most notable victory when he outpointed former heavyweight champion Jack Sharkey in 1933, three months after Sharkey had lost his title to Primo Carnera. Even more impressive was a ten-round decision over former light heavyweight champion Tommy Loughran in 1931. The Kingfish also fought two other heavyweight champions, losing three times to Max Baer, and once to Joe Louis. The latter fight took place in Chicago in 1935, two years before Louis won the heavyweight championship from James J. Braddock. Knocked senseless by Louis in the first round, Levinsky was still dazed as he walked out of Comiskey Park in Chicago with his then manager, Joe Jacobs, several hours after the fight had ended as rain began to fall. Turning to Jacobs, Levinsky, whose purse depended to a considerable extent on box office receipts—the gate, as such receipts are known—said, "Joe, do you think the rain will hurt the gate?" Jacobs, aware that his fighter was still in a state of semiconsciousness and apparently unaware of what had happened in the ring against Louis, replied, "I forgot to tell you, King. The fight's been called off."

aged Dempsey during most of his career, along with a number of other champions including Attell, Archie Moore, Joey Maxim, Mickey Walker, and Jackie Fields; and Billy Gibson, the only manager to have guided two fighters, Benny Leonard and Gene Tunney, who retired as undefeated champions.

Unlike baseball managers who devise and then implement strategy during games, boxing managers have virtually nothing to do with their fighter's training or their actual strategies in a bout. Those responsibilities lie with trainers, who usually had been fighters. Gibson, for one, sounded prideful when he often said that he actually knew little about the finer nuances of boxing. Before a bout involving one of his fighters, he usually limited his advice to "Take care of yourself" as his tiger was about to climb through the ropes and into the ring. Except for Kearns, most other managers rarely said much more, well aware that their principal tasks were to nurse their fighters along carefully, avoiding pitfalls in the form of superior boxers who might derail their chances of getting title fights, and getting as much money for a fight as possible.

For these responsibilities, higher-echelon managers like Morgan, Kearns, and Gibson were well rewarded, since, in most states at the time, they earned a third of their fighters' purses, although some, like Kearns, usually took more. To some fighters, a manager evolved into a father figure, who counseled them not only on their boxing careers but on a diverse array of other aspects of their lives. In that respect they could overstep their bounds, as Dempsey thought Kearns did in trying to polish the Manassa Mauler's manners and speech and even trying to exert control over what clothes Dempsey wore. At least Dempsey listened to Kearns's advice. Tunney, by contrast, seemed barely able to abide his managers, going through three of them early in his career.

The Dempsey-Levinsky fight was held on November 6, 1918, at the Olympic Club in Levinsky's hometown of Philadelphia. Not only was Levinsky outweighed by twenty pounds and overmatched, he was also under-trained. The Battler had already served a year in the Army as a boxing instructor at Camp Devens in Massachusetts, while continuing to box professionally, and now was working as a mechanic in a defense plant in Bridgeport, Connecticut. He had not fought for two and a half months, an eternity for a fighter who in January of 1914 had fought nine times, including three times in one week on two occasions.

Like many managers when their fighters are in over their heads, Morgan played down Dempsey's abilities. "He's been beaten four times, and the last time I saw him he looked terrible," said Morgan, not mentioning when he had last seen Dempsey. "But you can't tell; he might have improved."

Actually, Dempsey had lost four times in fifty-six fights, but only once in the last two years. "I'll take a chance," Levinsky said, feeling he had nothing to lose, since he would still be the light heavyweight champion regardless of the outcome. Taking leave of his defense plant job, the Battler now had all of two weeks to get ready for the man they were calling the Manassa Mauler.

The Olympia Club, which had a capacity of about five thousand, was packed, with several hundred standees in the rear, eager to exhort on their hometown favorite, Levinsky, and at the same time get to see the knockout artist from Colorado. It was a classic matchup—a young slugger against a veteran boxer, generally the best type of fight. But it was also a classic mismatch as Dempsey floored Levinsky for a nine count in the second round and then knocked him cold in the third with a vicious right to the jaw. Defense was Levinsky's trademark, but he could not hold off the stalking Dempsey.

Four years and fifty-four fights after winning the light heavyweight title, Levinsky finally defended it for the first time against France's "Orchid Man," Georges Carpentier, in Jersey City on October 12, 1920. Like the Dempsey fight, it was no contest, with Levinsky unable to counter Carpentier's unrelenting pressure and losing his title when Carpentier knocked him both out of the ring and down for the count of ten in the fourth round.

Besides losing his world title, Levinsky also seemed to lose interest in fighting. He fought just once more during 1920 and only eight times in 1921, winning four of those fights by decision, losing three times—twice on fouls—and fighting two no-decision bouts and one draw. By then, the Battler had had more than two hundred fights and most certainly was showing signs of slipping after sixteen years in the ring.

Maybe the end was near as far as Levinsky's ring career was concerned. But he felt he still had a lot left, including a surfeit of experience, and, hey, he now had a family and still loved what he was doing. Fortunately for Levinsky, Tex Rickard knew that he was still both popular and marketable even though his best days were behind him. And Rickard was about to come up with a new idea—and a new title— that he thought just might interest both Levinsky and that young and unbeaten New Yorker, Gene Tunney.

Hearst's star sportswriter and reporter Damon Runyon. NATIONAL BASEBALL HALL OF FAME AND MUSEUM, INC.

I f there was one defining characteristic in Tunney's makeup, it was a supreme confidence in everything he did. With that came an iron will, steely nerves, and a fierce determination. Where these qualities came from is difficult to discern. Certainly not from his father, who never expected to rise above being a rank-and-file longshoreman, and never did. At least some of it, though, may have come from his strong-willed and outspoken mother, who, like Jack Dempsey's mother, was the dominant parent, forever telling her seven children that, despite the family's straitened circumstances, they could achieve whatever they wanted to if they put their minds to it. Mary Jean Lydon Tunney, a tall, sturdily built woman, knew she may have been stretching things a bit, but felt that a little blarney might just help inspire her brood, or at least some of them.

From what Tunney said in later years, it appears that, as with many young people who grow up poor, his determination and his iron will came from within. In whatever he did from the time he was a child—whether it be in a game of marbles, in a spelling bee in elementary school, or in a foot race—he was determined to win. Once he got through a literally painful adolescent period when, because of his frail physical appearance, he was constantly being set upon by neighborhood hoodlums, young Gene's confidence grew, to a considerable extent because of his athletic talents. A book on willpower also came into play. Tunney was to say that the book, whose title he had forgotten in later years, had inspired him from the time he was fifteen, providing him with ideas on how best to become resolute and determined, which he put in practice in virtually everything he did. One thing he did occasionally as a teenager to steel his resolve and strengthen his willpower was to stare at the sun for up to three minutes, a regimen that no doubt would be strongly discouraged by ophthalmologists.

Though he was the best athlete in his neighborhood age group in his early teens, Tunney did not manifest a self-assurance until he had proven he could hold his own, and even fare better, in occasional street fights. Being better spoken than almost all of his friends, at least in part because of his avid reading habits, further fostered his youthful confidence. His good looks also helped. By his mid-teens, Tunney was strikingly handsome, and the flattering attention he was shown by girls his age and even older certainly didn't hurt his self-image.

That youthful confidence was bolstered further when he showed promise as a boxer before going into the Marines and then winning the American Expeditionary Forces light heavyweight championship. Beyond that, his performance in the boxing ring since his discharge had further buttressed his self-esteem. In twenty-two fights since returning home, Tunney had won sixteen by knockout, including ten inside of two rounds and had fought six no-decision bouts, all of which he appeared to have won.

After breaking his left thumb in one of his last fights in 1920 and with his oft-injured right hand also hurting, Tunney decided to get far away from boxing and from New York, but with the intention of staying physically active. A friend recommended that he go to a lumber camp in Ontario, where he could work as a logger, a physically taxing job but one that would not put undue pressure on his tender hands. So it was that from late December until the end of March, Tunney spent three months at a lumber camp, rising at 5:00 A.M. each workday, and then, armed with an axe and saw, tramping into densely wooded forests with his fellow workers to fell trees and then cut up the trunk and branches. With his left thumb still not sufficiently healed to resume sparring, he then spent a month and a half in Poland Spring, Maine, where an old Marine friend had a business, and where Tunney put in eight hours a day shoveling coal. When he returned to New York, Tunney weighed 185 pounds, fifteen pounds more than when he had left for Ontario. Obviously, the outdoor life, if not the laborious coal-shoveling, had helped bulk Tunney up to a heavyweight.

While Tunney was away, Dempsey was preparing to defend his title for the third time on July 2 at Boyle's Thirty Acres in Jersey City against Georges Carpentier, whose knockout of Battling Levinsky seven months earlier had helped gain him a shot at Dempsey and his championship. With his hands in relatively good shape, Tunney began training as soon as he returned for two fights that Doc Bagley had arranged, the first against a pedestrian fighter named Young Ambrose on June 28 at the Pioneer Athletic Club in Manhattan, and the second against Soldier Jones of Canada in the semifinal of the Dempsey-Carpentier card only four days later. Anxious to fight again, Tunney was particularly ecstatic about the second bout, aware that he would be fighting in front of a huge crowd, already being projected at more than one hundred thousand.

As Doc Bagley expected, Young Ambrose's chin posed no danger to Tunney's healed right hand and left thumb as the Fighting Marine rendered him unconscious when he caught Young Ambrose flush on the jaw with his left one minute into the first round. With Tunney's semifinal appearance in Jersey City only four days away, Bagley was happy with the quick ending.

Accustomed to fighting in small arenas in front of several thousand spectators or less, Tunney was in awe when he came down the aisle of Boyle's Thirty Acres to enter the ring for his fight against Soldier Jones, a fairly good heavyweight. By then, about an hour before the Dempsey-Carpentier bout was scheduled to start, around sixty thousand spectators already were in the wooden bleachers of the stadium that promoter Tex Rickard had had built in a New Jersey swamp across the Hudson River from Manhattan especially for what, in a not uncommon flight-of-word fancy, he had billed as "The Fight of the Century" between Dempsey and Carpentier.

Far too heavy at 185 pounds and still not in good fighting shape, Tunney was also nervous because of the size of the crowd, which would swell to slightly more than eighty thousand by the time Dempsey and Carpentier entered the ring. At the start of the eight-round bout, Tunney was tentative and surprisingly slow against Jones, one of six "Soldier Joneses"—presumably all veterans of the Great War—fighting in North America in the early 1920s. But Tunney needn't have worried—or so Bagley figured, since he was not about to risk Tunney's career in front of a huge crowd and every influential sportswriter in the country.

Awkward and swinging wildly from both sides, Jones made Tunney look bad during the early rounds, connecting with a number of solid shots to the head that jolted Tunney. Only Tunney's ring generalship and some snappy combinations, along with a few wicked right crosses to the jaw, finally wore down the Canadian and prompted the referee to stop the fight in the seventh round. It was hardly an impressive performance, and Tunney knew it. Certainly, he felt, no one in the huge crowd who had bothered to watch any of the semifinal match would have regarded Tunney as a potential challenger for Dempsey's heavyweight title—assuming Dempsey was to beat Carpentier—especially Tex Rickard or any other experienced boxing observers. Luckily for Tunney, few people seemed to pay any attention to the fight, which is usually the case for a preliminary bout before a big fight when most spectators spend the time socializing or, in the 1920s, making bets with one another on the main event.

After his fight, Tunney had his gloves and tape removed, put on a robe, and then knelt in a corner at ringside to watch the Dempsey-Carpentier fight. As it developed, he was to notice something that would in due time change his life forever.

Tunney finished the year with six more victories, all in New York and the last four by knockouts, two of them in Madison Square Garden. Perhaps Tunney's most memorable fight during that stretch was a one-sided bout on Staten Island. Having already knocked down his opponent, Eddie Josephs, nine times, Tunney eased up in the twelfth and final round, refusing to throw a punch because of Josephs's woeful condition, which included several broken ribs and cuts about his face. Tunney became irate when the pro-Josephs crowd inexplicably began to scream at Tunney for holding back. It was to be the first of several times when Tunney, in doing so, earned the wrath of bloodthirsty crowds, which he never could understand and never would appease. That victory, along with the five others—and especially the two in Madison Square Garden—after his unimpressive performance against Soldier Jones, led most New York boxing writers to wonder whether Tunney, now twenty-four, might be something special after all, even if he was a little too gentlemanly in the ring and obviously lacked a killer image.

Dempsey, meanwhile, had taken the rest of the year off. Still hurt by the boos he had heard, along with cries of "Slacker!" as he entered the ring to fight Carpentier—whom he had knocked out in the fourth round—Dempsey would not fight again until the Fourth of July of 1923. That would give him ample time to deal with allegations that he had been duplicitous during the Great War by accepting a draft deferment that more than a few people thought he did not deserve.

If Dempsey wasn't fighting, he was going to the fights occasionally, and, to Tunney's surprise and delight, was at ringside on October 14 when Tunney made his Madison Square Garden debut in a main event fight against Jack Burke, another fairly good but not outstanding young fighter. The Manassa Mauler had heard about the young light heavyweight from Greenwich Village but had never seen him fight, although he may have recalled the chance meeting aboard the ferry two years earlier. Tunney, who had been determined to do well in his first Garden fight now had an even greater incentive, to impress the great Dempsey, who was introduced before the scheduled eight-round bout. And he did. Clearly demonstrating that he was more than just a boxer, Tunney was more aggressive than usual and hurt Burke often with sharp combinations and several punishing right-hand leads while rarely allowing Burke to penetrate his defense before the one-sided bout was stopped in the third round.

Since his discharge, the unbeaten Tunney had won sixteen of his twenty-one fights by knockout, including the last two in main events at boxing's mecca, Madison Square Garden. Though his fights were being covered by the New York papers, he rarely saw himself mentioned between fights. When he asked Bagley if he knew why, his manager, wise in the ways of many of New York's best sportswriters and columnists, told Tunney that in order to get better coverage, it usually required paying off some of the writers. Naive about such payoffs, which were common in the 1920s, Tunney was taken aback, feeling that his steadily improving performances in the ring should suffice to get more space in the sports pages. The writers got paid for writing about fighters, didn't they? True, Bagley replied, but then pointed out to Tunney that promising fighters who paid some writers found themselves written up more often and more flatteringly.

Bagley thereupon reeled off a list of well-known fighters, including Dempsey and Benny Leonard, who, he told Tunney, owed much of their popularity and success to writers who were in effect on their payrolls. Grudgingly, Tunney, who was always tightfisted with money and whose purses still tended to be less than a thousand dollars per fight, agreed to let Bagley go ahead and work out financial arrangements with several writers, reportedly including Damon Runyon and Bill Farnsworth, the sports editor of the *New York American,* a Hearst paper for which Runyon was both the star news reporter and star sportswriter. Under the arrangement, Bagley told Tunney, the writers signed on each would receive 5 percent of Tunney's purses. Not only that, but Bagley told Tunney that it would be a good idea if they doled out financial "gifts" to some other prominent sportswriters after Tunney's fights. That, too, Bagley informed a somewhat incredulous Tunney, was also common practice, and could help Tunney get more main event appearances in places like Madison Square Garden, not to mention far more stories in the New York papers and elsewhere, too, since writers like Runyon were syndicated throughout the country. Sure enough, Tunney found out, as soon as Bagley began paying off the writers Tunney began to get more space in some of the New York dailies, and, in the case of stories written by syndicated writers like Runyon, in some other big-city papers around the country.

Though not yet famous, as he eventually would become, mainly because of his colorful and often exaggerated descriptions of sports events and his popular short stories about Broadway gamblers and their variegated associates, Runyon was a man in perennial search of a buck. Or at least he was before he became famous after some of his make-believe Broadway characters became immortalized in the hit musical *Guys and Dolls.* Barney Nagler, one of the most highly respected boxing writers over a period that extended from the 1930s to the 1980s, was known to become almost apoplectic when he would hear a young sports reporter wax reverentially about Runyon's work. "He was the crookedest writer around, with his hand in every promoter's pocket and in a lot of managers' and fighters' pockets, too," the usually mild-mannered and soft-spoken Nagler once suddenly thundered.

Indeed, Runyon had been on the take of promoters and fight managers since he was a young sportswriter on the *Pueblo Chieftain* in Colorado, where he grew up after his family moved to Colorado from Manhattan, Kansas. Early in his journalistic career, Runyon found out that managers and promoters were willing to pay a sportswriter or sports editor to ensure that their fighters got what they considered adequate space on the local sports pages. Taking a cue from some older writers, Runyon also bought, or was given, part ownership of some fighters in Pueblo and Denver, both good fight towns in the early part of the twentieth century. By owning a piece of a fighter, a sportswriter was even more inclined to write often and favorably about a fistic prospect.

Runyon's ethical misbehavior went even further. In his 1991 biography of Runyon, Jimmy Breslin said that while running an annual Milk Fund boxing benefit at Madison Square Garden for the wife of William Randolph Hearst, Runyon was inclined to skim off some of the gate receipts—in effect, as Breslin put it, stealing money from the babies of indigent New York families. But by then some of Runyon's best friends were well-known New York gangsters whose scruples also left much to be desired.

Then, too, Runyon may have been a pupil of onetime Colorado

sports writing colleague, Otto Floto, the sports editor of the *Denver Evening Post*. The colorful, heavyset Floto not only wrote about fighters in his newspaper; he also promoted some of their fights in Denver, Pueblo, and some other Colorado towns, including some of Jack Dempsey's early bouts. Naturally, Floto was not likely to write disparagingly about those fighters, whom he may also have partially owned. But then the top editors of the *Denver Evening Post* knew that Floto moonlighted as both a fight and wrestling promoter and apparently had no objection to his dual role of promoter and sports editor–fight writer. Floto probably felt underpaid, and his superiors at the *Post* probably agreed that he was. So if Otto could make a little extra money on the side, and thus be happy, why, that was fine, even if it was a flagrant conflict of interest.

The top editors at the *Post* had another reason to make allowances for Floto's prolific outside boxing work. In 1899, the new co-owners of the *Post*, Harry Tammen and Fred Bonfils, started a circus, which they named the Sells-Floto Circus, using Floto's name because of its mellifluous tone along with his portrait on advertising billboards. "Tammen was in love with the name, Floto," Gene Fowler, who began his celebrated newspaper career in Denver, once wrote. Despite the widespread use of his name to advertise the circus—which Jack Dempsey was to perform with briefly while he was the heavyeight champion—Floto was given neither an interest in the circus nor paid anything for the circus using his name. So far as is known, Floto did not complain, as long as he was able to continue writing about fights that he himself was promoting and sometimes about fighters he at least partially owned.

Aware that Georges Carpentier was not about to come to the United States to defend his world light heavyweight title, Tex Rickard decided that he could create his own title in the 175-pound weight class and call it the American light heavyweight championship. Naturally, the wily Rickard had two fighters in mind to compete for the new title—Tunney and Levinsky. After all, Rickard reasoned, Carpentier himself had held contrived titles such as the French welterweight championship and the European welterweight and middleweight titles and even the European heavyweight title, although he never fought at more than 170 pounds—and usually much less—and thus was never a full-fledged heavyweight.

Then, too, promoters in the past had even established racial and ethnic championships for fighters who for reasons ranging from prejudice to inferior talent had not been able to challenge for legitimate world titles. Before he finally got a shot at the world heavyweight championship in 1908 after eleven years as a virtually unbeatable professional, Jack Johnson held the Negro, or colored, heavyweight title for years during an era when many talented black fighters had a difficult time getting title fights within the conventional boxing establishment. For one thing, promoters did not like matching popular champions with large followings against good black boxers, since they ran the risk of diminishing a white fighter's stature, and thus his drawing appeal to the financial detriment of many promoters. Second, at least during the first three decades of the twentieth century, not many black fans attended championship fights, primarily for economic reasons, and therefore, the promoters knew, black champions—even great ones like Joe Gans, who reigned as the lightweight champion from 1900 to 1908—were not good gate attractions.

Conversely, although for more specious reasons, so-called Great White Hopes like Fireman Jim Flynn, who was knocked out twice by Johnson, and Ed "Gunboat" Smith—both leading, but certainly not outstanding, heavyweights—found themselves, along with other white fighters, fighting for "world white heavyweight championships," to which virtually no one except a few promoters gave any credence whatsoever. Johnson himself often attended such fights, sitting at ringside and smiling. He didn't have to say it, but everyone looking at him knew what he was thinking: he could take these guys on, one after the other, or maybe even both at the same time, and knock them out whenever he wanted to.

In matching Tunney against Levinsky, Rickard knew all too well that he ran the risk of staging a dull fight, since both fighters were counterpunchers, meaning they tended to box reactively and not proactively, although Tunney definitely tended to be the more aggressive of the two. As a rule, the best fights are those between punchers and counterpunchers, fights where one boxer is the aggressor and the other counters his offensive attack, and those involving two punchers.

Matching counterpunchers against each other, by contrast, usually was certain to produce a slow-paced fight with a premium on defense. It could be pretty to some boxing purists, but it was almost always anathema to those spectators who showed up, and usually not many did. But Rickard was sure they would turn out for a Tunney-Levinsky fight, knowing that while Levinsky, always popular in New York, would most assuredly stay on the defensive, Tunney, on the way up and wanting to impress friends and sportswriters, would fight aggressively, which he had already shown he was more than capable of doing.

Before the largest crowd ever to see a fight in the second Garden—a capacity gathering of more than fourteen thousand—Tunney received a huge ovation when he entered the ring, while Levinsky drew a moderate response, largely in tribute to his long career and his trademark durability. From the opening bell, it was evident that Tunney was the far superior fighter and that Levinsky, after so many ring battles over so many years, had little left. Pressuring Levinsky throughout, Tunney was the aggressor from the outset and had little trouble landing a wide variety of punches.

By the seventh round, it had become merely a battle for survival for Levinsky. With cheers from the pro-Tunney crowd, he fought back and held his own in the eighth and ninth rounds of the twelve-round fight. But by the tenth round, he could do little but retreat and hold on the rest of the way. By the final bell, Tunney had won all twelve rounds on the scorecards of the referee and two judges. Later, Tunney told how Levinsky, totally spent, had asked Tunney at the start of the last round not to knock him out and to let him finish the fight. Tunney agreed and proceeded to let up as a concession to Levinsky's pride and his long and distinguished career.

"Then, lo and behold, the Battler lets me have it right on the jaw with a right-hand punch," recalled Tunney. "I felt so foolish, and actually laughed, realizing I had been had by a great old pro. But I declined to respond in kind and let him finish the fight."

Feeling he was financially secure and aware that his best days as a boxer were far behind him, Levinsky, though only thirty years old, announced his retirement a few months after the Tunney fight. But like so many fighters, Levinsky, devoid of any business acumen, made a number of poor investments and, running low on cash, returned to the ring in 1926 at the age of thirty-five. The four-year layoff did not help, and like scores of other former champions who have made comebacks, Levinsky, now a full-grown heavyweight, was nowhere near the fighter he had been. Fighting primarily in the Northeast, but only once in New York, Levinsky won eighteen fights, lost six, fought six no-decision bouts, and had one draw against an array of second-rate fighters.

His finish was ignominious. Approaching his thirty-eighth birthday, and twenty-four years after his boxing career had started, Levinsky was disqualified in the fifth round of a fight in Grand Rapids, Michigan, when, showing no inclination to fight, he refused to heed the referee's command to throw some punches. Against the advice of his manager, Ai Lippe, to retire, Levinsky entered the ring for the last time in Hagerstown, Maryland, on January 15, 1929, against Herman Weiner, a journeyman boxer whom he had outpointed in an eight-round fight four months earlier. Only seconds into the fight, Weiner knocked Levinsky down with a right cross. After two more knockdowns, the referee stopped the fight midway through the opening round.

Returning to his wife and two children in Philadelphia after having fought an estimated five hundred fights, Levinsky invested his comeback earnings in real estate only a few months before the Wall Street collapse, which occurred in 1929, the year of his second and final retirement from the ring. Shortly before the stock market implosion, Levinsky, his wife, their seven-year-old son, Stanley, and three-year-old daughter, Harriet, moved to Manhattan where the old Battler opened a boxing gym. "When the stock market crashed, my father lost everything," Levinsky's daughter, Harriet Solodky, later said.

Back in Philadelphia, Levinsky became a real estate agent for about a decade, ran a gymnasium for a few years, and then worked in a shipyard as a steelworker during World War II. It was while working in Cramp's Shipyard that Levinsky and his wife got word that their son, then a twenty-two-year-old private in the Army, had been killed during the Battle of the Bulge in France in January of 1945.

"That devastated my father for the rest of his life," Harriet Solodky said. Levinsky died in 1949 of complications from pneumonia following an automobile accident. He was fifty-eight years old. "He was a wonderful father who hardly ever talked about his days as a boxer," his daughter said.

After beating Levinsky, Tunney was hardly content to rest on his laurels. He was now unbeaten in thirty-eight consecutive fights, and, at long last, he seemed to be getting noticed, both because of his victory over Levinsky and because of the two sports columnists now on his payroll. Following four more victories, three by knockouts, Billy Gibson and Tex Rickard felt that Tunney was ready for his most difficult test yet: a defense of his American light heavyweight title against the Pittsburgh Windmill, Harry Greb.

Tunney had never been in a ring with anyone resembling Greb, in style or talent. And although Greb, as a middleweight, fought at around 158 pounds, he had already beaten more than a few light heavyweights and even heavyweights weighing more than 200 pounds. Win or lose, Tunney was guaranteed not to forget the experience of being in a boxing ring with Harry Greb. Then, too, Greb might not know what to expect from the unbeaten and supremely confident young light heavyweight from Greenwich Village, who was now perhaps the hottest prospect in boxing. That he had also served as a marine during the Great War, and was handsome and intelligent, made him all the more appealing, if somewhat unusual for a fighter. But in Greb, Tunney would not only be matched against a quintessential ring brawler but against the "King of Dirty Tricks," a title Greb was particularly proud of. Gene Tunney would need more in the ring than his supreme confidence to beat the Pittsburgh Windmill.

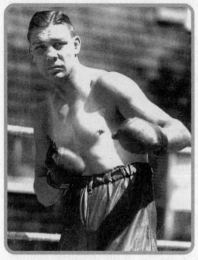

Harry Greb, the Pittsburgh Windmill.
THE STANLEY WESTON COLLECTION

EIGHT

The Pittsburgh Windmill

Amateur psychologists, and perhaps some real ones, too, were sometimes inclined to attribute Jack Dempsey's killer instinct in the boxing ring to a hardscrabble boyhood followed by an early manhood spent largely among hoboes, prostitutes, gamblers, hard-drinking miners and railroad workers, and sleazy boxing promoters, the latter of whom often took advantage of both his indigence and his naïveté.

Dempsey never did claim that those harsh experiences accounted for his unbridled ferocity in the ring, although he sometimes hinted that, subconsciously, they may have had something to do with it. If that was the case, it would have been understandable, since life, for Dempsey, right into his early twenties had been a constant struggle for survival, in and out of the ring. Not that he would have been an exception. Over the years, a legion of fighters have used boxing not only as a means of making a living but also to bolster their self-image or vent their wrath against society for reasons ranging from unhappy childhoods to real or perceived discrimination by employers, biased judges, and juries.

Harry Greb was certainly not one of them, although he fought with the intensity of a man who frequently had been wronged and was out to get even. There may never have been another fighter like Greb. His style, if you could call it that, was a helter-skelter mélange of rapid-fire punches, both legal and illegal, some of which were thrown from seemingly impossible angles and at times while Greb seemed to be airborne. He rarely ever trained, yet got stronger and more effective as a fight wore on, even if it lasted twenty rounds. And all the while he lived every day as if it might be his last, savoring a wide variety of worldly pleasures and racing expensive cars at breakneck speeds, often resulting in both wrecked cars and hospitalization. Despite, or perhaps because of, that lifestyle, Greb may have been the most popular athlete in Pittsburgh in the second and third decades of the twentieth century, rivaled only by the great Pittsburgh Pirates star shortstop, Honus Wagner.

Greb had grown up in a middle-class neighborhood in Pittsburgh, the second son of a German-born father, a stone mason and good provider for his Irish-American wife and their two sons and four daughters. Apart from his father's rigid opposition to him becoming a fighter, nothing in Greb's background would seem to have been responsible for his comportment inside a boxing ring, where he would flail away with a dizzying array of punches and utilize illegal tactics, such as thumbing, heeling, head-butting, biting, holding, and hitting at the same time, and even tripping and kneeing opponents. As one of the best fighters of all time, a natural middleweight who usually weighed between 150 and 158 pounds and often fought and beat men 40 and 50 pounds heavier, Greb did not have to rely on such unseemly tactics. But to Greb, boxing was a form of warfare, a battle for survival, and everything and anything went, even when he already had a fight won. "Prizefighting ain't the noblest of arts," he once said, "and I ain't the noblest artist."

What he indisputably was, though, was one of the most colorful fighters ever, a roistering sybarite who, despite his frenetic style of living, often fought three or four times in one week. In a milieu of womanizers, Greb also may have been the undisputed champion, to the point of "entertaining," as he would put it, one or even two women in his dressing room before a fight. While it was hardly regarded as a sensible pre-fight ritual by boxing trainers, who usually barred wives and girlfriends from training camps on the ground that sex was so physically draining, let alone right before a fight, Greb's handlers went along with his dressing room peccadilloes since they did not seem to affect his subsequent performance in the ring.

If Greb got mussed up at all during his pre-fight trysts, it hardly showed when he got into a boxing ring. Tough as he was, he was also exceedingly vain, slicking down his pompadoured, dark hair with Vaseline, covering his face with talcum powder—which he thought enhanced his appearance in or out of the ring—and usually carried a comb, pocket mirror, and powder puff in his robe so that he could spruce up between rounds, if necessary. If no one was ever going to see Harry Greb give less than his best in the ring, tainted though Greb's best might be, he also wanted to make sure he didn't look anything but his best before, during, and after a fight. As with Benny Leonard, nothing could trigger Greb's anger faster than a fighter who had the temerity to muss up his hair. Punch him in the face, fine. But muss his hair, be prepared for some rough retaliation.

What made Greb all the more remarkable was his aversion to conventional boxing training. Rarely did he go through the time-honored fighter's rituals of doing roadwork before dawn and then punching the light and heavy bags, skipping rope, and sparring in a gym. His argument against traditional training routines was convincing. What was the point of him training, Greb would ask when pressed about his rare appearances in a gym between fights, when he usually fought several times a week? In 1919, for example, he fought an amazing forty-four times, only five fewer times than Rocky Marciano fought during his professional career. "If I'm going to leave my fighting anywhere, it'll be on a beauty rest with some skirt," he said in the early 1920s. "I'm open to suggestions if anybody can name a pleasanter way."

Although he was only twenty-eight years old when he fought Tunney, Greb already had a recorded 229 fights—friends and close associates said he probably had had as many as a hundred more—and had beaten such good fighters as Al McCoy, George Chip, Jack Dillon, and Battling Levinsky, along with most of the top-ranked heavyweights. In a remarkable demonstration of rapid-fire, and unrelenting, punching, he outclassed Jack Dempsey in two sparring sessions in 1920, the year after Dempsey had won the heavyweight title and outweighed Greb by about thirty-five pounds. Over a ten-year span, he had lost only ten fights, but had avenged almost all of them in subsequent bouts.

It is unlikely that any great fighter had more nicknames. The Pittsburgh Windmill may have been the most appropriate and the most often used, but Greb was also called the Human Windmill, the Iron City Express, the Smoky City Bearcat, the Rubber Man, and the Wildest Tiger. He also was described as a buzzsaw, a whirlwind, a human dynamo, and perpetual motion in action, along with such unflattering terms as King of the Alley Fighters and the dirtiest fighter in boxing history. The best description of Greb's idiosyncratic fighting style, though, may have come from perhaps the preeminent sportswriter of the 1920s and 1930s, Grantland Rice, who wrote that Greb "comes upon an opponent like a swarm of bees" and was "a cross between a wildcat and a hornet's nest." Rice also described Greb as "one of the most remarkable athletic products in the history of the world." True, that was written in 1926, but by then Rice had already covered such notable athletes as Jim Thorpe, Jack Dempsey, Babe Ruth, Ty Cobb, Red Grange, Bill Tilden, and Bobby Jones. As for Greb's boxing ability, Rice wrote, "He is not only remarkably fast on his feet, but a streak of lightning with either hand. He can hit a man oftener from more different directions than any man that ever lived. I have seen him, when almost completely off-balance, hit a good boxer three times before a return was made." Damon Runyon found Greb fascinating for another reason. Well aware of Greb's penchant for women and nightlife in general, Runyon wrote, "The most remarkable thing about this truly remarkable man is how he musters the stamina to even slip through the ring ropes."

Though scandal was never attached to his name, Greb bet heavily on his fights, usually the entire purse, even when he got to the point where he was making almost forty thousand dollars for a fight. "No fighter ever sent it in more than Greb," Runyon said, alluding to his tendency to bet on himself. Greb also had a unique method of manipulating odds on his fights so that he would be less of a favorite and thus, if he gambled on himself and then won, which he practically always did, he would pocket more money. To tip the odds against himself in a big fight, he was apt to turn up drunk in front of boxing people, especially sportswriters and gamblers, the day before or even the day of a fight. In July of 1925, for example, Greb was favored to beat welterweight champion Mickey Walker, who was going after Greb's middleweight title at the Polo Grounds in New York. Aware that most of the city's best-known sportswriters and columnists often congregated at Billy LaHiff's restaurant on West 48th Street, Greb, accompanied by two women, got out of a taxi in front of the restaurant and staggered into LaHiff's appearing to be drunk less than ten hours before his fight with Walker.

Gamblers who had already bet heavily on Greb blanched at the sight of him, as did a number of the sportswriters who had picked, and bet on, Greb to win. Not surprisingly, they switched their bets as quickly as they could, prompting the odds on Greb to drop. Greb, as it turned out, had been drinking nothing stronger than ginger ale, which he would continue to drink at LaHiff's, a popular gathering place for sports and entertainment figures and politicians. Later that day, on July 2, Greb—a moderate drinker at best, who usually preferred soft drinks to hard liquor—would decisively defeat Walker in a bout in which referee Jack Purdy was knocked down twice, not unusual in a Greb fight. Thanks to his impressive impression of an inebriated drinker, Greb made far more money on his hefty wager than he would have otherwise.

By the time Greb was born on June 6, 1884, in the middle-class neighborhood called Bloomfield, Pittsburgh was already best known for the steel mills that were the city's economic bedrock. Though Pittsburgh had been a good fight town since the 1880s, major league baseball was the main recreation in the early 1900s for the tens of thousands of factory workers. As the new century began, Pittsburgh's brightest sports star was Honus Wagner, who came to be known as "The Flying Dutchman," and would lead the National League in batting eight times. Greb's father, Pious, idolized Wagner, both because of his playing ability and because they shared a German heritage. Hoping that his son would one day grow up to be a Pirate, Pious Greb spent hours playing catch with little Edward Henry and taking him to Pirate games. But during the games of catch, Pious found young Edward Henry a reluctant participant who not only had trouble throwing and catching a baseball but also struggled just to pay attention.

Like Tunney, Greb was small for his age and also tried to avoid street fights as a boy. When neighborhood bullies harassed him, he would run away rather than fight it out with someone older and heavier. Young Harry, as he was called, reached a breaking point one day in his early teens when he was accosted by four older boys in full view of his father, who looked on as the boys tied his son to the wheel of a wagon. "He broke loose, ran them down and whipped them so thoroughly that I never saw them in our neighborhood again," Pious Greb said. That may have been one of the few times, if indeed not the only time, Pious Greb was proud of his son as a fighter.

It may also have convinced young Harry Greb that he was better with his fists than with a bat and glove. Taking up the sport with a vengeance at one of the many boxing gyms in Pittsburgh, Greb, at eighteen, won the Pennsylvania amateur welterweight champion, and, a month later, made his professional debut in Pittsburgh, winning a six-round decision. When he told his parents he had become a fighter, the reaction from Pious Greb was not unexpected. Staring at his son, his face red with anger, Pious said, "No boy of mine who engages in it can live under my roof. Now get out." Knowing that there was no point in remonstrating with his father, young Harry turned to kiss his sobbing mother. Annie Greb had lost one son much too early in his life and did not want to lose another, even in the figurative sense, while he was only eighteen years old. But she, too, knew there was no point in arguing with her stubborn and domineering husband. And even if Pious Greb did change his mind, his wife knew that if their son continued fighting, life for him in the Greb household would be a hell on earth.

It would be an estrangement that would last for years.

Out on his own at the age of eighteen, which was not uncommon with young men from working-class families in 1913, Greb lived with friends for several years while continuing to work as a tinsmith's apprentice at the Westinghouse plant in Pittsburgh. But away from the job, due to his all-out, gung ho style of fighting and his refusal to give any quarter, Greb soon became a favorite among raucous Pittsburgh fight crowds.

Over the next six years, Greb would fight almost two hundred times, losing only a few no-decision fights, which most of his bouts were, and beating some of the best light heavyweights and heavyweights. But neither Mike O'Dowd nor Johnny Wilson, back-to-back middleweight champions, were willing to risk their titles against Greb, who by 1920 was recognized as one of the best fighters in the world. When Greb finally did get to meet O'Dowd in 1918, he beat him in a ten-round, nontitle bout in O'Dowd's hometown of St. Paul, Minnesota.

After about 150 fights, Greb finally made it to Madison Square Garden in New York in 1918. By now twenty-four years old, Greb fought a six-round exhibition against highly ranked heavyweight Ed "Gunboat" Smith, who had beaten Jess Willard before Willard won the heavyweight crown from Jack Johnson. Boxing was still illegal in New York on May 24, 1918, when the program was staged as a wartime benefit for the Red Cross, and thus all the fights were billed as exhibitions with no decisions rendered. A capacity crowd of about twelve thousand packed the Garden to watch Greb, Smith, and such prominent fighters as Battling Levinsky, Ted "Kid" Lewis, Lew Tendler, Jack Britton, and Johnny Dundee box six- and four-round bouts. In his account of the Greb-Smith fight, George Underwood of the *New York Sun* summed up the opinion of most boxing writers covering the bouts when he wrote that "Greb's youth and strength counterbalanced the ring craft of the veteran Smith. Greb was entitled to the verdict."

Five days after his Madison Square Garden debut, Greb was back in the ring at a minor league ballpark in Toledo, Ohio, where he won a fifteen-round newspaper decision. Three weeks later, Greb fought again in the Garden where he won a six-round decision over Zulu Kid, a highly rated middleweight whom Greb had already beaten twice. As if that weren't enough activity, Greb was in a Bridgeport, Connecticut, boxing ring four days later, winning another fifteen-round decision. That meant that in exactly one month, Greb had fought four times and a total of forty-two rounds, more than many fighters nowadays fight in an entire year.

By now, Greb had become a big draw at fight clubs throughout the Northeast and in the Midwest, primarily because of his hyperkinetic style of fighting and his consistent winning. Wherever the Windmill went, it seemed, he managed to find a girl or two or three, often catching the eye of one while he was fighting. His manager, Red Mason, told of how during a fight in Cleveland, Greb came back to his corner and asked Mason if, during the following round, he would ask the blonde with the permanent wave in the second row off to the left— "the one with the grapefruit knockers," Greb specified—if she'd be agreeable to having a drink with Greb after the fight. Greb, of course, had more than just a drink in mind, especially since he rarely drank, and Mason knew it. Mason demurred on the ground that he had enough to do during the fight, but, at Greb's insistence, finally consented. To Mason's surprise, the blonde agreed to have a drink with Harry. It was not to be the only time Greb would ask him to be his post-fight matchmaker.

In keeping with his vanity, Greb was rarely ever seen in public without a suit, tie, white shirt, and dress shoes. True, boxing intruded as often as five times a month, but if he loved the lights of nights, especially those of Manhattan, he loved to fight, too. The question among some people, Red Mason one of them, was whether he could combine high living and boxing and still win a championship someday. Or would Greb's at times out-of-control style of living, including his recklessness behind the wheel of a car, eventually prove disastrous. Greb had a ready response to criticism of his lifestyle. Hadn't anyone noticed, he would say, that he always had plenty of energy in the ring and gave fans their money's worth, if not more? Having a good time, he was certain, was having no effect whatsoever on his boxing career. And who could argue with him? Well, maybe Pious Greb. Whenever friends asked him about his son's celebrity status, Pious, who never went to any of Harry's fights, even at his beloved Forbes Field, would say, "He was a good baseball player. He should have stuck to baseball."

While serving in the Navy as a boxing instructor for a little more than a year during World War I, Greb still managed to get in nineteen fights, thanks to the Navy's generous policy toward professional athletes. By late 1918, while Greb was still on active duty, what many regarded as the unthinkable occurred: Harry Greb fell in love. The girl was eighteen-year-old Mildred Reilly, a pretty brunette from Beaver Falls, a Pittsburgh suburb, and on January 13 they were married at the Church of the Epiphany in Pittsburgh in the biggest wedding of the year in what was then called the Smoky City.

Over the next two years, Greb lost only two of forty-six fights and became, in the opinion of most boxing experts, the best middleweight in the world. Greb would make an even bigger impression on the boxing establishment during two sparring sessions in September of 1920. The Pittsburgh Windmill was in Benton Harbor, Michigan, for a fight with a fairly good light heavyweight named Chuck Wiggins, whom Greb had already beaten all three times they had met. The bout was to be on the undercard of Jack Dempsey's first title defense, against Billy Miske, on Labor Day.

Dempsey was already in training in Benton Harbor, and his manager, Jack Kearns, got the idea of asking Greb to spar with Dempsey. Kearns's reasoning was that Greb—like Miske more of a boxer than a puncher—would provide the Manassa Mauler with a good workout. With scores of sportswriters among the spectators looking on, Greb gave Dempsey more than a good workout. For three rounds, Greb darted in and out, peppering Dempsey with punches and eluding whatever blows Dempsey threw at him. If anyone had kept score, Greb would have won all three rounds handily. When it was over, Dempsey was left embarrassed and also angry at Kearns for inviting Greb to spar with him. As for the sportswriters who witnessed the session, they had a field day reporting how Greb—five inches shorter and thirty-five pounds lighter—had boxed the ears off the great Dempsey.

Upset over the newspaper accounts of the sparring session, Dempsey asked Kearns to try to get Greb back in the ring with him so that he could save face by knocking out the Pittsburgh Windmill.

Kearns did not think much of the idea, fearing that Greb would embarrass Dempsey again. But Dempsey insisted and Kearns, not surprisingly, found Greb eager to box with Dempsey again the next afternoon. Kearns was right; it was a mistake. Dempsey, trying desperately for a knockout, found nothing but air with most of his punches. Meanwhile, Greb, so much quicker and faster afoot than Dempsey, peppered the champion at one juncture with about fifteen unanswered punches. Kearns, realizing that the large corps of sportswriters at ringside were again likely to write how Dempsey had looked absolutely awful against Greb, let the round go for almost five minutes, feeling that the Manassa Mauler inevitably would land a haymaker that would knock out Greb. Dempsey never even came close, and, finally, Kearns signaled an end to the round and to the sparring session.

Dempsey's embarrassment was palpable as he left the ring. And when Greb sought a fight with Dempsey several years later, Kearns said, "The hell with that seven-year itch. We don't want any part of him."

If his performances against Dempsey were uplifting to Greb, even more so was the birth of his and Mildred's daughter, Dorothy, in 1920. She would be their only child, and, sadly, Mildred would not live to see her daughter grow up. A year later, in 1921, Mildred, only twenty-one at the time, would be stricken with tuberculosis and, late in the year, confined to a sanitarium while Harry's oldest sister, Ida, and her husband took care of little Dorothy. The birth of his daughter and his wife's illness had a profound effect on the heretofore carefree and at times irresponsible Greb. Concerned about Mildred's illness, which grew increasingly worse, he toned down his night-crawling while on the road, where he was most of the time, and called her almost daily.

Greb's next fight, on August 29, 1921, in Pittsburgh, was memorable both for its ugliness and its physical impact on the Pittsburgh Windmill. Greb's opponent was Kid Norfolk, the "Black Thunderbolt," as he was called, who fought as a light heavyweight and heavyweight and who on the night of the fight outweighed Greb by eighteen pounds. Greb knew that Norfolk was a rough customer and could thumb, gouge, and butt with the best of them, including Greb himself.

In a bruising battle marred by flagrant fouling, Greb, enraged by a head butt, deliberately thumbed Norfolk in his previously injured left eye. In the following round, Norfolk reciprocated by sweeping his left thumb across Greb's right eye. Partially blinded, Greb had difficulty seeing out of the damaged eye for the rest of the fight, which Norfolk clearly won on a newspaper decision. As it turned out, Greb had lost more than a fight; he had suffered a detached retina and by the end of the year he would have lost virtually all of the sight in his right eye.

Blindness, more than punch-drunkenness, has always been the bête noir of most fighters. The great Sam Langford would end up blind because of eye injuries sustained in the ring. So did Pete Herman, a Hall of Fame bantamweight champion both before and after World War I. Marvin Hart, one of only two fighters to outpoint Jack Johnson before he won the title, was blind in one eye when he beat Jack Root to win the heavyweight championship in 1904 following the retirement of champion James J. Jeffries. By the end of 1921 Kid Norfolk also would be blind in the eye further aggravated by Greb. Now Harry Greb, in his prime at the age of twenty-seven, was, for all intents and purposes, blind in one eye. As it developed, hardly anyone would be aware of it until after he died.

Despite his worsening right eye, Greb fought, and won, six more times in 1921, including his second bout in Madison Square on November 4 in which he outpointed Charley Weinert, a ranking heavyweight, in a fifteen-round bout. It turned out to be the last time Greb would be able to see an opponent out of his right eye. By Christmas, it had failed completely. So it was that, starting in 1922, when he would face his most difficult opponents yet, Harry Greb would be a one-eyed fighter.

Greb told practically no one—and why would he? Despite his monumental handicap, he was on a roll. He had lost only one of twenty-one fights in 1921, the vicious brawl with Kid Norfolk, and he most certainly did not want anyone, especially promoters, to know about his bad eye, since he knew most of them would become wary of booking him. Also, opponents would take advantage of his diminished sight in a variety of ways, such as moving constantly to their left so that he would have trouble seeing them.

Though now fighting with one eye, Greb would have a remarkable year in 1922. He would fight only eleven times, but his opponents would include the top-ranked heavyweight contender, Tommy Gibbons; the eventual light heavyweight champion, Tommy Loughran; and the reigning American light heavyweight titleholder, Gene Tunney, who was unbeaten in thirty-nine professional fights.

A natural light heavyweight, Gibbons had not lost any of his eighty-five professional fights and had won fourteen of his last fifteen bouts by knockouts coming into his fifteen-round bout against Greb at Madison Square Garden on March 13, 1922. In light of that record, an eight-pound weight advantage and a four-inch-longer reach, Gibbons was a 12-to-5 favorite to beat Greb. But on this night Gibbons could not avoid Greb's unrelenting barrage of punches, thrown, as usual, from every conceivable angle. When the fight was over, Gibbons had won only three of the fifteen rounds.

Gibbons had no complaints about the decision. Indeed, he was surprised to hear that he had won any rounds at all. "I seemed to have run into a solid wall of leather," he said. "I never saw so many boxing gloves in my life. Harry's a human buzzsaw. His punches seemed to come from everywhere—from the gallery, from under my shoes, from behind my back. If Harry had a real punch, I'd never have finished on my feet."

For his virtuoso performance, Greb received his biggest purse yet—seventeen thousand dollars, more than double the amount he had received for any previous fight. Considering that the Windmill took a big advantage of the 2-to-1 odds against him, he actually made considerably more—close, friends said, to twice more than his purse. Among the many spectators impressed by Greb's performance were Dempsey—who, after his own experience with the Windmill in a the sparring sessions three years earlier, knew how Gibbons must have felt trying to get untracked against the gyrating Greb—and twenty-four-year-old Gene Tunney.

Tunney had never seen anyone like Greb, and, while leaving the Garden, he was glad to know that the Windmill was no threat to his title. After all, Greb was a middleweight and Tunney already was thinking of moving on into the heavyweight ranks so that he could fight Dempsey, whom he was sure he could beat. What with his helter-skelter style of fighting and his great speed, Greb could be another matter. Still, Tunney had heard talk about Rickard matching him against the winner of the Greb-Gibbons bout. Because of that possibility, Tunney was hoping Greb would win. He felt that, given Gibbons's punching power, he was not ready for him at this stage of his career. And had he known that Greb was now fighting with only one eye, Tunney would have had even more reason to fight him rather than Gibbons.

As it turned out, Tunney got his wish. Highly impressed by Greb and the emotions he aroused, Tex Rickard matched Greb against Tunney for Tunney's North American light heavyweight title on May 23, 1922, at Madison Square Garden. Greb would have to give away about fifteen pounds, five inches in height, and several inches in reach to Tunney, but what else was new? Neither his new manager, George Engel, nor the 5' 8" Greb could last remember when, if ever, the Windmill had fought anyone lighter or smaller than him.

While the negotiations were going on, Engel booked Greb to fight Al Roberts, a reputable light heavyweight who had given Tunney one of his toughest fights two years earlier, in Boston only eleven days before the Tunney bout. Roberts, he felt, would be no trouble, and Tunney wouldn't be that much harder. The close proximity of the two fights did not bother Greb in the least. Roberts, as Greb expected, turned out to be an easy knockout victim. Now it was the unbeaten Tunney's turn. And in New York, Greb's favorite party town.

No one who saw the fight would ever forget it.

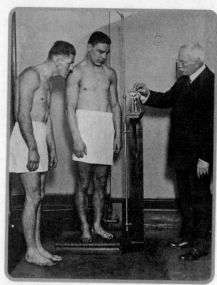

*Tunney, left, and Greb weigh in for their first fight,
with commissioner William Muldoon.*
BOXING HALL OF CHAMPIONS

W hen he agreed to Tex Rickard's proposal for a fight between
Harry Greb and Gene Tunney, more than a few smart boxing people thought that Tunney's manager, Doc Bagley, was
making a mistake, and a big one at that. Everyone seemed to
agree that Tunney was a very good prospect, but was not ready for
Greb. The Pittsburgh Windmill, they figured, was likely not only to
outfight Tunney but to rough him up with tactics unfamiliar to the
young and ethical boxer. Such a fight, they said, might even destroy
Tunney's confidence. After all, young Gene Tunney was going to go
into the ring with the King of the Alley Fighters.

Of course none of them knew that Harry Greb was now fighting
with one eye. Despite that handicap, Greb was confident of beating
Tunney. Meanwhile, Tunney had taken six weeks off since knocking
out Jack Burke for the second time. To prepare for Greb, Tunney spent
a month at what, for the next three years, would become his favorite
training site: a dairy farm owned by a close friend, Barry McCormack,

in Red Bank, New Jersey, about forty-five miles from Manhattan. Though he was a city boy by birth and upbringing, Tunney had become more and more attached to country living since spending the three months at the lumber camp in Ontario during the winter of 1921. Unlike many fighters who chafed at the spartan training quarters in a country setting, Tunney reveled in the farm's rustic charm and the tranquillity of the surrounding area.*

Hiring sparring partners who could emulate Greb's style was difficult, simply because virtually no one else fought like the Pittsburgh Windmill. Doc Bagley did the best he could, though, and brought in several fighters renowned for, if not much else, their roughhouse tactics. Most sportswriters who watched Tunney at Red Bank were impressed, but the more perceptive writers like W. O. McGeehan, Hype Igoe, and Damon Runyon knew that Tunney's sparring partners were pale imitations of Greb. If any of them could fight like the Windmill, they certainly wouldn't be sparring partners, whose ranks mainly constituted fighters on the downhill side of their careers or journeymen boxers who preferred the fairly steady employment that the job offered to one who was good at simulating another fighter. Demeaning as it might seem, serving as a sparring partner could be a lot better than dealing with unscrupulous managers and living a nomadic existence for very little money. Then, too, if you were a sparring partner for a champion, you often got to hang out with him and probably get your name in the papers more than when you were fighting in tank towns for small purses. Moreover, if you were still relatively young, sparring with top-ranked fighters could become a form of on-the-job training that could improve you as a boxer and even jump-start your career, as it did for eventual heavyweight champion Jimmy Braddock. After all, you may have taken a daily pounding from a Jack Dempsey—who would play cards with you in the morning and then try to knock you senseless in the afternoon—but you would be learning from the very best in the business. After such sparring sessions, fighting far less talented fighters in conventional bouts could sometimes be a lot easier, and compared to, say, Dempsey, a lot less dangerous.

*Such settings seemed to be requisite for boxers until gambling casinos became the most common venues for boxing in the 1970s and boxers were obliged to train there for their fights.

Greb had never seen Tunney fight, but, no matter, because he fought everybody the same way in his helter-skelter, buzzsaw fashion. He rarely ever watched opponents in advance, feeling it was a waste of time. Tunney, by contrast, did whenever he could, looking for flaws of which he might take advantage.

In advance of the fight, Dempsey, in an interview with Hype Igoe, had some cautionary words for Tunney about Greb. Obviously remembering his frustrating sparring sessions with the Windmill twenty months earlier, Dempsey said of Greb, "Funniest hitter in the world. He makes you think you're in a glove factory and shelves of them are tumbling down on you. He can slap you to death, I tell you. I found that the best way to get him was at close quarters. Getting close to him, however, isn't the easiest thing in the world."

Dempsey, of course, never had during his sparring sessions with Greb.

As always on the night of a big fight, the ornate lobby of the second Madison Square Garden was enveloped in smoke and made both raucous and boisterous by clamorous, even bellowing, fight fans, the boxing managers and trainers and promoters; the former fighters, many of them down and out and in either the early or late stages of dementia; the mobsters, politicians, grifters, and others who reveled in the noise, the smoke, the anticipation, and what passed for camaraderie. During the preliminary bouts, hundreds of gamblers, many in garish sports jackets, made wagers on Greb or Tunney, either with one another or with bookmakers who conducted business openly in full view of security guards in what had long been a pre-fight ritual at the second Garden and would continue to be at the third Garden at Eighth Avenue and 50th Street after it opened in September 1925.

Most of the five hundred or so members of a Pittsburgh contingent that had arrived by train the night before put their money on Greb— but then so, too, did most savvy boxing fans. By fight time, Greb was a 3-to-1 favorite to win, even though Tunney outweighed Greb by twelve pounds, was five inches taller, and had a five-inch-longer reach, which is often decisive for a skillful boxer such as Tunney.

Even though he was an avid boxing fan and his son had become one of the hottest prospects in the sport, John Tunney still had never seen him fight. Knowing how much his father liked boxing and how he himself had tried to pattern himself after his father's favorite fighter of the past, James J. Corbett, Gene kept hoping that his dad would eventually come to see him fight, perhaps against Greb in his biggest fight yet.

Following his first fight in 1915 when he knocked out Bobby Dawson in the seventh round, Tunney asked his father why he had not come to the bout.

"Do you think I would be happy seeing you bleeding?" John Tunney replied.

"No," Gene, then eighteen, said, "but I didn't get a scratch."

"But how was I to know that beforehand?" John Tunney said. "Take your mother's and my advice and do not do this thing anymore. Just consider yourself lucky in getting away without a scratch this time. This kind of luck won't continue if you make further attempts."

It would prove to be a prophetic comment.

John Tunney never did come to one of his son's fights, much to Gene's chagrin. Yet he knew that, in not wanting to see him fight, his father was no different from most other immigrants whose sons became fighters, although John Tunney's rationale was probably different.

As always, Greb, upon entering the ring, was the picture of confidence. With his dark hair slicked down and parted down the middle and his face heavily powdered, he had the appearance, as one writer put it, of "a street corner Dan Juan." Tunney could not have looked more different, a clean-cut yin to Greb's slick-looking yang. After receiving a far louder ovation, Tunney stood quietly in his corner, tall, square-jawed, and handsome, with his light brown hair in a modified crew cut.

From the opening bell, it soon became evident that whatever confidence Tunney had—and he had a surfeit of it—was unfounded against Harry Greb. Certainly, Tunney never expected what was to befall him. Neither did most of the sportswriters at ringside, among them Grantland Rice, Damon Runyon, and Westbrook Pegler. From the opening to the closing bells, Tunney, as Rice put it in his story the following day,

"fell into a hornet's nest last night and came near being stung to death."
Indeed, even those Greb supporters who had to wager fifteen dollars to
win five dollars never expected that the bout would be so one-sided.

Because of a cut on the left eyebrow that Tunney had sustained two
weeks before, Dr. Robert Shea, a friend who had been in Tunney's
training camp at Red Bank, injected Adrenalin Chloride into the eyebrow in the dressing room before the fight. He also injected Novocain
into the knuckles of both of Tunney's hands, which, once again, had
been sore during his sparring sessions. As it happened, Tunney would
need a lot more Adrenalin Chloride before the fight was over.

Charging across the ring at the opening bell, Greb immediately
landed a right to the jaw, followed by a chopping left that landed
flush on the bridge of Tunney's nose. The blow—some ringside observers said it actually was a head butt—broke Tunney's nose in two
places and unleashed a geyser of blood that would flow through the
round and through most of the rest of the fight. Greb, darting in and
out and then around Tunney, then landed a left and right to the stomach. That flurry of punches set the tone for the fight, demonstrating
that the swift and unorthodox Greb was easily able to penetrate Tunney's defense, which up to now had been perhaps the hallmark of his
boxing arsenal.

The crowd was stunned by the early ferocity of Greb's attack. The
pace was fast and furious during the first three minutes of the fight,
with Greb raining an unrelenting torrent of punches at Tunney and
easily winning the round. As the bell sounded, Greb headed toward his
corner with a smile on his face. There was no way, he must have felt,
that this kid could possibly beat him. In Tunney's corner, Doc Bagley
and his assistants quickly inserted a heavy dose of Adrenalin Chloride
into Tunney's broken and bleeding nose.

For Tunney, it would only get worse. Round after round, Greb, as
Hype Igoe would write in his account of the fight, "came at Tunney
from every angle with a thousand gloves laced to each piston-like
arm." It was an apt description, as Greb swarmed all over Tunney, refusing to give him adequate punching room and battering him almost

at will, to the astonishment of much of the crowd and in particular Tunney's hundreds of supporters from Greenwich Village.

It was quintessential Greb, reeling off punches in barrages, often grabbing and hitting at the same time, cuffing and slapping, butting Tunney in close-quarter exchanges, and constantly being warned, to absolutely no avail, by the frustrated and blood-soaked referee, Kid McPartland, who let the Windmill get away with everything short of kicking Tunney in the groin. Unfazed by an ongoing chorus of boos from the pro-Tunney crowd, Greb could not restrain himself from digging into his good-sized bag of dirty tricks. It was, of course, the only way he knew how to fight.

Bleeding from the nose throughout, despite the constant application of Adrenalin Chloride by his cornermen, Tunney began to bleed even more in the sixth round when, during some furious infighting, Greb, either with a punch or a butt—it was not clear which—opened up the cut on Tunney's left eyebrow, the area where Tunney had been cut during a sparring session. By the end of the round, McPartland's white shirt and pants were, as Damon Runyon put it in his story, "dyed scarlet," making McPartland look "as if he had been painting a house with red paint while under the influence of hard cider."

Indeed, throughout the fight, as Tunney continued to bleed, amid cries of "Stop it!" from many spectators, McPartland repeatedly stepped in between Tunney and Greb to wipe the blood from their gloves. If the bleeding was bad, it got worse in the ninth round when Greb opened up a cut over Tunney's right eye. By now, he was bleeding from the nose, both eyes, and his mouth, and the ring canvas had taken on the appearance of a slaughterhouse floor. Making matters worse, Tunney's corner had run out of Adrenalin Chloride to restrict the flow of blood from his broken nose. Aware of that, Abe Attell, who was a friend of Doc Bagley's, dispatched a Garden employee to a nearby drugstore to get more.

Anticipating that he might be butted and cut like never before, Tunney had concocted a mixture of half brandy and half orange juice and had Bagley bring it into the ring before the fight, so that it would be available if Tunney became weak from a loss of blood. By the end of the twelfth round, Tunney took a huge swallow of the mixture. It may have helped stem the flow of blood somewhat, but it also made Tunney so dizzy that, as he was to say, he saw "two red opponents" in front of him and the ring whirling around when Bagley and his other cornermen literally pushed him out of his corner when the bell rang. "How I ever survived the thirteenth, fourteenth, and fifteenth rounds is still a mystery to me," he was to say years later.

Remarkably, Tunney did survive the fifteen rounds. Remarkably, too, he had not won a single round. Remarkable, also, was the fact that Tunney never went down despite the punishment he absorbed. Of all the bouts Grantland Rice had seen, this one, he wrote, was "perhaps the bloodiest fight I ever covered." He added: "Greb handled Tunney like a butcher hammering a Swiss steak. By the third round, Gene was literally wading in his own blood."

At the end, not only was the Pittsburgh Windmill unmarked, but his plastered-down hair had not been disturbed. Tunney, on the other hand, was a bloody, and ghastly, mess. Shaking hands with Greb after the final bell sounded, Tunney said, "Well, Harry, you were the better man tonight." Tunney's emphasis was on the last word—"tonight." Badly beaten as he had been, he was already convinced that, in a return fight, he would beat the Pittsburgh Windmill. Certainly no one else in Madison Square Garden that night felt the same.

Wobbly and dazed, Tunney had to be assisted to his dressing room by Bagley and his aides. As he was, to his surprise, most of the Garden crowd gave him a rousing ovation for his courageous stand. Tunney had heard the roar of a crowd before, but always while he was winning a fight. None of those cheers, though, had ever been as loud as this one at Madison Square Garden on what for Gene Tunney had been a disastrous night.

Besides losing the fight and his American light heavyweight championship—in itself, no great loss—Tunney had also lost about two quarts of blood. Weak and exhausted, he finally collapsed as he approached his dressing room, and had to be carried. Bagley, Barry McCormack, and several close friends who were with Tunney urged him to go to a hospital. Barely able to talk, he steadfastly refused while Dr. Shea reset his broken nose, stitched the cuts over both eyes, and did the same to his lacerated lip. Another doctor, William Walker, the brother of Jimmy Walker, used a stomach pump to remove the mix of blood, Adrenalin Chloride, brandy, and orange juice that had made Tunney ill. While Tunney was being administered to, Abe Attell came into the room, brimming with excitement. Given his battered condition, Tunney found it hard to grasp Attell's excitement.

"Kid, you're the gamest fighter I ever saw," said Attell. "I lost twenty-five hundred dollars on you, but to hell with it."

Attell, who would raise eyebrows by turning up later at several of Tunney's training camps, then leaned over and kissed Tunney's lacerated face. "Doc," Attell said to Bagley, "will you sell your contract with this kid to me? He certainly will be the next heavyweight champion of the world."

Certainly precious few others felt that way. The prevailing view was perhaps best expressed by W. O. McGeehan of the *New York Tribune*. "A nice boy, that Tunney, and a good soldier, as the entire AEF (American Expeditionary Forces) will testify, but he has not the instincts for this kind of fighting, nor has he the speed," McGeehan wrote. "That dream of any kind of a boxing champion from the AEF (American Expeditionary Forces) vanished in the crimson mists at Madison Square Garden last night."

After more than two hours of being treated and resting in his dressing room, Tunney, aided by Bagley, McCormack, and several others, was helped out a back door of the Garden and into a taxi. At Bagley's suggestion, the cab driver headed for Central Park. Bagley and some of the others in the car thought the air might do Tunney some good on this lovely May night. Later, Tunney checked back into the hotel where he had stayed the night before. He had planned to go home to Greenwich Village, but there was no way that he would ever let his mother and father see him looking the way he did. As it was, Tunney returned the next day to Barry McCormack's New Jersey farm, where he had trained for the fight, to recuperate.

Before he left for Red Bank, Tunney, along with Bagley, went to the Manhattan offices of the State Athletic Commission to file a challenge to Greb for a return bout, accompanied by a $2,500 check. There, the commission chairman, William Muldoon, looking at Tunney's bruised face and his stitched-up eyes, mouth, and nose, said, "Son, why don't you forget about Greb. He's not a normal fighter. There's no point for you to fight him again." But Tunney insisted, telling a very dubious Muldoon he was convinced that he would beat Greb in a rematch.

"I discovered through the early part of the fight that I could lick Harry Greb," he was to say years later. "As each round went by, battered from pillar to post as I was, this discovery gradually became a positive certainty in my mind."

That comment, besides being baffling, demanded the question as to why Tunney didn't do what he apparently felt he knew he had to do to beat Greb during the fight. Tunney never did say, leaving the impression that while he was convinced he could beat Greb, he knew it wasn't going to happen that May night.

Greb, on the other hand, went out on the town after the fight with several friends, visiting several Manhattan speakeasies to drink—ginger ale, of course—and dance the night away until almost dawn. At one speakeasy, a friend pointed out that the fistic Pride of Pittsburgh had decisively beaten Tunney though handicapped by height, weight, reach, and to a lesser extent in age. To which Greb's close friend Hap Albacker, who had had more than a few drinks, added, "and by one eye."

Furious, Greb turned to Albacker, one of the few people who knew Greb's secret, and angrily said, "What the hell are you talking about?" Albacker, realizing his colossal faux pas, quickly blurted out, "I was just kidding." Albacker's quick recovery barely managed to save a lifelong friendship.

If most sportswriters and spectators thought Greb's victory had been an easy one, the Pittsburgh Windmill begged to differ, as he told more than a few people while celebrating his new championship that night. "It wasn't an easy fight; it was my hardest," he said at one point. "I was so arm-weary and leg-tired from trying to knock Gene out, I was in almost as bad shape as he was. Would you call an opponent a soft touch if you had to hit him as hard as you could for fifteen rounds and seldom made him stagger? I was in there with a guy tonight who has an iron jaw and an iron will, and I don't look forward to our next meeting."

Tunney would, though, and for good reason.

Legendary boxing promoter Tex Rickard with Jack Dempsey. AP IMAGES

TEN

The Faro Dealer from the Klondike

With his ego almost as badly bruised as his face, Tunney spent the month after the Greb fight resting and recuperating at Barry McCormack's farm in Red Bank, reading one of Shakespeare's most difficult works, *Troilus and Cressida,* and, after a week of total idleness, began doing some mild calisthenics and running several miles each morning. Despite his resounding and painful defeat, Tunney remained convinced that he would beat Greb in their rematch and, eventually, Dempsey. That attitude seemed to bespeak a self-confidence that had no foundation, especially after the Greb debacle.

In the aftermath of the fight, Tunney was being praised by New York sportswriters for his courage in surviving a veritable carnage, but dismissed as a potential threat to Georges Carpentier's world light heavyweight title. And most certainly no one was giving any thought to Tunney as a possible rival for Dempsey, who, having virtually run out of legitimate contenders for his heavyweight title, would spend several months traveling and partying in Europe.

Reading about the Greb fight the day after, John Tunney, by now retired at the age of sixty-two and in failing health, was deeply upset, not so much because of his son's one-sided defeat, but because of the beating he had absorbed, which was not only detailed graphically in sportswriters' accounts in all twelve New York City dailies but also depicted in photographs that accompanied the stories. During a phone conversation later that day, Tunney assured his father that he was all right, that the sportswriters had exaggerated his injuries, and that he had decided to return to Red Bank for a brief vacation.

"How could you let him do that to you?" John Tunney asked.

Touched by his father's solicitude, Tunney told him that he had simply been overwhelmed by Greb's highly unorthodox style and unrelenting aggressiveness, along with several well-placed head butts. He also assured the old stevedore that he would certainly get even with the Pittsburgh Windmill. Tunney then tried to assuage his mother's fears that he had been seriously hurt during the fight, telling her that he had merely sustained a few cuts around the eyes and mouth, and the ensuing bleeding had made it look much worse than it really had been. He would be home soon, he assured both of his parents, and they would be able to see for themselves that he was just fine. Of course, he looked awful right now, his face a mass of cuts, bruises, and welts, but John and Mary Tunney didn't have to know that, and they most certainly would not get to see their oldest son looking that way.

While Tunney was training for his first fight with Greb, Jack Dempsey was, in his words, having "a ball" in Europe. With no challengers in sight and not having fought since knocking out Georges Carpentier in July of 1921, Dempsey had hardly been busy, apart from shooting a movie serial in Hollywood and appearing in some touring vaudeville shows.

Dempsey and his friends mingled with royalty, high government officials, and socialites, among others, while visiting England, France, and Germany. "We just had a good time—lots of cafés, dancing, going to the race tracks, receptions, and laughs," Dempsey later recalled.

Also, apparently, plenty of compliant women. Dempsey never was into kiss-and-tell, but even he had to admit that he did not have a hard time finding female company, especially in Paris. "You should of seen it in 1922—especially if you could have been my age and heavyweight champion of the world," he said.

The trip aboard the *Aquitania* was Dempsey's first on an ocean liner and his first visit to Europe. It was made during the heyday of ocean-crossing passenger ships that, if you were fortunate and wealthy enough to travel first class, provided virtually every amenity, from beauty parlors to a gymnasium and even a movie theater. Dempsey, who had never been aboard a ship, could not believe the elegance and luxury of the majestic liner. At first, though, Dempsey, who still loved the wide open spaces of the Old West where he had grown up, felt constrained. On the ship's first day out, Damon Runyon—who had gone along on assignment for the Hearst-owned King Features Syndicate—wrote that Dempsey prowled the *Aquitania* like "a big animal investigating a new cage. He went bounding about nosing into every nook and corner."

By the second day, Dempsey had settled down and, thereafter, seemed to enjoy the ocean voyage immensely. During his week at sea, the heavyweight champion was a familiar figure throughout the ship—on deck, in the restaurants and bars—and drew far more attention among the approximately 1,500 passengers than such show business celebrities as D. W. Griffith, who had produced and directed Hollywood's first epic film, *The Birth of a Nation,* and the Dolly Sisters, who were perhaps the best-known singing and dancing act of the time. Each day, Dempsey ran about five miles on the ship's deck, worked out with weights, skipped rope, and sparred a few rounds with Joe Benjamin, a lightweight boxer and close friend. Out on deck, Dempsey playfully boxed with children and chatted with their parents and other passengers, who were charmed by his affability, gentleness, and willingness to mix with just about everyone on board.

In London, Dempsey stayed at the luxurious Savoy Hotel, went to the races at Epsom Downs, visited Buckingham Palace, and saw Big Ben and the Tower of London. One afternoon, Dempsey was the guest of honor at a luncheon given by Lord Northcliffe, the owner and publisher of *The Times* of London and the *Daily Mail*, at his town house outside London. Apparently at Kearns's suggestion, Dempsey bought a cutaway coat and striped pants to wear to the luncheon. As he was preparing to leave his hotel for the luncheon, decked out in the cutaway coat and striped pants, Damon Runyon said, "I'm going with you."

"I thought you said you weren't invited," Dempsey replied.

"I wasn't, but I'm going with you," said Runyon, never known to be a shrinking violet.

"They don't do things like that over here, Damon," said Dempsey, who had first met Runyon when he was starting out as a fighter in Colorado and Runyon was a sportswriter in Denver. "It's a private party. If you want to go, go ahead. But I'm not inviting you."

Dempsey finally left for the luncheon, alone. At Lord Northcliffe's town house, he found himself being introduced to members of royalty, government leaders, and high-ranking military officials. To say the least, he was ill at ease. For one thing, he was self-conscious about his high-pitched voice, which, as he said, made him sound like a girl. But Dempsey soon sensed that everyone seemed to go out of their way to make him feel comfortable.

As he had feared, Dempsey was called on to say a few words. Though he had already appeared in movies and on the vaudeville stage, Dempsey was not comfortable speaking in public. But he handled himself well and seemed to win over his audience. "I feel like the Irishman who was asked to do something special for the guests at a very fancy affair," Dempsey said to the assembled guests. "The Irishman said, 'I can't sing, I can't dance, and I can't tell a story. But I will tell you what I will do. I'll fight anybody in the house.'"

The guests roared, Dempsey said, 'Thank you,' and then sat down.

At one point during the luncheon, Northcliffe, summoned by a butler, went to the front door. There stood Damon Runyon.

"I'm Damon Runyon. I'm covering Jack Dempsey's trip abroad, and I'd like to take in this luncheon," said Runyon, certain that Lord Northcliffe had heard of him.

As Dempsey recalled, Northcliffe "looked at our great sportswriter like he was a roach or something. Then he said, 'I'm very sorry, but this is a private party for Mr. Dempsey. Good afternoon.' "

Dempsey, who had overheard the conversation, said Runyon never got over the slight. "And he had known me since I was a hobo," Dempsey said.

The next day a story appeared in *The Times* of London in which the writer, believed to have been Lord Northcliffe, wrote about the luncheon. He said he had expected Dempsey to be "loud of voice, loud in dress, and loud in manner." Instead, the anonymous writer said, he found a man who was "quiet spoken, almost excessively modest" and with "perfect manners." Reading the story that morning, Dempsey was delighted. It made him realize how far, literally and figuratively, he had come from the hobo jungles out West.

For all the hospitality shown him in England, Dempsey was more comfortable in France, especially in Paris. "It was more in tune with our crowd," Dempsey was to say. French government officials gave the champ a banquet, at which he was decorated with a medal. That Dempsey had demolished their biggest sports hero of the era, Georges Carpentier, less than a year earlier at Boyle's Thirty Acres in Jersey City, seemed to have been forgotten, perhaps because Carpentier still held the world light heavyweight title. In Paris, Dempsey had a warm reunion with the Orchid Man during a boxing show at which Dempsey refereed a fight while wearing a dinner jacket. Carpentier had taught Dempsey enough French so that he would be able to communicate with the fighters and proclaim the winner at the end of the bout.

"When the fight ended, I climbed into the ring, held up the hand of a guy named Billy Balzac and yelled, 'Le victor, Monsewer Billy Balzac,' " Dempsey later recalled as Carpentier, at ringside, burst out laughing. "I wasn't sure he won or not. But there was't much I could do. The other guy's name was Maurice Prunier or Proxineaux [it was Prunier] or something like that. How the hell could I have given it to him?"

In Paris, there were parties every night, mainly in Montmartre, the heart of Parisien nightlife. At one nightclub, Dempsey was persuaded to dance with Yancsi Dolly, one of the Dolly Sisters who had been aboard the *Aquitania,* while Irving Berlin played piano accompaniment. During the day, Dempsey and his friends went to the races at Longchamps, the famous Parisien track; to the top of the Eiffel Tower and to the Louvre; visited the Arc de Triomphe, the Cathedral of Notre Dame, and Napoleon's Tomb; strolled along the River Seine; and walked along the Champs-Elysées, followed by hundreds of adoring Parisiens.

Before leaving Paris, Dempsey was asked to compare the City of Light with London. "Paris was better," Dempsey said. "More girls. More action." And, he could have added, it afforded even more adulation than he received in England. Indeed, no American fighter, nor any other athlete, had ever been accorded such a reception in all the years since the Manassa Mauler took Paris by storm in the spring of 1922.

From Paris, Dempsey and his group went by train to Berlin, where, once again, he was greeted and treated royally. Arriving at the Berlin train station, he found a crowd of about seven thousand, which engulfed him when he got off the train. Dempsey was stunned by the reception, mainly because boxing had been practically unknown in Germany until after the Armistice, and that had only been four years ago. Yet here he was being greeted as a sports hero. If boxing was relatively new to Germany, the Germans turned out to be about a half-century ahead of the United States in one aspect of the sport—female boxing. At Kearns's suggestion the Dempsey party went to a cabaret where women boxers were appearing. Dempsey had assumed the boxing would be in a comic vein. But he was wrong. During several bouts, the women boxers went at one another with a vengeance, resulting in several bloody bouts, at least one broken jaw, and a number of knockdowns. Kearns and the others in Dempsey's party seemed to enjoy the bouts, but Dempsey was appalled by it all and could not wait to leave. "Women punching women—I hated it," he said.

Arriving back in New York on May 19, Dempsey told reporters he was prepared to fight any available contenders, including Harry Wills, the "colored heavyweight champion" whom some sportswriters called the "Dark Menace" or the "Brown Panther." The first term conjured visions of Jack Johnson's reign, implying that, should Wills win the title, it would "menace" the heavyweight division by keeping away fans who still might be averse to interracial boxing bouts, and there apparently were many. The second term, though, was not meant in a pejoratively racial sense, but rather much like the appellation "Brown Bomber" that was applied to Joe Louis in the 1930s and 1940s. To many boxing people, and certainly black newspapers such as the *New York Amsterdam News* and the *Chicago Defender,* the most logical contender was Wills, who was generally regarded as the second best heavyweight in the world. The problem was that Willis was black and no black fighter had fought for the heavyweight title since Jack Johnson had knocked out Tommy Burns to win the championship fourteen years earlier. Blacks had fought for and won some lighter weight championships, but not the far more prestigious heavyweight title. And so long as Tex Rickard was Dempsey's promoter, there was no way Wills was going to get a shot at Dempsey's title. The reason, essentially, was Johnson; not because of the way he fought—he had been a superb boxer with a big punch—but because of his flamboyance and defiance of white society and its customs and mores. In the opinion of Rickard, and indeed most whites, America wasn't ready for another black champion. One had been more than enough.

In truth, the 6′ 4″, 225-pound Wills was no Johnson, either in his lifestyle or his ability. Still, he had not only beaten Sam Langford anywhere from seven to twelve times in eighteen fights, depending on which records one checks, but also had defeated most of the best white and black heavyweights.

The vast majority of Wills's fights, like Langford's, had been against other black fighters. Most good white fighters—or at least their managers—wanted no part of Wills or Langford, which was a testament to their stature as boxers. That was also true of other good black heavyweights, most of whom fought each other as many as twenty-five times, since they could not get fights with white boxers. Langford, for example, once fought Jeff Clark four times in one month in 1918 when Langford was thirty-five years old and at least half-blind.

After he had won the heavyweight title in 1919, Dempsey had said he would never defend it against a "Negro" fighter. But by 1922,

Dempsey, who had fought a number of blacks on the way up, apparently had had a change of heart and said he would be glad to accept a challenge from a black fighter. That is, any black fighter but Sam Langford. "They always said I wasn't afraid of any man," Dempsey said years later. "The hell I wasn't. I was afraid of Sam Langford because I knew he would flatten me."

After visiting his mother at the house he had bought for her and the rest of the family in Los Angeles, Dempsey went on a month-long stage tour with Kearns, during which he sparred briefly with someone brave enough to box with him for a round or two and Kearns told some stories about his colorful, and somewhat checkered, career. In a good week, they could make as much as a thousand dollars, good money in 1922 but not what Dempsey was accustomed to making in the ring.

Despite their similar backgrounds, Kearns did not like Rickard. Perhaps it was because he knew he could not outsmart him, as he could other promoters, managers, and fighters. But he felt that if he and Dempsey were going to make any big money, Rickard would have to be the promoter. He was the best one around as he had demonstrated in staging the first "million-dollar gate" fight between Dempsey and Carpentier at Boyle's Thirty Acres in Jersey City. But during much of 1922 Rickard had much more on his mind than promoting fights. He had become enmeshed in a scandal that threatened not only to cut short his career as a promoter, but to send him to prison for a long time. Until the trial stemming from the scandal had been played out, Rickard was not about to promote any fights, not even one of Dempsey's.

Fifty-one years old, married, and with two children, George Lewis "Tex" Rickard had, by the early 1920s, become the best known boxing promoter in the world after having promoted Dempsey's fights with Jess Willard, Bill Brennan, and Georges Carpentier along with an epochal bout involving Jack Johnson in 1910. Though he himself was relatively reserved, Rickard's background was more colorful than that of most of the fighters whose bouts he promoted. Rickard had been born around 1870 on a Missouri farm that abutted the home of Zerelda James, the mother of the infamous James brothers, Jesse and Frank, and was orphaned at eleven. By then his family had moved to Texas and young George was already a trail cowboy and wrangler. At twenty-four he was elected town marshal of Henrietta, Texas, where he was paid $2.50 for every person arrested and a dollar for each dog impounded. When arrests were slow, Rickard hired teenage boys whom he would pay twenty-five cents for each dog they could round up, while he kept the rest. Henrietta generally was a peaceful town, and in later years old-timers there recalled that Rickard was a lot better at drawing a full house than a gun.

While he was a sheriff, Rickard married his first wife, Leona, but a year later—in 1895, the year Dempsey was born—she and their baby died. Rickard then headed to Alaska, where he became a bartender and faro dealer in the mining town of Circle City on the Yukon River. There he picked up the nickname "Tex," which would last for the rest of his life. A few months later, word reached Circle City that gold had been found in the Klondike, and Rickard, along with hundreds of others, headed further north and staked out a claim in the tent city of Bonanza Creek. After spending a brutally cold winter hacking away with a pick ax and coming up empty, Rickard sold his claim to an Englishman for sixty thousand dollars.

The following spring, he moved to the boomtown of Dawson in the Klondike, where, with his stake-claim money, he opened a gambling house and saloon. Not long after, he lost it to prospectors who had prospered at the gambling house's roulette table. Back working as a bartender and faro dealer in the Yukon, he established a sizable nest egg, mostly from poker and roulette, and moved to Nome, where, propitiously, he bought a saloon called the Northern a few days before a gold strike in the area. In a few year's time, he either made close to a half-million dollars or went broke, depending on which version he told in later years.

Deciding it was time to move on after seven years in Alaska, Rickard, now about thirty-one, went searching for diamonds in South Africa, half a world away, but his stay was both short and unprofitable. Returning to the American West in 1904, and again following the lure of gold dust, he opened a bar in Goldfield, Nevada—also naming this one the Northern Saloon—in the midst of another gold rush. Of all his moves during a nine-year odyssey in search of instant wealth, it turned out to be his best one yet. For it was in the southwestern Nevada town of Goldfield that Tex Rickard finally found his calling: he became a fight promoter.

Goldfield soon became another boomtown. One gold mine alone turned out more than $5 million worth of gold-bearing ore in three months. As the town continued to thrive on its bonanza of gold, local boosters began to look for a way to attract tourists and even new residents to aptly named Goldfield. The year was 1906 and it was time for a meeting to discuss Goldfield's future and, for that matter, to make sure it had one. At a gathering that included local businessmen, bankers, restaurant and gambling house proprietors, brothel operators, and saloon owners like Rickard, there was no lack of recommendations as to how Goldfield, and especially its businessmen, could continue to prosper. Suggestions ranged from a man-made lake on Main Street that would be stocked each morning with beer to a racetrack whose racers would not be Thoroughbreds or trotters but camels imported from the Sahara. After listening, incredulously, to the pie-in-the-sky suggestions, Rickard finally spoke up and suggested a prizefight. Ears perked up, whereupon Rickard made a compelling case for staging not just a prizefight, but a world championship prizefight, which, he said, would not only draw thousands of people to Goldfield but, with the attendant publicity, put the town on the map throughout the United States and perhaps even beyond.

Rickard could not have been more persuasive, and by the time he had finished his presentation and answered questions, his listeners were sold. Within an hour's time, the local wahoos—in truth, more interested in attracting business than just tourists to Goldfield—had formed the Goldfield Athletic Club, raised more than fifty thousand dollars, and designated Rickard as the club's treasurer and promoter. To Rickard, promoter sounded nice, but treasurer sounded even nicer.

With no connections in boxing but with a fifty-thousand-dollar bankroll—a huge amount for a promoter to have at his disposal— Rickard looked around to see which outstanding fighters A) would be amenable to coming to Goldfield to fight, B) would be apt to draw both national publicity and spectators—especially national publicity, and C) needed money. Rickard, after scouring newspapers and talking to everyone he knew even remotely connected with boxing, settled on Joe Gans, who, after having relinquished the world lightweight championship in 1904, had recently won the world welterweight title.

Gans seemed to be a perfect choice. He was probably the best all-around fighter in the world—he was famous—and, because of an unscrupulous manager, he was broke, even though he hadn't lost a fight in three years. He was also a rare breed—a black champion, and the first black to win the lightweight title, and third overall to win a world championship.*

Tracking down Gans in San Francisco, Rickard wired him an offer of twenty thousand dollars, which Gans accepted immediately without even knowing who he was going to fight. It turned out to be Battling Nelson, a native of Denmark who was known as "The Durable Dane" even though he had never fought in Scandinavia, or even Europe. A roughhouse brawler, with a reputation as a dirty fighter, Nelson gladly absorbed three punches to get in one hard shot and was impossible to knock out. To get Nelson, who had won the lightweight title a year before, Rickard had to offer more than he had offered Gans—thirty thousand dollars, and did so even though it exhausted his treasury. Not to worry, though, Rickard figured Goldfield was still a boomtown, and his colleagues in the Goldfield Athletic Club—who would be ecstatic at the fight their fellow club member had arranged—would be glad to up the ante and provide more funds for the club treasurer to ensure that the bout would be held and bring Goldfield the attention its boosters craved.

When Rickard announced that the fight—to the finish, no less, as in olden days—would be held on September 3 of 1906 in Goldfield, Nevada, not everyone was quite sure where Nevada was—it had not been admitted to the union until 1864—let alone Goldfield. Not yet having availed himself of such talented writers as Gene Fowler to pub-

---

*The others to accomplish this feat were George Dixon and welterweight Joe Walcott. Dixon had won the bantamweight championship in 1890 and the featherweight title in 1892 and again in 1898 to become the first fighter ever, black or white, to win championships in two different weight classes. Walcott won the welterweight crown in 1901 and is regarded as one of the best welterweights (147-pound weight limit) of all time. A latter-day heavyweight champion, Jersey Joe Walcott, whose real name was Arnold Cream, said he took the name of the long-ago welterweight titleholder because the old boxer was his father's favorite fighter.

licize his fights, or to pay off some sportswriters to do so, as he would later on, Rickard had to come up with ideas of his own to convince people it was worth their while to make the trip to the Nevada desert to see two of the best lighter-weight fighters in the world battle in the heat to the finish. Then Rickard got a brainstorm. From his saloon, he walked to the bank next door and got bank officials to place in the bank's front window all of the purse money—fifty thousand dollars (the equivalent today of about a half-million dollars)—in stacks of gold coins with a poster publicizing the impending fight. Bank officials, as anxious as other local businessmen for the fight to draw attention to Goldfield, cast aside decorum and agreed to do it. Rickard thereupon notified the local newspaper, which took pictures of the stacked-up gold coins in the bank window. The pictures then were picked up by the Associated Press and sent around the world, bringing instant, if ephemeral, fame to Goldfield.

In the days leading up to the fight, newspapers throughout the country and even abroad reported how several thousand people were descending on the tiny Western mining town of Goldfield, whose main street had been turned into a veritable midway of attractions that ranged from cakewalks to bull-sticking, and where Rickard had erected an eight-thousand-seat outdoor arena for the fight. Before a punch had been thrown, Rickard had put Goldfield on the map and the town already was profiting from an influx of fight-goers who, in the days before the title bout, were visiting Goldfield's restaurants, saloons, gambling houses, and its gold mines, and, in some cases, its brothels. If they wanted to, they also could watch both Gans and Nelson work out in the 90-plus-degree heat, free of charge.

Among those who did were several hundred women, most of them from the Goldfield area. That was because of Rickard's promotional acuity. In 1906, boxing, where it was allowed at all, was still held in low repute, and spectators were almost exclusively men. It was at Goldfield that Rickard set out to change a boxing crowd's makeup. In an effort to introduce women to the sport, he staged special training sessions for what some writers then referred to as "the fair sex," so that they could watch Gans and Nelson spar and shadowbox, careful to ensure that the sparring sessions the ladies saw were relatively tame and most definitely bloodless. After staging such "ladies' days," Rickard told sportswriters that "nearly every society woman in Goldfield would see the fight." Rickard knew he was referring to a very small segment of the rough-hewn area's female population. Nevertheless, he constructed screened-in boxes in the jerry-built stadium, far enough from the ring that they would be unable to see any blood that might be spilled and could not perceive the power of well-placed punches to the head and the visible impact it could have on the fighters. To the surprise of many writers and others, but not Rickard, about three hundred women turned out for the fight, most of them dressed in finery more befitting an afternoon tea or cocktail party than a boxing bout. Word of the fairly large female turnout made it into a lot of newspapers, and, thereafter, the number of women attending major fights grew, incrementally but lastingly.

With Goldfield in a holiday mood and with thousands of outsiders from as far off as California on hand, the arena built by Rickard was filled to overflowing for the much anticipated bout on the scorching hot Labor Day afternoon of 1906. At least thirty-two years of age, and possibly more, Gans gave away at least ten years to the twenty-two-year-old Nelson. But it made no difference: Gans was still a magnificent fighting machine. With his trademark left jab finding Nelson's face constantly, Gans repeatedly danced away from Nelson's bull-like charges while landing telling counterpunches. As the fight dragged on in the blistering heat with Gans in complete control, Nelson became frustrated and resorted to head-butting, rabbit-punching, and other illegal tactics that the Marquess of Queensberry had hoped he had outlawed a half-century earlier. Finally, in the forty-second round, after two hours of virtually nonstop action, Nelson drove a left uppercut into Gans's groin, prompting referee George Siler to stop the fight and award it to Gans on a flagrant foul.

Though he lost, Nelson wound up with more money than Gans. The Durable Dane, who had proved not as durable as Gans, received $23,000 (the equivalent of about $250,000). Gans got only $11,000 of the $20,000 he had expected, but also won Nelson's lightweight title. The gate, by the standards of the era, was huge, totaling $69,715, tax-free—the largest in boxing history at the time. The fight also was notable for other reasons: it was the last championship fight scheduled on a fight-to-the-finish basis ever held in the United States and the longest fight ever to end in a foul.

After paying off $23,000 in expenses, Rickard wound up with $13,715 for himself and the other members of the Goldfield Athletic Club, big money in 1906, especially in a small town like Goldfield, Nevada. The fight, by drawing thousands of people, had generated a lot of business, boosted the morale of townspeople, and granted Goldfield publicity the world over. Not that the publicity mattered much; Goldfield never did change after the fight. It certainly did not become a destination resort as Las Vegas did about twenty years later. Nor did it attract many, if any, new residents or businessmen. As a matter of fact, by the end of the following year, 1907, the gold mines had been depleted and closed and Goldfield became a ghost town. It eventually revived, however, and although it never became a boxing mecca, hosted occasional fights, including one in 1915 that featured a nineteen-year-old heavyweight prospect from Colorado named Jack Dempsey.

By 1907, when Goldfield had fallen on hard times, Rickard had long since left town. He had found his niche now, and his days of buying and selling gambling houses and saloons and prospecting for gold and diamonds were over. Before he was done, he would promote 234 fights over a twenty-two-year period, including five of the sport's most famous. But to Rickard, none would be more significant than the Gans-Nelson fight, which, in addition to providing him with invaluable experience, would launch him on a career that would make him the most famous boxing promoter of all time.

Rickard's record gate at Goldfield would be broken four years later—and almost four-fold, at that—in another fight in Nevada that would be promoted by him. The second fight, in Reno on July 4, 1910, would far overshadow the Gans-Nelson bout in Goldfield, for it would pit heavyweight champion Jack Johnson against former champion Jim Jeffries, who had not fought in six years.

The thirty-five-year-old Jeffries had retired undefeated in 1904 at the age of twenty-nine after the seventh successful defense of title, which he won when he knocked out Bob Fitzsimmons at Coney Island in the first heavyweight title bout ever staged in New York, on June 9, 1899. Two of those title defenses were knockout victories over James J. Corbett, who had preceded Fitzsimmons as the heavyweight title-holder. Having ballooned from his fighting weight of around 215 pounds to over three hundred, Jeffries was enjoying life on his alfalfa farm in Kansas and had no desire to return to the ring. But the clamor for "The Boilermaker" (he once had held such a job) to come out of re-tirement to try to re-place the heavyweight championship into the hands of a Caucasian had grown in intensity. One of the arguments made for such a bout was that Johnson did not deserve the title of heavy-weight champion since Jeffries had never been beaten. That reasoning, of course, was not only specious, it was illogical. But all the prodding—along with a guarantee of $100,000, far more than Jeffries had ever made in the ring—finally managed to get Jeffries to change his mind.

James J. Jeffries thus became the first Great White Hope. That racial label did not denote a groundswell of American racial prejudice against black boxing champions in general—after all, black champions like Joe Gans, Joe Walcott, and George Dixon had enjoyed a certain amount of popularity among white boxing fans, as had outstanding black boxers like Sam Langford—but the fact that the heavyweight champion of the world was Jack Johnson, who had gone out of his way to scorn white society and had infuriated many whites in the process.

After having won the "colored heavyweight championship" in 1903, while primarily fighting other outstanding black fighters such as Sam Langford, Sam McVea, and Joe Jeannette, Johnson won the world heavyweight title when he knocked out Tommy Burns, a 5′ 7″ Cana-dian native, in, of all places, Rushcutters Bay, a suburb of Sydney, Aus-tralia, on the day after Christmas in 1908. In other words, Johnson, though obviously the leading challenger to Burns's title, would have to go the ends of the earth to get a shot at that title. He most certainly would never get it in the country of his birth, the United States.

With Johnson seven inches taller and twenty pounds heavier, the fight was a mismatch from the start. Johnson knocked Burns down in the first round and no doubt could have knocked him out whenever he wanted. But instead he chose to toy with and taunt the diminutive heavyweight champion, hitting him with ease while Burns lunged at Johnson almost comically. Finally, in the fourteenth round, Johnson floored the badly worn-out Burns with a right-hand punch. Burns got up, whereupon Johnson began to batter him at will. At that point, several Australian police officers jumped into the ring to stop the fight, apparently to save Burns from further punishment. Referee Hugh McIntosh, a former newspaper editor, member of the Australian Parliament, and theatrical producer who had done some amateur boxing and thus should probably have known enough to stop the fight much earlier, then declared Johnson the winner and new champion. Through it all, Johnson, who may well have been the first major trash-talker in sports, had infuriated most of the twenty thousand spectators by taunting and humiliating Burns, then turning and laughing at the all-white crowd. But then Burns may have asked for both the taunting and the punishment that Johnson inflicted on him with the racist comments he directed at Johnson throughout the fight.

That a black man—and especially one like Johnson—should win sport's most coveted championship was deeply disturbing to many Americans, and, no doubt, to many others. Among those patently disturbed by Johnson's victory over Burns was novelist Jack London, who covered the fight for the *New York Sun.* "One thing remains," London wrote in his account of the fight, "Jeffries must emerge from his alfalfa farm and remove that smile from Johnson's face. Jeff, it's up to you!"

Despite such racially motivated comments Johnson kept right on flashing his gold-toothed smile while seemingly enjoying life to the hilt, spending far more time in nightclubs and in an array of sleek and fast cars than in gymnasiums. The more Johnson won, the greater the clamor for a White Hope who could dethrone him as champion. More than his taunting of white opponents in the ring, Johnson tended to incur the wrath of many whites because of his affinity for white women (he married two of them in an era when mixed marriages were exceedingly rare) and his extravagant lifestyle, which some whites felt was intended to antagonize white society, although Johnson never gave any indication that that was his purpose.

In deciding on the site of what would become as much a morality play as a boxing bout, Rickard told reporters, "Boys, it's got to be Reno because more railroads junction there."

Though he did not train particularly hard, Jeffries did go on a strict diet and lost about seventy-five pounds in the weeks leading up to the fight. Even William Muldoon, the fitness guru, former world wrestling champion, occasional Shakespearean actor, and eventual chairman of the New York State Athletic Commission, got involved because of the interracial bout. Muldoon, an overpowering figure, both physically and verbally, saw fit to make the four-day train trip to Reno to meet with Jeffries and tell him that he was, in effect, representing the white race in his fight with Johnson. In his sonorous and booming voice, he sought to convince "Old Jeff" that he had become the Great White Hope against the brash and unbridled black man who, for the sake of Caucasians the world over, had to be deposed as heavyweight champion. Bad enough, Jeffries thought, that he had had to take off so much weight and return to fight perhaps the best heavyweight champion ever after being out of the ring for six years, he also had to represent the entire white race.

Rickard reveled in the fight's nationwide press coverage even though most of the stories focused on race, reflecting the deep divisions between blacks and whites in the country. By now, he was the country's best-known boxing promoter—not necessarily a lofty honor, since the sport was still illegal in most states and held in low repute by most of American society—and apparently decided he needed a distinguishing appendage. In Rickard's case, it was a gold-tipped Malacca cane, which he was never without in public. Like almost all men of the era, he wore a hat—in his case a wide-brimmed gray fedora—and conservative suits, usually of gray, brown, or blue hues. Though crude at times, he was rather bland but a calm and persuasive negotiator who kept his light blue eyes fixed directly on whoever he was talking to. He drank sparingly, though at times, especially after a long negotiating session that went late into the day, he would sit up all night drinking bourbon and branch water with sportswriters, managers, and trainers, and never give any indication by morning that he had been drinking at all.

Determined again to attract women spectators, Rickard—who would serve as the referee—roped off a special section of box seats in the twenty-thousand-seat stadium he had built in Reno, complete with curtains for privacy. In a move that would thereafter be standard procedure at big fights, he arranged to have about a dozen famous fighters—including John L. Sullivan—introduced in the ring before the fight.

Paying up to fifty dollars for ringside seats, a crowd of 15,760, drawn from throughout the country, turned out for the bout. It was a colorful mélange that included captains of industry, bankers, cattle barons, actors and others from the entertainment world, big gamblers from both coasts, cowboys, cattle rustlers, world-class pickpockets, and Native Americans. Inexplicably, Jeffries, despite his long absence from the ring, was a 2½-to-1 favorite over perhaps the best fighter in the world and who, at thirty-two, appeared to be in his prime.

Johnson was fit and muscular as always. Jeffries, by contrast, looked wan and tired, probably because he had lost so much weight so quickly. He also looked worried. Perhaps he was thinking about what William Muldoon had told him—how he was representing the white race and had to strip this black menace of his title.

The fight was scheduled for forty-five rounds, but within minutes of the opening round it was obvious it would end much sooner. Slow and awkward, Jeffries, whose low crouch and long pawing-like left-hand jab were his trademarks, never had a chance. Johnson picked off and blocked almost every punch Jeffries threw while peppering the old former champion with a variety of blows. Both to thwart Johnson's attacks and to conserve his energy, Jeffries clinched often and held on. That prompted Johnson to say, loud enough to be heard in the ringside seats, "Now, stop lovin' me like that, Mr. Jeff."

Johnson, in turn, endured a stream of ugly racial epithets that were hurled at him by Jim Corbett, whom Rickard had recruited as Jeffries's manager and trainer, perhaps because Jeffries, while the heavyweight champion, had knocked out Corbett twice and thus Corbett was bound to know a lot about him as a fighter. Even many ringsiders pulling for Jeffries were appalled at Corbett's vicious remarks, which Johnson seemed to ignore. At one point, Corbett, trying to ridicule Johnson's hit-and-dance-away tactics, called out loudly, "Fight like a man." Johnson, smiling, turned to Corbett and replied: "I'm just doin' like you used to do, Mr. Corbett." And he essentially was, since Corbett, like Johnson, was a classic boxer. In truth, if Johnson had elected to fight as Corbett had tauntingly suggested, he probably could have knocked out Jeffries in the first round. But as usual, he chose to display his superb boxing skills, knowing he was in no danger of losing.

Winning every round with ease, Johnson finally put an end to the dull bout in the fifteenth round when he unleashed a fusillade of unanswered blows that sent Jeffries to the canvas three times. About halfway through his count after the third knockdown, Rickard stopped, walked over to Johnson, and put his right hand on his shoulder to signify that the fight was over.

Thirty-seven years later, sportswriter Dan Daniel wrote in *The Ring* magazine that Johnson had agreed in advance to take a dive in the fight "simply because he could not have had the match on any other terms." All the while, according to Daniel, Johnson intended to win, knowing that he could do so easily because Jeffries "was altogether unfit to put up a decent fight." Fortunately for Johnson, the mob had not yet made inroads into boxing, as it did, particularly, in the 1930s, 1940s, and 1950s, or, if Daniel's account was accurate, he might have had to pay the consequences for failing to go into the tank as he had agreed to do.

For Johnson, it was his biggest payday ever—$120,000. At $270,715, the gate was considerably less than the half-million Rickard had forecast, but it was still the largest in boxing history. Though it still had to be regarded as a financial success, Rickard, who finally became disturbed by the racial bitterness the fight engendered, vowed afterward that he would never again promote a fight between black and white fighters. One had been more than enough. But the fight had positioned Tex Rickard even more firmly as the most famous boxing promoter in the country.

Tough and cynical as he was, even Rickard cringed at some of what happened in the aftermath of the fight. Within hours after the daytime bout ended, racial rioting attributed to Johnson's victory broke out in several Southern cities. In Shreveport, Louisiana, three blacks were attacked and killed by whites, while two blacks were set upon and killed by whites in Little Rock, Arkansas. In Roanoke, Virginia, six blacks were severely beaten by a white mob, and in Pueblo, Colorado, thirty people, both black and white, were injured in what was described as a race riot. The violence also extended to the North, including New York City, where several white gangs roamed through black neighborhoods, wantonly assaulting blacks. One black man was beaten to death during the attacks and about thirty other blacks were hurt. In every instance, the violence was attributed to Johnson's victory over Jeffries.

In what would turn out to be his last fight in the United States, on July 4, 1912, Johnson knocked out Fireman Jim Flynn in the ninth round in Las Vegas, New Mexico. That Flynn, a journeyman fighter at best, could even get a shot at Johnson's title demonstrated two things: one was the paucity of good heavyweight challengers—that is, white challengers—and the second was Johnson's disinclination to defend his title against black heavyweights such as Sam Langford, Harry Wills, Joe Jeannette, and Sam McVea, who were, after Johnson, in fact the most formidable heavyweights in the world and whom he already had fought a collective total of thirteen times. Johnson knew he was better off sticking to white fighters; such fights drew more spectators, and, thus, larger gates, and were apt to be far less risky.

Reviled both in the press and in other forums, Johnson was indicted in Chicago in the fall of 1912 for violating the Mann Act for having transported a white teenager named Lucille Cameron across state lines for immoral purposes. The charge seemed to be part of a vendetta by the white American establishment to punish Johnson for his lifestyle and his scorn for convention, especially his dalliances with white women. In this case, the woman was his secretary when the alleged crime was committed and she married Johnson before the trial began, thus disqualifying her from testifying for the prosecution. Nevertheless, Johnson, who by now had become a hero to many blacks, was convicted and given a one-year prison term. But Johnson skipped bail and, accompanied by Lucille Cameron, fled to Europe by way of

Montreal, which, he was to say, he did by posing as a member of a black baseball team owned by Rube Foster, who later founded the Negro baseball leagues. Living mostly in France, where he was well received, Johnson defended his title twice—against a lightly regarded black fighter named Battling Bill Nelson and Frank Moran, a well-regarded heavyweight from Pittsburgh—and also fought several exhibitions.

In an effort to resuscitate the heavyweight division, and possibly boxing in general, American promoters not only began looking for White Hopes they would then recognize as "white champions," but began staging tournaments to create such ersatz titleholders. Among those recruited to participate were such journeymen as Carl Morris, Ed "Gunboat" Smith, Fireman Jim Flynn, Wild Bert Kenny (who would become best known for having been disqualified twice during a tour of Ireland for kicking opponents after he had knocked them down), and Bombardier Billy Wells of England, whose physical makeup included a chin of pure porcelain, which caused him to be knocked out ten times during his fifteen-year career. It was not an impressive lot, and Johnson took a sardonic pleasure in witnessing the attempt to crown a white heavyweight champion, since he had held the title of "colored heavy-weight champion" from 1903 until 1908 when he won the world title.

Well aware of boxing's depressed state, and sensing that there was not much money, if any, to be made by promoting heavyweight fights, or any others for that matter, Rickard decided in 1914 that it was a good time to move on again—this time to South America, where he would spend almost five years in Bolivia and Paraguay raising cattle and making a small fortune. By the time he returned to the United States, Jack Johnson was no longer the heavyweight champion, and boxing, though still illegal in most states, was beginning to show signs of being rejuvenated because of a sensational young knockout puncher named Jack Dempsey.

It is possible to perceive Johnson as a precursor of Muhammad Ali, whose braggadocio and showboating in the ring antagonized millions of American whites when he became the heavyweight champion in 1964 by knocking out Sonny Liston. Yet Johnson was disliked, at least by most whites, more than the surly onetime union head-buster Liston

and far more than Ali. But then America wouldn't have been ready for
Sonny Liston or Muhammad Ali in the early part of the century either,
and perhaps not even for the soft-spoken Joe Louis.

Some boxing historians believe that, in his prime, Johnson could
have beaten Dempsey and Ali and perhaps even Louis. He was a better
boxer than Dempsey and Louis, and could punch almost as hard, if not
as hard. And though not as fast, he was as good a boxer as Ali and a
much harder hitter.

Like Ali, he was also a controversial showman, both in and out of
the ring. Fittingly, his most notable victory—his one-sided knockout
of a washed-up Jim Jeffries—was promoted by the Phineas T. Barnum
of boxing, Tex Rickard, who, in a way, was just getting started.

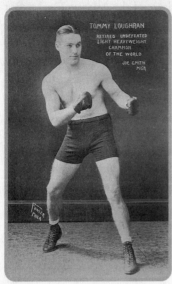

Philadelphia's beloved Tommy Loughran.
PHOTO BY FOWLER. COURTESY OF PHILLYBOXINGHISTORY.COM

■

ELEVEN

Tunney-Greb II
and Sadness
for Both

A fter a month of rest, some light training, an occasional swim off the Jersey Shore, and a few rounds of golf during the spring and early summer of 1922, Gene Tunney told Doc Bagley that he was ready to fight again. That was good news to Bagley, who knew that his relationship with Tunney had become shaky, since Tunney felt, in the wake of the Greb fight, that he had not been properly prepared for a fighter of Greb's caliber. Realizing that Tunney's confidence would have to be restored, Bagley booked him against Fay Kaiser, who had been one of the few doughboys to have beaten Bob Martin, the heavyweight champion of the American Expeditionary Forces boxing tournament, who went on to have an undistinguished professional career.

Tunney knew what to expect from Kaiser, having fought and beaten him four months earlier. Kaiser was no Harry Greb, either in style or in talent, and Tunney was confident he would beat him again in their rematch on July 6 in an outdoor arena in the Rockaway section of Queens in New York City on the shore of the Atlantic Ocean. But the fight did not quite go as expected. Kaiser, taking a cue from Harry Greb, decided to use his head, literally. Despite being warned by the referee several times, Kaiser continually banged his head against Tunney's face in the early round, opening up cuts on Tunney's nose and chin. For the first time in his career, Tunney—already renowned for his impeccable ring behavior—was enraged at an opponent, and decided to respond by rubbing his gloves near Kaiser's eyes, aware that blindness was the greatest fear on the part of most fighters. The butting stopped, and Tunney coasted to a twelve-round victory. Fully healed, and with his confidence restored, Tunney easily won two more fights in August. But his third fight that month, against a nineteen-year-old Tunney doppelgänger named Tommy Loughran—who had done much better against Greb on July 10 than Tunney had two months before—was another story.

Although it had been a good fight town since before the turn of the twentieth century, Philadelphia had produced only one champion—Philadelphia Jack O'Brien, who won the light heavyweight title in 1905 when he scored a thirteen-round knockout over Bob Fitzsimmons, the first fighter to win championships in three weight classes, but was then well past his prime at forty-two. If Philadelphia was to produce another champion, the best prospect in 1922 was Tommy Loughran, a swift, skillful boxer whose left jab was to become one of the most effective punches in boxing history.

Loughran, though five and a half years younger than Tunney, already had had forty-two professional fights—four less than Tunney—and all but two of them in the Philadelphia area. Since official decisions in professional boxing bouts in Pennsylvania could not be rendered, as had been the case in New York state for many years, most of Loughran's fights were newspaper decisions, almost all of which he had won. One that he had not won was his last bout, against Harry Greb, who, in the eyes of most sportswriters judging the fight, had narrowly outpointed Loughran only six weeks before Loughran's fight with Tunney.

Like Tunney, Loughran was Irish and handsome, did not drink or smoke, was unfailingly courteous and polite, and, overall, was an exemplar of clean living. Like Tunney, too, Loughran was a classic stand-up boxer, though not as hard a puncher, and who, at 160 pounds, gave away twelve pounds to the twenty-five-year-old Tunney. Also like Tunney, Loughran had learned how to fight out of necessity on the street—in his case in an Irish and Italian neighborhood of South Philadelphia where newsboys often had to fight to protect their street corner selling sites.

Almost all fighters shadowbox in training, a routine wherein they box against an imaginary opponent by dancing around, throwing punches, and ducking to avoid illusory blows. Loughran carried shadowboxing a step further, doing it with mirrors. Much like Tunney, he studied opponents' styles, both by watching them in person whenever possible and by obtaining as much information about them as he could. Then he would shadowbox in front of a set of mirrors he had rigged up in the basement of his parents' home in South Philadelphia, using the strategy he had mapped out for his next opponent. That way, he was able to see for himself what he would look like to his opponent—in effect, seeing himself as his opponent would see him.

The bout on August 24, 1922, matched perhaps the two best-looking fighters in the country at Baker Bowl, then the bandbox home of the Philadelphia Phillies baseball team, before a capacity crowd of around twenty-two thousand. At the outset, it appeared that the Philadelphia wunderkind's handsome profile might be sullied in quick time, and that, indeed, he might not make it past the first round. As Loughran moved in on Tunney early in the round, snapping his patented left jab at him in staccato-like fashion, Tunney suddenly unleashed a straight right cross that caught Loughran on the left side of his jaw, sending the Philadelphia teenager toppling to the floor. Dazed and obviously hurt, Loughran barely made it up at the count of nine and, seemingly feeding off the frenzied crowd, managed to elude Tunney for the remainder of the round.

Thereafter in the eight-round bout, Tunney never landed a punch to match the one that floored Loughran, although he did cause

Loughran's knees to wobble several times with jarring blows. But the elusive Loughran avoided far more punches than Tunney landed, while scoring often with his left jab and occasional right-hand punches to the head.

Not many boxers could outbox Tunney at this stage of his career, but Loughran was one of them. Aware of that, Tunney tried hard to knock out Loughran, but never came close after the opening round, and the fight appeared to have been even by the end. While there could be no official decision, the majority of sportswriters at ringside—most of them from Philadelphia-area newspapers—gave their verdicts to Loughran.

"Tommy Outclasses Gene in Sensational Bout After Weathering a Storm in First Round," read the somewhat misleading sub-headline in the following day's *Philadelphia Inquirer.* As it was, it went into the record books as a no-decision fight. Tunney himself knew it had been close, but felt that he had won the bout, as did virtually all the New York sportswriters who were present.

Loughran would get better—much better—eventually winning the world light heavyweight title in 1927 and then successfully defending it five times until he relinquished the title in 1929 in order to compete as a heavyweight. As a heavyweight who never weighed more than 192 pounds, Loughran beat most of the best fighters in the division, including eventual champions Max Baer and Jimmy Braddock, and a former champion, Jack Sharkey, along with most other leading heavyweights in the early 1930s. But in his only crack at the heavyweight title, on March 1, 1934, in Miami, he was outpointed by Primo Carnera, who outweighed Loughran by seventy-five pounds and used that weight advantage to lean on, step on, wrestle, and, in general, overwhelm the much lighter Loughran. Strangely enough, although Tunney and Loughran continued to fight as light heavyweights for several more years, they never fought each other again.

Having been badly beaten by Greb in May and then losing—at least in the eyes of some sportswriters at ringside—to Loughran three months later, Tunney had at least two good reasons to begin losing confidence in himself. In the days immediately after the Loughran bout, he began to wonder if he was as good as he thought he was. For three years he had maintained the overarching conviction that he knew how to beat Jack Dempsey. But Tunney was also sure that Dempsey was not exactly quaking in his boots about the prospect of losing his title to the former AEF light heavyweight champion.

But the Greb and Loughran fights had a salutary effect on Tunney, convincing him that he was still a work in progress. What he had going for him, in addition to his considerable skills as a fighter, was his capacity to learn from his mistakes, as he was sure he had while taking a beating from Greb and then trying too hard to knock out Loughran. Whether he had learned enough to beat the Windmill in their return bout seemed highly unlikely, especially after his performance against Loughran. Loughran, after all, was good, but he was no Harry Greb.

Finding himself once more in the position of having to prove himself after losing only one of forty-seven professional fights, Tunney fought three more times in 1922, winning one fight by decision and the last two by knockout. In his second fight, he had, for the first time, gone into the ring with the intention of hurting an opponent. Tunney had heard, secondhand, that the boxer, Jack Hanlon, also a New Yorker, had been disparaging him as a fighter and as a person. As a result, he went after Hanlon in a fury at the start of their fight and knocked him out one minute into the first round with what he later said was the hardest punch he had ever landed. As it was, though, the sight of an out-of-shape Hanlon lying on the floor with his jaw broken and blood flowing from his mouth haunted Tunney for months. Tunney never would enjoy seeing an opponent hurt, or even bleeding, and, after the fight, he felt remorseful about his avowed intention of hurting Hanlon, especially after finding out that Hanlon hadn't fought in almost two years and had won only two of his sixteen professional bouts. Never again would he go into a ring determined to do so.

Cruel as boxing can be, and given the nature of the sport—two men trying to render each other senseless—it is surprisingly rare for a fighter to be antagonistic toward an opponent. An emotionally overcharged Mike Tyson said in advance of his fight with the gentlemanly Briton Lennox Lewis in August of 2002 that he wanted to crush Lewis's skull and drive part of the skull bone into the brain. Not only was the comment repellent, but it was out of character for a boxer, if not for the mercurial and paranoiac Tyson.

The former middleweight champion Jake La Motta, one of the toughest and most durable fighters of all time, perhaps summed up the attitude of most boxers toward opponents. "It's a job. You have nothing against your opponent," said La Motta, who was knocked down only once in 106 professional fights. "And there's usually a respect for each other."

That seems to be how most great fighters of the past have felt. Like Tunney, Carmen Basilio also disliked only one opponent. Basilio, one of the most popular champions in the 1950s, who was never knocked off his feet in seventy-nine fights, seemed to have had good reason for his animosity. As Basilio recalled, he was in New York to fight at Madison Square Garden during the summer of 1954. The night before his fight, Basilio, by then a highly ranked welterweight, was walking in Times Square with his wife when they saw a crowd cluster around a pink Cadillac that had pulled up to a curb on Seventh Avenue. Basilio then saw Sugar Ray Robinson get out of the Cadillac with several other people. "Right away, I walked over to Robinson and introduced myself," Basilio said. "I figured he would know who I was because by then I was ranked. But he looked at me and walked right past without saying a word; in other words, he brushed me off. I was embarrassed and so was my wife. I vowed right then and there that if I ever got a chance to fight him in the ring, I'd get even."

It took three years, but Basilio did.

After winning the world welterweight championship in 1955, losing it in 1956, and then regaining it later that year, Basilio met Robinson for Robinson's middleweight title on September 23, 1957, in the third Madison Square Garden. It's doubtful that Robinson remembered slighting Basilio three years earlier, but the former onion farmer from Canastota in upstate New York, a heavy underdog in the fight, sure remembered the incident. In perhaps the best performance of his career, the craggy-faced Basilio, an aggressive brawler who was the antithesis of the slick and stylish Robinson, won a fifteen-round decision and his second world title. Asked forty-seven years later whether the slight on a Times Square street corner in 1954 had been a factor in his victory, Basilio said, "It certainly helped, I remembered how arrogant he was, and I was determined to get even, and I did."

The victory would be the pinnacle of Basilio's career. Six months later, he would meet Robinson in a rematch in Chicago, and Sugar Ray would regain his middleweight title. "He was the hardest puncher I ever fought and probably the best fighter, too," Basilio said. "But I never liked him, in or out of the ring."

Perhaps more than any other fighter, even the bizarrely deviant Mike Tyson, Dempsey was the personification of rage, intent on hurting an opponent as soon as possible when he was in a boxing ring, whether it was during a fight or against a sparring partner with whom he had been playing cards a few hours earlier. With his baleful stare, his brooding intensity, and his unbridled savagery, Dempsey seemed to harbor a deep resentment toward anyone in the ring with him, save perhaps the referee, while outside the ring he was unfailingly polite, gentle, and immensely likable. But Dempsey said his demeanor in the ring reflected his boxing persona—"It's the only way I know how to fight, whether it's in the gym or during a fight," he once said. "It's not because I dislike the guy I'm fighting."

That could be why, years later, Dempsey surprised Bill Gallo of the New York *Daily News* when Dempsey brought up the matter of an afterlife.

"You know what I'd like to be if I came back, Bill?" Dempsey said to Gallo.

"No, what, Jack?" Gallo recalled a quarter-century later.

"A lion," Dempsey replied.

"Why a lion, Jack," Gallo asked.

"Because," Dempsey responded, "a lion is the king of the jungle."

Probably most reflective of how most fighters respect one another is the way they often embrace, even hug, each other, at the end of a fight, all the more so if the bout has been an especially brutal one. Only fighters can understand the seemingly inexplicable bond that develops between two men while they are punching away at each other, a bond that is publicly manifested when the final bell sounds and, cut, bruised, and exhausted, they fall into each other's arms in a show of respect. True, in some cases the embrace is mere ritual, but more often than not it appears to be sincere and deeply meaningful, a tribute to each other's courage.

As Joyce Carol Oates, the poet and writer who has had a longtime fascination with boxing, wrote, "One might wonder if the boxing match leads irresistibly to this moment: the public embrace of two men who otherwise, in public or private, could never approach each other with such passion."

Athletes in some other sports, such as tennis and golf, will shake hands at the end of a match or round, but they will rarely hug one another. And even in the case of the handshakes, they are often perfunctory. Among boxers, though, the embraces seem to be heartfelt manifestations of respect.

Tunney's last fight of 1922, against Charley Weinert in Madison Square Garden, which he won by a fourth-round knockout, drew only eight thousand spectators and attracted little interest in the New York papers. Having been soundly beaten by Harry Greb and then thoroughly extended by the Philadelphia teenager Tommy Loughran, Tunney was no longer considered a hot prospect. Beating the likes of Jack Hanlon and Charley Weinert did not impress boxing insiders, many of whom felt that Tunney had gone as far as he could up the fistic ladder.

Feeling that Doc Bagley, his manager, was at least partially to blame for the beating he absorbed from Greb and his poor performance against Loughran, Tunney decided to sever relations with him after the Weinert fight. To do so, Tunney would have to buy out his contract from Bagley for five thousand dollars, a hefty sum, but, Tunney felt, well worth it. His next manager would be his best and his last. In Billy Gibson, Tunney found just what he wanted—someone who had maneuvered Benny Leonard to the lightweight title, was an intimate of many leading New York political figures, and was close to scores of boxing promoters, managers, referees, and boxing judges, along with more than a few well-known underworld figures.

After working in his father's Bronx butcher shop as a young man, Gibson opened a restaurant in the East Bronx that soon became a favorite gathering spot for lawyers, judges, entertainers, and political, sports, and mob figures. At the suggestion of influential friends, Gibson later opened the popular Fairmont Athletic Club in the Bronx, which became one of the most popular boxing clubs in New York. Though he was the first to admit that he knew little about boxing, Gibson promoted fights at his club and, later, at Madison Square Garden and in Havana.

That Gibson had little expertise in boxing did not faze Tunney. "Billy was very smart and resourceful about the business of managing boxers, though he never thoroughly understood boxing technique," Tunney was to say sometime later. Like many good fighters Tunney was convinced that he knew far more about boxing than any manager. It was Gibson's business acumen and connections that impressed Tunney and convinced him to sign a three-year contract that guaranteed Gibson a third of Tunney's future boxing earnings, typical for a manager at the time. Before their meeting, Gibson had misgivings about working with Tunney. He had heard that Tunney was difficult to manage, ignoring his managers' suggestions far more often than heeding them. But after meeting with Tunney, Gibson was not only highly impressed, but concluded that they could make a lot of money for each other. Still, as had been the case with Tunney's previous managers, Billy Roche and Doc Bagley, his relationship with Gibson would be a symbiotic one. In any event, it would be amicable enough to last for the rest of Tunney's career.

After his first two fights under Gibson in early 1923, Tunney again retreated to Barry McCormack's farm in Red Bank to prepare for his rematch with Harry Greb on February 23 at Madison Square Garden. To assist Tunney, Gibson brought in Benny Leonard, both to counsel him and occasionally to spar. One of boxing's most perceptive fighters, Leonard had seen the first Greb-Tunney bout and had quickly concluded, as he soon told Gibson, that Tunney had made a number of crucial mistakes, the most serious being his persistence in aiming almost all of his punches at Greb's head and ignoring the body. It was sage advice that Tunney was to remember when he went into the ring for the second time against Greb.

Greb had far more on his mind than beating Tunney again. The condition of his twenty-two-year-old wife, Mildred, had worsened and she had returned to their home in Pittsburgh from a nearby sanitarium. There was now no hope, and, Greb was told in early February, death could come almost any day. For all of his toughness in the ring, Greb found his young wife's imminent death unbearable. Still, he decided to continue fighting.

Prior to the Tunney rematch, Greb fought six times in six weeks, starting on New Year's Day of 1923. Two of Greb's six fights were victories over Tommy Loughran—the first a ten-round newspaper decision in Pittsburgh, the second a fifteen-round decision in Greb's first defense of his American light heavyweight title fifteen days later in Madison Square Garden. Although his impending fight with Tunney was only twenty-three days after his third fight with Loughran, Greb fought two twelve-rounders on February 5 and 16, winning both by decision. That meant he had only one week to prepare for Tunney or to rest. Not surprisingly, he chose to return to Pittsburgh by train to spend most of his time with Mildred, who was now fading fast. Returning to New York two days before the Tunney fight at Madison Square Garden, Greb was shaken and overwrought. But he knew that once the fight started, he would be totally focused on Tunney.

Despite his one-sided loss to Greb in their first fight, Tunney had been a slight favorite in the days leading up to the rematch, but then a heavy influx of Greb money in the hours before the fight sent him into the ring as a slight favorite. As expected, Greb charged out of his corner at the opening bell, but he was met by a series of sharp body blows that prompted the Windmill to clinch for the first of what would be many times. Seated at ringside, Benny Leonard smiled. Young Tunney was doing what he had suggested: going for the body.

Most effective in the early rounds was Tunney's left hook to the midsection, which on several occasions seemed to take the wind out of Greb. But Greb, undaunted as always, kept coming at Tunney from different angles with punches in bunches, and then constantly grabbing Tunney in an effort to forestall more body blows.

Apparently determined to let Greb know early on that he was prepared to respond in kind to roughhouse tactics, Tunney, nine pounds heavier at 174 pounds, grabbed Greb during a close-quarter exchange marked by some Greb rough stuff in the second round and wrestled him to the floor. But Greb was not about to change his ways, nor be intimidated by anyone. Still, because of his effective body attack, Tunney seemed to have won most of the first six rounds. Clearly, it was a totally different fight from the first one nine months earlier.

But then Tunney seemed to slow down in the middle rounds while Greb, who had missed most of his punches early on, began to find the range. As the fight wore on, Tunney appeared to tire—he said later that he had been battling the flu and had virtually been exhausted from the sixth through the eleventh rounds. Fortunately for him and for his betting backers, he somehow regained his strength with four rounds to go.

"They told me in my corner I was losing," Tunney said later, "and that if I wanted to win, I would have to capture the remaining rounds or knock him out."

That warning seemed to rejuvenate Tunney, who realized that a second straight loss to Greb, no matter how good the Pittsburgh Windmill was, would probably be a devastating blow to his career and would end his hopes of ever fighting Jack Dempsey. Summoning up energy from deep down within that he seemed to have exhausted, Tunney became far more aggressive in the remaining four rounds. Despite his strong finish, Tunney was uncertain who had won.

When ring announcer Joe Humphreys proclaimed that Tunney had regained the American light heavyweight title, there were cheers from the crowd, but they were mixed with boos and catcalls from hundreds of Greb supporters. Greb, furious, jumped up and down in his corner while screaming at referee Patsy Haley, who had cast the deciding vote for Tunney. Under the Walker Law as it then existed, if both judges agreed on a winner, the referee's scorecard was academic and not even revealed. However, if the judges disagreed, the referee's verdict decided the outcome. In the Tunney-Greb rematch, one judge, Charles Miles, had Greb as the winner, while the second judge, Charles Meegan, scored the fight for Tunney. So did Haley, which gave Tunney the split decision.

Of the writers at ringside surveyed by the *New York Tribune,* four voted for Greb while the same number had Tunney ahead at the end. Five others scored the bout as a draw. Grantland Rice was among those who thought Greb had won. "Greb did most of the fighting, most of the hitting, and most of the holding," Rice wrote in the *New York World.* "He used his head repeatedly, but even considering the number of points he lost in this way, he still deserved the decision."

Jim Halliday of the *Staten Island Advance* went even further, writing, "A vital blow at boxing in New York State was delivered last night in Madison Square Garden when Gene Tunney, badly beaten in 13 of the 15 rounds fought, was awarded the decision over Harry Greb."

But Hype Igoe of the *New York World,* perhaps the city's most respected fight writer, was among those who thought the decision was a fair one. "Greb's unsportsmanlike tactic probably went a long way toward bringing the title back to Gene Tunney," Igoe wrote. "Greb's hard head, used generously but ungloriously, caused storms of disapproval. Discounting Greb's rough-housing, his eternal clinching, the butting and holding, the clear work, straight hitting and honest fighting was done by Tunney."

Pittsburgh sportswriters covering the fight disagreed en masse with Igoe. Indeed, some were downright apoplectic about the decision. Writing in the *Pittsburgh Post,* Regis Welsh, the paper's "sporting" editor, said that Tunney had been "the beneficiary of the most highhanded robbery ever seen anywhere in the fistic world."

Greb agreed. "I was jobbed," said Greb, much of whose body was covered with welts from Tunney's body attack. "It was all fixed for the title to be handed back to Tunney. I won the majority of rounds, but Tunney gets the decision. It is a pretty cheaply won honor."

Returning to Pittsburgh the day after the fight, Greb found that his wife's condition had become grave. Pneumonia had set in, and now, doctors told Greb, it was a matter of days, and nothing could be done. He remained at her side almost constantly, while spending more time than he had ever done in the past with Dorothy, now three and a half years old and barely able to understand what her father did for a living or what was happening to her mother.

For all his hell-raising, Greb had become a good family man and remained deeply religious and attached to the Roman Catholic Church. While home that March, Greb would pray daily at St. Joseph's Church that Mildred would pull through. She would not. On March 18, at the age of twenty-two, she died with Greb and a few other family members at her side. Devastated by the death of his wife at such a young age, Greb remained in Pittsburgh for two months to spend time with little Dorothy and his sister, Ida, who, along with her husband, had cared for Dorothy since Mildred had become ill and would continue to do so for years to come.

For Tunney, 1923 also would be marked by sadness. By the end of the year, his father had died at the age of sixty-three. And just as John Tunney, out of fear of seeing Gene hurt during a bout, had never gone to any of his son's fights, so Harry Greb's father, Pious, who wanted so very much for his son to become a big league baseball player, would never see his son inside a ring either.

TWELVE

The Sack of Shelby

Downtown Shelby in 1923, before the Dempsey-Gibbons fight.
THE MARIAS MUSEUM OF HISTORY AND ART, SHELBY, MONTANA

A ware that his American light heavyweight title was a spurious championship, created by Tex Rickard as a promotional device designed to convince potential spectators that the fight had special significance, which it really did not, Tunney felt that to validate his credentials in the 175-pound weight class, he had to win the world title. But he had no more luck than Harry Greb did when Greb tried to do that after winning the American title from Tunney in their first fight.

Greb had hoped to capitalize on his decisive victory over Tunney by meeting the world light heavyweight champion, Georges Carpentier of France, who had gone back to fighting boxers in his own weight class after having been knocked out by Jack Dempsey. But Carpentier and his crafty manager, François Descamps, had heard enough about Greb not to risk the Orchid Man's title against the Pittsburgh Windmill, especially in the States. They may as well have, though. In the second defense of the title he had won from Battling Levinsky in 1920, Carpentier was knocked out in the sixth round by Battling Siki of Senegal on September 24, 1922. The irony of that loss was that Carpentier and Descamps thought Siki would be a lot easier to beat than Greb.

For Tunney, though, the quest for the world title was more logical since he was a legitimate light heavyweight, while Greb was a middleweight. With a lucrative and attractive title fight with Carpentier now out of the question, Tunney decided it was time to move up to the heavyweight division and start getting ready for Dempsey. Maybe he could barely beat a 165-pound Harry Greb, but Tunney was still certain that he could take the measure of the 190-pound Dempsey, something that Greb had done during two sparring sessions with the Manassa Mauler in 1920.*

By far the biggest fight during the summer of 1923 was scheduled to be held in a place hardly anyone had ever heard of—Shelby, Montana, an oil boomtown and key railroad junction about thirty miles south of the Canadian border. An out-of-the-blue offer to Dempsey's manager, Jack Kearns, in the late winter of of 1923 to defend his title in Shelby came at an opportune time for Kearns and Dempsey, who were determined to get Dempsey back in the ring after a two-year layoff. Any hope Dempsey and Kearns may have had for a big-money fight in New York had been dashed on February 4, 1923, when William Mul-

---

*Though Georges Carpentier would not defend his world light heavyweight title against Harry Greb, Johnny Wilson agreed to risk his somewhat shaky middleweight crown against the Pittsburgh Windmill. One of the least distinguished of the middleweight champions, Wilson waited three years before making a title defense at the Polo Grounds in New York on August 31, 1923. By then he had been labeled a "cheese champion," a derogatory term in boxing that implies a fighter is not worthy of his title, which in Wilson's case was no doubt true as long as Greb was around. In one of the roughest and dirtiest title bouts ever held in New York, Greb won thirteen of the fifteen rounds to capture the title. Incredibly, Greb, one of the best middleweights of all time, had had to take on almost two hundred opponents, and beat almost all of them, before getting a shot at the 160-pound titleholder. Now he was not only king of the alley fighters, but also king of the middleweights. And no one would ever call Harry Greb a cheese champion.

doon, the chairman of the New York State Athletic Commission, announced that unless promoters lowered their purses for heavyweight title fights and reduced prices for spectators attending those fights, there would be no heavyweight title bouts staged in New York. Boxing had become much too commercialized by "money-mad promoters and managers" and newspaper coverage of heavyweight fights had become excessive, said Muldoon, who at the age of seventy-eight was not only still taut, fit, and alert, but ran one of the most successful physical culture centers, as he called them, in the Westchester County suburb of Purchase. Moreover, Muldoon asked, how could anyone justify a heavyweight fighter making more money in one fight than the president of the United States makes in four years?

Cynics felt that Muldoon's pronouncement actually had nothing to do with fighters, promoters, and managers making too much money, but everything in the world to do with making certain that Harry Wills did not get a shot at Dempsey's title, at least in New York state. For if he did and won, the world would again have a black heavyweight champion, which was anathema to Rickard—and, many thought, to Muldoon.

But Edward Van Every, a New York sportswriter, was to write in his biography of Muldoon that the boxing commissioner had made his announcement not of his own volition, but on "orders from a very high place," presumably Washington, although Van Every did not say. Whatever the reason, Muldoon's announcement put him in the position of being in control of boxing in the country's most populous state, which had the nation's biggest sports arena (Madison Square Garden) and two of the largest stadiums (the Polo Grounds in Manhattan and Ebbets Field in Brooklyn), with a third stadium (Yankee Stadium) scheduled to open in April, and yet lamenting that its participants were making too much money and that the sport was getting too much publicity.

What made Muldoon's comments all the more ironic was the fact that there had not been a heavyweight title fight in New York since December 14, 1920, when Dempsey knocked out Bill Brennan in Madison Square Garden. And at that, the Dempsey-Brennan bout had been the first title fight in the state since March 25, 1916, when Jess

Willard retained his championship in a ten-round bout with Frank Moran. That meant that over a period of seven years there had been two heavyweight championship fights in New York state. And there hadn't been many elsewhere either, since Dempsey had not defended his title in two years, and had put it on the line only three times in the three and a half years he had held sport's most coveted championship.

Given Muldoon's virtual ban on heavyweight title fights in New York, Kearns decided to wire an acceptance of the Shelby offer that guaranteed Dempsey $200,000 (the equivalent of slightly more than $2 million today) for the fight, which was set for July Fourth. According to John Kavanagh, the retired publisher of the *Shelby Promoter,* a weekly newspaper, the offer was made after his uncle, James W. "Body" Johnson, and a colleague, Mel McCutcheon, saw a newspaper story in February of 1923 reporting that a Montreal boxing promoter had offered $100,000 to Dempsey if he would make a title defense in the Canadian city. Furthermore, they were aware of the worldwide publicity that tiny Goldfield, Nevada, had received from the Joe Gans–Battling Nelson lightweight title fight in 1906 and the attention that had been drawn to Reno in 1910 by the Jack Johnson–Jim Jeffries heavyweight championship bout. So, Johnson and McCutcheon collectively reasoned, Why can't we offer even more than the Montreal promoter and put Shelby on the map. It would strictly be a publicity stunt designed to focus attention on Shelby and, quite possibly, help enrich Johnson and McCutcheon in their real estate business. They were anxious to sell both land and houses to outsiders who had never heard of the town, which had only been incorporated since 1914. Apart from a lack of money, there were at least three other sizable problems that seemingly would preclude a Dempsey title fight from being held in Shelby: 1) there was no place in town to hold a big fight; 2) no thought had been given to a prospective opponent; and 3) neither Johnson nor McCutcheon knew anything about boxing, let alone how to promote a fight.

But that hardly mattered. "It was strictly a publicity stunt to publicize Shelby and to get people to move into the area," Kavanagh said in October of 2005. "They had no inkling of actually having the fight in

Shelby." Thus, Kearns's acceptance stunned Johnson and McCutcheon and just about everyone else in Montana. But once the story broke, they decided to press on, hopefully with the help of local boosters, along with the oil prospectors and real estate men who had made a bee-line for Shelby as soon as oil was unearthed in what became known as the Kevin-Sunburst oil field just north of the town in the spring of 1922.

Besides raising $200,000, building an arena, and getting a suitable opponent, there were other problems. Under Montana law, a fight could not be held without the support of a service organization. Johnson and McCutcheon then managed to get the backing of the local post of the American Legion, whose state commander, Loy Molumby, had denounced Dempsey as a "notorious slacker" once the announcement of the Shelby fight offer was made. The Legion post, which had staged a few small fight cards the previous winter, grudgingly gave its support. Then, in an ironic twist, Molumby, a lawyer in Great Falls, Montana, was asked by Johnson and McCutcheon to meet with Kearns in Chicago, both to sign a contract and to give him a down payment of $100,000. Molumby, who had been a pilot in the Army Air Corps during World War I, surprisingly agreed, perhaps because of the fee he had been guaranteed and suggestions by Johnson and McCutcheon that he might be asked to be the promoter of the fight. By then, at the suggestion of Lyman Sampson, who had been designated as the local Legion post's boxing matchmaker, an opponent had been selected: Tommy Gibbons, a highly rated heavyweight from St. Paul, Minnesota.

Before it went any further, Johnson's father, James A. Johnson, who had been elected Shelby's first mayor in 1914 and still held the post, convinced his son to get the blessing on the proposed fight from Montana governor Joe Dixon, an old friend of the mayor's. After listening to the proposal at the state capitol in Helena, the governor turned to the younger Johnson and said, "Body, just where are you going to get $200,000? Hell, man, there isn't that much money in the whole state of Montana." That prompted Body Johnson to bring the governor up to speed on the oil boom just outside Shelby, and the "fast-working oil men up in that country who will be glad to help us out to finance the fight."

Dubious, but impressed with Johnson's vision and optimism, Governor Dixon gave his blessing while recommending he first check things out with the state's attorney general, which Johnson did, even though he never expected the fight to take place. It was, after all, just a publicity-grabber to let people know about what local boosters were advertising as "the Tulsa of the West," while appearing to ignore the fact that Tulsa was, in most people's opinion, also in the West.

Johnson and Molumby finally got to meet with Kearns in mid-April in Salt Lake City, where Kearns said he wanted $100,000 when the contract was signed and the remaining $100,000 before Dempsey stepped into the ring. Two weeks later, Molumby, carrying a certified check for $100,000, went to Chicago to close the deal with Kearns at the Morrison Hotel. In a city accustomed to strange happenings, something very strange apparently occurred. For when Molumby returned to Shelby, he notified Johnson, McCutcheon, and Johnson's father, the mayor—who would become a major financial backer of the fight—that he had had to sign a contract guaranteeing Dempsey (and, of course, Kearns) $300,000—$100,000 more than he had been authorized to guarantee—or Kearns said there would be no fight in Shelby.

"Kearns apparently threw a wingding of a party and may have gotten Molumby drunk and then convinced him to sign the contract," John Kavanagh was to say eighty-two years later. "Maybe Kearns provided him with a woman. Who knows? Otherwise, why would an intelligent lawyer, who had very strict instructions to offer only $200,000, do what he did?"

So Shelby—where many people doubted backers of the fight could come up with $200,000—was now obliged to somehow mine another $100,000. After hearing Molumby contend that Kearns had demanded another $100,000, Johnson said, "We decided there was nothing to be done but buckle down and try to live with it."

So it was that a nondescript cattle town and distributing point on the Great Northern Railroad, which had morphed into an oil boomtown, was faced with coming up with $200,000 for a fight that might never even be held. And oh yes—the town now had to build a stadium for the fight, and a very big one, at that.

Newspaper readers around the country gaped at the news. Before the oil strike, Shelby had been so obscure that it had not even been listed in the U.S. Census until 1920 when it had grown to a town of 525 residents. Three years later, in 1923, the population had risen to just under one thousand with many of the newcomers oil prospectors, oil drillers, contractors, and real estate men, all looking to make a killing.

While the oil strike had made a lot of people wealthy in a hurry and had sent real estate values in Shelby soaring, the town was generally unknown outside Montana, except, perhaps, for riders on the Great Northern Railroad, some of whose trains stopped in Shelby. What few business establishments there were on its unpaved Main Street included one hotel, two banks, a few stores, several saloons, King Tut's Dance Hall, and Aunt Kate's Cathouse, which featured the biggest and most prominent sign on Shelby's main drag.

Years later, Kearns, asked to describe Shelby, said, "It's one of those wide-open towns. Red Dog saloon, gambling halls—you know, like you see in the movies."

It was an apt description. A little less apt, perhaps, but more entertaining was the comment by Arthur "Bugs" Baer, a humor columnist for Hearst's King Features syndicate, who, after spending a few days in Shelby, wrote, "This place is so tough the canaries sing bass."

Collectively ecstatic at the thought of the great Jack Dempsey, a product of the West himself, defending his title in Shelby, Johnson and McCutcheon decided that Gibbons would be an ideal opponent. He was a good fighter, although, at thirty-four, probably on the downside of a twelve-year career. Still, he had only lost two of his last twenty-four fights—one to Harry Greb and the other on a foul to Billy Miske—and was one of the best heavyweights around.

The $300,000 purse that Molumby agreed to equaled what Kearns and Dempsey had received for the Carpentier fight in Jersey City. But that fight, featuring the two biggest names in boxing at the time, was held right across the Hudson River from Manhattan and drew more than eighty thousand. Who knew, Kearns wondered, how many people would come to Shelby, Montana—even to see the great Dempsey fight? Who knew, too, how the remaining $200,000 would be raised?

If Kearns had worked out a sweetheart deal with Loy Molumby, Gibbons would soon find out that he most likely would be fighting for Dempsey's title, but nothing else. Molumby offered Gibbons's manager, Eddie Kane, 50 percent of the gate receipts for the fight over $300,000 and up to $600,000, and 25 percent of everything above that, and Kane accepted the offer. Kearns knew immediately that Gibbons would be fighting for nothing. There was no way, he realized, that a cow town like Shelby, even if did have good railroad connections, was going to produce anywhere near a gate of $300,000—let alone $600,000.

When Kearns told Dempsey he had agreed for a fight against Gibbons in Shelby, Dempsey said, "I never heard of it." And Dempsey was from the West.

"It ain't a big place," Kearns said, practicing considerable understatement, "but the money's there. Some oil fellows out there want to put the town on the map and sell some oil stocks."

"I don't want to fight in no place named Shelby," Dempsey replied. "It's crazy."

"They're going to give us two-fifty and fifty percent," Kearns said in referring to the guaranteed purse, which he seemed to have devalued. But then, omissions like that were not uncommon on the part of managers in the 1920s and well afterward.

"Well, okay," Dempsey said. "But I'm going to hold you responsible for the money." Letting a manager be responsible for the money due a fighter was not always a smart business decision in the 1920s. But Kearns had done relatively well for Dempsey—he had gotten him a shot at the heavyweight title and a lucrative purse for the Carpentier fight. Kearns hadn't done much for him over the last two years, but Dempsey trusted him—to a certain degree.

Under the terms of the contract, Dempsey and Kearns were to receive the remainder of their guarantee in $100,000 payments on June 15 and on July 2—two days before the fight. If the Shelby group failed to make any of the three payments, the fight would be canceled, with Dempsey and Kearns keeping whatever had been paid. When Kearns received a certified check for $100,000 from Molumby in Chicago, he had good reason to believe that Johnson, McCutcheon, and their presumably prosperous Shelby colleagues would make good on all the payments. By then, Johnson had enlisted the financial assistance of a number of Shelby businessmen, a few oilmen, some bankers, and, most important, his father, who had added to his financial success as a rancher through oil leases and as president of the First State Bank of Shelby. Suddenly, what had begun as a publicity stunt had evolved into a can-do effort in a somewhat bedazzled community whose civic and business leaders, not to mention real estate agents and oilmen, felt that, hey, maybe we can pull this off after all.

But then what appeared to be a quixotic venture was dealt another blow when a small plane carrying Body Johnson, Molumby, and two other men crashed while distributing tickets to the fight to American Legion posts in Montana. Molumby and two of the men escaped serious injury, but Johnson was critically hurt and hospitalized for ten days.

In late May, Dempsey set up training camp in a former beer garden in Great Falls Park just outside of Great Falls, Montana, about eighty-five miles from Shelby. A crowd of several hundred, including the local high school band, greeted Dempsey when his train arrived in Great Falls, and many of the greeters followed his motorcade through town. Dempsey quickly endeared himself to the townspeople when, at one point, he jumped out of his moving convertible to march with the band, even going so far as to borrow the drumsticks from one band member so that he could beat the big bass drum.

Further endearing himself to the locals shortly after his arrival in Great Falls, Dempsey not only attended a cattle breeders show, but bought a Hereford bull there and, later, purchased a cow and a wolf cub to go with the bulldog and Persian kitten he had brought with him from Salt Lake City, which he still called home. Dempsey also raised several hundred dollars for a Great Falls orphanage by boxing a three-round exhibition with Bombardier Billy Wells, a sparring partner and former British heavyweight champion, and mingled freely with spectators who came to his workouts.

Dempsey did not look impressive in the sparring sessions. Several times he was jarred and hurt by sparring partners Jack Burke and George Godfrey, both of whom were among the better heavyweights in the 1920s. In one sparring session, Burke—whom Gene Tunney had knocked out in the ninth round fifteen months earlier—floored Dempsey twice, with a right to the jaw and a left hook. Never before having seen a world-class fighter up close, most of the Montanans who came to watch the Manassa Mauler spar for free had no idea whether he was paying the price for the two years he had spent away from the ring. But veteran sportswriters like Heywood Broun, Damon Runyon, Grantland Rice, and Hype Igoe noticed that the champ was reacting slower than in the past to punches and also moving considerably slower. Still, no one thought Gibbons, good as he was, had a chance against Dempsey.

The first sign that the fight was in trouble came on June 15, when the second $100,000 payment was due under Kearns's agreement with Johnson, McCutcheon, and Molumby. Not only was the Shelby group short of money—it was short by 98 percent, Kearns was told during a meeting with members of the group in Great Falls.

"We're having a little difficulty coming up with the hundred thousand dollars," said Mayor Johnson. "We mailed out a great many tickets to various parts of the state and all over the country, but they haven't been paid for yet. And expenses have been unexpectedly large. To tell the truth, there's only about sixteen hundred dollars on hand."

Kearns exploded, incredulous that tickets for the fight had been sent to ticket brokers without being bonded, "Well, that's a helluva note," he said angrily. "But as I told you when we signed for the fight, if the terms aren't met, no fight."

Mayor Johnson, realizing the fight was in jeopardy, had an idea.

"Mr. Kearns, would you consider taking fifty thousand head of sheep in place of the hundred thousand dollars?" he said.

Kearns looked at Johnson in disbelief. "Now just what the hell would I do with fifty thousand sheep in a New York apartment?" he asked.

At that point, George Stanton, the president of a bank in Great Falls, who had come to the meeting at the request of the citizens committee, had another suggestion. "Why don't you take over the promotion and ticket sale?" he asked Kearns. "From all I can see, you own the fight right now."

"Damned if I'll promote it," Kearns thundered. "These guys are the promoters, I'm trying to train a fighter. Just let them get up the money or there won't be any fight. That's all I've got to say." Kearns then stormed out of the hotel room.

Several hours later, he was summoned back to the hotel for a meeting with Stanton, now essaying the role of the state of Montana's deus ex machina. "Mr. Kearns," Stanton said sternly, "the money will be raised. We people in Great Falls are getting behind the fight. We'll see that every nickel is raised."

Having been informed of Stanton's stature as perhaps the leading financier in Montana, Kearns felt reassured. He had good reason to. By five o'clock the next afternoon, Stanton, at a press conference he had called, handed Kearns a check for $100,000. Stanton seemed to imply that he had come up with the money on his own, but in fact most of it had come from Mayor Johnson, through land and oil leases from his estate. So the fight was back on, at least for now, with the third and final $100,000 due two days before the scheduled fight. It would not be the last crisis to befall the biggest scheduled fight in years in a place hardly anyone had ever heard of.

By mid-June, many of the country's best-known sportswriters had descended on Great Falls and Shelby. They spent most of their time with Dempsey in Great Falls while occasionally making the two-and-a-half-hour trip by automobile or train to Shelby, both to watch Tommy Gibbons train and to talk to some of the local principals in the promotion in an effort to sense whether the fight would actually take place. Many of them also had a field day describing the old cow town and its unsophisticated inhabitants, along with the wildcat oil prospectors and real estate hustlers who had moved in to make financial killings from the oil strikes. Like Dempsey and Kearns, most of the big-city writers thought that the fight would never come off, at least not in Shelby.

If Dempsey and Kearns were both larger-than-life figures in the eyes of most Montanans, Gibbons was a distinct counterpoint—a quiet, unassuming family man. He was also the "people's choice" in the fight because of his approachability and because he was from the Northwest. With his wife and three young children, Gibbons, who was staying in Shelby, was a familiar figure in town, pushing his infant daughter around in a stroller, doing grocery shopping, and stopping to talk to everyone who approached him and wished him well in the fight.

As time went on, Dempsey and Kearns became the heavies in the eyes of Montanans, mainly because of Kearns's repeated threats that he and Dempsey would leave Shelby if they did not get all of the guaranteed $300,000 by July 2. To the locals, the guarantee was both astronomical and ridiculous for a fight in a town of slightly over a thousand people, who, for the most part would not make that much money in their lifetime. If there was a villain in the piece, it was the dyspeptic forty-five-year-old Kearns, who, dressed in tight-fitting pin-striped suits, vest, tie, and black patent-leather shoes, strutted about both Great Falls and Shelby with an incongruous touch of sartorial splendor and an arrogance that only further alienated him from the local townspeople, who regarded him as a shifty and untrustworthy New York popinjay.

Though far more likable, Dempsey eventually became Public Enemy Number Two in the eyes of many Montanans, even though, unknown to the locals, he would gladly have fought for much less money. But Kearns, perhaps fearing for his personal safety in a town where most of the men carried pistols—which some of them fondled conspicuously whenever Kearns came into sight—never let on that he, and he alone, handled Dempsey's financial affairs. Thus many Montanans thought it was Dempsey who was being greedy during the crises over the money shortage. Dempsey sensed his drop in popularity in the grimness of the few spectators who turned up at his training sessions and by the glares he encountered whenever he went into downtown Great Falls.

To more than a few Montanans, Dempsey and Kearns were picaroons, prepared to hightail it out of the state under cover of darkness before the scheduled fight with the $200,000 they had already received on the ground that the local promoters had not kept their end of the bargain. That seemed especially likely when talks broke down briefly on July 3 and Kearns announced that the fight was off. Kearns later was to say that on that day Frank Walker, a lawyer from Butte who had come to Shelby to try to salvage the fight and who later would become postmaster general under Franklin Roosevelt, shook his fist at Kearns and warned him not to leave town until after the fight had been held. Like many others, Walker felt that Shelby, if indeed not all of Montana, was being taken for a very expensive ride by Kearns, and that the state's honor was at stake.

Despite the hundreds of nouveaux riches created by the 1922 oil strike and the subsequent emergence of Shelby as a mini-boomtown, it soon became evident that the citizens committee was having trouble raising the last $100,000. Though not even a member of the citizens committee, George Stanton, the prominent Great Falls banker who had persuaded Mayor Johnson to produce the second $100,000 payment, came up with a plan to raise the money. The plan: Stanton said that twenty lifelong friends in Montana each had acceded to his request to put up $5,000—ergo, a grand total of $100,000—to meet the final payment. "I am determined to save the honor of Montana," Stanton said, adding, "Kearns would like to get out of this fight if he could."

Stanton wasn't the only one in Montana who thought that should the citizens committee fail to come up with the final payment, Kearns and Dempsey would—as, under their one-sided agreement, they could—leave Shelby and Great Falls, unannounced, with the $200,000 they had already received. On July 2, it looked very much like that would happen. That morning, Stanton announced that only eight of his twenty friends had pledged the $5,000, leaving the committee $60,000 short. "I guess that the fight will have to be called off," he said.

When Kearns heard the news, he made what he called his "final offer"—he would give the citizens committee until noon the next day, July 3, to come up with $50,000 and he would take the remaining $50,000 from the gate receipts. But after a day-long effort to raise the money, Loy Malumby, now reinstated as the citizens committee's principal negotiator, informed Kearns that there was no way that the committee could make that deadline, if indeed any deadline before the Fourth of July. Thus, Malumby said, the fight apparently was off.

"All right," Kearns told Malumby acridly at the end of a meeting that ended shortly after midnight on the morning of July 3, the day before the scheduled fight. "That goes for me. The fight is off."

By now, the on-again, off-again status of the fight had become front-page news in many newspapers across the country. On July 3 it even made the front page of the *New York Times.* "The fight is off," read Elmer Davis's lead at the top of the fold on page one. That Elmer Davis would be assigned to cover the Dempsey-Gibbons bout demonstrated how important the story had become throughout the United States and even beyond its borders. If the *Times* had a star reporter in the early 1920s, it was Davis, a former Rhodes Scholar who was fluent in Latin, Greek, and German. With the *Times,* he had served as a foreign correspondent, as well as a political, editorial, and sportswriter. Davis was so highly thought of by the paper's hierarchy that he was chosen by publisher Adolph Ochs to research and then write a book entitled *History of the New York Times, 1851–1921.*

For all of that, Davis also breached a long-standing byline barrier at the *Times.* No matter how big the sports story, *Times* sportswriters, unlike their competitors at other New York newspapers, did not get bylines. But Davis's stories from Shelby, several of which ran on the front page, had his name at the top, ending the tradition wherein *Times* sportswriters toiled in anonymity. After covering numerous major news stories, including several more world championship fights, Davis went on to become a successful author—two of his books, *But We Were Born Free* and *Two Minutes to Midnight,* both about the McCarthy era, were bestsellers—and a radio commentator for CBS News and, later, ABC News. During World War II, President Roosevelt named Davis the head of the then new Office of War Information.

Unlike the florid tales of writers like Rice, Runyon, Ring Lardner, Heywood Broun, and W. O. McGeehan, Davis's stories leading up to the fight were gracefully written but relatively subdued. Still, Davis vividly conveyed the kaleidoscopic chain of events in Shelby while describing the hardscrabble nature of the old cow town and some of its more colorful characters and others who had traveled to Shelby for the fight. "Not since the time when President Wilson went into the silences to commune with his soul and decide what to say to the Germans about the *Lusitania* has there been such feverish tension as existed in Great Falls tonight when the populace waited till midnight to see whether Jack Kearns was going to weaken or hold to his determination of no last hundred thousand, no fight," Davis wrote in his July 3 story from Great Falls, where the last-ditch negotiations were taking place.

That was about as hyperbolic as Davis would wax in the thousands of words he filed via Western Union to the *Times*. In his front-page story the following day, he reported that the fight apparently would take place after all, but only because Kearns had agreed at 2:30 A.M. to take the remaining $100,000, or whatever there was, from the gate receipts on the day of the fight. Everyone, Kearns included, knew that the gate receipts would not reach that level, and that, thus, he and Dempsey would be settling for far less while Gibbons would—as it had appeared for some time—fight for nothing. It was not supposed to turn out that way, of course, but it was now inevitable. "For that, however, only their own mismanagement and fatuous optimism is responsible," Davis wrote in referring to the citizens committee.

Given the contentious negotiations that had made it uncertain right up until the day of the fight whether it would come off, things hardly seemed to have been able to get worse. But then, of course, they did.

The throngs of spectators from throughout the upper Midwest and even the Pacific Coast never did materialize, in large measure because of the uncertainty surrounding the fight, which prompted the Great Northern and other major railroads to cancel more than twenty special trains from Chicago, Seattle, and other Western cities. As it was, the only extra trains from out of state that carried passengers to Shelby for the fight were two from St. Paul, Minnesota—Gibbons's hometown—and one from Spokane, Washington. All of the rest were from within Montana, and there were less than a half-dozen of those. Most out-of-towners who did travel to Shelby for the fight did not arrive until July 3 or the day of the fight, and the vast majority were from Montana. Most of the tents that had been erected in Shelby parking areas, complete with sleeping cots, stayed empty, as did the ten thousand parking spaces set aside for visitors and the cots set up to handle an anticipated overflow in Shelby's two hotels.

In the days right before the fight, the rutted Main Street, Shelby's main drag, took on a carnival air from the heart of town to the forty-thousand-seat octagonal-shaped wooden outdoor arena, with its eighty-five rows of seats, built in an astonishing four weeks on a twenty-acre site. A number of tent shows were set up, including one that featured a Wild West show of local Blackfoot Indians, two others where simultaneous rodeos were held, and one in which a lady phrenologist held court. In addition, there were a score of concessions whose merchandise ranged from miniature boxing gloves to field glasses.

With few large indoor arenas in the United States—and with none of them holding more than fourteen thousand people—outdoor fights produced the largest gates since they could be held in stadiums holding as many as eighty thousand, as was the case with Dempsey's bout against Georges Carpentier in Jersey City in 1921. The downside, though, for both fighters and spectators, was that, because of the absence of floodlights—which were not installed in most large stadiums until the 1930s—bouts had to be staged during the afternoon and usually in the summer. That was the case with the Dempsey-Gibbons fight, which was scheduled for mid-afternoon.

Already baked by a week-long heat wave that had sent temperatures as high as 100 degrees, Shelby awoke to yet another scorcher on the Fourth of July. Dempsey and his entourage of cornermen and two bodyguards arrived in town about 11:00 A.M. aboard a private car attached to a train that carried several hundred spectators from Great Falls. Seeing several thousand people awaiting Dempsey at the Shelby station, many of them with small-scale artillery at their sides, Dempsey's chief bodyguard, Wild Bill Lyons, a colorful character from New York who wore two pearl-handled pistols, told the engineer to discharge the passengers and then, after uncoupling the rest of the cars, to run the Dempsey car to a siding near the arena about a mile from the railroad depot whose track had been laid expressly for the fight. Hundreds of people ran alongside Dempsey's private car, some cheering for the champion and others screaming imprecations. Because of fears for Dempsey's safety, four more burly bodyguards boarded his special car when the train from Grand Falls pulled into Shelby.

As some of the crowd grew more menacing, Lyons alighted from the train and dashed over to the ticket window where Kearns and about a dozen deputy sheriffs were hawking tickets.

"They got it [the private car] on the siding, but I don't like the looks of the crowd around the car," Lyons, sweating and obviously worried, said to Kearns. "They're too quiet and sullen."

Kearns, by now used to hostile Montanans, told Lyons, "You and Trant"—Mike Trant, a Chicago detective who was moonlighting as a bodyguard for Dempsey—"go down there and see nobody gets on that car. Have the engineer keep it moving up and down the siding."

Lyons, concerned for Kearns's safety and the gate receipts he was collecting, suggested that he stay to protect the manager-turned-ticket-seller. Kearns, inured to the glares and menacing looks directed his way, told Lyons he could get along without a bodyguard.

"Get going," he told him. "There ain't enough people in Montana to take this money away from me."

As it turned out, Kearns was right; Dempsey needed Lyons for protection more than Kearns did. When Dempsey finally got off the train, he was unable to get into the arena, which had not yet opened, as the crowd pressed around him, some within a few feet. Surrounded by his bodyguards, Dempsey, a startled look on his face, had to take refuge at an outside concession stand for a half-hour while being alternately heckled and cheered by the boisterous crowd around him.

Dempsey, who had become increasingly annoyed at Kearns's intransigence over their guarantee, which had exacerbated an already inflammatory situation, couldn't help but wonder why in the world he had ever agreed to go along with a title fight in what had become an extremely hostile area. Indeed, in the week leading up to the fight, the proceedings surrounding the bout and the fight itself had become a sort of medieval morality play, with Dempsey in the role of the archvillain and Gibbons cast as the defender of family values and the frontier spirit in general.

"For the first and only time, I was more worried about getting hurt by the crowd than by the guy I was fighting," Dempsey was to say later.

According to the Internal Revenue agents on hand to make sure that the government got its proper share of tax money from the gate revenues, only 7,202 people actually paid to get in. And many of those entered only after Kearns, alarmed over the small crowd, cut the ticket prices—pegged at fifty-five dollars for ringside seats and twenty dollars for seats in the far reaches of the stadium—to ten dollars about an hour before the fight started, then dropped the price even further to eight dollars. That increased the crowd to around ten thousand. Then, as the bout was about to start, after a delay of almost an hour while Kearns tried to induce more people to buy cut-rate tickets, several thousand more people surged into the stadium when a barbed wire fence many of them had been leaning on gave way. That brought the overall crowd to about twelve thousand, leaving about twenty-eight thousand empty spaces in the wooden bleachers.

Tanned to the color of leather, uncharacteristically clean-shaven, and appearing calm and collected, Dempsey was greeted with far more boos and hisses than cheers when he entered the ring, surrounded by about a dozen handlers and bodyguards. By contrast, Gibbons, pink-skinned, with a marmoreal complexion, and at 174 pounds, fourteen pounds lighter than Dempsey, drew a huge ovation from the crowd as he climbed the steps into his corner.

By fight time, the temperature had reached 95 degrees. From the outset, it was evident that two years of inactivity had left Dempsey rusty. Aggressive as always, he focused on Gibbons's body during the first few rounds in the hope of wearing down the challenger and forcing him to drop his guard to cope with the body assault. But Gibbons thwarted Dempsey's aggression by clinching repeatedly and, as the fight wore on, eluding most of Dempsey's punches. However, Dempsey, far stronger than Gibbons, took advantage of the numerous clinches to inflict rabbit punches—blows to the back of the neck—while also roughing up Gibbons inside. Gibbons's manager, Eddie Kane, aware of Dempsey's penchant for such tactics, had asked that they be prohibited, as they were in most states. But Kearns had demanded as a precondition to any contract that both rabbit and kidney punches be permitted. And as in almost every other demand he made, he had his way.

As good a boxer as Gibbons was, his jabs and punches were ineffective against Dempsey, who crowded and overpowered him throughout, sometimes with blows to Gibbons's midsection, which drew shouts of "foul" from the crowd. With Kearns's Philadelphia friend Jim Daugherty as the referee, there was little, if any, chance that Dempsey was going to be disqualified for a low blow, short of a punch to the groin that might incapacitate Gibbons. By the middle of the fight, it was evident that Gibbons's main objective was to survive the fifteen rounds without enduring any severe punishment, and he did. Not only did he become only the second fighter to go beyond ten rounds against Dempsey—Bill Brennan had been the first—but Gibbons maintained his streak of never having been knocked down in eighty-nine fights.

Most ringside observers felt that Dempsey had won thirteen of the fifteen rounds, losing only the fifth and ninth rounds. Still, it was hardly an impressive performance. Most of the cheers that greeted Daugherty's decision seemed to be directed toward Gibbons for having lasted the fifteen rounds with the Manassa Mauler. Dempsey, still an avaricious ogre in the eyes of most of the crowd, was booed and taunted as he hurriedly left the ring, anxious to depart Shelby as soon as possible.

Most writers felt that Gibbons's reluctance to mix it up with Dempsey and his clinching and constant backpedaling made it a dull bout. But Damon Runyon, for one, saw it in a different light, calling it "one of the greatest battles of recent years in the prize ring." It was not only a sad commentary on the better fights in the past few years, but also an embroiderized version of what had actually happened. "Gibbons was the coyote, one of the wisest, fastest and shiftiest animals of the plains, on which this game was played; Dempsey, the greyhound, strong, speedy, alert, dangerous," read Runyon's hyperbolic story in the July 5 edition of the *New York American* and in many other newspapers across the country. "Running, twisting, doubling, Gibbons, the coyote, got safely home to cover at the end of the long chase, panting a little, bleeding a little—but safe."

Dempsey also seemed to have impressed Otto Floto, the sports editor of the *Denver Evening Post,* who was an old friend of the man from Manassa and the only writer present who had covered the last bare-knuckle heavyweight title bout thirty-four years earlier when John L. Sullivan knocked out Jake Kilrain in the seventy-fifth round in Richburg, Mississippi. One of the illusions the bout dispelled, Floto wrote, "was the cry that Dempsey is a short-round fighter, and anyone sticking with him five or six rounds has a chance to beat him. He was stronger at the finish than he was at the start. And he was faster in the closing rounds than in the beginning. He was hitting with more accuracy, was gaining momentum, and was outboxing the clever Gibbons from every angle."

Barely marked, apart from a cut on his mouth and a number of red welts on his body, Gibbons, surrounded by his handlers and friends, left the stadium in his ring attire and walked the quarter-mile to the nearby cottage he had shared with his wife and three children for the past month. Like some fistic Pied Piper, Gibbons was trailed all the way home by hundreds of cheering supporters yelling "Tommy! Tommy!" and, whenever possible, shaking his hand or patting him on the back.

There was no such glorious exit for Dempsey, even though he had retained his title. Within an hour after the fight, Dempsey, his father, two brothers, and the rest of his entourage, except for Kearns, who remained behind to count up the gate receipts under the watchful eyes of the revenue men, boarded his special railroad car, which was then attached to a Great Northern train carrying spectators back to Great Falls.

Gate receipts totaled approximately $80,000, of which the revenue men reportedly took the government's share of 10 percent. That left Kearns, and, of course, Dempsey, with about $72,000, bringing their total purse to $272,000. Not bad, considering that Gibbons had reportedly fought for nothing but a shot at Dempsey's title.

"Tommy had often said 'I'll fight Dempsey for nothing,' " Dempsey was to say later, "and that's just what they gave him." There was a trace of sadness in Dempsey's voice when he made the comment, since he liked Gibbons, knowing that, besides being a good fighter, he was a solid family man and a good person. Kearns, though, cynical as ever, felt that for him it was a justified case of schadenfreude. Years later, John Kavanagh, the retired publisher of the *Shelby Promoter* newspaper, said that a ledger sheet documenting expenses from the fight showed that Gibbons had in fact been paid $7,500.

Kearns had been scheduled to meet after the fight in a saloon with some members of the local citizens committee and civic officials to officially bid good-bye to Shelby. But given the temper of most Montanans over Kearns's inflexibility on Dempsey's purse, along with the collective chagrin on the part of many people who had thought the fight would be a boon to the town, Kearns decided it would be in his best interest to leave immediately with his friend, Dan McKetrick, a veteran boxing promoter who had been assisting Kearns in the run-up to the fight. Had he gone to the meeting, Kearns felt, he might not have been able to leave town with all of the seventy-two thousand dollars collected at the box office that day. Kearns had good reason to think that most members of the group had been drinking and, as the liquor flowed, their collective anger and rage toward him had risen. Thus, Kearns felt, making an appearance in the saloon might not be a prudent idea.

However, there was a problem about making a precipitous departure from Shelby, since the last train of the day had already left for Great Falls. That did not stop Kearns from hurrying to the Shelby train depot with McKetrick, each of them carrying a suitcase filled with cash. As luck would have it for Kearns and McKetrick, a locomotive with an attached caboose was on the track, with the engineer on the platform talking with another railroad man. Kearns promptly asked the engineer if he would be willing, for five hundred dollars in cash, to transport him and McKetrick to Great Falls as soon as possible. Apparently with nothing else pressing, the engineer agreed, whereupon Kearns extracted five hundred dollars in cash from one of the suitcases he and McKetrick were carrying and gave it to the engineer. As he did, sportswriter Hype Igoe came walking somewhat erratically along the platform playing his ukulele and singing. Igoe obviously had finished composing his opus on the fight and, like some other writers, was not leaving Shelby until the next day. With time on his hands, Igoe apparently had been unwinding with some bootleg booze.

"Hey, Hype," Kearns called out. "This is the New York express. Hop aboard."

Igoe, secure in the knowledge that his luggage was in Great Falls, where he had been staying, immediately clambered aboard with the aid of Kearns and McKetrick.

Concerned that some of the disillusioned members of the Shelby citizens committee might come looking for him, Kearns spent the night in the basement of a Great Falls barber shop, along with McKetrick. The next day, July 5, Kearns joined Dempsey in a private car aboard a train bound for the champion's hometown, Salt Lake City. As they boarded the train, a man—no doubt expressing the sentiments of many Montanans—called out, "Don't hurry back." Kearns smiled and replied, "Don't worry, brother—we won't."

Gibbons received a tumultuous reception when he and his family returned to St. Paul. "From the time he stepped from the train at the station this morning until late Saturday afternoon, Gibbons, whom Jack Dempsey, world's heavyweight champion, could not knock out, was given an almost continuous ovation," the *Chicago Tribune* reported on July 7. "His machine [car] was literally showered with flowers."

Regardless of whether he had received any money for fighting Dempsey, Gibbons became one of the few people to profit from the Shelby debacle. As the only fighter to have lasted fifteen rounds against the Manassa Mauler, Gibbons, suddenly a hot property, spent two months on the Pantages vaudeville circuit—a small theatrical operation that served as a training ground for big-league shows—in the Mid- and Far West, sparring on stage, talking about the fight, and earning around ten thousand dollars.

In his story for the North American Newspaper Alliance, which appeared throughout the country, Heywood Broun, the widely known sports columnist and drama critic who covered the fight, said that at the end of the bout the crowd had "cheered the victory of Montana over the newspapers. That was the big thing in the mind of almost everybody in the arena. Dempsey and Gibbons were secondary. It was Montana fighting for its life against the experts and the funny men from the big town papers. Everything in Shelby, from its climate to its financial judgment, had been held up to ridicule by the articulate visitors with portable typewriters. Wednesday, Montana answered back."

If Montana had achieved a "victory," as Broun claimed, it was a Pyrrhic one. For over the next month, when Shelby could have used another oil strike, financial disaster struck instead. On July 9, the Stanton Trust & Savings Bank of Great Falls, owned by George Stanton, who had become the key figure in ensuring that the fight would be held, went out of business. Stanton said the fight had no bearing on the closing, which he attributed to postwar conditions in general. That explanation seemed odd, since the war had ended almost five years before. Eventually, reports circulated that Stanton's eleventh-hour association with the fight's promotion had caused a run on his bank, which he could not meet because of the $70,000 he had withdrawn from his own account to help meet the second $100,000 payment to Kearns.

While in Great Falls to take over the Stanton bank, the state banking examiner, L. Q. Skelton, made a side trip to Shelby to take over Mayor Johnson's First State Bank of Shelby, which had also gone under on July 10. Johnson had been forced to stop payment to depositors on that day, mainly because he had pledged $150,000 of his own money toward the fight and turned out to be the biggest loser in the ill-fated venture.

The banking situation only got worse. On July 11, the First State Bank of Joplin, Montana, which was affiliated with Stanton's bank in Great Falls, shut down. According to newspaper reports, the closing, like the first two, was attributed to the Dempsey-Gibbons fight. That still wasn't the end of it. Just over a month later, on August 16, the First National Bank of Shelby was ordered closed by its board of directors after withdrawals of more than $100,000 since the fight. The closing left Shelby without a bank and with practically no assets. To make matters worse, the oil boom collapsed shortly thereafter and Shelby returned to being a quiet Western cow town, as it had been before the oil strike and the fight. To help make ends meet, at least for the lumbermen and contractors responsible for building it, the stadium was torn down and the more than one million feet of lumber used was salvaged by the mortgage holders.

In a parting eulogy to Shelby, Elmer Davis wrote in the *New York Times* of July 7, 1923, "It is impossible not to admire the courage and determination of the tiny little town. Its citizens realized long ago that they were well hooked, but they hung on grimly to the end. They never mentioned the word 'quit' and they never lost hope, even in the darkest days. They deserved a better reward, but these people undoubtedly will look back on the bout with regret, but they can do so without shame. Shelby played the string right through to the count of ten."

Some other observers thought that Shelby was to blame for its misfortune. "It was the booster spirit that got Shelby into trouble—the frontier booster spirit, which seems to have been a particularly red-blooded and chuckleheaded variety," John Lardner, a well-known sportswriter and the son of Ring Lardner, wrote years later. As Lardner put it, Shelby "opened the relationship [with Kearns] by begging to be taken." And of course, it was.

For Kearns, it was also a sort of retribution. He had told of how, before he was born, his father, John Philip McKernan, had made about $100,000 from a gold mine he owned in Montana in the 1870s, only to lose it all when the president and secretary of the bank where he had deposited all his mine earnings absconded with everything, including McKernan's profits. In his autobiography, *The Million Dollar Gate*, Kearns said his and Dempsey's financial raid was "satisfactory revenge on the state of Montana for this early fleecing of my father. They took him for $100,000. I got it back some forty-five years later with two hundred percent compound interest." Obviously, Kearns had shed no tears over the bank closings that had stemmed from "the Sack of Shelby," as John Lardner called it. From his perspective, George Stanton and the other bankers had got their just desserts, even though they had nothing to do with Kearns's father's financial misfortune.

More than eighty years after the fight, in 2005, a new breed of Shelby boosters was planning to build a small park on the site where the 1923 bout was held. To be called Champions Park, it was planned to be a replica of the forty-thousand-seat arena and include larger-than-life bronze statues of Dempsey, Gibbons, and Jack Kearns's handpicked referee, Jim Daugherty. By then, Shelby, grown to a population of 3,400, was thriving with an employment rate of 98 percent. Agriculture—primarily wheat and barley—had become the major employer followed by oil and gas production, transportation, since Shelby was still a major railway distribution point between Chicago and Seattle and north to Canada and some other points, and a privately run maximum-security prison, which employed more than five hundred.

Main Street, now paved and with Aunt Kate's Cathouse long gone, includes about twenty retail stores, three banks, a movie theater, four restaurants, and five bars, one of which, the Alibi Bar, features a number of photos of the Dempsey-Gibbons fight. Nearby, the gloves that Gibbons wore, along with other memorabilia from the bout, are on display at the Marias Museum of History and Art. Over the years, Gibbons returned to Shelby with his wife several times—once to present a blanket to the first winner of the Tommy Gibbons Handicap Thoroughbred horse race at the Marias Fair, which became an annual event. Obviously willing to forgive if not forget, Shelby officials also invited Dempsey back, but the old Manassa Mauler never did return.

"The fight's never been forgotten here," Shelby mayor Larry J. Bonderud said eighty-two years later, "and we're trying to create even more interest by establishing Champions Park, which we hope will draw tourists to Shelby. It can only help our town, which is already doing very well."

In the years after the Dempsey-Gibbons fight, Jack Kearns reveled in recounting how his and Dempsey's inglorious but profitable expedition had led to the closing of a number of banks, including two in Shelby. Some two decades later, during a gathering of fight managers, trainers, sportswriters, and others connected with boxing, one of the managers recalled the "Sack of Shelby."

"Remember Shelby, Doc?" one of the managers asked, with a trace of envy in his voice. "You and Dempsey broke three banks in Montana."

"Not three," Kearns replied with a sly smile. "We broke four."

THIRTEEN

*Luis Angel Firpo knocks Jack Dempsey
out of the ring.* AP IMAGES

The
Wild Bull
of the
Pampas

Eight days after Dempsey's unimpressive victory over Tommy Gibbons, a crowd about four times as large as the one at Shelby—approximately 80,000 in all—jammed Boyle's Thirty Acres in Jersey City, the wooden stadium that had been built in a Jersey City swamp for the Dempsey-Carpentier "Battle of the Century" in 1921. The size of the crowd—the biggest ever at the time to watch a boxing bout, or any other sporting event in the United States—was remarkable in that the participants were a forty-one-year-old former heavyweight champion who had not fought in three years and an awkward and wild-swinging twenty-eight-year-old fighter from Argentina whom Damon Runyon had nicknamed "The Wild Bull of the Pampas."

The former champion was Jess Willard, who had knocked out Jack Johnson in 1915 to win the heavyweight title—that is, assuming that Johnson did not take a dive—but then lost it four years later to Dempsey in what was only his second title defense. After that, Willard retired and did not fight again until he stopped a journeyman named

Floyd Johnson in New York at the beginning of what was to be a short-lived comeback. His opponent was the dark-haired and ruggedly handsome 6′ 3″ Luis Angel Firpo, an unskilled but powerful fighter who had lost only two of twenty-nine professional fights and had scored twenty-three knockouts, most of them in South America where he had become a heroic figure of epic proportions. Since coming to the United States in early 1922, Firpo had knocked out ten of eleven of his opponents, including Bill "K.O." Brennan in the twelfth round, three months after Brennan had given Dempsey a scare. With an Italian surname—his father had emigrated to Argentina from Italy—Firpo soon became a huge fan favorite in the United States, because of his aggressive style of fighting and his powerful right-hand punch, not to mention that Italians comprised one of the three largest ethnic boxing fan bases in the country. Latin Americans living in the United States, along with thousands of Firpo supporters from South America who had come to New York for the fight, also rallied to Firpo's side, feting him at parties and other events at Hispanic nightclubs and restaurants in Manhattan.

Given the styles of Willard and Firpo—both punchers with little foot speed—their fight did not portend a classic boxing bout. However, in promoting the fight, Tex Rickard was convinced that Firpo would prove too strong for an over-the-hill Willard and that Firpo, largely because of his good looks, his strength, and his punching power, could be portrayed as an ideal challenger for Dempsey. He was right on both counts. Ponderous and slow-moving, Willard proved to be an easy target for Firpo, who was three inches shorter than the 6′ 6″ "Pottawatomie Giant."

Nowhere near the fighter who had beaten Johnson, Willard landed several left uppercuts—his best punch and the one that he always said had knocked out Jack Johnson—but they were few and far between. Though he missed far more punches than he landed and seldom threw a left, Firpo still managed to batter the plodding Willard with round-house right-hand punches that staggered the former champion. Finally, he caught Willard with a right-hand chop to the jaw that sent him down on his knees, two minutes into the eighth round. Both hurt and dazed, Willard tried to hoist himself up with the aid of a middle rope strand before falling back to the canvas and being counted out.

Tex Rickard was elated at the fight's outcome. So was Jack Kearns, who told him after the bout that a Firpo-Dempsey fight would be a huge success, at least at the gate. Though they did not like each other, Rickard and Kearns were two of the smartest people in boxing, and, although they realized that Firpo was an unpolished and unskilled fighter whose only weapon was a strong right hand, they also knew he was highly marketable.

Kearns agreed to accept 37.5 percent of the gate, while Firpo, who did his own negotiating, settled for 12.5 percent. It would turn out to be a satisfactory arrangement for everyone. For Dempsey and Kearns it eventually meant a purse of slightly more than $500,000, while Firpo ended up with almost $200,000 (the equivalent today of more than $5 million for Dempsey and about $2 million for Firpo).

In keeping with his established practice of fighting rather than training, Firpo booked three fights in July and August, even though he was to meet Dempsey on September 14. Rickard, concerned that one of his opponents might get lucky and knock out or at least cut up Firpo, tried to talk him out of the fights, but the Argentine insisted on going ahead with them on the grounds that they would make him a better fighter and, thus, a stronger opponent for Dempsey.

To the relief of Rickard and Kearns, Firpo, fighting only two weeks after beating Willard, knocked out two of his opponents easily and won a decision from the third. But while the three fights enhanced his résumé and his bankroll and thrilled his legion of admirers, both in North and South America, they did not appear to have made him a better fighter. Sportswriters who watched him spar at an Atlantic City racetrack against the few sparring partners that he had hired saw that he was still as awkward and wild as ever, but that his looping right-hand punch was a potentially lethal weapon; when it landed, it hurt and even floored some of his practice partners. Aware, though, that Dempsey tended to feast on big, slow-moving heavyweights, virtually none of them gave Firpo any chance of beating the Manassa Mauler.

Training outside Saratoga Springs in upstate New York, Dempsey was impressive against a half-dozen very good sparring partners. (Kearns always made it a point to bring in good fighters as sparring partners, even highly ranked heavyweights.) But his strangest sparring partner for the Firpo fight turned out to be Paul Gallico, a young sportswriter for the New York *Daily News.* In a daring and somewhat rash effort at participatory journalism, Gallico approached Dempsey and asked him if he would spar a round or two with him.

Somewhat taken aback, yet amused at Gallico's pluck, Dempsey looked him over and said, "What's the matter, son? Don't your editor like you no more?"

Gallico then explained that he thought being in the ring with Dempsey, and perhaps even being knocked down by him, would give him a better perspective on boxing, and especially on boxing the best heavyweight in the world. Gallico also knew that getting in the ring with Dempsey, and then writing about the experience, probably would impress his editors.

"I think I understand, son," Dempsey replied in his high-pitched voice as they sat on a porch at Thomas Luther's White Sulphur Springs Hotel a week before the Firpo fight. "You just want a good punch in the nose." That was not exactly what Gallico had in mind, but he nodded anyway, and Dempsey told Gallico to show up at ringside on the following Sunday, five days before the Firpo fight.

When Kearns heard about the agreed-upon sparring session, he became alarmed. He did not know Gallico, but had seen him around and had noticed that he was about 6′ 3″ and weighed around 190 pounds, about the same weight as Dempsey, and looked like an athlete, which he had been at Columbia, where he had been a member of the varsity crew and its co-captain only two years before. What, Kearns wondered, if he was a ringer posing as a sportswriter, who had been dispatched to Dempsey's training camp to try to butt and cut up the champion? Kearns asked Damon Runyon and Hype Igoe about Gallico, and, though they knew he was a sportswriter, they pretended they did not know Gallico, and, twitting Kearns, they said, yes, he did have the look of a ringer. Kearns then tried to get Dempsey to call off the sparring session, but he refused.

As Sunday drew near, Gallico understandably began to have second thoughts. Perhaps, he thought, his venture into participatory journalism with Dempsey wasn't such a good idea after all. The sports editor at the *Daily News,* though, thought it was a superb maneuver. When Kearns called him to check on whether Gallico was indeed a sportswriter for the newspaper, the editor not only confirmed that he was a bona fide member of the sports staff but, like many fight managers who use the plural "us" in talking about their fighters, told Kearns that he and Gallico wanted Dempsey "to hit us hard as he can because we want to know just how a knockout feels." That, of course, would have been news to Gallico, who wanted Dempsey to do no such thing. Indeed, when asked about his upcoming sparring session by Hype Igoe, Gallico said, somewhat wistfully, "We're just going to fool around. Dempsey's going to take it easy." Whereupon Igoe looked at Gallico ruefully and replied, "Son, don't you know that man can't take it easy."

On the afternoon of his scheduled ring session with Dempsey, before a crowd of about three thousand, Gallico sensed that Dempsey—who had just knocked out his first sparring partner of the day—appeared to be irritated at Gallico's presence. If he was, it was because Dempsey regarded anyone who got into a ring with him as a mortal enemy. Gallico, of course, posed no threat whatsoever to Dempsey's well-being, but once a fight or a sparring session started, Dempsey was not about to show any sympathy to anyone, even a twenty-four-year-old sportswriter who had never been in a boxing ring in his young life.

As soon as the bell for the first round rang, Gallico saw Dempsey coming right at him with a menacing look on his face. Moving to the center of the ring in a straight-up stance to meet the champion, Gallico stuck out a weak left jab, more as a protective measure than as a weapon. To his astonishment, Dempsey walked right into the jab, which landed on Dempsey's nose. *Maybe I shouldn't have done that so fast,* Gallico thought, as Runyon, Igoe, Grantland Rice, and the rest of the assembled press corps looked on in amazement. Their young colleague had guts, all right, maybe too much guts for his own good.

Flushed with his early success, Gallico tried a few more jabs, and they, too, landed, but that was the last thing that Gallico remembered about the sparring session. He opened his eyes to find himself in a sitting position on the floor and Kearns, acting as the referee, standing over him and counting. Somehow he managed to get to his feet at the count of eight—"like an idiot," as Gallico was to recall. At that point, Damon Runyon, apparently sensing that Gallico's life might be in danger and also feeling guilty about not telling Kearns that he was indeed a young sportswriter, shouted to Kearns, "Hey, Doc, tell Dempsey to take it easy. It's a gag. Gallico really is from the *Daily News.*"

Kearns's response was to merely smile at Runyon. It was much too late for any compassion on Dempsey's part now, Kearns thought. Or was it? Suddenly, and uncharacteristically solicitous after having floored Gallico with a right to the jaw, Dempsey went into a clinch with him and said, "Hang on and wrestle around until your head clears, son." But even as he spoke to Gallico, Dempsey, out of habit, struck him on the back of the neck with a few relatively light rabbit punches, which gave Gallico both more material for his story and more pain. The rabbit punches also sent Gallico to the canvas again, where, unconscious, he was counted out by Kearns.

The sparring session had lasted a minute and a half and left Gallico with a bloody nose, a cut lip, and a headache. To some of his sportswriting colleagues it stamped him as courageous while others were inclined to question his sanity. But overall it certainly earned him a considerable amount of respect from the writers at ringside who had watched the sparring session, hoping against hope that Dempsey would take it easy on Gallico. But, as Hype Igoe had told Gallico, Dempsey was unable to "take it easy" when he was in the ring, no matter who the opponent was.*

---

*Gallico's escapade into participatory sports journalism made him a pioneer in the genre. More than three decades later, it inspired George Plimpton to write a series of Walter Mitty–ish articles and books based on his brief experiences as a faux rookie quarterback for the Detroit Lions football team, a three-round boxing session opponent with light heavyweight champion Archie Moore— who, unlike Dempsey against Gallico, took it easy on Plimpton, apart from bloodying his nose— and as a baseball pitcher facing major league hitters.

Largely because of Rickard's promotional talents and overwhelming newspaper coverage, aided in part by Rickard's weekly paychecks to about a dozen New York City sports editors and sportswriters, the Dempsey-Firpo fight became the talk of both North and South America. To some writers, the bout was not only between a celebrated former champion and an unpolished young knockout puncher, but also involved cultures. Incredibly even such a reasoned and respected newspaper as the *New York Tribune* ran stories that said Firpo was a "disbeliever in Nordic supremacy" and that even if Firpo were to beat Dempsey, another member of the Nordic race would certainly appear on the boxing scene to overcome the Latin threat. Going even further, Bruce Bliven, writing in the *New Republic,* which normally did not cover boxing bouts, explained why he was going to be at ringside. "We are here to see the Nordic race defend itself against the Latin," Bliven wrote.

Even though the New York State Athletic Commission had set a $27.50 limit on ticket prices, the gate surpassed $1 million the day before the fight. That made it the second fight to earn more than $1 million, and both of them involved Dempsey, as would the next three. What tickets remained were sold within an hour and a half after they were put on sale at the Polo Grounds the afternoon of the fight, some of them to fans who waited in line since the day before. Tens of thousands of people—estimates ranged as high as 35,000—were turned away when the box offices closed at 6:00 P.M. By then, 86,228 tickets had been sold for a fight in a stadium that seated about 55,000 for baseball, but far more for a boxing bout, since thousands of chairs were set up on both the infield—where the ring was erected—and the outfield grass.

What transpired during the three minutes and fifty-seven seconds

---

Not that other writers have not sparred with champions. Norman Mailer sparred occasionally with his friend, light heavyweight champion José Torres, who himself became a writer on boxing matters, and Budd Schulberg sparred several times with Archie McBride, a highly rated heavyweight in the 1950s, at Schulberg's farm in New Hope, Pennsylvania, and once sparred briefly with a top-ranking middleweight, Roger Donoghue, who also had sparred with Mailer. Of Schulberg's boxing style, Donoghue said, "He gets very close to the ground, in a huddled sort of crouch, and he peers up at you over the rim of his gloves like a woodchuck looking out of a hole." As for Mailer, Donoghue said, "He's not bad, but he's a much better writer."

that the fight lasted was to linger in the memories of those nearly ninety thousand spectators for a long time, if indeed not forever.

At the start, Dempsey rushed across the ring in his familiar crouch and threw a left hook to the head, which Firpo, to the surprise of most of the crowd, ducked away from. Firpo then caught Dempsey with a solid right to the face, followed by another right to the temple. Dempsey was clearly stunned by the ferocity of Firpo's attack. He then literally was stunned when the rangy Argentine pounded a wicked right to Dempsey's abdomen, which sent Dempsey sagging to the canvas on his knees, triggering an uproar from the huge crowd, which was shocked at seeing the Manassa Mauler go down only ten seconds into the scheduled fifteen-round fight. Grabbing Firpo by the legs, Dempsey pulled himself up before referee Jack Gallagher could begin a count and immediately drove a left hook to the jaw that put Firpo down on his back. Like Dempsey, Firpo arose without a count and, rushing at the champion, rocked him with a right to the body. Slightly over a minute had transpired, but by now virtually everyone in the ballpark was on their feet and would remain there until the fight was over.

Though obviously hurt, Dempsey responded with another left hook to the jaw that again sent Firpo crashing to the canvas, this time on his hands. But again the challenger clambered to his feet before Gallagher could start a count and quickly drove a right to the body before falling into a clinch. As Gallagher broke the clinch, Firpo dropped his arms while stepping back in accordance with Gallagher's instructions. It was a huge mistake. Dempsey immediately ripped across a left uppercut to the head that sent Firpo reeling to the canvas for a nine-count, as thousands in the crowd, particularly the Argentine's fans, let out a chorus of boos. It was the third time Firpo had been knocked down, and, if the fight had taken place about a dozen years later, it would have automatically been stopped, since, by then, a three-knockdown rule, which summarily ended a fight, would have taken effect. But there was no limit to the number of knockdowns a fighter could endure in the 1920s.

With Dempsey standing right over him—a violation of the neutral corner rule in New York, which had been placed in effect earlier that year and which Gallagher, the referee, failed to enforce during the fight—Firpo's gloves had barely left the canvas at the count of nine when the champion dropped him again with a right uppercut near the heart. Again, a chorus of boos, and, finally, a warning from Gallagher to Dempsey to go to a neutral corner following a knockdown. But Dempsey did not. Instead, he circled behind Firpo, and as Firpo struggled to his feet wondering where Dempsey had gone, Dempsey nailed him from behind with a right to the head that put the Argentine down for the fifth time.

Battered and bleeding from the mouth and nose and becoming more and more enraged by Dempsey's tactics as the round wore on, Firpo went after Dempsey in a fury, landing a chopping right to the head at close range that sent the Manassa Mauler to the floor on his knees. Rising before Gallagher could start a count, Dempsey, obviously dazed and hurt, tore after Firpo. Refusing to give ground but showing virtually no defense, Firpo stood there and absorbed a fusillade of blows that put him down again. Once again, Firpo sprang up without a count, despite the screams of his trainer, Jimmy DeForrest—"Stay down! Stay down!"—cries that Firpo should have heeded. That became evident when the slow-moving Firpo, his legs wobbly by now, promptly ran into a right uppercut that put him on the canvas for the seventh time.

This time, a badly hurt Firpo just barely beat the count of ten. To the astonishment of the crowd, Firpo, rather than grab Dempsey into a clinch or move away to further clear his head, charged at Dempsey in a rage, throwing a right from over his head—an extraordinary punch—that sent Dempsey reeling into the ropes, evoking a cascade of cheers and screams from the thousands of Latins in a crowd that was now in a collective state of disbelief.

Then it happened—the most spectacular knockdown in boxing history (the most controversial would come several years later). Only this time, it was Dempsey who went down, or, more correctly, who went tumbling head over heels out of the ring in what he later conceded was the most frightening episode of his career.

Trapping Dempsey against the ropes, Firpo unleashed a barrage of rights to the head and body—the last one a right-hand blow that was half-punch and half-push which caught an off-balance Dempsey on the left collarbone and sent him between the top and middle ropes, headfirst into the press row at ringside, leaving the crowd stunned, as much by the bizarre knockdown as by Firpo's remarkable comeback. As Gallagher began his count at the inner edge of the ropes, Dempsey was given what turned out to be the biggest lift of his career—and a literal one, at that. The champion had landed, headfirst, on the portable typewriter of Jack Lawrence, the boxing writer for the *New York Tribune,* with his feet tangled in the bottom of the three ropes. By virtually all accounts, Lawrence, aided by Perry Grogan, a Western Union telegrapher who was sitting next to him, pushed Dempsey upward into the ring, where he regained his footing as Gallagher's count reached nine with about thirty seconds left in the round.

As Lawrence recounted the incident, Dempsey, after landing on Lawrence's typewriter, called out, "Help me back in there." And Lawrence did the best that he could, if for no other reason than to get 192 pounds off his portable typewriter. If that were the case, Firpo should have immediately been declared the winner and new heavyweight champion, since no one, in or out of a ring, is allowed to help a downed fighter get up. But Dempsey insisted that he got back in the ring on his own.

"First, let me say that Lawrence's grabbing me to help me back into the ring did not assist me at all," Dempsey told sportswriter Dan Daniel of the *New York Journal.* "I know the writers meant well, but they hindered me. I was able to navigate and knew what I was doing." Yet in the same interview, Dempsey said he had no recollection of what had happened in the fight from the first time he was hit by Firpo. "I was knocked out by the Argentinian's first punch and went right on fighting in my sleep," he told Daniel.

With the Polo Grounds crowd in an uproar—apart from those who had bet heavily on the heavily favored Dempsey and looked on incredulously, realizing that if they were on the verge of losing their money, Dempsey was in imminent danger of losing his title—Firpo again charged at the champion, throwing a barrage of rights, almost all of which missed, while Dempsey, dazed and groggy, tried unavailingly to clinch. Bobbing and weaving in an effort to avoid Firpo's charge, Dempsey got in several blows just before the bell, and about three more after the bell had sounded and Firpo had dropped his hands to his side, eliciting yet more boos from Firpo supporters.

Incredibly, there had been ten knockdowns in the round, and Dempsey, though down only three times compared to seven times by Firpo, had come the closest to being knocked out.

As Dempsey staggered back to his corner, Kearns emptied a pail of cold water on the champion, while his cornermen, Jerry Luvadis and Joe Benjamin, looked frantically for smelling salts, which Kearns eventually found in his pants pocket.

A groggy Dempsey, resting on his stool, finally turned to Kearns and said, "What round was I knocked out in?"

"You just slipped," Kearns replied, a white lie that he felt was necessary at the moment. "You're coming out for the second."

Dempsey, always at his best after he had been hurt, appeared rejuvenated as the bell rang for the second round and the crowd began cheering before a blow had been struck "My head was now clear and I could now think," he recalled later. "I went out after him again, but this time with respect. I wasn't going to get nailed again."

For all of its drama, the fight had degenerated into a brawl, much like some of the winner-take-all saloon fights that a hungry young Dempsey had engaged in not too many years ago. Defense? There was none whatsoever by either fighter. It was a troglodytic struggle, and someone obviously was going to get knocked out—and, it appeared, soon.

Rushing across the ring to encounter Firpo, Dempsey pounded a series of lefts and rights to Firpo's body before going into a clinch. As Gallagher broke them, Dempsey grabbed the 216-pound Firpo and, in a throwback move to the bare-knuckle, everything-goes days, threw him to the canvas. As soon as he got up, Dempsey connected with three hard left uppercuts to the body that sent Firpo down again for a count of five.

After Dempsey's narrow escape near the end of round one, the tide seemingly had turned, sending Dempsey backers into a screaming frenzy. Moments later, Dempsey ripped a left hook to the Argentine's midsection followed by a right to the jaw that sent him to the floor on his back. After lying motionless until Gallagher's count had reached six, he rolled over onto his stomach, with his long arms and legs spread-eagled on the canvas while Dempsey stood in a neutral corner for only the second time. Finally, fifty-seven seconds into round two, Gallagher intoned ten, ending perhaps the most action-packed two-round—or any number of rounds, for that matter—fight in history.

The fight had lasted only three minutes and fifty-seven seconds, but there had been twelve knockdowns; Firpo had gone down nine times—not counting the time he was thrown to the canvas by Dempsey in the second round—and Dempsey three times. Not surprisingly, the fight, short as it was, generated controversy from sports columns to editorial pages to church pulpits. To many, the patent brutality that characterized the fight was in itself a strong argument to those who felt that boxing should again be outlawed, at least in New York, where it had been legalized only three years before. If Dempsey still hadn't gotten over the bad publicity he'd received in connection with his last fight, against Tommy Gibbons in Shelby, he was in for an even worse time in the aftermath of the Firpo battle. More than a few prominent members of the boxing world felt that Dempsey had dealt a grievous wound to a sport still viewed in disrepute by some of his actions in the fight, such as punching Firpo twice when he had his hands down, refusing repeatedly to go to a neutral corner after knocking Firpo down, and knocking him down again as he staggered to his feet after several of his nine knockdowns.

Several days after the fight, Dempsey apologized to Firpo for hitting him as soon as he got up, claiming he was so dazed he didn't know what he was doing. To which Firpo, likable and with a wry sense of humor—and whose varied business interests would make him one of the richest men in South America—replied, "There were three of us in the ring, Jack, so if you didn't know what you were doing, why didn't you hit the referee?"

As was the case in Shelby, Dempsey also was roasted by many writers and others for the size of his purse—a half-million dollars. Hardly anyone—not the president of the United States, and certainly not anyone in the sports or entertainment worlds—was making anywhere near that amount. Babe Ruth's salary that year was $50,000, and he had to play 152 games to receive it while leading the American League in home runs, runs batted in, total bases, slugging average, runs scored, and walks, and while batting .393, his highest average ever, only to finish second to Harry Heilmann's .403.

Among those critical of Dempsey's purse—Firpo earned $156,000—was the *Christian Science Monitor,* which said in an editorial that American men who fought in the Great War must have been left to wonder "at the national temperament that leaves them to shift the best they may for a livelihood while giving $500,000 and unbounded adulation to a pugilist who carefully avoided the trenches."

There it was again—the old slacker charge, which Dempsey thought had been put to rest, but which would still surface from time to time. When it did, it would hurt Dempsey even more than one of Firpo's right-hand punches.

Even Grantland Rice thought that referee Jack Gallagher had good reason to disqualify Dempsey for punching Firpo after a clinch-break in the first round and after the bell had rung. Those, Rice wrote, were "actions for which he might have been disqualified then and there." But Rice conceded that "it is quite possible that Dempsey was so badly hurt by Firpo's terrific wallops that he was in a mental daze—completely out of his head."

Both Nat Fleischer and Dan Daniel thought that Firpo should have been declared the winner because of Dempsey's egregiously illegal blows, his refusal to heed Gallagher's directives to go to a neutral corner, and his being helped back into the ring.

"Firpo should be wearing the crown," Fleischer said after the fight, while Daniel, some years later, wrote, "Firpo was cheated; by all rights, he should have been the champion." Firpo, of course, agreed. "I won it four times on fouls and bad refereeing," he said. "One, when Dempsey hit me low, two times when he hit me while I was getting up"—most ringside observers thought it happened about five times— "and once after I knocked him out of the ring. So many American writers pushed him back into the ring it looked like he was getting a back massage."

Because of the assistance Dempsey received in getting back into the ring, the rule relating to such rare incidents was changed. At the time of the fight, the rule had said that a fighter had to return to the ring immediately or be counted out, but set no time limit. The new rule specified that a fighter had to return to the ring within ten seconds under his own power. It also was amended to make it clear that a referee was not to begin a count until a fighter had gone to the farthest neutral corner, something that Dempsey never could remember in the heat of battle, having stood over so many fighters after knocking them down. And his forgetfulness in just such a situation would prove costly in the future.*

Despite the criticism in the press, pulpit, and elsewhere about Dempsey's foul tactics and the savageness of the fight, Dempsey came out of it more popular than ever. Few fans, it seems, were offended by his tactics; indeed, they were far more impressed with his surviving three knockdowns, and being able to withstand a torrent of Firpo's powerful punches, including the one that knocked him out of the ring. In the eyes of most sports fans, he was now the biggest sports hero in the United States, and perhaps the world, and that was saying a lot, considering the presence of Babe Ruth, Ty Cobb, and a host of other sports giants of the time.

However wealthy he had become under Kearns's guidance, Dempsey felt that his manager had taken advantage of him financially, and not only because he took half of Dempsey's earnings, compared to the customary one-third that most managers kept. Kearns also owed Dempsey money that the champion had put up for an apartment complex they had bought in Los Angeles in both their names. Fearful that he would not get his fair share of his purse from the Firpo fight—slightly over $500,000—Dempsey told Rickard after the fight that he himself would pick up his check at Rickard's Madison Square Garden

*So noteworthy and unusual was the knockdown that George Bellows, the noted artist, drew a crayon lithograph of it, showing Dempsey hurtling out of the ring and landing in the press row. The lithograph, far and away boxing's most famous, has hung at the Metropolitan Museum of Art on and off since 1925 when it was completed and given to the museum at Fifth Avenue and 86th Street in Manhattan. Some of the 103 prints of the Bellows lithograph were being auctioned for between fifteen thousand and thirty thousand dollars more than eighty years after the fight.

office the next morning. Rickard told Dempsey that would be fine, and gave him the check.

Expecting to pick up the check himself later that morning, as he usually did, Kearns flew into a rage when Rickard—who never liked Kearns—told him he had given it to Dempsey. "Well, damn you," Kearns thundered. "I'm the manager. You should have given it to me." Rickard, savoring Kearns's tantrum, merely shrugged. Rickard had suspected that Kearns was taking more than his rightful share from Dempsey's purses and felt that in this instance he was getting his just desserts.

Kearns was even more enraged when he went to Dempsey's hotel room in Times Square. "You got that money," he screamed at Dempsey.

"Yeah," Dempsey said calmly while proceeding to count out less for Kearns than the manager expected, since Dempsey had deducted what Kearns owed him for the California apartment house they had bought and jointly owned.

Furious, Kearns said, "What are you going to do with that money?"

"Well, I'm putting two hundred thousand dollars in a trust fund," Dempsey replied calmly.

"At what interest?" Kearns said in a demanding tone.

"I don't know," Dempsey said, trying to remain calm in the face of his manager's rage. "Three, four, five percent. Whatever I'm going to get."

"You damn fool," Kearns shouted. "I could get you fifteen percent."

Dempsey, looking Kearns directly in the eye, then let his old manager know clearly that he no longer trusted him. "Doc, I'm going to put that money where I know I'll have it when I'm old," he said.

It was, in a sense, the beginning of the end of a long relationship that had led Dempsey to the heavyweight championship and to riches both for him and for the onetime Klondike faro dealer who had become the most famous, and richest, boxing manager in the world.

Though in his prime at twenty-eight, Dempsey would not defend his title again for three years, but would remain very much in the public eye while earning over $2 million, most of it from appearing in movies, mostly serials aimed at teenage boys. First, though, he was upset over the controversy surrounding his conduct in the ring. While he was a hero to many, he knew that hardly anyone looked at him as a paragon of sportsmanship and that many people perceived him to be both brutish and savage in the ring. That bothered him, and the more he read critical stories about his unethical, and even illegal, behavior during the Firpo fight, he realized he had to get far away from New York and its newspapers and, for that matter, from just about everyone.

Over the next three years, Dempsey fought only a few profitable exhibition fights, usually for around five thousand dollars, against opponents who had no chance in the world to beat, or even hurt, him. Most of the exhibitions, usually four-round bouts, during which, fortunately for his opponents, Dempsey rarely extended himself, were tied to appearances Dempsey was making with Kearns in the early part of 1924 on the Pantages vaudeville circuit. The vaudeville contract, which was negotiated by Kearns, called for Dempsey to chat briefly with Kearns and then to shadowbox and punch the heavy bag—longtime training camp rituals. Later, after his and Kearns's act had been polished, they toured a number of cities in the Northeast with the Loews vaudeville circuit, one of the biggest and best known in the country. In New York, Dempsey's appearance on Broadway drew around seventy-five thousand people in one week and broke box office records for a vaudeville show. Because of his star power, and certainly not for his stage presence, Dempsey was paid $7,500 a week—very high for a vaudeville entertainer—over a five-week run.

Most of 1924 and 1925 was spent in Los Angeles, which Dempsey by then regarded as his home and which he later was to call "easily the most important city in my life." Having made $500,000 for the Firpo fight and about $1 million for his work in Hollywood, Dempsey felt no need or desire to fight. And in truth, given the dearth of legitimate contenders, it would be difficult for a promoter, even a crafty one like Tex Rickard, to come up with an attractive opponent for Dempsey. Sam Langford, though still beating up on most opponents on the so-called chitlin circuit of black fighters, was at least forty years old, and Dempsey had flat out said he would not fight Langford. That Langford was black had nothing to do with Dempsey's disinclination to fight him; what did was Dempsey's conviction that, even at forty, Langford would beat him.

As it was, there was only one viable contender, and that was another, younger black fighter, Harry Wills, who had lost only one of fifty-three fights in the last nine years, and who, at thirty-three years of age, was running out of time. But although Wills, a soft-spoken, light-hitting heavyweight from New Orleans, was the antithesis of the flamboyant Jack Johnson, neither Tex Rickard nor Kearns wanted Dempsey to run the risk of losing the heavyweight title to a black fighter. Rickard had three reasons. First, he remembered the racial riots triggered when Johnson knocked out Jim Jeffries in the title fight he promoted and refereed in Reno in 1910. Second, he did not feel the country was ready for another black heavyweight champion. Third, he was convinced that Wills, as a heavyweight champion, would be an economic disaster for boxing, especially for promoters like himself.

Far more lucrative than appearing on the vaudeville stage and fighting exhibitions was the time Dempsey spent in Hollywood during 1924 and 1925. Dempsey had already done an earlier stint in Hollywood—in 1920, a year after he had won the heavyweight title, Pathé Studios paid him about twenty-five thousand dollars to star, to use the word loosely, in a twelve-part serial entitled *Daredevil Jack,* which was completed in the astonishingly swift time of three months. In the simplistic formula used in each of the fifteen-minute films, Dempsey was a sports hero, usually a fighter, who would come to the rescue of an endangered beauty. To make Dempsey's ruggedly handsome but somewhat marred visage more suitable for the silver screen, Lon Chaney, a masterful makeup artist who later would achieve fame as a fright-inducing actor, used putty and other ingredients to restructure Dempsey's ears, nose, and beetle-brows. Almost entirely because of Dempsey's stature as an American sports icon, *Daredevil Jack,* to the amazement of film critics, was a mild commercial success, even though Dempsey conceded he was no actor. "When I started, I was really bad, and I never got any better," he said.

That didn't stop Universal Pictures in 1924 from signing Dempsey to a million-dollar contract under which he made ten silent films—the era of talking pictures did not start until the release of *The Jazz Singer* starring Al Jolson, a friend of Dempsey's, in 1927—that once again cast him in a variety of heroic roles. Released as serials entitled *Fight to Win* and *All's Swell on the Ocean,* the films drew millions of Dempsey idolators, most of them teenage boys, to Saturday afternoon matinees throughout the country. No matter how hard his directors tried, Dempsey never came close to becoming an accomplished actor. Wooden in front of the camera, Dempsey, feeling like a fish out of water, often was on the verge of backing out of his contract. But Kearns, who still got half of everything Dempsey earned, convinced him to continue with his short-lived acting career. Fortunately for Dempsey, all of his movies were silent pictures, which meant that moviegoers would not be taken aback by hearing the heavyweight champion's incongruous falsetto.

Popular among movie people because of his stature as a world-famous fighter who was better known than most of Hollywood's leading men, Dempsey loved the adulation he received in the burgeoning film capital from such film luminaries as Douglas Fairbanks, Charlie Chaplin, and Harold Lloyd. During his Hollywood days, Dempsey enjoyed having the respect of most segments of the film colony, particularly female stars who were attracted to a masculine, ruggedly handsome athlete who also happened to be rich. Even if they never got into a serious romantic entanglement with Dempsey, just to be seen, and hopefully photographed, with the heavyweight champion was almost guaranteed to get them publicity. At first, Dempsey felt uncomfortable at parties, feeling both out of place and self-conscious.

"They talked over my head a lot," he once said. "No snubs, really. Nobody snubs the heavyweight champion of the world. It was just that I'd get a feeling now and then that I didn't know what they were talking about. It wasn't much comfort to tell myself that maybe they didn't, either."

Convinced that he wanted to stay in Los Angeles, Dempsey persuaded his mother, sister, and two brothers to leave Salt Lake City and move there where he had bought a luxurious home for them and himself at 24th Street and Western Avenue. Celia Dempsey, while appreciating her famous son's gesture, never felt at home in Los Angeles, missing her Mormon friends and finding it difficult to get a good night's sleep in a house where Dempsey cronies, including sportswriters, former fighters, and others connected with boxing, often stayed up through the night, drinking and talking loudly well after she, Dempsey, and the rest of the family had gone to bed. In less than a year, aware that his mother was unhappy in L.A. and wanted to return to Utah, Dempsey bought her a farm near many of her old Mormon friends, where she remained for the rest of her life.

After a number of affairs with some of Hollywood's most glamorous stars—Dempsey was never a kiss-and-teller, but he was rumored to have had flings with Clara Bow and Barbara Stanwyck, among other actresses—Dempsey once again fell in love, this time with an actress named Estelle Taylor, never a big star but good enough to have received top billing in three films in 1919, 1920, and 1922. A striking and luminous brunette who was both temperamental and outspoken, Taylor had been discovered by producer William Fox when she was nineteen years old. She had been in Hollywood for four years when she was introduced to Dempsey in 1924 when she was twenty-five years old—four years younger than Dempsey—while making *The Alaskan*. For Dempsey, one look at the sensual actress from Wilmington, Delaware, and the heavyweight champion of the world was smitten. Like many women who are attracted to famous athletes, Taylor had no common interests with Dempsey, but seemingly liked him because of his gentleness, warmth, and generosity, all characteristics that seemed paradoxical in light of his ferocity and killer instinct in the boxing ring.

"She was more than a beautiful movie star," Dempsey said years later. "She had wit, a fast mind, and a sense of humor like a razor. She put me into another world."

That Dempsey was one of the most famous people in the country and thus could attract attention to Taylor, whose career was floundering, could have made him all the more appealing to Taylor. The passionate romance that ensued provided grist for the tabloids of the day and transformed Taylor from a little-known movie actress into a nationally known celebrity. Dempsey had had his share of one-night stands with many beautiful and famous women, but close friends knew that he was happiest when he had a close relationship with one woman, even someone like Maxine Cates, and in Estelle Taylor he was convinced he had found the love of his life. So much so that he wanted to marry her within weeks after they met. But there was a problem. Taylor was already married.

The marriage was not difficult to dissolve. Taylor, a teenage beauty queen in Delaware and later a model in New York, had married a Philadelphian named Kenneth Malcolm Peabody when she was fourteen, but they had not lived together for the past four years. Peabody contested Taylor's divorce action and sued Dempsey for alienation of his wife's affections, which in truth had not been affectionate for years. The suit was thrown out, and on February 7, 1925, Dempsey and Taylor were married at the First Presbyterian Church in San Diego in a ceremony attended by only a handful of close friends.

Taylor's pet name for Dempsey was "Ginsberg," which puzzled most people when they heard her call him that. She started to do so after he told her that while he was Irish, as most fight fans had always thought, he also was part Cherokee and also had a Jewish strain since one of his father's great-grandmothers had been Jewish. Once that news got out, Dempsey had more fans than ever. Irish boxing fans knew he was Irish, but Native Americans, or at least most of them, did not know he was part Cherokee. And no one, it seems, knew that he had a Jewish strain. It seemed yet another way for Dempsey to be acclaimed as a true people's champion.

From the time Taylor first met Jack Kearns, she despised him, a sentiment that was mutual. She not only thought Kearns had taken unfair advantage of Dempsey financially—a very valid point—but also found him coarse and crude and knew that he had tried to discourage Dempsey from marrying her. Like many managers—and some fighters, such as Gene Tunney—Kearns was convinced that professional boxing and marriage did not agree. All the more so, Kearns felt, when the woman was as independent, outspoken, and intelligent as Estelle Taylor. He had found that out when, after Dempsey had broken the news of their engagement to him by phone, he traveled to Los Angeles by train to try to keep Dempsey from going through with the wedding.

During dinner at a Hollywood restaurant with Dempsey, Taylor, and Teddy Hayes, a friend of the champion's, Kearns made some crude remarks about Taylor in a loud voice that could be heard throughout the restaurant. Dempsey was shocked but said little, even when Kearns threatened to reveal some salacious information he claimed to have unearthed about Taylor, who was rumored to have had affairs with a number of upper-echelon movie executives who happened to be married. Finally, an irate Taylor and an embarrassed and upset Dempsey left the restaurant. Back at Taylor's apartment, she exploded into a rage, furious at Dempsey for not responding to Kearns's demeaning and abusive remarks, which had embarrassed them both. She gave him a choice: end his relationship with Kearns or she would call off their wedding. Dempsey told her he was through with Kearns. Maybe, but the actual breakup would not take place for almost another year when Kearns refused to go along with a demand by Dempsey—possibly instigated by Taylor—that henceforth he would have to settle for 35 percent of Dempsey's earnings, which had surpassed a half-million dollars in 1924 even though the only fighting he had done was a few exhibitions.

Dempsey was not surprised when Kearns, who now also was managing welterweight champion Mickey Walker, declined the offer. He would continue to receive 50 percent of everything Dempsey earned, including his income as an actor, or nothing at all. It would turn out to be nothing at all; the most successful boxer-manager relationship in the sport's history was essentially over, although Kearns would go on trying to collect at least a third of Dempsey's income for the rest of Dempsey's career.

The young couple took a honeymoon trip to Europe in May, where, as in 1922, Dempsey was warmly greeted everywhere he went—in this case to London, Paris, Berlin, Cologne, and Vienna. He also fought several lucrative exhibition bouts, which he said, only partly in jest, were necessary to help pay for all of the shopping Estelle was doing. Soon after returning to the States in July of 1925, Dempsey and Taylor moved into a new and spacious house in the Hollywood Hills. While her marriage to Dempsey had brought her more publicity and fame than any of her screen roles had, Taylor's movie career continued to spiral downward. In an effort to rejuvenate his wife's career, Dempsey bought the screenplay of *Manhattan Madness* from Douglas Fairbanks and his wife, Mary Pickford, and financed the making of the movie in which he co-starred with Taylor. Despite the pairing of the world heavyweight champion and his beauteous wife, the movie did poorly at the box office and Dempsey lost a considerable amount of money.

It was to be Taylor's final starring role. As her career stalled, Taylor began to blame Dempsey for it. After Paramount Pictures refused to renew her contract in 1925, she told Dempsey that several actor friends, notably Lupe Velez, ironically a onetime paramour of Dempsey's, had said that being married to a fighter—even the world heavyweight champion—was hurting her in Hollywood. Dempsey, who was well liked by just about everyone in Hollywood, found that hard to believe. And he was right. Estelle Taylor, it seemed, was just looking for an excuse for her failure to get decent roles.

Still, Dempsey conceded that Taylor's career had begun to go south soon after their marriage. "She wasn't a great actress. Her only real weapon was her great beauty," Dempsey was to say years later. "I guess everybody looks around for somebody to blame his failures on, and I was her nearest target. It began to be my fault if she didn't get a part. She explained to me that social contacts play an important role in the success or failure of Hollywood stars, and being married to a pug hurt her socially and therefore hurt her career."

If Estelle wasn't going to be working much—her career eventually would rebound—Dempsey certainly didn't want to go on acting, although he was to appear briefly in three more movies from 1927 to 1958, and perhaps even upstage his wife. Besides, he now missed the ring. It had been almost three years since he had last defended his title. And though he was through with Kearns, it was time to start training and fighting again. That Dempsey was beginning to get some bad press—even from a few New York writers he considered friends—may have had something to do with his urge to return to the ring. Grantland Rice had written, not long after Dempsey's marriage to Estelle Taylor, that because of his long inactivity from boxing, Dempsey had come to rank with Jack Johnson as being the most unpopular heavyweight champions of all time.

If he did want to resume fighting, the big question was against whom? It most certainly would not be against old friends Billy Miske and Bill Brennan. Miske, after hanging on to fight twenty-four more times after his title shot against Dempsey in September of 1920 while suffering from Bright's disease, had died on New Year's Day of 1924 at the age of thirty-nine. Brennan, who like Miske had fought Dempsey twice, died three months later when he was shot and killed outside a bar he owned in the Washington Heights section of Manhattan for refusing to buy beer from a mob-controlled distributor. Ironically, in what was to be the last fight for both of them, Miske had knocked out Brennan in the fourth round in Omaha.

Little did Dempsey realize that, though he would fight again soon, his acting career also was still not over. Except that the next time he would be a leading man, it would be on the stage in a play that would co-star Estelle and that would eventually reach Broadway. The downside was that by then, although he would only be in his early thirties, he would no longer be the heavyweight champion of the world.

Tunney, right, and France's "Orchid Man,"
Georges Carpentier. STANLEY WESTON COLLECTION

FOURTEEN

A
Dream Fight
(for Women Fans)

W hile Jack Dempsey frequently was being photographed with beautiful women, even before his romantic entanglement with Estelle Taylor, Gene Tunney rarely was seen in public with a female companion. Though he was nowhere near as famous as Dempsey in the early 1920s, Tunney had a lot of appeal. He was the more handsome of the two, a veteran of the Great War, far more articulate (although he already had begun to speak in an affected and pedantic manner), more polished in his manners, and possessed of a much wider breadth of interests.

As his victories mounted, he got more newspaper space, in large measure because of the payoffs to Damon Runyon and Bill Farnsworth and a number of other sportswriters and sports editors who were on Tex Rickard's payroll and thus were inclined to play up Rickard's fights, no matter how badly mismatched they might appear to be. Tunney also had become well known enough to have his picture occasionally show up in at least some of the New York papers. Also, more and more women were turning up at his fights, attracted as much, if not more so, by his good looks, his well-sculpted physique, and his refined demeanor. Tunney was, as the saying went, a catch and one of New York's most eligible bachelors. But Tunney himself had indicated publicly that he was not about to enter into a serious romantic relationship—not as long as he was fighting. Like Doc Kearns, from whom he could not possibly be more different, Tunney believed that boxing and marriage did not mix, especially if you aspired to a championship.

In a somewhat odd turn of phrase, Hattie Fithian Cattell, a writer for the *New York Journal,* described Tunney as "manly beauty and brains with a fighting instinct," while, in his syndicated column, the socialite Cornelius J. Vanderbilt, Jr., called Tunney an "Adonis."

So where were all the women when Tunney was not in training at Barry McCormack's farm in New Jersey or wielding an axe in northern Maine or Canada? Certainly some attractive females had caught his eye. And they had, but then Tunney, who still lived at home into his late twenties—not uncommon among young men at the time, especially young Irish men- -was circumspect about his dating. When Dempsey and Greb and many other big-name boxers were in New York, they would often be seen at LaHiff's, Delmonico's, Texas Guinan's, the Silver Slipper, and other popular restaurants and nightclubs where movie and stage stars, socialites, well-known underworld figures, sportswriters, and newspaper columnists tended to gather, both to dine and drink illicit gin, scotch, and some of the finest French wines from sterling silver flasks. Tunney, though, never a night owl to begin with, and who, like Dempsey, rarely took so much as a beer during his fighting days, was never seen at any of them. And he most certainly never turned up at any of the tonier speakeasies, such as Jack and Charlie's at 21 West 52nd Street, which following repeal of the Prohibition amendment in 1933 became known as the "21" Club and developed into one of Manhattan's most exclusive restaurants.

When Tunney did go out with a woman, it usually would be to a small and relatively unknown restaurant in Greenwich Village or mid-Manhattan, where he might be recognized by some people but not photographed or mentioned in any of the gossip columns that had begun to become popular in some of the New York newspapers in the mid-1920s. A budding intellectual, Tunney, along with his craving for at least some literary classics, also was developing an interest in art and the theater, and often he and his female companions would turn up unnoticed at Manhattan museums and at Broadway theaters, where members of the boxing establishment who might recognize him were unlikely to be.

Much as he remained convinced that he, and maybe he alone, could beat Jack Dempsey, Tunney still had to prove that he could beat a much smaller fighter, the indomitable Harry Greb. True, he had regained his ersatz American light heavyweight title with a fifteen-round decision over Greb in February of 1923. But Tunney, who had been decisively thrashed by Greb nine months earlier, had not been particularly impressive in winning the closely contested rematch.

Since they had split their first two fights, and given the inherent hero-villain appeal of their confrontations (which became a trademark of Tex Rickard's matchmaking), Rickard knew that a rubber match would be a big attraction. He did not have to work hard to convince Tunney and Greb and their managers that a third fight would be lucrative for everyone concerned, and the bout was set for December 10, 1923, again at Madison Square Garden.

The fight was especially significant to Tunney, now twenty-six, since he was growing into a heavyweight. Thus he felt that the third Greb bout might be his last as a light heavyweight, since he was having trouble making the 175-pound maximum weight limit. For Greb, the fight was far less important. If Tunney was evolving into a heavyweight, Greb was a natural middleweight with no aspirations of moving up into the light heavyweight ranks on a full-time basis, although he still harbored the hope of getting a shot at Dempsey's heavyweight title.

Apart from being convinced that he could beat Dempsey—which still seemed highly unlikely—Tunney had good reason to want to move into the heavyweight division, since there was a decided dearth of worthy challengers. Tommy Gibbons may have been the best of the lot, but though he had gone fifteen rounds with Dempsey, he had been beaten decisively and a rematch made no sense. And even though Luis

Angel Firpo had knocked down Dempsey twice and through the ropes on another occasion, he had demonstrated that he had a powerful right-hand punch but nothing else, including no defense, and was not likely to dethrone the Manassa Mauler.

Looking around, Tunney, like Dempsey and Tex Rickard, could not spot another worthy challenger except for Harry Wills, no doubt the best of a relatively weak assortment, but whose pigmentation would deny him a shot at Dempsey's title. Tunney never would fight Wills either. Nor would he ever fight a black boxer as a professional. Dempsey, by contrast, fought about a dozen, and maybe more, black fighters. Tunney was not known to be a racist, but conceded that, as a thirteen-year old boy, he was "as heartsick as any other Caucasian when Jack Johnson whipped and humbled the great white paladin, the big Fellow, James J. Jeffries." Referring to his virtually all-white Greenwich Village neighborhood, Tunney said years after his career had ended that "Nowhere was there a more vociferous demand that the paler sub-species of the human race be vindicated by the gloved knuckles of Jeff." Tunney may have been exaggerating. The "demand," no doubt, was even more vociferous in some other parts of the country.

While Tunney had not boxed for four months because of his thumb injury, Greb had fought six times since winning the middleweight title. Those six fights had been held over an eight-week span, meaning that on average he had fought once every week and a half. And the last of those six fights was a middleweight title defense in Pittsburgh, a week before his third Tunney bout. Even in an era when fighters like Greb sometimes fought several times a week, Rickard was furious; indefatigable as Greb was, he could be cut or otherwise injured and force postponement of a fight that was certain to draw well. Fortunately for Rickard, Greb emerged unscathed.

Despite his decisive loss in the first fight and the closeness of the second, Tunney entered the ring as a 2-to-1 favorite, meaning a bettor favoring Tunney had to put down two dollars to win one dollar, while a Greb supporter needed only to bet one dollar to win two dollars. Tunney was supremely confident; he felt that, after two fights with Greb, he knew exactly what he had to do: concentrate on his body.

Greb, feeling that he had already beaten Tunney twice, was as sure, if not more so, that he would whip Tunney.

To the surprise of the raucous crowd, which again included hundreds of Greb supporters from the Pittsburgh area, Greb eschewed many of his customarily rough, and even illegal, tactics he had used during the first two fights, and which he felt may have cost him the decision in the second fight. Indeed, the fight was remarkably clean, with Tunney continuously repelling Greb's whirlwind attacks and ripping punishing blows to his body. Still, there was considerable booing when ring announcer Joe Humphreys proclaimed that Tunney had retained his American light heavyweight title. Most boxing writers had Tunney well ahead—Jack Lawrence, who had pushed Dempsey back into the ring three months earlier after he had been sent sprawling out of it—gave Greb only three of the fifteen rounds, scored three even, and gave the remaining nine to Tunney. Fred Keats of the *New York Herald* had it even more one-sided, crediting Tunney with eleven rounds. Referring to the negative response from much of the crowd, both Lawrence and Keats made the valid point that most boxing fans—particularly those far from ringside—place too much credence on punches to the head, where Greb landed most of his blows, none of which appeared to hurt Tunney, and fail to take into account the damage done by solid punches to the body. That Greb, as always, finished strong, winning the last two rounds, also appeared to have had a considerable impact on the crowd, as strong finishes usually do in boxing.

Tunney and Greb would fight twice more—in Cleveland on September 17, 1924, and in St. Paul, Minnesota, on March 27, 1925. By the Cleveland fight, Tunney had developed into a full-grown heavyweight, coming in at 180 pounds, seventeen pounds heavier than Greb. Again, the fight was close, and a poll of sportswriters was split, resulting in a draw newspaper decision.

If the second, third, and fourth fights between Greb and Tunney were close, the outcome in St. Paul was crystal-clear: Tunney won easily before a capacity crowd of around nine thousand. With Greb again outweighed considerably—this time by fourteen pounds—Tunney was more effective than he had been in the first four bouts with his unrelenting body attack, which in the opinion of most boxing writers enabled him to take eight of the ten rounds.

In later years, many boxing historians erroneously reported that, after losing the first fight to Greb, Tunney had won the next four to avenge the initial defeat four-fold. In reality, Tunney had won three of the fights and lost one, with one bout ending in a draw. Considering that he was facing one of the best boxers of the era in Tunney, it was a commendable achievement by Greb—especially given that, in all five fights, he was fighting with only one eye.

Impressive as Tunney was in his last fight against Greb, he would be even more imposing in his next bout, accomplishing something that not even Jack Dempsey could do, and in the process establishing himself as a viable contender for Dempsey's heavyweight title. Greb, meanwhile, would hold on to his world middleweight title until February 26, 1926, when, obviously slipping after more than 275 fights, and perhaps as many as three hundred, he would lose a split fifteen-round decision to Theodore "Tiger" Flowers, a soft-spoken church deacon from Georgia who would become the first black to win the 160-pound title. Six months later, in what would turn out to be his final fight, Greb would also lose a rematch to Flowers. Two months later, at the age of thirty-two, Harry Greb would be dead. Ironically, one year later, Flowers would die at the same age under remarkably similar circumstances to Greb.

One of Greb's pallbearers would be his most bitter antagonist, Gene Tunney, who by then would have become a better heavyweight than almost everyone in the boxing world could ever have imagined. In their five fights, Greb butted Tunney often, cuffed him with illegal punches, and committed numerous other fouls. Yet Tunney never complained about Greb's tactics. That was the way Harry Greb fought, and no one was going to change his style, any more than anyone was going to convert Jack Dempsey from a puncher to a boxer. Tunney understood that and, rather than hold any animus toward the Pittsburgh Windmill, he would always view him with considerable respect, perhaps because he had given the Golden Boy from Greenwich Village a licking in the ring that Tunney would never forget.

Between his third and fourth fights with Greb, Tunney would win seven straight fights. By far his most significant victory would come on July 24, 1924, over Georges Carpentier, the defrocked light heavyweight champion, who was making his second appearance in the United States since being knocked out by Jack Dempsey in 1921. Though the Orchid Man was still a formidable boxer, it seemed evident to boxing writers who had covered him for years that he was slipping and had lost some of the skills that had enabled him to knock out Battling Levinsky to win the light heavyweight title four years earlier or even the fighter who had thrown a brief scare into Jack Dempsey when the elegant Frenchman made a bid for Dempsey's heavyweight championship. Carpentier was only thirty—three years older than Tunney— but he had been fighting professionally since he was fourteen and had had 105 professional fights compared with only sixty-two for Tunney.

In an obvious effort to attract attention to the fight—ticket sales were lagging, in large measure because of Carpentier's loss to Tommy Gibbons seven weeks earlier—promoter Jimmy Johnston arranged for lawn parties for both Carpentier and Tunney, perhaps the first, and maybe the only, time that had been done for two boxers. But then Carpentier and Tunney were hardly typical boxers. If anything, they were the diametric opposites of what most people perceived boxers to be. They were both good-looking, intelligent, well mannered, and even charming, and could be comfortable in drawing rooms and even lawn parties. They also tended to show compassion for opponents they had grievously hurt in the ring.

The first of the lawn parties, held at the Long Island estate where Carpentier was both staying and training, attracted an eclectic mixture of boxing people, Broadway entertainment figures, socialites, both sports and society editors, and, in particular, a large number of women, including Mrs. Oscar Hammerstein, the wife of the composer, and Mrs. Sam Harris, whose husband, the well-known Broadway producer, had become involved in boxing for years as the sponsor of several prominent fighters. To the delight of many of the women present, Carpentier served as a waiter, dispensing drinks and snacks and engaging in conversation with the guests in a setting that could have inspired *The Great*

Gatsby, which F. Scott Fitzgerald would set in the very same exclusive and wealthy Long Island South Shore. Several days later, Johnston did the same for Tunney, holding a cocktail party at Barry McCormack's farm in Red Bank, New Jersey, that attracted many of the same people who had attended the soiree for Carpentier, along with a considerable number of Broadway *Follies* and *Vanities* dancers. Tunney, far more reserved than Carpentier, mingled with the guests for a while and then retired to the guest house where he was staying, to the disappointment of many of the *Follies* and *Vanities* beauties, whom Johnston had had transported to the party on the banks of the Shrewsbury River. Many of the women had not seen Tunney before and were struck by his good looks, his obvious intelligence, and his pleasant manner. True, Carpentier was also good-looking, but why, some of the female guests wondered, hadn't anyone told them that Tunney was even more handsome?

A crowd of around forty thousand turned out for the fight at the Polo Grounds between the most handsome practitioners of what Pierce Egan, the eighteenth-century British boxing historian, had described as "The Sweet Science of Fistiana." That was about half of the eighty thousand that had attended Carpentier's "Battle of the Century" against Dempsey at Boyle's Thirty Acres in Jersey City three years before and far less than the nearly ninety thousand that had watched the Dempsey-Firpo epic at the Polo Grounds a year earlier. But both of those fights had featured the magnetic Dempsey, and were for the heavyweight title. Still, a crowd of forty thousand for a light heavyweight fight was pretty good.

Like the last big fight at the Polo Grounds, between Dempsey and Firpo ten months before, this one also would generate controversy in its aftermath. From the beginning, it became apparent that Carpentier's only chance of winning was to knock out Tunney with his right, as had been the case with Firpo against Dempsey. But Carpentier's dazzling boxing skills had obviously deteriorated, particularly his defense, and Tunney raked him easily with a wide variety of punches, most of them to the body, throughout the fight, which was scheduled for fifteen rounds.

Carpentier won only one of the first nine rounds and was on the verge of being knocked out in the tenth when Tunney put him down twice with left hooks to the jaw. When Tunney continued to batter Carpentier with unanswered blows to the head and body, referee Andy Griffin tried to intervene to stop the bout, but the Frenchman waved him away. Moments later, after Tunney had rocked Carpentier with a left hook to the head, manager François Descamps jumped onto the ring apron and waved a sponge at Griffin while imploring the referee to stop the fight. Eager to continue, Carpentier screamed at Descamps to back off shortly before the bell rang.

The end, for all intents and purposes, came in the fourteenth round when, after a furious exchange in mid-ring, Carpentier forced Tunney into the ropes, whereupon Tunney unloaded a wicked left uppercut to the midsection that sent the Orchid Man to the canvas with about a half a minute left in the round. Clutching his groin and writhing in apparent pain, Carpentier looked up at Griffin, grimacing and claiming he had been hit below the belt and thus fouled. Appearing confused, Griffin never did begin a count after Tunney had gone to a neutral corner. Seconds later, the bell sounded, ending the round, after which Descamps and Carpentier's trainer, Gus Wilson, dragged their fighter to his corner.

The scene at the start of the fifteenth and final round was both bizarre and memorable. Still clutching his groin and wobbly-legged, Carpentier moved toward the center of the ring, aided by Descamps and Wilson. After leaving his corner to begin the round, Tunney stopped in his tracks, confused and, with his hands at his side, looking on incredulously. He became even more incredulous when, from a semi-crouch position, Carpentier sagged to the canvas as Tunney backed off, while Descamps continued to scream "Foul!" After about thirty seconds of utter confusion, Griffin finally waved Tunney to his corner and ring announcer Joe Humphreys climbed into the ring and raised Tunney's right hand, signifying that the fight was over. The controversy over the fourteenth-round knockdown, though, was not.

Some ringside observers thought that one of Tunney's knees, and not a blow to the midsection, had done the damage that sent Carpentier to the floor in the fourteenth. Among them was the un-bylined writer of the *New York Times*, who wrote in a front-page story: "What really seemed to have happened was that Carpentier rushed Tunney against the ropes in the fourteenth round and was struck in the groin by Tunney's knee." Neither the *Times* reporter nor anyone else who subscribed to that theory said which of Tunney's knees was to blame.

The day after the fight, perhaps after reading the *New York Times* account, Descamps changed his tune and said that Tunney's knee—he didn't specify which one, either—had "incapacitated Carpentier" in the fourteenth round and apparently not a low blow, as he had originally charged.

That one of his knees, and not one of his fists, had put Carpentier down, and in pain, was news to Tunney. "The blow which Carpentier claimed as a foul was a left uppercut right in the pit of the stomach," Tunney said. "I am certain that the blow was not low."

Despite the controversy, there would be no rematch. For one thing, Tunney, whose career was obviously on the rise, had decisively beaten a Carpentier whose best days in the ring were long past. Second, Tunney now planned to fight exclusively as a heavyweight. He had been adding weight, almost all of it muscle, and had had to lose eight pounds in training in order to get down to under 175 pounds—the agreed-upon maximum for the fight.

Tunney's favorite sportswriter, W. O. McGeehan of the *New York Herald Tribune* (the *Herald* and *Tribune* merged in 1926), who also had become a friend, wrote that Tunney should have knocked out Carpentier, but apparently did not because he lacked the will to do so. The most unkind cut, though, came from the typewriter of Joe Williams, the syndicated sports columnist for the Newspaper Enterprise Association, who wrote, "Tunney has little genuine class, and talk of matching him with Dempsey is ridiculous. He is a fair body puncher with a neat left hook, but is ordinary at long range. He is not a natural hitter, and his punches lack the snap and kick that come with perfectly delivered, well-timed blows."

Carpentier begged to differ. Tunney, he said through swollen lips, was a very good fighter, certainly one of the best around. The Orchid Man still insisted that he had been fouled, but was sure the foul was ac-

cidental. Tunney, he said, was much too much the gentleman to deliberately hit him below the belt. Carpentier also never mentioned being
struck by one of Tunney's knees.

In the aftermath of the fight, Tunney was left wondering what he
could do to gain more respect. No one seemed to think he had any
chance of beating Dempsey. And who had he beaten? A washed-up
Battling Levinsky. Harry Greb in two fights, which many boxing experts thought Greb had won, and an over-the-hill Georges Carpentier,
whom Tunney outweighed by about twenty pounds.

What, Tunney wondered, did he have to do to gain acceptance as a
challenger to Dempsey's title? Perhaps beat the best heavyweights
around. Apart from Dempsey and Harry Wills, the "colored heavyweight champion," that would seem to be an aging Tommy Gibbons.
He had lasted fifteen rounds with Dempsey in Shelby and he had decisively beaten Carpentier. Maybe an impressive victory over Gibbons
would quiet the skeptics who didn't think Tunney would have a
chance in the world against Jack Dempsey—if such a fight ever came
about.

Rickard with his third wife (at far left), their baby, held by Gene Tunney, and their nanny.
STANLEY WESTON COLLECTION

FIFTEEN

Tex Rickard's Worst Possible Nightmare

By the spring of 1925 Tunney no longer had to worry about getting down to 175 pounds. Eight months after knocking out Carpentier, Tunney had fought Greb for the last time—in March of 1925—and, now weighing just over 180 pounds, announced he would fight only heavyweights, with the intention of convincing Tex Rickard that he, more than any other heavyweight, had the best chance of beating Jack Dempsey. Fortunately for Rickard, by that time he was free to worry about such things, as everyone seemed to have gotten over the scandal of three years earlier that had threatened not only to end his career as a boxing promoter, but to send him to prison for a long time. Well, almost everyone.

The scandal, big even by New York standards at a time when politicians, judges, and others who had been associated with Tammany Hall were still going to prison on a fairly regular basis, broke not long after Rickard had emerged as one of the country's best-known sports figures,

and, most certainly, the best-known promoter of any sport. Besides promoting the first fight to draw more than $1 million, he had turned the
second Madison Square Garden into a profitable operation by staging
not only major boxing bouts, but college basketball games, wrestling
matches, horse and dog shows, circuses, and six-day bicycle races. But
on January 22, 1922, New Yorkers awoke to see front-page headlines in
the city's half-dozen morning dailies proclaiming that Rickard had been
arrested on charges of having sexually abused a number—it would eventually reach seven—of young girls, ranging in age from eleven to fifteen.
The accompanying stories and the trial that followed caused a sensation.
Through it all, Rickard's lawyer, Max Steuer, claimed that the famed promoter had been set up—"framed," as he put it—although no one on the
defense side of the trial ever did say who might have tried to frame
Rickard.

With the world's most famous fighter, Jack Dempsey, still haunted
by recurrent charges that he had been a slacker during World War I, the
arrest of the world's best-known promoter in a sport that was constantly under attack as being barbaric and corrupt was hardly what
boxing needed.

In testimony to a grand jury and later in court, the girls, who all
knew one another, said they had met Rickard—who was married and
lived on Madison Avenue—at a private pool at Madison Square Garden and that he had, on a number of occasions, taken them to his suite
in the Garden tower and to two different apartments in a building on
West 47th Street, where he took sexual liberties with them. To substan-
tiate their charges, they provided detailed descriptions of the apartments and the tower suite.* That the girls, all from relatively poor
families, could describe the apartments and the Garden's tower suite
with such precision seemed very damaging to Rickard's case.

A number of intriguing events added to the drama of the grand jury
proceedings and the subsequent trial in March of 1922. First, one of the
girls who had been sought for questioning in the case was kidnapped

---

*It was here that Stanford White, the famed architect who had designed the second Madison Square
Garden, had had his dalliances with the teenage Broadway dancer Evelyn Nesbit, which ultimately
led to White's shooting death by Nesbit's millionaire husband, Harry Thaw, on June 25, 1906, and
one of the most celebrated murder trials of the twentieth century.

from her Brooklyn home on January 27 by a former fighter, Nathan Pond, an acquaintance of Rickard's, and taken to a farm in Wappinger Falls in upstate New York. Acting on a tip, police found the girl, Nellie Gasko, on the farm two weeks later, along with Pond, who was arrested on bribery and kidnapping charges. Pond was alleged to have offered the Gasko girl a bribe so that she would not testify against Rickard during the trial. The girl previously had signed an affidavit alleging that Rickard had attempted to attack her on three occasions in one of the West Side apartments.

Shortly thereafter, Walter Fields, a box office worker at Madison Square Garden, who held the leases on the two apartments where the girls said Rickard had molested them—and who was expected to be called to testify by the prosecution—disappeared. To make matters worse, seemingly, for Rickard, Harry Verch, the janitor of the apartments, told the grand jury that indicted Rickard that the promoter had told him before he was arrested that if anyone was to seek him (Verch) for questioning to "Keep quiet. Keep your mouth shut." Under cross-examination during the trial, Rickard admitted he had instructed Verch to remain silent, but said it was in a different context and related to his liquor supply in one of the apartments.

"I didn't want to lose it," Rickard testified, referring to the liquor, which he said he had bought before Prohibition took effect in the fall of 1919. Further, Rickard told the court, the discovery of liquor belonging to him could have been embarrassing.

By the time he was put on the witness stand by the prosecution, Verch, the janitor, seemed to have developed a memory lapse. Asked by prosecutor Ferdinand Pecora about his grand jury testimony that Rickard had told him to remain silent if authorities started to ask any questions relating to the apartments, a nervous Verch said he suffered from a poor memory and didn't remember a thing, whereupon he was dismissed.

At the start of the trial, Pecora focused heavily on Rickard's past, alleging that he had made a fortune during his entrepreneurial days in the Klondike and Nevada by rigging roulette wheels, cheating at cards, and operating brothels that employed girls barely into their teens.

Rickard both blanched and stiffened as Pecora went on to charge in a courtroom packed with men—women were excluded from the trial proceedings, apparently in the belief that some of the salacious testimony would be too sensitive for them to hear—that Rickard had seduced a young girl in Rawhide, Nevada, where he had run a gambling casino, and then been beaten with a whip by the girl's mother, who then committed suicide.

"Were you not, in the long and the short of it, Mr. Rickard," Pecora said, "a cad and a cheater, and to get to the heart of this affair, sir, an abuser of young women—a pedophile?"

Visibly shaken, Rickard, who was confined to jail during the weeklong trial, steadied himself and softly replied, "No, I was not."

In Rickard's defense, Steuer brought out that several of the girls who had made the accusations against Rickard were older than they claimed—the eleven-year-old, for example, turned out to be fifteen—and that a few had been arrested for theft, robbery, forging checks, begging, and a variety of other offenses. Steuer also produced an impressive list of witnesses who vouched for Rickard's character, including Kermit Roosevelt, the son of the former president Theodore Roosevelt; Anthony Drexel Biddle, the wealthy Philadelphia sportsman and philanthropist; and Charles Herron, an Alaska newspaper publisher and industrialist who testified that he had known Rickard since his gold rush days in Alaska and said that Rickard's reputation there had been and still was impeccable.

Under questioning by Steuer, Rickard appeared to hold the jury and spectators mesmerized as he recounted his early days as a cowhand, a Texas sheriff at the age of twenty-three, a gold prospector, a gambling house owner in Alaska and Nevada, a cattle rancher in South America, and of course, a boxing promoter. Rickard also told how, before his arrest, he had met one of the girls in somewhat strange circumstances. According to Rickard, the girl, fifteen-year-old Sarah Schoenfeld, and her mother had come to his office at Madison Square Garden during the previous summer, unannounced, and had asked him to help get the girl's brother released from jail in Wisconsin, where he was serving a sentence for burglary. Rickard testified that he had never met either the Schoenfeld girl or her mother and had no idea why they had turned to him for help, but agreed to write to the governor of Wisconsin in an effort to help them.

That the Schoenfeld woman and her daughter would show up at Rickard's office to plead for help, without Rickard knowing them, and that the promoter then would agree to try to help get Sarah Schoenfeld's brother out of a Wisconsin jail did seem somewhat strange, to say the least. In an obvious effort to buttress Rickard's account of the inexplicable meeting, a Madison Square Garden employee, William Money, testifying for the defense, confirmed that Mrs. Schoenfeld and her daughter had indeed come to the Garden on that summer day and that he, without first contacting Rickard, took them to his office, where Rickard agreed to meet with them.

Pecora tried to discredit Rickard's story, saying that Rickard did not try to intercede for the Schoenfelds until after he had become acquainted with the girl, who testified that Rickard had sexually attacked her.

In his cross-examination, Steuer sought to contradict testimony by two of the girls that they had been with Rickard in one of the apartments on the afternoon of Saturday, November 12, by contending that Rickard had spent that afternoon at the Polo Grounds watching a Dartmouth-Pennsylvania football game with two Garden associates. Both of the associates testified that Rickard had indeed been at the game, as did Bill Farnsworth, the sports editor of the *New York American* and one of the New York sports journalists who received weekly checks from Rickard.

But under cross-examination, Rickard said he could not remember who won the game—which he said was the first football game he had ever attended—nor what color uniforms the teams wore. That seemed highly unlikely to many people, but not to others who knew that it was not uncommon for some spectators to spend more time socializing than paying attention to the event itself, especially if they were not particularly interested in the sport.

As it was, it took the jury only an hour and a half to return a not guilty verdict on March 27. Hearing the verdict, Rickard grabbed the railing in front of the defense table as his knees sagged and the courtroom erupted into cheers. Later, Rickard told reporters, "I've shot craps for $30,000 a throw, but I never went through anything like this last hour."

Regardless of the not guilty verdict, Rickard's reputation was tarnished. Near the end of the trial, Steuer said in court that Rickard was through as a promoter, and would devote all of his energies to tracking down whoever was behind what his lawyer had referred to as a "frame-up." But after lying low for a few months and staying away from anyone connected with boxing, Rickard eventually returned to the Garden as its promoter of boxing and just about everything else. Not only would Rickard survive as a promoter, but he would go on to stage two of the biggest fights in boxing history, build a third Madison Square Garden on Eighth Avenue in Manhattan and another Madison Square Garden in Boston (which came to be known as the Boston Garden) in 1928. The Boston Madison Square Garden was to be the second of seven Gardens in the country that Rickard envisioned, but the last to be built.

So in early June of 1925, Rickard was free to put together the best heavyweight fight he could think of: Gene Tunney against Tommy Gibbons, who, since going the fifteen-round distance against Dempsey in Shelby, Montana, two years before, had won all eleven of his fights, all but one by a knockout. One of Gibbons's knockouts had been over Kid Norfolk, one of only two fighters—Tunney was the other—to beat Harry Greb twice.*

---

*A black fighter from Norfolk, Virginia—hence his name—Kid Norfolk also had knocked out Tiger Flowers, who eventually would beat Greb to become the first black middleweight champion, and Battling Siki, who had knocked out Georges Carpentier to capture the light heavyweight championship. Like many young black fighters, Kid Norfolk—whose real name was William Ward—had started fighting in "Battle Royals," the demeaning spectacles wherein as many as two dozen black boxers, often blindfolded, would crowd into a boxing ring and fight until only one was left standing. At the end, spectators would reward the winner by throwing change into the ring. The Battle Royals were staged almost exclusively in the South, including one on the undercard of a Dempsey fight in Atlanta on July 6, 1918. Among the black fighters who had started out in Battle Royals were Jack Johnson, Tiger Flowers, and Beau Jack, the great lightweight champion of the 1940s and 1950s. Beau Jack, who was born Sidney Walker in Augusta, Georgia, once said that while fighting blindfolded he knew a Battle Royal was over and that he had won when he heard the last fighter fall to the canvas. Like most of the other Battle Royal fighters, Jack was prescient enough to make sure how many were in the ring when the bell sounded for the one and only time (there were no rest periods, as in a conventional fight). "When I heard the last kerplunk," Jack once said, "I knew I had won." The Battle Royals continued into the early 1940s, leaving as their sole redemptive legacy the term itself, usually defined as a fierce free-for-all.

Harry Wills, like most other good black heavyweights, had trouble getting top-ranked white fighters into the ring with him. And no wonder. Through 1924, he had lost only six of sixty-six fights, with all six losses coming against black fighters, including two of the world's best heavyweights at the time, Sam Langford and Sam McVea, both of whom beat Wills twice. And no fighter ever did better against Langford, still regarded as one of the best fighters of all time, than Wills did. In eighteen bouts between the two boxers, Wills won thirteen, lost only two, while three were no-decision fights. Moreover, he had won his last eleven bouts, which included victories over Luis Firpo and well-established white heavyweights Bartley Madden and Charley Weinert.

As with Carpentier and Greb, Rickard knew that Tommy Gibbons, at thirty-four, and maybe as much as three years older, was past his prime. But lasting fifteen rounds against Dempsey without ever being knocked down—as he never had in sixty-one professional fights—still made him an attraction. Tunney, who regarded Gibbons as the best fighter in the world after Dempsey, did not hesitate in agreeing to the fight. Nor did Billy Gibson, who felt that such a bout, like the Carpentier fight, was a perfect showcase for Tunney. Rickard, convinced that the fight would be a big draw, decided to stage it at the Polo Grounds on June 5, 1925.

With Dempsey showing no sign of wanting to defend his title in the foreseeable future, and Harry Greb apparently past his prime, and Benny Leonard retired—although he would make a comeback in 1931—boxing had grown short on marquee names and had few good championship prospects. The best in early 1925 definitely was Gene Tunney. And to Rickard's delight—and in some cases because of his financial largesse to a number of sportswriters and editors—the sporting press was suddenly paying more attention to Tunney and even touting him as the best challenger for Dempsey's title, if he was ever going to defend it.

What also pleased Rickard about Tunney was that as he became better known, more and more women were coming to his fights. Having been the first promoter to persuade women to attend major fights,

Rickard prided himself on the fact that since the Dempsey-Carpentier bout the number of women turning up at Madison Square Garden and at New York ballparks for big fights had been increasing markedly. Maybe Tunney didn't have the panache of Carpentier, but he was better-looking, and Rickard knew that counted for something.

On an unseasonably hot and humid early June night, with the temperature in the low nineties, a crowd of about forty thousand turned out for the fight at the Polo Grounds. Considering that it was not a title fight and Gibbons was past his prime, the size of the crowd was considerable. Gibbons had not a clue that Tunney had been studying him and collecting information about his style for the last two years from two of his former sparring partners. But when Tunney entered the ring against Gibbons, he knew that the veteran from St. Paul's most effective tactic was to feint twice with his right hand, as if he were to throw a right, and then, with his opponent protecting his head, Gibbons would move his left foot forward, drop his head and whip across a powerful left hook to the head or to the body. But Gibbons soon found that Tunney was anticipating not only his lethal left off the double-feint, but almost everything else he planned to do.

As a result, the fight was surprisingly one-sided, with Tunney winning every round but one before Gibbons was knocked down for the first time in his career by a right uppercut to the ribs just under the heart followed by a right to the jaw in the twelfth round. Though badly hurt, Gibbons rose groggily at the count of seven. Tunney, reluctant to hit the wounded Gibbons, gave him time to raise his gloves to defend himself. As Tunney was to say later, "I hate to hit in a situation like this, but the game calls for a finish, so I put just enough power in the right-hand clip to the jaw to sink Tom once again on his haunches." This time, Gibbons was counted out.

Far more aggressive than he had been in any previous fight and hitting with more power than in the past, Tunney elicited rave reviews from most sportswriters. Calling Tunney's performance "a brilliant exhibition of boxing," Grantland Rice wrote, "it marks the approach of a new heavyweight challenger who is on his way." Writing in the *New York Times*, which was now starting to byline some of its sportswriters,

James Dawson said, "Tunney's victory is expected to pave the way for a heavyweight championship bout between the Greenwich Village boxer and Jack Dempsey." Maybe Dawson knew something that no one else did—that Dempsey actually planned to defend his title someday.

Quick to point out that he had done something to Gibbons that Dempsey could not—knock him out—Tunney said after the fight that "I think I have established my right to the championship match with Jack Dempsey tonight. Now I want Dempsey."

The fight, only Gibbons's fourth defeat against fifty-seven victories, turned out to be his last. A few days later, he announced his retirement after fifteen years in the ring. So the fight both served as a coda for Gibbons and as a major stepping-stone toward a title shot for Tunney. But even though Tunney had now clearly emerged as one of the leading contenders for Dempsey's title, it mattered little if Jack Dempsey, now married to Estelle Taylor, continued making movies in Hollywood and hanging out with his show business friends. Dempsey had all the money he needed, and although he would say from time to time that he missed fighting, more and more boxing people were beginning to wonder if he would ever come back.

Tunney, twenty-eight, spars with his father's
boxing idol, fifty-nine-year-old former
heavyweight champion James J. Corbett
(right). ANTIQUITIES OF THE PRIZE RING

SIXTEEN

Dempsey Decides to Come Back

Now a full-fledged heavyweight at 189 pounds, Tunney closed out 1925 with victories over four more heavyweights. After the third fight, a twelve-round newspaper decision over highly ranked Johnny Risko in Cleveland on November 18, Tunney got to meet his father's favorite fighter, James J. Corbett, who was appearing on stage at a Cleveland theater. Corbett, after watching Tunney fight for the first time, then turned up, unannounced, in his dressing room. Tunney was both surprised and delighted. Even more memorable for Tunney than that meeting was a sparring session between the two a month later.

Viewed by only a handful of people atop the Putnam Building in Times Square in New York, the sparring session was arranged by Grantland Rice, who was writing and producing a series called *Sportlight*, whose segments were to be shown in movie theaters. Wearing long white pants, the fifty-nine-year-old Corbett astonished the twenty-eight-year-old Tunney with his feints, snapping jabs, quick and sharp left hooks, and his swift movement. The session included three two-minute rounds—eight minutes in all—and Corbett more than held his own with the much younger Tunney.

No one got hurt, of course. It was a classic sparring session, evocative of the ones held in London in the eighteenth and nineteenth centuries, when aristocrats and even members of the nobility, under the tutelage of boxing masters, often former fighters, danced around, throwing light punches in tests of skill, much like fencers wielding foils with no intent of injuring one another.

Later, Tunney, still in awe of Corbett's boxing skills in his sixtieth year, said, "I honestly think he's better than Benny Leonard. It was the greatest thing I've ever seen." Indeed, Corbett had been one of the greatest. Thirty-three years earlier, he had knocked out John L. Sullivan to win the heavyweight title in 1892. In the Sullivan bout, the first held under Marquess of Queensberry rules, with both fighters wearing four-ounce gloves (boxers nowadays use eight and ten-ounce gloves, depending on their weight division), Corbett, outweighed by thirty-four pounds, raked Sullivan with a torrent of swift jabs and solid blows to the head and body while remaining virtually untouched because of his swift footwork and agile head moves, which totally perplexed the plodding, wild-swinging Sullivan. Corbett's scientific approach—the very antithesis of Sullivan's roughhouse, brawling style—dramatically changed boxing, putting a greater emphasis on defense, footwork, and all-around boxing skills, and earned him the title "Father of American Boxing." In fact, the bout, and Corbett, gave boxing in the United States a patina of respectability, since the sport's most exalted title was now held by a personable and articulate boxer who, for at least a while, demonstrated that a scientific approach could be the most effective in the most dangerous of sports.

Though he is best remembered as the first outstanding boxer in the post-bare-knuckle era, Corbett was proudest of his acting career. During his nine-year professional boxing career, Corbett had only nineteen fights—Harry Greb had more fights than that in six different years. And during four of those years, Corbett did not fight at all. But his career as an actor spanned thirty-eight years, beginning in 1891, his third year as a professional boxer, and lasting until 1930 when he was sixty-four years old, three years before he died in New York City, where he had settled down after a fashion. As an actor, Corbett was good enough to star in about a half-dozen plays, including *Cashel Byron's Profession*, the George Bernard Shaw work about a boxer. At first, Corbett, like most other fighters who appeared on the stage, drew people into theaters because of his celebrity status as a boxer. But as the years went on and Corbett became more skilled as a thespian, he attracted theatergoers because of his talent as an actor.

By contrast, Sullivan's appeal on the stage owed solely to his bluster and larger-than-life persona. Still, the Boston Strong Boy succeeded financially as an actor, drawing thousands to his performance as a blacksmith in a play entitled *Honest Hearts and Willing Hands*, which ran for almost two years, in 1890 and 1891. Later, Sullivan was to portray Simon Legree in *Uncle Tom's Cabin*. Quite often, before the curtain would go up on one of his performances, Sullivan would stride to the front of the stage and bellow out his trademark boast of "I can lick any man in the house." Given the zeitgeist of the 1890s and his popularity, the boast almost always elicited a wave of cheers and laughter. Sullivan may have been crude and even tasteless at times, but in an era of few sports heroes, he was perhaps the most outstanding, particularly in the eyes of most Irish boxing fans.

Other champions who tried acting on stage included Jim Jeffries, who starred, though woodenly, as Davy Crockett; and Bob Fitzsimmons, who appeared in a vehicle entitled *The Slugging Blacksmith*, which had a reasonably long run. Much later, Max Baer, for all of his flamboyance in and out of the ring, failed as a song-and-dance man in vaudeville in the 1930s and in a starring role in a movie entitled *The Prizefighter and the Lady*. However, Baer did acquit himself fairly well in a supporting role in the 1956 film *The Harder They Fall*. Max Schmeling, a former heavyweight champion who Baer knocked out in 1933, did even better. Hugely popular in Germany, Schmeling reportedly received fifty thousand dollars, plus royalties, for his appearance in *Love in the Ring*, a film made in his homeland in the 1930s.

For the most part, though, fighters who consented to appear on stage—including Jack Johnson and Primo Carnera—merely sparred for a few meaningless and generally bloodless and awkward rounds until the novelty wore off in the 1930s, although Johnson also appeared—in a nonsinging role—in the opera *Aïda*. After that, whatever acting fighters did tended to be in front of movie cameras and not audiences, as was the case with Muhammad Ali.

Usually when the marquee-name fighters were merely called on to spar—or, in the case of melodramas or other performances, appear to knock out villains—things went according to the script. But not always. Shortly after he retired, Jack Dempsey co-starred with his wife, Estelle Taylor, in a play entitled *The Big Fight* directed by the theatrical impresario David Belasco. In the play's climactic fight scene, Dempsey, portraying an imaginary fighter named Jack Dillon, knocked out a former club-fighter-turned-actor named Ralph Smith with a lightly thrown right-hand punch in the first round. Smith, who was almost seven feet tall and weighed about 275 pounds, took his nightly dive with aplomb.

"Every night as he hit the deck, I marveled at the way he did it," Dempsey said. "He was a real artist at being knocked down. Sometimes I wondered whether he had learned this on the stage or in the ring. Wherever he learned it, old Ralph could really dive. Every time he went down for the count, shaking the stage and the scenery, the audience thought I had knocked him out for good."

In fact, it was the rare instance where Dempsey was able to restrain himself and go easy with a punch and yet make it look legitimate. One night in New Haven, Dempsey threw the right-hand punch, as called for in the script, but Smith, instead of going down, retaliated with a right to the head that shook Dempsey. As Dempsey was to recall, "Somebody had sense enough to ring the bell."

The script did not call for a round two, but there was one because of Smith's surprising refusal to follow the script in round one. There was also a round three, four, and five. In the fourth round, Dempsey, exasperated at Smith, got him into a clinch and said, "Hey, you bum. Go down. You're ruining the show." Still recalcitrant, Smith broke free of the clinch and kept on fighting. Dempsey, forcing Smith into a clinch again, warned Smith that unless he went down soon he would knock him out for real, which he finally did in the fifth round.

"I hit him on the side of the head with a right and down he went, just like he used to when he was acting," Dempsey said. "Only this wasn't acting."

After the show, Dempsey stormed into Smith's dressing room and yelled, "What the hell were you trying to do out there—fight?"—which, of course, is what the audience thought he was supposed to be doing.

"I'm sorry, Jack," Smith replied while rubbing his sore jaw where Dempsey's hard right had finally put him on the canvas. "But you hit me so hard in that first round that I didn't know where I was from then on." Somehow Smith survived his memory lapse and stayed on as Dempsey's nightly foil.

Dempsey received a thousand dollars a week, more than three times as much as Estelle. But then Dempsey was the big attraction. And as Dempsey said years later, his wife, though a professional, "was almost as bad an actress as I was an actor, and I wasn't any actor at all."

By the beginning of 1926, Jack Dempsey had had his fill of acting. He had made several movies and appeared in vaudeville more times than he cared to remember during the last three years. For those ventures he had been well paid, perhaps more than he would have earned if he had made a few title defenses during that period, since, apart from Harry Wills, there were no viable challengers who could help produce big paydays. Other reasons for his disinclination to return to the ring included his marriage to Estelle Taylor, who hated boxing; and his breakup with Jack Kearns, whom Taylor hated even more than she disliked boxing; and his contentment—at least until the end of 1925—with the good life he was savoring in Hollywood.

Estelle Taylor had noticed his growing restlessness in the latter part of 1925, and was hardly taken by surprise when Dempsey told her that he wanted to get back in the ring. Dempsey said he owed it to his fans, and to the country in general, to return and defend his title after an absence of three years. He was now thirty years old—relatively old for a fighter at the time—and could not wait much longer. He knew that Estelle wanted to continue with her film career, and he told her that he wanted her to go on making movies, and that they could still spend most of their time together. Persuasion was not a strong suit for the Manassa Mauler, but his words were obviously genuine and sincere, and he was able to convince Estelle that he had to get back in the ring.

First, he would have to find a new manager. There was no chance of a reconciliation with Kearns. That relationship had been both long and profitable, but it was all over. Or was it? Ever vigilant when it came to Dempsey's dealings with Kearns, Estelle noticed that Jack had signed a three-year "agreement" in 1923 that did not end until August 9, 1926.

"Whatever you do, don't agree to fight until after the agreement ends," Estelle told her husband at their Los Angeles home. "Otherwise, Kearns will say he deserves half of what you make." Dempsey had learned long ago that his second wife was not only beautiful, but also very smart.

Informed by Dempsey that he wanted to come back and defend his title, Tex Rickard decided that the most attractive opponent would be Tunney, and that the fight should be held in New York, either at Yankee Stadium or the Polo Grounds. However, the New York State Athletic Commission, by a two-to-one vote in July of 1926, ruled that if Dempsey was to defend his title in New York, it would have to be against Wills. Subsequently, however, and perhaps because of political pressure, commissioner George Brower reversed himself in late July and voted for a Dempsey-Tunney match in New York, as had commissioner William Muldoon. But the third member, James J. Farley, who would go on to become postmaster general under President Roosevelt and one of the country's most powerful Democrats, remained steadfast, voting for a Dempsey-Wills fight in New York. Some people thought it was to curry favor with blacks in New York, since there was a good chance that Al Smith, who was serving his third of four terms as governor in 1926 (gubernatorial terms in New York at the time lasted two years), would seek the Democratic presidential nomination in 1928.

That seemed to clear the way for Dempsey and Tunney to fight in the state, at either Yankee Stadium or the Polo Grounds. But there was still one obstacle: Dempsey was not licensed to fight in New York. Granting him one, most figured, would be a mere formality. But it was not. In a surprise development, the state License Committee, a separate entity from the Athletic Commission, on August 16 denied a license to Dempsey unless he would agree to fight Wills first. Dempsey had satisfied one of the State Athletic Commission's requirements when he picked Gene Normile, a longtime acquaintance, as his manager to succeed Kearns, even though he had no boxing background whatsoever and knew very little about the sport. But then lack of knowledge about boxing hardly kept Tex Rickard from becoming the most successful promoter in boxing history.

Knowing his limits, Normile had nothing to do with counseling Dempsey on boxing. That was fine with Dempsey, who, feeling he had been taken advantage of by Doc Kearns, wanted to be his own manager. "The years with Kearns, the years of never having much to say about myself, now made me want to handle everything myself," Dempsey said later. "It wasn't very smart, but I guess it was natural."

Dempsey might have been right on the second point, but he definitely was right on the first. For all of the rancor between Kearns and Dempsey at the end of their long association, Dempsey knew he owed Kearns a lot. "I doubt if I would have become heavyweight champion if it hadn't been for Kearns," Dempsey said. "He was a great manager, a great judge of fighters." No one could ever say that about Gene Normile, who had been a telegrapher and a newspaper reporter and later handled the books for a friend of Dempsey who owned a Manhattan nightclub.

"When he was around," Dempsey said of Kearns, "he was invaluable in the business of preparing me for a fight. His most important contribution was his knowledge of boxing styles. He could spot a weakness or a strength in an opponent before anybody else could. He was the greatest expert I ever met. He was never wrong."

Never wrong, that is, except when he insisted on half of everything Dempsey earned in or out of the ring—and when he verbally assaulted Estelle Taylor in a Hollywood restaurant the year before.

At Dempsey's urging several months later, Rickard, whom Dempsey trusted implicitly, reluctantly agreed to promote a Tunney-Wills fight, although he was opposed to it, fearing that if Wills beat Tunney and then won the title the repercussions would be severe, triggering racial unrest and a diminished interest in the heavyweight division. As it developed, Wills's manager, Paddy Mullins, rejected a $250,000 offer to fight Tunney—with the winner to meet Dempsey for the title—on the grounds that Wills, as the top-ranked contender, at least in Nat Fleischer's eyes, was entitled to fight Dempsey without having to beat Tunney.

But Dempsey knew that a fight with Wills was out of the question. For Dempsey, it was nothing personal against Wills—it was strictly business. "He was gypped out of his crack at the title because people with a lot of money tied up in the boxing game thought that a fight against me, if it went wrong, might kill the business," said Dempsey, who was convinced he could beat Wills easily.

As the bickering between Rickard and the two state agencies went on, officials of the Sesquicentennial Exhibition in Philadelphia, along with Mayor W. Freeland Kendrick and Pennsylvania governor Gifford Pinchot began to take notice of Rickard's difficulty in staging a fight between Dempsey and Tunney. Commemorating the country's 150th birthday anniversary in the city where the Constitutional Convention had been held and where the Declaration of Independence was signed in 1776, the exhibit—touted by Sesquicentennial officials as a mini–world's fair—failed to draw anywhere near as many people as expected and was in danger of drowning in a sea of deep red ink. Some of the events were being held in a concrete horseshoe stadium that had a capacity of almost 150,000 people, but was never even half-filled. In the eyes of the exposition's officials, it was the perfect place for the Dempsey-Tunney fight, if for no other reason than it would focus attention on the financially strapped Sesquicentennial and some of its exhibits outside the stadium. Moreover, Philadelphia had always been a good fight town.

For all the talk about the possibility of the fight being shifted to Philadelphia, Tunney was still hopeful that it would be held in New York. And that was understandable. It was his hometown, and it would give him the opportunity to become the first boxer from New York to win the world heavyweight championship and to do it in New York. Also, he felt his chances of beating Dempsey would be better in New York, where championship fights were scheduled for fifteen rounds, compared with a ten-round limit in Pennsylvania. Tunney's reasoning was that the longer his fight with Dempsey lasted, the better it would be for him, since he believed he was in better condition and Dempsey would tire if the bout went beyond ten rounds.

In mid-August it appeared that Tunney might get the opportunity to win the championship in his hometown after all, when New York State attorney general Albert Ottinger ruled that Dempsey was entitled to a license despite the License Committee's ruling. But the committee stood firm, ignoring Ottinger's legal opinion and refusing to grant Dempsey a license. That left Rickard with one last resort—appealing the License Committee's ruling to the courts, as Ottinger had suggested. But Rickard, to the surprise of Ottinger, the License Committee, and many others, did not do so. Others were not so surprised. They knew Rickard felt that if he took the matter to court, a judge might wind up not only ruling against him, but suggest that the state legislature repeal the Walker Law, which had legalized professional boxing six years earlier. Even if the Dempsey-Tunney fight would go elsewhere, Rickard was the main boxing promoter in New York, and he certainly did not want that to happen.

Thus, with New York out of the question as a site for the fight, and with a lucrative financial offer having been made by officials of the Sesquicentennial Exhibition in Philadelphia, it made sense to take the fight ninety miles south, and Rickard did. As the *New York Times* said in an eight-hundred-word editorial on August 20, the move "was New York's loss and the gain of Philadelphia." The editorial went on to say that "the stadium will be a gold mine on the night of Sept. 23. What similar area of soil in any other industry could be so productive in the few hours to be given to the production." As developments were to show, the *Times*'s editorial writer had been prophetic.

If the fight wasn't going to be in New York, New York's mayor Jimmy Walker would still be at ringside rooting for his old Greenwich Village neighbor, even though there had been rumors that Walker owned a piece of Wills and had been pushing for a Dempsey-Wills fight.

As for Dempsey, he was furious at the License Committee, and vowed that he would never again fight in New York. "As far as New

York is concerned, I am through," Dempsey said on learning that the fight had been moved to Philadelphia because of the License Committee's refusal to grant him a license. It was a vow that he would break within the next ten months.

For Tunney, meanwhile, the opportunity he had been looking forward to since he was an unknown Marine boxer seven years before was finally going to present itself. The question was: Could he take advantage of it?

Tunney with his friend George Bernard Shaw.
AP IMAGES

SEVENTEEN

■

Gene Who?
You Must
Be Kidding

W hen the Dempsey-Tunney fight was announced in late July,
the response was not surprising. Almost everyone in the
country knew who the world heavyweight champion was,
although some people could not be blamed for wondering
whatever happened to him; after all, he hadn't fought in three years.
But even those who knew a lot about Tunney—mostly boxing insiders
and some sportswriters, most of them from New York—felt that Tunney was in over his head, not to mention in potential danger, against
the heavier, more experienced, and harder-hitting Dempsey. And why,
asked Nat Fleischer and some other highly respected sportswriters,
wasn't Dempsey fighting Harry Wills?

But if boxing people thought the fight was going to be a hard sell,
they did not reckon with the promotional wizardry of Tex Rickard.
Before he even arranged the match, he had the theme in place: the fight
would be a morality play involving a handsome, clean-cut former marine from the sidewalks of New York whose boxing skills reminded

old fight fans of James J. Corbett, and a no-holds-barred roughneck with a menacing scowl and a deadly punch who had been labeled a slacker for accepting a deferment during the Great War. In offering Tunney a shot at Dempsey's title, Rickard told him that Dempsey was not only out of shape, but, after three years of inactivity in the ring, would be easy pickings. Then, in explaining why he thought Tunney would make a good opponent for Dempsey, he told the champion that Tunney was a good light heavyweight, but couldn't possibly hurt him and would be lucky to get past the second round. It was a quintessential Rickard con, and both fighters knew it.

Even sportswriters who weren't on Rickard's payroll bought Rickard's plot line, seizing on it with gusto at a time when the best-known sportswriters, such as Damon Runyon, Grantland Rice, and Ring Lardner, thrived on sports events that involved conflict, especially when the stories pitted a powerful team or individual against an underdog. Or a hero-type against a villain, which had become a Rickard staple. In the case of Dempsey and Tunney, they also had cultural and personal differences. In Dempsey, you had the rugged individual from the Western frontier, who had worked the gold, silver, and copper mines of Colorado as a young man, traveled from town to town clinging to the underside of freight cars while living a hobo's existence, and, as a teenager, had fought men far bigger and older than him for winner-take-all purses in saloons before becoming a professional fighter. But if Dempsey had grown up poor, so had Tunney, and both had left school early to help support their families. But while Dempsey had gone looking for fights to make desperately needed money as a teenager, Tunney had tried to avoid them through the dexterous use of his hands and feet when he was set upon by neighborhood bullies.

Indeed, the two fighters could hardly be more different. Dempsey from the West, Tunney from the East; Dempsey the slugger who fought out of a crouch and stalked opponents relentlessly, Tunney the standup, manufactured boxer. Dempsey, a truculent and fiercely aggressive knockout artist who seemed to feel that every opponent was intruding in his domain and who embodied a combination of rage and ruthlessness. Tunney, a skillful, albeit methodical boxer who regarded boxing as more of a chess match than a life-or-death struggle. Dempsey, who relaxed by playing cards and checkers, listening to jazz records and roughhousing with sparring partners he would often punish cruelly and unnecessarily in the ring. Tunney, an incipient intellectual, with a rococo speech pattern who spent much of his spare time reading the classics and who tended to withdraw whenever he hurt a sparring partner.

If Dempsey felt, as he often said, that his objective was to kill the other fighter before his opponent had a chance to kill him, Tunney's goal was just to win, preferably without hurting the other fighter and no matter if the fight went the distance. "I found no joy in knocking people unconscious," Tunney was to say some years later. "The lust for battle and massacre was missing." Indeed, in both the Carpentier and Gibbons fights, Tunney had refrained from hitting his opponents when they were in serious trouble. Dempsey, by contrast, loved fighting with a passion, so long as the bout didn't last too long—which is where the differences between them got interesting. If a fight went on more than a few rounds, Dempsey began to worry about losing and getting hurt. Tunney, on the other hand, never worried about getting hurt; he was too elusive and too good a boxer for that to happen—or so he thought. But Tunney also had sensed Dempsey's fear: the longer a fight went, Tunney felt, the more worried Dempsey became about getting hurt. Tunney believed, correctly as Dempsey was to concede years later, that Dempsey actually was afraid of getting hurt and dreaded the thought of losing his eyesight as so many fighters had. Indeed, Tunney thought that the killer image that Dempsey and some other fighters projected was a facade, and that in fact it was designed to shield their fear.

While Dempsey knew very little about Tunney, Tunney knew an awful lot about him. He had seen Dempsey fight Carpentier, Bill Brennan, and Luis Firpo in person, and had watched, over and over, films of about a half-dozen of his other bouts. But saying that he watched the films understates the case; he had studied them assiduously, looking for moves Dempsey made before throwing a hook or an uppercut or any other type of punch. One thing he was convinced he had spotted was Dempsey's vulnerability to a straight right-hand punch. In both the Carpentier and Firpo fights, he had been jarred—and even knocked down by Firpo—by right-hand blows to the jaw.

Tunney also knew that Dempsey, like Joe Louis and Rocky Marciano in later years, was not going to surprise an opponent. He was going to keep stalking you, trying to get you to fight at close quarters, where he was most dangerous. It was the only way he knew how to fight, and it most certainly had been successful, especially against fighters who chose to mix it up. Tunney knew that Dempsey was not about to change, not now, not after all his success. Maybe you never knew what to expect from a fighter like Harry Greb, but you knew exactly what you were going to get from Dempsey. Deep down, Tunney was convinced that he not only knew what to expect, but how to cope with it in a way that would surprise the champion.

Before the fight was announced to the public, Rickard suggested to Billy Gibson and Tunney that they try to reach out to people who might be able to put pressure on the State Athletic Commission and the State License Committee to keep the bout from being held outside New York. Gibson had excellent contacts, one of whom was Tim Mara, a well-known bookmaker—bookmaking was legal in the prepari-mutuel betting days—and the founder and owner of the New York Giants, who had started playing in the National Football League the year before. Sure, he would try to help, said Mara. All he wanted, he told Gibson and Tunney, was 25 percent of whatever Tunney's earnings would be if the fight were held in New York, and the same percentage of Tunney's future earnings in the event he won the title. Tunney thought Mara's demands were outrageous, but Gibson said it was best to go along with them; Mara, he told Tunney, had a lot of political clout. Mara, Gibson knew, also owed him a favor. When Joe Carr, the commissioner of the fledging National Football League, decided he wanted a franchise in New York, he was referred to Gibson in 1925 because of his political connections, and offered him one for five hundred dollars. But Gibson declined the offer—he was too busy guiding Tunney toward a shot at the heavyweight title—and referred Carr to Mara, who agreed to accept the franchise. "I felt that, for five

hundred dollars, I had nothing to lose," Mara said years later of a franchise that became one of the most valuable in professional sports.

After signing to fight Dempsey, Tunney went to California by train
to film a serial movie entitled *The Fighting Marine.* Tunney spent nine
weeks in Hollywood doing the serial, his only venture into movie-
making. A quick study, Tunney usually wrapped up his scenes in one
take—to the delight of the Pathé Moving Picture Company, which was
making the silent picture. Tunney conceded that he was never comfortable in front of the cameras, and his stiff style of acting showed it. Yet
the serial, like Dempsey's *Daredevil Jack* serials aimed at teenagers,
fared well at the box office. While shooting, Tunney lived at the Hollywood Athletic Club, mainly because it had a gym where he was able
to work out daily, which he had to do early since he had to be on the
lot by 7:45 every day.

Unlike Dempsey, Tunney had no desire the savor Hollywood's
nightlife, or spend much time with members of the cast or others associated with the film industry. Some friends and the film company's
public relations people tried to match him with a number of starlets
who were more than anxious to be seen with the handsome, athletic,
and well-spoken celebrity. But Tunney would not be enticed. For the
most part, when he wasn't on the film lot, he read and worked out, although he occasionally had dinner with Bill Russell, an actor who had
been a chaplain with the Army when they met during the Great War,
and a few other friends he knew in Los Angeles.

When efforts to hold the fight in New York collapsed in mid-
August, Rickard—who by then had been negotiating with officials of
the Sesquicentennial in Philadelphia, along with Governor Pinchot
and Mayor Kendrick—announced on August 18 that the bout would
be held at the Sesquicentennial Stadium five weeks later, which was remarkably short notice for just about everybody. That made what was
to transpire on September 23 all the more surprising.

Dempsey and Tunney already had begun training by the time the date
and site were announced—Dempsey in Los Angeles, New York,
and in Saratoga Springs, and Tunney in the tiny upstate New York
hamlet of Speculator. Under the terms of the contract, Dempsey was to

get $700,000 (the equivalent today of about $7.5 million) and Tunney $200,000 (slightly over $2 million). For both fighters, it would be by far their largest purses to date.

From the time the fight was announced, Dempsey was the favorite, even though he hadn't fought in three years; during that span Tunney had had nineteen fights and won them all. Though Dempsey had been a professional fighter a year longer than Tunney, he had had, according to most record books, only four more fights—eighty-one to seventy-seven—but most likely far more than were recorded. And Tunney had actually boxed far more rounds—513 to 320. But then Dempsey had knocked out most of his opponents early, including twenty-five in the first round, while scoring fifty knockouts overall. Still, that was only six more knockouts than Tunney, who was considered a boxer and not a knockout artist.

Contrary to reports that Dempsey had let himself go physically during his long stay in Hollywood, he looked fit and said he was only a few pounds over his fighting weight of 190 when he began training in Los Angeles in July. In the ring against his sparring partners, he seemed to be the same snarling fistic assassin bent on mayhem. Most sportswriters were impressed and were quick to predict that Tunney would fall within five rounds. After all, he was an overgrown light heavyweight with brittle hands and not much of a punch. In fact, Tunney, like Dempsey, had won most of his fights by knockout, but not many writers seemed to have noticed. As predictions of a Dempsey knockout grew, so, too, did the odds on Dempsey winning. It was hard to find a writer or an ex-fighter who expected Tunney to win. One of them, though, was Harry Greb, who had said after losing decisively to Tunney in their fifth and final fight that Tunney could beat Dempsey and had bet on his old rival. "You can set me down as a looney when I tell you I've put two grand on Tunney to win," Greb said. "I know what Tunney can do through personal experience. And I've got a line on Dempsey. When I boxed him, I had no trouble hitting him, for he hasn't got the speed stuff now that made him so dangerous. He can't break through Tunney's guard, and Tunney is a far harder puncher than people give him credit for."

Greb, though, was among a distinct minority. But none of the adverse predictions bothered Tunney. Over the last year, not only had he put on about 12 pounds—he weighed 186 pounds when he began training for the fight and would be the same at the weigh-in on the day of the fight—but his shoulders were broader and his neck thicker. And no longer did he have to worry about his once fragile hands. Working in lumber camps had certainly helped build them up, as had his daily habit of squeezing small rubber balls for hours at a time.

To train, Tunney chose a small resort hotel in the Adirondacks in the village of Speculator, about seventy-five miles northwest of Albany, which was owned by an old Marine buddy. Like his New Jersey training retreat in Red Bank, Speculator could hardly be more peaceful. Following his daily training regimen, Tunney often would go canoeing on nearby Lake Pleasant, then read for hours in the shade of a large tree or on the hotel veranda. While doing his early morning roadwork, Tunney would shadowbox for about ten minutes and also, from time to time, jog backward while throwing punches, then stop suddenly and throw a straight right-hand punch. It was the punch, Tunney was convinced, that would win the fight for him, not necessarily by knocking Dempsey out, but by jarring him and sending a message that would remain with him as long as the fight lasted. And running backward was not new for Tunney. During the previous winter, while playing golf in Florida with Tommy Armour, one of the game's greatest players, Tunney would, as Armour later recalled, suddenly run backward down a fairway, throwing punches and repeatedly saying "Dempsey, Dempsey, Dempsey." And that was before the fight had been set. But if reading a novel or a classic helped to relax Tunney, reading the New York papers did not. Always curious as to what the leading New York sportswriters were saying about the fight, he read about a half-dozen newspapers every day. Almost every account he read not only forecast a Dempsey victory, but a knockout. Confident as he was about beating Dempsey, the negative stories—especially the ones predicting that he would be badly beaten—began to exact a toll on Tunney, particularly at night. About a week after setting up camp at Speculator, Tunney began having recurring nightmares, during which he was lying on a ring floor, bloodied, badly beaten, and being counted out, with Dempsey hovering nearby, ready to pounce on him should he get up.

"One night at the beginning of my long training period, I awakened suddenly and felt my bed shaking," Tunney later said. "It seemed fantastic. Ghosts or what? Then I understood. It was I who was shaking, trembling so hard that I made the bed tremble. I was that much afraid—afraid of what Dempsey would do to me. The fear was lurking in the back of my mind and had set me quaking in my sleep, the nightmare thought of myself being beaten down by Dempsey's shattering punches.

"The vision was of myself, bleeding, mauled and helpless, sinking to the canvas and being counted out. I couldn't stop trembling. Right there, I had already lost that ring match, which meant everything to me—the championship. I had lost it—unless I could regain it," Tunney recollected. "I got up and took stock of myself. What could I do about this terror? I could guess the cause. I had been thinking about the fight in the wrong way. I had been reading the newspapers, and all they had said was how Tunney would lose. Through the newspapers I was losing the battle in my own mind."

At the time, Tunney told no one, not Gibson, McCabe, Jimmy Bronson—another handler he had met in France—or anyone else about the nightmares. "When the nightmares persisted, despite my inner conviction that I knew how to beat Dempsey, and indeed would, I decided to stop reading the sports pages, and did until after the fight," Tunney said. "I simply had to close the doors of my mind to destructive thoughts and divert my attention to other things."

If Tunney was a city boy who loved the country, Dempsey was the product of small, dusty frontier towns in Colorado and Utah who, in adulthood, felt most at home in big cities like New York and Los Angeles. Returning to New York occasionally from Saratoga Springs in July and early August in his effort to get a New York license, Dempsey worked out a number of times at Stillman's Gym, boxing's best-known training facility, which was situated on the second and third floors of a grimy building on Eighth Avenue between 54th and 55th Streets in Manhattan, just four blocks north of the third Madison Square Garden, which had opened the previous September and was far less ornate than the second Garden. There, in a cavernous room on the second floor that reeked of sweat, liniment, and cigar and cigarette smoke, champions such as Benny Leonard sparred, shadowboxed, and punched the speed and heavy bags alongside washed-up fighters who had never made it to a main event and never would and young boxers just starting out.

In one session at Stillman's on August 10, before a crowd of several hundred managers, trainers, former fighters, publicity men, sports-writers, and boxing fans who had heard that he was going to be work-ing out and paid the 25-cent admission to get in, Dempsey was at his most menacing, seemingly boiling over with rage. Over a twenty-minute span, the Manassa Mauler knocked out two sparring partners inside of two minutes, both with left hooks, and fought three full rounds—one round with one fighter and two rounds with another be-fore climbing a stairway to the third floor to skip rope and dig vicious uppercuts into the stationary heavy bag.

The following day, the *New York Times* account of the workout said it reflected "the fury of the champion in action more than any pre-vious workout since Dempsey undertook training while awaiting dis-position of his license application." Some observers felt that the uncertainty as to whether he would be granted a license, along with newspaper criticism that he was avoiding Harry Wills, had combined to make Dempsey even more ferocious in the ring than usual. And that was saying a lot.

While training in the Adirondacks, Tunney inadvertently underwent an experience that would invite ridicule from many sportswriters for years to come and create within a deep resentment of the boxing es-tablishment. As Tunney recounted the experience, he was returning from his morning roadwork when he found a reporter standing out-side his cabin. The reporter, Brian Bell, told Tunney that he had been sent to Speculator from the Albany bureau of the Associated Press to do a story about the challenger's training regimen. Consenting to an interview, Tunney invited Bell into the cabin, something he was un-likely to have done if it were one of the big-city sportswriters who had been demeaning his chances of beating Dempsey.

During the interview, Bell noticed a copy of Samuel Butler's classic *The Way of All Flesh* on an end table. Tunney had bought the book several months before at a secondhand bookstore in Los Angeles for fifty cents, both because of what he called its "provocative title" and because George Bernard Shaw had described it as a masterpiece during the book's literary reincarnation in the early 1920s.

"Are you reading that?" the alert thirty-six-year-old reporter asked about the book, a nineteenth-century novel about the dreary life among English curates and deacons in a small, and depressing, English town.

"Yes," Tunney replied. "It's a great book."

"So you like to read?" Bell inquired.

"Yes, very much so," Tunney responded, having no idea as to the ultimate impact of what, to him, appeared to be a minor diversion from the subject being discussed—his training routine and how he felt about the impending Dempsey fight. In truth, Tunney had been reading some of the so-called classics for years, often as a way to unwind while training for a fight. Before his fight with Battling Levinsky, for example, he had relaxed between workouts by reading Victor Hugo's *Les Misérables.* That was certainly a break from tradition, since most fighters at the time spent most of the long hours between early morning roadwork and afternoon training sessions playing pinochle or checkers, or listening to jazz records, or, of course, sleeping. With no interest in pinochle and checkers, and with a long-developed passion for reading, Tunney preferred to relax that way. "By doing so," he once said, "I forgot all about a forthcoming fight, even when reading on the actual day of the fight."

Brian Bell was bright enough to know that he had hit upon a very good story, one that would be far better than a piece on Tunney's training regimen. For the next hour or so, Bell asked Tunney questions about his reading habits and found him eager to respond, especially when the talk got around to Shakespeare. By the time the interview had ended, Bell, who later became the Associated Press bureau chief in Washington, knew that Tunney had been introduced to Shakespeare by a fellow marine on the way to France and that his favorite Shakespeare play was *Troilus and Cressida,* not one of the Bard's best-known works but one that Tunney particularly enjoyed because it involved constant conflict, and since the warriors in the drama, in Tunney's eyes, were similar in attitude to great boxers of his day.

But not even Bell had any inkling as to the eventual impact the story he was to write—which would appear in newspapers throughout the world—would have on the fight, on the rest of Tunney's boxing career, and, indeed, on the rest of his life.

With the fight now set for Philadelphia, both Dempsey and Tunney had to leave upstate New York and set up training camps nearer Philadelphia. The sites they picked reflected their personalities. For Dempsey, it was a dog track in Atlantic City, New Jersey, which was by then one of America's most popular summer resorts, while for Tunney it was the Glen Brook Country Club in Stroudsburg, Pennsylvania, in the Pocono Mountains, which featured a golf course, where Tunney would spend much of his time before the fight. If their training sites fit their personas, so, too, did the atmosphere at their training camps. Dempsey's camp, during his afternoon sparring sessions, resembled a raucous outdoor version of Stillman's Gym in New York, replete with scores of boxing managers, trainers, and former fighters, along with boxing hangers-on with at most a tenuous connection to the sport, well-known gamblers, gaudily dressed women—most of them with blond hair of dubious authenticity—and on average a hundred or so Broadway characters right out of a latter-day Damon Runyon story. All that was missing was the gamy and stale smell of Stillman's Gym and the cigarette and cigar butts that littered the gym's dirty floors.

In sharp counterpoint, Tunney's training camp was businesslike and almost downright sedate. The main pre-Revolutionary building, built of wood and stone, bespoke a genteel past. And while his workouts drew thousands of spectators and a large number of sportswriters, although nowhere near as many as Dempsey did, there were virtually no boxing hangers-on, like the ones drawn to Dempsey's camp, few managers and trainers, and certainly no flashy blondes. But there were women, hordes of women and teenage girls, who came to stare at and even get to meet the handsome Tunney.

"Every day at the improvised ringside there are as many women as there are men," the society writer Cornelius J. Vanderbilt, Jr., scion of one of America's best-known and wealthiest families, wrote in his syndicated column after a visit to Tunney's training camp. "And the majority of them are youngsters in their teens. Gene is the hero of 'Young Americana.' "

That might have been stretching it a bit, unless Vanderbilt was referring to "Young Female Americana." Vanderbilt went on to say that hotels and boarding houses in the Stroudsburg area had never before had as many young women as guests. "Hundreds of girls who take their vacations in September have come to the country to get a peep at their hero," he wrote. "And Gene has a smile for all, a handshake, too, and his signature when he cannot do otherwise."

They may not have squealed as teenage girls did several decades later during stage appearances by Frank Sinatra and Elvis Presley, but most of the young women gazed adoringly at Tunney's handsome features. Jimmy Bronson, Lou Fink, and other longtime boxing people had never seen anything like it and kidded Tunney incessantly about the female adoration.

"It would be difficult to find a more perfect Adonis type, every feature being correct," Vanderbilt wrote. "In a measure, his photographs reveal this; and perhaps that is another reason why he is the recipient of such an extraordinary amount of 'mash' mail. From all parts of the country, they write him, with some of his admirers being most persistent."

Asked about the letters, Tunney said some merely asked for autographs or signed photographs, while some others "might be considered proposals." Obviously proposing marriage to the handsome former marine was not the right approach. "When I am ready to get married, I don't want the girl to propose," Tunney said in referrence to the written proposals. "I hope to do that myself."

Damon Runyon, Grantland Rice, Ring Lardner, W. O. McGeehan, and scores of other writers came by occasionally to watch the Fighting Marine work out, and were suitably impressed by his sparring sessions with Jimmy Delaney, a well-respected heavyweight, and two other fighters who had worked for Dempsey in the past. Tunney not only sparred with Dempsey's old boxing workhorses, but later would sit with them by the hour, trying to pick their brains to elicit memories of Dempsey weaknesses or other distinctive traits in the ring that they could recall.

After that, Tunney usually took a brief nap and then played nine or eighteen holes of golf. Then it was time for *The Way of All Flesh,* alone and in peace. To the east, in Atlantic City, Dempsey might be playing pinochle or checkers or roughhousing with some of his sparring partners, which hardly would have been unusual. Even out of the ring, Dempsey could be rough, occasionally and inadvertently. At one point, while roughhousing with trainer Gus Wilson, he delivered what he thought was a playful blow to the side that sent Wilson to the hospital, where a damaged kidney had to be removed.

Outdoor training camps were common at the time, as they had been for many years, and would remain popular in advance of outdoor fights into the 1960s. The reason, of course, was that it made sense for a fighter to train outside for a fight that would be held outdoors. Dempsey, a sun worshipper who almost always seemed to have a deep tan, and Tunney, who loved the outdoors, thrived in such training milieus, but some fighters did not.

"The birds' singing drives you nuts," complained Tami Mauriello, a latter-day heavyweight, while training "in the country," as he described it, for a title fight with Joe Louis in 1946 in which he failed to last a round. Another city boy, Rocky Graziano (né Thomas Rocco Barbella), who grew up in Manhattan, found the peace and quiet of the country unnerving. "There's nothing to do at night but listen to the lousy crickets," Graziano lamented while training at Pompton Lakes in New Jersey, a well-known training camp where Louis and many other leading fighters prepared for major fights in New York.

By the time Tunney opened camp in Stroudsburg, virtually everyone connected with boxing, and a lot of people who weren't, had become aware of Tunney's taste for the classics. "The fight's in the bag, Jack," said bodyguard Mike Trant. "The so and so is reading a book."

At first, Tunney found himself being asked as many, if not more, questions about his reading habits than about Dempsey. Tunney explained that it was really nothing new; he had loved to read since he was at St. Veronica's, and had started reading Shakespeare while in the Marines. So, Tunney tried to stress, it was no big deal. But to the writers it was. A fighter—any fighter—reading a book was news. And a fighter reading a book—and a classic at that—while training to fight Jack Dempsey. Well, that was a very big deal, and a very good story.

As time went on, Tunney grew tired of answering questions about his reading. Yet he also seemed to invite such questions by showing up at his daily news briefings with a book. Early on, Tunney sensed that some of the writers, including such giants of the era as Lardner and Paul Gallico, thought he was putting on airs by carrying a literary classic to his meetings with reporters, and then, under questioning, talking about his literary tastes at length. To make matters worse, Tunney had a tendency—perhaps because of his reading—to express himself didactically and with polysyllabic words when simpler ones would have sufficed. Even worse, he spoke in convoluted sentences, often in what appeared to be blank verse, and in what most certainly appeared to many to be an effort to impress his listeners. That not only made him a literary poseur in the eyes of some writers, but also a phony highbrow, if not worse, and those opinions began to find their way into print.

Twenty-eight years later, Tunney reflected on that negative perception of him. "Of course there were some who thought it was all a pose," he told Associated Press sports columnist Will Grimsley. "It wasn't, I assure you. I had loved to read since I was a small boy in Greenwich Village. I belonged to three libraries and read everything I could get my hands on."

Tunney was too proud, and too reluctant, to recount that love of literature to the mass of writers who descended on his training camps—first in the Adirondacks and later in the Poconos. He felt that he did not have to justify his affinity for the classics. If they thought he was being a poseur, then so be it. Meanwhile, he would go right on reading in between and after his daily workouts. Once, when pressed, Tunney, somewhat exasperated, blurted out, "I don't think you have to be illiterate to be a boxing champion." The remark, if anything, only further alienated some sportswriters, who took it to insinuate that most champions were just that—illiterate.

Single, handsome, intelligent, always with his nose in a book and about to earn more money in one night than he had made in seven years as a professional fighter, Tunney seemed to the outside world to have not a care in the world while training for the biggest fight of his life. Dempsey, on the other hand, was being hounded by lawyers and process servers employed by Jack Kearns, his former manager, who had filed three lawsuits against Dempsey for money he claimed that he was owed by the champion for services during the three years he had been inactive in the ring. Of that amount, $333,333.33 was for what Kearns claimed was his share of a Dempsey-Wills fight that was never held—Kearns's reasoning was that it should have been—and for the Dempsey-Tunney bout, which had not yet been held. All told, the three suits asked for around three-quarters of a million dollars. Ironically, all of the suits asked for a third of Dempsey's earnings, the customary percentage of a fighter's boxing earnings that managers generally received. Kearns, of course, always kept half of whatever Dempsey made—in the ring, on the vaudeville stage, or wherever—but obviously felt it was best to ask for only a third in his suits, since keeping half of a fighter's purses was illegal almost everywhere, and so to demand that large a share could both raise eyebrows and get Kearns in trouble.

While Kearns turned up at Dempsey's training camp in Atlantic City to hold court with writers, mainly to state his legal claims against Dempsey, his lawyers filed suits in courts in Philadelphia and Atlantic City, seeking injunctions that would prevent Rickard from paying any of the $700,000 Dempsey was guaranteed until Kearns got what he claimed was owed to him. The lawyers finally succeeded in persuading a judge in Atlantic City to force Dempsey to post a bond of $100,000 on the grounds that Kearns was entitled to a third of Dempsey's purse in the Tunney fight since the contract for the fight was signed before Kearns's contract with Dempsey expired. In addition, the judge granted a motion for the appointment of a receiver to handle all of Dempsey's proceeds from the bout in the event the courts decided that Kearns was entitled to a share of the champion's earnings.

As if Kearns's suits weren't creating enough stress for Dempsey, the Manassa Mauler encountered even more legal troubles. A week before the fight, B. C. Clements, the head of the Chicago Coliseum Club in Illinois, arrived in Philadelphia with several lawyers and an injunction that had been issued by an Indiana judge preventing the Dempsey-Tunney fight from being held because, Clements maintained, Dempsey had agreed to meet Harry Wills in Indiana a year earlier. Clements had taken over for Floyd Fitzsimmons, the original promoter of the projected Dempsey-Wills bout for which Dempsey was supposed to have received $1 million. Dempsey, however, had backed out when Fitzsimmons was unable to come up with a suitable down payment and insisted that no contract had been signed. Clements begged to differ and produced a document purporting to be a contract for the projected fight in a city and on a day that never were determined.

Stories about Kearns's and Clements's legal maneuvers were front-page news in Philadelphia, New York, and Atlantic City. Dempsey, an avid newspaper reader, saw them, and although he declined to discuss the suits, close associates said that the constant legal wrangling in the days leading up to the fight was having an adverse effect on the champion. News of the bond and the receiver were particularly upsetting to Dempsey, as was the subpoena delivered to him at his training camp three days before the fight. Aides said that, in general, Dempsey was hurt by Kearns's claims that he had failed to pay the manager money due, especially since Dempsey hadn't fought in three years and in light of the fact that Kearns had handled all of the champion's financial affairs since they began their partnership.

Both Tunney and Dempsey, in addition to using several professional sparring partners, each had one ranking fighter in camp to spar against. Tunney boxed several rounds each day with Jimmy Delaney, whom Tunney had barely outpointed in a ten-round bout in Chicago three years before and then defeated again in another close ten-rounder a year later in Delaney's hometown of St. Paul, Minnesota. Delaney had also fought a draw with Philadelphia's Tommy Loughran, who was serving as a sparring partner for Dempsey, and who had beaten a number of the better heavyweights around. Leading fighters traditionally had made it a point to spar against at least one or two boxers whose styles resembled their next opponent. And if not a Tunney facsimile, Loughran was close. A slick, hard-to-hit boxer, he had beaten Harry Greb among others, and, in the opinion of some sportswriters, had gotten the best of Tunney during their eight-round bout in Philadelphia in 1922. Loughran, who was to win the light heavyweight crown in 1927, also had won a ten-round newspaper decision over a fading Georges Carpentier only three months earlier.

Delaney, although not quite in Loughran's class, fought out of a crouch like Dempsey, and, like the champion, had a good left hook. During a number of spirited sparring sessions, Delaney landed more than a few good blows, particularly to the body, but never got the best of Tunney, although he drew blood several times. Loughran, on the other hand, was more effective against Dempsey, especially with his left jab. In perhaps the best encounter between the two fighters, on September 15, Loughran bloodied Dempsey's reconstructed nose— which was a cause for concern in the Dempsey camp and a source of amusement for some writers—and blackened his left eye with a sharp left hook.

Some writers, though, thought Dempsey was holding back, especially while sparring with Loughran because Tommy was a leading light heavyweight and Dempsey did not want to hurt the popular Philadelphian. "That was a laugh," Paul Gallico of New York *Daily News* was to write. "Dempsey, who never went easy on anybody, would have broken Loughran in two if he could have caught him." Gallico, of course, had found that out firsthand when he got into the ring with the Mauler three years earlier.

Robert Edgren, the sports columnist and sports cartoonist whose cartoons first drew Tunney's attention to boxing when he was a young boy, was among those who were impressed by Dempsey's sparring sessions. "There is no doubt that Dempsey has done the impossible," Edgren wrote in the *New York Evening World* on September 18, "and that through a determined grind covering several months, he has overcome the effect of a three-year layoff and come back to fighting form." Yet Edgren, who had seen a number of Tunney's fights and had watched him train, was one of the few writers who thought he had a good chance to beat Dempsey.

Some other writers were far less impressed. Several said it was obvious that Dempsey missed having Kearns in his corner. Of Dempsey's current handlers, Davis Walsh, a writer for the *Philadelphia Inquirer,* said, "I can't think of a more inept combination, and neither can Dempsey, according to reports." Walsh was referring to Gene Normile, Dempsey's manager—who, Walsh said, was "a race track man who can tell you how a race can be run, but not how a fight should be fought"— and Dempsey's trainers, Gus Wilson and Jerry Luvadis. In fact, Wilson had trained Carpentier before joining the Dempsey camp, and Luvadis had been with the champion for years.

For all of his faults, Kearns knew how to run a training camp extraordinarily well. "When it came to managers, there was no one like Doc," Dempsey had said. Now, the champ found, there was also no one like Doc Kearns when it came to filing suits. Even worse, perhaps, Kearns, in between causing Dempsey legal trouble, was telling writers that Dempsey was not a great fighter and never had been and that he was worse now because he essentially had become his own manager. In essence, Kearns was saying that Dempsey had succeeded only because of his managerial skills. Dempsey's response was that if Kearns was such a brilliant manager, then how come none of the twenty or so fighters in his stable over the last fifteen years had won any championships? In truth, for at least a while, Kearns had managed Abe Attell, the former featherweight champ, and would, in the future, manage world champions Jackie Fields, Mickey Walker, Archie Moore, and Joey Maxim.

As the day of the fight neared, it was turning into perhaps the most publicized and anxiously awaited sports spectacle ever, both because of Dempsey's return to the ring after a long absence and the sense that Tunney posed at least a threat to his title. Largely because of Rickard's skill as a promoter, Dempsey was being portrayed as the villain for having evaded service during the Great War and not having defended his title for three years, while Tunney, the handsome, clean-cut former marine, was being cast as the hero.

In the days before the fight, Dempsey was more tense than veteran boxing writers had ever seen him. At times, he was sullen and unusually quiet; at other times he seemed nervous and looked drawn. Maybe he had heard all the glowing reports about Tunney's workouts. Or maybe it was because of all the suits that had been filed against him by Kearns, who had become his bête noir. Or perhaps he just missed his wife, Estelle Taylor, who had left Los Angeles by train on September 20 after some work in Hollywood and wasn't due in Philadelphia until the day after the fight. Among the few former fighters picking Tunney to win was Abe Attell. "Tunney showed me enough to convince me," said Attell, who had arranged to get much needed Adrenalin Chloride for Tunney when he was badly cut up in his first fight with Harry Greb. "I'll place four thousand dollars on Gene to win."

Greb, of course, had also bet heavily on Tunney. "I know that he is not a natural fighter, and does not look like a fighter," said Greb, who had failed to regain his middleweight title from Tiger Flowers a month before. "But at the same time nobody beats him much. He is one of those fellows who will not be beaten." Except by Greb himself, it went without saying.

Benny Leonard picked Dempsey to win, but that may have been to try to increase the odds on Dempsey, since Leonard thought Tunney could win and planned to bet on the challenger. "He's a marvel at taking punishment, and I don't think there's a man alive who can survive in a ring after Dempsey crashes that fearful left hook to the chin or the right hand to the body," said Leonard—or, more accurately, his ghost writer, who had been writing daily columns for the Philadelphia *Bulletin* in advance of the fight.

What made Leonard's prediction surprising was that, at Billy Gibson's request, Leonard had sparred a few times with Tunney at his training camp and showed him how to elevate his left jab so that it would be more apt to open cuts around Dempsey's eyes. Leonard had used such a jab for years to inflict eye cuts on opponents. Moreover, Leonard had been impressed with Tunney.

Among the few writers who thought Tunney would win were W. O. McGeehan of the *New York Herald Tribune,* Harry Grayson, a highly respected sports columnist for the Newspaper Enterprise Asso-

ciation, Perry Lewis of the *Philadelphia Inquirer,* and Frank Mc-
Cracken of the Philadelphia *Public Ledger.* But most of the big jour-
nalistic guns, including Rice, Runyon, Ring Lardner, Paul Gallico, and
Westbrook Pegler, picked Dempsey to knock out Tunney.

Tunney was hardly surprised. But in an interview with old friend
Ed Van Every of the *New York Evening World,* he oozed confidence.
"Think this over carefully," he told Van Every. "What has Dempsey
done since he fought Bill Brennan back in 1920? It took him twelve
rounds to bring Bill down, and then he had to resort to the use of so
foul a punch as the rabbit blow. If Jack could not bring Bill down inside of ten rounds, how does he figure to fare any better against me in
ten rounds? I think I can say without boasting that I am a better boxer
than Dempsey, who must have been close to his best six years ago and
yet could do nothing with Brennan in ten rounds. That is one of my
reasons for feeling that it is in the cards for me to win."

That hardly sounded like a scared fighter, which many of Dempsey's
opponents had been in the past when they got in the ring with the Man
Killer. And if Tunney was nervous the day before the fight, it did not
show on the golf course. Playing eighteen holes the day before the
fight at the Shawnee Country Club not far from his training camp,
Tunney carded a 92, his best round of the year and a highly respectable
score for an occasional golfer on a tough course. "The day's golf gratified me exceedingly," Tunney, lapsing once again into an extravagant
speech pattern, told writers after his round with Reggie Worthington,
a member at Shawnee and a longtime friend, and Bill McCabe, one of
his closest friends, whom he had met while McCabe was in charge of
the Knights of Columbus boxing program for American servicemen in
France during the Great War.

McCabe, a sixty-five-year-old golfing novice, said later that Tunney had spent much of the round helping him with his game—giving
him solicited advice on his grip, swing, and other facets. "And I kept
telling myself that this is the lad that is going to fight the great Jack
Dempsey tomorrow," McCabe said. "Well, I might be worried about
it, but he certainly isn't." After his round of golf, Tunney finally re-
lented when asked for a prediction. "I am confident that I will win. I
do not despise the abilities of my opponent, but I have unlimited con-

fidence of my own, and tomorrow night's fight will show that I was justified in it." Convoluted, yes, but a typical Tunney sentence.

Surprisingly, years later, Tunney said that "on the whole the Strouds-burg experience was unpleasant." He wrote that there had been "much disloyalty and dissension among the members of my camp." It seems that word had gotten back to Tunney that several of his sparring part-ners had told friends that Tunney had no chance against Dempsey, mainly because he couldn't hit hard enough. In fact, Tunney, as always, focused more on defense during sparring sessions and held back from punching hard and risking injury to his sensitive hands or to his spar mates. If Dempsey beat up on sparring partners unmercifully, no mat-ter if they already had been hurt, Tunney always refrained from trying to hurt a sparring partner, feeling that it served no purpose. Thus he felt a sense of betrayal when he got wind that some of his sparring part-ners, apparently unaware that he was holding back to protect his hands and them, had denigrated his chances of winning.

No golfer, apart from a round he had played with Georges Carpentier, Dempsey started off the day before the fight with a four-mile hike in Atlantic City. He spent the rest of the day relaxing, playing checkers with bodyguard Mike Trant, the Chicago detective, and sitting on the porch of his cottage reading the sports pages and listening to jazz records. Smiling and appearing relaxed, Dempsey told reporters, "I'm going in there to make a short fight. I'll be tearing after Tunney from the sound of the first gong, and I'll be trying to knock out Tunney with the first punch if I can because I know he will be trying to do the same to me. One thing is certain. I'm in excellent condition, and ready for the battle of my life." Dempsey also got some good news. One of the legal weights that he had been bearing in the month before the fight was lifted when a three-judge panel in Philadelphia dismissed a move for an injunction by B. C. Clements, the Chicago promoter who had tried to stop the title bout. In Common Pleas Court, the three judges ruled that Clements failed to produce any proof that the Chicago promoters were prepared to go ahead with a projected title fight between Dempsey and Harry Wills the previous year. Nor, the judges ruled, had the promoters complied with the terms of an alleged contract by giving Dempsey a

$300,000 advance. Jack Kearns's suits were still pending, but it looked more and more as if they also would be dismissed.

Strangely enough, two days before the fight, Dempsey said that he expected to lose eventually and that Tunney was the type of fighter he preferred to lose to. In one of the final columns Dempsey—really his ghost writer, believed to be sportswriter Frank Menke—wrote for the *Philadelphia Inquirer*, Dempsey said that when it came time to lose, he would prefer that "my successor would be some fine, clean American who would stand for and uphold the highest ideals of the boxing game . . . some one of the type of Gene Tunney." Dempsey, or his ghost, quickly added, however, that he did not expect to lose to Tunney.

The day before the fight, a rumor spread that Tunney planned to fly to Philadelphia the morning of the fight. Not many people were traveling by plane in 1926—Charles Lindbergh would make his historic solo flight across the Atlantic eight months later—and certainly not fighters on the day of a big fight, and the Dempsey-Tunney bout was looming as the biggest ever in terms of attendance and worldwide attention. Tunney himself tried to dismiss the rumor. "No, I certainly am not going to fly to Philadelphia," he told Mary Dixon Thayer of the *Philadelphia Inquirer* during an interview at the Glen Brook Country Club. "If Tex Rickard believes this crazy rumor, he will be up here after me with a machine gun, and I wouldn't blame him." Tunney added that he was unsure whether he would make the trip by train or car, but did say, "I think it will be by motor with Wade Morton, a Philadelphia friend." Tunney's comment was reassuring to Tex Rickard, who had heard the rumor and, while he was convinced that Tunney would never do such a thing, found it disquieting.

Most writers assigned to cover Tunney in Stroudsburg had left by late afternoon after being told that the challenger would be leaving for Philadelphia by car the next morning. The *New York Times* once again diverted its star reporter, Elmer Davis, from the world beat and assigned him to the fight. Already in Philadelphia the day before the bout, Davis filed a front-page story that forecast Dempsey and Tunney would square off "before the largest crowd of any kind since the games in the Roman Circus Maximus were called on account of the darkness

of the dark ages." Davis did not say how big the crowds were at the
Circus Maximus games, but he was probably right when he said the
gathering at the Dempsey-Tunney fight would at least be as large.

Before dinner during his last day at Stroudsburg, Tunney went
through a most unusual and unscheduled sparring session witnessed
only by his trainers, Lou Fink and Lou Brix, confidant Jimmy Bronson, and one lone writer—Jackie Farrell of the New York *Daily News*.
During the session, Tunney boxed three sparring partners for one
round apiece while never throwing a single punch. For nine uninter-
rupted minutes, without any rest, Tunney let his opponents attack him
at will while he merely parried all of the blows, either by dodging or
blocking the punches. By the time the nine minutes were up, not a single punch had landed on Tunney. Farrell, a veteran boxing writer, later
said it was the best boxing exhibition he had ever seen. Still, Farrell
picked Dempsey to win the fight.

As most fighters do on the night before a fight, both Dempsey and
Tunney went to bed early, around ten o'clock. Dempsey had dined
with Gene Normile and Philadelphia Jack O'Brien, whom he had
hired as his new chief second a few days earlier, while Tunney had a
light dinner at the Glen Brook club with his brother, Tom, his close
friend Bernard Gimbel, Jimmy Bronson, and the movie actor and
longtime friend Bill Russell.

After dinner, Tunney saw his manager, Billy Gibson, in an animated
conversation with Abe Attell in the club's foyer. Attell's unsavory reputation was known to Tunney, but he had learned to accept him being
around because of his close friendship with Gibson. Tunney had heard
how Attell, the world featherweight champion from 1906 until 1912
and a member of the Boxing Hall of Fame, had probably thrown more
fights than all of the other champions of his era put together. Since retiring from the ring, Attell had stayed active as a gambler, mainly on
horse racing and boxing, and he had put a bundle on Tunney to win.
But what in the world, Tunney wondered, was he doing at the Glen
Brook Country Club the day before the Dempsey fight talking to Billy
Gibson? Quite a few boxing people who knew all about Attell would
have wondered the same thing, but along more sinister lines.

*Tunney with retired lightweight champ Benny
Leonard (left) and Tommy Gibbons (right).*
STANLEY WESTON COLLECTION

EIGHTEEN

Rich Men,
Poor Men,
Beggar Men,
and Thieves

R arely, if ever, have so many people descended on an American
city in a single day as happened on September 23, 1926. The
city was Philadelphia, and by most accounts more than a hundred thousand visitors, including about seventy-five thousand
from New York and New Jersey alone, arrived by train, automobile,
and bus in the City of Brotherly Love on that early fall day.

Railroad officials said about sixty thousand riders had boarded regularly scheduled and chartered trains at New York's Pennsylvania Station alone on the day of the Dempsey-Tunney bout, while another
fifteen thousand departed on trains leaving from Jersey City, most of
them between 1:00 and 5:00 P.M., for the two-hour train ride. "Never,
according to station officials, has the Pennsylvania Station held so
many men celebrated for wealth or achievement or both, as it did during these four hours yesterday afternoon," the *New York Times* was to
report. "Faces made familiar by the rotogravure sections could be seen
not singly, nor in small groups, but in hundreds."

Among the thousands leaving New York by private rail car were some of the biggest panjandrums on Wall Street and from the business, banking, and manufacturing worlds and show business. Indeed, no other sporting event, or any other event for that matter, had ever attracted such an assemblage of the rich and famous. From New York, in addition to Astors and Vanderbilts, came Irving Berlin; future New York governor and president, Franklin Delano Roosevelt; the late President Theodore Roosevelt's three sons, Theodore, Kermit, and Archie; publisher William Randolph Hearst; W. Averell Harriman; Condé Nast, the magazine publisher; theatrical producers Florenz Ziegfeld, David Belasco, George White, and William Brady (who had managed James J. Corbett); the noted horseman George D. Widener (with a party of nine); Gertrude Ederle (who earlier in the year had become the first woman to swim the English Channel); Walter Chrysler, the head of the Chrysler Corporation; Tammany Hall leader George Olvany; Jacob Ruppert, the owner of the New York Yankees and its star player, Babe Ruth; John McGraw, the manager of the New York Giants; Wilbur Robinson, the owner and manager of the Brooklyn Robins (later to become the Dodgers); Mayor Jimmy Walker; James J. Farley, the chairman of the New York State Athletic Commission, who had fought to keep the fight out of New York; George Walker, donor of golf's Walker Cup; socialites Anne Morgan (daughter of the late J. Pierpont Morgan), Alice Roosevelt, and Harry Payne Whitney; and the actress and socialite Peggy Hopkins Joyce, who once publicly proclaimed that Dempsey was her "lover," only to have the champion respond by saying that the first he knew of the relationship was when Joyce made the announcement.

"If holding hands with her once makes me her lover, then I guess I am," Dempsey said in squelching any talk about a romantic entanglement.

Additionally, the New York contingent included scores of Wall Street financiers, banking leaders, captains of industry, real estate moguls, merchant princes like Ellis Gimbel; Leopold Stokowski, the renowned conductor, who at the time conducted the Philadelphia Symphony orchestra; Mrs. Douglas MacArthur, the wife of the general; the presidents of the Pennsylvania Railroad, the New York Central Railroad, and the Central Railroad of New Jersey; and Broadway characters such as One-Eyed Connolly, the illustrious gate-crasher, who would not only succeed in gaining entry without a ticket but would get as close as the press section before being ushered to a seat more distant from the ring.

Coming from the Far West, also by rail and partying during much of the five-day cross-country trip in their private cars, were such Hollywood film stars as Charlie Chaplin, Tom Mix (Dempsey's cowboy film hero and friend), Mae West, Norma Talmadge, Hope Hampton, comedian Eddie Foy, and another cowboy star of the silver screen, William S. Hart. From the Midwest came top executives of the country's major auto and steel companies; J. Ogden Armour, the meatpacking magnate; Harry Sinclair, the oil baron; Barney Oldfield, the famous race car driver; William Wrigley, Jr., the head of the chewing gum company and owner of the Chicago Cubs baseball team; several prominent newspaper publishers, including Joseph Pulitzer; the mayors of a half-dozen cities, and a host of big-city political bosses and lesser politicians, along with such gangland figures as Al Capone and some of the country's other large-scale bootleggers.

The Washington establishment also was well represented. Because of Philadelphia's proximity to the nation's capital, cabinet officials, including Secretary of the Treasury Andrew Mellon, the secretaries of the Navy and War departments, members of Congress, and hundreds of others, including a large number of foreign diplomats, descended on Philadelphia, as did the governors of eight states, including Al Smith of New York, who in the past had openly expressed a dislike for boxing but felt it politically and socially necessary that he attend the fight since one of his constituents, Tunney, was one of the stars of this glittering show.

Philadelphia society also was out in full force, including some of the city's most distinguished families, such as the Biddles, Drexels, and Shibes, along with Charles Schwab, chairman of the board of the Bethlehem Steel Company, and Samuel Vauclain, the president of the Baldwin Locomotive Works, who purchased about 2,500 ringside tickets at a cost of $67,000. Also seated at ringside were Bobby Jones, the golfer, and George Von Elm, who, six days earlier, had ended Jones's two-year run as the United States amateur champion at Baltusrol in Short Hills, New Jersey.

In his lead story in the *New York Times,* the day after the fight, Elmer Davis estimated that the crowd, which he described as "the most opulent and most distinguished that ever saw a fight," included an "estimated" 2,000 millionaires. "In fact," Davis wrote, "almost everybody who professes to be a person of prominence and who was able to get down to Philadelphia at this particular time was on the premises."

Never had a sports event in the United States drawn such a diverse mélange of well-known, affluent, and influential people. And never had so many women attended a boxing bout, with the *Philadelphia Bulletin* estimating that at least 10,000 of those in the crowd of about 135,000 were women, many of them socialites from New York, Philadelphia, Boston, and Chicago. So much so that most of Philadelphia's six newspapers assigned society writers to the fight, as much to see what some of America's most prosperous women wore, where they and their husbands or other companions sat (virtually all were at the expansive ringside) and with whom; how they comported themselves; and, when possible, how they reacted, both to the fight and to the overall atmosphere. Tex Rickard had made boxing respectable for women as far back as 1906, but no fight had ever drawn anywhere near as many women as the one about to break attendance and gate receipts records in Philadelphia.

Most of the women, and perhaps a majority of the men on hand, had never seen a boxing bout before. But the Dempsey-Tunney fight had come to transcend sport and become more of a happening than a sporting event, in part because it marked Dempsey's return and in part because of the sharp contrast between the Manassa Mauler and the handsome ex-marine who read Shakespeare. At least some of the women, no doubt, had come to the fight to see whether this boxing "Adonis," as Cornelius Vanderbilt, Jr., had described Tunney, really was as good-looking as Vanderbilt said.

What made the size and composition of the crowd particularly remarkable was the event itself—a prizefight. Only seven years before, boxing had been banned in New York, Pennsylvania, and in most other states and most countries, as it had been during almost all of the nineteenth century and during most of the first two decades of the twentieth. Riddled with corruption whenever it had been legalized in the United States, the sport had been tarnished by fixed fights and gangster infiltration, and it had appealed mainly to the lowest element of society. But now here in Philadelphia, one of America's most genteel cities, some of the country's most prominent citizens were brushing against one another on their way to their ringside seats to witness a boxing bout that had evolved into an event of epic proportions. In the process, they had bestowed a simulacrum of respectability to the sport.

In the eyes of many Philadelphians, securing the Dempsey-Tunney fight had been a huge achievement. The City of Brotherly Love may have been the site of the Constitutional Convention and the signing of the Declaration of Independence, but it was always overshadowed by New York, only about ninety miles away. It may have had the Liberty Bell, a major seaport, a renowned symphony orchestra, two big-league baseball teams, and a number of other attractions, both historical and cultural, but New York had Broadway, the Metropolitan Opera, Times Square, the Wall Street financial district, the world's most famous the-atrical district, the the Statue of Liberty, Madison Square Garden, and three big-league baseball teams. All of that was enough to give Philly, as it was known, a collective inferiority complex. But now it was stag-ing the biggest sports attraction ever held before the largest sports crowd of all time.

Despite an accurate forecast of rain, it had become obvious by early evening that the crowd would break all attendance records for a prizefight. Sesquicentennial Stadium had seventy thousand seats, but Rickard had practically doubled that capacity by installing a tempo-rary grandstand at the open end of the huge horseshoe-shaped con-crete bowl along with thousands of folding chairs on the stadium surface. By 6:00 P.M., four hours before the fight was scheduled to start, the crowd had already numbered about seventy-five thousand, and by nine all seventy thousand permanent seats were filled, along with most of those in the temporary bleachers and on the stadium grass and run-ning track that surrounded the playing field.

Much of the pre-fight conversation among the spectators centered on how Tunney, in a startling and unannounced move, had indeed flown —through a thick fog, no less—from Stroudsburg in Pennsylvania's Poconos to Philadelphia that morning in a small plane piloted by the well-known stunt flier Casey Jones. Neither Gibson nor Rickard nor hardly anyone else connected with the fight knew of Tunney's audacious plan.

Rickard, aware that more than a hundred thousand tickets had been sold by the day before the fight and that another $1 million gate was assured, was chatting with a group of sportswriters in front of the Bellevue-Stratford Hotel in Philadelphia the morning of the fight when one of the writers broke the news. "Hear the latest, Tex?" the writer asked the promoter. "We just got word that Tunney's flying into town for the weigh-in."

Rickard, who had been in a jovial mood, blanched. "Goddam that son of a bitch," he blurted out. "What's he trying to do to me?"

To which Bill McGeehan of the *New York Herald Tribune* responded, "To you? What about himself?"

Apparently no one except Jimmy Bronson, Bernard Gimbel, and Tunney's brother, Tom, knew of Tunney's plan to fly to Philadelphia, apart from Casey Jones and race car driver Wade Morton, who had finished fourth in the Indianapolis 500 race on the previous Memorial Day, then referred to by most people as Decoration Day. Tunney knew Morton, and had made arrangements through him to have Jones, whose exploits at air shows had made him the best-known pilot in the country, fly him to Philadelphia on the morning of the fight. Both Jones and Morton were sworn to secrecy about the flight. Though he denied it at the time, Tunney's intention, as he admitted years later, was to show Dempsey that he not only did not fear him, but had no fear of flying, even in a single-engine plane on the very day of their fight, which had taken on epic proportions throughout the country. As it developed, it was not a very good idea.

As Tunney was leaving the Glen Brook Country Club at about 10:00 A.M., to the cheers of a small group of guests and staff workers, he thanked everyone for their support, then evoked a collective gasp when he told everyone—including about a dozen reporters—that he was flying to Philadelphia. As several of the writers ran for telephones to call their newspaper sports desks, Morton pulled up in his Duesenberg to drive Tunney to the Shawnee Country Club, about five miles away, where Tunney had played eighteen holes of golf the day before.

Tunney then spoke briefly to the small group around the third tee of the golf course, where Jones was waiting in his plane. "I had to keep it a secret," he said of his flight. "Billy Gibson would have had a recurrence of his hay fever if he knew I was going to fly, and Rickard would have been down here with handcuffs. But you know it's really the sensible thing to do. First, I'll have a little diversion which will keep my mind off the fight. And second it will be much quicker than by train or motor car, and there won't be that continuous bumpy motion that is very hard on the nerves." Little did Tunney realize that the flight would be much worse.

With Tunney and Morton squeezed together in the front cockpit seat, wearing heavy leather flight jackets over their suits, and Jones, wearing goggles and an aviator's helmet, in the rear, the biplane took off at ten minutes before noon, leaving a swirl of dust in its wake as the group gathered on the ground at the Shawnee golf course looked on incredulously. After circling the golf course twice, the plane finally headed east toward Philadelphia. As it did, the mist grew thicker, eventually evolving into a thick fog, which caused Jones to lose his bearings.

Confused—this was in the pre-radar days when pilots flew with a limited amount of navigational aids—Jones found himself lost high above the Poconos for about a half-hour until the fog began to lift. If Tunney really thought that by flying he would avoid the "continuous bumpy motion" of a car or train, he found he was badly mistaken. As it was, the rapid ascents and descents necessitated by the fog not only made the flight "bumpy," but also made Tunney airsick. Growing increasingly nauseated as the flight continued, Tunney threw up twice.

By the time Tunney's airsickness had set in, word of his flight was big news in Philadelphia and in radio broadcasts across the country. The flight itself would be front-page news in many newspapers, including the *New York Times,* the day after the fight.

If Tunney was sick during and after his flight, Rickard and Gibson were sicker. When Jones finally made a smooth landing at the Philadelphia Naval Flying Field an hour and a half after taking off on an eighty-five-mile flight that should have taken less than an hour, he did so in front of a crowd of about a hundred people, including a score of reporters and photographers, a contingent of marines, and the commandant of the field. Climbing down from the plane, Tunney, who had sported a tan throughout his stay in Stroudsburg, looked pale and fatigued. As Jones struggled to get out of the cockpit in the rear, he smiled and asked his famous passenger, "How did you like it, Gene?"

Tunney, still feeling nauseated, was not about to tell Jones how he really felt in earshot of the reporters. "Oh, it was grand, Casey," he said with a smile. "I enjoyed it a lot."

From the naval flying field, Tunney, still airsick, was driven to the offices of the Pennsylvania State Athletic Commission in the Drexel Building to be weighed in. Sportswriters and others at the weigh-in thought that Tunney looked very pale. Frank Wiener, the chairman of the Athletic Commission, thought he had an explanation for Tunney's pallor. "I have just weighed Gene Tunney, and I never saw anybody so scared," he told Tunney's close friend Bernard Gimbel a short while later. "He is as white as a sheet. I hope he doesn't die from fright between now and ring time."

"He's not frightened," Gimbel replied. "It must be because of the flight." Gimbel was right; Tunney's pale complexion had nothing to do with the fight, but everything to do with his wretched air experience. Wiener remained steadfast in his belief that, as the fight drew closer, Tunney had become frightened at the prospect of stepping into the ring against Dempsey.

"I tell you he is scared to death," Wiener said emphatically.

"We will see tonight," responded Gimbel.

Tunney may have looked scared to Frank Wiener, but Dempsey looked nervous when he was weighed in at 190 pounds at his rented house in Atlantic City at about the same time Tunney was getting on the scales in Philadelphia.

Dempsey's trip to Philadelphia was nearly as rough as Tunney's. Accompanied by Philadelphia Jack O'Brien, Gus Wilson, Jerry Luvadis, and three bodyguards, Dempsey arrived at the Broad Street train station in Philadelphia at 6:40 P.M. aboard a private car. Along the way, Dempsey began to feel weak and queasy, and by the time he got to the Adelphia Hotel, he felt worse and vomited several times. By then, he looked as pale as Tunney had at his weigh-in, and Gene Normile and the others in his party were concerned. Alone in his room, Dempsey relaxed for about an hour, dozing off briefly, before leaving for Sesqui-centennial Stadium, feeling considerably better.

Dempsey chalked up his discomfort and the vomiting to something he had eaten, maybe the olive oil he took each morning before break-fast. Eventually, conspiracy theories abounded. One, propagated in late November by an Atlantic City police captain named Charles Mab-butt, who had been in charge of the police detail at Dempsey's training camp, was that Dempsey had been poisoned. According to Mabbutt, "a poisonous substance" had been placed in a cream pitcher that Dempsey had used the morning of the fight. How Mabbutt knew about the alleged poisoning he never did say, and virtually no stock was put into his account. For one thing, bodyguard Mike Trant said that Mabbutt never ate with Dempsey, and so how would he know that Dempsey had even used the cream that morning?

Years later, another conspiracy theory came to the fore when Jerry Luvadis reportedly told Normile that Dempsey became ill after Trant gave him his usual morning dose of olive oil. That theory seemed to have at least a grain of substance since Normile fired Trant the day after the fight, although he said it was because of Trant's association with gamblers and not because he suspected the Chicago detective of poi-soning Dempsey. Dempsey himself never gave credence to any of the conspiracy theories, speculating that he may have had ptomaine poi-soning brought on by something he ate.

As if his dizzying plane ride hadn't been enough to unnerve and phys-ically upset him on the day of the fight, Tunney endured another upsetting incident late that afternoon, about the time Dempsey started feeling ill. Having gone to a friend's house to rest after the weigh-in, Tunney had a steak as his pre-fight dinner about 4:00 P.M., then lay down to take a nap. About a half-hour later, Tunney was awakened by a knock on the bedroom door. When he opened the door, he found Billy Gibson, Max "Boo Boo" Hoff, and a man who turned out to be Hoff's lawyer.

Furious at being awakened from a deep sleep, Tunney asked Gibson what in the world was going on. Trying to calm his fighter down, Gibson said, "It is very important that you witness a paper to make sure we get our dough." Gibson said the document solely related to an agreement that Gibson had entered into with Hoff, and seeing nothing wrong with it, and anxious for Gibson, Hoff, and the lawyer to leave, Tunney agreed to sign it. Hoff's lawyer then drew a paper from his briefcase and handed it to Gibson, who then said to Tunney, "This one, too" while asking him to sign it. Glancing at the document, Tunney saw that it was a long-term contract between Gibson and Tunney. Irate at Gibson for trying to have him sign a contract only a few hours before the biggest fight of his life, Tunney threw the contract at Gibson, Hoff, and the lawyer and demanded that they leave.

Feeling that Gibson had tried to take advantage of him, Tunney, enraged and upset, never did get to finish his nap. Years later, Tunney wrote that Hoff and his lawyer were "trying to assure themselves of something in case I lost by a knockout. They had undoubtedly bet that way." Tunney never did say what assurances Hoff and his lawyer were seeking and why they sought them about five hours before the Dempsey fight was to begin.

Some people close to Gibson said later that Gibson had become concerned on the afternoon of the fight that the bout might be "stolen" from Tunney and offered Hoff a share of Tunney's purse so that he could exert whatever influence he had to protect Tunney's—and of course his own—interests. Supposedly, in the event Tunney was knocked down during the fight, Hoff was prepared to have a ringside doctor jump into the ring to award the fight to Tunney on a foul. Thus Gibson's eleventh-hour concern may have been the reason he interrupted Tunney's pre-fight nap to let him know about the "protection" they had been guaranteed by Hoff and his lawyer. Whether Tunney ever signed a document agreeing to such an arrangement never was determined, but the "protection" issue would linger, and to a degree embarrass Tunney, well beyond the fight in Philadelphia.

By the time Dempsey and Tunney arrived at the stadium, shortly before 9:00 P.M., it was cool, around fifty degrees, and overcast, with a forecast of rain within the hour, becoming heavy thereafter for the rest of the evening. Once the fight started, it could not be halted because of weather conditions—heavy rain, winds, whatever—except for lightning. Estimates of the vast crowd by sportswriters and Philadelphia police officials ranged as high as 145,000. Glancing around from his front-row seat in the press section, Ring Lardner did not appreciate the presence of some of those seated nearby at ringside—least of all that of Arnold Rothstein, the New York racketeer, who had engineered the fixing of the 1919 World Series during which eight members of Lardner's beloved Chicago White Sox, including the legendary hitter Shoeless Joe Jackson, conspired to throw the Series to the Cincinnati Reds.

Making Lardner doubly unhappy, his pre-fight glance also took in a key figure with plenty of connections to Rothstein: Abe Attell. Nearby, too, at ringside was Boo Boo Hoff. But then as the *Times* said in a front-page sidebar to its main story the day after the fight, the vast assemblage was a diverse one, including "rich men, poor men, beggar men and maybe even thieves." Lardner, among others in the press rows, most certainly would agree that the qualifier "maybe" was unnecessary in that sentence, since Rothstein, Attell, and Hoff alone were not only thieves but a lot worse.

Moving around at ringside greeting acquaintances and celebrities he recognized, Rickard was far more impressed than was Lardner with the bankers, industrialists, railroad tycoons, movie stars, Broadway producers, socialites, and other members of America's elite in the huge crowd. At one point, taking a seat alongside Hype Igoe, the ukulele-playing boxing-writer-cartoonist for the *New York World,* Rickard turned to look at the vast assemblage and said, "Hype, I ain't never seed nothing like it." Grammar was not Rickard's strong suit, but promotion was, and on this night he was promoting the most lucrative fight before the biggest crowd in boxing history. Now, if only the rain could hold off.

NINETEEN

■

The
Manassa Mauler
and the
Manly Marine

Pioneer sportscaster Graham McNamee
broadcasts the Dempsey-Tunney fight in
Philadelphia on September 23, 1926.
NATIONAL BASEBALL HALL OF FAME AND MUSEUM, INC.

By the time Dempsey and Tunney arrived at Sesquicentennial Stadium, they had both shaken off their respective ailments. Tunney's stomach had settled down and Dempsey's mysterious
queasiness had gone away. In their cavernous and bleak dressing
rooms in the bowels of the stadium, they were a study in contrasts.
Dempsey, as always in the hours before a fight, was fidgety and nervous,
anxious to get into the ring. Tunney, meanwhile, appeared almost super-
naturally calm, smiling and discussing the weather forecast—it had not
yet begun to rain—with Jimmy Bronson and Billy Gibson. Shortly after
nine o'clock, a half-hour before he was due in the ring, Tunney stretched
out on a training table and, in a few minutes, was sound asleep.

For the second time in less than five hours, a Tunney nap was interrupted. This time it was by Tommy Reilly, who had just found out that
he was going to referee the fight, and the Pennsylvania athletic commissioner Frank Wiener, who at the weigh-in had misconstrued Tun-

ney's airsickness-induced pallor for fright. Wiener introduced Reilly to Tunney, saying that the veteran referee wanted to discuss the rules with him. Tunney thought that was odd, as he told Wiener, since Billy Gibson and Jimmy Bronson had already gone over the rules with Gene Normile and Philadelphia Jack O'Brien the day before.

"You have read the rules, haven't you?" Reilly asked Tunney.

"I am very well acquainted with the rules," Tunney replied. "Is there any change? And how about the rabbit punch?"

"Barred," Reilly responded.

"How about the kidney blow?" Tunney inquired.

"Barred," Reilly replied again.

"Then are you going to enforce these rules?" Tunney asked Reilly.

"Yes, I am going to enforce them," Reilly said. "I want you to know that this isn't going to be a pink tea. This fight is going to be an honest one, and I don't want any complaints or alibis from the loser."

"What do you mean?" said Tunney, becoming increasingly annoyed at the tone of Reilly's questioning.

"I'm telling you that I'm in there to have an honest fight, and you both will be treated as though you are strangers to me," Reilly, his face reddening, said.

"Well, you are a stranger to me," Tunney said. "And what is more, you go and tell Mister Dempsey just what you told me." (Reilly and Wiener eventually did.)

Reilly, obviously annoyed at Tunney's suggestion, turned and headed for the door, followed by Wiener. As they did, Gibson, Bronson, and Billy McCabe looked at Tunney and then one another and laughed. Tunney, belatedly seeing a certain humor in Reilly's line of questioning, broke into a smile and went back to sleep, wondering why, at the last minute, Reilly and Wiener had come into his dressing room and why the referee had felt it necessary to go over some rules. Maybe it was because Wiener knew that Abe Attell and Boo Boo Hoff had been hanging around with Gibson at Tunney's training camp in Stroudsburg the night before the fight. Maybe Wiener also had heard how Gibson and Hoff had interrupted Tunney's earlier nap that afternoon. Those get-togethers with unsavory figures like Attell and Hoff would seem to provide good reasons for Wiener to have become suspicious. Or then maybe Wiener just wanted to see whether Tunney still looked scared to death, as the commissioner had said after the weigh-in.

Late in arriving at the stadium because of the choking automobile and bus traffic in the area, Dempsey had been more nervous than usual and in no mood for a nap. "Jack, for God's sake, hurry up," Tex Rickard said to the champ as he walked in with his entourage.

"Don't worry about the rain," Dempsey replied. "This guy ain't going over two rounds anyway."

Rickard, ecstatic over the crowd and a gate that he knew had already surpassed that of the first $1 million fight between Dempsey and Carpentier, told both Dempsey and Tunney that the crowd outside was the biggest ever for a fight or any other sports event in the United States and maybe even the entire world. Dempsey had been guaranteed $400,000, but with a gate of more than $1.5 million the champion now stood to make as much as $750,000. No fighter—indeed, no athlete—had ever made anywhere near that much money for a year's work, let alone one night's.

At 9:25 P.M., Tunney was awakened, again. This time it was by a security man, calling on the challenger and his cornermen to follow him to the ring, a walk of about a hundred yards. Just before leaving, Tunney turned to Gibson and said, "This is what you want me to do, Gib, isn't it?" Tunney then let loose a swift right-hand punch, missing Gibson's chin by a few inches.

"Yeah, that will do the trick," replied Gibson, a bit shaken.

"Watch me," Tunney said calmly. "Let's go."

An astonishing crowd—far bigger than even Tex Rickard ever anticipated—was waiting when Tunney, wearing purple trunks and a scarlet robe with blue trimming and the Marine Corps emblem of a globe and anchor on the back, began the long walk to the ring. As Tunney, looking straight ahead and with a trace of a smile on his face, came into view, cheers and applause grew louder and louder as he walked toward the ring. He had heard cheers before, but nothing like this. Cool and composed as Tunney seemed to be, the cheering eventually reached a point where it sent a chill up and down his back.

As Tunney climbed into the ring, the ovation reached a crescendo. Some writers thought much of the cheering had been evoked by Tunney's robe and the Marine insignia, which, they speculated, reminded many people in the crowd that Tunney had joined the Marines during the Great War while Dempsey had received a deferment and had kept on boxing. Whether it was a psychological ploy or not, Dempsey kept Tunney waiting for four minutes, a long time in boxing.

That did not help the champion's cause or do anything for his popularity. When Dempsey came down an aisle, wearing a white sweater (a common accouterment for fighters in the 1920s) and with a white towel draped over his left shoulder, and, finally, at 9:34, stepped into the ring, he heard as many boos as he did cheers. Most sportswriters were still in thrall to Dempsey; he was friendly and cooperative, the very epitome of a heavyweight champion. With a few exceptions like Nat Fleischer, the writers did not seem to mind that Dempsey took a three-year hiatus from the ring while holding on to the heavyweight title and living the high life in Hollywood and Europe. But many fans did.

Looking down at the first few rows of ringside while waiting for Dempsey, Tunney saw the faces of most of America's most famous sportswriters, including Rice, Lardner, Runyon, McGeehan, Gallico, Westbrook Pegler, and Heywood Broun. Also at ringside were Graham McNamee and Major J. Andrew White, whose radio broadcast of the fight would be carried throughout the United States, to South America, and to England, where the fight would begin at 2:45 A.M. local time.*

As Dempsey entered the ring and headed for his corner, Tunney got up from his stool, walked toward Dempsey, and said, "Hello, champion."

---

*McNamee and White had combined to broadcast the first major fight, the so-called Battle of the Century between Dempsey and Georges Carpentier in 1921. To a large degree because of his frenetic delivery, McNamee, a onetime concert baritone singer, would become the best-known radio announcer of the 1920s and 1930s, broadcasting championship fights, political conventions, and other major news stories. His frenzied, rapid-fire style, which placed higher premiums on excitement and imagery than accuracy in describing a sports event, set the tone for other sportscasters in radio's early days, such as Bill Stern and Clem McCarthy, and made his one of the most familiar voices in the United States. It also earned him the opprobrium of some sportswriters, who, hearing McNamee's description of a fight, sometimes wondered if they were watching the same sports event.

"Hello, Gene," replied Dempsey, somewhat taken aback.

When ring announcer Joe Griffo then introduced Dempsey as "the heavyweight champion who has defended his title for the past six years," there was a roar of boos that rocked the whole ampitheater. Griffo's introduction obviously was wrong, since Dempsey hadn't defended his title in three years, although he had held it for seven years. Dempsey had still not gotten over being booed, while Carpentier, a Frenchman, was cheered before their fight at Boyle's Thirty Acres five years before, so he was hardly surprised at the adverse reception he was receiving in Philadelphia. Griffo, though, had only made matters worse.

After receiving their pre-fight instructions from referee Tommy Reilly in mid-ring while surrounded by their cornermen, Dempsey and Tunney turned toward their corners as a light rain began to fall. As they did, Tunney said to Dempsey, "May the better man win, Jack." Dempsey, taken off stride by the comment, mumbled something like, "Yeah, yeah."

Such a moment, just before the bell sounds for the start of a big fight, and especially a heavyweight bout between two outstanding fighters, is far and away the most dramatic period of time in any sport. Tension is tangible and extends from the ring throughout the crowd, particularly close-up at ringside, where sportswriters and others get to see and hear the force of a punch and its impact on an opponent, which cannot be discerned far back in a stadium or arena and rarely, if ever, on television. Indeed, the suspense is far greater than during the minutes before the opening kickoff of a Super Bowl game or before the first pitch of a World Series. Everyone knows the football game is going to last sixty minutes, if not longer, and a baseball game at least nine innings, so long as rain does not intrude. But a fight can end in a minute or even less.* Spectators who take their eyes off the fighters for a split second run a real risk of missing a split-second knockout punch. And when Dempsey and Tunney advanced toward each other at the first

---

*In what is acknowledged to be the shortest fight ever, Al Couture, a journeyman welterweight from Lewiston, Maine, knocked out Ralph Walton in ten and a half seconds of the first round on September 24, 1946, in Lewiston. Less than a second into the fight, according to records of the bout, Couture nailed Walton with a right to the jaw that put him down for the count of ten. Thus the elapsed time, including the referee's count, was ten and a half seconds.

bell in Sesquicentennial Stadium in Philadelphia, more than a few people thought that the bout could be over very, very fast.

As expected, Dempsey went right after Tunney, who, also as expected, retreated. As Tunney would say later, he hoped that by backing up he would make Dempsey believe that he was afraid of him. "I wanted him to become a little overconfident," he said.

As Tunney retreated, Dempsey threw the first punch of the night, a wild right that missed by about a foot. Tunney then initiated the first of what would be many clinches, again to lead Dempsey into believing he was afraid to mix it up. After Reilly had broken up the clinch, Dempsey kept on coming, and again Tunney clinched. With a minute gone, neither fighter had landed a punch, apart from several left jabs by Tunney and some light and ineffective blows in the clinches by both fighters. Now in mid-ring, Tunney planted his feet firmly on the wet canvas and feinted twice with his left hand. Then, as Dempsey dropped his left slightly before throwing a left hook—something Tunney had spotted by closely watching film of Dempsey's fights with Carpentier, Firpo, and Bill Brennan—Tunney threw the punch he had worked on surreptitiously for months—a quick right-hand lead, which caught Dempsey on the left cheekbone, just as Carpentier had done with his swift and powerful right five years before. Tunney had hoped to land the blow on the jaw. Still, the punch had landed, solidly, and it had buckled Dempsey's knees. And Tunney knew from the look on Dempsey's face that the punch had both hurt and shaken him.

"He was stopped in his tracks and his knees sagged," Tunney said sometime later. "Perhaps if the punch landed on Jack's jaw, I might have knocked him out."

Tunney knew that a hard punch to the jaw had far greater impact than one to the cheekbone, since it often transmits a shock wave that results in a concussion, and, in boxing, a knockout. A microsecond after his first sneak right-hand punch, Tunney landed another right, which also landed on the low-crouching Dempsey's cheekbone. Dempsey, meanwhile, kept stalking Tunney, throwing right-hand leads and his patented left hook, but few of the blows pierced Tunney's defense, whether he stood toe-to-toe with Dempsey or danced away in a clockwise fashion to avoid the Manassa Mauler's dangerous left.

But by midway through the three-minute round, Tunney was fighting with an increased confidence and exchanging punches with Dempsey at close range, to the amazement of sportswriters at ringside and many others in the vast crowd, who felt that Tunney was courting disaster. Anyone in the past who dared mix it up with Dempsey at close range, and, in effect fight his fight, had not lasted long. The difference was that Tunney's punches—mostly combinations of lefts and rights—were landing and Dempsey's, from relatively long range, were not.

By the time the bell sounded, the round had been one-sided in Tunney's favor. Most writers and spectators were incredulous at what they had seen, mainly Tunney's temerity in daring to slug it out with boxing's Man Killer. Turning to one another, spectators, both the knowledgeable and the boxing neophytes, were equally surprised at how inept Dempsey had looked, missing most of his punches by a foot or more and offering virtually no defense during the opening round. It did not take an expert to tell that the champion looked bad.

Unfortunately for Dempsey, his cornermen, and his supporters, it was a pattern that would continue throughout the fight. The opening round had set the tone. More confident with each passing round, Tunney continued to dance rings around Dempsey, usually moving to his left so Dempsey could not land his powerful hook, but also becoming more aggressive by taking the fight to Dempsey. And the challenger was finding Dempsey an easy target, while most of the champion's punches hit nothing but air. But Tunney knew that Dempsey was always dangerous, and that it took only one of his solid blows to knock out an opponent.

The rain, which began just before the opening round as a drizzle, continued to intensify until it became a downpour by the ninth round of the ten-round bout. By round five the canvas floor in the ring was soaking wet and slippery. Such conditions are more likely to affect a boxer like Tunney than a puncher like Dempsey, because the boxer relies more on footwork, and in wet conditions can find it difficult to get traction. But a slippery ring can also hinder a puncher, since the puncher finds it more difficult to get set and establish leverage before throwing a hard punch.

Tunney, though, did not seem to be slowed by the wet and slippery canvas. Nor, for that matter, did Dempsey, who kept wading in looking for an opening that never came. Late in the fight, knowing that he needed a knockout to win, Dempsey rushed headlong at Tunney only to be met by a barrage of fast combinations of lefts and rights to either the head or body.

Following the third round, Graham McNamee told his vast radio audience, "We will have to tell you that Tunney has now won three rounds." That was stunning news to most listeners since the consensus was that Dempsey was likely to dominate the early rounds and probably knock out Tunney during the first five rounds. "He is outboxing the champion from start to finish," McNamee went on. "Dempsey is absolutely unable to get going. He seems to have nothing, except that now and then he shoots over a left."

Nearby sportswriters, who had grown accustomed to McNamee's hyped-up and exaggerated versions of a fight, realized that this time they could not disagree with McNamee. His assessment was right on the money.

It would only get worse for Dempsey. As McNamee said in his staccato fashion halfway through the fourth round, "Dempsey seems to be satisfied to take all the punches, anything to get in on Tunney, while standing flatfooted in the middle of the ring." Late in the round, McNamee added, "It is a very tame round, and once again Tunney shows his superiority. Tunney has now won four rounds in succession." Again, there would be no disagreement from the nearby writers, most of them stunned by Dempsey's inept showing against the fast-moving Tunney and his rapid-fire assault of punches, most of which were landing and turning Dempsey's face into a mass of welts and bruises.

By the fourth round, Tunney's swift and accurate left jab had opened a cut under Dempsey's right eye. But that may have been Dempsey's best round, which several writers at ringside thought he had won. In the round, Dempsey landed three good left hooks, the most damaging and hurtful of which was one to Tunney's larynx.

"Nobody gets to Jack's body as a rule and stays on his feet," Tunney was to say after the fight. "But I tried, and in the wink of an eye

Dempsey uncorked his left hook. It missed the button, but landed on my larynx. It all but paralyzed my throat and I was hoarse for a week afterward from the effects of that mighty wallop."

At the end of the round, McNamee said, excitedly, "Gene is landing, I should say four or five blows for every one that the champion lands, and they have more steam than the champion's blows."

The pattern continued for the rest of the fight, with Dempsey, snarling and snorting loudly while stalking Tunney—fighters have to snort for air since their mouthpieces prevent them from breathing through their mouths—but rarely landing a punch, while Tunney countered Dempsey's rushes with quick combinations and sharp left hooks and uppercuts and right crosses, almost all of which connected. At the end of round eight, McNamee told his audience, "Jack is showing no defense. The only thing he has been showing is an ungodly number of jolts on the jaw without worrying about it." Again, McNamee's reporting was right on target. Surprising as it was, Tunney, focusing almost entirely on the head, seemed to be peppering Dempsey at will.

By the eighth round Dempsey could barely see out of his blackened and cut right eye. Making matters worse, a chopping right by Tunney opened up a cut along his left eye. By then, blood also flowed freely from Dempsey's mouth. By the end of the round, the result seemed to be a foregone conclusion. Dempsey's only chance at that juncture was to knock Tunney out. But by then, Dempsey, slowed by the battering he had endured, seemed to have little left. His strategy over the final two rounds was to crowd Tunney, as he had tried to do throughout the fight, and unload left hooks and right crosses. Most of those blows, however, were wild and Tunney had little trouble eluding them.

At ringside, between rounds, some writers with early deadlines already began to write the leads of their stories and pass them on to nearby Morse operators to send to their newspapers and news agencies. Almost every story being typed out on wet copy paper in the cramped press area—everyone including the writers was uncovered, and thus soaked to the skin—contained the adjectives "stunned," "shocked," and "upset."

By the end of the eighth round, if not earlier, Tunney had to know he had won practically every round, which he had in the opinion of the two judges, and could have played it safe by spending the rest of the fight trying to avoid a knockout. But while still cautious, Tunney, rather than clinch repeatedly, kept countering Dempsey's wild offensive assaults by raking him with an assortment of punches to the head and body, ending the fight with a left-right combination to the face and two left jabs to the head.

By the time Dempsey came out for the last round, there were cuts around both of his eyes, his left eye was closed, his face bruised and swollen, and blood flowed from his mouth. By contrast, Tunney, apart from a slight cut along his right eye, was virtually unmarked. Before the final bell sounded, Major White told his and McNamee's radio audience, including several thousand Tunney supporters in smoke-filled Madison Square Garden, "There is a new champion in the making" and that Dempsey is "a hollow shell of what he was." White, however, seemed to have missed a salient point: that Tunney had had a lot to do with Dempsey's showing. If he appeared to be a "hollow shell," it could well have been because he had never faced such a brilliant boxer, who, contrary to popular thought, was also a punishing puncher.

Before Joe Griffo announced the decision of the two judges—referee Tommy Reilly's scorecard would only come into play if the judges disagreed on the winner—thousands of drenched spectators had already headed toward the exits. They did not have to hear Griffo tell them that Tunney had won. Not only had Tunney become the first New Yorker to win the world heavyweight championship, and the first heavyweight to do so by a decision, but he had won all ten rounds on the scorecards of both judges.

After Griffo's announcement, Dempsey, his face a puffy mass of cuts and bruises, walked quickly to Tunney's corner, put both arms around Tunney, and congratulated him. "Good boy, Gene," Dempsey said through his bruised and swollen lips. "You were too good for me."

"Thanks, Jack. You've been a great champion," Tunney responded.

Dempsey, wearing his sweater and with a white towel draped across his head, then hurriedly left the ring, accompanied by Jack O'Brien, Gene Normile, Jerry Luvadis, and Gus Wilson. Barely able to stay conscious, Dempsey was tended to by two doctors, who needed six stitches to close the wound over his left eye, and treated his blackened and cut right eye and bloodied lip. Quiet and seeming distraught, the deposed champion was eventually driven to his hotel room, still in his boxing trunks, and still silent.

Expecting to be serenaded with boos and catcalls as he made the long walk down an aisle leading to his dressing room, Dempsey was surprised when he heard cheers and applause, rising in pitch as he walked along. In victory, Dempsey had seldom been cheered—apart, perhaps, when he survived three knockdowns before knocking out Luis Angel Firpo, but even Dempsey knew those cheers were based on his remarkable comeback from near-disaster. The cheering startled Dempsey and brought tears to his eyes. Dempsey knew that the sight of him, bloodied, bruised, and beaten, had aroused a wave of sympathy among many in the huge crowd at Sesquicentennial Stadium.

"The people were cheering for me, clapping for me, calling out my name in a way I had never heard before," Dempsey said later. "I never realized how much I had hungered for a sound like that, and now here it was—on the night I blew my title."

Surprisingly, since he had entered the ring as the clean-cut former marine with virtually no chance of beating Dempsey, who had been labeled a draft-dodger, Tunney's ovation was more subdued as he left the ring. Rickard may have been one of the few people who was not surprised. He also was delighted. The crowd's reaction convinced him that, one-sided as the fight was, there would be a rematch.

In the dressing room, surrounded by a small group of friends, along with the ubiquitous Abe Attell, Tunney said that, in his opinion, the fight was essentially over from the moment he rocked Dempsey with a straight right-hand punch in the first round. "That blow won the fight," he said. "Dempsey was dazed for the rest of the battle, and I was a certainty to outpoint him for the championship. Jack was battered and worn out at the end, and I may have knocked him out if the bout went a few rounds more."

Later, Tunney issued a statement that paid high tribute to Dempsey. "Dempsey fought like the great champion that he was," the statement said. "He had the kick of a mule in his fists and the heart of a lion in his breast. I never fought a harder socker nor do I hope to meet one. Dempsey fought like a gentleman and never took an unfair advantage in the ring. Once or twice he may have hit me a little low, but always it was by accident. He never meant it."

Indeed, in the fifth round some writers at ringside noticed Tunney had said something to Dempsey. Asked later what it was, Tunney replied: "I said, 'Keep them up, Jack,' " an obvious reference to what Tunney had considered a low blow or two. To which, Tunney said, Dempsey replied, "Sorry, Gene." Dempsey always had been gracious to an opponent at the end of a fight—for example, helping lift the massive Firpo off the floor after he had knocked him out. And he showed the same grace at the end of the Tunney fight. "When the gong rang at the end of the fight, he threw his arm over my shoulder and said: 'You fought a great fight, Gene. You deserve to win,' " Tunney said after the bout. "I don't care what they say about him, he is certainly a man in the ring."

Later, Dempsey also issued a statement, which was both gracious and terse.

"I have no alibis to offer," the statement said. "I lost to a good man, an American—a man who speaks the English language. I have no alibis."

That seemed to suggest that Dempsey might not have been as gracious, or as willing to accept defeat, if he had lost previous title defenses to two foreigners, Georges Carpentier and Luis Angel Firpo. Both spoke the "English language," Carpentier much better than Firpo, but the fact that they were not Americans seemingly would have bothered Dempsey much more than losing his title to Tunney.

In New York, hundreds of supporters, including friends, gathered in Abingdon Square in Greenwich Village for a spontaneous rally to honor the neighborhood hero, even though Tunney had moved his family—his mother, sisters, and brother, Tom—to a house on Arlington Avenue in the affluent Riverdale section of the Bronx in the northwestern end of New York City. Thousands more had gathered to hear the fight and watch reports on the bout as they were flashed across the famous news scroll on the Times Tower in Times Square. Of the approximately eight thousand people who heard the broadcast of the fight at Madison Square Garden, the crowd's support seemed to be split, and the decision was met with a mix of cheers and boos.

That seemed surprising since Tunney had been born and raised in New York and still lived in the city. But it may have demonstrated the latent support that Dempsey had, which had been overshadowed by the slacker charge, the ensuing trial on whether Dempsey had misled the government in obtaining a deferment during World War I, and the fiasco in Shelby, Montana, where Dempsey had been portrayed as an avaricious millionaire athlete. The truth of the matter was that most boxing fans related more to Dempsey than Tunney. They could admire outstanding boxers like Benny Leonard and other champions in lighter weight classes, but as for heavyweights, well, they were supposed to be avatars, capable of knocking out opponents with one punch—not winning on points. Tunney may have been a clean-cut guy, and a veteran to boot, but he did not have a killer instinct and rarely knocked anyone out with one punch as Dempsey could and often did, and which in the view of many boxing fans heavyweight champions were supposed to do.

Nursing his assorted cuts and bruises, Dempsey never left his hotel room that night after returning there after the fight. Sullen and quiet, he lay on a rubbing table for a half-hour while Jerry Luvadis tried to soothe his battered body with a rubdown and Mike Trant tried, but failed, to lift his badly dampened spirits. Dempsey's flagging spirits got a lift a short while later when he received a telegram from his wife, Estelle Taylor. "Jack, boy, so sorry I can't be with you now," the wire read. "Cheer up and wire me where to come to you."

Estelle had been in Los Angeles for several weeks in connection with a movie project, and Dempsey was glad that she was not around to see him after the fight. But she would be tomorrow. Taylor had been determined not to find out the outcome of the bout until she reached Philadelphia the afternoon after the fight. And there was a good chance she would not, since she was on an eastbound train with the wife of fight promoter Floyd Fitzsimmons. However, when the train, the *Pennsylvania Limited,* made a stop in Fort Wayne, Indiana,

Taylor heard a newsboy on the train platform outside her compartment call out, "Extra! Extra! Tunney beats Dempsey by decision." That prompted Estelle to send another telegram to her husband, asking how he was and saying that she was anxious to see him.

Fitzsimmons, a close friend who was with Dempsey, promptly wired a response, which read: "Dear Estelle. Jack is fine. Lost in a rainstorm. No disgrace. Don't worry."

Saying Dempsey was "fine" was stretching things, since, in fact, he was both devastated and badly cut and bruised. But then, Dempsey didn't want to upset his wife. She'd been having enough trouble getting good roles, and their marriage had become shaky.

Before the night was over, Dempsey had already heard talk about a rematch. But after taking another look at himself in a bathroom mirror, he felt that maybe he should go back to making movies. It certainly was safer and far less painful. One fight with a brilliant boxer like Gene Tunney was quite enough. Or was it?

TWENTY

Grantland Rice, perhaps the best sports-writer from the genre's golden age.

"*Honey, I Forgot to Duck*"

Most Americans who hadn't heard the radio broadcast of the Dempsey-Tunney fight were shocked to wake up the next day and find out that Dempsey, the ultimate boxing warrior and archetypal heavyweight champion, had been beaten, and very decisively at that, by an overgrown light heavyweight who gave the impression that he would much rather be lying in a hammock reading something by Shakespeare or Victor Hugo than in a boxing ring.

An intellectual heavyweight champion? That was not only unheard of, it just wasn't right. Heavyweight champions were supposed to be like Dempsey—an aggressor who knocked out almost everyone he had ever fought and whose best defense was a fierce, even ferocious, offense. Tunney was an anomaly, sui generis among heavyweight champions, a slick boxer in a milieu of punchers. Moreover, he was the first fighter to win the heavyweight championship by decision and not a knockout. That didn't seem right, either.

Tunney, too, was struggling with the night's events. He may have been able to take a nap in his dressing room before his epochal fight with the heavily favored Dempsey, but in the quiet of his hotel room in Philadelphia he lay awake most of the night; and, like most sports fans, he was unable to accept the fact that he had won the title.

He had gone to bed after a celebration with a small group of friends, including his cornermen, and his brother, Tom, during which he sipped on a cup of hot tea. But tired as Tunney was after a day that began with a daring plane ride and ended with a victory party of sorts, sleep was hard to come by. Finally, at 7:00 A.M., he got up, still wondering, he later said, whether his victory over Dempsey had indeed been nothing but a very pleasant dream. Enjoying the solitude in his hotel room, Tunney finally called room service for breakfast and the morning papers, including whatever ones from New York that the hotel might have.

The new heavyweight champion would not be overjoyed at what he was to read, although he was pleasantly surprised that his hometown's most prestigious paper, the *New York Times,* had run a three-column banner headline on its front page, along with twenty-five stories, including six on the front page alone, and a two-column photograph on page one of the new world heavyweight champion from Greenwich Village. All of the writers who had predicted that Dempsey would knock out Tunney now seemed to be saying that Tunney had obviously beaten an over-the-hill and poorly conditioned Dempsey, who had apparently taken the challenger too lightly, had lost his vaunted punch, and who was stale after three years of inactivity. Some also cited the rumors that Dempsey may have been poisoned the morning of the fight or several days before. That prompted Nat Fleischer, the editor and publisher of *The Ring* magazine, to say that if Dempsey was the victim of any poisoning, he had been "poisoned by worry" as a result of Kearns's suits and the process servers he had been dodging leading up to the fight. That "worry" would linger for some time to come. A few writers also thought Dempsey may have been bothered by the rain and the soaking wet canvas floor in the ring.

Tunney found that amusing. "Did they think my side of the ring was dry?" he said on the day after. "As a matter of fact, the heavy rain probably saved Jack from being knocked out. I had him in bad shape one or two occasions, and the falling rain quite likely had a reviving effect."

Some writers also speculated that Dempsey was at a disadvantage fighting without a legitimate boxing manager—Gene Normile knew little about boxing and his main function was handling Dempsey's business affairs—and especially fighting without Jack Kearns in his corner.

The boxing press, apparently, was giving Dempsey a free pass, not to mention a plethora of excuses for having lost to a boxer who, presumably, would not have had a chance against the Manassa Mauler in his prime. The reference to Dempsey's "prime" seemed to be a stretch, since, at thirty-one, he was only two years older than Tunney, whose name many writers kept prefacing with the adjective "young."

Mainly because of Boo Boo Hoff's friendship with Billy Gibson and Abe Attell's presence at Tunney's training camp site in the Poconos, rumors had been rife that the fight might not be on the up and up. Ed Van Every, a sportswriter for the *New York Evening World* and a friend of Tunney since childhood, had written the day before the fight that there were "doings in the vicinity of the Tunney camp that did not look any too well on the face." Van Every went on to say in his day-after-the-fight story that Attell had been "close to Billy Gibson, up to the last few hours of the fight" and was in Tunney's dressing room after the bout.

In the month leading up to the fight, Dempsey had been a prohibitive favorite at odds ranging as high as 4-to-1, meaning a Dempsey bettor had to put up, say, four hundred dollars to win a hundred dollars. But on the day of the fight, as thousands of New Yorkers descended on Philadelphia, a flood of money was wagered on Tunney, dropping the odds to 12-to-5 on Dempsey. Some "betting commissioners," as the *New York Times* referred to major bookmakers, said "they had never seen anything like the change of heart on the part of bettors that took place today." According to Van Every, Attell claimed that Tunney supporters had held back until the last minute to take advantage of the larger odds after delegating Attell "to pass judgment as to his opinion of Tunney's chances." Attell, of course, thought Tunney's chances were very good indeed, and, like Tim Mara and Boo Boo Hoff, had bet heavily on the challenger.

Amid the sundry speculations, the one by Ring Lardner seemed to be the most illogical. In a letter to Scott and Zelda Fitzgerald, close friends of Lardner and his wife, who were in Europe, Lardner wrote that the fight was a "fake, a very well done fake." Lardner's conclusion was based on a conversation he had after the fight with Benny Leonard. The former lightweight champion had always been close to gamblers and told Lardner he suspected the fight had been fixed. That may explain why the Great Bennah had picked Dempsey to win by a knockout in a newspaper column before the fight, but then bet heavily on Tunney to win.

Lardner's reaction may have stemmed from his belief that Dempsey epitomized what a heavyweight champion should be, while Tunney was a powder-puff puncher (Dempsey, for one, would have disagreed with that assessment) and an intellectual poseur. There was no way, in a fair fight, Lardner thought, that Dempsey could lose to Tunney.

Because of the risk of a libel suit, Lardner could not write that the fight was fixed, or even that he thought it was, unless he had ironclad proof. So, to get the matter off his chest, Lardner set it down in his letter to the Fitzgeralds. Apparently by saying it was a "very well done fake," Lardner suggested that Dempsey had made it look legitimate by going the distance, even though that meant taking a beating. Yet Lardner knew that fighters who agree to throw a fight almost always go down early in a bout and are counted out. Apparently Lardner, if he really did believe that Dempsey had taken a dive, felt that Dempsey was too proud a fighter to feign being knocked out, and thus had agreed to lose, but to last the ten rounds if he could and absorb whatever punishment Tunney might administer, which turned out to be substantial.

In his letter to the Fitzgeralds, Lardner said he had bet $500 on Dempsey, giving 2-to-1, meaning the most he could win was $250. "The odds ought to have been seven to one," he went on to say, adding that "the championship wasn't worth a dime to Jack; there was nobody else for him to fight, and he had made all there was to be made out of vaudeville and pictures." In fact, there still were other fighters for

Dempsey to fight—perhaps even Tunney again—and if there was no more money to be made by Dempsey in vaudeville and the movies (actually, there still was), there was still plenty to be made in the ring.

Back at their hotel room after the fight, Grantland Rice told Lardner that, though he filed his morning-paper story from ringside, he had both a sore throat and hangover and didn't know how he was going to be able to file his piece for the next day's afternoon papers. "I intended to give Tunney a fitting tribute in my overnight story on that historic night. And I intended to go as easy on Dempsey as I could. I did neither," Rice recalled years later in his autobiography, *The Tumult and the Shouting.*

"Take a slug of bourbon and lie down," Lardner told Rice, who was already stretched out on a bed. "I'll file your overnight." For one writer to write a colleague's story was common at the time when many writers' motors ran on alcohol—bootleg hooch, as it was called during Prohibition. So it was that one of America's best-known sportswriters, Ring Lardner, who was familiar with Rice's grandiloquent style of writing, wrote a story about the Dempsey-Tunney fight with the byline of an even better-known sportswriter, Grantland Rice, on top.

Taking some literary license, Lardner—already an acclaimed short story writer who had published eight books—roasted both Dempsey and Tunney for putting on what he thought was a lousy fight, which many people thought it was. Then he phoned it in without Rice seeing it.

"Neither [Dempsey or Tunney] spoke to me for several months," Rice was to say later. "I couldn't blame either, but I couldn't open my mouth. I had a ghost." Rice did not hold Lardner's ghosted story against him. For years, they had been best of friends, although all they had in common were fondness for bridge, poker, golf, and gambling and the fact that they were probably the two best-known sportswriters in the country. But the contrasts between them were many and pronounced. Lardner liked to knock arrogant sports heroes off pedestals while Rice tended to glorify athletes. Rice was outgoing and talkative, Lardner reserved and quiet. Rice was an optimist, Lardner a pessimist.

Still, they had a great respect for each other and were close. Indeed, if the 1920s was the Golden Era of Sport, it was also the Golden Era of Sportswriting. Rice and Lardner, along with Runyon, Gallico, Pegler, Broun, and McGeehan, among others, represented a group of sportswriters whose collective talent has not been equaled since. At a time when sportswriters rarely ventured into a locker room, they concentrated on the event, and they did so with vivid and colorful prose, painting word pictures of major fights, baseball and football games, horse racing, golf, and tennis. One disadvantage of their approach was that they tended to get close to many of the athletes they covered, especially while riding trains where they ate, drank, and played cards together. That closeness made them less inclined to be critical than latter-day sportswriters, who, in addition to being more distant from the multi-millionaire sports figures they cover, find themselves forced to be more enterprising in their coverage and harsher in their assessments because of competition from television and at times, perhaps, because of the huge salaries most top-level professional athletes earn today.

In his story on the fight for the *New York American* and King Features Syndicate, Damon Runyon—who like Lardner achieved his greatest fame as a writer of short stories and screenplays—suggested that Dempsey showed that he was washed up as a fighter. "They all go the same way," Runyon said in his lead. "Another once great champion joined the big parade of the has-beens, the never-ending parade." Runyon, always one of Dempsey's staunchest supporters, went on to say that Dempsey was "so badly out-boxed and outclassed" that toward the end of the bout "he seemed more of a third-rater than one of the greatest champions that ever lived." It was one of several stories that particularly hurt Dempsey.

The *New York Times* ran two main front-page stories on the fight: Elmer Davis did the lead piece, which began on the first right-hand column, and James Dawson, the *Times*'s main boxing writer, wrote that Tunney "was complete master from first bell to last. He out-boxed and he out-fought Dempsey at every turn. All the evidences of the old Dempsey were merely that: only faint evidences, indications, unim-

pressive flashes, save for their expressions of futility, of helpless hope-
lessness, of utter ineffectiveness."

That was a harsh assessment, but it was essentially true. After all, in
the opinion of most of the three hundred–plus sportswriters covering
the fight, Tunney won all ten rounds. "In defeat, Dempsey was revealed as an overrated fighter, a man who was good, but never great,"
Dawson said. "It sounds uncharitable in view of his courageous stand
to say he had nothing save heart, but that verdict must be uttered.

"Those who accept this view theorize as follows: Dempsey won the
title from a cumbersome hulk in Willard"—it might be noted that this
was the same Willard who had knocked out Jack Johnson, one of the
greatest heavyweights of all time—"he beat a broken man in Miske,
and a comparative middleweight in Carpentier; he couldn't do anything with a brainy fighter like Gibbons; he battered an unschooled
floundering giant in Firpo, and fell when he faced his first real opposition from a man who was determined and unafraid and who could
fight as well as box."

Dempsey was both stunned and hurt when he read what Dawson,
whom he considered a friend, had written. What made Dawson's be-
lated denigration of Dempsey somewhat inexplicable was that he had
written glowingly of Dempsey in the past, and had picked him to beat
Tunney.

If he knocked Dempsey while he was figuratively down, Dawson
also failed to give Tunney any credit for his strong performance, saying, "Tunney is not a really great fighter." If he was, Dawson reasoned,
"he would have knocked out Dempsey." There, again, Tunney was
being denigrated for not having a killer instinct. Just being a great
boxer wasn't enough.

Dempsey, while refusing to offer any alibis, dismissed much of the
criticism about his performance and especially suggestions that he may
not have tried to win. "Let me tell you, I was licked by a darn good
fighter, and I only wish that some of the guys who say Tunney can't hit
could sample the first smash I got at the very start of the fight,"
Dempsey said. "There was plenty on that sock, and I never really got
over it through the rest of the fight."

As to insinuations that he may not have gone all-out to win, Dempsey recoiled in anger. "That is the one thing that hurt me more than any of Gene's punches," he said. "Some of the guys who I thought were my pals said things in their stories that cut me deep. There's always a lot of funny talk after a big fight, but some of the boys I have in mind"—Ring Lardner, no doubt, was one—"ought to know me well enough to know that I'd give my right arm to keep the championship."

Dempsey remained in his suite at the Adelphia Hotel most of the day after losing his title, bruised and despondent. His spirits were lifted, though, when his wife arrived. She knew her husband had lost decisively, but when she looked at his badly bruised face she blanched. "What happened, Ginsberg?" she asked, using her pet name for her husband.

Dempsey's answer, when it appeared in the newspapers, made him sport's most endearing figure: "Honey, I forgot to duck."

The pithy quote became a sports classic and elevated Dempsey's popularity to a level it had never before reached. Ironically, the expression also summed up his simple approach to fighting. You hit an opponent and you ducked when he tried to hit you. Unfortunately for Dempsey, he did neither very well against Tunney.

Late that afternoon, Tunney, on the spur of the moment, decided to call on Dempsey, unannounced, and arrived at the Adelphia Hotel about an hour after Estelle had gotten there. "I decided that although the world might have started forgetting the king that was, I would drop in sometime during the day to pay my respects to the fellow that had been so thoughtful and considerate to the kid on the ferryboat one day back in 1920," Tunney said.

Even Tunney was taken aback when he saw the bruises, welts, and cuts on Dempsey's face when Dempsey, obviously surprised to see Tunney, greeted him warmly. After some lighthearted conversation that left both fighters laughing, Tunney said, "I always thought you were a great champion, and I want to say now that you're a first-class opponent and fought as clean and game a fight as any man who has been in a ring." That was an especially gracious comment, since Dempsey had, on more than a few occasions when they were in a clinch, pounded punches against the rear lower part of Tunney's neck—the illegal and damaging rabbit punch.

Dempsey thanked Tunney profusely. "Gene, I'm sorry to lose the title, but I'm glad you were the one to win it from me," Dempsey said. "I want to wish you every bit of luck and hope you make a million dollars out of the title."

Even though the Dempsey-Tunney fight had drawn the biggest crowd ever to a sports event, along with a record gate of $1,895,723, Tex Rickard was hardly ecstatic after the fight, even though his share was close to a half-million dollars. Talking to a group of friends, including a number of writers, in his hotel suite, Rickard said, "I never thought it could happen to him." Him, of course, was Dempsey. Since Dempsey's split with Kearns, Rickard and Dempsey had become close, with Rickard helping to advise Dempsey. When a writer asked Rickard what he might do next now that Tunney was the heavyweight champion, he replied, "I don't know. This other fellow ain't ever been a drawing card. Dempsey was the one who drew them in."

There had now been three million-dollar-plus fights, and they had two things in common: Rickard had promoted all three, and Dempsey had been the main draw in each. Yet on this big night, the biggest in American sports history at the time, the old faro dealer from Texas by way of the Yukon and Goldfield, Nevada, among other places, seemed to be feeling low.

He should not have. As the *New York Times* and other newspapers stressed the day after the fight, the Dempsey-Tunney fight, apart from drawing a record crowd for a sports event, had succeeded in attracting many of the country's most prominent people. It also had drawn more women than any sports event in the past. And it was because of the promotional genius of Tex Rickard, who, as he had in his first two million-dollar fights, managed to convince people high up on the country's social ladder that it was perfectly acceptable, not to mention exciting, to go to a big fight, and to see and be seen by others of equal social status. Once scorned as disreputable, corrupt, and a vestige of barbarism, and attended primarily by roughnecks from the bottom of the social ladder, boxing—or at least a big fight—had taken on a cachet of its own and was now as respectable as going to the theater.

But one thought buoyed Rickard. Despite the one-sidedness of the fight, he still felt that a rematch was a possibility. Sportswriters already had enumerated a laundry list of reasons, if not excuses, as to why Dempsey had lost, and Rickard knew he could capitalize on those rationales. Besides, there were no other worthy challengers—or none that Rickard felt would draw another million-dollar-plus gate by fighting Tunney. Harry Wills was still listed by the estimable Nat Fleischer as the leading heavyweight contender. But after the contretemps over Wills that helped keep the Dempsey-Tunney fight out of New York—and, of course, the fact that Wills was black—Rickard wanted nothing to do with him. Neither, apparently, did Tunney, who, though he would never fight a black boxer, never gave any indication of being biased against blacks, and in later years would say that his favorite fighters were Sugar Ray Robinson and Archie Moore, both of whom were black and outstanding boxers, as, of course, was Tunney.

"Somehow it seems to me that it is not for the best interest of boxing that heavyweights, and champions, in particular, shall clash in mixed matches," Tunney was to say a few days after beating Dempsey. That may have sounded like a prejudiced comment, but in fact it was a pragmatic one: Tunney, like Rickard, felt that having another black heavyweight champion would hurt boxing economically. And Tunney was very attuned to the economic aspect of the sport.

Obviously ambivalent about his future, Dempsey told reporters in New York several days after the Tunney fight, "Gene Tunney is the best man I ever fought, but if we ever meet again I'll beat him. There's no maybe about that, either. He's a grand man and a a great fighter, but I know I can stop him." Suddenly, it did not sound as if Dempsey was ready to quit.

But given the decisive loss Dempsey had suffered to Tunney, a rematch did not seem to make sense. Rickard knew that, but who else was out there in the way of legitimate challengers? Rickard knew the answer: not much. The best prospect was probably Jack Sharkey, a cocky and talkative twenty-three-year-old who had won his last nine fights. Like Tunney, Sharkey was more of a boxer than a puncher, who had knocked out (or at least stopped) only six of twenty-nine professional opponents, and four of those knockouts were in his first five fights. Also like Tunney, Sharkey sometimes gave the impression that he wasn't particularly fond of prizefighting.

Rickard, like most everyone else with an intimate knowledge of boxing, knew that a fight between two boxers was usually boring. Thus, Rickard was hardly keen on a bout between Tunney and Sharkey, a former sailor whose nickname was "The Boston Gob," even though he was from Binghamton, New York, where he had been born Joseph Paul Zukauskas to Lithuanian parents.

Eventually, Rickard got another one of his highly imaginative and overarching ideas: Why not let Sharkey and several other high-ranking heavyweights fight it out and then match the ultimate winner with Dempsey? The Dempsey fight probably would draw another million-dollar-plus gate, as would a second Tunney-Dempsey title bout, if Dempsey won the qualifying fight. Rickard's logic was unassailable. Under his plan, he could conceivably have Dempsey involved in two more million-dollar-gate fights, whereas if he merely matched Dempsey against Tunney, and Dempsey was again beaten decisively, Dempsey would be through—and Rickard would miss out on another million-dollar gate.

On Saturday, September 26, Tunney returned to New York to be honored in his hometown, and thousands turned out to greet him at Pennsylvania Station. Accompanied by a motorcycle police escort, Tunney's motorcade headed down Seventh Avenue under a blizzard of confetti and through the new champion's old Greenwich Village neighborhood before swinging eastward to New York's City Hall, where Mayor Jimmy Walker hosted a brief reception.

From City Hall, Tunney's motorcade went to the Biltmore Hotel in mid-Manhattan, where a luncheon arranged by Tim Mara—who had won more than $150,000 on the fight but would wind up suing Tunney for breach of contract—was held in his honor and where Tunney received a number of effusive tributes.

After paying tribute to Dempsey, Tunney could not resist a dig at

New York sportswriters, many of whom were in attendance. At first, Tunney praised the writers, saying "many of them I count among my closest personal friends." That prompted some of the writers to look at one another and smile, wondering who in the world Tunney was talking about. But then Tunney indelicately recalled how he had once asked a former leading heavyweight, Frank Moran, how he had felt about some harsh criticism he had received after a fight. "When I mentioned it, he merely replied, 'Consider the source, Gene,' " Tunney said. Tunney's anecdote got a big laugh from the crowd, but not from any of the twenty or so sportswriters on hand.

But he was not done. "As a matter of fact, I have always baffled the newspaper men. They have always made me a short-ender, and for this I am grateful on behalf of the boys in the Village," Tunney said, alluding to his old Greenwich Village neighborhood. "They have profited handsomely, since in betting on me, they have always been able to get the best prices."

It was not exactly a scathing criticism of the sportswriting press, but Tunney's comment was enough to further alienate at least some of the New York writers, who thought that Tunney, in the afterglow of winning the heavyweight championship, could have been more gracious, but now turned out to be something of a sore winner.

"I made the error of criticizing their attitude toward my victory in a smarty-smarty manner," he was to say six years later. "This may have been justified, but it certainly was unwise. Practically overnight, I became the most unpopular of all the heavyweight champions. I could have been a more gracious winner. I goaded and gloated, and I deserved what I got."

Tunney may have become almost instantly unpopular with some fans and writers, but a multitude of people, including many war veterans and active servicemen, were glad Tunney had won. Dempsey, of course, had hardly been a fighting champion at the time and, although plenty of fight fans liked his roughhouse style, a lot of people did not. Then, too, many Americans still resented the draft deferment Dempsey had obtained during the war, which enabled him to keep fighting and to earn hundreds of thousands of dollars while young men his age were dying in battle in France. Unless you were a sportswriter or a member of the boxing establishment, Tunney, by contrast, was easy to like. He was handsome, intelligent, had served in the Marines during the war, was close to his family, and, unlike Dempsey, did not appear to be bent on hurting an opponent in the boxing ring. And he loved to read, which many parents were quick to point out to their sports-minded sons. To many parents, he also seemed like the kind of young man they would like to see their daughters marry. And thousands, if not more, young women, both in the United States and elsewhere in the world, adored Tunney, mainly for his looks and his physique, but also for his obvious intelligence.

With no challengers on the horizon, Tunney decided that he would take a long break from the ring, and probably would not fight again until the summer of 1927. He wasn't sure who his first challenger would be, but Tunney had a strong hunch that it would be Dempsey. Meanwhile, offers began to pour in to Gibson for Tunney's services, ranging from performances on the vaudeville stage and in a circus. One of the first offers was from the King Features Syndicate, owned by the Hearst Corporation, which wanted Tunney to write—or at least have a ghost writer write—a brief serialized autobiography that would appear daily in Hearst newspapers throughout the country. The financial offer was good, and all Tunney had to do was spend a few hours with Gene Fowler, then a star reporter and columnist for Hearst, who was assigned to write the series, which would appear under Tunney's byline. In his farewell column, Tunney—or, really, Fowler—touched on marriage, declaring that, so long as he held the heavyweight title, he would not marry, and, looking ahead, would not marry for at least four years. He went on to lament that he could not be seen in public with a woman "without having it fly thick and fast the next day that I am to wed." But then Tunney seemed to leave the door open to getting married before the four-year deadline he had set earlier. After saying that he admired a woman "who is clean, wholesome, and worthy of motherhood," he added, "If love should come to me—and the chances seem remote to me—I cannot predict with certainty what I shall do. Perhaps I shall be taken off my feet. Who knows?"

Gene Tunney and Greenwich heiress Polly Lauder. AP IMAGES

TWENTY-ONE

The Prizefighter and the Heiress

T housands of American women feasted on Tunney's words about the girl of his dreams, hoping that perhaps they would be the chosen one who would sweep Tunney off his feet. Unfortunately, they would be hoping against hope, since America's most eligible—and perhaps handsomest—bachelor was in the process of falling in love, and with an heiress to the Andrew Carnegie fortune, at that. Several months before the Dempsey fight, Tunney had met Mary Josephine (Polly) Lauder through her older sister, Katherine Dewing. Tunney had previously been introduced to Katherine by Sam Pryor, Jr., a wealthy businessman from Greenwich whose family was close to the Lauders. Impressed with Tunney's intelligence, manners, and good looks, Kay Dewing, as she was known, told her sister, then twenty, about the twenty-nine-year-old Tunney and asked if she would like to meet him.

Like her sister, who was four years older, Polly Lauder had never met a prizefighter and most certainly had never gone to a boxing bout.

But based on what her sister told her, she agreed to meet the handsome boxer, whereupon Kay Lauder Dewing and her husband, Ed, an insurance executive, arranged a dinner party at their apartment in Manhattan in the spring of 1926. Out of that meeting came one of the great, and most surprising, romances—and love stories, as a number of magazines and tabloid newspapers were to describe the relationship—of the Roaring Twenties.

Subsequently, Sam Pryor, Jr., threw a dinner party at his parents' house on Long Island Sound in Greenwich in the summer of 1926 shortly before his marriage that September. "One day at our place in Greenwich, I had a small get-together to which I invited Polly and Gene," Pryor wrote in a brief and limited-edition autobiography that was published in the early 1980s. "I had no intention of playing matchmaker; things just turned out that way."

Apparently things had turned out that way even before Pryor's dinner party.

To say that Gene Tunney and Polly Lauder were an unlikely couple understates the case. The beauteous Polly was a grand-niece (or a first cousin, second removed, as her family referred to the familial tie) of Andrew Carnegie, the industrialist and philanthropist, and had grown up on the family's Greenwich estate amid affluence and opulence. She had gone to exclusive private schools, including the Lenox School in New York and the Finch School, a junior college, which she attended in New York and Versailles, France. She also was a member of the junior leagues of New York and Greenwich and was listed in the Social Register. Her father, George Lauder, Jr., a nephew of Carnegie, had inherited his father's fortune, gone to Yale, and become a director of Presbyterian Hospital and the Manhattan Eye and Ear Hospital in New York. An expert yachtsman, he had died of pneumonia at the age of thirty-seven.

George Lauder, Jr.'s, father had grown up with Carnegie, a first cousin, in a small Scottish town near Edinburgh, and, at Carnegie's request, had followed him to the United States in the latter part of the nineteenth century and become a partner in the Carnegie Companies. After accumulating considerable wealth—estimated to have been more than $50 million—Lauder later became a vice president of the J. P.

Morgan Company in 1908 after Carnegie had sold Carnegie Steel to U.S. Steel, which had been created by J. P. Morgan, for $260 million and became the largest steel producer in the United States. The sale made Carnegie one of the richest men in the world, if indeed not the richest.

Like many wealthy young women in the Greenwich area, Polly Lauder, whose parents had moved to Greenwich from Pittsburgh a year before she was born, sailed on Long Island Sound, rode horseback with Sam Pryor, Jr., and other friends in Greenwich's wealthy "North Country," and attended debutante balls in New York and in Fairfield and Westchester counties. Most of her friends were from some of the wealthiest families in Fairfield County in Connecticut and Westchester County in New York, directly across the Connecticut border—one, Faith Rockefeller, was the daughter of John D. Rockefeller, Jr.—and it is unlikely that any of them ever had dated the son of a longshoreman from a poor neighborhood in Greenwich Village. Their boyfriends tended to have gone to prep schools like Phillips Academy in Andover, Massachusetts, or Phillips Exeter Academy in New Hampshire, and then, more often than not, to Yale, Harvard, or Princeton.

Certainly, in her social and academic circles, Polly Lauder had never met anyone like Gene Tunney, the son of Irish immigrants, who had dropped out of high school at fifteen to take a job as a shipping clerk to help support his large family and had become a professional prize fighter at nineteen. If the relatively tall—about 5′ 7″—and elegant Polly Lauder found a certain fascination in Tunney's almost diametrically opposite background, his love of learning, his high aspirations, and his love of the classics, he in turn was enchanted with her vivacious personality, her breadth of knowledge, her wit, her athleticism (she was both an accomplished equestrian and an excellent swimmer), her love of the outdoors, and, no doubt, her striking beauty.

For two years after they first met, they would see each other occasionally, almost exclusively at the Lauder estate in Greenwich, but also at the homes of both Sam Pryor, Jr., and his father, and at her sister and brother-in-law's homes in West Hartford, Connecticut, and Manhattan. Occasionally, too, Tunney would travel to the Lauders' summer home, a private retreat on Johns Island, about one mile off the coast of South Bristol in Maine. Although rumors of romantic entanglements often surfaced after Tunney had won the heavyweight title, they had always proven unfounded. And yet, the romance between Tunney and Polly Lauder flourished privately, unknown to the outside world, for more than two years. As it deepened, Polly tried to convince Tunney to abandon boxing. Though she knew little about the sport, she knew it was dangerous and feared that the man she had fallen in love with might get hurt. Eventually, as they became more serious, Tunney promised he would leave the ring, but, as he told Polly, he could not until after the rematch with Dempsey, and, assuming he retained his title, one more fight he was obliged to take under his contract with Tex Rickard.

In an attempt to assuage her fears of him being hurt, Tunney told Polly he was convinced that in his second fight with Dempsey, as in the first, he would rarely get hit, and most certainly would not get hurt. In truth, Tunney knew deep down that when you fought Jack Dempsey, there was always a chance you might get hurt, and badly at that. By then, though, Tunney knew that if he continued fighting beyond one post-Dempsey bout he would probably lose what had become the great love of his life. Indeed, Polly had already hinted at that.

Despite Tunney and Polly Lauder's successful quest for privacy, there had been clues to the relationship, but no one had picked up on them. Less than a week after beating Dempsey in Philadelphia, Tunney spent several days in Greenwich. A story in the *New York Times* on September 28 reported that Tunney had been in the Fairfield County town the day before visiting friends. After first paying a call on the Pryor family, the *Times* said, Tunney went to the home of Mrs. George Lauder, Jr., "where he was a luncheon guest." No doubt Mrs. Lauder's daughter Polly was at the luncheon and was the main reason for Tunney's visit. And so the romance would go for two years, with Polly Lauder dying to introduce Tunney to her friends, far more because of his intelligence, charm, and good looks than the fact that he was the heavyweight boxing champion of the world, which she knew they would find to be a remarkable paradox.

While Tunney was being swamped with offers for winning the heavyweight title, not many were coming in for Dempsey. For the most part, Dempsey's mood remained dark. Kearns's suits still bothered him, as did the beating he had taken from Tunney. A few days after the fight, he had told Rickard during a phone conversation that he was sure he did not want to fight again.

"I've had it, Tex," he told Rickard. That was not what Rickard wanted to hear. The promoter had become aware that, in losing, Dempsey, never universally popular, had become more popular than ever. He pointed this out to Dempsey and told him not to be too hasty in making a decision. There was a dearth of good heavyweights around, and, in Rickard's eyes, Dempsey might still be the best of the lot.

Two weeks after their fight, Dempsey and Tunney were reunited at the third, and new, Madison Square Garden, where they had been invited by Rickard to attend a boxing card. What happened before the main event fight was more significant than the fight itself. When Dempsey climbed through the ropes to be introduced by Joe Humphreys, he was cheered for more than two minutes. That had never happened before, and Dempsey was deeply touched. Yet when Tunney, the native New Yorker, got into the ring to receive a championship belt from the Metropolitan Boxing Writers Association, he heard far more jeers and boos than cheers. Dempsey, standing in the ring with Tunney, felt embarrassed for the new champion.

"That was an outrage," Dempsey angrily said later. "I felt just as badly as Gene did."

Tunney said later that he was not totally surprised. He knew that, when it came to heavyweights, most boxing fans preferred aggressive punchers like Dempsey, not the backpedaling fancy-dan boxer types like him. Maybe Tunney was not surprised, but the boos—in his hometown, no less—hurt.

To Rickard, the reception Dempsey received convinced him that Dempsey was still boxing's biggest attraction. There was no way, he told himself, that he was going to let the Manassa Mauler fade away into the sunset. Not when he was apparently more popular than ever and not when there was so much money to be made with him in the ring.

Disturbing as the boos at Madison Square Garden had been to Tunney, he was to feel far worse later that night. He was told that his old ring rival, Harry Greb, had died earlier that day in Atlantic City. Greb, only thirty-two years old, had decided to have elective surgery at the Atlantic City Hospital to repair an injury to his nose that was restricting his breathing. Greb had suffered the injury in a car accident shortly after losing again to Tiger Flowers at Madison Square Garden on August 19, five weeks before the Dempsey-Tunney fight. Tunney thought that Greb, always vain about his appearance, had had the surgery for cosmetic reasons, mainly to straighten out his nose, but doctors said that was not the case. Apparently Greb had suffered a cerebral hemorrhage shortly after coming out of the anesthesia that had been administered before the operation. Ironically, Flowers, a year older than Greb, was to die thirteen months later, also after an operation, in his case for the removal of scar tissue, only four days after his last fight.

Doctors who operated on Greb were astonished to learn that he had fought for five years with the sight of only one eye. His badly damaged right eye had been removed about a week before the Dempsey-Tunney fight and replaced with a glass eye. That accounted for the patch he had worn while attending the fight and betting on Tunney. When word got out following his death that Greb had been fighting for five years—and during that time beating Gene Tunney and then winning the middleweight title—with only one eye, everyone connected with boxing was amazed.

"He was the gamest fighter I ever knew," Tunney said on learning of Greb's death. Two days later, Tunney, deeply affected by Greb's death, went to Pittsburgh to be a pallbearer at the funeral of the Pittsburgh Windmill. Because of his rough, and even illegal, tactics in the ring, Greb did not make many friends in boxing. Yet Tunney and Greb had established a close bond. "Harry and I remained the best of friends, with not the slightest bit of anger or ill will," Tunney said following Greb's death.

Even though Greb had embarrassed Dempsey during two sparring sessions in 1921, the year he lost the sight in his right eye, Dempsey was saddened by his death at such a young age—only a year younger than he was. That Greb had lost an eye fighting also had a considerable impact on Dempsey. One of Dempsey's greatest fears was being blinded in the ring, and after the severe damage around both of his eyes in his fight with Tunney, he had become even more apprehensive. Now, the revelation about Greb having lost the sight of an eye at the age of twenty-seven gave Dempsey further pause about fighting again.

That did not help Rickard's cause when, during a luncheon with Dempsey four days after Greb's death, he tried to persuade Dempsey to fight a tune-up during the coming summer and then be rematched with Tunney in September. Rickard used all his wiles in making his pitch, citing the crowd reaction to Dempsey's introduction at Madison Square Garden two weeks after he had lost his title as evidence of Dempsey's increased popularity, and claiming that Dempsey's three-year absence from the ring was no doubt a factor in his loss to Tunney. But Dempsey seemed uninterested in fighting again, and Rickard realized it was best not to apply too much pressure. Estelle Taylor, meanwhile, was anxious to get back to the West Coast to try to capitalize on the new phenomenon of talking pictures, and so in late November, Dempsey and his wife, trying to keep their shaky marriage together, boarded a train at Grand Central for the five-day trip to their home in the Hollywood Hills.

On October 30, Tunney left by ship for a ten-day trip to Bermuda, where he was to spend most of his time playing golf and sailing, two sports that were of little, if no, interest to most boxers. A week after his return, his name was back in the news when, during a visit to Youngstown, Ohio, Tunney sought to defend remarks he made that seemed to disparage George Bernard Shaw's novel about a prizefighter entitled *Cashel Byron's Profession.* Claiming that he had been misunderstood, Tunney was responding to a comment by Shaw in London in which the author and playwright had said that if Tunney could rewrite the novel and do a better job of it, then, as far as Shaw was concerned, he was welcome to try. Tunney, in response, said he merely had meant that Shaw's novel would have to be changed somewhat for a screen adaptation, which was being considered in Hollywood.

"I would not attempt to advise him how to finish a work of literature any more than I would expect him to advise me how to box an opponent," Tunney said.

Little did Tunney know that his comments on Shaw's book would lead to a long and close friendship between the prizefighter and the playwright.

Under terms of his vaudeville contract, Tunney was to receive seven thousand dollars a week for eight weeks of appearances at theaters in a number of cities, starting in Manhattan on November 29. All Tunney had to do under the contract, which was negotiated by his friend, William Morris, the head of what would become one of the world's best-known entertainment agencies, was to spar for two rounds on stage and then talk briefly to the audience.

During Tunney's sparring sessions—each of the two rounds lasted two minutes—he demonstrated his quickness, his superb defense, and his fast hands. His sparring partner was merely a foil whose main objective was to make Tunney look good, and, above all, not try to hurt him, not that he probably could have if he tried. After sparring, Tunney spoke briefly to the audience, touching on his boyhood in Greenwich Village, his military service, his professional boxing career, and his passion for physical fitness, which he tried to impart to his sizable audiences. The sport of boxing, only recently having gained some widespread respectability, could not have had a better advertisement.

Tunney's first gig was a one-week stay at the Loews State Theatre on Broadway and 45th Street in the heart of Times Square. For thirty-five cents during the afternoon and fifty cents at night, customers could, as newspaper advertisements put it, see "Gene Tunney in Action," along with the silent movie *The Temptress,* which featured a twenty-one-year-old Swedish ingenue named Greta Garbo.

Tunney's contract called for him to make four appearances a day, each of which lasted about fifteen minutes. Referring to Tunney's stage debut, The *New York Times,* in a story that briefly covered the newest vaudeville acts in town, said "Loew's State has an important attraction this week in the person of Gene Tunney, heavyweight champion. He drew a large audience"—the *Times* did not say how large—"yesterday for whom he gave, among other things, a brief sparring exhibition."

What the review did not mention was that Tunney and two sparring partners, who were part of his onstage stint, were arrested, along with the manager of the theater, after his second appearance in the afternoon on charges that the new champion was engaging in an unlicensed boxing exhibition. The new champion, along with his two spar mates and the theater manager, were then taken to a West Side precinct, where they were formally charged and released on bail of $500 each. Both annoyed and undeterred, Tunney, along with his sparring partners, immediately returned to the Loews State Theatre for two evening performances "without further difficulty," as the *New York Times* was to report in a front-page story the following day.

Tunney became livid when he learned that the arrests were made at the request of James J. Farley, the chairman of the New York State Athletic Commission, who said later that night that theater officials and the New York City Police Department had been told in advance by the commission that Tunney's sparring on stage violated a state law that required theaters to obtain a license for "boxing exhibitions."

But the next day the two other members of the State Athletic Commission, William Muldoon and George Brower, told reporters at the commission's offices that Farley had acted on his own and they were opposed to his actions since they did not believe Tunney had violated any law. While Muldoon and Brower were in effect repudiating the action of their fellow commission member, Tunney's lawyer, Dudley Field Malone, said in the West Side court that the arrests had been inspired by personal "animus" on the part of Farley, who had been the only member of the three-man commission to oppose a Dempsey-Tunney fight in New York. Malone also pointed out that a number of prominent fighters, including Jim Jeffries, Tiger Flowers, and Tom Sharkey, a leading heavyweight around the turn of the century, had given sparring exhibitions on the stages of New York theaters without any action having been taken against them.

"Chairman Farley, as everybody knows, did his utmost to prevent Tunney from meeting Dempsey and to compel Dempsey to meet Wills," Malone told the court. "He argued that Tunney was no match for Dempsey and that Wills was the only man." Malone went on to point out that Tunney turned out to be too tough for Dempsey and Wills proved easy pickings for Jack Sharkey. "Farley has been more or less of a laughing stock since then, and his anger has taken the form of this petty persecution of Tunney, who is a New York boy and a great popular favorite," Malone, one of Manhattan's most prominent lawyers, said.

Positing Tunney as a "great popular favorite" may have been stretching the truth, but Malone was on target with most of what he said in court. Farley was furious at Dempsey for not agreeing to fight Wills in New York. But Dempsey had nothing to do with Tex Rickard's decision to match him against Tunney. And neither did Tunney. If Farley, who many thought had been trying to court the black vote in New York by proposing a Dempsey-Wills title fight, should have been angry at anyone, it was the New York State License Committee, which practically forced Rickard to look elsewhere for a site when it refused to give Dempsey a New York license.

Tunney continued to do his four-a-day stage appearances at Loews State during the trial, which ended with Tunney, his sparring partners, and the theater officials being cleared of all charges.

Within a few weeks Tunney began to find the vaudeville routine boring, repetitive, unchallenging, and demeaning. If Tunney had been asked to recite a few passages from one of Shakespeare's works during his vaudeville act, he no doubt would have relished the idea and done it enthusiastically. However, no one was prescient enough to realize that the new heavyweight champion of the world was not your typical boxer and that he would have reveled in being able to show a theatrical audience that being a prizefighter did not preclude having cultural interests beyond the boxing ring. By the time Tunney's act got to Boston, he asked William Morris if he could buy himself out of his contract. Having already noted that Tunney was drawing good audiences, which were heavily populated by young women, Morris in effect told Tunney that a deal was a deal, especially when the deal was financially productive for the William Morris Agency. Tunney's—and his father's—idol, James J. Corbett, may have loved appearing onstage, but then Corbett had become an accomplished actor in plays that usually ran about two hours, although he, too, had started by sparring onstage. Tunney, by contrast, felt uncomfortable and was happy when his eight-week run ended in late January of 1927.

Tunney, after finishing his vaudeville run, saw a lot of Polly Lauder, played golf, and did some roadwork and occasional sparring. Turning author, he also wrote an article for the March 1927 issue of *American Legion Monthly* in which he defended his reading habits.

"Being a boxer, my reading attracts attention," Tunney understatedly wrote. "Some think I am high-hatting the boys when I talk literature. I am not. I didn't begin to talk about books. Others did it to make conversation. Many put me through a cross-examination, a quiz to test my literary knowledge, as if I were an infant prodigy of eleven applying for admittance to college. I answer out of politeness' sake."

That obviously was an allusion to written remarks by some of the country's best-known sportswriters who, in challenging Tunney's literary interest, suggested that he was a literary "poseur," and even a "phony highbrow," as one writer put it. Contending that his interest in reading went back to grade-school days, Tunney also noted that he was not the first heavyweight champion with a cultural bent. "It is a hobby with me, just as Jem Mace, a bare-knuckle champion of the 1860s played the violin and Jem Ward, another prize ring title holder, painted pictures," Tunney wrote, while adding a comment he had made previously to sportswriters before the Dempsey fight. "Because a man is a boxer it doesn't follow that he has to be illiterate." It was an artful literary defense of his literary habits, but, alas to Tunney, his interest in classical literature would continue to be questioned or ridiculed.

Only two weeks after Tex Rickard virtually wrote Harry Wills off as a contender for Tunney's new title, Wills eliminated himself as a viable challenger when he lost on a disqualification to the hottest heavyweight prospect around, Jack Sharkey. Despite a twenty-six-pound weight advantage, Wills "was battered around the ring from the start," the Associated Press said in its account of the fight on October 12 at Ebbets Field in Brooklyn, the home of the Brooklyn Robins baseball team. Frustrated and badly beaten, Wills resorted to illegal backhand blows, which prompted referee Patsy Haley to disqualify him in the thirteenth round of the scheduled fifteen-round fight.

Even black newspapers, which had accused Dempsey of avoiding Wills for years, and, after he had won the title, had urged Tunney to fight the Brown Panther, agreed that Wills had now been marginalized as a contender. Only a week before Wills met Sharkey, the *New York Amsterdam News,* the city's most prominent black newspaper, said that Tunney had adopted "the dodging tactics of Jack Dempsey" and was "hiding behind the color line" by not agreeing to fight Wills. Actually, Tunney was not thinking of fighting anyone, at least until the following summer. But Wills's one-sided loss to Sharkey, who at twenty-four was thirteen years younger, made it all the more unlikely that Tunney, or any other future champion, would fight Wills. As the *Kansas City Call,* a popular African-American paper, said after the Sharkey fight, "Harry Wills is through," and "no more will he be the subject of heated controversy as to whether he 'can' or 'can't,' could or couldn't."

One thing was certain: Tex Rickard would no longer have to keep coming up with reasons, most of them specious, as to why Wills was not getting a shot at the world heavyweight title.

By mid-April, Dempsey, after three months of chopping down trees and doing daily roadwork and occasional sparring in the Ventura Mountains in southern California, under the guidance of trainer Gus Wilson, told Rickard he was ready to return. Rickard thereupon announced that he would match Dempsey against the winner of a May 20 fight between Sharkey and Jimmy Maloney, who already had fought each other three times, with Maloney winning the first fight and Sharkey the next two.

Dempsey and Tunney were among the crowd of forty thousand that turned out for the Sharkey-Maloney bout. A much better fighter than when he had been floored seven times in two rounds by Maloney two years before—or maybe he was just trying harder, you never knew with Sharkey—Sharkey easily outboxed and outpunched his fellow Bostonian, knocking him down three times before referee Lou Magnolia stopped the bout in the fifth round. Both Tunney and Dempsey were impressed. Sharkey had boxed brilliantly and punched harder than they expected. There was no doubt in their minds that Sharkey was a possible heavyweight champion in the making. Most writers felt that Dempsey had good cause for concern in his impending fight against Sharkey, who was fast, with a swift and snapping left jab and an excellent defense. Besides all that, Sharkey, perfectly proportioned at six feet and 195 pounds, had become a more powerful puncher. Based on his performances against Harry Wills and Jimmy Maloney, Sharkey would be much more than just a tune-up for Dempsey.

Three weeks after the Sharkey-Maloney fight, Rickard announced that Sharkey and Dempsey would meet at Yankee Stadium on July 21, with the winner to fight Tunney, probably in September. Rickard was happy about the outcome, aware that Sharkey was not only a better fighter than Maloney, but also more colorful, not to mention emotional, and that his fight with Dempsey would earn more than $1 million. Still, he was hopeful that Dempsey would not only knock out Sharkey but would be impressive in beating him to make a return bout with Tunney a viable return match, which everyone seemed to be hoping for.

At his first press conference since before the Tunney fight nine months earlier, Dempsey told reporters in New York why he really had decided to come back. "I want to be convinced I'm wrong and that my ring days are over," he said. "Maybe Sharkey can convince me."

For the Sharkey fight, Dempsey had a new manager and a third trainer. His new manager was Leo Flynn, a veteran who had managed a number of heavyweights, including Bill Brennan. The prevailing consensus among boxing insiders was that Flynn was picked by Rickard, with whom he was close. Rickard, like many others, felt that Dempsey's failure to have an astute manager in his corner for the Tunney fight may have cost him the title. In addition, apparently also at Rickard's suggestion, Billy Duffy, a veteran manager, trainer, and nightclub owner, also joined the Dempsey brain trust. Duffy, a convicted felon, would later be part of the cabal that engineered Primo Carnera's bizarre rise to the world heavyweight title by fixing practically all his fights. But then Rickard was not so much concerned about Duffy's police record as he was about the fistic gravitas that Flynn and Duffy could impart to Dempsey, who hadn't really had much since his breakup with Doc Kearns.

On July 2, nineteen days before the Sharkey fight, Dempsey was relaxing on the porch at Tom Luther's resort in the Adirondacks shortly before noon when he received a phone call that left him in shock. The call was from Schenectady, only twenty miles from Dempsey's training camp. There, his brother Johnny, who had come east hoping for a reconciliation with his twenty-one-year-old wife, had killed her and himself when she refused to return west with him and their two-year-old son.

A heroin addict whom Dempsey had helped support for years after trying to help him get started as an actor in California, Johnny Dempsey had only recently been released following a month's treatment for his addiction at a hospital in Salt Lake City, where a doctor had declared him cured. Mainly because of his problems with drugs, Edna Dempsey had broken up with him several months before and took their son to Schenectady, where she had relatives. Johnny had followed in early June, hoping for a reconciliation with Edna, but his efforts failed.

That July 2 morning the landlady in the rooming house where Johnny Dempsey's estranged wife was staying heard loud voices followed by three shots. She later told police that she rushed to the room to find Johnny Dempsey dead on the floor and Edna Dempsey shot and wounded. By the time an ambulance arrived, Edna Dempsey was dead as well.

After the violent death of his youngest sibling, Dempsey, who now was left with two older brothers, Bernie and Joe, felt at least partially responsible for Johnny's death, since he had persuaded him to move to Hollywood. Red-eyed from crying, Dempsey told reporters at the training camp, "Johnny wanted to be a fighter. He was a year older than I was and one of the handsomest guys you ever saw, wonderful personality, smile and all that. He could box as good as anybody, but the second he was tagged, the fight was over."

Early the next morning, Dempsey told Flynn that he would resume training immediately and that he would be prepared to fight on July 21.

On the day of the fight, Sharkey was an 8-to-5 favorite. Dempsey was hardly surprised. Sharkey had been much more active and had been impressive in his last few fights. He was also eight years younger, almost as good a boxer in the opinion of some boxing experts as Tunney, very fast, and, on top of all that, brimming with confidence. Sharkey was certainly better than Billy Miske, Bill Brennan, and Luis Firpo, all of whom Dempsey had knocked out in title defenses, and most likely better than Jess Willard, from whom Dempsey had won the title, and Tommy Gibbons, who had extended Dempsey through fifteen rounds. Indeed, the only fighter Dempsey had faced who was probably better than Sharkey was Tunney. The major difference between Sharkey and Tunney was that while Tunney was a highly intelligent and collected boxer, Sharkey could be emotional and even headstrong in the ring. Tunney, without a doubt, was the smarter fighter.

Given Dempsey's poor performance against Tunney and, before that, his three-year absence from the ring, the crowd at Yankee Stadium that night—estimated at eighty thousand—was astonishing. Describing the bout as Dempsey's "fight of his life," James Dawson of the *Times* wrote in that day's paper, "The magnet of Dempsey, combined with the popularity Sharkey has attracted to himself through his rush to heavyweight prominence, is expected to make this the greatest nonchampionship battle in pugilistic history."

It most definitely was not, although it would end both dramatically and controversially.

The first round set the tone for the first five rounds as Sharkey, in defiance of his cornermen, elected to stand at close quarters and slug it out with Dempsey. Even more surprisingly, Sharkey seemed to easily absorb several of Dempsey's patented left hooks to the head and body. If Sharkey wasn't heeding his corner's advice, neither was Dempsey. The former champion had been told time and again by Leo Flynn that Sharkey was most vulnerable with body punches, yet Dempsey aimed most of his blows at the head during the early rounds, with most of them missing badly.

Gaining more confidence with the passing of each round, Sharkey appeared to have clearly won the first five rounds, both outboxing and outhitting Dempsey, who was slow afoot, awkward, and off-balance much of the time, and wild with most of his punches. Finally, in the sixth round, Dempsey, with cuts over both his eyes and his face smeared with blood, made it a fight by focusing on Sharkey's body, digging in a number of good body blows in a round that appeared even.

Continuing to attack the body, Dempsey pounded a number of punches to the body at the beginning of the seventh round. Then Sharkey, after absorbing four straight blows that appeared to have been below the belt, momentarily turned to referee Jack O'Sullivan to complain. It was a fatal mistake. As he swung his head back to face Dempsey, the Manassa Mauler shot across a powerful left hook that traveled no more than ten inches but caught Sharkey solidly on the left side of the jaw. Sharkey sank to the canvas slowly, much like a snowman sinking to the ground under a hot midday sun. As O'Sullivan began his count, Sharkey first grabbed his groin with one glove, then the left side of his jaw where the knockdown punch had landed. By ten Sharkey was on all-fours, crawling toward his corner. Dempsey immediately went to his side to help him to the corner, where Sharkey's handlers managed to get him to sit on his stool.

The huge crowd, almost overwhelmingly for Dempsey, erupted with a roar that carried well beyond the cavernous stadium in the Bronx. Dempsey had looked bad for five rounds, fair for only one, and perhaps may have been disqualified for hitting low, but he had won the fight, and a rematch with Tunney now was a virtual certainty.

With cuts over both eyes, on his mouth and on his nose and another under his left eye, along with welts and bruises across his face, Dempsey looked more loser than winner while Sharkey was virtually unmarked. Had any of his blows been low? Dempsey was asked later, amid the bedlam of the New York Yankees' locker room. "The right hand blows I drove home were fair and square to Sharkey's body," Dempsey told reporters. "The left hook to the jaw was the finisher. There can be no question about the finisher of that punch."

That was true. But many ringsiders, including about half of the sportswriters covering the fight, thought Sharkey had been fouled by Dempsey's body punches in the climactic round and thus should have been disqualified. In the lead front-page story in the *New York Times*, James Dawson said of the controversial Dempsey blows to Sharkey's midsection that "they were unmistakably low punches, four of them, although concededly unintentional." Dawson was joined in his opinion by, among others, Grantland Rice, Damon Runyon, W. O. McGeehan, Joe Williams, and Bill Corum of the *New York Journal*. But just as many other writers thought that Dempsey's controversial body punches were above the belt, including Paul Gallico, Robert Edgren, Hype Igoe, Westbrook Pegler, and Ed Sullivan, later to become the widely known Broadway columnist and television personality.

Sharkey, who would go on to win the heavyweight title in 1932 from Max Schmeling, after having lost to Schmeling on a foul during an attempt to win the title two years earlier, did not complain. At the age of twenty-four, he knew he still had plenty of time. "It's all in the game," he said of the controversial ending before heading back to Boston by car with his wife the day after the fight. Some cynics thought it was also "all in the game," and prearranged, when Sharkey lost his title to Primo Carnera on a knockout on what appeared to be a very inept left hook by the Ambling Alp on June 29, 1933.

Asked after the fight why he had hit Sharkey when Sharkey turned his head to complain to O'Sullivan, Dempsey smiled and said, "What was I going to do—write him a letter?" It was classic Dempsey, if not exactly sportsmanlike. To Dempsey, you dropped your guard at your peril. If your opponent wasn't paying close attention to you and you belted him in the jaw, well, what did he expect?

Tunney was one of the few ringsiders who was impressed with Dempsey's showing. "His punches were short, but they were snappy and forceful," said Tunney. "I might even say that I never saw Dempsey in a better fight."

Some cynics felt that Tunney was either trying to be gracious or trying to hype what obviously was going to be a rematch between him and Dempsey. Jim Dawson's appraisal may have been closer to the truth. "He was revealed as a shell of his former self, a man whose fighting spirit and effectiveness have left him," Dawson wrote in the *Times*. "He has nothing now but the will to fight, minus even the desire. Of him, it can truly be said that his spirit is willing, but the flesh is weak."

Tex Rickard cringed when he read those words the next morning. But overall he had a number of reasons to be happy. First of all, the of-

ficial crowd of 72,283 produced a gate of $1,083,530—the largest ever
for a nontitle fight. And second, Rickard was delighted that Dempsey
had emerged the winner. Not many people would be excited about a
fight between Tunney and Sharkey, if for no other reason than they
were both boxers. Rickard knew that a return bout between Dempsey
and Tunney, the paragon of punchers against perhaps the best boxer in
the world, would draw far more interest. Rickard also knew that, on
the strength of the knockout—which may or may not have followed a
series of illegal punches by Dempsey—he could now justify a return
bout between Dempsey and Tunney.

By late September the Sharkey fight would long be forgotten,
Rickard felt, and the Dempsey-Tunney rematch would be huge, maybe
even drawing more than the 135,000 spectators who saw the first fight
in Philadelphia, and perhaps becoming the first fight to draw more
than $2 million at the gate. Rickard knew that Dempsey had slipped
and had not looked good against Sharkey. But he still could knock an
opponent out with that left hook. And so long as he could do that, he
could still draw a crowd. He might be outboxed, as he had been by
Tunney and Sharkey, but his appeal lay in the undeniable fact that, as
against Luis Firpo and Sharkey, he might appear to be badly beaten,
even knocked out of the ring, but he could still wind up winning by a
knockout. It was all part of the Dempsey mystique. There had never
been anything like it in boxing, and Rickard was determined to keep it
going as long as he could.

TWENTY-TWO

The Long Count

Jack Dempsey refuses to heed referee Dave Barry's command to go to a neutral corner after knocking down Gene Tunney during their "long count" bout in Chicago.

O nce again, as in the aftermath of his fights with Luis Firpo and Gene Tunney, a Dempsey fight was the talk of the country the day after. Whether he won or lost, and even if he looked bad in winning, the Manassa Mauler seemed to be involved in controversy. But his newfound popularity seemed undiminished. And if there was a benefit of the doubt in the Sharkey fight, in the eyes of most sports fans, the benefit went to Dempsey.

But the controversy soon became academic. Within the next two days, Tex Rickard had gotten both Dempsey and Gene Tunney to agree to a rematch at Soldier Field, an elegant year-old coliseum in Grant Park in Chicago along Lake Michigan. Rickard had quickly ruled out New York, both because of the $27.50 maximum that he could charge for ringside seats and because Yankee Stadium, the largest outdoor facility in the city, could not match Soldier field in capacity. A third, lesser reason was Rickard's continued antipathy toward James J. Farley. Making New York all the more undesirable to Rickard—and to Dempsey and Tunney—was the action of the New York State License Committee, which had denied Dempsey a license to fight in New York a little more than a year ago.

Immediately after the Dempsey-Sharkey fight, George Getz, a millionaire coal operator from Chicago and the head of a booster committee that had been set up by Mayor William "Big Bill" Thompson, contacted Rickard and strongly recommended that the Dempsey-Tunney rematch be held at Soldier Field. Getz made a good pitch. Among the points he made, and which Rickard particularly liked, were that Soldier Field could hold as many as 160,000 spectators for a boxing bout and that Getz and his committee would guarantee that ringside-seat tickets could be priced at $40. Certain that the fight would attract more than a hundred thousand people, Rickard thereupon guaranteed Tunney $750,000—about what Dempsey received for their first fight—and Dempsey $400,000, plus a share of the gate for both of them if it surpassed $2 million, which Rickard felt it would. Both sides accepted, and the fight was set for the Windy City, or, as Carl Sandburg, a Chicagoan, called it, "City of the big shoulders . . . hog butcher for the world." And of course, in the 1920s, Chicago was also the bailiwick of Al Capone, the transplanted Brooklynite, and a host of his enemies and friends, many of those friends in high places, including, it was rumored, in the mayor's office.

Not everyone was happy about the thought of Jack Dempsey—he of the Great War draft deferment—fighting at Soldier Field, which had been built to honor American servicemen. At least four Chicago aldermen and a number of American Legion posts in the Midwest objected to having Dempsey fight there, contending that it would be a defilement of a structure built in tribute to American doughboys of the Great War and those who had fought for their country in other wars. But once the deal had been struck, it was clear that the fight would be held at Soldier Field on September 22, and the outcry over Dempsey fighting there soon subsided.

For all of the attention it would get, many boxing people felt that the rematch made no sense. Tunney had won all ten rounds of the first bout, and it was obvious that if the fight had been scheduled for fifteen rounds, Dempsey, who was fading badly at the end, would have been knocked out. And against Sharkey, Dempsey clearly had been outboxed and outfought over the first five rounds and maybe had even lost the sixth round before he took advantage of a momentary lapse by Sharkey. Indeed, Dempsey had knocked him out with what in effect was a sneak punch that followed several questionable body punches, which many ringsiders thought were below the belt.

It also had become clear that Dempsey, at the still young age of thirty-two, was either slipping or could not hold his own with superior boxers like Sharkey and Tunney, no doubt the best fighters he had ever gone up against. Meanwhile, Tunney, good as he was, was obviously getting better. Still, because he was Dempsey, a lot of people, including more than a few boxing experts, felt that Dempsey would have a good chance against Tunney. But hardly anyone could have expected that the fight in Chicago would be a fight for the ages and, arguably, the most memorable boxing bout ever.

Tunney spent much of the spring and early summer of 1927 in Greenwich, ostensibly visiting his good friend, Sam Pryor, Jr., but, in fact, seeing a lot of Polly Lauder, with whom he had become totally entranced. Since Tunney was determined to keep the burgeoning romance a secret, he and Polly rarely went out in public together; rather they would spend much of their time together at the Lauder estate, at the homes of Pryor and his father, and at the Lauder family's private island in Maine.

With the Pryors and any other friends who became privy to the romance sworn to secrecy, no one else seemed to know about it, except for Tunney's mother, his brother, and his sisters. Before beginning training in July for his rematch with Dempsey, Tunney also visited Polly on Johns Island. There, in seclusion, they were able to be alone on the private beach along the cool waters of the Atlantic Ocean. By then, Gene Tunney was in love, but was not yet about to let the world know it. For Polly Lauder, the secrecy of their romance only served to enhance, and even enrich, their relationship and give it an aura of mystery.

Tunney's welcome in Chicago on September 2 was both tumultuous and, to the champion, heartwarming. The Midwest was Dempsey territory—as indeed was most of the country—and thus Tunney was amazed when several thousand Chicagoans, along with a squad of marines, turned out to greet him at the LaSalle Street Station following his eighteen-hour train trip from New York, and then even more people hailed him as his motorcade headed to City Hall, where he was to be greeted by Mayor Bill Thompson—who was reportedly linked to Capone and some other gangsters—other city officials, and George Getz, the nominal promoter of the impending fight. Under Illinois rules governing professional boxing, a promoter had to be a resident of the state. Everyone connected with the fight knew, though, that Tex Rickard actually would run the show.

In the *Chicago Herald-Examiner*, Warren Brown wrote, "There was a touch of Lindbergh about the Tunney reception, a hint of Armistice Day, or the return of the heroes from the war." That may have exaggerated the welcome the handsome young champion received, but Chicago newspapers of the time, forever involved in newspaper circulation wars—which, like Chicago gang fights, often turned violent—had found that hyperbole sometimes was the most effective weapon.

Asked about the coming fight at the City Hall reception, Tunney smiled and said, "If there is to be a fight, I know nothing of it. I don't like fighting, but I do like boxing, and as far as I know this is going to be a boxing contest."

Everyone laughed. Certainly the new heavyweight champion was kidding. But he wasn't. To him, it was indeed going to be a contest involving planning, strategy, guile, and intelligence, as much as it would involve anything else. To Dempsey, by contrast, it was going to be a fight. So far as Dempsey knew, he had never been in a "boxing contest" in his life.

Dempsey had slipped into Chicago unobtrusively with his entourage in mid-August and gone directly to his training site. Once again reflecting their personalities, Dempsey trained at a racetrack and Tunney at a country club. Dempsey's base was Lincoln Fields, a year-old Thoroughbred racing facility in Crete, Illinois, about thirty-five miles from Chicago, while Tunney set up camp at the new Cedar Crest Country Club in Lake Villa, fifty-two miles from the Loop, the heart of Chicago's downtown section.

Estelle Taylor, who had stayed far removed from Dempsey's training camp a year ago, was close by at the fashionable Edgewater Beach Hotel in downtown Chicago with a nurse named Viola Watson, who served as both a companion and medical adviser. Estelle, who had already made twenty-four movies, including the original 1923 silent film version of *The Ten Commandments,* in which she had a leading role as Miriam, the sister of Moses, also had portrayed Lucrezia Borgia in *Don Juan,* which was released in 1926, and appeared in *New York,* which had just come out. Hollywood wanted to hold on to actresses like Taylor, who were not only beautiful but whose voices lent themselves to talkies. In 1928 alone, the first year that talking pictures blossomed, Taylor was in five films, and by the time her career ended when she was fifty-one, she was to have made sixteen talking pictures and forty-three movies in all, ending with Jean Renoir's *The Southerner* in 1945.

Taylor spent most of her time at the hotel with Watson or alone. Occasionally, accompanied by Watson, she visited her husband at Lincoln Fields, usually only staying for lunch and leaving before Dempsey's sparring sessions began. Dempsey in turn went in to Chicago several times to join Estelle for dinner. But their marriage, shaky for years, was only getting worse, and Dempsey knew it. Those close to Dempsey felt that the marital discord weighed heavily on Dempsey while he trained for the rematch. As the rematch neared, he became tense, which was bad news for his sparring partners. Dempsey was mean enough in the ring when things were going well; when he was upset, he took it out on his spar mates. Fortunately for them, the old Manassa Mauler was missing far more punches than he was landing, even during the sparring sessions, and also seemed to be even slower afoot than he had been in Philadelphia the year before.

Most writers who had covered Dempsey in the past were not particularly impressed with his sparring sessions. The left hook was still a lethal weapon and rocked several of his sparring partners, but then none of them could be mistaken for Gene Tunney in fighting ability. Dempsey looked especially bad against Dave Shade, a good middleweight and several cuts above an average sparring partner. As with Tommy Loughran before the first Tunney fight, Dempsey found Shade hard to hit and in turn had trouble against Shade's quick jab and swift combinations. That, of course, did not augur well for Dempsey, since Shade's style was similar to, though not as effective as, Tunney's.

Some boxing people speculated that that was why Leo Flynn, after two weeks at Lincoln Fields, decided to have Dempsey spar at night, rather than in the afternoon, and to close workouts to the public. Tunney, meanwhile, continued to box, and without customary headgear at that, during the warmth of mid-afternoon, and his training sessions remained open to the public. Just about everyone, including most boxing writers, was impressed, and those who had seen Tunney train at Stroudsburg a year ago thought he looked even better, both moving faster and hitting harder, which was not exactly what Dempsey's people wanted to hear. As for the lack of headgear—usually de rigueur during sparring sessions—Tunney felt he was prone to be less careful while wearing it, and that if and when he got hit by a sparring partner where his head was exposed, it would better prepare him to absorb Dempsey's powerful blows, if indeed the champ was able to land any.

Despite how one-sided the first fight had been, the rematch seemed to arouse greater interest throughout the country and abroad, even though the consensus among boxing writers was that Dempsey had slipped while Tunney was better than ever and still improving. One line of reasoning, which Rickard kept stressing to sportswriters, was that, unlike the first fight, which followed three years of idleness by

Dempsey, Dempsey was coming off a tough bout against a very good heavyweight in Sharkey. Then there was the legion of Dempsey adherents who were convinced that the Manassa Mauler would change his tactics and perhaps focus more on Tunney's body and try to "cut off the ring," a boxing term denoting a fighter's ability to restrict an opponent's movement by pinning him in a corner, preferably against the ropes. Most astute boxing people thought that was wishful thinking. There was only one way Dempsey knew how to fight, and that was to stalk an opponent and fire away at the head and body—mostly at the head. It was unreasonable to think, most veteran Dempsey watchers felt, that after thirteen years as a professional fighter he was going to recalibrate his style of fighting.

By mid-September, Rickard was assured of an unprecedented $2 million gate. By then, more than a hundred thousand tickets had been sold, including most of the forty thousand forty-dollar ringside seats. In fact, most of those seats were a long way from ringside, extending back 113 rows. The cheapest tickets, which cost five dollars, were going far more slowly, perhaps because most of them were almost six hundred feet from the ring, from where spectators would need binoculars to see what was happening. But given the hype the fight was receiving, Rickard was convinced that most of those distant seats would sell out, too.

What wasn't good for the fight, though, were rumors of a fix that popped up periodically. Less than two weeks after Tunney arrived in Chicago, a report in the *New York Journal* said that he had been offered $1 million by the same cabal that had fixed the 1919 World Series—Rothstein, Attell, and a few other New York mobsters—to take a dive. Tunney denied that he had been approached by Rothstein or Attell, and largely because of his clean-cut image, most people believed him.

Still, the *Journal* report and other rumors had the effect of dropping the odds on Tunney from 9-to-5 to about 7-to-5, and they would drop even more by the night of the fight, which had many people wondering about the legitimacy of the rematch. They wondered even more when Al Capone told some newspaper reporters that he had bet fifty thousand dollars on Dempsey, and then winked, as if to suggest that he was betting on a sure thing. Capone made his wager after hearing that Davey Miller, a well-regarded referee who ran a speakeasy, was going to be named to referee the fight, and that Miller's brother had wagered heavily on Dempsey. Thinking there might be a connection, Capone bet on Dempsey, too.

Tunney, Gibson, and Bronson had also heard the report about Capone's big bet on Dempsey, which was cause for concern in Chicago, where Capone's power and influence dwarfed that of the mayor and just about everyone else. Years later, Ed Sullivan, who covered Dempsey's camp for the New York *Daily News,* wrote that five of Capone's henchmen had turned up at Dempsey's training site and said Capone was prepared to have "the right man" referee the fight if Dempsey's brain trust paid a fee of fifty thousand dollars. That, of course, was a lot less than the $1 million Rothstein and Attell were alleged to have proffered to Tunney to throw the fight. It's unclear if Capone was having a worse year than Rothstein and his associates, or if Scarface Al wasn't positive he could bribe a referee.

Dempsey, Flynn, and company of course turned down the proposal. For one thing, the offer did not make sense. As Dempsey was to point out, a referee—whether crooked or honest—was not apt to help him, since it was highly unlikely that he would outpoint Tunney. "I've got to rely on these," Dempsey said, holding up his fists. Nevertheless, Dempsey sent Capone a handwritten note asking him to back off and let the fight go on in a sportsmanlike, and honest, fashion. The next day, Estelle received a huge bouquet of flowers with a note that said, "To the Dempseys in the name of sportsmanship." The note was unsigned, but there was no need for it to have been signed. Dempsey had a pretty good idea who had sent the flowers.

Perhaps because of the swirl of rumors about a fight that had been fixed by either Capone or Rothstein and Attell, Dempsey's camp began to worry about his food. To make sure that no one would tamper with anything on Dempsey's menu, Leo Flynn brought in his wife, Katherine, to cook for the former heavyweight champion. Up until then, because of the suspect olive oil or coffee cream that Dempsey had ingested before the first Tunney fight, Jerry Luvadis was designated to sample whatever Dempsey was going to eat. That prompted W. O. McGeehan of the *New York Herald Tribune* to write, "As long as the Greek lived, Dempsey could eat."

In between rumors of fixes, crooked referees, and other possible chicanery, Dempsey or someone in his camp—most likely Leo Flynn—sent an "open letter" to the *Chicago Herald-Examiner* that alleged Tunney had conspired with Billy Gibson and Boo Boo Hoff to fix the first fight in Philadelphia. The letter, which ran on the newspaper's front page three days before the rematch and started "Dear Tunney," said that Dempsey had been told that "somebody with some sort of political power—or power in boxing affairs in Philadelphia" was going to ensure that a referee and one of the two judges would see to it that Tunney won if the fight went the distance. In the letter, Dempsey went on to say that "if I hit you at any point lower than the top of your head and dropped you, that somebody would yell 'foul' in your behalf" and that "a doctor would jump in and find that you were fouled."

Dempsey, or whoever wrote the letter, went on to say that Tunney had won the fight "fair and square" but that he felt it was time for Tunney to say what part Hoff and Attell had played in the alleged plot, why Tunney had met with Hoff and Gibson only five hours before the fight, and why Gibson "would have to borrow twenty thousand dollars from Hoff on fight night."

Responding with a letter of his own to "My dear Dempsey," which ran alongside the "Dear Tunney" missive, Tunney said his first reaction was to ignore the letter and "its evident trash completely." Tunney went on to say he thought the Dempsey letter was "a very cheap appeal for public sympathy," and added a postscript: "I might add that I wrote this letter myself."

The day after Dempsey's open letter to Tunney appeared in the *Herald-Examiner,* the *Chicago Tribune* published a copy of an ostensible contract that seemed to bear out Hoff's claim that he was entitled to a share of Tunney's ring earnings. Hoff's lawyer had incorrectly listed Tunney as Eugene Joseph Tunney, rather than James Joseph—his real name—and so Tunney had signed it as listed on the contract, which both he and Gibson later claimed was invalid. Indeed, Hoff's lawyer drew up a slightly different contract the day after the Philadelphia fight, but both Gibson and Tunney refused to sign it.

Hoff eventually would go to court to demand $200,000 from Tunney's purse in the first fight. That was hardly 20 percent, but more like 100 percent. Meanwhile, Tim Mara had filed a suit claiming Tunney owed him $400,000 from the first fight. Obviously Hoff and Mara either hadn't paid attention to how much Tunney got for the fight in Philadelphia or were deficient in arithmetic, since the total of their monetary demands was three times what Tunney got for winning the title. But then it was hardly the first time a fighter was expected to pay out more money from his purse than he had actually received.

Indeed, right up until the opening bell of the rematch, suspicions lingered about whether the fight was on the level. The referee was not to be picked until just before the bout started, so that mobsters would have a difficult time getting to the referee in time to bribe him. Or then maybe someone connected with the Illinois Athletic Commission, which was to appoint the referee and two judges, just might tip off a gambler or a mobster for a hefty price as to who the referee and the judges were to be. In Chicago, in the 1920s, anything was possible. If a group of New Yorkers could convince eight members of the Chicago White Sox not to do their best, and thus throw the 1919 World Series to the Cincinnati Reds, then it was conceivable that they could persuade one boxer to take an early dive for $1 million beyond the $1 million already was guaranteed.

A few days before the fight, Edward Neil, a writer for the Associated Press, quoted Tunney as having told him during an interview at his training camp that he looked with disfavor on marriage and never expected to marry, which might have come as jarring news to Polly Lauder back east. However, according to Neil, Tunney allowed in the interview that "fate, he believes, may some time bring across his path the woman destined to be his mate." In fact, Tunney was convinced that he had already found that woman and, to protect his intensifying romance with her, he had merely sent up another smoke screen. If Polly happened to see Neil's story, he knew she would understand.

Amid the rampant fix allegations involving not only the impending fight but even the first one, there came a curious development during one of several meetings involving representatives of the Tunney and Dempsey camps, their lawyers, the nominal promoter, George Getz, and the Illinois Boxing Commission. Most of the time was spent on the commission's relatively new rules—boxing had only been legalized again in Illinois in 1926, and then only in cities where it had been approved at referendums. This had of course occurred in Chicago, where, as in New York until passage of the Walker Act in 1920, bootleg boxing had flourished for years.

To the surprise of everyone present, Dempsey's manager, Leo Flynn, had insisted—according to what Tunney claimed he had been told by Getz and which several sportswriters reported—that the referee of the fight had to enforce the rule which prescribed that, in the event of a knockdown, the fighter scoring the knockdown must go to a neutral corner. Most of those present were taken aback at Flynn's concern about enforcement of the rule, which was based on one put into effect in New York in 1922, since it was generally felt that if there were to be a knockdown it most likely would be registered by Dempsey and that Tunney's corner would be the most concerned about a violation of the neutral corner rule. But Flynn's insistence on adherence to the neutral corner rule suggested that the Dempsey camp was worried about their man being floored by Tunney, or that perhaps Dempsey—whom Tunney also had been convinced was lacking in confidence—had insisted that the rule be enforced. That the issue was brought up turned out to be both prophetic and ironic.

Despite all its precautions, the Athletic Commission did not seem to trust anyone who had influence over the fight. Rather than have the referee and judges give their decisions to the ring announcer, the commission said the cards of the three officials would first have to be handed to the commissioners at ringside. In the event that the commission felt that the ultimate decision was unfair, they would reserve the right to reverse it—which would be unprecedented—or decide not to have a decision rendered at all. Both the Dempsey and Tunney camps were incredulous at such a possibility, but then again they remembered this was Chicago, where strange things were known to happen.

On the day before the fight, Dempsey left Lincoln Fields in mid-afternoon for Chicago where he checked in at the Hotel Morrison, not far from the Edgewater Beach Hotel, where Estelle was staying. Tunney, though, did not depart from the Cedar Crest Country Club until eleven o'clock the day of the fight. Tunney had spent much of his last afternoon at Lake Villa reading Somerset Maugham's *Of Human Bondage.**

Before going to bed the night before the fight, Tunney asked his friend Sam Pryor, Jr., to bring him a nearby bottle of water. Noticing that the bottle was half-empty, Tunney, said, "Sam, I don't think I had better drink that. Why don't you go down and get me a fresh bottle." Pryor thereupon went downstairs to get a fresh bottle of water from a padlocked icebox.

"Because the Capone era was at its height, and racketeers had become involved in boxing, only I had the key to a padlocked icebox that Gene used," Pryor said years later. "We never did find out why the water bottle was only half full or whether anything had been added."

No doubt Tunney had remembered the stories about how Jack Dempsey's olive oil or coffee cream allegedly had been laced with a mysterious, and perhaps even poisonous, substance the morning of their first fight and wasn't about to take any chances. Not when Al Capone had reportedly bet fifty thousand dollars on Dempsey.

Remarkably, by the morning of the fight the betting was at even money and, at some betting establishments, Dempsey was a slight favorite because of a heavy influx of money placed on the Manassa Mauler by supporters freshly arrived from points west of Chicago, including the ex-champion's native state of Colorado. That seemed to make little sense, since Dempsey had not been impressive in his sparring while Tunney had, and in light of Tunney's complete dominance of Dempsey in their first fight. Tunney was bemused when he read of the shift in the odds, which by mid-afternoon were reportedly at even

*A few years later Tunney met Maugham and thanked him for writing the book, explaining how it had enabled him to relax and forget about the upcoming fight. Maugham smiled and said he had good reason to thank Tunney, too. Alluding to references to the book by sportswriters covering Tunney, Maugham said, "My dear fellow, I want to thank you for the most free advertising I ever had."

money and would stay that way until the fight began. He was even more amused to read an "exclusive" by the Hearst Hollywood gossip columnist, Louella Parsons, which said that "no matter how the fight goes, he [Tunney] will enter a monastery and study for the priesthood." Parsons, who never let over-verification ruin a juicy item, went on to say that "women don't interest Gene in the slightest. Ask any feminine reporter who has tried to interview him. Anyhow, Gene wants to be a priest."

If Tunney's mother saw the Parsons column, it might well have lifted her spirits; after all, she had been hoping since Gene was a boy that he would become a priest. As for Polly Lauder, the Parsons column, if she got to read it, no doubt would have given her a laugh.

In no other sport is the stress and strain of waiting as pronounced as it is in boxing. As a rule, a main-event fighter has to wait about fourteen hours, or even longer, from the time he gets up in the morning until he climbs into the ring. Most fighters try as hard as they can to keep their minds off the fight, and especially off the opponent. In most cases, the more a fighter thinks about an opponent, the more fearful he becomes. Thus it's best to try to occupy your mind in other ways. Playing cards and, later, watching television are perhaps the most popular diversions.

Carmen Basilio, the former welterweight and middleweight champion, once said he liked to have his wife by his side the day of a fight. "She would help me relax," said Basilio, a relentlessly aggressive fighter who won the welterweight title from Tony DeMarco in 1955 and the middleweight championship from Sugar Ray Robinson two years later. "But no matter what I did—read, watch TV, talk to my wife, I'd be very keyed up all day. I'd usually have lamb chops for dinner about half past four in the afternoon and lay down to take a nap, but I never could fall asleep, so I'd just rest for a while."

Jake La Motta, the onetime middleweight champion and, like Basilio one of the few fighters to have beaten Robinson during his prime, said, "I'd be a little on edge all day, and couldn't wait to get into the ring. But I was never nervous while waiting, and I certainly was never worried. Good fighters have no fear, and if you've worked hard in training, there's no reason to be worried. And the night before a fight,

I'd sleep like a baby. Then in the afternoon, after the weigh-in, I'd eat some pasta and take a nap. A lot of my fights were in New York, where I live, so I had the advantage of being able to spend the day at home. I think that's a lot better than having to spend the day at a hotel."

Not all fighters enjoy La Motta's equanimity. "I'd get nervous a few days before a fight and would be on edge the day of the fight," Larry Holmes, the former heavyweight champion, said in June of 2004. "I always had a plan, so I knew if I followed my plan, I would be okay once the fight started. The worst part, though, is the long wait. A lot of my fights were in Vegas, so I'd be able to get my mind off the fight by playing blackjack and shooting dice during the day. That helped me relax, even more so when I won at the tables. Then late in the afternoon, after a spaghetti dinner, I'd put on some soft music and doze off for a while. The music definitely helped."

Then, of course, there was Harry Greb, who often took his mind off a fight that night by spending much of the day, and even the early evening, with a woman or two or three.

Like Jake La Motta and Larry Holmes, Gene Tunney claimed that he never had trouble taking a nap before a big fight. Dempsey, on the other hand, always did. For the Manassa Mauler, the long hours of waiting on the day of a fight were agonizing. It wasn't as bad earlier in his career, when most of his big fights were held in the afternoon. But waiting for the late night fights to start—most title bouts start around 10:00 P.M., and sometimes as late as 11:00—was, for Dempsey, torturous. And it was all of that for the Manassa Mauler on Thursday, September 22, 1927, in Chicago, as he passed the time reading the Chicago sports pages, having a steak at four in the afternoon, then trying but failing to take a nap, talking on the phone several times with Estelle—whom, in courtly fashion, he still referred to as Miss Taylor—while awaiting the short ride to Soldier Field.

To this day, no other sports event has ever drawn as many famous people, from so many diverse fields, as the second Dempsey-Tunney fight in Chicago. Trains from New York and Los Angeles, in particular, along with about fifty private planes—twenty from Curtiss Field on Long Island alone—brought in some of the country's best-known citizens. Arriving from Hollywood the day before the fight were such movie notables as John Barrymore, Charlie Chaplin, Gloria Swanson, and Norma Talmadge, as well as Douglas Fairbanks and Al Jolson, both friends of Dempsey and who, inexplicably, had sparred with him on several occasions. Also on hand were Tom Mix, Jackie Coogan, producers Adolph Zukor and Joseph Schenck; theatrical owner Sid Grauman, gossip columnist Louella Parsons, and movie czar Will Hays, Hollywood's first censor in an era when not even "hell" or "damn" could be uttered on the silver screen.

From New York, aboard private cars attached to regularly scheduled passenger trains, or in some cases specially chartered trains, came George M. Cohan, David Belasco, and James J. Corbett; John Ringling, a longtime financial backer of Tex Rickard; Irving Berlin; newspaper magnate Roy Howard, magazine publishers Condé Nast and Richard Berlin, financier Bernard Baruch, and newspaper publishers Joseph Pulitzer and Ogden Reid; Mrs. Vincent Astor; theatrical producer and Boston Red Sox owner Harry Frazee, maligned to this day by Boston Red Sox fans for having sold Babe Ruth to the New York Yankees in 1920; Alfred Sloan, the president of General Motors; and Walter Chrysler; Admiral Richard E. Byrd, the first person to fly over the North Pole and who led five expeditions to Antarctica; Gerald Swope, the president of the General Electric Company; New York Giants manager John McGraw; and New York Yankees owner Colonel Jacob Ruppert.

Other prominent spectators included chewing gum magnate William Wrigley, Jr., baseball star Ty Cobb, baseball commissioner Kenesaw Mountain Landis; Dr. Charles Mayo, one of the Mayo brothers from the famed Mayo Clinic in Rochester, Minnesota; Marshall Field, the department store tycoon, and his wife; the presidents of the nation's six biggest railroads, including the New York Central and Union Pacific; presidents of some of America's largest industrial companies, including Carnegie Steel; Texas newspaper publisher Amon Carter; nine United States senators; a dozen congressmen; the mayors of sixteen large cities (but not Jimmy Walker, who was on his way back to New York from Europe); department store magnates, heads of a half-dozen oil companies, the presidents of more than a dozen large banks,

scores of stockbrokers, millionaires by the dozen, and countless socialites who rarely, if ever, had been drawn to a boxing bout. Also at
ringside were more than a few Rockefellers, Vanderbilts, Harrimans,
and Astors.

Royalty also was well represented. At ringside was the Marquis de
Blandford, whose mother, the Duchess of Marlborough, was the former Consuelo Vanderbilt; the Marquis de Douglas and Clydesdale,
heir of the Duke of Hamilton and a friend of Tunney; and Princess
Xenia of Greece, who flew in from New York with five other people
on a trimotor plane piloted by the princess's husband, William Leeds,
a licensed pilot for all of one month. Also present in a close ringside
seat was Dempsey's father, Hyrum, wizened and thin and now in his
mid-seventies.

Tex Rickard, aware of the cachet and imprimatur that such a distinguished array of spectators gave to the fight, made certain that all of
them were seated close to the ring, but not too close. For the squea-
mish and those uninitiated to the intrinsic brutality of boxing, sitting
close to a boxing ring is not highly recommended. Rickard knew that
getting sprayed by the fighters' sweat, and sometimes blood, does not
necessarily add to the pleasure of watching a prizefight, especially one
involving heavyweights, who usually hit the hardest. And he certainly
did not want to offend the sensibilities of those of his distinguished patrons who were not accustomed to the occasional brutality of the prize
ring.

The setting for the fight was befitting of the crowd. If many of the
rich and famous in attendance had never been to a prizefight, or to any
big sports event, they had to be in awe of Soldier Field, then the ne
plus ultra of American sports stadiums. Now primarily known as the
still elegant but somewhat modernized home of the Chicago Bears of
the National Football League, Soldier Field was in 1927—and may
still be—the country's most majestic stadium. Its signature feature
was, and still is, the classic Doric colonnades atop the grandstand that
rose one hundred feet above the grass surface where the ring had been
set up and evoked sporting venues of ancient Greece and the Roman
Colosseum.

Opened the year before, the oval-shaped stadium, built of concrete with granite-textured cast stone, covered a seven-acre area. It already had hosted a crowd of more than a hundred thousand for its first big sports spectacle, the Army-Navy football game the previous November, but the gathering for the Dempsey-Tunney rematch was far greater.

The night of the fight was chilly and overcast, with the temperature in the mid-50s. A light rain fell early in the evening, but, unlike the first fight in Philadelphia, this one would be fought in dry weather. By 9:00 P.M., an hour before the main event was scheduled to start, there were more than a hundred thousand people in the stadium, and by fight time, there would be about forty-five thousand more.

Though pleased, Rickard still wasn't completely satisfied. He had envisioned a sellout, which would have meant the sale of almost 175,000 tickets, an almost unimaginable number for any type of event. Three days before the fight, he had blamed the scheduled radio broadcasts of the fight for holding down ticket sales. "I'll never be foolish enough again to let these radio fellows to come in and broadcast a championship fight of mine without paying something, if it's only a cent a listener for the privilege," Rickard said. Rickard, of course, neglected to concede that such broadcasts just might generate more interest in boxing and induce many listeners to attend major fights of his in the future.

Walking around at ringside shortly before the rematch began, Rickard beamed, not only at the size of the gathering, estimated at around 145,000, but at the dazzling number of the rich and famous. Stopping to chat with a sportswriter, Rickard said, "Kid, if the earth came up and the sky came down and wiped out my first ten rows it would be the end of everything because I've got in those ten rows all the world's wealth, all the world's big men, all the world's brains and production talent. Just in them ten rows, kid. And you and me never seed nothing like it."

On a prearranged signal, six referees took their seats at ringside at 8:00 P.M. Five would officiate the preliminary bouts and the last one left sitting would referee the main event. None of the six, according to Illinois Athletic Commission chairman John Righeimer, knew which one had been chosen by the commission to handle the Dempsey-Tunney fight. It came down to Dave Barry when he remained the only referee sitting by the time the semifinal fight preceding the title bout began at nine. Maybe the Illinois Boxing Commission picked Barry, a highly regarded referee and onetime lightweight fighter, as a birthday present—he turned forty-four the day of the fight.

No fewer than five Chicago radio stations were covering the fight. But as with Dempsey-Tunney I, the biggest audience would belong to Graham McNamee of the National Broadcasting Company, who had a hookup of seventy-four stations and whose broadcast, it was said later by NBC officials, had been heard by more than 50 million people in the United States and Canada and a dozen other countries in Europe and Latin America. That number seemed high, since, according to Frank Hinman in the *Chicago Tribune* the day after the fight, "Conservative estimates place fifteen million of the country's twenty million listeners within hearing range of the seventy-four stations which put the battle on the air."

The fighters strode down an aisle and entered the ring—first the deeply tanned Dempsey, draped in a white robe with the initials "J.D." on the front and wearing black trunks, and then, several minutes later, Tunney, wearing his scarlet and blue robe with the Marine Corps insignia on the back. At thirty-two, Dempsey still possessed what Paul Gallico was later to describe as "the most beautifully proportioned body ever seen in a ring" with "the wide sloping shoulders of the puncher, a slim waist and fine symmetrical legs." Since Illinois boxing rules did not mandate that a fighter enter a ring bereft of any facial hair, as Pennsylvania's did, Dempsey reverted to his customary unshaven gladiatorial appearance, which, with his battle-tested scowl, made him look all the more menacing. Tunney, though trim and lithe, looked pale by comparison, his skin a pinkish white color that was accentuated by the klieg lights that shone down on the ring from above and floodlights from atop the stadium's colonnades.

The ovation for Dempsey was huge, rising to a crescendo that could be heard a mile away. Tunney, while cheered by many of the spectators, received a far more subdued reception. That was a sharp contrast to their first fight, when the cheers for Tunney were far greater than for Dempsey, who was making his first appearance in a boxing ring in three years and was resented for that and, to a lesser degree, because more than a few sportswriters had played up Tunney's military service. Then, Tunney was looked upon as the handsome, intelligent, well-read young man who had joined the Marines during the war and was a prohibitive underdog to the scowling and menacing Dempsey, who had been capitalizing on his heavyweight title by making movies and stage appearances but not fighting. By now, though, the slacker innuendos that had been lodged against Dempsey were forgotten. So, too, apparently was his three-year hiatus from the ring. Best remembered now were his knockout of Jack Sharkey, only two months earlier, and his graciousness after losing his title to Tunney a year ago. That he was also the consummate prizefighter, unrelenting and unyielding and who relied solely on an aggressive offense, made him, in the eyes of most sports fans, the epitome of a heavyweight champion. Tunney, meanwhile, had gone from hero to villain for a few reasons: many people felt he had won the title with an assortment of slick and mechanical boxing maneuvers; some were put off by his affected manner of speaking in public; and plenty of fans bought into what Paul Gallico said was the popular perception of him as "a priggish, snobbish, bookish fellow, too proud to associate with common prizefighters."

Dancing around the ring and waving to friends and sportswriters he knew, Dempsey seemed loose and relaxed. When Tunney climbed through the ropes several minutes later, Dempsey turned to him and said, "How are you, Gene?"

"Quite well, Jack, and you?" Tunney replied with a smile, before walking to his corner, appearing calm and collected. Their polite words spoke volumes about how much they respected each other.

Following the introduction of Jim Corbett, Jack Johnson, Benny Leonard, Jim Jeffries, Battling Nelson, and a number of other past and present champions, Dave Barry was introduced as the referee and two wealthy Chicago businessmen—George Lytton, a former amateur boxer, and Sheldon Clark, a Sinclair Oil Company executive—as the judges.

Most of Barry's pre-fight instructions seemed to be aimed at Dempsey.

"In the event of a knockdown, the man scoring the knockdown must go to the farthest neutral corner," Barry said in a clear, forceful voice.

"Is that clear, Jack?" Barry asked Dempsey.

The Manassa Mauler nodded.

Turning to Tunney, Barry repeated his question. "Is that clear, champ?"

Tunney nodded in the affirmative.

"Now, in the event of a knockdown, unless the boy scoring it goes to the farthest corner, I will not begin the count until he does," Barry said. "Is that clear, Jack?"

"Yes," Dempsey replied.

"Is that clear, champ?"

Tunney again nodded in the affirmative.

Barry also stressed that both rabbit and kidney punches, for which Dempsey was notorious, were forbidden. Both Dempsey and Tunney again nodded in affirmation.

"Good luck to you both," Barry finally said while waving the fighters to their corners.

In the fleeting moment before the bell sounded for the fight to begin, Leo Flynn reminded Dempsey to look out for Tunney's sneakily quick right hand, which had stunned him at the start of the first fight. And across the ring, Jimmy Bronson was once more cautioning Tunney to circle to the left as often as possible to avoid Dempsey's powerful left. In both instances, the fighters, who were hearing old refrains, stared straight ahead, well aware of what they had to do.

At 10:08 P.M. Central Daylight Time, the bell sounded. As the fight began, quite a few of those in the vast assemblage could not help but wonder: Is the fight going to be on the level? After all, this was Chicago, "City of the big shoulders," and, some worried, maybe of the big fix, too.

Dempsey charged right at Tunney, to the delight of his backers, who, it soon became evident, vastly outnumbered Tunney's supporters. Dempsey's strategy again was obvious: to force Tunney to fight at close quarters and to pound his crushing uppercuts to the body, forcing Tunney to lower his guard so Dempsey could then unleash his powerful left hook, or a right cross to the jaw.

Tunney expected that, but still, unlike in the first fight, he stood his ground and either tied up the onrushing Dempsey or met his charges with sharp left jabs to the head or swift left-right combinations, punches thrown rapid fire, one after the other. And oftentimes, Tunney, obviously confident, was the aggressor, going after Dempsey with swift barrages of punches and, on several occasions, driving Dempsey into the ropes. There was no way, and Dempsey and Tunney both knew it, that Jack Dempsey was going to outpoint Gene Tunney. If he was to win, it would have to be by a knockout, and for all of the force of his body punches, the knockout would have to be achieved by a punch—or, more likely, a series of punches—to the head.

The pattern of the fight was remarkably similar to their first encounter—Dempsey constantly stalking Tunney, bobbing and weaving, his head tucked behind his left shoulder, making his chin a difficult target, while Tunney peppered the former champion with lightning-fast punches and then danced away, usually to the left, making it more difficult for Dempsey to hit him with his patented left hook, or clinching when he felt in any danger. But it was during the clinches that Dempsey did most of his damage, albeit illegally, with rabbit punches.

Though he had made it clear during the pre-fight instructions that such punches were illegal, and despite shouted verbal protests from Tunney's corner, and occasional complaints by Tunney himself, Barry seemed oblivious to the illegal blows. However, he did, on several occasions, warn Dempsey of punches that appeared to have been low.

As in Philadelphia, Tunney was in total command, appearing to clearly win the first five rounds. Dempsey, while both slow afoot and with his punches, fought better than he had in the first fight, but what few punches he landed during those rounds seemed to have little impact on Tunney. The champion, by contrast, jolted and hurt Dempsey several times in the early rounds, particularly in the fourth, when he staggered Dempsey with a left-right combination to the head, and then two sharp rights to the jaw. By the end of the round, Dempsey needed both a dose of smelling salts and repair work for a cut under his right eye.

Dempsey did, finally, get in a good left hook, which shook Tunney at least momentarily, midway through the fifth round, but Tunney responded with with several sharp rights to the head as he continued to outbox and outslug Dempsey. By then, Gibson, Bronson, and the other seconds in Tunney's corner had only one main concern: their fighter was getting too aggressive.

"Don't take chances, Gene," Bronson said after the fifth round. "You're winning by a mile. Don't slug with him." Tunney nodded, acknowledging that he had perhaps begun living dangerously by slugging it out with Dempsey.

At the end of the fifth round, Sergeant Bill Smith, one of two Chicago police officers who had been assigned as bodyguards to Tunney from the time he began training at the Cedar Crest Country Club, became so agitated over Dempsey's rabbit punches that he leaped onto the apron of the ring near where referee Dave Barry was standing, and screamed at Barry, "You son of a bitch, if you don't stop those rabbit punches, you'll be carried out of here dead." In Chicago, in the 1920s and 1930s, even the cops sometimes sounded like bad guys, and sometimes they were.

By the end of that round, Dempsey's face was bloodied from cuts near both eyes and badly bruised from Tunney's unerring jabs and combinations. By then, too, Dempsey seemed to have slowed down. Dempsey finally appeared to have an edge in a round in the sixth when he ripped a half dozen punishing hooks to Tunney's body, but by the seventh round it was evident to even the most loyal Dempsey backers that time was running out for the former champion. Though the huge crowd was enthralled at the outset by the high drama of the fight—the veteran warrior, Dempsey, trying to regain his title from the younger, book-loving Fancy Dan—it seemed to become subdued the more that Tunney outthought and outboxed the most popular heavyweight champion of all time. Seemingly, it would take a miracle for a tiring Dempsey to beat this unmarked boxing paragon, who seemed to know when and where every punch was coming from.

But then the tenor of the fight changed dramatically in the seventh round, which, more than three-quarters of a century later, is still recalled as not only the most memorable round in boxing history, but among the most controversial episodes ever in sports. Less than a minute into the round, as Tunney began to shoot another left jab at Dempsey, the challenger beat him to the punch with a roundhouse right that caught Tunney on the left side of the head and knocked him off-balance. Instantly, Dempsey followed that blow with a crushing left hook that sent Tunney reeling into the ropes just to the left of Dempsey's corner.

With Tunney helpless and obviously hurt, Dempsey pounced, firing five lightning-fast left- and right-hand punches to the head, the last two or three of which landed as Tunney began to slowly sink to the canvas, almost as if in slow motion, before landing on his back. Dazed as he was, Tunney somehow had the presence of mind to grasp the middle rope with his left hand and, in a matter of seconds, pull himself up to a sitting position.

The pro-Dempsey crowd exploded with a roar that could be heard through most of the nearby Loop in downtown Chicago and perhaps halfway across Lake Michigan. Fifteen hundred miles away, in the living room at the elegant home of Mrs. George Lauder, Jr., in Greenwich, Connecticut, there were probably gasps from Mrs. Lauder and her daughters, Kay and Polly, as they listened to Graham McNamee bellow, "Tunney is down! Tunney is down from a barrage of lefts and rights to the face!" If they had the radio on—and how could they not have?—it had to be Polly Lauder's worst nightmare: that the handsome young man with whom she had fallen in love might get badly hurt in his second fight with the fighter they called the Man Killer—Jack Dempsey, the hardest puncher in boxing.

All of sudden, Dempsey's pre-fight prediction that he would "win by a knockout in about seven rounds" seemed astonishingly prophetic, for here, in the seventh round, Gene Tunney had been knocked down with a withering assault of punches and was obviously badly hurt.

Describing the scene, James Dawson in the *New York Times* wrote, "Society's bluebloods forgot decorum and yelled excitedly. Kings of finance and princes of industry were mingling their yells with those of governors, mayors, representatives in Congress, senators, lawyers, doctors, theater and movie folk and just plain ordinary people."

In the next day's *New York Herald Tribune*, Grantland Rice would write, "There were 145,000 crazy human beings on their feet yelling and screaming, for unless a miracle happened, Jack Dempsey had proved for the first time in the heavyweight kingdom that they can come back. He had his foot upon the lost trail, the ghostly road leading back to the top of the golden hill."

For Tunney, being knocked down was a new experience. Over a twelve-year professional boxing career that had encompassed seventy-five fights and a grand total of 488 rounds, Tunney had never been knocked off his feet. It was fitting, of course, that if anyone was going to do it, it was going to be Jack Dempsey. But if it was the first and only time that Tunney would be knocked down, it also was to become the most controversial knockdown in boxing history.

As soon as Tunney landed on the floor, Barry prepared to start a count, but then realized that Dempsey was standing against the ropes within a few feet of the down and dazed Tunney and close to Dempsey's corner. With the Soldier Field crowd in an uproar, Barry called out to Dempsey to go across the ring to a neutral corner. But either because of the crowd noise or his own personal confusion, Dempsey did not move. Finally, Barry, turning away from the supine Tunney, screamed at Dempsey and succeeded in waving him to the farthest neutral corner.

As soon as Tunney hit the floor, the timekeeper, Paul Beeler—whose job it was to begin counting as soon as a fighter was knocked down—began a verbal count which had reached four by the time Tunney had righted himself into a sitting position on the floor, with his left hand still draped across the middle rope. Ignoring Beeler's count, Barry began his own: *One . . . Two . . . Three . . .* , in effect, boxing's version of the last rites.

When Barry's count reached two, Tunney, still looking dazed and glassy-eyed, looked up at Barry, seemingly aware of what was happening. The question was: Could Tunney get up before Barry intoned ten?

Tunney claimed later he was convinced from the time he heard Barry count two that he could get up, but also realized it was in his interest to stay down, to rest and plot his strategy, until the count got to nine.

"When I regained full consciousness, the count was two," Tunney was to say later. "I knew nothing of what had gone on and was only aware that the referee was counting two over me. So I knew I had eight seconds in which to get up."

As Barry called out nine, Tunney bounced to his feet, whereupon Dempsey charged at him, obviously going for the kill. Considering how badly he had hurt Tunney, and with almost two minutes still left in the round, most Dempsey supporters were virtually certain that the Manassa Mauler would knock out Tunney. As he lay on the canvas, Tunney, as he was to say later, knew that he had three options once he was up: he could grab and clinch the charging Dempsey; he could stand firm and try to counter his charge with a knockout punch of his own; or he could retreat for the rest of the round, or at least until he felt strong enough to throw some punches of his own. Being Tunney, the smart, and now levelheaded, master boxer, he chose the latter course.

Bouncing up from the floor just as Barry was raising his right hand and preparing to intone ten, Tunney realized that his legs were all right. "*Your legs are fine*, was the first thought I had after rising," Tunney was to recall. Indeed, they were better than Dempsey's, which seemed to have slowed to a slog. Tunney, though still somewhat shaky, eluded Dempsey's first charge by dancing backward. With almost two minutes left in the round, Dempsey had plenty of time, but he simply could not catch up with the retreating Tunney.

As Tunney continued to retreat, thousands of Dempsey supporters in the crowd, enraged at Tunney's defensive tactics, began to scream imprecations at the champion, defying him to stand his ground and fight. "Stand up and fight, you yellow coward!" bellowed one burly man. "Fight, you son of a bitch!" screamed another ringsider. Of course, Dempsey's legion of supporters in the crowd knew that was not going to happen, not against the menacing Manassa Mauler. Maybe he wasn't the Dempsey of three or four years ago, but, as he had just demonstrated, he could still knock down the man who had taken away his heavyweight title.

They also knew that if the roles were reversed, Dempsey, on getting up after a knockdown, would have charged at Tunney, as he had after he had been knocked down with the first punch of the Firpo fight. Retreat? Jack Dempsey? Never.

When Dempsey did manage to close in on the retreating Tunney, the increasingly clearheaded champion grabbed Dempsey's arms, both to clinch and to prevent Dempsey from banging him on the back of his neck with rabbit punches. Surely, Dempsey's fans, both in the vast stadium and listening to radios across the country, felt that he would eventually catch up with Tunney and knock him out. But he could not. Finally, in his abject frustration, Dempsey stopped in his tracks, dropped his gloves to his side and then, with his face contorted into a malevolent sneer, waved at Tunney with his left glove to come forward. He muttered, "Come on and fight, you son of a bitch."

Seated in the first row at ringside with Dempsey and Tunney right in front of him, Paul Gallico saw what he was to describe as "a glance of bitter, biting contempt for his opponent." In his story, Gallico, only in his twenties but already one of the best and brightest sportswriters in the country, wrote, "I thought that little bitter laugh that came from his throat when he dropped his hands to his sides after pursuing Tunney twice around the ring was half contempt for the man who would not meet him toe to toe, and half resignation, amusement, at himself. Here he was, Jack Dempsey, the greatest hitter in the ring, with his man licked, broken and dizzy, and he couldn't finish him, couldn't summon that final vicious urge from deep down in him to whip at this man again and again until he went down the way the others had gone down before him—so they could count fifty over them if they wanted to."

Dempsey's gesture, urging Tunney to come on and fight, was futile, of course, as Dempsey knew it would be. Years later, Dempsey would say, "That seems pretty silly, when I look back at it, though a lot of guys wrote some nice things about it. Why should he do what I wanted him to do?"

By late in the round, Tunney, an extraordinarily conditioned athlete, had recovered sufficiently to fight back and land several good combinations—left- and right-hand punches in succession—as Dempsey appeared to tire, as much, apparently, from pursuing Tunney around the ring as from the assault of punches that had knocked Tunney down. Just before the bell, Tunney rocked Dempsey with a right to the chest, just above the heart, which Dempsey was to say was "the hardest blow I have ever received. I thought I was going to die after that punch. I couldn't get my breath."

As Grantland Rice was to write, "Dempsey wore himself down in a futile pursuit of the faster man. At this moment, it was the wounded lion chasing the antelope, and the antelope got away." Rice may have had the wrong fighter wounded, since Tunney, at least when he got off the floor, appeared to have been far more wounded than Dempsey, but his analogy was both colorful and accurate enough. Dempsey had had his chance in the seventh round, but it had been squandered, both because of his inability to corner Tunney after the knockdown and because of Tunney's masterful boxing skills, even when under duress, and his superb physical condition. "He had let the big crowd roar and rave and jeer as he danced away, a ghost that Dempsey couldn't reach," Rice wrote with great perspicacity.

It was the first round that Dempsey had clearly won in seventeen rounds with Tunney, although some writers such as Damon Runyon inexplicably gave Dempsey four of the first seven rounds in the second fight. But then Runyon was a huge Dempsey booster, and a close attachment to a fighter can color a reporter's observation in scoring a fight. Rice and most other writers thought Dempsey had won only two of the first seven rounds, and some felt he had only won the seventh. But he had won the round solely because of the knockdown. Even after the knockdown, and especially in the last minute of the round, Tunney had outboxed, and certainly outwitted, Dempsey. By the eighth round, it was obvious that Dempsey was spent. Refreshed after his minute rest in his corner, Tunney seemed totally rejuvenated.

In total control and easily eluding Dempsey's wild swings, Tunney dropped Dempsey with a right to the head midway through the round, the one and only time he would knock down Dempsey over twenty rounds. In a move that would raise eyebrows, Barry immediately began a count before Tunney had even had a chance to head for a neutral corner. Could, some boxing cynics immediately wondered, Boo

Boo Hoff and some other racketeers who'd bet heavily on Tunney
somehow have managed to bribe Barry before the fight? No matter,
for before Barry reached two on his premature count, Dempsey
jumped up. It was typical Dempsey. To Dempsey, a fight in the ring
was like the winner-take-all fights he had had in Colorado saloons
when he was a hungry teenager. Just about anything went, and if you
got knocked down you got up as soon as you could; the hell with resting on the floor. It had nothing to do with machismo or trying to show
that you could take it and weren't hurt. You just got up as quickly as
you could and went right at the guy who knocked you down.

Which Dempsey did now and with utter futility. For the remainder
of the eighth round and over the last two, Dempsey, slow and tired,
pursued Tunney doggedly, but never came close to landing an effective
punch, while Tunney pummeled him repeatedly with snapping left
jabs that opened a second cut near Dempsey's left eye. In Dempsey's
corner, Leo Flynn continued to scream, "Lead! Lead! Lead!," unavailingly trying to get Dempsey close enough to unload a left hook or
right cross that might lead to another knockdown. Dempsey heard
Flynn, loud and clear, but, tiring by the minute, he knew he had nothing left. For all intents and purposes, the fight had ended in the seventh
round—ironically, the only round Dempsey had clearly won.

More out of frustration than anything else, Dempsey wrestled Tunney to the floor early in the tenth and final round, and then, his face a
bloody mask, was battered about the ring by an assortment of swift
punches to the head. It was a fitting coda to what, for the most part,
had been another one-sided bout between Dempsey and Tunney, but
that would forever be remembered for the seventh-round knockdown
and its alleged "long count."

As the final bell sounded, McNamee said into his microphone, "It
is all over and Dempsey is practically out on his feet, and I think there
is no question now who is the champion." McNamee, who never reported Dempsey's initial refusal to go to a neutral corner, and the de-
layed count that ensued, then said, "Ladies and gentlemen, I assure you
there were no fouls in this fight. There was nothing questionable that I
saw." How McNamee, an experienced sports broadcaster, could have
missed seeing the dozens or so of rabbit punches that Dempsey had

thrown—at least forty by Tunney's count—or not mention the "long count" was unfathomable. And so it was that millions of listeners had no inkling of the controversy over Dave Barry's count—or, for several seconds at least, lack of a count. They would have to wait until they read the morning newspapers the next day to learn about the "long count" controversy, which would become the biggest sports story of the year—bigger even than Babe Ruth becoming the first major league baseball player to hit sixty home runs in a season—more than any of the other seven teams in the American League in 1927.

The announcement that Tunney had retained his title was anticlimactic, but still elicited almost as many boos as cheers from the crowd. Meanwhile, in the ring, Tunney, speaking into the NBC microphone, said, "Hello, everybody. It was a real contest all the way through. I want to say hello to all my friends in Connecticut and elsewhere. Thank you." Tunney was even more precise during a brief post-fight interview with Major Andrew White, who had broadcast the fight for CBS, when he said, "Hello to my good friends in Greenwich, Connecticut."

In the Lauder family home in Greenwich, Polly Lauder no doubt had recovered from the shock caused by Tunney's knockdown in the seventh round, and if she was indeed listening, had to know that she was one of the "friends in Connecticut" to which Tunney had referred during his radio interviews. One can imagine the collective sense of ecstasy among the Lauders in knowing that not only had Tunney retained his title but also had not been hurt.

As the Lauders, Pryors, Gimbels, Eagans, and other Tunney supporters exulted, tens of thousands of people streamed out of Soldier Field convinced that Jack Dempsey had unfairly been denied a justified knockout victory. Disappointment also set in at many homes and other places where the fight was heard via radio. Listening to Graham McNamee's account at a friend's house on Grand Avenue on Chicago's North Side, only a few miles from Soldier Field, fifteen-year-old Studs Terkel let out a yell when Dempsey knocked Tunney down in the seventh round. "We were all for Dempsey," said Terkel, the renowned author, years later. "To us, he was a real fighter, a working-class type of guy, while Tunney was a phony intellectual. And when he knocked down Tunney, we thought, 'Dempsey is back, and he's won it.' "

Thrilled at what he had just seen, sixteen-year-old Nat Rosoff jumped up from his ringside seat, as did his father, "Subway Sam" Rosoff, whose firm had built two New York City subway lines in the early part of the twentieth century. "My dad knew Dempsey, and we were both rooting for him," Rosoff recalled seventy-nine years after the "long count" fight. As for the first Dempsey-Tunney fight in Philadelphia, the Rosoffs had traveled from New York to Chicago aboard a chartered train. "I clearly remember the knockdown and how Dempsey was hovering over Tunney near where we were sitting about ten rows back from the ring," Rosoff, in his mid-nineties, said. "When Tunney got up, we were sure Dempsey would knock him out, but Tunney got on his bicycle and Dempsey never could catch him."

In his syndicated story for the Hearst newspapers, Damon Runyon wrote that, because of the "long count," "arguments are bound to ring through the fistic world." And he was right, only he didn't realize how long they would "ring." To Dan Daniel of the *New York Journal,* Dempsey's "bullheaded attitude doubtless lost the title for him" and deprived him of becoming the first heavyweight ever to regain his title. Nat Fleischer wrote, "Gene Tunney was Jack's superior in everything but the punch, and even in this Gene was excelled by a slight margin." Fleischer—who clocked Tunney as having been down for fourteen seconds—went on to point out that, by his count, Tunney landed almost twice as many punches as Dempsey did, and three times as many over the last two rounds.

Dempsey's manager, Leo Flynn, and his other cornermen, along with untold thousands of sports fans, and some sportswriters who should have known better, claimed that Dempsey had been robbed— that he had knocked out Tunney, yet had lost the fight. Immediately after the fight, Flynn announced that he would file an appeal with the Illinois Athletic Commission asking it to reverse the decision. "Intentionally or otherwise, I was robbed of the championship," said Dempsey in his dressing room, with cuts along both eyes, blood oozing from the mouth, a cut on his left ear, and his badly bruised face. "In the seventh round, Tunney was down for a count of fourteen or fifteen. Every stopwatch around the ring caught the time as about fifteen seconds, and the inefficiency of the referee or the timekeeper, or both, deprived me of the fight.

"Everybody knows I am not a whiner," Dempsey went on, as several hundred reporters took down his every word. "When Tunney beat me last year, I admitted that he was the better man that night. I am not an alibi artist, but I know down in my soul that I knocked Tunney out tonight, and what's more chased him all around the ring and should have won on points at least."

Asked if he wanted to fight Tunney again, Dempsey said, "You bet your life. I beat Tunney tonight, and I will beat him again any time he wants to get into the same ring with me. I am not ready to retire by a long shot—not before I've had another crack at Tunney."

If Dempsey was an angry loser, Tunney was hardly a gracious winner. "I have boasted that fellow for eight long years, but it is all over now," Tunney said just a few hours after the fight, while rubbing a lump the size of an egg on the back of his neck. "He hit me below the belt on several occasions, and he butted me with his head like a goat. In the clinches he twisted my arms and was apparently trying to wrench or break them by bending them backward. And those rabbit punches kept banging the base of my skull."

Realizing that Tunney had nothing to do with the "long count," Dempsey had a different perspective once he had calmed down several hours after the fight. Once again, as at Philadelphia, he lauded Tunney. "There's not much for me to say except that I was beaten again tonight by a man who demonstrated beyond all question of doubt that he is the better man," he said. "I felt in the seventh that the championship had come back to me, that I had shattered that old stuff that they can't come back. I take my hat off to him. He's a real champion, worthy of the name and title."

Like his droll explanation to his wife about his badly bruised face after the Philadelphia fight, that gracious statement would add to Dempsey's stature and make him even more popular than he had been before the rematch—and he already had been the most popular athlete in the world.

Even those who agreed with Dempsey that he had indeed knocked out Tunney felt that his actions, or inaction, after the knockdown had cost him the fight. And virtually no one agreed with Dempsey that, having failed to win by a knockout, he deserved to have won the fight by decision. The Dempsey camp also contended that Dave Barry, the referee, should have picked up the count of the timekeeper, Paul Beeler, once Dempsey had finally gone to a neutral corner, rather than start at one. But Beeler explained that once he saw that Dempsey had not gone to a neutral corner, he stopped his count at four, and then restarted it at one in conjunction with Barry after Dempsey had finally gone across the ring.

Both Barry and Beeler appeared to have been right. One of the Illinois Athletic Commission members, Paul Prehn, told reporters at ringside after the fight that the commission's rules provided for a restart of a count once a fighter reaches a neutral corner after at first, as was the case with Dempsey, he had refused to do so. Arthur Mercante, who refereed more than one hundred title fights, including the first Muhammad Ali–Joe Frazier bout, said seventy-five years later that Barry had acted improperly. "He should have picked up the time-keeper's count," Mercante, a member of the Boxing Hall of Fame, said. Mercante, though, was probably thinking of the rules in New York, where that was the policy.

Estimates of how long Tunney had been down ranged from fourteen to eighteen seconds. More important, though, was whether Tunney could have gotten up before a count of ten had Dempsey immediately gone to a neutral corner.

Tunney said he definitely could. At different times, he told varying accounts of when he might have been able to get up. The day after the fight, Tunney told a group of sportswriters in his suite at the Hotel Sherman, "I can say that I could have arisen after one second had I wanted to." To most ringsiders near Dempsey's corner, where Tunney was knocked down, that seemed highly unlikely, especially if he was referring to the initial count, which Barry halted at two when he saw that Dempsey had not gone to a neutral corner. It also appears that he could not have gotten up at one, or even two, on the film of the fight.

Days after the fight, Tunney said on several occasions that he had not become aware of the referee's count until it had reached two, which was after he had been down for at least six seconds and possibly longer. In an interview with *New York Journal* sportswriter Frank Graham in 1961, Tunney said he had no idea how long he was down. "I only know that when I began cerebrating I heard the referee count two. By nine my head was clear and I got up."

At other times, Tunney said he might have gotten up earlier, but that Billy Gibson and Jimmy Bronson, in his corner, had yelled to him to stay down until the count of nine, which of course he did. Tunney also said right after the fight that Jimmy Bronson, his chief trainer, had warned him between the sixth and seventh rounds not to get careless. "But I thought Dempsey was weak and wobbling," Tunney said in conceding that he had ignored Bronson's advice.

Glad as he was that Tunney managed to survive the knockdown, Bronson laced into Tunney verbally when he returned to his corner after the fateful seventh round. "I told him plenty before the eighth round started," Bronson, Tunney's most trusted cornerman, said. "I had just warned him to keep away from that one-two punch when he walked right into it. When he came back, I called him everything I could think of, and all he could say was, 'I'm all right, Jimmy, don't worry.' And he was. He showed that by fighting the smart battle that he did."

Tunney vaguely remembered the first punch that started the assault which led to the knockdown. "I started a left lead, and Dempsey crossed his right over it," Tunney said. After that, though, everything was a blur. "I didn't see the left coming," he said. "So far as I was concerned, it came from out of nowhere. That embarrassed me more than anything else, not to mention the damage done."

Of the left hook, Tunney said, "It was the hardest of the seven blows and the one that prepared me for the five others and, incidentally, for a much discussed but pleasant fourteen seconds' rest on the canvas."

As to whether he could have gotten up without the benefit of the "long count," Tunney said, "I don't know. I can only say that at the count of two I came to and felt in good shape. I had eight seconds to go. Without the long count I would have had four seconds to go. Could I, in that space of time, have got up? I'm quite sure that I could have. When I regained consciousness after the brief period of blackout, I felt that I could have jumped up immediately and matched my legs against Jack's, just as I did."

In another of Tunney's writing ventures, he explained why he stayed down until the count reached nine. "Realizing as do all professional boxers that the first nine seconds of a knockdown belong to the man who is on the floor, I never had any thought of getting up until the referee said nine," Tunney said years later. "Only dazed boxers who have momentarily lost consciousness and 'show-offs' fail to take the nine seconds that are theirs. My signal to get off the floor was the count—nine. The action of the referee in not taking up the count immediately when I went on the floor, regardless of where Dempsey was, is another question."

Not that Tunney was about to second-guess Dave Barry, who wrote in *The Ring* magazine two months later that he thought Tunney had "regained his senses in three or four seconds" after being knocked down.

As for Dempsey, years later he paid tribute to Tunney for what he did. "I'll never know whether he could or could not have gotten up during what should have been the first section of the count," Dempsey said in suggesting that Barry should have continued counting even though Dempsey was hovering nearby. "Gene has often told me he could have, and I have no reason not to believe him. Gene's a great guy. He took the count, whatever it was, and that's what any smart fighter would have done."

Rickard, of course, reveled in the controversy, knowing it could lead to a groundswell for a third fight between Dempsey and Tunney. Such a fight, Rickard was sure, would break the $3 million barrier. As it was, the fight at Soldier Field had had gate receipts of $2,658,660, the equivalent of more than $28 million today, the largest in boxing history, and had drawn a paid crowd of 104,943. That paid attendance was less than the 120,757 who had paid to see the first fight. But in both cases, the crowds appeared far bigger, and no doubt were, since some spectators had received complimentary tickets. The crowd at Sesquicentennial Stadium had been estimated at around 135,000, but many sportswriters and others experienced at estimating crowds thought that the gathering at Soldier Field was larger—about 145,000—which would have made it the biggest crowd ever to have seen a sports event in the United States to this day.

If those were record crowds, so, too, were the fighters' purses. Dempsey got $425,000 (the equivalent today of about $4.5 million), the biggest purse ever at the time for a losing fighter. Tunney's share was an astonishing $990,445.54 (more than $11 million). But Tunney had an idea. He told Rickard he didn't want a check for that amount—he wanted one for a million dollars. So he wrote out a personal check for $9,554.46 and Rickard handed him one for a million, making Tunney not only the first fighter, but the first athlete—perhaps even the first person—ever to receive $1 million for one night's work.

The big question in the immediate aftermath of the second fight was whether there would be another rematch. Dempsey said, within an hour after the fight, that he wanted to fight Tunney again. But a little while later that night he conceded that Tunney had demonstrated "beyond all question of doubt that he is the better man." That statement hardly seemed to justify a third fight between the two great rivals. But given Dempsey's near knockout of Tunney, there seemed to be more justification for a third fight than there was for a second one after Tunney had won all ten rounds in completely dominating Dempsey the first time around.

It was generally assumed that Tunney, only thirty years old, would fight again. But then, hardly anyone knew that the handsome boxing champ had fallen in love, and that the love of his life might have some bearing on whether he would.

*Old rivals Gene Tunney and Jack Dempsey
with Polly Lauder Tunney at Dempsey's
popular New York restaurant.*

STANLEY WESTON COLLECTION

Greenwich
Village
to
Greenwich,
Connecticut

O n September 23, 1927, the Greenwich, Connecticut, *News and
Graphic* reported that a dinner-dance at the Greenwich Country Club the previous night had attracted a "large society gathering" during which "returns were received over the radio
on the Tunney-Dempsey fight." The membership of the soigné club,
founded in 1892, consisted of Greenwich's beau monde, mostly old-
moneyed millionaires, Wall Street financiers and stockbrokers, bankers,
and corporate executives. Many of the members were in the Social Register, and the club seemed an unlikely place for the radio broadcast of a
boxing bout to be blaring during a dinner-dance, even one for the
heavyweight championship of the world. But then Gene Tunney had
been turning up more and more in the affluent New York City suburb,
ostensibly to visit his friend, Sam Pryor, Jr., and had even spoken at the
Greenwich Rotary Club. Thus Tunney had become something of a
sports favorite in a community whose wealthy residents had paid boxing very little, if any, heed in the past. Tennis, golf, and polo were the

most popular sports among members of the Greenwich Country Club, and boxing still carried the stigma of a corrupt and brutal sport patronized mainly by the lower classes. It most certainly was hardly popular in Greenwich, then and now the quintessence of a wealthy New York City suburb.

Because of Tunney's friendship with the Pryors and the fact that Sam was in a ringside seat at Soldier Field for the champ's rematch with Dempsey it was possible that some of the club's members had requested that the fight broadcast be played during the dinner-dance. Then, too, maybe some members of the Greenwich Country Club had gotten wind of a burgeoning romance between the handsome boxer with a literary bent and the beautiful heiress Polly Lauder. And just perhaps, those who had found out about the romance had used the dinner-dance, and the fight broadcast, as an appropriate occasion to spread a bit of gossip among fellow members, while first extracting pledges to keep the little secret within the club or at least within the members' social circle.

Whatever the reason for the interest in the fight, many of the several hundred partygoers at the club cheered when Tunney was declared the winner, and then cheered even louder when he said he sent his best wishes to his "friends in Greenwich, Connecticut."

Fifteen hundred miles to the west, Tunney was entertaining a group of friends, including Pryor, Pryor's classmate Ed Dewing (Polly Lauder's brother-in-law), Bernard Gimbel, who also lived in Greenwich, and Father Francis Duffy, the chaplain of the celebrated "Fighting 69th" Army regiment from New York City, in Tunney's penthouse suite at the Hotel Sherman, along with Chicago Mayor Big Bill Thompson—who had pretty much allowed Capone and other gang leaders to have free rein in the city—and some other people he hadn't met in the past.

On the day after the fight, more newspapers ran stories about the rematch on the front page than had done so after the first fight, mainly because of the controversy over the "long count." People who had never paid attention to boxing found themselves interested in why and

how Tunney was able to remain on the floor at Soldier Field for perhaps as long as seventeen seconds without being counted out. After all,
almost everyone knew that if you were down for ten seconds in a boxing bout you were out. Indeed, "down and out," like many boxing expressions, had long been used in everyday conversation for years.

Mainly because of some poor reporting, the consensus across the
United States and elsewhere was that Dempsey had been robbed from
regaining his title. Even editorial writers, ignorant of the Illinois rules
relating to knockdowns, inveighed against referee Dave Barry's handling of the knockdown, while contending that Dempsey had actually
knocked out Tunney and should have been declared the winner.
Everyone, it seemed, had an opinion, one way or the other, on perhaps
the biggest sports controversy ever in the United States.

One of the few people, it seemed, who did not dispute Barry's conduct after the knockdown was Dempsey. Asked again about the "long
count" the day after the fight, Dempsey said he was not disposed to
"squawk" about it, but would sign an affidavit protesting Barry's actions and Tunney's victory if his manager, Leo Flynn, chose to file a
formal protest with the Illinois Athletic Commission. Flynn, to no
one's surprise, did just that the afternoon after the fight, claiming that
Dempsey had in fact knocked Tunney out in the seventh round, and
that Tunney had been down for "from thirteen to seventeen seconds"
and yet was permitted to continue fighting. The protest, as expected,
was summarily rejected by the commission's chairman, John Righeimer,
who said it would not even be considered by the commission, both because Flynn did not have a contract with Dempsey, and because the
fight had been conducted in accordance with the commission's rules.

Remaining in Chicago for another two days, Tunney faced a barrage
of questions about the "long count" and his retreating tactics in the
seventh round.

"I take it that many people are annoyed with me because I kept
away from Dempsey after he had knocked me down," Tunney said to
reporters. "Undoubtedly that nettled him, but his gesture to me to
come in and fight was merely theatrical. I could see that he was puz-

zled by my tactics, and the sensible thing for me to do was to keep him that way. In a way, Dempsey had the breaks in both of our fights because they happened to be ten-rounders. At Philadelphia he was through in the last round, and he certainly wasn't going much further in this latter fight."

Maybe Dempsey had won only one of the twenty rounds against Tunney, but Tex Rickard already was envisioning a third bout. After all, Rickard was quick to point out, Dempsey had come close to knocking Tunney out in the second fight. Rickard also knew that perhaps millions of people thought that Dempsey had indeed done just that, but had been deprived of a victory because of a referee's poor judgment.

There was one big hitch in Rickard's long-range plan for a third fight. After a few weeks of reflection and talking things over with his wife, Dempsey decided to retire. Rickard, who had become a close personal friend, tried to talk him out of it, convinced—at least he told Dempsey he was convinced in a bit of dissembling—that Dempsey would knock Tunney out the third time out. Finally, Rickard got a telegram from Dempsey that said, "Count me out, Tex." This time, Rickard realized that Dempsey really meant it and gave up all thoughts of a $3 million third fight.

Tunney, who was not surprised at Dempsey's retirement, speculated that Dempsey was quitting because he had sustained severe cuts around both eyes during the two fights and feared going blind. Dempsey never admitted that that was the reason, but Nat Fleischer, who knew Dempsey well, said that an eye specialist had told Dempsey that he risked dangerous impairment to his eyes if he continued to fight.

While he understood Dempsey's apparent rationale for retiring, Tunney was disappointed. He knew that because of the "long count" controversy, questions lingered over the legitimacy of his victory over Dempsey. Thus he was anxious to fight Dempsey again, both because of the enormous purse he would be guaranteed, and so that he could vindicate himself from aspersions that he actually should have been counted out at Soldier Field.

The day after the fight, two friends of Tunney's from Greenwich Village had run into Al Capone at the LaSalle Street railroad station. During a brief conversation, Capone told Tunney's friends that he had lost forty-five thousand dollars betting on Dempsey, but didn't care since Tunney, like Capone, was from New York—in Capone's case, Brooklyn—as if that really mattered to Scarface Al. Then, too, forty-five thousand dollars was a mere drop in the bucket for Capone, whose bootlegging business and myriad other rackets were flourishing in the Chicago area and elsewhere, bringing in millions in ill-gotten booty annually.

Capone went on to say that he had been told by friends that Tunney's training camp had been run by "a couple of college guys"—an apparent reference to relatively recent Ivy League graduates Eddie Eagan and Bernard Gimbel—and that Tunney had been spending as much time reading as training; therefore, the Capone informers said, Tunney, despite his one-sided victory over Dempsey a year ago, had no chance against Dempsey. Based on that information, Capone said, he had bet on Dempsey.

According to what Tunney's friends had told him about their chance encounter with Capone, the notorious gang leader had gotten word about five hours before the fight that the Illinois Athletic Commission had switched referees and that Davey Miller, believed to be in league with Capone, was not going to referee the fight. By then, Capone told Tunney's friends, it was too late to change his bet, even though it was unlikely he would do so. Dempsey, after all, was Capone's kind of fighter, a "man-killer," who felt that an opponent was a deadly enemy to be destroyed as quickly as possible. Tunney? He was a sissy who hit you and then ran away. Not Scarface Al's kind of guy. In Capone's world, you might hit an enemy or a gang informer on the head with a baseball bat, but then you'd walk away, not run.

Tunney's long boxing hiatus gave him more time to spend with Polly Lauder, in Greenwich, in New York (at small dinner parties at her sister, Kay's, apartment), and on Johns Island off the Maine coast.

Along the way, Tunney was to endear himself all the more to the Lauders and Pryors—and what few others who may have known about the Lauder-Tunney romance—with an appearance at Yale in the spring of 1928.

While vacationing in Miami Beach in December of 1927, three months after the "long count" fight, Tunney had met William Lyon Phelps, who for many years taught a course in Shakespeare at Yale. Phelps had read about Tunney's fondness for Shakespeare's works, and, during a round of golf, asked Tunney if he would be willing to speak to his class on Shakespeare during the coming spring semester. Tunney agreed, but asked Phelps not to publicize his appearance. He also assumed that the students would want to hear about his boxing career, physical conditioning, and the connection between reading the classics and training for a fight. But that was not what Billy Phelps had in mind.

When Tunney arrived in New Haven to speak to Phelps's class on April 23, 1928, Phelps asked him if he could focus on Shakespeare during his talk. Though unprepared to do so, Tunney agreed. Tunney then got a second surprise when he walked into a lecture auditorium in Harkness Hall and, rather than face only Phelps's Shakespeare class of 250 students, encountered a standing-room-only gathering of about 500 students, along with a number of newspaper reporters, since by then word of Tunney's appearance had gotten out.

Somewhat taken aback, and admittedly nervous at first, Tunney soon decided to focus on *Troilus and Cressida*, one of Tunney's favorites, in part because it involves a fight between Hector, whom Phelps described as "the heavyweight champion of the Trojans," and Ajax, whom the Greeks matched against Hector after Achilles, regarded as the Greeks' best fighter, refused to fight. Speaking without notes for half an hour, Tunney held his overflow audience spellbound.

Tunney said he was well aware that he had been invited to Yale because he was the heavyweight champion and "surely not because I have anything important to say about Shakespeare." But then he proceeded to show that he had plenty to say, quoting flawlessly not only from Shakespeare but also from Thomas Carlyle, the British historian and novelist, and British philosopher and writer Herbert Spencer. In talking about *Troilus and Cressida,* he jokingly compared Ajax, the boastful Greek warrior, with Jack Sharkey, whose repeated challenges had annoyed Tunney. "Now Ajax was a big powerful man without much brains, just like Jack Sharkey," said Tunney.

Professor Phelps, sitting off to one side in the auditorium, beamed at the comparison and was delighted with Tunney's talk. When it was over, the students stood and applauded, then besieged Tunney for autographs. Tunney's talk at Yale was front-page news around the country, and even beyond. A front-page story in the *New York Times* ran for more than a thousand words and included extensive quotes from Tunney.

"I believe every newspaper in the world contained some kind of report of Tunney's address," Professor Phelps was to write in his autobiography eleven years later. "Press cuttings were sent me from India, New Zealand, Alaska, Japan—indeed from everywhere. For the moment, Tunney found himself more famous for having lectured at Yale than for having defeated Dempsey, and," said Phelps, "I found myself more famous for having invited him than for any book I had written or any professional work I had done." Delighted at the response he received, Tunney was to say later that to deliver a lecture on Shakespeare at Yale as the heavyweight champion of the world was "the height of the fantastic."

The next morning in Greenwich, Polly Lauder and her family were thrilled when they read in the *New York Times* about Tunney's appearance. And as members of the Yale alumni, Sam Pryor, Jr., Eddie Eagan, and Ed Dewing were delighted at Tunney's performance at their alma mater. Once again, Tunney had shown that he was the best advertisement boxing could possibly have.

But if Tunney thought it might gain him more support and respect from the boxing establishment and most of its fans, he was wrong. Will Rogers, the popular humorist, probably best summed up the reaction of most of the boxing public when he said of Tunney's talk at Yale, "Let's have prizefighters with harder wallops and less Shakespeare." Rogers, a highly intelligent humorist with a vast populist appeal, probably was just trying to be funny, but his pithy quote would resonate with most boxing fans. In Tunney, the boxing world had a paladin as its heavyweight champion, but an unappreciated one—and Tunney knew it better than anyone.

By April, Tunney had long since told his mother, brother, and sisters that he had fallen in love with Polly Lauder. Shortly thereafter, he drove his mother and two of his sisters from their home in Riverdale in the northern Bronx to Greenwich, only about thirty miles away, to meet Polly, her mother, her sister, Kay, and her seventeen-year-old brother, George. Having grown up in relatively straitened circumstances in Ireland, and then having lived in a poor, predominantly Irish neighborhood in Greenwich Village, Mary Tunney was shocked by WASPy Greenwich—and especially the Lauder estate. Tunney, of course, had told his mother and sisters not to be nervous or apprehensive—that Polly, her mother, and sister had already embraced him warmly and would do the same to them, which they did.

Under terms of a contract that Tunney had signed with Tex Rickard a few days before the "long count" fight, Rickard would promote at least one more fight for Tunney, provided that he beat Dempsey, for which Tunney would be guaranteed at least a half million dollars. The list of viable contenders was short, and, with Rickard's approval, Tunney himself picked his opponent—Tom Heeney, a heavyweight from New Zealand who was known as "The Hard Rock from Down Under." A crude brawler, Heeney's best fighting trait seemed to be his ability to take a punch. In forty professional fights, he had lost eight times but had never been knocked out.

Heeney was far from impressive at his training camp on the Jersey Shore. Indeed, his sparring partners seemed to have no trouble hitting the Hard Rock from Down Under, whose nickname, it soon became obvious, reflected his ability to absorb punishment. He looked especially bad while sparring four rounds with a promising twenty-two-year-old New Jersey light heavyweight named James J. Braddock, who, seven years later, would win the heavyweight championship and the nickname "Cinderella Man" by upsetting Max Baer.

After one sparring session, writers gathered around Jack Dempsey, who was working for Rickard to publicize the fight. "How does he look to you, Jack?" one of the writers asked Dempsey.

"Heeney, in my opinion, has better than an even chance of winning," Dempsey said. "Only a superman can beat him. He looks to me to be in great shape. He is strong and rugged and apparently has lots of stamina. He can take a punch and also punch hard. If you can do that, you've always got a chance."

Looking at one another and trying to avoid the gaze of what they were certain to be an embarrassed Dempsey, the writers wondered if Dempsey was talking about the fighter they had just seen battered by his sparring partners and stumbling about the ring. Unfortunately he was. One of the reasons virtually all the sportswriters liked Dempsey was because of his naturalness and honesty. Thus, most of those who had just heard what Dempsey said became furious at Rickard for using Dempsey to shill for Heeney, regardless of the substantial amount of money he probably was paying the former champ. None of the writers believed a word Dempsey said, and they knew he didn't either, but felt they had to include his comments in their stories.

For a fight needing a boost, the Tunney-Heeney match got one the day before the bout when word spread that Dempsey would be in the New Zealander's corner. According to the rumor, believed to have been spread by Rickard, Dempsey was to apply for a second's license that afternoon. Late editions of several newspapers carried the report on their front pages. Apparently, if Rickard could no longer get Dempsey in the ring to fight, maybe he could get him in the ring to give advice to a challenger who could use all the help he could get and perhaps draw more people to the fight.

Among those who heard the report was Frank Menke of King Features, the Hearst syndicate that usually carried stories with Dempsey's byline but that were written by Menke in advance of Dempsey's title fights. Menke immediately sensed the inherent dangers in such a scheme: Heeney, a foreigner, trying to take the title away from a former marine who had served in the Great War, with Dempsey, who had fought the war in boxing rings, in his corner. Menke quickly realized that if that happened, Dempsey's war record, or lack thereof, as well as the slacker charges, were bound to surface again.

Soon, bells began to ring in Menke's and even Rickard's ears. Eventually, they also began to ring in newspaper offices. Paul Gallico recalled getting a phone call that afternoon. "Hello, Paul. This is Jack. Jack Dempsey. The story about my acting as a second to Heeney. Ridiculous. Nothing to it," Dempsey told Gallico, the only writer brave enough to have gotten into the ring with Dempsey. "Don't know how it got started. I wouldn't dream of it. I'm an American first and last. Get me, kid? You can say I wouldn't go in Heeney's corner if they asked me."

As it turned out, the only time Dempsey was to get into the ring on July 26, 1928, was to be introduced before the fight. Thereafter, he sat at ringside pulling, though not overtly, for his fellow American, Tunney.

From the time the gates opened at Yankee Stadium in late afternoon, it was apparent that the gate receipts would be well below the $1 million for which Rickard had hoped, but had not necessarily anticipated. Still, the crowd was around forty-five thousand, which was not bad for a fight involving a brawler from New Zealand who was given virtually no chance of winning.

Climbing into the ring, Dempsey received a thunderous ovation from the crowd, far louder than the one given to Tunney, the first New Yorker to win the heavyweight championship and who was fighting in his home state as the champion for the first time.

The fight, as expected by boxing writers who had watched Heeney spar, was one-sided throughout. Heeney, whose fearlessness overshadowed both his talent and judgment, threw a steady barrage of punches, and some, but not many, landed. By contrast, Tunney found Heeney almost as easy a target as a punching bag, connecting often to both the head and body until referee Ed Forbes stopped the fight with eight seconds remaining in the eleventh round.

Appearing to punch harder than he had in the past, Tunney rocked Heeney repeatedly with powerful blows to the head interspersed with punishing uppercuts to the body that had the New Zealander wincing in pain. At one point, Heeney was temporarily blinded by a Tunney punch, whereupon the champion stepped back and asked Forbes to see if the New Zealander was all right, a rare gesture by a fighter, but not Tunney. Along the way, Tunney clearly demonstrated that he was now as strong a puncher as he was a masterful boxer.

For Tex Rickard, the fight was a financial failure, his first after so much success since promoting the fight in Goldfield, Nevada, between Battling Nelson and Joe Gans twenty-two years earlier. Gross receipts for the fight totaled $674,950, a far cry from the $2,658,660 that the second Dempsey-Tunney bout had drawn in Chicago. Of that amount, the federal government took 25 percent and state taxes 5 percent, leaving Rickard with a net of less than $550,000. Out of that, the promoter had to pay Tunney $525,000 (slightly more than $5 million today) and Heeney $100,000 (just under $1 million), along with around $75,000 for the rental of Yankee Stadium. That left Rickard in a position he had never been in before—in the red, to the tune of more than $150,000 (about $1.5 million) and possibly much more given other expenses.

One of Rickard's greatest attributes as a promoter had been his ability to cast one fighter as a hero and the other as the villain. Of Rickard's heroes and villains, Dempsey was the only fighter who had played both roles. So it was that all five of Rickard's million-dollar-gate fights had matched a hero-type against a villain, and in all five Dempsey had been either the hero (three times) or the villain (twice). In the Tunney-Heeney fight, Rickard knew that it was not possible to cast one as the hero and the other as the villain. Maybe a lot of fans and writers thought Tunney was a phony highbrow who felt that members of the boxing establishment were beneath him, but he was an American, and a war veteran at that. And even if he wasn't a knockout artist, he was a very good fighter. So how could he be the villain in a fight against a foreign fighter from New Zealand, of all places? He wasn't. And when Joe Humphreys raised his hand in victory, most of the crowd cheered Tunney louder than he had ever been cheered before.

In the days after the Heeney fight, Rickard realized there was no logical contender to fight Tunney. So who could he match Tunney against next? Jack Sharkey was damaged goods and of no interest to Rickard. And young Max Schmeling, the German knockout artist, had severely hurt his chances when he was knocked out by a journeyman fighter Gypsy Williams only five months before the Tunney-Heeney fight. Both Schmeling's and Sharkey's times would come, but neither was a viable opponent for Gene Tunney over the next year. So Rickard, in the week after the Heeney fight, struggled to come up with a worthy challenger. He needn't have done so. On Tuesday, July 31, Tunney made Rickard's quest for a challenger academic when, at a luncheon honoring William Muldoon, the eighty-two-year-old mandarin of the New York State Athletic Commission, Tunney stunned Muldoon, Rickard, James J. Farley, and even his manager, Billy Gibson, when he announced that he was retiring. The Heeney fight, as he had promised Polly Lauder, was the grand finale of his brilliant career in the ring.

In explaining why he was retiring, Tunney touched on Rickard's concern when he indicated that the main reason was a dearth of contenders. "There is no contender at the present time who appears capable of attracting real public interest," Tunney said while declining to note that that could have been said of Tom Heeney. "If there were I might delay my retirement long enough to face him in the ring, but it looks as if it might be two or three years before a dangerous opponent is developed. That is too long to stand and wait."

It sounded like a good reason to quit. But it wasn't the real reason. The real one, which Tunney wasn't about to disclose, was that he had proposed to Polly Lauder and she had accepted—with the understanding that Tunney would never fight again. Not only that, but the couple had decided to marry during the coming fall. Furthermore, as he conceded years later, Tunney felt he had nowhere to go but downward, and that if he continued fighting he would eventually have been beaten by a younger fighter. And like Dempsey, he feared losing his eyesight or suffering brain damage in the ring.

Exactly when Tunney popped the question to Polly Lauder is uncertain. He once said that it was well before the Heeney fight. But his close friend, Sam Pryor, Jr., said the proposal was made the night he beat Heeney. After the fight, according to Pryor, he and Tunney went from Yankee Stadium to their room at the Biltmore Hotel near Grand Central Terminal. There, Pryor said, Tunney told him he was going to go through with two of the most important decisions of his life: ask Polly Lauder to marry him and then retire from the ring. According to Pryor, Tunney then left the hotel to meet with Polly, who was with her mother at the Lauders' Manhattan apartment. "At about two in the morning, he burst into the room," Pryor said, and exulted, "Sam, I'm the happiest man in the world. Polly said yes."

Whatever version is right, Polly Lauder, the Greenwich socialite and heiress to a large part of the Carnegie fortune, had agreed to marry the handsome heavyweight champion of the world. And with close to $2 million of his own in the bank, no one could say that he was marrying Polly Lauder for her money.

Often ridiculed for his love of good literature, Tunney now found himself criticized for retiring in his prime. Some boxing people, including a few prominent writers, said Tunney owed it to boxing to defend his title at least a few more times. But Tunney did not think he owed boxing anything. He had seen too many great fighters lose part, or all, of their sight, like Sam Langford and Harry Greb. He had also seen more than a few ex-fighters walking around with rubbery legs or shaking their heads uncontrollably or stuttering or mumbling incoherently, all because of boxing—which, if anything, he thought, owed them something for probably staying with the sport much too long. Still, Tunney later admitted that he was at his physical peak and still improving when he retired and probably could have continued to fight at a high level for a few more years.

Most well-known sportswriters were restrained in their comments about Tunney. To most of them, even after beating the great Dempsey twice, he was still an enigma. As John Kieran, the erudite and scholarly sports columnist for the *New York Times*—the paper's first—wrote, "He didn't look like a prizefighter; he didn't talk like a prizefighter; he didn't act like a prizefighter (except in the ring)." Even Kieran, who could not only quote Shakespeare but Cicero, Homer, and Socrates, among others, didn't sound like he was going to miss the Manly Marine despite their mutual love of classical literature.

On August 8, the *New York Times* and a number of other New York papers ran front-page stories reporting that Tunney had become engaged to Polly Lauder. The reports gained credibility when the Greenwich socialite, asked about them in telephone queries sent to Johns Island in Maine by boat—the island did not have telephone service—declined to say if they were untrue. Adding further substance to the published reports, Miss Lauder's secretary, Floyd Barbour, the head of the commercial department at Greenwich High School, told the Associated Press that reports of an engagement were "on the right track."

The story titillated readers, who had been totally unaware, as had just about all journalists, that the former heavyweight champion had been courting the heiress. They would be titillated even more the next day when newspapers across the country announced that the rumors were true and that Tunney and Miss Lauder were indeed engaged and were to be married in the coming fall or winter, and most likely in New York. The engagement announcement came in the form of a telegram sent to the mainland by boat for delivery to the Associated Press reporter waiting on a South Bristol, Maine, dock.

Reflecting the newsworthiness of the announcement, the *New York Times* carried its story on the front page alongside a story that reported a far more epochal event: the first transmission of a television broadcast, wherein moving pictures were transmitted on radio waves from the television laboratory of the Westinghouse Electric and Manufacturing Company in East Pittsburgh. Significant, and indeed historic, as the test was, the Tunney-Lauder engagement announcement attracted more attention.

And of course, the Tunney-Lauder engagement also was the talk of the town in Greenwich. That a young Greenwich socialite was to marry a former prizefighter, no matter how wealthy or handsome, came as stunning news to many of the town's affluent residents, accustomed as they were to their young women marrying stockbrokers or professional men of comparable, if not greater, family wealth.

Perhaps to ease the blow of the announcement to some of its readers, the *Greenwich Press,* one of the town's two weekly newspapers, pointed out in a front-page story that Tunney had been "the most scholarly and cultured of pugilistic champions" and had retired from the ring with more than $2 million. Further enhancing Tunney's image in the eyes of incredulous Greenwich readers, the *Press* noted, too, that Tunney and Miss Lauder would live in a pre-Revolutionary-era Colonial house on two hundred acres in Stamford that they had bought. Still, to many people in Greenwich who knew the Lauders, and their high social station in the town, the general reaction was: Polly Lauder marrying a prizefighter? How could she?

Five days after the engagement was announced, Tunney returned to New York from Johns Island by train. First, he tried to elude reporters in Maine by wearing dark glasses, pulling his coat collar up to shield part of his face, and pulling his hat brim down. Then he left the train at the 125th Street station in Harlem to avoid a phalanx of waiting media members at Grand Central Terminal. The next morning, photographs of Tunney and Polly Lauder that somehow were taken on Johns Island were spread across the front page of the New York *Daily News* and scores of other newspapers in the United States and even abroad. The engagement had become the biggest love story of the year, if not the decade, and Americans were devouring every word and picture of it that appeared in print.

A few days later, Tunney, accompanied by W. O. McGeehan, his sportswriting friend, and another man, boarded the liner *Mauretania,* which was bound for Southampton. "Tunney, Sailing, Is Lionized at Pier," read a front-page headline in the *New York Times* the following day.

"Giggling girls, longshoremen, and hundreds of others saw the former champion off at a Hudson River pier on 14th Street," not far, the *Times* pointed out, from "where Tunney once played shinny and baseball as a poor kid of the neighborhood." There was no doubt that the large crowd had been drawn by the hope of seeing Polly Lauder, who had not yet been seen by the general public. As the *Times*'s story noted, "There were more cameramen at the pier than had met the Prince of Wales, or Queen Marie, or President Wilson when he came home from Versailles." Polly Lauder, though, was nowhere to be seen.

Tunney was scheduled to go on a walking tour in France and Germany with Thornton Wilder, the American novelist and playwright, and to attend several banquets in England. For reasons never made clear, the walking tour with Wilder never took place, although Tunney did spend some time with Wilder at his home outside London. Before his return, Tunney would also meet a number of other noted writers, such as George Bernard Shaw, H. G. Wells, Ernest Hemingway, Arnold Bennett, and F. Scott Fitzgerald, whose latest book, *The Great Gatsby*, had been published the year before. Tunney was pleasantly surprised to find out that most of the literary lions he met on his trip had an interest in boxing, apparently because they equated boxers with ancient warriors of the past.

In London, about a week after his arrival from New York, Tunney was the guest of honor at a dinner arranged by Sir Harry Preston, a popular and wealthy British sportsman, that attracted about fifty guests, including Bennett and a number of other British writers and several members of the British nobility. Tunney was flattered at the composition of the guest list. Among those invited who could not make it were the Prince of Wales and George Bernard Shaw, who sent a letter from the Riviera expressing his regret at being unable to be present.

Called on to speak, Tunney delighted the other guests with his obviously well-informed references to Shaw's *Cashel Byron's Profession*, Fielding's *Tom Jones*, William Hazlitt's *The Fight*, and Victor Hugo's *The Man Who Laughs*, all of which dealt with boxing. Tunney may have disdained the publicity about his impending marriage, but he was delighted the following day to see references to his talk on the front page of several London newspapers.

Thrilled at having received a letter of regret from Shaw, Tunney wrote back to the playwright to continue a correspondence—most of it epistolary—that would last for twenty-eight years. In December Tunney and Polly Lauder Tunney would meet Shaw and his wife for the first time in London. Meanwhile, Tunney, in his last few weeks as a bachelor, continued to be in demand at dinners and other social functions in London. Even the Prince of Wales invited him to St. James's Palace for a chat.

Despite the good press Tunney was receiving in England, he chafed when reporters asked him about his coming wedding and, especially, when they raised questions about Polly Lauder and their drastically different backgrounds. Apparently because of Tunney's reactions, *Editor and Publisher,* the newspaper trade magazine in the United States, seemed to suggest in an editorial that perhaps newspapers should begin to ignore Tunney, whose departure from boxing, it said, had left "a very small vacancy in the public's sports gallery.

"Further, we do not believe that the public cares two whoops for Mr. Tunney's future plans, nor for details of his courtship conduct obtained by peephole reporting," the editorial continued. "Let him get married in peace and retire to banking, Shakespeare, philosophy, or whatever unadventurous career at last claims him."

The editorial, which seemed to reflect the sentiments of the boxing establishment toward Tunney, most certainly did not reflect the opinion of most newspaper readers. In truth, most American newspaper readers, and many abroad, too, seemed to be feasting on news of Tunney's romance, and could hardly wait for the next day's papers to read about the coming wedding and when and where it would be held.

En route to Italy aboard the liner *Saturnia,* Polly Lauder—accompanied by eleven relatives and friends, including Faith Rockefeller—had no idea where or when she was to be married. Indeed, she did not find out until the *Saturnia* docked in Naples on October 2 and Tunney hurried aboard and told her that they were to be married the next day in Rome.

Before a gathering of fewer than two dozen people, mostly Lauder relatives and friends, including Thornton Wilder and the Irish tenor John McCormack, Tunney and Polly Lauder were married in a salon at the Hotel de Russie in two ceremonies, one civil and one Roman Catholic. For whatever reason, neither Tunney's mother nor any of his siblings attended. Whether it was because Tunney, a Catholic, was, in Polly Lauder, marrying an Episcopalian was never made clear, although that seems to have been an unlikely reason. Perhaps none of them wanted to make such a long ocean voyage, which usually took at least five days and sometimes longer.

Following a lunch and reception at the hotel, Tunney and his bride, escorted by policemen, left the hotel and were engulfed by photographers. Several cameras were smashed during their dash toward the car, which quickly sped away, bound for Perugia. As the *New York Times* reported the next day, "The result was the rather unpleasant scene in which angry words were exchanged when the car left."

Despite Tunney's efforts to keep the wedding both private and secret, it was front-page news in many newspapers around the world, complete with photos taken outside the Hotel de Russie. Somehow, Tunney failed to realize that he was still a famous public figure and that his marriage to a beautiful socialite climaxed a rags-to-riches saga and was a major news story to millions of readers, many of whom had no interest in boxing whatsoever. As in dealing with sportswriters in the past, Tunney's tactlessness hurt him and made his attempts to ensure privacy for him and his wife even more difficult.

For more than fourteen months, the couple would remain in Europe, touring Italy, Spain, Yugoslavia, and England. Royally greeted wherever they went, Tunney and his wife spent much of their time attending the opera and the theater, visiting museums, reading, swimming, and attending dinner parties whose guest lists included writers, diplomats, and members of royalty, along with banquets held in the former champion's honor.

Much of the honeymoon also was spent on the island of Brioni in the Adriatic Ocean, where Tunney often took long walks with George Bernard Shaw, who had become something of an intellectual mentor for Tunney. Shaw, by then in his early seventies, was fascinated by Tunney, and he found the curious young athlete a pleasant diversion from literary people. Tunney, meanwhile, was in awe of Shaw's knowledge, not only of literature, but of art and music and, in particular, Wagnerian operas, many of which Tunney and his wife later were to attend at the Metropolitan Opera in New York. Tunney also was surprised to learn of Shaw's interest in boxing—pugilism, as both he and Tunney called it—and to hear that, in his youth, the playwright had enjoyed "sparring," as the British referred to a gentlemanly form of boxing.

In 1930, following Tunney's return to the United States, Hollywood wanted to know if Tunney was interested in performing the title role in a movie version of Shaw's *Cashel Byron's Profession*. Tunney thereupon wrote to Shaw to ask for his opinion. Shaw, never fond of the novel, responded by saying that Hollywood "would spoil it by putting a championship fight into it," which is precisely what Hollywood producers planned to do, making Byron a heavyweight champion portrayed by Tunney. In his letter to Tunney, Shaw went on to say that "you are one of the few men on earth who cannot be filmed in a sham fight, because you have been filmed in no less than three real ones of the first order, and a stage one after that would be unbearable."

Taking Shaw's advice, Tunney told Hollywood he wasn't interested.

Over the next two decades, Tunney would visit Shaw occasionally when he was in Europe on vacation with his wife or on business. They also continued to exchange letters. In his final letter to Tunney in 1948, Shaw wrote, "I hope you are all well at home, as I hold you in affectionate remembrance. I am damnably old (92) and ought to be dead." Two years later, Shaw was dead, passing away at the age of ninety-four. Theirs had been an odd relationship, but one that both men seemed to have savored and that had a significant impact on Tunney's intellectual development and his literary pursuits.

If Tunney wasn't interested in acting, Jack Dempsey was, if only because he was trying to save his floundering marriage with Estelle Taylor. When producer David Belasco, who had attended both of the Dempsey-Tunney fights, offered Dempsey the starring role as a fighter named Jack "Tiger" Dillon, and Taylor a lesser part in a play called *The Big Fight*, she told him to take it, since Belasco guaranteed that the show would reach Broadway.

Dempsey was reluctant to take the part. "Honey, I know how much this means to you, but I can't act," Dempsey said to Estelle after the offer was made. "You ought to know that. You saw me in those serials I made."

Estelle had already made twenty-seven movies, most of them silent pictures, and mostly in secondary roles, but the only time she had appeared on Broadway was as a chorus girl in 1918. *The Big Fight* was an opportunity to show what she could do in a melodrama.

"David Belasco can make a good actor out of *anybody,*" Taylor said.

To save the marriage, he agreed. The play opened in Philadelphia before a capacity audience in early September, then moved to Broadway for a four-week run. Hundreds of Dempsey fans jammed the sidewalk outside the Majestic Theatre on West 44th Street on opening night, September 18. Policemen had to clear a path for celebrities like Mayor Jimmy Walker, Ethel Barrymore, Will Rogers, Bebe Daniels, Tex Rickard, and former Dempsey nemesis James J. Farley. From New York, the play moved on to Boston and then New Haven, drawing well on opening night in both cities, but poorly thereafter before closing in early November and marking an end to Dempsey's acting career. Belasco, it turned out, could not make an actor out of everybody, as Dempsey found out while performing in a stilted fashion while uttering his few lines in what Brooks Atkinson, the drama critic for the *New York Times,* called "a somewhat piping voice."

During the next decade, the Tunneys would raise three sons—Gene Lauder, who became an assistant district attorney in Alameda County in the San Francisco Bay Area; John Varick, who would become a three-term United States congressman and then a one-term U.S. senator from California; and Jonathan, a businessman specializing in Far Eastern affairs—and a daughter, Joan. Like many of Tunney's friends, Gene Lauder Tunney and John Tunney did their undergraduate work at Yale before going to law school, while Jonathan went to Stanford.

As a father, Tunney inculcated the values of learning and knowledge to his children from the time they were toddlers. Not wanting them to grow up in the shadow of a famous father, he rarely spoke of his exploits as a fighter and kept scrapbooks and what little memorabilia he had saved out of their sight. Indeed, there was practically nothing in the Tunney household evocative of his fighting days.

Though he most certainly did not want his sons to become fighters, Tunney did provide them with boxing gloves when they were very young so that they could box with one another, more in the tradition of the old British spar sessions than to actually fight. Sometimes, though, the fraternal boxing sessions became intense. In one session, with Tunney looking on, Gene, the oldest son, responded vigorously to a sharp left jab from his youngest brother, Jonathan, known as Jay, with a flurry of hard body blows. Feeling that young Gene was taking advantage of his youngest brother, Tunney himself put on a pair of gloves, confronted his oldest son in a boxing pose and said, "Okay, Gene."

Taken aback, young Gene told his father that there was no way he was going to box with him. In response, Tunney senior pointed out that he and his father—who had given him his first boxing gloves at the age of ten, mainly so that he could learn to protect himself—sometimes sparred when he was a boy.

"But your father wasn't the heavyweight champion of the world," young Gene replied.

That drew a smile from Tunney—by all accounts a warm and caring father who was determined to see that his sons were well educated and successful—who promptly took off the gloves while, at the same time, admonishing young Gene Tunney to go easy on his youngest brother when they boxed.

For years the Tunneys would also raise hundreds of Hereford cattle and sheep on their sprawling estate, which they would call Star Meadow Farm. There, too, the Tunneys would play hosts to writers like Wilder and John Marquand; Lowell Thomas, a nationally known newscaster; David "Carbine" Williams, the inventor of the M-1 carbine rifle used by the U.S. Army starting in World War II; and Prescott Bush, a United States senator from Connecticut, who lived in Greenwich and whose son and grandson both became U.S. presidents; operatic and theatrical stars and symphony conductors; and longtime friends such as Bernard Gimbel (by then chairman of the board of Gimbel Brothers department stores), Eddie Eagan, and Sam Pryor, Jr.

From early in his career as a fighter, Tunney was drawn to men who were both well educated and successful. All the more so if they had been good athletes. Gimbel and Eagan were classic examples. Both had attended Ivy League schools—Gimbel had gone to the University of Pennsylvania and Eagan to Yale, Harvard Law School, and to Oxford—and had done well afterward, Gimbel in the family business and Eagan as a lawyer and, later, as chairman of the New York State Athletic Commission. Gimbel also had been a boxer and football player at Penn, while Eagan boxed at Yale. Both Gimbel and Eagan—and especially Eagan—were good enough to spar with Tunney, and in later years remained close to Tunney socially. Like Sam Pryor, Jr., Gimbel also was a business adviser to his longtime friend, while Eagan, particularly in their later years, frequently met Tunney for drinks after work at the men's bar at the Biltmore Hotel, the New York Athletic Club, and the exclusive Union League Club (of which Tunney, no doubt, was the first and only former boxer to become a member). Their discussions usually covered politics and business, and, to a lesser degree, sports. The two men, along with Sam Pryor, Jr., would remain Tunney's best friends until Tunney's death.

"In social gatherings with Gene, the conversation practically never turned to boxing," said Bill Stack, a former corporate executive and football captain at Yale who became a friend of Tunney after they had spent time together as officers in the Navy during World War II. "He was much more interested in talking about literature, music, and current affairs. His friends rarely brought up his boxing career, apparently because they knew he didn't particularly want to talk about it, especially when Polly and other women were around."

Of his father, John Tunney once said, "He revered learning and was keen on good literature and operatic music. He enjoyed dialogue with first-class academic and artistic minds, and he was a shrewd investor and a formidable success in business. He had a damned good sense of humor and was loved by many men in all walks of life. As a son, I found it hard to believe that someone who had grown up in such disadvantaged economic conditions could have evolved into such a cultured man."

For more than a year after returning from his prolonged honeymoon, Tunney spent most of his days and nights reading an eclectic mix of literature, ranging from H. G. Wells's *History of the World* to Edward Gibbons's *Decline and Fall of the Roman Empire,* along with books on philosophy, psychology, and economics. A superb all-around athlete, he also kept fit by playing golf, tennis, and softball, swimming, skiing, skating on the pond in the rear of his home, and deep-sea fishing in Florida.

Eventually, and inevitably, Tunney, still in his early thirties, realized that he had too much energy and enthusiasm to devote most of his time to reading and studying. He had to find something else to do, something challenging. Although it wasn't the challenge he was look-ing for, one thing he did have to do after returning from Europe was contend with two long-standing suits by Tim Mara and Boo Boo Hoff. Mara had sued Tunney for $405,000, which he claimed was owed him for services rendered before the first Dempsey fight and for an agreed-upon percentage of his purses for both Dempsey bouts and his final fight, with Tom Heeney. Hoff dropped his suit after he was unable to prove that he had provided any services to Tunney in advance of the first Dempsey-Tunney fight that had warranted $450,000, or any sum for that matter. Mara fought his suit to the end, but came up a loser in court. Like Hoff, Mara was unable to demonstrate that he had been of any assistance in getting Tunney a shot at Dempsey's title. Finally, by 1932, Tunney was free of any court suits. "In later years, my father and Gene became good friends, and Gene often came to our apartment on Riverside Drive," Wellington Mara, who succeeded her father as owner of the New York Giants, said in 2003.

Also in an effort toward keeping busy, Tunney had no trouble find-ing lucrative positions in the business world. He knew all too well that he was not in demand because of his business acumen, which had con-sisted primarily of being involved in negotiating contracts for his last half-dozen fights and in arranging his marriage in Rome. Companies wanted Tunney, either in executive capacity or on their board of direc-tors, because of his stature as an intelligent and articulate former heavy-weight champion. At any rate, Tunney soon plunged into business, finding in the corporate world the discipline, challenges, decision-making, and competition he had found lacking while spending most of his days reading at Star Meadow Farm. Many of his friends were top-level corporate executives and, with their help, Tunney soon would be a board member of almost a dozen blue chip companies. Eventually, he also would become president of a major distillery company, chairman of the board of a conglomerate that controlled a number of rubber products companies, and head of a Stamford-based building firm that constructed more than five hundred houses on a tract along the Stamford-Greenwich border in Connecticut, mainly for veterans after World War II. For a while he also was the boxing editor of the *Encyclopaedia Britannica* and sports editor of a magazine called *The Connecticut Nutmeg*.

Always interested in politics, Tunney was considered a potential candidate for the United States Senate from Connecticut in the 1930s, but discouraged efforts to get him to run. As an ardent Democrat, he spoke out in support of Franklin Delano Roosevelt when he ran for, and was elected, president in 1932 and 1936. But he turned against FDR—whom Tunney had met while Roosevelt was governor of New York in the late 1920s and Tunney was the heavyweight champion—in 1940 when he successfully sought an unprecedented third term as president on the ground that no president was entitled to seek a third term. "Even Washington didn't run for a third term," Tunney said in throwing his support in 1940 to the Republican presidential candidate, Wendell Wilkie, who became a close friend. Following that political apostasy, Tunney did not vote for a Democratic presidential candidate until his friend Joe Kennedy's son, John Fitzgerald Kennedy—like Tunney a Roman Catholic—ran in 1960.

Tunney's life as a businessman and dilettante was interrupted in 1941 when he was asked by Navy Undersecretary James Forrestal, who later served as defense secretary, to accept a commission as a lieutenant commander and start up a physical fitness program for student pilots in the Navy. After the United States entered the war in 1941, Tunney was named director of the physical fitness program for the entire Navy with the rank of captain. A lifelong fitness buff, Tunney was ideally suited for the task and reveled in it until he left the Navy at the end of the war in 1945.

As time went on, Tunney distanced himself more and more from boxing. He turned up often at fights in the 1930s, 1940s, and 1950s, but seldom after that, apart from the first bout between Muhammad Ali and Joe Frazier in 1971. That night, ironically, Tunney, virtually a forgotten champion, was introduced, but the iconic Dempsey was inadvertently overlooked by ring announcer Johnny Addie, who eventually made amends. Tunney may have been the quintessential paladin of boxing, but Dempsey got the bigger ovation. But then, many in the crowd knew that Tunney had long since abandoned the sport, while Dempsey had never really gone away.

"They're always inviting me to major fights, with all expenses paid for my wife and I, but I have no interest in going," he said in the mid-1960s. "And when I turn down the invitations, they seem to hold it against me. I just don't see any point in me being introduced in the ring before a fight. After all, I haven't fought in more than thirty years. Why should anyone be interested in seeing me in a boxing ring now?"

Life for Gene Tunney in late middle age seemingly could not have been much better. Successful in business and with a large and growing family, an estate in Stamford, an apartment on Park Avenue in New York, a summer retreat on Johns Island in Maine—which President John F. Kennedy visited with some friends at the Tunneys' invitation in 1962 for a few days of sailing and recreation—a home in Hobe Sound, Florida, and a farm on Delaware's Eastern Shore, Tunney was a contented man. But then what appeared to be an idyllic life was wracked by tragedy in late March of 1970 when his daughter, Joan Tunney Wilkinson, was accused of killing her husband, Lynn Carter Wilkinson, with an axe as he lay sleeping in their cottage about twenty-five miles north of London.

Mrs. Wilkinson, who was thirty, then drove to a friend's house, where, police said, she tried to commit suicide by inhaling fumes from her car's exhaust. Meanwhile, she had left her two daughters, five and three, in the cottage with her mother-in-law. Found by police a short while later, she readily admitted to killing her thirty-one-year-old husband. After hearing testimony that Mrs. Wilkinson had been suffering from schizophrenia for years, a judge in London ordered her committed to a hospital for the criminally insane on June 12, 1970. She subsequently was released and returned to the United States and remarried.

The event absolutely overwhelmed the family, but at least part of the pain from that family tragedy was assuaged later in the year when Tunney's middle son, John Varick, was elected to the United States Senate from California at the age of thirty-six—making him the youngest member of the Senate—when he defeated the Republican incumbent, George Murphy, a former movie actor best remembered for his roles as a song and dance man. Six years earlier, John, in his first foray into politics, had, at the age of thirty, upset a veteran Republican congressman, Pat Minor Martin, in a predominantly farming district in the California desert east of Los Angeles. In that race, John, who had only lived in the Riverside area for a few years, after serving in the Air Force nearby, and had to contend with the image of a carpetbagger, had some impressive assistance. Among those who campaigned for Tunney were his University of Virginia Law School roommate, U.S. senator Edward "Ted" Kennedy; his father; and Jack Dempsey. (Gene Tunney had known Kennedy's father, Joseph Kennedy, for years, and that association led to the friendship between their sons.)

By then, Gene Tunney and Jack Dempsey had developed a warm friendship, seeing each other occasionally in New York, where Dempsey had settled after retiring to run a popular restaurant in midtown Manhattan. Told by Tunney that his son was involved in a tight congressional race, Dempsey offered to campaign for him. When Tunney told his son, John Tunney, understandably, welcomed the help of the old Manassa Mauler. Tunney and Dempsey subsequently appeared at a number of campaign rallies for John Tunney, drawing crowds of more than one thousand at three barbecues where films of the Dempsey-Tunney fights were shown, with commentary afterward by the old fistic adversaries. As it developed, Tunney won the election in an upset by only nine thousand votes in a district of about a half-million people, and many observers felt that Dempsey's campaign appearances made the difference. The following January, Dempsey, at John Tunney's invitation, traveled to Washington with Tunney's father to attend his swearing-in ceremony.

While Tunney made a relatively easy transition from prizefighter to businessman and country squire, Jack Dempsey hit some rough spots after retiring from the ring following the second Tunney fight.

After his last theatrical venture in *The Big Fight,* Dempsey was hired by Tex Rickard to be his co-promoter on a fight between Young Stribling and Jack Sharkey in Miami, where Rickard had recently bought a home and where he had invested heavily in real estate on Miami Beach. Even Dempsey knew that Rickard, with whom he had become close, had hired him to try to draw attention to a fight that had generated little interest. Shortly before the fight, on January 5, 1929, Rickard died in a Miami hospital when an infection set in following surgery for a gangrenous appendix, with his third wife and Dempsey at his bedside. He was fifty-nine, or maybe even older. No one knew for sure. Seven months before he died, Rickard said he was worth about $2.5 million, but after his death, Dempsey, who knew him as well as anyone, claimed the old faro dealer from the Klondike left a lot less.

"Tex was my best pal for twelve years," Dempsey said. "His word was better than a gold bond. He never went back on it."

Later that week, during a two-day wake, about twenty-five thousand people filed past his bier in the third Madison Square Garden, where the boxing ring usually was erected and where the ice was set down for New York Rangers hockey games, the team Rickard launched—and which he named for his Texas background—in the fledgling National Hockey League in 1926. Thousands more filled the arena for his funeral service on January 9, with several thousand more lined up outside the Garden on Eighth Avenue to watch as his coffin was placed in a hearse for the trip to Woodlawn Cemetery in the Bronx, where another old sheriff from the west, Bat Masterson (who had become a New York sportswriter in the early part of the twentieth century), also had been buried. It was an unprecedented tribute to a fight promoter, whom the *New York Times,* in an editorial after his death, called "one of the great showmen of all time."

Later in 1929, the year Rickard died, Dempsey was to lose almost everything he had, roughly $3 million, in the stock market crash. Fortunately, Estelle Taylor was still making movies during the last few years of their rocky marriage. Like Benny Leonard, who had also been wiped out by the Wall Street collapse, Dempsey considered making a comeback at the age of thirty-five. First, though, in need of immediate income, he fought almost two hundred exhibitions across the country, sometimes as many as four in one night, and winning almost all of them by knockouts, usually against local area amateurs. The exhibitions earned Dempsey about $200,000 and, as sort of a trial run toward a possible comeback, he fought ranking heavyweight Kingfish Levinsky in Chicago in 1932 when Dempsey was thirty-nine. Levinsky, one of the better of a poor lot of heavyweight contenders, easily warded off most of Dempsey's punches and found the old champ an easy target during their four-round bout. Realizing he had nothing left, the exhibition ended any thoughts Dempsey had of making a comeback.

Over the next seven years, Dempsey appeared in several movies and, still hugely popular, refereed scores of fights and wrestling matches to which he often was the biggest attraction. As a boxing referee, Dempsey, not surprisingly, was somewhat lenient, to say the least. If a young fighter turned to him to complain about an opponent's roughhouse, even foul, style of fighting, Dempsey was apt to say to the complainant, "Never mind that, son. Let's just keep fighting and have ourselves a nice little fight."

The money Dempsey earned, especially from his exhibition bouts, was enough to put him back on his feet and financially able in 1935 to open a restaurant on Eighth Avenue across from the third Madison Square Garden, which later was moved to the west side of Broadway in Times Square where it remained open until 1975. In between he managed to enlist in the Coast Guard in 1942 at the age of forty-seven after first being rejected by the Army because of his age. Given a commission, Dempsey headed the physical fitness program at a Coast Guard base in New York, then saw service in the Pacific, including at Okinawa by which time most of the fierce fighting on the island had ended. Pictures of Dempsey standing in a landing craft as it approached Okinawa, wearing a battle helmet and with a machine gun in his left hand, appeared in newspapers throughout the world. The picture appeared to have been staged just like the photos of Dempsey in striped work clothes and cap wielding a riveting gun while ostensibly working in the Hog Island Shipyard in South Philadelphia during World War I.

Years later, referring to his wartime experiences in the Coast Guard and the slacker charge that had been leveled against him during World War I, Dempsey said, somewhat ruefully, "They said I was a slacker in World War I and a hero in World War II. They were wrong both times."

Dempsey ran his popular restaurant, which at its second location became a prime Manhattan tourist attraction, with a hands-on approach. For years he greeted awestruck customers at the door, near where he usually sat by the large front window. If he knew a patron well, he would personally lead him to a table. "And you march in, proudly, under escort," Paul Gallico, an occasional visitor, would write. "It feels like being presented at court."

To no one's surprise, he and Estelle Taylor divorced in 1932 after five years of marriage. His third marriage, to Hannah Williams, a singer, lasted ten years. It also produced Dempsey's only children, two girls, Joan and Barbara, of whom he was awarded custody and on whom he doted. Dempsey married for the fourth time in 1958 to Deanna Piattelli, the owner of a Manhattan jewelry store, whose daughter, Barbara Lynn, he adopted. It was the most enduring and happiest of his four marriages and lasted until his death following several strokes at the age of eighty-eight on May 31, 1983.

In between his third and fourth marriages, Dempsey had a brief reconciliation with Jack Kearns at a dinner in New York on January 30, 1950, at which Dempsey was honored by the Associated Press as the greatest fighter of the half-century, and at which Kearns was an honored guest. Forgetting, at least for the night, that Kearns had harassed him for years with legal claims and had kept around half of his earnings until their split in 1926, Dempsey told the assembled guests that he was grateful to Kearns "for making me a champion" and for earning him $1 million. It was a graceful and noble acknowledgment and drew a burst of applause. Kearns in turn told the audience that "Everybody has always known that my heart belonged to Dempsey." That comment took a lot of people, including Dempsey, by surprise. Nevertheless, Dempsey and Kearns shook hands warmly. "As of that night, I forgave Doc for a lot of things—even though I could never forget," Dempsey said more than a quarter of a century later.

About a dozen years after that meeting, Kearns, down on his luck, came into Dempsey's restaurant, and while having lunch with his most famous fighter, asked Dempsey for a five-hundred-dollar loan. "I gave him the dough and for the first time in all the years I had known Doc, I pitied him, which made me feel pretty awful," Dempsey was to say. It was the last time they would meet. Kearns was to die about a year later, on July 7, 1963 at the age of eighty-one.

Six months after Kearns's death, Dempsey's sympathy for his former manager turned to anger when *Sports Illustrated* ran a story in January 1964 claiming that Kearns had put plaster of paris on the wet gauze that he applied to Dempsey's hands before he knocked out Jess Willard to win the heavyweight title. That, of course, would have made Dempsey's gloves rock-hard and a far more lethal weapon than they usually were. The story carried the joint byline of the deceased Kearns and Oscar Fraley, who had collaborated with Kearns on his autobiography, *The Million Dollar Gate*, which would be published two years later without the plaster of paris allegation.

Enraged as he was by the charge, Dempsey took heart when it became obvious that virtually no one believed the story. Skeptics, medical experts, and others pointed out that had the gauze beneath Dempsey's gloves been "loaded" with plaster of paris, he probably would have broken every bone in Willard's face and in Dempsey's own hands, too, and that it also probably would have shattered the gloves. Dempsey eventually sued the magazine on the grounds that the article had damaged his reputation and name and had resulted in a loss of income. That last element of Dempsey's suit was something of a stretch, since no one seemed to believe the story; his restaurant continued to thrive; he remained much in demand at various functions; and his stature as an American sports icon stayed intact. As it developed, Dempsey was to say, an out-of-court agreement with *Sports Illustrated* was reached and an apology printed by the magazine. It was bad enough that Kearns had hounded Dempsey for hundreds of thousands of dollars long after they had ended their fighter-manager relationship. Now, even in death, Kearns was still causing him trouble.

Two years later, in 1966, when he was seventy-one, Dempsey made an emotional return to his birthplace of Manassa, Colorado, where the house in which he was born had been removed, turned into a museum, and relocated to a park named for the town's most illustrious son. Five thousand people gathered for the dedication ceremony, a parade through the town of about one thousand residents, which included Dempsey astride a horse, and a barbecue. It was the first time in four decades that Dempsey had been in Manassa, and, as he told the big crowd, he was deeply touched by the honor. The museum's curator, Michelle Richardson, said in July of 2005 that visitors had since come to the out-of-the-way, difficult-to-reach museum from as far off as South Africa and Denmark. "It's amazing where some of them come from," she said.

As it developed, Dempsey's fists remained formidable even after the Manassa museum had opened. In his early seventies, Dempsey was riding home one night when his taxi stopped at a light in midtown Manhattan. As it did, two young men opened the back doors on both sides of the cab, obviously bent on mugging Dempsey. Leaping out of the taxi, Dempsey hit one of the would-be muggers with a right cross from out of the past and then flattened his accomplice with his old patented left hook. Ironically, Dempsey was to say that he felt sorry for the young men having to resort to mugging tactics. "They obviously thought they saw a perfect victim—a well-dressed, older man who would fork over his money right away," he was to say. Obviously the young men both thought wrong and picked the wrong man to try to mug.

Tunney, with whom Dempsey's name would be forever inextricably linked, had preceded Dempsey in death by five years, dying in 1978 at the age of eighty-one of a blood infection. Dempsey's death had been reported on the front page of the *New York Times,* along with a three-thousand-word obituary by sports columnist Red Smith in the sports section along with a number of secondary sidebar stories. At his fourth wife's request, Dempsey, the Manassa Mauler from Colorado who spent most of his adult life in Los Angeles and New York and was, above all, a man of the people, was buried in Southampton on Long Island, a summer retreat for the wealthy close by the Atlantic Ocean and hardly Dempsey's kind of town.

Tunney's death, by contrast, was reported on page 22 of the *Times* in the form of an unbylined obituary that ran about 750 words, with a four-column headline that read: "Tunney, Boxing Champion Who Beat Dempsey, Dies." Tunney may have decisively beaten Dempsey twice, but Dempsey still got top billing, even in death, and, indeed, even got mentioned in headlines about Tunney's death. But then, it has been Dempsey, far more than Tunney, whose memory and accomplishments have remained green. Since Dempsey retired in 1927, there have been—at last count—twenty-two fighters named for him, including nineteen "Young Jack Dempseys," one "Mexican Jack Dempsey," one "Little Jack Dempsey," and one "Sailor Jack Dempsey." By contrast, so far as is known, no other fighter has ever taken the name of Gene Tunney.

Though Dempsey remained the more popular of the two after they had both left the ring, Tunney did become more appreciated as time went on. About seven years after his last fight, Tunney was asked by Paul Gallico, then the sports editor of the New York *Daily News,* if he would referee a series of bouts at Yankee Stadium between a team of amateur fighters from England and a group of Golden Gloves champions from New York. Tunney was reluctant at first, both because he had become so far removed from boxing and, apparently, because he was unsure of how the crowd would react to him. But he finally agreed, and when he stepped into the ring and was introduced, the crowd of fify thousand gave him an ovation that lasted about ten minutes. As Gallico said, the cheering was a little late in coming, but Tunney was deeply touched. After all, he had never heard cheering for him like that before.

In 1968, ten years before Tunney died, Jim Murray, the brilliant sports columnist for the *Los Angeles Times,* wrote that Tunney should have been a living legend, "the toast of every Irish bar on two continents." Instead, Murray, who also was Irish, said, "They never called him 'Champ.' He was unloved, underrated, shunned by his own people, rejected by history. Still, he was the best advertisement his sport has ever had." Murray went on to write that "he was an austere man, pedantic, bookish, autocratic and aloof. He always acted as if he were slumming in pugilism. His fights were solo recitals. His opponents were just pianos, canvasses, spear-carriers. Something to practice his art on. He was the artist. He was like no Irishman you ever saw, but he was the greatest Irish athlete who ever lived. If you don't think so, tell me who was."

How would Tunney have done against the best heavyweight champions who followed him? Bert Randolph Sugar, the boxing historian and author, thought Tunney would have beaten Joe Louis and Rocky Marciano. Red Smith, the highly respected sports columnist, once wrote that Tunney "would have handled Muhammad Ali like breaking sticks." Sugar found such a hypothetical matchup between two of the best defensive heavyweights of all time tough to call, since, as he speculated, "they might fight fifteen rounds without either one landing a punch," although he thought that Ali eventually would "out-fast" Tunney. Budd Schulberg, who began watching prizefights in the 1920s, also thought Tunney probably would have beaten Louis, who, Schulberg noted, "always had trouble with good boxers like Billy Conn and Bob Pastor."

When the Associated Press chose Dempsey as the best boxer of the first half of the twentieth century, Tunney was asked his opinion of the AP's choice, which was based on a survey of sportswriters and sportscasters. That was fine with Tunney, who often said he thought the Manassa Mauler was the best fighter of all time. Since he had beaten Dempsey twice, that left some people wondering where Tunney stood. When asked, he declined to say.

With just a trace of gray in his full shock of light brown hair, and with none of the physical badges carried by many former fighters, apart from a slightly disfigured left ear, Tunney continued commuting to work in New York on a fairly regular basis into his seventies. Spinal surgery in 1969 slowed him down considerably, and then in 1978 a blood infection developed in his legs. The infection gradually worsened, and on November 7 of that year he died in Greenwich Hospital.

If Tunney had any regrets, it apparently involved his adverse relationship with sportswriters in the last few years of his boxing career. "As I look back on it, I was too hard on them," he once said. "In fact my attitude was juvenile. I did not take cognizance of the fact that they were only trying to do a job. I was irritated at the way they received me. They had been my derogators. And my reaction was expressed in a manner ascribable to my Irish temperament."

Eventually, though, most sportswriters who had covered Tunney realized they had both misunderstood and been unfair to him. Westbrook Pegler and Tunney and their wives even dined together in Manhattan restaurants, and, years after Tunney retired, Gallico visited Tunney at his home. "Probably no athlete has had to take the public beating that fell to Tunney on his way to realizing his ambitions," Gallico, one of Tunney's severest "derogators" in the late 1920s, wrote in his book *Farewell to Sport* in 1939. "He was caught groping for light, serenity, and education and ridiculed for it. He probably never knew it, but he was paying the penalty for violating a popular concept—that of the pugilist."

Gallico, who gave up sportswriting in the late 1930s to write such novels as *The Snow Goose* and *The Poseidon Adventure,* went on to say that "in our blind and stubborn defense of the Dempsey image, we picked up the wrong story and missed the far more thrilling one that was being enacted under our very own noses"—the six-year stalking of Dempsey and the "painstaking preparation" to beat him and "win the right to wed an heiress."

"When we should have been cheering him to the echo for the perfection of his profession, we hated him instead for practicing his deceitful arts upon that hero image of ourselves, caveman Dempsey." As it turned out, Gallico said, "many fine people genuinely liked Gene because he was a likeable personality."

Unfortunately for Tunney, not enough people knew that when he was beating the ears off perhaps the most popular prizefighter of all time, Jack Dempsey. None of that seemed to bother Tunney much over the years, mainly because life, for the most part, had been very good to him. Still, he conceded that he should have been more tolerant of criticism and shown a sense of humor when he was mocked for his reading habits.

"A little more chance to be spoiled by popularity would have been welcome," he once said. "Not that I was particularly keen for applause. But it was no spiritual gratification to know that I was an unpopular champion."

Yet that he could sit on a commuter train in his sixties unnoticed and unbothered by other riders was just fine with Tunney, who thrived on the anonymity, or at least the privacy he was accorded by his fellow commuters. Even in the years after he lost his title to Tunney, Dempsey was usually called "Champ." But even though he had taken away Dempsey's title and then beaten him in a rematch, Tunney rarely was addressed that way. Don Russell, a radio and television newsman and announcer at the time, recalled how he had called Tunney "Champ" one morning while riding with him on a commuter train from Stamford. "Later, as we were walking through the concourse at Grand Central Terminal, Tunney half-whispered to me, 'Do me a favor, if you will, and don't call me Champ,' " Russell said. " 'I don't like to draw attention to myself.' " And he practically never did after he left the ring.

On the days he wasn't driven to New York by the family chauffeur, Tunney would drive the ten miles from the Stamford train station to his beloved Star Meadow Farm. Driving into the garage, he would see a framed copy of the million-dollar check he had been given by Tex

Gene Tunney's grave marker.
JOHN A. CAVANAUGH III

Rickard after the "long count" fight in Chicago in 1927, which had hung there for many years.

After Tunney's death, Polly Lauder Tunney—who drove a car into her mid-nineties—often visited her husband's grave, situated on the same winding country road as Star Meadow Farm. Locating Gene Tunney's gravesite in the relatively small and isolated Revolutionary-era Long Ridge Union Cemetery is not easy. Large headstones abound in the cemetery, but Tunney's grave, shielded by a six-foot-high, twenty-foot-long hedge and situated in the rear of the cemetery, has only a small concrete marker—about eighteen inches wide and about eight inches from top to bottom—in the ground. On it is the legend:

JAMES JOSEPH TUNNEY
1897–1978
WORLD WAR I—FRANCE
PVT. U.S. MARINE CORPS
WORLD WAR II—CAPT. U.S. NAVY

That's it. No mention that James Joseph Tunney was known worldwide as Gene Tunney, and that he was a former world heavyweight champion. In death as in life, Gene Tunney, the most enigmatic and intellectual of heavyweight champions, asked no favors of the sport that had made him famous.

ACKNOWLEDGMENTS

■

Setting out to write a biography of a seemingly all-but-forgotten, albeit fascinating, former heavyweight champion who never seems to have gotten his due is a formidable task. All the more so when that former champion fought more than three-quarters of a century ago, making it difficult to find and interview contemporaries who have seen him fight. Fortunately, such great writers—who also happen to be boxing buffs—as Budd Schulberg and Studs Terkel were not only still around but still going strong in their nineties, when I interviewed them. So was Nat Rosoff, a marine lieutenant colonel in World War II who as a boy sat at ringside at both Dempsey-Tunney fights with his father, who came to be known as "Subway Sam" Rosoff, the builder of two New York City subway lines in the early part of the twentieth century. More than seven decades later, Nat Rosoff's memory, in his midnineties, was both sharp and crystal clear. Another vigorous nonagenarian and boxing authority who contributed to my project was Truman Gibson, who as president of the International Boxing Club during the middle of the twentieth century was a major figure in the sport, and who continued practicing law until his death at the age of ninety-three, in December 2005.

What was most remarkable, though, was the help I got from a number of people who were not even born when Gene Tunney beat Jack Dempsey to win the heavyweight championship, and then again in their rematch. Little did I know that there was a cult of Tunney admirers throughout the United States and abroad who collected memorabilia about perhaps the most underrated heavyweight champion of all time and who were delighted to learn that a book was to be written about boxing's most enigmatic and intelligent champion. Indeed, when I placed an advertisement in *The Ring* magazine four years ago entitled "Has Anybody Here Seen Tunney?" seeking boxing fans who may have seen Tunney fight—a very long shot, since you almost assuredly would have had to be in your nineties to have done so—or who had met the former heavyweight champion or had any memorabilia about him, I was stunned by the response.

The ad elicited e-mail messages, phone calls, letters with photos, newspaper and magazine clippings, posters, and other souvenirs from a diverse group of Tunney admirers from as far off as New Zealand. Among them were J. J. Johnston, a former amateur boxer from Chicago and a longtime actor who has appeared on the Broadway stage, in movies, and in television shows; Father Ted Schmitt, the pastor of St. Monica Roman Catholic Church in Chicago and a longtime boxing fan who boxed recreationally for years; Al Arilotta, a retired letter carrier from Rochester, New York; and Toby Weston Cone, the daughter of the late Stanley Weston, an accomplished artist, writer, and boxing historian who once owned *The Ring* magazine after having published several other boxing magazines. Then, too, there were the Harry Greb cultists, such as Ed Cahill (another actor) and Jim Cashman, a trader on the Chicago Board of Trade, who, like the Tunney admirers, felt that the Pittsburgh Windmill—the only fighter to beat Tunney, and one of the most colorful, and best, boxers ever—had been too long forgotten, and who both provided me with a cornucopia of materials about their boxing idol. Additional information about the "King of the Alley Fighters" came from Greb's great-granddaughter, Jennifer Wohlforth. In many instances, in addition to contributing materials on Tunney, many of my sources referred me to others whom they felt could also help in my endeavor and usually did.

All of my source-searching and research wouldn't have been necessary if my agent, Andrew Blauner, hadn't seen the promise in such a book and afforded so much good advice for my proposal, and if Jonathan Karp, then a vice president and senior editor with Random House, had not been so enthused about the project. Jon's counsel and advice at the start were invaluable, as were his patience and encouragement during the three years we worked together. Like Jon, Mark Tavani, who guided me along the rest of the way, was both a joy to work with and did a brilliant job in editing my manuscript. To both of them, I am deeply indebted.

Like many book ideas, mine came about by chance. Though I had known about Tunney most of my life and, as noted in my Introduction, had met him on a commuter train many years ago, I never seriously considered writing a book about him until I interviewed the Boxing Hall of Fame referee Arthur Mercante for a story I was doing about him for the *New York Times* while he was still working championship fights at the age of eighty. During the interview at Mercante's Long Island home, he recounted how he and many other boxing figures—mainly fighters, but also some trainers and former boxers like Mercante—had been recruited by Tunney to serve as athletic instructors when Tunney headed the Navy's physical fitness program during World War II. "Tunney fish," they were called, as Mercante, who refereed the first Muhammad Ali–Joe Frazier bout, along with more than a hundred other title fights, was to tell me. As we continued to talk about Tunney, it dawned on me that while at least a half dozen books had been written about Dempsey, none, at least in recent years, had been done about the classic boxer, patron of the arts, and friend of some of the world's best-known writers, who had walked away from the ring in his prime, after beating the great Dempsey twice, to marry a beautiful heiress to the Andrew Carnegie fortune. Mercante agreed that it was odd, especially given Tunney's uniqueness as a fighter who went on to become a highly successful businessman and gentleman farmer on his Connecticut estate. Thus, fortuitously, the idea for this book was born.

I had help from scores of people, including some like W. C. Heinz, the former sportswriter and novelist, who was in his early nineties when I spoke with him on several occasions in 2005 and 2006, and Bill Stack, a Yale football captain in the mid-1930s and later a corporate executive, both of whom knew Tunney well for years after he had retired from the ring. Then there were longtime Tunney family friends like Hope Gimbel Solinger, the daughter of Tunney's close friend Bernard Gimbel; Ann Forsberg; and Sam Pryor, III, whose father, Sam Pryor, Jr., was instrumental in bringing Tunney and Polly Lauder together.

No one could have been more helpful than the aforementioned Toby Weston Cone, who contributed scrapbooks and photos from her father's voluminous files, and Steve Lott, the president of Boxing Hall of Champions in New York, which has perhaps the largest collection of old fight films in the world. Steve provided whatever fight films I wanted, going back to the turn of the twentieth century, along with some hard-to-find still photos. Invaluable, too, was my longtime friend Bert Randolph Sugar, boxing's premier historian and a gifted writer, editor, and raconteur, whose books, *The 100 Greatest Boxers of All Time* and its sequel, *Boxing's Greatest Fighters,* were indispensable resources. Sugar also provided a plethora of hard-to-find articles that enhanced my manuscript and invariably held the answers to whatever boxing questions, no matter how arcane, I asked.

Others who contributed vital background information were Corey Lavinsky, a California boxing memorabilia collector who produced a wealth of material on his namesake and boxing idol, Battling Levinsky, who, unlike Corey, was not a genuine Levinsky, having been given his *nom de boxe* by legendary manager Dumb Dan Morgan; John Dempsey, a longtime boxing activist in Philadelphia and a member of the Ring One Veterans Boxing Association in that city, who was equally generous in providing background material on another former light heavyweight champion from the City of Brotherly Love, Tommy Loughran—arguably Philadelphia's premier fighter—who gave Tunney one of his toughest fights; and Chuck Hasson, a veritable encyclopedia of boxing in Philadelphia and its environs, who provided a list of the leading boxing writers for Philadelphia papers in the 1920s.

Thanks also go out to Harold Blake, a volunteer worker at the century-old St. Veronica's Church in Greenwich Village, himself an alumnus of St. Veronica's school, which Tunney attended and where he developed his passion for reading. A lifelong resident of the Village, Blake was my guide on a tour of Tunney's old neighborhood, which included visits to two of the three tenement buildings where the Tunney family had lived. Blake also recounted what life was like in the poor and predominantly Irish neighborhood in the 1920s and '30s, and the strict, and at times even harsh, regimen students had to follow at the school.

Of inestimable assistance was Anne Preston, a distant cousin of Tunney's, who has operated an excellent Tunney website and was a font of information on the Tunney family's life in County Mayo in Ireland and on John and Mary Tunney's early days in New York. Also helpful was another Tunney cousin, Andrew Lydon, and his wife, Jeanne.

Given the secrecy that surrounded Tunney's courtship of Polly Lauder, it is difficult to unearth information on how they met and how and where they fell in love in what became perhaps the most romantic love story of the 1920s. Fortunately, I was able to do so, in large measure through the cooperation of Sam Pryor, III; his brother, Tap (who lives in the Cook Islands in the South Pacific); and their sister, Tay Thomas, all of whom regarded the Tunneys as sort of surrogate relatives to the extent that they referred to them as "Uncle Gene" and "Aunt Polly."

For the inside story on how the mob was able to "guide" the inept and naive Primo Carnera to the heavyweight title in the 1930s, I turned to Budd Schulberg, who converted the real-life tale of the tragic Carnera fistic saga into perhaps the best book ever written about boxing, *The Harder They Fall,* a roman à clef that was made into a movie starring Humphrey Bogart and Rod Steiger. Budd, who often segued from superb novelist to first-rate boxing writer during his distinguished writing career, also furnished anecdotes and other information about his father's idol, Benny Leonard, and some of the other outstanding Jewish fighters of the 1920s and '30s, some of whom he saw fight while going to boxing cards at the old Hollywood Legion boxing arena in Los Angeles with his father, the Paramount Pictures production chief B. P. Schulberg, in the 1930s.

As any writer of historical nonfiction will attest, librarians can be crucial to a book's success. In my case, they were essential in coming up with old, even nearly archaic, books and microfilm of long-ago newspapers, many of which are now defunct. At the top of the list is Susan Madeo at the Westport, Connecticut, library, who procured whatever microfilm or books I was after. Another staff member at the Westport library, Debbie Celia, also was quick to respond to some arcane requests. Helpful, too, was Lynne Swanson at the Wilton Library, also in Fairfield County in Connecticut, who obtained a number of relatively obscure books, some of them from far-off libraries, through the indispensable interlibrary loan network. In addition, thanks go to staff workers in the microfilm rooms at the Ferguson Library in Stamford, Connecticut and at the Greenwich Library, also in Connecticut. The New York Public Library's main branch on Fifth Avenue and the Denver Public Library also were immensely helpful, as were staff members at the DiMenna Nyselius Library at Fairfield University, and Linda Miller, the indomitable secretary in the English Department office at Fairfield U. I am indebted to the Philadelphia Free Library, the Chicago and San Francisco public libraries, and the Abraham Lincoln Presidential Library in Springfield, Illinois, for supplying microfilm of long-ago newspapers. Pertinent information and materials, along with local history, also were provided by Michelle Richardson, curator of the Jack Dempsey Museum in his hometown of Manassa, Colorado, and Evelyn Tibbits, the Manassa town clerk.

Others who helped, in one way or another, were boxing memorabilia collectors Harry Shaffer, the proprietor of Antiquities of the Prize Ring, who contributed a number of the photos that appear in the book; Pete Ehrmann, who loaned me a hard-to-get book on light heavyweight boxers; Tracy Callis, Don Scott, Mike Silver, and Hank Kaplan, the founder and co-publisher of the website CyberzoneBoxing.Net, probably the best record-keeping boxing source in existence. Assistance also came from Marian Tuba at the New York Historical Society; Brother Luke Salm of the New York District Christian Brothers, who provided the photo of Tunney's eighth-grade graduating class at St. Veronica's parochial school; Sister Marguerita Smith, an archivist at the St. Joseph's Seminary in Yonkers, New York; Toby Smith of the *Albuquerque Journal,* in New Mexico, the author of *Kid Blackie,* a detailed and well-written account of Jack Dempsey's early days in Colorado, who donated several photos from his personal collection; Leslie Dean of the National Railway Historical Society, who explained how Dempsey was able to survive while riding "the rods" beneath freight trains in his early days; Megan Heuer of the Metropolitan Museum of Art, in New York, who provided a copy of the famed George Bellows painting of Dempsey being knocked out of the ring by Luis Angel Firpo; Rebecca Weiss of the Swann Galleries, also in New York; Bill Steinman, the sports-information director emeritus at Columbia University; Dean Hellinger, the vice president of the Marias Museum of

History and Art in Shelby, Montana, the site of the 1923 title fight between Jack Dempsey and Tommy Gibbons; John Kavanagh, the retired editor of the *Shelby Promoter* newspaper in Shelby; Harriet Solodky, daughter of Battling Levinsky; Max Baer, Jr., who turned to acting, not fighting, and proudly reminisced about his colorful father, who also did some acting; Dick Romeniecki of the Pennsylvania Historical Society; Roger Cleveland of the Waterbury, Connecticut, *Republican-American* sports staff, who provided clips on what Battling Levinsky and some others claimed was the Battler's third fight on New Year's Day of 1915; Marianne Rissolo, who was an au pair for the Tunneys at their Stamford, Connecticut, estate in the 1960s, and Ralph Grasso, a gardener at the estate for years, both of whom spoke glowingly about Gene and Polly Tunney as employers and as people in general; Patricia and Don Knickman, former owners of the Glen Brook Country Club, in Stroudsburg, Pennsylvania, where Tunney trained for his first fight with Dempsey; Bob Bennett, the superintendent of the Southampton Cemetery on Long Island; Paul Mazik, former caretaker of the Long Ridge Union Cemetery in Stamford, Connecticut; and Aase van Dyke, my Francophile neighbor, who translated materials—written in French—about Tunney's Marine brigade's base in Gièvres, France, during World War I that were sent to me by Marion Fourestier, communications director for the French Government Tourist Office in New York City. Valuable information about Tunney's service in the Marines, along with a photo used in this book, came from Bob Aquilina of the History and Museums Division of the U.S. Marine Corps.

Generous, too, was George Rugg, the curator of the Joyce Sports Research Collection at the University of Notre Dame, who contributed materials from what has become a treasure trove of boxing publications, newspaper and magazine stories, and other esoteric information about the sport from the middle of the nineteenth century onward. From Yale University, research archivist Judith Ann Schiff provided background material on William Lyon Phelps, the school's legendary English professor, who invited Tunney to speak to his class on Shakespeare while he was still the heavyweight champion, and Yale sports archivist Jeff Zonder supplied information on Eddie Eagan, an outstanding amateur boxer and Yale alumnus who was one of Tunney's closest friends.

Others who contributed, in one way or another, were Sean Curtin, a veteran referee and former Illinois state boxing official; the late New York Giants' owner Wellington Mara, whose father, Tim, the founder of the team, reconciled with Tunney after a long legal battle between the two; former boxing trainer, manager, and television commentator Gil Clancy; Tony Mazzarella of the Ring Eight retired boxers organization in Queens, New York; Gary Micheli, a fire inspector for the Pueblo, Colorado, Fire Department, who supplied background information on Fireman Jim Flynn, who was both a Pueblo fireman and a fireman on the Denver & Rio Grande Railroad before he became the only fighter to knock out Jack Dempsey; Peter Hope, the president of the Old Bristol Historical Society in Maine, and Kristine Poland, the town administrator for Bristol, who filled me in on the history and provided other information on Johns Island, the privately owned isle off the coast of Maine where Tunney and Polly Lauder spent time together before their romance became one of the biggest stories of 1928; Jeff Brophy of the Boxing Hall of Fame, in Canastota, New York; Dempsey's stepdaughter, Barbara Piattelli Dempsey Phillips, who recounted the old champ's gentleness and love of family, especially in his later years; Ed Knoblauch, the webmaster of the New York History website, who provided some fascinating information about what Manhattan was like when Tunney was growing up in the West Village; my longtime friend Dave Anderson, the Pulitzer Prize–winning sports columnist for the *New York Times,* for his remembrances of Jack Dempsey; the late Joe Durso, whose elegant writing graced the sports pages of the *Times* for many years; and Bill Gallo, the talented sports cartoonist and columnist for the New York *Daily News,* who was a close friend of Dempsey's; and Jim Zamora of the *San Francisco Chronicle,* who enabled me to track down Max Baer, Jr. Deep appreciation also goes to my young computer guru, Paul McLaughlin of Wilton, Connecticut, without whose expertise in times of technical emergencies this book might never have been finished, and to Professor Laurence Hogan of Union County College in New Jersey, who supplied scores of newspaper clippings about black boxers who fought during the early part of the twentieth century.

Three of my Stamford friends—Don Russell, John Considine, and Jack Moriarty—also provided interesting anecdotes about Tunney. Russell, the former longtime "morning man" on the Stamford radio station and later a network broadcaster, recalled how Tunney disliked being called "champ" after his retirement from the ring, while Considine, the former Stamford police chief, and Moriarty, a retired deputy police chief in the city, related an incident involving a fall Tunney took at his North Stamford home many years after he had retired. Responding to a call from the Tunney household, officer Floyd Dujack, who patrolled the area and knew Tunney quite well, found the former heavyweight champion on a bathroom floor.

"Champ, you're down!" a concerned Dujack exclaimed.

"Yes, Floyd," Tunney replied with a smile, "but only for the second time."

The first time, of course, had been many years before in the famous "long count" fight in Chicago. Tunney may have long distanced himself from boxing but most certainly had never forgotten the most dramatic episode in his glorious ring career. Nor, it seems, had most of my multitude of sources, many of whom felt that "The Fighting Marine" deserved better than he got from the sports world while he was fighting and that the story of his fascinating life had long been waiting to be told.

Jack Dempsey (William Harrison Dempsey)

BORN: Manassa, Colorado, June 24, 1895
DIED: New York, May 31, 1983
KEY: **W** indicates a win.
KO indicates a win by knockout.
TKO indicates a technical knockout wherein the fight was stopped.
ND indicates no decision.
L indicates a loss.
WF indicates a win by foul.
LF indicates a loss by foul.
"KO by" indicates a loss by knockout.
A number following the outcome code indicates the number of rounds in the bout.

1914	OPPONENT	CITY/TOWN	OUTCOME
Aug. 17	Young Herman	Ramona, Colo.	Draw 6
Nov. 2	One-Punch Hancock	Salt Lake City	KO 1
Nov. 30	Billy Murphy	Salt Lake City	KO 1
1915			
Jan. 1	Battling Johnson	Salt Lake City	KO 1
Feb. 2	Joe Lyons	Pocatello, Idaho	KO 9
Feb. 26	Chief Geronimo	Pocatello, Idaho	Draw 4
March 3	Johnny Pierson	Salt Lake City	KO 7
April 1	Chief Gordon	Salt Lake City	KO 6
April 5	Jack Downey	Salt Lake City	L 4
April 26	Anamas Campbell	Reno, Nev.	KO 3
May 31	Johnny Sudenberg	Goldfield, Nev.	Draw 10
June 13	Johnny Sudenberg	Tonopah, Nev.	Draw 10
Aug. 1	Fred Woods	Montrose, Colo.	KO 4
Oct. 7	Andy Malloy	Durango, Colo.	ND 10
Oct. 23	Andy Malloy	Montrose, Colo.	KO 3
Nov. 19	George Copelin	Cripple Creek, Colo.	KO 7
Dec. 13	Jack Downey	Salt Lake City	Draw 4
Dec. 20	Two-Round Gillian	Salt Lake City	KO 1
1916			
Feb. 1	Johnny Sudenberg	Ely, Nev.	KO 2
Feb. 21	Jack Downey	Salt Lake City	KO 2
Feb. 23	Boston Bearcat	Ogden, Utah	KO 1
March 9	Cyril Koehn	Provo, Utah	KO 4
March 17	George Christian	Price, Utah	KO 1
April 8	Joe Bonds	Ely, Nev.	W 10
May 3	Terry Kellar	Ogden, Utah	W 10
May 17	Dan Ketchell	Provo, Utah	KO 3

May 30	Bob York	Price, Utah	KO 4
June 24	Andre Anderson	New York	ND 10
July 8	Wild Bert Kenny	New York	ND 10
July 14	John Lester Johnson	New York	ND 10
Sept. 28	Young Hector Conrew	Salida, Colo.	KO 3
Oct. 7	Terry Kellar	Ely, Nev.	W 10
Oct. 16	Fighting Dick Gilbert	Salt Lake City	W 10
Nov. 29	Young Hector Conrew	Salida, Colo.	KO 2

1917

Feb. 13	Fireman Jim Flynn	Murray, Utah	KO by 1
March 21	Al Norton	Oakland, Calif.	Draw 4
March 28	Willie Meehan	Oakland, Calif.	L 4
April 11	Al Norton	Oakland, Calif.	Draw 4
July 25	Willie Meehan	Emeryville, Calif.	W 4
Aug. 1	Al Norton	Emeryville, Calif.	KO 1
Aug. 10	Willie Meehan	San Francisco	Draw 4
Sept. 7	Willie Meehan	San Francisco	Draw 4
Sept. 19	Charlie Miller	Oakland, Calif.	KO 1
Sept. 26	Bob McAllister	Emeryville, Calif.	W 4
Oct. 2	Ed "Gunboat" Smith	San Francisco	W 4
Nov. 2	Carl Morris	San Francisco	W 4

1918

Jan. 24	Homer Smith	Racine, Wis.	KO 1
Feb. 4	Carl Morris	Buffalo, N.Y.	WF 6
Feb. 14	Fireman Jim Flynn	Fort Sheridan, Ill.	KO 1
Feb. 25	K. O. Bill Brennan	Milwaukee, Wis.	KO 6
March 16	Fred Saddy	Memphis	KO 1
March 25	Tom Riley	Joplin, Mo.	KO 1
May 3	Billy Miske	St. Paul, Minn.	ND 10
May 23	Dan Ketchell	Excelsior Springs, Colo.	KO 2
May 29	Arthur Pelkey	Denver	KO 1
July 1	Tommy "Kid" McCarthy	Tulsa	KO 1
July 4	Bob Devere	Joplin, Mo.	KO 1
July 6	Dan "Porky" Flynn	Atlanta	KO 1
July 27	Fred Fulton	Harrison, N.J.	KO 1
Aug. 26	Terry Kellar	Dayton, Ohio	TKO 5
Sept. 13	Willie Meehan	San Francisco	L 4
Sept. 14	Jack Moran	Reno, Nev.	KO 1
Nov. 6	Battling Levinsky	Philadelphia	KO 3
Nov. 18	Dan "Porky" Flynn	Philadelphia	KO 1
Nov. 28	Billy Miske	Philadelphia	ND 6
Dec. 16	Carl Morris	New Orleans	KO 1
Dec. 30	Ed "Gunboat" Smith	Buffalo, N.Y.	KO 2

1919

Jan. 20	Big Jack Hickey	Harrisburg, Penn.	KO 1
Jan. 23	Kid Harris	Reading, Penn.	KO 1
Jan. 29	Kid Henry	Easton, Penn.	KO 1

Feb. 13	Eddie Smith	Altoona, Penn.	KO 1
April 2	Tony Drake	New Haven, Conn.	KO 1
July 4	Jess Willard	Toledo, Ohio	TKO 3
	(World heavyweight title fight)		

1920

Sept. 6	Billy Miske	Benton Harbor, Mich.	KO 3
Dec. 14	K. O. Bill Brennan	New York	KO 12
	(World heavyweight title fight)		

1921

July 2	Georges Carpentier	Jersey City, N.J.	KO 4
	(World heavyweight title fight)		

1923

July 4	Tommy Gibbons	Shelby, Mont.	W 15
	(World heavyweight title fight)		
Sept. 14	Luis Angel Firpo	New York	KO 2
	(World heavyweight title fight)		

1926

Sept. 23	Gene Tunney	Philadelphia	L 10
	(World heavyweight title fight)		

1927

July 21	Jack Sharkey	New York	KO 7
Sept. 22	Gene Tunney	Chicago	L 10
	(World heavyweight title fight)		

Total bouts: 81 / Won: 60 / Lost: 6 / W by KO: 50 / W by decision: 9 / W by foul: 1 / Draw: 9 / No decision: 6

Gene Tunney (James Joseph Tunney)

> BORN: New York, May 25, 1897
> DIED: Greenwich, Connecticut, Nov. 7, 1978

1915

July 2	Bobby Dawson	New York	TKO 8
Aug. 7	Battling Genrimo	New York	KO 3
Aug. 28	George Lahey	New York	KO 2
Dec. 11	Billy Rowe	New York	ND 6

1916

July 21	K. O. Jaffe	New York	ND 10
Dec. 8	Young Guarini	New York	TKO 8
Dec. 15	Young Sharkey	New York	KO 6
Dec. 29	Sailor Wolfe	New York	KO 2

1917

Feb. 2	Victor Dahl	New York	ND 10

| Oct. 2 | K. O. Sullivan | New York | ND 10 |
| Dec. 21 | Young Joe Borrell | New York | KO 2 |

1918

| Jan. 15 | Hughey Weir | New York | KO 2 |
| July 9 | Young Guarini | Jersey City, N.J. | KO 1 |

1918-1919

Tunney had approximately twenty bouts while based in France with the U.S. Marines for slightly more than a year. Tunney won all of his fights and captured the American Expeditionary Forces light heavyweight title before resuming his professional career in late 1919.

1919

| Dec. 16 | Dan O'Dowd | Bayonne, N.J. | ND 8 |
| Dec. 29 | Bob Pearce | Newark, N.J. | TKO 2 |

1920

Jan. 1	Whitey Allen	Bayonne, N.J.	KO 2
Jan. 20	Bud Nelson	Bayonne, N.J.	KO 1
Jan. 26	Jim Monahan	Jersey City, N.J.	TKO 1
Feb. 2	Al Roberts	Newark, N.J.	KO 8
March 4	Ed Kinley	Jersey City, N.J.	KO 5
April 5	K. O. Sullivan	Newark, N.J.	KO 1
April 9	Jack Clifford	Binghamton, N.Y.	KO 3
June 7	Jeff Madden	Jersey City, N.J.	TKO 2
June 28	Ole Anderson	Jersey City, N.J.	TKO 3
Oct. 22	Ray Smith	Camden, N.J.	TKO 2
Oct. 25	Paul Samson-Koerner	Paterson, N.J.	ND 10
Nov. 25	Leo Houck	Philadelphia	ND 6
Dec. 7	Leo Houck	Jersey City, N.J.	ND 8

1921

June 28	Young Ambrose	New York	KO 1
July 2	Soldier Jones	Jersey City, N.J.	TKO 7
Aug. 4	Martin Burke	New York	W 10
Aug. 18	Eddie Josephs	New York	W 12
Sept. 26	Herbert Crossley	New York	KO 7
Oct. 14	Jack Burke	New York	TKO 3
Oct. 25	Wolf Larsen	New York	TKO 7
Dec. 22	Eddie O'Hare	New York	KO 6

1922

| Jan. 13 | Battling Levinsky | New York | W 12 |

(For newly-created North American light heavyweight championship)

Feb. 11	Jack Clifford	New York	TKO 6
Feb. 14	Whitey Wenzel	Philadelphia	TKO 4
March 3	Fay Kaiser	Grand Rapids, Mich.	ND 10
April 10	Jack Burke	Pittsburgh	TKO 3
May 23	Harry Greb	New York	L 15

(For North American light heavyweight championship)

| July 6 | Fay Kaiser | New York | W 12 |
| Aug. 4 | Ray Thompson | Long Branch, N.J. | KO 3 |

Aug. 17	Charley Weinert	Newark, N.J.	ND 12
Aug. 24	Tommy Loughran	Philadelphia	ND 8
Oct. 27	Chuck Wiggins	Boston	W 10
Nov. 3	Jack Hanlon	New York	KO 1
Nov. 29	Charley Weinert	New York	KO 4

1923

Jan. 29	Jack Renault	Philadelphia	NC 4
Feb. 3	Chuck Wiggins	New York	W 12
Feb. 23	Harry Greb	New York	W 15

(For North American light heavyweight championship)

May 7	Jack Clifford	Detroit	TKO 8
May 16	Jimmy Delaney	Chicago	ND 10
July 31	Dan O'Dowd	New York	W 12
Dec. 10	Harry Greb	New York	W 15

(For North American light heavyweight championship)

1924

Jan. 15	Harry Foley	Grand Rapids, Mich.	ND 10
Jan. 24	Ray Thompson	West Palm Beach, Fla.	KO 2
Feb. 15	Martin Burke	New Orleans	W 15
March 17	Jimmy Delaney	St. Paul, Minn.	ND 10
June 26	Erminio Spalla	New York	TKO 7
July 24	Georges Carpentier	New York	TKO 15
Aug. 18	Joe Lohman	Columbus, Ohio	TKO 8
Sept. 17	Harry Greb	Cleveland	ND 10
Sept. 27	Ray Neuman	Ebensburg, Penn.	W 10
Oct. 27	Barry Foley	Memphis	KO 1
Nov. 10	Buddy McHale	Memphis	KO 2
Dec. 8	Jeff Smith	New Orleans	W 15

1925

March 27	Harry Greb	St. Paul, Minn.	ND 10
June 5	Tommy Gibbons	New York	KO 12
July 3	Italian Jack Herman	Kansas City, Mo.	KO 2
Sept. 25	Bartley Madden	Minneapolis	KO 3
Nov. 18	Johnny Risko	Cleveland	ND 12
Dec. 29	Dan O'Dowd	St. Petersburg, Fla.	KO 2

1926

Sept. 23	Jack Dempsey	Philadelphia	W 10

(World heavyweight title fight)

1927

Sept. 22	Jack Dempsey	Chicago	W 10

(World heavyweight title fight)

1928

July 26	Tom Heeney	New York	TKO 12

(World heavyweight title fight)

Total bouts: 77 / Won: 58 / Lost: 1 / W by KO: 44 / W by decision: 14 / No decision: 17 / No contest: 1

SELECTED BIBLIOGRAPHY

■

Allen, Oliver E. *New York, New York: A History of the World's Most Exhilarating and Challenging City.* New York: Atheneum, 1990.

Andre, Sam, and Nat Fleischer. *A Pictorial History of Boxing.* New York: Bonanza Books, 1981.

The Baseball Encyclopedia, eighth edition. New York: The Macmillan Publishing Company, 1990.

Blady, Ken. *The Jewish Boxers Hall of Fame.* New York: Shapolsky Publishers, 1988.

Bodner, Allen. *When Boxing Was a Jewish Sport.* Westport, Conn.: Praeger, 1997.

Breslin, Jimmy. *Damon Runyon.* New York: Ticknor & Fields, 1991.

Delaney, Edmund T., and Charles Lockwood. *Greenwich Village: A Photographic Guide.* New York: Dover Publications, Inc., 1976.

Dempsey, Jack, Lt. *How to Fight Tough.* Boulder, Col.: Paladin Press, 1943.

Dempsey, Jack, with Barbara Piattelli Dempsey. *Dempsey.* New York: Harper & Row, 1977.

———, with Bob Considine and Bill Slocum. *Dempsey, by the Man Himself.* New York: Simon & Schuster, 1960.

Durso, Joseph. *Madison Square Garden: 100 Years of History.* New York: Simon & Schuster, 1979.

Eagan, Edward P. F. *Fighting for Fun: The Scrapbook of Eddie Eagan.* New York: The Macmillan Company, 1932.

Fair, James R. *Give Him to the Angels: The Story of Harry Greb.* New York: Smith and Durrell, 1946.

Fields, Armond. *James J. Corbett: A Biography of the Heavyweight Boxing Champion and Popular Theater Headliner.* Jefferson, N.C.: McFarland & Company, Inc., 2001.

Fowler, Gene. *Beau James: The Life and Times of Jimmy Walker.* New York: Viking Press, 1949.

———. *Timber Line: A Story of Bonfils and Tammen.* Garden City, N.Y.: Garden City Books, 1947.

Gallico, Paul. *Farewell to Sport.* New York: Alfred A. Knopf, 1938.

Goldman, Herbert G., ed. *The Ring Record Book and Boxing Encyclopedia.* New York: The Ring Publishing Corporation, 1985.

Goldstein, Ruby, with Frank Graham. *Third Man in the Ring.* New York: Funk and Wagnalls, 1959.

Heller, Peter. *In This Corner . . . !: Forty World Champions Tell Their Stories.* New York: Simon & Schuster, 1973.

Johnson, James W. *The Fight That Won't Stay Dead.* Shelby, Mont.: Promoter Publishing Company, 1989.

Kearns, Jack, with Oscar Fraley. *The Million Dollar Gate.* New York: Macmillan, 1966.

Lardner, John. *White Hopes and Other Tigers.* Philadelphia: J. B. Lippincott, 1951.

Lardner, Ring, Jr. *The Lardners: My Family Remembered.* New York: Harper & Row, 1976.

Leighton, Isabel, ed., *The Aspirin Age: 1919–1941.* New York: Simon & Schuster, 1949.

Levine, Peter. *Ellis Island to Ebbets Field: Sport and the American Jewish Experience.* New York: Oxford University Press, 1992.

Mills, Freddie. *Forward the Light-Heavies.* London: Stanley Paul and Company, 1956.

Mullally, Frederic. *Primo: The Story of "Man Mountain" Carnera.* London: Robson Books, Ltd., 1991.

Oates, Joyce Carol. *On Boxing.* Garden City, N.Y.: Dolphin/Doubleday, 1987.

Plimpton, George. *Shadow Box: An Amateur in the Ring.* New York: G. P. Putnam's Sons, 1977.

Ribalow, Harold U. *The Jew in American Sports.* New York: Bloch Publishing, 1966.

Rice, Grantland. *The Tumult and the Shouting: My Life in Sport.* New York: A. S. Barnes and Company, 1954.

Riess, Steven, ed. *Sports and the American Jew.* Syracuse, N.Y.: Syracuse University Press, 1998.

Roberts, Randy. *Jack Dempsey: the Manassa Mauler.* Baton Rouge, La.: Louisiana State University Press, 1979.

Ross, Barney, with Martin Abramson. *No Man Stands Alone: The True Story of Barney Ross.* Philadelphia: Lippincott, 1957.

Sammons, Jeffrey T. *Beyond the Ring: The Role of Boxing in American Society.* Urbana, Ill.: University of Illinois Press, 1988.

Smith, Toby. *Kid Blackie: Jack Dempsey's Colorado Days.* Ridgway, Col.: Wayfinder Press, 1987.

Sugar, Bert Randolph. *Boxing's Greatest Fighters.* Guilford, Conn.: The Lyons Press, 2006.

———. *The 100 Greatest Boxers of All Time.* New York: Bonanza Books, 1984.

Tunney, Gene. *A Man Must Fight.* Boston and New York: Houghton Mifflin Company, 1932.

Tunney, Gene. *Arms for Living.* New York: Wilfred Funk, Inc., 1941.

Van Every, Edward. *The Life of Gene Tunney: The Fighting Marine.* New York: Dell Publishing Company, 1926.

Ward, Geoffrey C. *Unforgivable Blackness: The Rise and Fall of Jack Johnson.* New York: Alfred A. Knopf, 2004.

Weston, Stanley. *The Best of the Ring: The Bible of Boxing.* Chicago: Bonus Books, 1992.

NOTES

∎

INTRODUCTION

xi "Isn't it ridiculous": Conversation with author, 1965.

xii "Pardon me for asking": Ibid.

xii "Tunney, he reads books": Jack Dempsey bodyguard Mike Trant, quoted in *Collier's*, March 21, 1927.

xiii "They're always asking me": Conversation with author, 1965.

xiv Ranked Dempsey as the ninth best: Bert Randolph Sugar, *Boxing's Greatest Fighters* (Guilford, Conn.: The Lyons Press, 2006).

xiv "No athlete ever succeeded in obscuring his own great skills so completely": Frank Graham, *Sports Illustrated*, December 3, 1961.

xvi "You could put them in robes": Author's interview with Bert Randolph Sugar, January 21, 2006.

xvii "I guess I could have handled it better": Conversation with author, 1965.

CHAPTER 1

4 After emigrating to the United States: *New York Times*, September 24, 1926.

5 Gift of boxing gloves on tenth birthday: James Kilgallen, Hearst Headline Service, September 23, 1966.

5 Become a priest: Ibid.

6 Learning from Willie Green: Edward Van Every, *The Life of Gene Tunney: The Fighting Marine* (New York: Dell Publishing Company, 1926); Gene Tunney, *A Man Must Fight* (Boston and New York: Houghton Mifflin Company, 1932).

7 Only fifteen dollars a week: Ed Fitzgerald, "Gentleman Gene—the Champion Nobody Understood," *Sport*, May 1950; Gene Tunney, "Gene Tunney's Own Story," King Features Syndicate, Inc., October 1926.

7 John Dos Passos and Willa Cather: Edmund T. Delaney and Charles Lockwood, *Greenwich Village: A Photographic Guide* (New York: Dover Publications, 1976).

7 City of just under two million: Oliver Allen, *New York, New York: A History of the World's Most Exhilarating and Challenging City* (New York: Atheneum, 1990).

7 St. Veronica's Church: *Fifty Year Celebration: 1953, St. Veronica's Millennium Campaign*, 2003; Reverend Thomas J. Shelley, *The History of the Archdiocese of New York* (Strasbourg: Editions du Signe, 1999).

8 "the good brothers would rap me on the knuckles": Fitzgerald, "Gentleman Gene—the Champion Nobody Understood."

8 "It was not uncommon": Author's interview with St. Veronica's parishioner and volunteer Harold Blake, March 2004.

9 A soldier's dive: Van Every, *The Life of Gene Tunney*.

9 Penchant for learning: Ibid; Tunney, "Gene Tunney's Own Story."

9 "Gene was such a simple-looking chap": Van Every, *The Life of Gene Tunney.*

10 Eager to take part in theatrical productions (at St. Veronica's School): Ibid; Tunney, "Gene Tunney's Own Story."

10 Young Tunney was able to recite the soliloquies of: Tim Cohane, "Gene Tunney Today," *Sport,* July 10, 1956.

10 Office boy at Ocean Steamship Company: Fitzgerald, "Gentleman Gene—the Champion Nobody Understood;" Van Every, *The Life of Gene Tunney;* Tunney, "Gene Tunney's Own Story."

11 Encountering Willie Green again: Van Every, *The Life of Gene Tunney;* Tunney, *A Man Must Fight.*

12 Boxing Willie Green at a smoker: Tunney, *A Man Must Fight.*

14 Bout with Leonard Ross: Ibid.

16 "No fighter I have ever known": Ibid.

17 First pro fight against Bobby Dawson: Fitzgerald, "Gentleman Gene—the Champion Nobody Understood;" Fitzgerald, "Boxing's Most Underrated Champ," *The Ring,* January 1982.

18 Fairmont A.C. and Billy Gibson: Ibid; *New York Times,* September 27, 1926.

19 No rush to fight again: Tunney, *A Man Must Fight; New York Times,* December 9, 1916.

CHAPTER 2

20 The original Jack Dempsey: The Nonpareil: Herbert G. Goldman, *The Ring Record Book and Boxing Encyclopedia* (New York: The Ring Publishing Corporation, 1985).

20 The ninth of eleven children: Jack Dempsey with Barbara Piattelli Dempsey, *Dempsey* (New York: Harper & Row, 1977); Jack Dempsey with Bob Considine and Bill Slocum, *Dempsey, by the Man Himself* (New York: Simon & Schuster, 1960); Toby Smith, *Kid Blackie: Jack Dempsey's Colorado Days* (Ridgway, Col.: Wayfinder Press, 1987); Jimmy Breslin, *Damon Runyon* (New York: Ticknor & Fields, 1991).

22 "I know the church is right": Smith, *Kid Blackie.*

22 "hard as iron anvils": Author's interview with Bill Gallo, May 21, 2005.

23 Saloon fights: Dempsey, *Dempsey, by the Man Himself.*

24 Riding the rods: Dempsey, *Dempsey, by the Man Himself;* author's interview with Leslie Dean of the National Railway Historical Society, October 29, 2003.

24 "Harry, I feel terrible": Dempsey, *Dempsey, by the Man Himself;* Smith, *Kid Blackie.*

25 Henceforth to be known as Jack Dempsey: Randy Roberts, *Jack Dempsey: the Manassa Mauler* (Baton Rouge, La.: Louisiana State University Press, 1979).

26 Fringe boxing figure Jack Price: Ibid; Roger Kahn, *A Flame of Pure Fire: Jack Dempsey and the Roaring '20s* (New York: Harcourt Brace, 1999).

26 The Boston Bearcat: Dempsey, *Dempsey;* Dempsey, *Dempsey, by the Man Himself.*

27 Dempsey's first fight in New York: Ibid; Roberts, *The Manassa Mauler; New York Press, New York American,* and *New York World,* June 25, 1916.

30 John "The Barber" Reisler: Dempsey, *Dempsey, by the Man Himself;* Kahn, *A Flame of Pure Fire.*

32 John Lester Johnson breaks three of Dempsey's ribs in Harlem bout: *New York Tribune* and *New York World,* July 17, 1916.

33 Tunney making seventeen dollars a week as a shipping clerk. Fights Kid Jaffe: *New York Tribune,* July 22, 1914.

34 Despite broken ribs, Dempsey back in ring two months later in Salida, Colorado: Smith, *Kid Blackie;* Dempsey, *Dempsey, by the Man Himself.*

34 Dempsey and Maxine Cates married October 9, 1916: Ibid; Roberts, *The Manassa Mauler;* Dempsey, *Dempsey.*

34 Tunney wins all four fights in December 1916: BoxRec website, 2006.

CHAPTER 3

37 Rejected by the Marines: Ed Fitzgerald, "The Man Who Licked the Fight Racket," *Sport,* March 1951.

37 Left job at Ocean Steamship: Tunney, "Gene Tunney's Own Story."

37 Lifeguard and bouncer: Author's telephone interview with Doug Foulks, town historian in Keensburg, New Jersey, May 15, 2004.

38 Tunney as a middleweight: Tunney, *A Man Must Fight.*

38 Job on Hudson River waterfront: Ibid.

38 Treatments for arm injury: Ibid.

39 Boxing soon intruded: "Use Your Head When You Hit," *The American Legion Magazine,* August 1926.

40 Following basic training: The 11th Marines, Marine Corps Reference Section, Biographical Files, Marine Corps Historical Center; author's telephone interviews with Robert Aquilina, assistant head of the reference section, History and Museums Division, Marine Corps Historical Center, June 15 and 17, 2003, March 3, 2006.

40 Marine company clerk and Shakespeare: "I Knew Jack Dempsey When," *Cosmopolitan,* July 1945.

41 "What are you doing?": Tunney, *A Man Must Fight.*

42 Germans surrender: Ibid.

42 Casualties sustained by American forces: Susan Everett, *History of World War I* (New York: Bison Books, 1980).

43 "Go on, get in there": Tunney, *Arms for Living;* Gene Tunney biography, Reference Section Biographical Files, Marine Corps Historical Center; Fitzgerald, "Gentleman Gene—the Champion Nobody Understood."

45 Tunney's reputation as a fighter in the Marines: "Use Your Head When Hit," *The American Legion Monthly,* August 1926; "Champion Is a State of Mind," *The Saturday Evening Post,* February 10, 1940.

46 The giant killer from Gièvres: *Stars and Stripes,* February 1919.

46 AEF tournament: Tunney, *A Man Must Fight;* Tunney, *Arms for Living;* Tunney, "Gene Tunney's Own Story."

48 Tunney wins AEF light heavyweight title: *New York Times,* April 27, 1919; *Stars and Stripes,* May 2, 1919.

49 Tunney's thoughts drifted: "The Long Road to Fame and Fortune," King Features Syndicate, Inc., October 1926; Tunney, *Arms for Living.*

49 Brother John shot to death: *New York Times,* June 30, 1919 and August 15, 1919.

50 Eagan the only athlete to win gold medals at both the Summer and Winter Olympics: Olympic Hall of Fame Sports Biographies, March 5, 2005.

51 Tunney takes quickly to Eagan: Edward P. F. Eagan, *Fighting for Fun: The Scrapbook of Eddie Eagan* (New York: The Macmillan Company, 1932); author's interview with Jeff Zonder at Yale University Sports Archives.

51 Tunney meets Marine Corporal Jack McReynolds: "I Knew Jack Dempsey When,"
    Cosmopolitan, August 1945.

51 If Dempsey were to lose: Tunney, *Arms for Living.*

52 "Jack the Giant Killer": Goldman, *The Ring Record Book and Boxing Encyclopedia.*

53 Tunney returns from France in July 1919: The 11th Marines, Marine Corps Histori-
    cal Center, August 6, 2003.

53 Seventeen pounds heavier: Tunney, "Gene Tunney's Own Story."

54 Back in Greenwich Village: Tunney, *A Man Must Fight.*

CHAPTER 4

57 "I can't believe it's him": "I Knew Jack Dempsey When," *Cosmopolitan,* July 1945;
    Tunney, "Gene Tunney's Own Story;" Arthur Daley, *The American Legion Maga-
    zine,* April 1965.

58 "Nice to meet you": Ibid.

58 Taking Tunney's, right hand: Ibid.

59 Former featherweight boxer Sammy Kelly: Tunney, "Gene Tunney's Own Story."

60 Meets Bernard Gimbel: Ibid.; Tunney, *A Man Must Fight.*

61 Dan O'Dowd fight: New York *Daily News,* November 15, 1919; Tunney, *Arms for
    Living.*

61 Delighted at Tunney's following: Tunney, *A Man Must Fight;* Tunney, "Gene Tun-
    ney's Own Story."

62 Al Roberts fight: *New York Times* and *New York Tribune,* February 3, 1920; Tunney,
    "Gene Tunney's Own Story."

63 Frank "Doc" Bagley again becomes Tunney's manager: Tunney, *A Man Must Fight.*

64 Leon See and Primo Carnera: Frederic Mullally, *Primo: The Story of "Man Moun-
    tain" Carnera* (London: Robson Books, Ltd., 1991); Budd Schulberg, *Sparring with
    Hemingway: And Other Legends of the Fight Game* (Chicago: Ivan R. Dee, 1995).

65 Leon "Boom Boom" Chevalier: Associated Press, April 14, 1930; author's interview
    with Budd Schulberg, May 12, 2004.

66 Ring death of Ernie Schaaf: Mullally, *Primo;* Schulberg, *Sparring with Hemingway;*
    New York Times, New York Herald Tribune, and New York *Daily News,* Feb-
    ruary 14, 1933.

67 Carnera wins heavyweight title: *New York Times, New York Herald Tribune,* June 20,
    1933.

67 "the champion who sprang full and overgrown from the fertile mind of the mob":
    Schulberg, *Sparring with Hemingway.*

67 Virtually broke: Ibid; Mullally, *Primo.*

68 Raise his knockout streak to eleven: *New York Times;* Goldman, *The Ring Record
    Book and Boxing Encyclopedia;* Tunney, *A Man Must Fight.*

CHAPTER 5

69 The first two Madison Square Gardens: Joseph Durso, *Madison Square Garden: 100
    Years of History* (New York: Simon & Schuster, 1979); author's interview with Joseph
    Durso, June 7, 2003.

71 Sullivan-Tug Wilson bout: *New York Times,* July 18, 1882.

73 Corbett exhibitions: Durso, *Madison Square Garden; New York Times*, February 17, 1892 and December 15, 1896.

73 Willard-Moran title fight: *New York Times,* March 26, 1916.

73 Walker boxing bill introduced: Ibid, April 27, 1920 and May 25, 1920; Gene Fowler, *Beau James: The Life and Times of Jimmy Walker* (New York: Viking Press, 1949); State Archives, New York State Assembly, Albany, New York.

74 Aware that Walker: Fowler, *Beau James.*

75 Walker pulls out all the stops: Ibid.

75 Letters and telegrams from Protestant ministers: Ibid; Kahn, *A Flame of Pure Fire.*

77 Tammany tabs Walker to run for mayor: Allen, *New York, New York;* Fowler, *Beau James.*

77 Walker inaugurated as New York's one hundredth mayor: *New York Times* and *New York Herald Tribune,* January 2, 1926.

79 "That's cheap. Think of what it would cost if I worked full time": Allen, *New York, New York;* Fowler, *Beau James.*

79 Love affair with Walker begins to wane: Allen, *New York, New York.*

79 Walker, under fire, resigns as mayor: *New York Times* and *New York Herald Tribune,* September 2, 1932.

79 "You are mistaken. What the world loves is a winner": Fowler, *Beau James.*

79 Marries actress Betty Compton in France after wife obtains divorce: *New York Times,* April 20, 1933.

80 Twenty thousand pass by Walker's coffin: New York *Daily News* and *New York Herald Tribune,* November 21, 1946.

80 Dempsey knocked out by Fireman Jim Flynn: *Denver Evening Post, Pueblo Chieftain,* and Associated Press, February 14, 1917.

81 Rumors that Dempsey had taken a dive against Flynn: Joe Williams's syndicated column in Newspaper Enterprise Association, March 10, 1930.

82 Dempsey accepts offer of new manager: Dempsey, *Dempsey* and *Dempsey, by the Man Himself.*

82 Telegram informing Dempsey that his youngest brother had been stabbed to death: Dempsey, *Dempsey, by the Man Himself.*

83 Jack Kearns offers to manage Dempsey: Ibid.

85 Evens score with Fireman Jim Flynn: Ibid; Associated Press, February 14, 1918; Roberts, *The Manassa Mauler.*

85 Public relations blunder: Associated Press, United Press, and International News Service, November 8, 1918.

86 Draft-dodging trial: *San Francisco Chronicle, San Francisco Examiner, New York Times,* and Associated Press, June 9–17, 1920.

88 Dempsey called slacker after fight with Bill Brennan: Dempsey, *Dempsey, by the Man Himself.*

88 "I wanted to die, and for some years after that, I wished I had": Ibid.

89 First title defense against Billy Miske: Associated Press, *New York Times,* and *New York American,* September 7, 1920; Kahn, *A Flame of Pure Fire;* Roberts, *The Manassa Mauler.*

89 "I knocked him out because I loved the guy": Dempsey, *Dempsey, by the Man Himself.*

90 Defends title second time versus Bill Brennan: *New York American, New York Times,* and New York *Daily News,* December 15, 1921.

91 Leaving Madison Square Garden: "Gene Tunney's Place in the Ring," *Collier's,* February 10, 1951.

CHAPTER 6

93 Al McCoy, real name Al Rudolph: Steven Riess, ed., *Sports and the American Jew* (Syracuse, N.Y.: Syracuse University Press, 1998).

93 Less than four hours: Nat Fleischer, *The Ring*, March 1935.

94 Third fight in one day?: *Waterbury Republican* (Connecticut), January 2, 1915.

94 "Levinsky set a record": Nat Fleischer, *The Ring*, March 1935.

95 Soon after, Buck Areton: Allen Bodner, *When Boxing Was a Jewish Sport* (Westport, Conn.: Praeger, 1997).

96 Daniel Mendoza: Ibid; Harold U. Ribalow, *The Jew in American Sports* (New York: Bloch Publishing, 1966); Ken Blady, *The Jewish Boxers Hall of Fame* (New York: Shapolsky Publishers, 1988).

97 By the second decade: Goldman, *The Ring Record Book and Boxing Encyclopedia,* 1985.

97 "You did it for money, no other reason": Author's interview with Danny Kapilow, June 2, 2003.

97 "As a kid growing up": Author's interview with Charlie Gellman, March 23, 2003.

98 Smart fighters: Author's interviews with Kapilow and Gellman, April 4, 2003.

98 "If Billy had a Jewish head": Peter Levine, *Ellis Island to Ebbets Field: Sport and the American Jewish Experience* (New York: Oxford University Press, 1992).

98 "Abe, when are you going to fight again?": Barney Ross with Martin Abramson, *No Man Stands Alone: The True Story of Barney Ross* (Philadelphia: Lippincott, 1957).

98 Benny Leonard related a somewhat similar experience: Levine, *Ellis Island to Ebbets Field.*

99 Into his nineties: Author's interview with Budd Schulberg, April 2, 2004.

99 Leonard's fight with Irish Eddie Finnegan: Author's interview with longtime sports publicist Irving Rudd, circa 1992.

100 Jack Britton fight: *New York Times, New York American,* and *New York Tribune,* November 27, 1922.

102 "In those days": Author's interview with Budd Schulberg, April 2, 2004.

102 Manny Seamon's explanation of Leonard loss: Bodner, *When Boxing Was a Jewish Sport.*

102 Name changes: Ibid.

103 Max Baer's claim of Jewishness resonated among Jews: Ibid; Sugar, *Boxing's Greatest Fighters;* author's interview with Bert Randolph Sugar, April 15, 2004; Riess, *Sports and the American Jew.*

103 "That made my father": Author's interview with Max Baer, Jr., January 7, 2006.

104 Battling Levinsky anglicizes his name: Riess, *Sports and the American Jew;* Bodner, *When Boxing Was a Jewish Sport;* author's interview with Harriet Levinsky Solodky, May 22, 2005.

104 Impossible to knock out: Freddie Mills, *Forward the Light-Heavies* (London: Stanley Paul and Company, 1956), Goldman, *The Ring Record Book and Boxing Encyclopedia,* 1985; *The Ring,* March 1930.

104 One of boxing's most colorful characters: Dan Morgan: *Dumb Dan* (New York: Tedson Publishing, 1953).

105 Flushed by Levinsky's success: Ibid.

106 The Dempsey-Levinsky fight: *Philadelphia Inquirer, Philadelphia Record,* and *New York Times,* September 17, 1918.

107 "He's been beaten four times": Morgan, *Dumb Dan.*

107 Besides losing his world title: Goldman, *The Ring Record Book and Boxing Encyclopedia,* 1985.

CHAPTER 7

109 From what Tunney said in later years: Gene Tunney, "Champion Is a State of Mind," *The Saturday Evening Post,* February 10, 1940.

110 Working at lumber camp in Ontario: "Gene Tunney's Place in Ring History," *The Saturday Evening Post,* February 10, 1951; Tunney, "Gene Tunney's Own Story."

111 As Doc Bagley expected: "Tunney's Hour of Travail," *Esquire,* June 1943.

112 Awkward and swinging wildly: *New York Times* and *New York Sun,* July 3, 1921.

112 Tunney kneels in corner to watch Dempsey-Carpentier: "Gene Tunney's Place in Ring History," *The Saturday Evening Post,* February 10, 1951; "The Man Who Licked the Fight Racket," *Sport,* March 10, 1951.

113 Madison Square Garden debut: Tunney, "Gene Tunney's Own Story;" *New York Times,* October 16, 1921.

114 Paying off sportswriters: Tunney, *A Man Must Fight;* conversation with Barney Nagler, circa 1985; author interview with Bert Randolph Sugar, April 14, 2004.

115 Become almost apoplectic: Author's conversation with Barney Nagler, circa 1978.

115 Runyon's part ownership of fighters in Pueblo and Denver: Breslin, *Damon Runyon.*

115 Stealing money from babies: Breslin, *Damon Runyon.*

115 Runyon may have been a pupil of Otto Floto: Ibid; Gene Fowler, *Timber Line: A Story of Bonfils and Tammen* (Garden City, N.Y.: Garden City Books, 1947); Dempsey, *Dempsey* (New York: Harper & Row, 1977).

116 Tex Rickard creates American light heavyweight championship: Tunney, "Gene Tunney's Own Story."

118 Before the largest crowd: *New York Times, New York Tribune,* and *New York American,* January 14, 1922.

118 "Then, lo and behold, the Battler lets me have it": Tunney, "Gene Tunney's Own Story;" Tunney, *A Man Must Fight.*

119 Against the advice: "Battling Levinsky Knocked Out, Quits Ring," *National Police Gazette,* February 16, 1929.

119 Returning to his wife and two children: Author's interview with Harriet Levinsky Solodky, May 22, 2005; Blady, *The Jewish Boxers Hall of Fame.*

119 Back in Philadelphia: Author's interview with Harriet Levinsky Solodky, May 22, 2005.

120 "He was a wonderful father who hardly ever talked about his days as a boxer": Ibid; *Philadelphia Inquirer, Philadelphia Record,* and *Philadelphia Daily News,* February 13, 1949.

CHAPTER 8

122 "Prizefighting ain't the noblest of arts": Rolfe Garrett, "Harry Greb—Windmill of the Ring," *Arena,* July 10, 1929.

123 "Entertaining" women in his dressing room before a fight: James Fair, *Give Him to the Angels: The Story of Harry Greb* (New York: Smith and Durrell, 1946).

123 "If I'm going to leave my fighting anywhere": Ibid.

124 "comes upon an opponent like a swarm of bees": Grantland Rice, *New York Herald Tribune,* May 26, 1926.

124 As for Greb's boxing ability: Ibid.

124 "The most remarkable thing about this truly remarkable man": Damon Runyon, *New York American,* May 15, 1922.

125 Greb staggered out of a cab and into Billy LaHiff's restaurant: Dan Parker, New York *Daily Mirror,* July 10, 1946.

125 Not surprisingly, they switched their bets: Ibid.

125 Referee knocked down twice during Greb–Mickey Walker fight: *New York Herald Tribune* and New York *Daily News,* July 3, 1925.

126 Greb's father idolized Pittsburgh Pirates' shortstop Honus Wagner . . . Hoping that his son would grow up to be a Pittsburgh Pirate: Harry Keck, *Pittsburgh Sun-Telegraph,* June 26, 1926; Fair, *Give Him to the Angels.*

126 "He broke loose, ran them down and whipped them so thoroughly": Garrett, *Arena,* July 10, 1929.

126 "No boy of mine who engages in it": Fair, *Give Him to the Angels.*

127 Over the next six years: Goldman, *The Ring Record Book and Boxing Encyclopedia, Pittsburgh Sun-Telegraph,* and *Pittsburgh Press.*

127 After about 150 fights: *New York Times, New York American,* and *New York Sun,* May 25, 1918.

128 Four fights involving forty-two rounds in one month: Goldman, *The Ring Record Book and Boxing Encyclopedia; New York American,* June 21, 1918; *Bridgeport Telegram* (Connecticut), June 25, 1918.

128 The blonde with the permanent wave: Fair, *Give Him to the Angels.*

129 "He was a good baseball player": Harry Keck, *Pittsburgh Sun-Telegraph,* September 14, 1943.

129 Sparring sessions with Jack Dempsey: Jack Kofoed, "The Human Windmill," *Fight Stories,* December 1929, January, February, and March 1930; Fair, *Give Him to the Angels.*

130 "The hell with that seven-year itch": Fair, *Give Him to the Angels.*

130 Birth of Greb's only child: Fair, *Give Him to the Angels;* Harry Cleavelin, "A Tale of Two Harrys," *Boxing Illustrated,* August 1960.

130 Greb's 1921 fight with Kid Norfolk: Ibid; John Lardner, "King of the Alley Fighters," *True,* March 1957.

131 By the end of 1921, Greb was blind in one eye: Lardner, "King of the Alley Fighters;" Cleaveline, "The Harry Greb Story," *Boxing Illustrated,* March 1950.

132 Greb would have a remarkable year: *Pittsburgh Sun-Telegraph, Pittsburgh Press,* and *New York Times,* March 14, 1922.

132 "I seemed to have run into a solid wall of leather": *New York Times* and *New York Tribune,* March 14, 1922.

CHAPTER 9

134 To prepare for Greb: Tunney, *A Man Must Fight.*

136 "Funniest hitter in the world": *New York World,* April 25, 1922.

136 Most of the: New York *Daily News* and *New York Tribune,* May 23, 1922.

137 "Do you think I would be happy seeing you bleeding?": Tunney, *Arms for Living.*

137 "a street corner Don Juan": Lardner, "King of the Alley Fighters," *True.*

138 Because of a cut: Arthur Mann, "Tunney's Hour of Travail," *Esquire,* June 1943.

138 Charging across the ring: Ibid; *New York Times, New York World,* and *Pittsburgh Post-Gazette,* May 24, 1922.

138 "came at Tunney from every angle": *New York World,* May 24, 1922.

139 "as if he had been painting a house with red paint": Damon Runyon, *New York American,* May 24, 1922.

139 Aware of that: Grantland Rice, *The Tumult and the Shouting: My Life in Sport* (New York: A. S. Barnes and Company, 1954).

140 "How I ever survived the thirteenth, fourteenth, and fifteenth rounds is still a mystery to me": Mann, "Tunney's Hour of Travail," *Esquire,* June 1943.

140 "perhaps the bloodiest fight I ever covered": Rice, *The Tumult and the Shouting.*

140 "Well, Harry, you were the better man tonight": Tunney, *A Man Must Fight.*

140 Besides losing the fight: Rice, *The Tumult and the Shouting;* Mann, "Tunney's Hour of Travail," *Esquire,* June 1943; Tim Cohane, "Gene Tunney Today," *Look,* July 10, 1956.

141 "Kid, you're the gamest fighter I ever saw": Cohane, "Gene Tunney Today," *Look,* July 10, 1956.

141 Aided by Bagley, McCormack, and several others: Mann, "Tunney's Hour of Travail," *Esquire,* June 1943; "Gene Tunney's Place in the Ring," *Collier's,* February 10, 1951.

141 Before he left for Red Bank: Fitzgerald, "Gene Tunney: The Man Who Licked the Fight Racket"; Cohane, "Gene Tunney Today," *Look,* July 10, 1956.

142 "I discovered through the early part of the fight": Fair, *Give Him to the Angels.*

142 Furious, Greb turned to Albacker: Lardner, "King of the Alley Fighters," *True,* March 1957.

142 "I was so arm-weary": Ibid.

CHAPTER 10

144 "How could you let him do that to you?": Tunney, *Arms for Living.*

144 "We just had a good time": Dempsey, *Dempsey, by the Man Himself.*

145 "You should of seen it in 1922": Ibid.

145 Dempsey prowling the Aquitania: *New York American,* April 14, 1922.

145 Dempsey's workouts aboard ship: Kahn, *A Flame of Pure Fire.*

145 Sightseeing in London: Dempsey, *Dempsey, by the Man Himself;* Dempsey, *Dempsey; New York American,* April 21 and 23, 1922; *New York Times,* April 25, 1922.

145 Luncheon given by Lord Northcliff: Dempsey, *Dempsey, by the Man Himself;* Kahn, *A Flame of Pure Fire.*

147 "It was more in tune with our crowd": Ibid.

147 "When the fight ended": Ibid.

147 There were parties every night: Roberts, *The Manassa Mauler.*

148 Dancing with one of the Dolly Sisters: King Features Syndicate, Inc.; Kahn, *A Flame of Pure Fire.*

148 "Paris was better. More girls, more action": Dempsey, *Dempsey, by the Man Himself.*

148 Women boxers in Berlin: Dempsey, *Dempsey, by the Man Himself;* Dempsey, *Dempsey;* King Features Syndicate, Inc., May 12, 1922; Kahn, *A Flame of Pure Fire.*

148 The "colored heavyweight champion": *New York Times, New York Tribune,* and *New York American,* May 20, 1922.

150 "They always said I wasn't afraid of any man": Dempsey, *Dempsey, by the Man Himself.*

150 Monthlong stage tour: Ibid; *New York Times,* May 20, 1922.

153 Rickard promotes his first fight: Ibid; Dempsey, *Dempsey; New York Times,* August 25, 1906, and September 3, 4, and 5, 1906.

157 With Johnson seven inches taller: *New York Sun* and *New York Times,* December 27, 1908.

158 "One thing remains": Jack London in *New York Sun,* December 28, 1908.

159 "Boys, it's got to be Reno": *New York Herald* and *New York Times,* May 25, 1910.

160 Rickard's second fight—Jack Johnson versus Jim Jeffries: Roberts, *The Manassa Mauler;* Dempsey, *Dempsey;* Dempsey, *Dempsey, by the Man Himself; New York Times* and *New York Tribune,* July 2, 3, and 5, 1910.

160 Corbett taunting Johnson: Randy Roberts, *Papa Jack: Jack Johnson and the Era of White Hopes* (New York: Free Press, c. 1983).

162 Racial strife in the aftermath of Johnson-Jeffries fight: Ibid; Roberts, *The Manassa Mauler; New York Times, New York Herald,* and *New York Sun,* July 6 and 7, 1910.

162 Johnson knocks out Fireman Jim Flynn: Associated Press, *Denver Evening Post,* and *New York Times,* July 5, 1910.

162 Johnson skips bail and flees to Europe: John Lardner, *White Hopes and Other Tigers* (Philadelphia: J. B. Lippincott, 1951).

163 "White" heavyweight champions: Ibid; Sam Andre and Nat Fleischer, *A Pictorial History of Boxing* (New York: Bonanza Books, 1981).

163 Rickard turns cattle raiser in South America: Hype Igoe, "Rickard in Retrospect," *The Ring,* January 1931; *New York Times* and *New York Herald Tribune,* January 7, 1929.

Chapter 11

165 Tunney knew what to expect from Kaiser: *New York Times,* July 8, 1922; Tunney, *A Man Must Fight.*

167 Tommy Loughran fight: Author's interview with John Dempsey, May 3, 2003; *Philadelphia Inquirer, Philadelphia Record,* and *New York Times,* August 25, 1922.

168 "Tommy Outclasses Gene": headline in *Philadelphia Inquirer,* August 25, 1922.

169 Revenge fight with Jack Hanlon: Tunney, "Courage is a Business," *The Saturday Evening Post,* June 1, 1940.

170 The former middleweight champion: Author's interview with Jake La Motta, September 12, 2003.

170 As Basilio recalled: Author's interview with Carmen Basilio, September 15, 2003.

171 "It's the only way I know how to fight": Paul Gallico, *Farewell to Sport* (New York: Alfred A. Knopf, 1938).

172 "One might wonder": Joyce Carol Oates, *On Boxing* (Garden City, N.Y.: Dolphin/ Doubleday, 1987).

172 Tunney severs relations with Doc Bagley and hires Billy Gibson: Ed Fitzgerald, "Gentleman Gene—The Champion Nobody Understood," *Sport,* May 1950; Tunney, *Arms for Living.*

173 Benny Leonard teaches Tunney how to deliver a cutting jab: Tim Cohane, *Look,* July 10, 1956.

174 Mildred Greb's condition worsens: Fair, *Give Him to the Angels;* author's interview with Harry Greb's granddaughter Jennifer Wohlforth, January 6, 2004.

175 "They told me in my corner I was losing": Tunney, "Gene Tunney's Own Story."

176 Returning to Pittsburgh: Author's interview with Greb historian Jim Cashman, January 10, 2004; *Pittsburgh Sun-Telegraph,* February 26, 1923.

177 Greb had become a good family man: Fair, *Give Him to the Angels;* author's interviews with Jim Cashman and Greb's granddaughter Jennifer Wohlforth, February 10 and 11, 2004; author's interview with Ed Cahill, Greb authority and documentary filmmaker, April 7, 2004.

CHAPTER 12

179 In one of the roughest and dirtiest: *New York American, New York Times,* and *New York Tribune,* September 1, 1923.

180 "money-mad promoters and managers": Roberts, *The Manassa Mauler.*

180 "orders from a very high place": Van Every, *The Life of Gene Tunney* (New York: Dell Publishing Company, 1926).

181 Offer from Shelby to Dempsey and Kearns: Author's interview with retired Shelby newspaper publisher John Kavanagh, October 14, 2005.

181 "It was strictly": Ibid.

182 "Hell, man, there isn't that much money in the whole state of Montana": Ibid.

183 Lloyd Molumby meets with Kearns in Chicago: Lardner, *White Hopes and Other Tigers.*

183 "Kearns apparently threw a wingding of a party": Author's interview with John Kavanagh, October 14, 2005.

183 "We decided there was nothing to be done": Ibid.

184 "It's one of those wide-open towns": Lardner, *White Hopes and Other Tigers.*

184 "This place is so tough": Humor columnist Arthur "Bugs" Baer on Shelby, King Features Syndicate, Inc., June 23, 1923.

185 "It ain't a big place": Dempsey, *Dempsey, by the Man Himself.*

186 Dempsey sets up training camp in Great Falls, Montana: *New York Times,* May 18, 1923; Lardner, *White Hopes and Other Tigers.*

186 Dempsey did not look impressive: King Features, Inc., June 5, 1923; *New York Tribune,* June 7, 1923.

187 "We're having a little difficulty": Lardner, *White Hopes and Other Tigers;* Rice, *The Tumult and the Shouting.*

187 "would you consider taking fifty thousand head of sheep": Jack Kearns with Oscar Fraley, *The Million Dollar Gate* (New York: Macmillan, 1966).

188 George Stanton's intervention in effort to save fight: Ibid; *New York Times,* July 2, 1923.

188 Gibbons was a distinct counterpart to Dempsey and Kearns: Ibid; Roberts, *The Manassa Mauler;* Kahn, *A Flame of Pure Fire; New York Times,* June 17 and 21, 1923.

190 George Stanton's plan to save the Dempsey-Gibbons fight: *New York Times,* King Features Syndicate, Inc., and *New York Tribune,* July 4, 1923; Lardner, *White Hopes and Other Tigers.*

191 "The fight is off": *New York Times,* July 3, 1923.

191 If the *Times* had a star reporter: Depauw University biography of Elmer Davis.

191 "Not since the time": Elmer Davis writing in *New York Times* on July 3, 1923.

192 The throngs of spectators never did materialize: *New York Times,* King Features Syndicate, Inc., *New York Tribune,* and *Denver Evening Post,* July 3 and 4, 1923; Lardner, *White Hopes and Other Tigers;* Kearns, *The Million Dollar Gate.*

192 In the days: Ibid.

193 Dempsey and his entourage arrive in Shelby on July 4: *New York Times, New York Sun,* and *New York American;* Lardner, *White Hopes and Other Tigers;* author's in-

terview with John Kavanagh, October 14, 2005; author's interview with Shelby museum curator Dean Hellinger, October 15, 2005.

194 "They got it [the private car] on the siding": Kearns, *The Million Dollar Gate;* Lardner, *White Hopes and Other Tigers.*

194 "Get going. There ain't enough people in Montana to take this money away from me": Ibid.

194 "For the first and only time": Dempsey, *Dempsey, by the Man Himself.*

195 Kearns tried to induce people to buy cut-rate tickets: *New York Times* and *New York American,* July 5, 1923.

195 Tanned to the color of leather: *New York Times,* July 5, 1923.

195 Dempsey, far stronger than Gibbons: Ibid; King Features, Inc., July 5, 1923.

196 Most ringside observers felt Dempsey had won thirteen of the fifteen rounds: *New York Times,* July 5, 1923.

196 "one of the greatest battles of recent years in the prize ring": Damon Runyon in King Features Syndicate, Inc., July 5, 1923.

196 "Gibbons was the coyote": Ibid.

196 One of the illusions the bout dispelled: Otto Floto, *Denver Evening Post,* July 5, 1923.

197 No glorious exit for Dempsey: *New York Times,* July 5, 1923; Lardner, *White Hopes and Other Tigers;* Kearns, *The Million Dollar Gate.*

197 Gate receipts totaled approximately $80,000: *New York Times* and *New York Tribune,* July 5, 1923; Kahn, *A Flame of Pure Fire.*

197 "I'll fight Dempsey for nothing": Dempsey, *Dempsey, by the Man Himself.*

197 Years later: Author's interview with John Kavanagh, October 15, 1923.

198 Kearns decided it would be in his best interest to leave town immediately: Lardner, *White Hopes and Other Tigers;* Kearns, *The Million Dollar Gate.*

198 Kearns gives engineer five hundred dollars for train trip to Great Falls: Kearns, *The Million Dollar Gate.*

198 "Hey, Hype": Ibid.

199 Man calls out "Don't hurry back": Ibid.

199 "From the time he stepped from the train": *Chicago Tribune,* July 6, 1923.

199 In his story: Heywood Broun for the North American Newspaper Alliance, July 6, 1923.

200 While in Great Falls: Lardner, *White Hopes and Other Tigers.*

200 The banking situation only got worse: Ibid; Kearns, *The Million Dollar Gate.*

200 Shelby Mayor Johnson asks Kearns for loan: Kearns, *The Million Dollar Gate.*

200 "What do you think?" Kearns asked Dempsey: Ibid; Lardner, *White Hopes and Other Tigers.*

200 "A few years later": Kearns, *The Million Dollar Gate.*

200 In a parting eulogy: *New York Times,* July 7, 1923.

201 "It was the booster spirit that got Shelby into trouble": Lardner, *White Hopes and Other Tigers.*

201 Retribution for Kearns: Kearns, *The Million Dollar Gate.*

201 "Sack of Shelby": Ibid; Lardner, *White Hopes and Other Tigers.*

201 More than eighty years after the fight: Author's interviews with John Kavanagh and Dean Hellinger, October 14 and 15, 2005.

202 "The fight's never been forgotten here": Author's interview with Shelby mayor Larry J. Bonderud, October 15, 2005.

202 "Remember Shelby, Doc?": Lardner, *White Hopes and Other Tigers.*

CHAPTER 13

204 Firpo-Willard fight: *New York Times* and *New York Sun,* July 13, 1923.

205 To the relief of: Associated Press and *New York Times,* July 28 and August 14, 1923.

206 Paul Gallico asks Dempsey to spar with him: New York *Daily News,* September 8, 1923.

206 "hit us as hard as he can because we want to know just how a knockout feels": Gallico, "My Fight with Jack Dempsey," *Reader's Digest,* July 1954; Gallico, *Farewell to Sport;* Dempsey, *Dempsey.*

207 "Dempsey's going to take it easy": Gallico, "My Fight with Jack Dempsey," *Reader's Digest,* July 1954; Gallico, *Farewell to Sport.*

207 "Son, don't you know that man can't take it easy": Ibid.

207 Gallico quickly tossed out a weak left jab: Ibid; *Reader's Digest,* July 1954; Dempsey, *Dempsey.*

208 The sparring session had lasted a minute and half: Ibid; Gallico, *Farewell to Sport.*

209 Firpo a "disbeliever in Nordic supremacy": *New York Tribune,* September 10, 1923.

209 Going even further: Bruce Bliven, *The New Republic,* September 1923.

209 Lines for tickets: *New York Times* and *New York Tribune,* September 15, 1923.

210 Description of Dempsey-Firpo: *New York Times, New York Tribune, New York Sun, New York American,* and *New York World,* September 15, 1923.

212 "Help me back in there": *New York Tribune,* September 16, 1923; "Best of the Ring," *The Ring,* October 1923.

212 "First, let me say": *New York Journal,* September 23, 1923.

213 "What round was I knocked out in?": Dempsey, *Dempsey* and *Dempsey, by the Man Himself;* Kahn, *A Flame of Pure Fire.*

213 "You just slipped": Ibid.

214 "There were three of us in the ring, Jack": *Esquire,* October 1958.

214 Criticism of Dempsey for his half-million-dollar purse: *Christian Science Monitor,* September 15, 1923.

215 Grantland Rice on disqualifying Dempsey: *New York World* and *New York Journal,* September 15, 1923; Nat Fleischer in *The Ring,* October 1923.

216 "I won it four times on fouls": Gallico, *Farewell to Sport.*

216 George Bellows lithograph of Dempsey knocked out of ring: Author's interview with Megan Heuer, Metropolitan Museum of Art, September 1, 2004.

216 Dempsey picks up check at Rickard's office day after fight: Dempsey, *Dempsey, by the Man Himself.*

217 Kearns flies into rage over Dempsey getting check: Ibid; Dempsey, *Dempsey.*

217 Dempsey's three-year hiatus from the boxing ring: Ibid; Roberts, *The Manassa Mauler.*

220 "They talked over my head a lot": Dempsey, *Dempsey, by the Man Himself.*

221 After a number of affairs: Kahn, *A Flame of Pure Fire.*

221 Dempsey falls in love with actress Estelle Taylor: Dempsey, *Dempsey* and *Dempsey, by the Man Himself;* Kahn, *A Flame of Pure Fire.*

221 "She was more than a beautiful movie star": Dempsey, *Dempsey, by the Man Himself.*

222 Taylor, a teenage beauty queen: Dempsey, *Dempsey, by the Man Himself;* Gallico, *Farewell to Sport;* Kahn, *A Flame of Pure Fire;* author's interview with Barbara Dempsey Phillips, July 9, 2005.

222 Jack Kearns's crude remarks about Estelle Taylor: Dempsey, *Dempsey;* Kahn, *A Flame of Pure Fire;* Dempsey, *Dempsey, by the Man Himself.*

223 Dempsey not surprised when Kearns declines cut in his percentage of Dempsey's earnings: Dempsey, *Dempsey, by the Man Himself.*

223 Honeymoon trip to Europe: Dempsey, *Dempsey* and *Dempsey, by the Man Himself; New York Times,* May 22 and 25, 1923.

223 Buy home in Hollywood Hills: Dempsey, *Dempsey* and *Dempsey, by the Man Himself; New York Tribune,* July 27, 1923.

223 Dempsey and Estelle Taylor star in *Manhattan Madness:* Kahn, *A Flame of Pure Fire;* Dempsey, *Dempsey, by the Man Himself;* Dempsey, *Dempsey.*

224 "She wasn't a great actress": Dempsey, *Dempsey, by the Man Himself.*

225 Deaths of Billy Miske and Bill Brennan: Kahn, *A Flame of Pure Fire;* Dempsey, *Dempsey, by the Man Himself; New York Times,* January 2, 1924 and April 15, 1924.

CHAPTER 14

227 "manly beauty and brains with a fighting instinct": *New York Journal,* September 20, 1926.

227 Cornelius Vanderbilt calls Tunney an "Adonis": *Liberty,* August 1926.

229 "as heartsick as any Caucasian": *The Saturday Evening Post,* June 1, 1940.

229 Tunney, a 2-to-1 favorite over Greb in second fight: *New York Tribune,* February 23, 1923.

230 Considerable booing when Tunney declared winner over Greb: *New York Tribune, New York World, New York Times,* and *Pittsburgh Sun-Telegraph,* February 24, 1923.

230 Tunney and Greb would fight twice more: *Cleveland Press, New York Times,* and Associated Press, September 18, 1924.

230 St. Paul fight: *Minneapolis Tribune* and Associated Press, March 28, 1925.

231 That was the way Harry Greb fought: Tunney, *Arms for Living.*

232 Promoter Jimmy Johnston arranges lawn parties for Carpentier and Tunney: *New York Times,* July 15, 1924; *New York Herald Tribune,* July 17, 1924.

233 Carpentier-Tunney fight: *New York Times, New York American,* and *New York Tribune,* July 3, 1924; Tunney, "Gene Tunney's Own Story."

235 Carpentier was "struck in the groin by Tunney's knee": *New York Times,* July 3, 1924.

235 "Tunney has little genuine class": Joe Williams, sports columnist for the Newspaper Enterprise Association, July 3, 1924.

CHAPTER 15

238 New Yorkers woke to front-page headlines about Tex Rickard's arrest: *New York Times, New York Tribune,* and *New York Sun,* January 22, 1922.

238 Testimony by young girls to grand jury and in court that Rickard molested them: *New York Times,* January 26, 1922.

238 Girl sought for questioning kidnapped and then found in upstate New York: *New York Times,* February 8, 10, and 11, 1922.

239 "Keep quiet. Keep your mouth shut": *New York Times,* March 23, 1922.

239 "I didn't want to lose it": Ibid, March 28, 1922.

240 Max Steuer's defense of Rickard: Ibid; *New York American,* March 25, 1922.

240 Rickard holds jury and spectators mesmerized as he recounts background: *New York Times* and *New York Sun*, March 25, 1922.

240 Impressive list of character witnesses: Ibid; *New York Tribune*, March 25, 1922.

240 "Were you not, in the long and short of it . . . a cad and a cheater": Ibid, March 28, 1922.

240 Schoenfeld girl and mother visit Rickard at Madison Square Garden: Ibid.

240 Several of the girls were older than they claimed: Ibid, March 27, 1922.

241 Rickard claims to have been at football game at Polo Grounds: *New York Times*, March 25, 1922.

241 Jury takes only an hour and a half to acquit Rickard: *New York Times* and *New York Tribune*, March 29, 1922.

242 "I've shot craps for $30,000 a throw": Ibid.

242 "When I heard the last kerplunk": Author's interview with Bert Randolph Sugar, June 10, 2005.

244 On an unseasonably hot and humid early June night: *New York Times*, *New York Herald Tribune*, and *New York Sun*, June 6, 1925.

244 "I hate to hit in a situation like this": Tunney, *Arms for Living*.

245 "Tunney's victory is expected to pave the way for a heavyweight championship bout": *New York Times*, June 6, 1925.

245 "I think I have established my right": *New York Herald Tribune*, June 6, 1925.

CHAPTER 16

246 Tunney gets to meet his father's favorite fighter, James J. Corbett: Rice, *The Tumult and the Shouting*.

247 "I honestly think he's better than Benny Leonard": Ibid.

248 Corbett as a successful actor: Armond Fields, *James J. Corbett: A Biography of the Heavyweight Boxing Champion and Popular Theater Headliner* (Jefferson, N.C.: McFarland and Company, Inc., 2001).

248 Sullivan's appeal on the stage: "Fighters as Thespians," Nat Fleischer, *A Pictorial History of Boxing* (New York: Bonanza Books, 1981).

248 Other champions who tried acting: Ibid; *The Ring*, November 1943.

249 Dempsey and his second wife, Estelle Taylor, in the play *The Big Fight*: Dempsey, *Dempsey, by the Man Himself.*

249 "Every night as he hit the deck": Ibid.

249 One night in New Haven: Ibid.

251 "Whatever you do, don't agree to fight until after the agreement ends": Ibid.

251 New York State Athletic Commission rules Dempsey must fight Wills: *New York Times*, July 9, 1926.

252 New York State License Committee denies license to Dempsey: Ibid, *New York Herald Tribune* and *New York Sun*, August 17, 1926.

252 "The years with Kearns": Dempsey, *Dempsey, by the Man Himself.*

252 "I doubt I would have become heavyweight champion": Ibid.

253 "He was gypped out of his crack at the title": Ibid.

253 Sesquicentennial officials and Philadelphia mayor show interest in Dempsey-Tunney fight: *New York Times* and *Philadelphia Record*, July 15 and 16, 1926; author's interview with Dick Romeniecki, Historical Society of Pennsylvania, February 10, 2004.

254 New York state attorney general rules Dempsey is entitled to license: *New York Times*, August 15, 1926.

254 "New York's loss and the gain of Philadelphia": Ibid, August 20, 1926.

254 "As far as New York is concerned, I am through": *New York Herald Tribune*, August 22, 1926.

CHAPTER 17

259 New York Giants' owner Tim Mara's involvement with Tunney and Gibson: Author's interview with Wellington Mara, January 8, 2003; Tunney: *A Man Must Fight*.

260 Tunney spends nine weeks in Hollywood making a serial movie: Tunney, "Gene Tunney's Own Story."

260 Efforts to hold fight in New York collapse: *New York Herald Tribune, New York Times*, and *New York Sun*, August 19, 1926.

261 Greb betting five thousand dollars on Tunney to win, *Philadelphia Record*, September 19, 1926.

262 Tunney begins having recurrent nightmares in training camp: *The Saturday Evening Post*, June 1, 1940.

263 "When the nightmares persisted": Ibid; Tunney, *A Man Must Fight*.

264 Dempsey knocks out two sparring partners within two minutes time: *New York Times*, August 11, 1926.

264 Tunney undergoes experience that would invite ridicule from sportswriters: Norman Vincent Peale, ed., *Faith Made Them Champions* (New York: Guidepost Associates, 1954); Harry Paxton, ed., *Sport USA: The Best from the Saturday Evening Post* (New York, Edinburgh, and Toronto: Thomas Nelson & Sons, 1961); Will Grimsley column for the Associated Press, March 31, 1954.

266 By contrast, Tunney's training camp was businesslike and almost sedate: *Philadelphia Public Ledger*, September 15, 1926; author's interviews with Don and Patricia Knickman, former owners of the Glen Brook Country Club on January 21, 2005.

266 Hordes of women attracted to Tunney's training camp in the Poconos: Cornelius Vanderbilt, Jr., New York *Daily Mirror*, August 24, 1926.

267 "It would be difficult to find a more perfect Adonis type": Ibid.

267 "When I am ready to get married": Mary Dixon Thayer in the Philadelphia *Bulletin*, September 23, 1926.

268 Dempsey, while rough-housing, sends trainer Gus Wilson to the hospital: Gallico, *Farewell to Sport*.

268 "The birds' singing drives you nuts": Tami Mauriello in the New York *Daily News*, September 10, 1946.

268 "There's nothing to do at night but listen to the lousy crickets": Rocky Graziano in the *New York Journal-American*, September 20, 1948.

269 Tunney reflects on negative perception of him: Will Grimsley, Associated Press, March 31, 1954.

269 "I don't think you have to be illiterate to be a boxing champion": Ibid.

270 Kearns's suits against Tunney: *New York Times* and *New York Herald Tribune*, August 10 and 17, 1926.

271 Injunction served on Dempsey in connection with proposed fight with Harry Wills: *Philadelphia Inquirer* and *Philadelphia Record*, September 17, 1926.

272 "That was a laugh": Gallico, *Farewell to Sport*.

272 "There is no doubt that Dempsey has done the impossible": *New York Evening World*, September 18, 1926.

273 "I can't think of a more inept combination": *Philadelphia Inquirer*, September 21, 1926.

274 "Tunney showed me enough to convince me": *Philadelphia Record,* September 19, 1926.

274 Benny Leonard picks Dempsey to win: Philadelphia *Evening Bulletin,* September 20, 1926.

275 Tunney was hardly surprised: *New York Evening World,* September 21, 1926.

275 Playing eighteen holes the day before the fight: *Philadelphia Public Ledger, Philadelphia Record, Philadelphia Inquirer,* and *New York Times,* September 23, 1926; *Sport,* September 1960.

275 McCabe, a sixty-five-year-old golfing novice: *Philadelphia Inquirer,* September 23, 1926.

276 "on the whole the Stroudsburg experience was unpleasant": Tunney, *A Man Must Fight.*

276 "I'm going in there to make a short fight": *Philadelphia Record,* September 23, 1926.

276 Dempsey also got some good news: *Philadelphia Inquirer* and *New York Times,* September 23, 1926.

277 "No, I certainly am not going to fly to Philadelphia": *Philadelphia Bulletin,* September 22, 1926.

277 "before the largest crowd of any kind": Elmer Davis in the *New York Times,* September 23, 1926.

278 Tunney goes through unusual sparring session night before first Dempsey fight: New York *Daily News,* September 23, 1926.

278 Gibson and Abe Attell in "animated conversation" night before fight: Tunney, *A Man Must Fight.*

CHAPTER 18

279 Railroad officials on crowded trains: *New York Times, New York Herald Tribune, Philadelphia Inquirer,* September 24, 1926.

280 An assemblage of the rich and famous: Ibid.

280 "If holding hands with her once makes me her lover": *New York Times,* May 20, 1922.

281 Coming from the West: *New York Times* and *New York Herald Tribune,* September 24, 1926.

282 "the most opulent and most distinguished that ever saw a fight": *New York Times,* September 24, 1926.

284 "We just got word that Tunney's flying into town for the weigh-in": *New York Herald Tribune,* September 24, 1926.

284 Tunney leaves Glen Brook Country Club: "Champion Is a State of Mind," *The Saturday Evening Post,* February 10, 1940; *New York Times* and *Philadelphia Inquirer,* September 24, 1926.

285 "I had to keep it a secret": Tunney, *Arms for Living.*

285 The flight would be much worse: *New York Times,* September 24, 1926; Gallico, *Farewell to Sport;* Fitzgerald, "Boxing's Most Underrated Champ," *Sport,* May 1950; Tunney, "Champion Is a State of Mind," *The Saturday Evening Post,* February 10, 1940.

286 "Oh, it was grand, Casey": *Sport,* September 1960.

286 "I never saw anybody so scared": Tunney, *A Man Must Fight.*

286 "He's not frightened": Ibid.

286 Dempsey's trip to Philadelphia: *Philadelphia Inquirer,* Philadelphia *Evening Bul-*

letin, New York Times, and *New York Herald Tribune,* September 24, 1926;
Dempsey, *Dempsey, by the Man Himself.*

287 Theory that Dempsey had been poisoned: *Baltimore News* and Associated Press, December 1, 1926; Dempsey, *Dempsey.*

287 Years later, another conspiracy theory developed: Roberts, *The Manassa Mauler.*

288 Furious at being awakened from a deep sleep: Tunney, *A Man Must Fight.*

288 Gibson was concerned the first Dempsey-Tunney might be "stolen": Van Every, *The Life of Gene Tunney.*

289 "rich men, poor men, beggar men and maybe even thieves": *New York Times,* September 24, 1926.

289 "Hype, I ain't never seed nothing like it": *New York World,* September 24, 1926.

CHAPTER 19

290 Tunney stretched out on training table before fight for a nap: *The Literary Digest,* October 16, 1926; Edward Van Every, "Tunney Tells How He Won the Title," *Popular Science Monthly,* December 1926.

291 Referee Tommy Reilly interrupts Tunney nap in dressing room: Tunney, "Gene Tunney's Own Story."

291 Gibson, Bronson, McCabe, and Tunney share laugh after Reilly leaves: Ibid; Tunney, *A Man Must Fight.*

292 Tunney lets loose with a right-hand punch that just misses Gibson's chin: *The American Legion Monthly,* March 1927.

293 "Hello, champion": Ibid; Tunney, *A Man Must Fight;* Tunney, "Gene Tunney's Own Story."

295 "He was stopped in his tracks and his knees sagged": *The Saturday Evening Post,* February 10, 1940; *Collier's,* February 10, 1951.

297 "We will have to tell you that Tunney has now won three rounds": NBC radio broadcast, quoted in *New York Times,* September 24, 1926.

297 "Dempsey seems to be satisfied to take all the punches": Ibid.

297 "Nobody gets to Jack's body as a rule and stays on his feet": Philadelphia *Evening Bulletin,* Philadelphia *Public Ledger,* September 24, 1926.

298 "Jack is showing no defense": Graham McNamee, NBC radio broadcast, quoted in *New York Times,* September 24, 1926.

299 "There is a new champion in the making": Major J. Andrew White, NBC radio network broadcast, quoted in the *New York Times,* September 24, 1926.

299 "Good boy, Gene. You were too good for me": *Philadelphia Inquirer,* September 24, 1926.

299 "Thanks, Jack. You've been a great champion": Ibid.

300 "The people were cheering for me": Dempsey, *Dempsey, by the Man Himself;* Arthur Daley, "The Dempsey-Tunney Long Count—A Living Legend," *The American Legion Magazine,* April 1965.

300 In the dressing room: *Philadelphia Inquirer, Philadelphia Record,* and *New York Times,* September 24, 1926.

300 "Dempsey fought like the great champion that he was": Ibid.

301 "Keep them up, Jack": *The American Legion Magazine,* March 1927.

301 "Sorry, Gene": Ibid.

301 "I have no alibis to offer": *Philadelphia Inquirer,* Philadelphia *Public Ledger, New York Times,* Philadelphia *Evening Bulletin,* September 24, 1926.

301 In New York: *New York Times,* September 24, 1926.

302 Telegram to Dempsey from his wife, Estelle Taylor: *New York Times* and *Philadelphia Inquirer,* September 24, 1926.

303 Taylor hears a newsboy call out that Tunney had beaten Dempsey: Associated Press, September 23, 1926.

303 "Dear Estelle, Jack is fine": Ibid; *New York Times,* September 24, 1926.

CHAPTER 20

305 "Did they think my side of the ring was dry?": *Philadelphia Record,* Philadelphia *Public Ledger,* September 25, 1926.

306 There were "doings in the vicinity of the Tunney camp that did not look any too well on the face": Edward Van Every in *New York Evening World,* September 22, 1926.

306 Some "betting commissioners": *New York Times,* September 24, 1926.

307 Ring Lardner's letter to F. Scott and Zelda Fitzgerald: Kahn, *A Flame of Pure Fire.*

308 "Take a slug of bourbon and lie down": Rice, *The Tumult and the Shouting.*

308 "Neither [Dempsey or Tunney] spoke to me for several months": Ibid.

309 In his story on the fight for the Hearst syndicate: Damon Runyon for King Features Syndicate, Inc., September 24, 1926.

309 Tunney "was complete master from first bell to last": *New York Times,* September 24, 1926.

310 Dempsey refused to offer any alibis: *Philadelphia Inquirer, New York Times,* and Philadelphia *Public Ledger,* September 24, 1926.

310 "Let me tell you": Ibid.

311 "What happened, Ginsberg?": Dempsey, *Dempsey, by the Man Himself;* Harry Carpenter, *Masters of Boxing* (New York: A. S. Barnes and Company, Inc., 1964); Kahn, *A Flame of Pure Fire.*

311 "Honey, I forgot to duck": Ibid.

311 Tunney calls on Dempsey at the Adelphia Hotel: *Philadelphia Inquirer,* Philadelphia *Evening Bulletin,* and *New York Times,* September 25, 1926.

312 "Gene, I'm sorry to lose the title": Ibid.

312 "I never thought it could happen to him": *Philadelphia Inquirer,* September 25, 1926.

312 "I don't know. This other fellow ain't ever been a drawing card": Ibid.

313 "Somehow it seems to me": Van Every, *The Life of Gene Tunney.*

313 "Gene Tunney is the best man I ever fought": *Philadelphia Inquirer,* September 26, 1926.

314 Tunney returns home to New York: *New York Times, New York Herald Tribune,* and New York *Daily News,* September 27, 1926.

314 Could not resist dig at New York sportswriters: Ibid.

315 But he was not done: Ibid.

315 "I made the error of criticizing their attitude": Tunney, *A Man Must Fight.*

316 Offers began to pour into Gibson for Tunney's services: *New York Times,* September 30, 1926.

316 One of the first offers was for Tunney to "write" a serialized autobiography: King Features Syndicate, Inc., October 1, 1926.

316 Tunney, through his ghost writer, touches on marriage: Ibid, November 10, 1926.

CHAPTER 21

317 Tunney had met Polly Lauder through her older sister: *Stamford Advocate*, September 23, 1928; *Greenwich News Graphic*, September 25, 1928; author's interview with Sam Pryor III, February 5, 2005.

318 Sam Pryor throws dinner party for Tunney and Polly Lauder: Sam Pryor, Jr., and John Burnett, *All God's Creatures: The Autobiography of Sam Pryor*, (New York Vantage Press, 1981). Interview with Sam Pryor III, February 5, 2005.

318 Polly Lauder had grown up amid affluence and opulence: *Stamford Advocate*, August 9, 1928; *Greenwich News and Graphic*, August 15, 1928.

318 George Lauder, Jr.'s, father had grown up with Carnegie: Pryor, Jr., *All God's Creatures;* author's interview with Sam Pryor III, March 10, 2005; *Stamford Advocate*, September 23, 1928; *New York Times*, August 8, 1928.

319 Like many wealthy young women in the Greenwich area: Ibid.

319 For two years after they first met: Author's interview with Sam Pryor III, April 15, 2005.

320 Tunney is a luncheon guest at the home of Polly Lauder's mother in Greenwich: *New York Times*, September 28, 1926.

321 "I've had it, Tex": Roberts, *The Manassa Mauler;* Dempsey, *Dempsey.*

321 Dempsey and Tunney reunited at the third Madison Square Garden: *New York Times*, October 23, 1926; Ed Fitzgerald, *The Ring*, January 1982.

321 "That was an outrage": Ibid.

322 Harry Greb dies at the age of thirty-two: *Pittsburgh Sun-Telegraph, Pittsburgh Press, Pittsburgh Post-Gazette*, and *New York Times*, October 23, 1926; Tunney, *Arms for Living.*

322 Tiger Flowers, who won Greb's middleweight title, dies thirteen months later: *New York Times* and *New York Herald Tribune*, November 17, 1927.

322 Doctors astonished that Greb had fought five years with one eye: *Pittsburgh Post-Gazette, Pittsburgh Press*, October 24, 1926; Fair, *Give Him to the Angels.*

322 "He was the gamest fighter I ever knew": *Collier's*, February 10, 1951.

323 Tunney leaves by ship for Bermuda: *New York Times*, October 31, 1926.

323 Tunney defends remarks about Shaw novel: Associated Press, November 19, 1926.

323 "I would not attempt to advise him how to finish a work of literature": Ibid.

324 Under terms of his vaudeville contract: *New York Times*, November 12, 1926.

324 Tunney's first gig: Ibid; *New York Herald Tribune*, November 29, 1926.

324 "Loew's State has an important attraction this week": Ibid, November 30, 1926.

325 Tunney and two sparring partners arrested after performance: Ibid; *New York Herald Tribune*, November 30, 1926.

325 Farley had acted on his own: Ibid, December 1, 1926.

325 personal "animus" on the part of Farley: Ibid.

325 "Chairman Farley, as everybody knows": Ibid.

326 Cleared of all charges: *New York Times*, December 15, 1926.

326 If he could buy himself out of his contract: Tunney, *A Man Must Fight.*

327 "Being a boxer, my reading attracts attention": *The American Legion Monthly*, March 1927.

327 Not the first heavyweight champion with a cultural bent: Ibid.

327 Harry Wills loses on disqualification to Jack Sharkey: Associated Press, October 12, 1926.

328 Tunney had adopted "the dodging tactics of Jack Dempsey": *New York Amsterdam News*, October 5, 1926.

328 "Harry Wills is through": *Kansas City Call*, October 14, 1927.

328 Told Rickard he was ready to return: Dempsey, *Dempsey, by the Man Himself*; Roberts, *The Manassa Mauler*.

328 Rickard thereupon announced: *New York Herald Tribune*, April 15, 1927.

328 Dempsey and Tunney were among the crowd: Ibid; *New York Times*, May 21, 1927.

328 Referee Lou Magnolia stopped the bout in the fifth round: Ibid.

329 Three weeks after the Sharkey-Maloney fight: *New York Sun* and *New York Times*, June 11, 1927.

329 "I want to be convinced": Ibid.

329 For the Sharkey fight: Dempsey, *Dempsey;* Breslin, *Damon Runyon.*

330 On July 2, nineteen days before the fight: Dempsey, *Dempsey;* Roberts, *The Manassa Mauler; New York Times*, July 3, 1927.

330 A heroin addict: Roberts, *The Manassa Mauler;* Dempsey, *Dempsey, by the Man Himself; New York Times*, July 3, 1927.

330 After the violent death: Dempsey, *Dempsey, by the Man Himself;* Kahn, *A Flame of Pure Fire.*

330 "Johnny wanted to be a fighter": Dempsey, *Dempsey, by the Man Himself.*

330 Dempsey tells Flynn he wants to resume training immediately: *New York Times*, July 4, 1927.

331 "fight of his life": Ibid, July 21, 1927.

331 It most definitely was not: *New York Times, New York Herald Tribune,* and *New York Sun,* July 22, 1927.

332 "The right hand blows I drove home": *New York Times,* July 22, 1927.

333 "they were unmistakably low punches": Ibid, *New York World* and *New York Journal,* July 22, 1927.

333 "It's all in the game": *New York Times,* July 23, 1927.

333 "What was I going to do—write him a letter?": Roberts, *The Manassa Mauler;* Kahn, *A Flame of Pure Fire.*

333 "His punches were short": *New York Times,* July 23, 1927.

333 Some cynics felt: Ibid, July 22, 1927.

334 Largest gate ever for a nontitle fight: Ibid, July 23, 1927.

CHAPTER 22

336 Within the next two days: *New York Times* and *New York Herald Tribune,* July 24, 1927.

336 Getz made a good pitch: Ibid, July 26, 1927.

336 Tickets could be priced at $40: Kahn, *A Flame of Pure Fire;* Roberts, *The Manassa Mauler.*

336 Rickard guaranteed Tunney $750,000: *New York Times,* August 10, 1927.

336 Not everyone was happy about Dempsey fighting at Soldier Field: *Chicago Tribune,* August 5, 1927; Roberts, *The Manassa Mauler.*

338 Tunney receives warm welcome in Chicago: *Chicago Herald-Examiner, Chicago Daily News,* and *Chicago Tribune,* September 3, 1927.

338 "There was a touch of Lindbergh": Warren Brown writing in the *Chicago Herald-Examiner*, September 3, 1927.

338 "If there is to be a fight": *Chicago Herald-Examiner*, September 3, 1927.

339 Dempsey's base was at a race track; Tunney's at a country club: *Chicago Tribune*, September 4, 1927.

339 Estelle Taylor staying at Edgewater Beach Hotel with a friend: Ibid.

339 Whose voices lent themselves to talkies: Thomas Staedeli, "Portrait of the actress Estelle Taylor," *International Silent Movie Mail*.

341 Rickard assured of boxing's first $2 million gate: *Chicago Tribune* and *New York World*, September 7 and 8, 1927.

341 Ringside seats extend back 113 rows from the ring: *Chicago Herald-Examiner* and *New York Herald Tribune*, September 8, 1927.

341 Report of fix: *New York Journal*, September 12, 1927.

341 Capone tells reporters he had bet fifty thousand dollars on Dempsey to win: *Chicago Herald-Examiner*, *Chicago Daily News*, and *Chicago Tribune*, September 10 and 11, 1927.

342 Ed Sullivan says five Capone henchmen turned up at Dempsey's training camp: New York *Daily News*, October 25, 1951.

342 "I've got to rely on these": Dempsey quoted in *The Ring*, June 1967.

342 Leo Flynn brings in wife to cook for Dempsey: *New York Herald Tribune*, September 12, 1926.

343 "As long as the Greek lived, Dempsey could eat": W. O. McGeehan in *New York Herald Tribune*, September 15, 1927.

343 Dempsey or someone in his camp sends an "open letter": *Chicago Herald-Examiner*, September 19, 1927.

343 "Dear Tunney": Ibid.

343 Tunney had won the fight "fair and square": Ibid.

343 "My dear Dempsey": Ibid.

343 An ostensible contract that seemed to bear out Hoff's claim: *Chicago Tribune*, September 20, 1927.

344 Tunney quoted as saying he looks with disfavor on marriage: Edward J. Neil, writing for Associated Press, September 19, 1927.

345 To the surprise of everyone present: Tunney, *A Man Must Fight*.

346 On the day before the fight: *Chicago Herald-Examiner* and *Chicago Tribune*, September 22, 1927.

346 A few years later, Tunney met Somerset Maugham: *Collier's*, February 10, 1951.

346 "Sam, I don't think I better drink that": Pryor, Jr., *All God's Creatures*.

346 "Because the Capone era": Ibid.

346 Remarkably, by the morning of the fight: *Chicago Herald-Examiner*, *Chicago Tribune*, and *New York Chicago Daily News*, September 23, 1927.

347 Tunney amused to read he was going to enter monastery: Louella Parsons column for Universal Service, September 21, 1927.

347 Carmen Basilio on relaxing the day of a fight: Author's interview with Basilio, June 24, 2002.

347 Jake La Motta, like Basilio, one of the few fighters to beat Sugar Ray Robinson: Author's interview with La Motta, June 12, 2002.

348 Not all fighters enjoy La Motta's equanimity: Author's interview with Larry Holmes, April 16, 2004.

348 For Dempsey, the hours of waiting were agonizing: Dempsey, *Dempsey, by the Man Himself.*

348 No other sports event has ever drawn so many famous people: *Chicago Tribune, New York Times, New York Herald Tribune,* and *Chicago Herald-Examiner,* September 23, 1927.

349 Arriving from Hollywood: *New York Times* and *Chicago Tribune,* September 23, 1927.

349 From New York: Ibid; *New York Sun* and *Chicago Daily News,* September 23, 1927.

349 Other prominent spectators: Ibid.

350 Royalty also was well represented: *New York Times,* September 23, 1927.

351 Though pleased with the crowd, Rickard wasn't completely satisfied: *Chicago Tribune,* September 20, 1927.

351 "I'll never be foolish enough": *Chicago Tribune,* September 27, 1927.

351 "Kid, if the earth came up and the sky came down": *New York World,* September 23, 1927; Bill Nack in *Sports Illustrated,* September 22, 1997.

352 That number seemed high: *Chicago Tribune,* September 23, 1927.

352 "the most beautifully proportioned body ever seen in a ring": Gallico, *Farewell to Sport.*

353 "a priggish, snobbish, bookish fellow": Ibid.

353 Dempsey turned to him and said, "How are you, Gene?": Tunney, *A Man Must Fight.*

353 "Quite well, Jack, and you?": Ibid.

354 Referee Barry's instructions: Ibid; *Chicago Herald-Examiner,* September 23, 1927; Rice, *The Tumult and the Shouting.*

356 "Don't take chances, Gene": Harvey Woodruff in *Chicago Tribune,* September 23, 1927.

356 "You son of a bitch": *Chicago Herald-Examiner,* September 23, 1927.

357 "Tunney is down! Tunney is down!": Graham McNamee on the NBC radio network, quoted in *New York Times,* September 23, 1927.

357 "Society's bluebloods forgot decorum": James Dawson in *New York Times,* September 23, 1927.

358 Grantland Rice would write, "There were 145,000 crazy human beings": *New York Herald Tribune,* September 23, 1927.

359 "When I regained full consciousness, the count was two": Isabel Leighton, ed., *The Aspirin Age: 1919–1941* (New York: Simon & Schuster, 1949).

360 "I thought that little bitter laugh": Paul Gallico in New York *Daily News,* September 23, 1927.

360 "That seems pretty silly, when I look back at it": Arthur Daley, *The American Legion Magazine,* April 1965.

361 "the hardest blow I have ever received": Roberts, *The Manassa Mauler.*

361 As Grantland Rice was to write: *New York Herald Tribune,* September 23, 1927.

361 "He had let the big crowd roar and rave": Ibid.

362 Leo Flynn continued to scream, "Lead! Lead!": *New York Herald Tribune,* September 23, 1927.

362 "It is all over and Dempsey is practically out on his feet": Graham McNamee on the NBC radio network, quoted in *New York Times,* September 23, 1927.

363 "Hello, everybody. It was a real contest all the way through": Tunney interview on the NBC radio network.

363 "Hello to my good friends in Greenwich, Connecticut": Tunney during a postfight interview with Major J. Andrew White on the CBS radio network.

363 "We were all for Dempsey": Author interview with Studs Terkel, June 20, 2003.

364 "arguments are bound to ring through the fistic world": Damon Runyon for *New York American* and Hearst Headline Service, September 23, 1927.

364 "Dempsey's "bullheaded attitude doubtless lost the title for him": Dan Daniel in *The Ring,* March 1962.

364 "Gene Tunney was Jack's superior in everything but the punch": *The Ring,* October 1927.

364 "Intentionally or otherwise, I was robbed of the championship": *Chicago Herald-Examiner, Chicago Tribune,* and *New York Times,* September 23, 1927.

365 "Everyone knows I am not a whiner": Ibid.

365 If Dempsey was an angry loser: *Chicago Herald-Examiner, Chicago Tribune,* and *Chicago Daily News,* September 23, 1927.

365 "There's not much for me to say": *Chicago Tribune,* September 25, 1927.

366 Beeler explained that once he saw that Dempsey had not gone: *Chicago Tribune, Chicago Herald-Examiner,* and *New York Herald Tribune,* September 23, 1927; author's interview with veteran trainer Gil Clancy, June 10, 2004.

366 "He should have picked up the timekeeper's count": Author's interview with Hall of Fame referee Arthur Mercante, March 30, 2005.

366 "I can say that I could have arisen": *Chicago Herald-Examiner, Chicago Tribune,* and *Chicago Daily News,* September 24, 1927.

367 "I only know . . . I heard the referee count two": Frank Graham in *Sports Illustrated,* December 4, 1961.

367 Bronson laced into Tunney verbally: Tunney, *The Atlantic Monthly,* June 1939.

367 Tunney vaguely remembered the first punch: Leighton, *The Aspirin Age.*

367 Of the left hook: Ibid.

367 "I can only say that at the count of two": Red Smith, *Press Box: Red Smith's Favorite Sports Stories* (New York: W.W. Norton & Company, Inc., 1976).

368 "Realizing as do all professional boxers": *The Ring,* November 1927.

368 "I'll never know whether he could or could not have gotten up": Dempsey, *Dempsey, by the Man Himself.*

369 Tunney wanted a check for $1 million: Ibid; Frank Graham in *Sports Illustrated,* December 4, 1961.

CHAPTER 23

371 Dinner dance at the Greenwich Country Club: *Greenwich News and Graphic,* September 23, 1927.

371 Fifteen hundred miles to the west: *Chicago Herald-Examiner* and *Chicago Tribune,* September 23 and 24, 1927; W. O. McGeehan in *New York Herald Tribune,* September 24, 1927.

372 Leo Flynn files formal protest over the outcome: Ibid; *Chicago Daily News, New York Times,* and *New York Herald Tribune,* September 23, 1927.

372 "I take it that many people are annoyed with me": *Chicago Herald-Examiner* and *Chicago Tribune,* September 24, 1927.

373 "Count me out, Tex": Dempsey, *Dempsey, by the Man Himself.*

374 Two friends of Tunney's run into Al Capone: Tunney: *A Man Must Fight.*

374 "a couple of college guys": Ibid.

374 The notorious gang leader had gotten word: Ibid.

375 Tunney meets Yale professor William Lyon Phelps: William Lyon Phelps, *Autobiog-*

raphy, with Letters (New York, London, Toronto: Oxford University Press, 1939); Tunney, *Arms for Living.*

375 Phelps asked Tunney to focus on Shakespeare during talk at Yale: Phelps, *Autobiography, with Letters;* Tunney, *Arms for Living.*

375 Tunney, addressing assemblage of five hundred at Yale, discusses *Troilus and Cressida:* Ibid; *New York Times* and *New Haven Register,* April 24, 1928.

375 Tunney quotes from Shakespeare, Carlyle, and Spencer: *New York Times,* April 24, 1928.

376 "I believe every newspaper in the world": Phelps, *Autobiography, with Letters.*

376 "Let's have prizefighters with harder wallops and less Shakespeare": Frank Graham, Jr., *Sports Illustrated,* December 4, 1961.

377 Tunney drove his mother and two of his sisters to the Lauder estate in Greenwich: *Greenwich Press,* August 10, 1928.

377 Heeney was far from impressive: *New York World,* July 18, 1928; *New York American,* July 20, 1928.

378 "Heeney, in my opinion, has better than an even chance of winning": Jack Dempsey quoted in *New York Times,* July 23, 1928.

379 Soon, bells began to ring in Menke's: Gallico, *Farewell to Sport.*

379 "Hello, Paul. This is Jack. Jack Dempsey": New York *Daily News,* July 25, 1928.

379 As it turned out: *New York World, New York Sun,* and *New York Times,* July 27, 1928.

379 Climbing into the ring: Ibid.

380 The fight was a financial failure: *New York Times* and *New York Herald Tribune,* July 24 and 25, 1928.

381 Tunney announces his retirement: *New York Times, New York Daily News,* and *New York Herald Tribune,* August 1, 1928.

381 "There is no contender at the present time": *New York Times,* August 1, 1928.

382 He was making two of the most important decisions of his life: Pryor, Jr., *All God's Creatures.*

382 "Sam, I'm the happiest man in the world": Ibid.

382 "He didn't look like a prizefighter": John Kieran, *New York Times,* August 11, 1928.

383 Reports that Tunney had become engaged to Polly Lauder: Ibid; *New York Herald Tribune* and *Greenwich News and Graphic,* August 8, 1928.

383 Reports of an engagement were "on the right track": Associated Press, August 7, 1928.

383 Tunney and Miss Lauder were indeed engaged: Ibid; *New York Times, New York Herald Tribune,* Stamford, Connecticut *Advocate,* August 9, 1928; *Greenwich News and Graphic,* August 15, 1928.

384 Tunney returned to New York from Johns Island in Maine by train: *New York Times, New York Daily News,* and *Greenwich Press,* August 14, 1928.

384 Tunney sails for Europe aboard the liner *Mauretania: New York Times,* August 17, 1928.

384 "Giggling girls, longshoremen, and hundreds of others saw the former champion off": Ibid.

385 Tunney met a number of noted writers abroad: Ibid, November 15, 1928; Tunney, *A Man Must Fight* and *Arms for Living.*

385 Called on to speak: Tunney, *Arms for Living.*

385 Tunney wrote back to the playwright: Ibid.

386 The newspaper trade magazine in the United States: *Editor and Publisher,* August 21, 1928.

386 "we do not believe that the public cares two whoops for Mr. Tunney's future plans": Ibid.

386 Polly Lauder herself had no idea where or when she was to be married: *New York Times*, September 22, 1928; *Greenwich News and Graphic*, September 25, 1927.

386 Tunney hurried aboard and told her they were to be married the next day in Rome: Ibid, October 3, 1928.

386 Tunney and Polly Lauder were married in a salon at the Hotel de Russie: *New York Times*, *New York American*, and Associated Press, October 4, 1928.

387 "The result was the rather unpleasant scene": *New York Times*, October 4, 1928.

387 Much of the honeymoon was spent on the island of Brioni in the Adriatic: Tunney, *Arms for Living;* "Gene Tunney—the Man Who Licked the Fight Racket," *Sport*, June 1950.

387 Shaw, by then in his early seventies, was fascinated by Tunney: *Collier's*, June 23, 1951.

388 Tunney thereupon wrote to Shaw: Tunney, *Arms for Living*.

388 Taking Shaw's advice: Ibid.

388 Shaw wrote, "I hope you are all well at home": *Collier's*, June 23, 1951.

388 Two years later, Shaw was dead: *American Heritage College Dictionary*, fourth edition (Boston: Houghton Mifflin, 2004).

388 Dempsey was reluctant to take the part: Dempsey, *Dempsey, by the Man Himself*.

389 "David Belasco can make a good actor out of *anybody*": Ibid.

389 Moved to Broadway for a four-week run: *New York Times*, September 19, 1928.

389 Policemen had to clear a path: Ibid, *New York Herald Tribune*, September 19, 1928.

390 Tunney put on a pair of gloves and confronted his oldest son: *Los Angeles Times*, January 31, 1971.

390 "But your father wasn't the heavyweight champion of the world": Ibid.

390 The Tunneys would play host to writers like Wilder: Author's interview with Sam Pryor III, April 12, 2005; Gallico, *Farewell to Sport;* author's interview with former Yale football captain Bill Stack, May 9, 2002; author's interview with Sam Pryor III, April 14, 2005.

391 Gimbel had also been a boxer and football player at Penn: Author's interviews with Gimbel's daughter, Hope Gimbel Solinger, November 5, 2003, and February 10, 2004.

391 "In social gatherings with Gene, the conversation practically never turned to boxing": Author's interview with Bill Stack, May 9, 2002.

391 "He was much more interested in talking about literature": Ibid.

391 John Tunney once said, "He revered learning": Author's interview with John Tunney, April 8, 2002.

392 Long-standing suits by Tim Mara and Boo Boo Hoff: Fitzgerald, "Gene Tunney— the Man Who Licked the Fight Racket," *Sport*, May 1950; Fitzgerald, "Boxing's Most Underrated Champ," *The Ring*, January 1982.

392 Finally, by 1932, Tunney was free of any court suits: Frank Graham, Jr., "Double Image of a Champion," *Sports Illustrated*, December 4, 1961.

392 Many of his friends were top-level corporate executives: Author's interview with Bill Stack, August 15, 2002; author's interview with Sam Pryor III, April 14, 2005.

393 Tunney was considered a potential candidate for the United States Senate: Gallico, "Gene Tunney—Then and Now," *Liberty*, February 28, 1931.

393 Turned against Roosevelt in 1940 when he ran for a third term: Author's interview with Sam Pryor III, February 5, 2005.

393 Did not vote for a Democratic presidential candidate until JFK in 1960: Ibid.

393 Asked by Forrestal to start a physical fitness program for navy pilots: Tunney, *Arms for Living;* author's interview with Bill Stack, August 15, 2002.

394 "They're always inviting me to major fights": Author's conversation with author in 1965.

394 Idyllic life wracked by tragedy: *New York Times,* March 30, 1970.

394 Joan Tunney Wilkinson ordered committed to mental hospital: *New York Times* and *Los Angeles Times,* June 12, 1970.

395 Tunney's middle son, John Varick, elected to the U.S. Senate: *Los Angeles Times* and *New York Times,* November 6, 1970.

395 Dempsey offered to campaign for the son of his old rival during congressional race: Dempsey, *Dempsey;* Tunney, *Arms for Living.*

395 Dempsey and Tunney appear at three campaign rallies for John Varick Tunney: Dempsey, *Dempsey; Los Angeles Times,* September 27, 1964.

395 Dempsey travels to Washington with Gene Tunney to attend swearing-in ceremony: *New York Times,* January 3, 1965; Dempsey, *Dempsey.*

396 Rickard had recently bought a home in Miami and invested heavily: *New York Times* and *New York Herald Tribune,* January 6, 1929; Dempsey, *Dempsey* and *Dempsey, by the Man Himself.*

396 Rickard died in a Miami hospital when an infection set in: *New York Times* and *New York Herald Tribune,* January 6, 1929.

396 "Tex was my best pal for twelve years": Ibid.

396 During a two-day wake: Ibid; *New York Herald Tribune,* January 6, 1929.

396 Thousands attended his funeral: Ibid, January 10, 1929.

396 Dempsey was to lose almost everything he had: Kahn, *A Flame of Pure Fire;* Roberts, *The Manassa Mauler;* Dempsey, *Dempsey, by the Man Himself.*

397 In need of income, Dempsey fought almost two hundred exhibitions: Dempsey, *Dempsey, by the Man Himself.*

397 He fought a ranking heavyweight, Kingfish Levinsky: Roberts, *The Manassa Mauler;* Kahn, *A Flame of Pure Fire; Chicago Tribune,* February 19, 1932.

397 Opened restaurant in mid-Manhattan in 1935: Kahn, *A Flame of Pure Fire; New York Times,* June 1, 1983.

397 Enlist in the Coast Guard in 1942 at age of forty-seven: Ibid; Roberts, *The Manassa Mauler.*

397 Dempsey headed fitness program at Coast Guard base in New York and landed at Okinawa in the Pacific: Dempsey, *Dempsey* and *Dempsey, by the Man Himself.*

398 "They said I was a slacker in World War I": Kahn, *A Flame of Pure Fire.*

398 "And you march in, proudly, under escort": Gallico, *Farewell to Sport.*

398 His third marriage produced Dempsey's only children: Dempsey, *Dempsey* and *Dempsey, by the Man Himself.*

398 Married for the fourth and last time in 1958: Ibid.

398 Brief reconciliation with Jack Kearns in 1950: *New York Times* and *New York Herald Tribune,* January 31, 1950.

398 Grateful to Kearns "for making me a champion": Ibid; Dempsey, *Dempsey.*

398 "Everybody has always known that my heart belonged to Dempsey": Ibid.

400 An emotional return to his birthplace of Manassa, Colorado: Author's interview with Dempsey museum curator Michelle Richardson, July 12, 2005.

400 "It's amazing where some of them come from": Ibid.

401 Twenty-two fighters named for Dempsey but none for Tunney: BoxRec website.

401 Tunney invited to referee amateur bouts at Yankee Stadium: Gallico, *Farewell to Sport.*

401 Tunney should have been a living legend: Jim Murray, *Los Angeles Times,* March 17, 1955.

402 "he was an austere man, pedantic, bookish": Ibid.

402 "would have handled Muhammad Ali like breaking sticks": Red Smith, *New York Times,* March 10, 1980.

402 "they might fight fifteen rounds without either one landing a punch": Author's interview with Bert Randolph Sugar, March 10, 2005.

402 Tunney probably would beat Louis: Author's interview with Budd Schulberg, April 2, 2005.

402 Tunney died in a Greenwich hospital of a blood infection: *New York Times* and *New York Herald Tribune,* November 8, 1978.

403 "As I look back on it, I was too hard on them": Lee Greene, "The Aristocrat of the Ring," *Sport,* June 12, 1962.

403 "Probably no athlete has had to take the public beating that fell to Tunney": Gallico, *Farewell to Sport.*

403 "A little more chance to be spoiled by popularity would have been welcome": Tunney, *Arms for Living.*

404 Tunney referred to as "champ" on New York–bound commuter train: Author's interview with former broadcaster Don Russell, February 15, 2006.

404 Tunney would see a framed copy of his million-dollar check from the "long count" fight: Frank Graham, Jr., "Double Image of a Champion," *Sports Illustrated,* December 4, 1961.

405 Polly Lauder drove a car into her nineties: Author's interview with friend Hope Gimbel Solinger, March 12, 2002.

INDEX

◼

Page locators that include an "n" indicate information that will be found only in the footnote on that page. Page locators that are in italics refer to photographs.

A

Adams, Laurel, 34
Addie, Johnny, 394
Aida (opera), 249
Albacker, Hap, 142
Ali, Muhammad, 63n, 99, 163–64, 366, 394, 402
Allen, Whitey, 62
All's Swell on the Ocean (movie), 220
Ambling Alp, *see* Carnera, Primo
American Expeditionary Forces (AEF) boxing tournament, 46–49
American light heavyweight title
  created by Rickard, 116, 178
  Tunney-Greb fight, 133–42
  Tunney-Levinsky fight, 116, 117–19
Anderson, Andre, 29
Aquitania (ocean liner), 145, 148
Arcel, Ray, 104
Areton, Buck, 95
Armour, J. Ogden, 281
Armour, Tommy, 262
Associated Press, honors Dempsey as greatest boxer of first half of twentieth century, 398, 402
Astor family, 280, 349, 350
Atkinson, Brooks, 389
Attell, Abe
  at first Dempsey-Tunney fight, 300, 306–7
  at first Tunney-Greb fight, 139, 141
  friendship with Gibson, 278, 291
  as Jewish boxer, 96, 98
  managed by Kearns, 106, 273
  managed by Morgan, 104

  Tunney watches his Madison Square Garden fights, 11
  as unsavory character, 278, 289, 291, 341, 342, 343
Avonia Athletic Club, Greenwich Village, 78

B

Baer, Arthur "Bugs," 184
Baer, Max, 66, 67, 103–4, 168, 248, 377
Baer, Max Jr., 104
Bagley, Frank "Doc"
  arranges fights for Tunney, 111, 134
  fired by Tunney, 172
  and first Tunney-Greb fight, 134, 135, 138, 139–40, 141, 165
  hired by Tunney, 63
  relationship with Tunney, 173
  suggests paying off sportswriters, 114
Baker Bowl, Philadelphia, 167
Balzac, Billy, 147
Barbella, Thomas Rocco, 268
Barbour, Floyd, 383
Barnum, P.T., 70
Barry, Dave
  photo, *335*
  as referee for Dempsey-Tunney rematch, 352, 353, 354, 355, 356, 358–59, 361–62, 363, 366, 368, 372
Barrymore, Ethel, 389
Barrymore, John, 349
Baruch, Bernard, 349
Basilio, Carmen, 170–71, 347
Battle of the Century (Dempsey-Carpentier fight), 112, 203, 233, 293n

Battle Royals, 242n
Bayonne Amusement Park, New Jersey, 62
Beau Jack, starts out in Battle Royals, 242n
Beeler, Paul, 358, 366
Belasco, David, 249, 280, 349, 388, 389
Bell, Brian, 264–66
Bellows, George, 17
Benjamin, Joe, 145, 213
Bennett, Arnold, 385
Berlin, Irving, 95, 148, 280, 349
Berlin, Richard, 349
betting, *see* gambling
Biddle, Anthony J. Drexel, 76–77, 240
Biddle family, 281
The Big Fight (play), 249–50, 388–89, 396
Biltmore Hotel, 314, 382, 391
black fighters
    and Battle Royals, 242n
    color line in boxing, 31n, 117, 148–50, 157, 219, 243, 313
    Tunney's view, 229, 313
    see also Flowers, Theodore "Tiger"; Gans, Joe; Johnson, Jack; Langford, Sam; Norfolk, Kid; Wills, Harry
Black Thunderbolt, *see* Norfolk, Kid
Blackie, Kid, 20, *20*, 24, 25
Blake, Harold, 8
Blandford, Marquis de, 350
Bliven, Bruce, 209
blue laws, 77
Bogart, Humphrey, 67
Bonderud, Larry J., 202
Bonfils, Fred, 116
Boston Bearcat, 26
Boston Garden, 242
Boston Gob, *see* Sharkey, Jack
Boston Strong Boy, *see* Sullivan, John L.
Bow, Clara, 221
boxers, respect for one another, 170–72
boxing, *vs.* fighting, 27, 338–39
boxing managers, 63, 105–6
Boyle, Gene, 9, 150
Boyle's Thirty Acres, Jersey City
    Dempsey-Carpentier fight, 111
    Willard-Firpo fight, 203
Braddock, James J., 105n, 135, 168, 377
Brady, William, 280

Brennan, Bill "K.O."
    death of, 225
    fights Dempsey, 68, 80, 88, 89–91, 150, 180, 196, 258, 275, 295, 331
    fights Firpo, 204
    fights Miske, 89, 225
    fights O'Dowd, 61
    managed by Leo Flynn, 329
Breslin, Jimmy, 115
Britton, Jack, 75, 100–101, 105, 127
Brix, Lou, 278
Broadway Social Club, Brooklyn, 93
Bronson, Jimmy, 278, 290, 291, 342, 354, 356, 367
Brotty's Liquor House, Greenwich Village, 78
Broun, Heywood, 187, 191, 199, 293, 309
Brower, George, 251, 325
Brown, Warren, 338
Brown Bomber, *see* Louis, Joe
Brown Panther, *see* Wills, Harry
Brown's Athletic Club, Manhattan, 93
Burke, Jack, 113, 134, 186–87
Burns, George, 95
Burns, Tommy, 80, 149, 157–58
Bush, Prescott, 390
But We Were Born Free (book), 191
Butler, Samuel, 264
Byrd, Richard E., 349

C
California Jewish Voice, 103
Callahan, Mushy, 102–3
Cameron, Lucille, 162
Cantor, Eddie, 95
Canzoneri, Tony, 103
Capone, Al, 281, 336, 338, 341–42, 346, 371, 374
Carbo, Frankie, 63
Carlyle, Thomas, 375
Carnegie, Andrew, 317, 318, 319, 382
Carnera, Primo, 64–67, 68, 103, 105n, 168, 329, 333
Carpentier, Georges
    comparison with Tunney, 232
    fights Dempsey, 111, 112, 113, 144, 147, 150, 179, 185, 193, 232, 258, 259, 293n, 294, 295, 301, 310
    fights Gibbons, 232

fights Levinsky, 107, 111, 179, 232
fights Tunney, 226, 232–36, 258
and Greb, 178–79, 179n
loses light heavyweight title, 179, 242n
photo, 226
title issues, 116–17, 143
Carr, Joe, 259
Carter, Amon, 349
Cashel Byron's Profession (play), 248, 323–24, 385, 388
Cates, Maxine, 34, 57, 81, 82, 84, 86–88
Cather, Willa, 7
Cattell, Hattie Fithian, 227
Champ, use of nickname, 401, 404
Champions Park, Shelby, Montana, 201, 202
Chaney, Lon, 219
Chaplin, Charlie, 220, 281, 349
cheese champions, defined, 179n
Chevalier, Leon "Boom Boom," 65
Chicago Coliseum Club, 271
Chicago Defender, 149
Chicago Herald-Examiner, 338, 343
Chicago Tribune, 343, 352
Chicago White Sox, 344
Chip, George, 124
Christian Science Monitor, 215
Chrysler, Walter, 280, 349
Church of Jesus Christ of Latter-day Saints, 21–23
Cinderella Man, *see* Braddock, James J.
Circus Maximus, 277–78
City Athletic Club, Manhattan, 59–60
Clark, Jackie, 45
Clark, Jeff, 149
Clark, Sheldon, 353
Clay, Cassius, 63n
Clements, B.C., 271, 276
Cobb, Ty, 124, 216, 349
Coetzee, Gerrie, 93
Cohan, George M., 349
Comiskey Park, Chicago, 105
Compton, Berry, 78, 79
Conn, Billy, 98, 402
The Connecticut Nutmeg (magazine), 393
Connolly, One-Eyed, 281
Coogan, Jackie, 349
Cooper, James Fenimore, 40

Copelin, George, 24
Corbett, James J. "Gentleman Jim"
background, 247–48
comparison with Tunney, 257
at Dempsey-Tunney rematch, 349, 353
idolized by Tunney's father, 3, 137
Irish pride in, 6
in Madison Square Garden, 73
photo, 246
racial remarks, 160–61
spars with Tunney, 246, 246–47
stage appearances, 326
Corum, Bill, 333
Cream, Arnold, 153n

D
Daniel, Dan, 161, 212, 215, 364
Daniels, Bebe, 389
Daredevil Jack (movie), 87, 219, 260
Daugherty, Jim, 195, 196
Davis, Elmer
covers Dempsey-Gibbons fight, 191–92, 200–201
covers first Dempsey-Tunney fight, 277–78, 282, 309–10
Dawson, Bobby, 17–18, 137
Dawson, James
covers Dempsey-Sharkey fight, 331, 332–33
covers Dempsey-Tunney rematch, 357–58
covers first Dempsey-Tunney fight, 309–10
suggests possibility of Dempsey-Tunney fight, 245
De La Salle Academy, New York City, 10
Decline and Fall of the Roman Empire (book), 391
DeForrest, Jimmy, 211
DeKalb troopship, 40
Delaney, Jimmy, 267, 271
Delmonico's (restaurant), 227
DeMarco, Tony, 347
Dempsey, Barbara, 398
Dempsey, Bernie, 22, 24–25, 330
Dempsey, Bruce, 82
Dempsey, Celia, 21–22, 86, 220–21
Dempsey, Edna, 330
Dempsey, Hyrum, 21, 22, 350

Dempsey, Jack
  background, 20–24
  beginning of association with Doc
    Kearns, 83–84
  beginnings as fighter, 22–24
  begins to fight professionally, 24–27
  birth of, 21
  as boxing referee, 397
  changes managers from Price to
    Reisler, 30
  comparison with Tunney, 26–27, 33,
    256–59, 263, 268, 273, 276, 290, 293,
    296, 304, 315–16, 394, 400–401
  criticism of, 85–86, 87, 214–15, 218, 224
  crowd response after his loss to Tun-
    ney, 300
  death of, 398, 400–401
  decides to retire, 373
  divorce and remarriages, 398
  draft deferment issue, 69, 85–88, 113,
    336–37, 353
  enlists in Coast Guard during World
    War II, 397–98
  exhibitions and vaudeville tours, 150,
    218, 397
  family problems, 82, 86–88
  fights Battling Levinsky, 105, 106–7
  fights Brennan, 68, 80, 88, 89–91, 150,
    180, 196, 258, 275, 295, 331
  fights Carpentier, 111, 112, 113, 144,
    147, 150, 179, 185, 193, 232, 258, 259,
    293n, 294, 295, 301, 310
  fights Fireman Jim Flynn, 80–81, 85
  fights Firpo, 203, 210–14, 229, 258, 295,
    301, 310, 331
  fights Gibbons in Shelby, Montana,
    179–202, 228, 310, 331
  fights Jack Johnson, 150
  fights Miske, 85, 88–89, 129, 310, 331
  fights Sharkey, 329–34, 337, 353
  fights Tunney, see Dempsey-Tunney
    fight; Dempsey-Tunney rematch
  fights Willard, 52, 56, 56–59, 86, 203,
    310, 331, 399
  first fight in Madison Square Garden,
    68, 80, 89–91, 180
  first meets Gene Tunney on Hudson
    River ferry ride, 56–59
  first New York fights, 27–33

  full name, 20
  in Hollywood, 218–24, 250–51, 323
  honored by Associated Press as great-
    est boxer of first half of twentieth
    century, 398, 402
  Jewish strain, 222
  lack of contenders after Firpo, 218
  later fighters named for him, 401
  licensing issues, 251–55
  life after boxing, 395–400
  loses fortune in 1929 stock market
    crash, 396–97
  as Manassa Mauler, 57
  marries Estelle Taylor, 221–22
  marries Maxine Cates, 34
  mugging incident, 400
  and "Negro" fighters, 149–50, 219
  operates restaurant in midtown Man-
    hattan, 395, 397, 398, 399
  parties in Europe, 144–48
  photos, 20, 56, 69, 143, 203, 335, 370
  popularity of, 216, 218, 302, 321,
    335–36, 365, 399
  post-retirement relationship with Tun-
    ney, 395
  reconciliation with Kearns, 398, 399
  returns to Colorado birthplace, 400
  role in rejuvenation of boxing, 163
  role in Tunney-Heeney fight, 378–79
  spars with Harry Greb, 129–30, 322
  as stage actor, 249–50, 388–89
  style of fighting, 26, 51–52, 121, 171
  takes nickname "Jack," 24, 25
  treatment of Tunney outside ring, 204,
    300–301, 311–12
  utters quote "Honey, I forgot to
    duck," 311
  voice of, 23, 146, 220
  watches Tunney-Burke fight in Madi-
    son Square Garden, 113
Dempsey, Jack ("The Nonpareil"), 20, 24,
  59
Dempsey, Joan, 398
Dempsey, Joe, 330
Dempsey, Johnny, 330
Dempsey-Tunney fight
  aftermath, 299–314, 321, 323
  attendance, 279–83, 289, 292, 312
  betting on, 306–7

crowd response to appearance of fighters, 292–93, 294
Dempsey travels to Philadelphia,
286–87
favorite to win, 261–62
gate, 292, 312
Lardner's concerns about a fix, 307–8
lead-up to, 286–89
licensing issues, 251–54, 259, 260
press accounts, 305–11
prominent spectators, 280–82
radio broadcast, *290*, 293, 297, 298,
299, 302
rematch possibilities, 313–14
response to announcement, 256
ten rounds, 294–99
training sites, 260–61, 262, 263–64,
266–70, 276
Tunney flies into Philadelphia, 282–86
Tunney's nightmares, 262–63
women attendees, 282
Dempsey-Tunney rematch
aftermath, 363–69, 371–73
agreement, 336–37
attendance, 351, 368–69
betting on, 341–42, 346
crowd response to appearance of fighters, 352–53
gate, 341, 368–69
greater interest in, 340, 371–72
long count, *335*, 358–60, 364–65,
366–68, 371–72, 405
photo, *335*
preparation for, 338–51
prominent spectators, 348–50
radio broadcasts, 351, 352, 371
rumors of fix, 341–44
ten rounds, 354–63
third bout possibilities, 373
training sites, 339–41
Denver Evening Post, 116, 196
Descamps, François, 179, 234, 235
Detroit Jewish Chronicle, 103
Dewing, Ed, 318, 371, 376
Dewing, Katherine (Kay) Lauder, 317,
318, 377
Dillon, Jack, 52, 81, 92, 124, 249
Dixon, George, 153n, 157
Dixon, Joe, 182, 183

Doessererick, Charlie, 62
Dokes, Michael, 93
Dolly Sisters, 145, 148
Don Juan (movie), 339
Donoghue, Roger, 209n
Donovan, Arthur, 67
Dos Passos, John, 7
Douglas and Clydesdale, Marquis de, 350
Downey, Jack, 24
Drexel family, 281
Duffy, Billy, 64, 329
Duffy, Francis, 371
Dumas, Alexandre, 40
Dundee, Johnny, 11, 127

E
Eagan, Eddie, 50–51, 374, 376, 390–91
Eagan family, 363
Ebbets Field, Brooklyn, 327
Ederle, Gertrude, 280
Edgren, Robert, 5, 272–73, 333
Editor and Publisher, 386
Egan, Pierce, 233
Encyclopedia Britannica, 393
Engel, George, 133
eyesight concerns, 131, 258, 323, 351, 382

F
Fairbanks, Douglas, 99, 220, 223, 349
Fairmont Athletic Club, the Bronx, 18,
27, 28, 29, 173
Farewell to Sport (book), 403
Farley, James J., 251, 280, 325–26, 336,
381, 389
Farnsworth, Bill, 114, 241
Farrell, Jackie, 278
female boxers, 148
Field, Marshall, 349
Fields, Jackie, 97, 106, 273
Fields, Walter, 239
fight clubs, 16, 18–19
The Fight (essay), 385
fight promoters, 150
    see also Bagley, Frank "Doc"; Kearns,
    Jack "Doc"; Rickard, Tex
Fight to Win (movie), 220
fighting, *vs.* boxing, 27, 338–39
The Fighting Marine (movie), 260
Fink, Lou, 278

Finnegan, Irish Eddie, 99–100
Finnegan, Mickey, 95
Firpo, Luis Angel
    background, 204
    fights Dempsey, *203*, 210–14, 229, 258,
        295, 301, 310, 331
    fights Willard, 203–5
    fights Wills, 243
    photo, *203*
Fitzgerald, F. Scott, 233, 307, 385
Fitzgerald, Zelda, 307
Fitzpatrick, James, 49
Fitzsimmons, Bob, 6, 157, 166, 248
Fitzsimmons, Floyd, 271, 302, 303
fixed fights, 63–67, 283, 307–8, 341–44
    see also taking a dive
Fleischer, Nat, 27, 30, 94, 215, 253, 256,
        293, 305, 313, 364, 373
Floto, Otto, 116, 196–97
Flowers, Theodore "Tiger," 231, 242n,
        274, 322
Flynn, Errol, 103
Flynn, Fireman Jim, 80–81, 85, 117, 162,
        163
Flynn, Katherine, 342
Flynn, Leo, 329, 330, 331, 340, 342, 343,
        345, 354, 364, 372
Forbes, Ed, 379, 380
Forrestal, James, 393
Foster, Rube, 163
Fowler, Gene, 116, 153–54, 316
Fox, William, 221
Foy, Eddie, 281
Fraley, Oscar, 399
Frawley Act of 1911, 12, 73, 77, 93
Frazee, Harry, 349
Frazier, Joe, 366, 394
Fulton, Fred, 81

G
Gains, Larry, 66
Gallagher, Jack, 210–11, 212, 213, 214,
        215
Gallico, Paul
    asks Tunney to referee series of ama-
        teur bouts, 401
    covers Dempsey-Loughran fight, 272
    covers Dempsey-Sharkey fight, 333
    covers Dempsey-Tunney rematch, 360
    covers first Dempsey-Tunney fight,
        275, 293
    as Dempsey's sparring partner, 206–8
    description of Dempsey, 352
    later view of Tunney, 403
    as one of best sportswriters of his time,
        309
    Tunney's concern about, 269
    visits Dempsey's restaurant, 398
Gallo, Bill, 22, 171
gambling
    betting on Dempsey-Tunney rematch,
        341–42, 346, 374
    betting on first Dempsey-Tunney fight,
        261, 306–7
    Greb bets on his fights, 124–25
    in Madison Square Garden, 136
    and newspaper decisions, 28–29
gangs of New York, 4
gangsters, *see* mobsters
Gans, Joe, 31n, 117, 153–55, 156, 157,
        181, 380
Garbo, Greta, 324
Gasko, Nellie, 239
Gavin, William, 74
Gellman, Charley, 97–98
Gentleman Jim (movie), 103
Gershwin, George, 95
Getz, George, 336, 338, 345
Gibbons, Edward, 391
Gibbons, Mike, 52
Gibbons, Tommy
    background, 132
    fights Carpentier, 232
    fights Dempsey in Shelby, Montana,
        179–202, 228, 310, 331
    fights Greb, 132, 133, 184
    fights Miske, 89, 184
    fights Tunney, 242, 243, 244–45, 258
    photo, *279*
Gibson, Billy
    background, 172–73
    contact with Hoff, 288, 306, 343–44
    and Dempsey-Tunney rematch, 342,
        356, 367
    and first Dempsey-Tunney fight, 243,
        259–60, 274, 290, 291
    friendship with Attell, 278, 306
    hired by Tunney, 172–73

as Leonard's manager, 102, 106, 172
response to Tunney's flying to match against Dempsey, 285
responsible for establishing Fairmont Athletic Club, 18–19, 28, 173
surprised by Tunney's retirement announcement, 381
as Tunney's manager, 106, 120, 316
Gillian, Two-Round, 26
Gilmore, Patrick, 70, 71
Gilmore's Garden, 70
Gimbel, Bernard, 60, 278, 286, 371, 374, 390–91
Gimbel, Ellis, 280
Gimbel family, 363
Godfrey, George, 186
Golden Era of Sports, 1920s as, 309
Golden Era of Sportswriting, 1920s as, 309
Goldfield, Nevada, 152–56, 181
Gophers (gang), 4
Gordon, Waxey, 102
Graham, Frank, 367
Grand Central Terminal, Manhattan, 70
Grange, Red, 124
Grauman, Sid, 349
Grayson, Harry, 274
Graziano, Rocky, 97, 268
Great Bennah, *see* Leonard, Benny
The Great Gatsby (book), 233, 385
Great White Hope, first, 157, 159
The Great White Hope (movie), 103
Greb, Annie, 126
Greb, Harry
  background, 125–28
  backs Tunney to beat Dempsey, 261, 274
  beaten twice by Kid Norfolk, 130–31, 242
  bets on his own fights, 124–25
  characteristics, 122–25, 128–29
  death of, 231, 322–23
  dressing room pecadillos on fight day, 123, 348
  eyesight issue, 131, 382
  fights Gibbons, 132, 184
  fights Loughran, 166
  fights Tunney, 120, 132–42, *134*, 173–77, 228, 229–31, 236

fights Wilson, 179n
full name, 126
illness and death of wife, 176–77
Madison Square Garden debut, 127–28
marriage and fatherhood, 129, 130
nicknames, 124
photos, *121*, *134*
spars with Dempsey, 129–30, 322
wins American light heavyweight title from Tunney, 140, 178–79
Greb, Pious, 126, 177
Green, Willie
  first spars with Tunney, 6
  role in Tunney's early professional fights, 16, 18, 19
  Tunney's gratitude toward, 7
  Tunney's sparring sessions with, 11–14, 15
  urges Tunney to accept professional fight club offer, 16
Greenfield, Alf, 72
Greenwich Country Club, 371
Greenwich Press, 383–84
Greenwich Settlement House, Greenwich Village, 15
Griffin, Andy, 234
Griffith, D.W., 145
Griffith, Emile, 31n
Griffo, Joe, 294, 299
Grimsley, Will, 269
Grogan, Perry, 212
Grupp's Gymnasium, Harlem, 30, 33
Guys and Dolls (Broadway musical), 115

H
Haley, Patsy, 100–101, 175, 327
Halliday, Jim, 176
Halper, Chuck, 97
Hammerstein, Mrs. Oscar, 232
Hampton, Hope, 281
Hanlon, Jack, 169, 172
Hard Rock from Down Under, *see* Heeney, Tom
The Harder They Fall (book), 67
The Harder They Fall (movie), 248
Harlem Sporting Club, 31, 32
Harriman, W. Averell, 280
Harriman family, 350
Harris, Harry, 96

Harris, Mrs. Sam, 232
Harrison, William Henry, 20
Hart, Marvin, 131
Hart, William S., 281
Haukop, Ed, 90
Hays, Will, 349
Hazlitt, William, 385
Hearst, William Randolph, 115, 280
   see also King Features Syndicate
Heeney, Tom, 377–80
Heilmann, Harry, 215
Hemingway, Ernest, 385
Herron, Charles, 240
Hinman, Frank, 352
History of the World (book), 391
Hitler, Adolf, 103
hobos *vs.* tramps *vs.* bums, 22
Hoff, Max "Boo Boo," 288, 289, 291, 306,
   307, 343–44, 362, 392
Hoffman, Ancil, 103
Holmes, Larry, 348
Honest Hearts and Willing Hands (play),
   248
Horton Act of 1896, 12, 77
Hotel de Russie, Rome, 386, 387
Houck, Leo, 68
Howard, Roy, 349
Hudson Dusters (gang), 4
Hugo, Victor, 385
Humphreys, Joe, 90, 101, 175, 230, 234,
   321, 380

I
Igoe, Hype, 206
   covers Dempsey-Gibbons fight, 187,
     198
   covers Dempsey-Sharkey fight, 333
   covers first Dempsey-Tunney fight,
     289
   covers Tunney-Greb fights, 135, 136,
     138, 176
   and Gallico-Dempsey sparring session,
     206, 207–8
   and Rickard, 198, 289
Illinois Athletic Commission, 344, 345,
   351, 364, 366, 372, 374
Inter-Allied Games, 50
Irish boxers, 3, 4, 6, 13, 20, 59, 97, 102,
   146, 222, 401–2

J
Jack, Beau, starts out in Battle Royals,
   242n
Jack and Charlie's (speakeasy), 227
Jackson, Shoeless Joe, 289
Jacobs, Billy, 16
Jacobs, Joe, 105n
Jaffe, K.O., 34
James, Jesse and Frank, 150
James, Zerelda, 150
Jamieson, Ted, 47–48
Jeannette, Joe, 162
Jeby, Ben, 97
Jeffries, James J.
   as actor, 248
   at Dempsey-Tunney rematch, 353
   fights Jack Johnson in Reno, 156–57,
     158–59, 160–62, 164, 181, 229
   retirement of, 131
Jersey City Armory, 62
Jewish boxers, 92, 95–108
Johansson, Ingemar, 93
John the Barber, *see* Reisler, John
Johnson, Floyd, 204
Johnson, Jack
   and color line in boxing, 31, 31n, 117,
     149
   comparison with Ali, 163–64
   comparison with Wills, 219
   at Dempsey-Tunney rematch, 353
   fights Dempsey, 150
   fights Fireman Jim Flynn, 80, 162
   fights Hart, 131
   fights Jeffries in Reno, 156–62, 164,
     181, 219, 229
   fights Johnson, 163
   fights Moran, 163
   fights Willard, 73, 127, 203, 204, 310
   flees to Europe, 162–63
   loses heavyweight title to Willard, 73,
     127, 203
   movie *The Great White Hope* about
     his career, 103
   on stage, 249
   starts out in Battle Royals, 242n
   unpopular as heavyweight champion,
     162, 224
   wins "colored heavyweight champi-
     onship," 117, 157, 163

wins world heavyweight title from
  Tommy Burns, 80, 149, 157–58, 163
Johnson, James A., 182, 183, 186, 187,
  188, 190, 200
Johnson, James W. "Body," 181–82, 183,
  184, 185–86, 187
Johnson, John Leonard, 31, 32
Johnston, Jimmy, 232–33
Jolson, Al, 95, 349
Jones, Bobby, 124, 281–82
Jones, Casey, 284–86
Jones, James Earl, 103
Jones, Soldier, 111, 112, 113
Josephs, Eddie, 113
Joyce, Peggy Hopkins, 280
J.P. Morgan Company, 319

K
Kaiser, Fay, 165–66
Kane, Eddie, 185, 195
Kansas City Call, 328
Kapilow, Danny, 97, 98
Kavanagh, John, 181, 183, 197
Kearns, Jack "Doc"
  absence felt, 273, 306
  background, 83–84
  beginning of association with
    Dempsey, 83–84
  breakup with Dempsey, 216–17, 223,
    250
  brings in Greb to spar with Dempsey,
    129–30
  during Dempsey-Firpo fight, 213
  and Dempsey-Gibbons fight in Shelby,
    Montana, 179–202
  files lawsuits against Dempsey, 270–71,
    274
  and Firpo-Willard fight, 204
  as manager, 60, 85, 88, 89, 105–6, 146,
    273
  reaction to Gallico as Dempsey's spar-
    ring partner, 206–7, 208
  real name, 83n
  reconciles with Dempsey, 398, 399
  and *Sports Illustrated* story about
    Dempsey's Willard fight, 399
  successor as Dempsey's manager, 252
  urges Dempsey to continue acting ca-
    reer, 220

vaudeville stage tour with Dempsey,
  150, 218
view of marriage and Estelle Taylor,
  222–23
Kearns, Soldier, 93, 94
Keats, Fred, 230
Kelly, John, 20
Kelly, Sammy, 59, 60
Kendrick, W. Freeland, 253, 260
Kennedy, Edward "Ted," 395
Kennedy, John F., 86, 393, 394
Kennedy, Joseph P., 393, 395
Kenny, Wild Bert, 29, 163
Kevin-Sunburst oil field, 182
Kid Galahad (movie), 103
kidney punches, 195, 291, 354
Kieran, John, 382
Kilbane, Johnny, 11
Kilrain, Jake, 196
King Features Syndicate, 316, 378
Knights of Columbus halls, 4, 6, 12–13
Krakow, Harry, 105n
Ku Klux Klan, 77

L
La Guardia, Fiorello, 79, 80
La Motta, Jake, 31n, 170, 347–48
Lahey, George, 35
LaHiff's (restaurant), 125, 227
Landis, Kenesaw Mountain, 349
Langford, Sam, 26, 31, 31n, 81, 131, 149,
  150, 157, 162, 218, 243, 382
Lardner, John, 201
Lardner, Ring
  comparison with Elmer Davis, 191
  concern that first Dempsey-Tunney
    fight was fixed, 307–8
  covers first Dempsey-Tunney fight,
    257, 267, 275, 289, 293, 311
  as one of best sportswriters of his time,
    309
  relationship with Rice, 308–9
  Tunney's concern about, 269
Lauder, George (brother-in-law), 377
Lauder, George Jr. (father-in-law), 318
Lauder, George Sr., 318–19
Lauder, Polly, *see* Tunney, Polly Lauder
  (wife)
Lauder family, 318–19, 363, 377

Lawrence, Jack, 212, 230
Lebrowitz, Bernard (Barney), 92, 104,
    105
    see also Levinsky, Battling
Leeds, William, 350
legality of professional boxing, 4, 12–13,
    53, 62, 71, 73–77, 127, 163, 282–83,
    325–26, 345
Leiner, Benjamin, 95
    see also Leonard, Benny
Leonard, Benny
    background, 94–96
    comparison with Corbett, 247
    death of, 102
    at Dempsey-Tunney rematch, 353
    at first Dempsey-Tunney fight, 274,
        279, 302, 307
    as Jewish fighter, 94–95, 96, 98–102
    loses fortune in 1929 stock market
        crash, 94, 99, 396
    occasional Tunney sparring partner,
        173, 274
    as popular fighter in early 1920s, 11,
        16, 62, 74, 75, 80, 106, 172, 243
    at Stillman's Gym, 264
    watches Tunney-Greb fights, 173, 174
Leonard, Sugar Ray, 31n
Levinsky, Battling
    background, 92–93, 104
    death of, 120
    fights Carpentier, 107, 111, 179, 232
    fights Dempsey, 105, 106–7
    fights Dillon, 52, 92
    fights Fireman Jim Flynn, 81, 82
    fights Tunney, 116, 117–19, 236
    as Jewish light heavyweight champion,
        92
    later in life, 119–20, 124, 127
    name changes, 92, 104, 105
    number of fights, 93–94, 105, 119
    photo, 92
Levinsky, Kingfish, 105n, 397
Lewis, Lennox, 169
Lewis, Perry, 275
Lewis, Ted "Kid," 96, 127
Lindbergh, Charles, 50, 277, 338
Liston, Sonny, 63n, 163
Little Jack Dempsey, 401
Lloyd, Harold, 220

Loew's State Theatre, 324, 325
Loew's vaudeville circuit, 218
London, Jack, 40, 158
long count, 335, 357, 358–60, 364–65,
    366–68, 371–72, 405
Long Ridge Union Cemetery, Connecti-
    cut, 405
Los Angeles Times, 401–2
Loughran, Tommy, 105n, 132, 165,
    166–69, 271–72
Louis, Joe, 67, 98, 105n, 149, 164, 259,
    268, 402
Love in the Ring (movie), 248
Luther, Thomas, 206, 330
Luvadis, Jerry, 213, 273, 286, 287, 299,
    302, 343
Lynch, Joe, 75
Lyons, Wild Bill, 193–94
Lytton, George, 353

M
Mabbutt, Charlie, 287
MacArthur, Mrs. Douglas, 280
Mace, Jem, 327
Madden, Bartley, 93, 94, 243
Madden, Owney "the Killer," 64
Madison Square Garden
    adds boxing to attractions, 72–73
    background, 69–71
    in Boston, 242
    Dempsey-Brennan fight, 68, 80, 89–91,
        180
    first Dempsey fight, 68, 80, 89–91, 180
    first Tunney fight, 113
    first two Greb fights, 127–28, 131
    on night of a big fight, 136
    radio broadcast of first Dempsey-
        Tunney fight, 299, 302
    and Rickard sex scandal, 238–39, 240,
        241
    Tunney-Greb fight, 132–42
    Tunney-Greb rematch, 173–76
    Tunney receives heavyweight title belt,
        321
    Tunney-Weinert fight, 172
    wake for Tex Rickard, 396
Madison Square Garden Bowl, 66
Magnolia, Lou, 328
Mailer, Norman, 209n

Malone, Dudley Field, 325–26
Maloney, Jimmy, 328–29
Man Killer, *see* Dempsey, Jack
The Man Who Laughs (book), 385
managers, *see* boxing managers
Manassa Mauler, 57
  see also Dempsey, Jack
Mandell, Sammy, 103
Manhattan Madness (movie), 223–24
Manhattan Transfer (book), 7
Manly Marine, *see* Tunney, Gene
Mann Act, 162
Mara, Tim, 259–60, 307, 314, 344, 392
Mara, Wellington, 392
Marchand, Henri "K.O.", 45
Marciano, Rocky, 123, 259, 402
Marlborough, Duchess of, 350
Marquand, John, 390
Marquess of Queensberry boxing rules,
  74, 155, 247
Martin, Bob, 45, 165
Martin, Pat Minor, 395
Mason, Red, 128
Masterson, Bat, 396
Maugham, Somerset, 346, 346n
Mauretania (ocean liner), 384
Mauriello, Tami, 268
Maxim, Joey, 106, 273
Mayo, Charles, 349
McArdle, Tom, 19, 28, 29
McBride, Archie, 209n
McCabe, Bill, 275, 291
McCarthy, Clem, 293n
McCormack, Barry, 134–35, 140, 141,
  143, 173, 227, 233
McCormack, John, 386
McCoy, Al, 93, 96, 102, 105, 124
McCracken, Frank, 275
McCutcheon, Mel, 181–82, 183, 184, 185,
  187
McGeehan, W. O.
  accompanies Tunney to England, 384
  comparison with Elmer Davis, 191
  covers Dempsey-Sharkey fight, 333
  covers Dempsey-Tunney rematch, 343
  covers first Dempsey-Tunney fight,
    267, 274, 284, 293
  covers Tunney-Carpentier fight, 235
  covers Tunney-Greb fights, 135, 141

  as one of best sportswriters of his time,
    309
  as Tunney's friend and favorite sports-
    caster, 235
McGraw, John, 280, 349
McIntosh, Hugh, 158
McKernan, John Leo, 83n
  see also Kearns, Jack "Doc"
McKetrick, Dan, 198–99
McLarnin, Jimmy, 95, 103
McNab, Gavin, 86
McNamee, Graham, *290*, 293, 293n, 297,
  352, 357, 362, 363
McPartland, Kid, 139
McReynolds, Jack, 51–53
McVea, Sam, 162, 243
Meegan, Charles, 175
Meehan, William, 85, 89
Mellody, Honey, 83, 83n
Mellon, Andrew, 281
Mendoza, Daniel, 96
Menke, Frank, 277, 378
Mercante, Arthur, 366
Metropolitan Boxing Writers Associa-
  tion, 321
Metropolitan Opera, 387
Mexican Jack Dempsey, 401
Miles, Charles, 175
Milk Fund boxing benefit, 115
Miller, Davey, 374
Million Dollar Gate (book), 399
Miske, Billy, 85, 88–89, 129, 184, 224–25,
  310, 331
Mitchell, Charlie, 72
Mix, Tom, 99, 281, 349
mobsters, 4, 64–67, 102, 115, 161, 281,
  283, 338, 344, 346
  see also Capone, Al; Hoff, Max "Boo
  Boo"
Molumby, Loy, 182, 183, 184, 185, 186,
  187, 190
Money, William, 241
Moore, Archie, 31n, 106, 208n, 273, 313
Moran, Frank, 73, 163, 181, 315
Morgan, Anne, 280
Morgan, Dumb Dan, 60, 104–5, 106, 107
Morgan, John Pierpont, 71
Mormons, 21–23
Morris, Carl, 84, 163

Morris, William, 324, 326
Morton, Wade, 277, 284, 285
Muldoon, William, 141–42, 159, 179–80,
    181, 251, 325, 381
Mullins, Paddy, 253
Murphy, George, 395
Murray, Jim, 401–2

N
Nagler, Barney, 115
Nast, Condé, 280, 349
National Hockey League, 396
Neil, Edward, 344
Nelson, Battling Bill, 153–55, 156, 163,
    181, 353, 380
Nesbit, Evelyn, 238n
neutral corner rule, 210–11, 214, 216, 345,
    354, 358, 361, 362, 366
New Republic, 209
New York American, 27, 114, 241
New York Amsterdam News, 149, 328
New York Athletic Club, 391
New York Daily News (newspaper), 206,
    207
New York Evening World (newspaper), see
    Edgren, Robert; Van Every, Edward
New York (movie), 339
New York Rangers, 396
New York State Athletic Commission,
    101, 102, 141–42, 180, 209, 251
    see also Farley, James J.; Muldoon,
        William
New York State Transit Commission, 79
New York Times (newspaper)
    coverage of first Dempsey-Tunney
        fight, 264, 277–78, 279, 282, 285, 289,
        305, 306, 309–10, 312
    coverage of Sullivan-Wilson fight, 72
    coverage of Tunney-Carpentier fight,
        235
    coverage of Tunney-Roberts fight, 63
    coverage of Tunney visit to Greenwich
        after first Dempsey-Tunney fight,
        320
    coverage of Tunney's initial vaudeville
        stage appearances, 324, 325
    editorial on move of Dempsey-Tunney
        fight from New York to Philadel-
        phia, 254

    editorial tribute to Tex Rickard, 396
    front-page story of Tunney's engage-
        ment, 383
    front-page story on Tunney's talk to
        Yale class, 376
    Kieran's view of Tunney, 382
    reports on Tunney's marriage, 387
    see also Davis, Elmer; Dawson, James
New York World (newspaper), 32
    see also Igoe, Hype
newspaper decisions, defined, 28–29, 32
    see also sportswriters
Norfolk, Kid, 130–31, 242, 242n
Normile, Gene, 252, 273, 278, 287, 291,
    299, 306
North American Newspaper Alliance,
    199
Northcliffe, Lord, 145–47

O
Oates, Joyce Carol, 172
O'Brien, Eddie, 16–17, 18
O'Brien, Philadelphia Jack, 31n, 76, 80,
    166, 278, 286, 291, 299
Ocean Steamship Company, 10, 11, 12,
    14–15, 33, 34, 36, 37, 39, 59
Ochs, Adolph, 191
O'Dowd, Dan, 60–61
O'Dowd, Mike, 127
Of Human Bondage (book), 346, 346n
Oldfield, Barney, 281
Olvany, George, 280
Olympic Club, Philadelphia, 106
One of Ours (book), 7
Orchid Man, see Carpentier, Georges
O'Sullivan, Jack, 332
Ottinger, Albert, 254

P
Page, Greg, 93
Palermo, Blinky, 63
Pantages vaudeville circuit, 199, 218
Papke, Billy, 81
parochial schools, 8
Parsons, Louella, 347, 349
Pastor, Bob, 402
Pathé Studios, 219, 260
Peabody, Kenneth Malcolm, 222
Pecora, Ferdinand, 239–40, 241

Pegler, Westbrook, 137, 275, 293, 309, 333, 403

Pennsylvania State Athletic Commission, 286

Perry, Bob, 65

Pershing, John, 47, 48

Phelps, William Lyon, 375

Philadelphia Bulletin (newspaper), 274, 282

Philadelphia Inquirer (newspaper), 168, 273, 277

Piattelli, Barbara Lynn, 398

Piattelli, Deanna, 398

Pickford, Mary, 223

Pinchot, Gifford, 253, 260

Pioneer Athletic Club, Manhattan, 111

Pittsburgh Windmill, *see* Greb, Harry

Plimpton, George, 208n

Polo Athletic Club, 34

Polo Grounds, Manhattan, 209, 233, 243–45

Pond, Nathan, 239

Poreda, Stanley, 66

Prehn, Paul, 366

Presley, Elvis, 103, 267

Preston, Harry, 385

Price, Jack, 26, 27, 29, 30, 31

The Prizefighter and the Lady (movie), 248

Prunier, Maurice, 147

Pryor, Sam Jr., 317, 318, 319, 337–38, 346, 370, 371, 376, 381–82, 390, 391

Pryor family, 363, 371

P.S. 41, New York City, Tunney as part-time athletic director at, 16, 17, 19, 34, 35, 38

pugilism (Tunney's phrase), 27, 387, 403

Pulitzer, Joseph, 281, 349

Purdy, Jack, 125

R

rabbit punches, 291, 354, 355, 356, 360, 362, 365

racketeers, *see* mobsters

Randolph, Al, 93

Ray, Johnny, 98

Reid, Ogden, 349

Reilly, Mildred, 129, 174, 176

Reilly, Tommy, 290–91, 294, 295, 299

Reisler, John, 30–33, 63

Reno, Nevada, as site of Johnson-Jeffries fight, 156–62, 164, 181, 219, 229

Rice, Grantland
comparison with Elmer Davis, 191
covers Dempsey-Firpo fight, 215
covers Dempsey-Gibbons fight, 187
covers Dempsey-Sharkey fight, 333
covers Dempsey-Tunney rematch, 358, 361
covers first Dempsey-Tunney fight, 257, 267, 275, 293, 308
covers Tunney-Greb fights, 137, 176
and Gallico-Dempsey sparring session, 207–8
interest in Greb, 124
as one of best sportswriters of his time, 309
photo, *304*
relationship with Lardner, 308–9
view of inactive Dempsey, 224
view of Tunney-Gibbons fight, 244
as writer and producer of *Sportlight* series, 246

Richardson, Michelle, 400

Rickard, Tex
aftermath of first Dempsey-Tunney fight, 312–14, 321, 323
attends Broadway opening of Dempsey in *The Big Fight*, 389
background, 150–52
becomes fight promoter, 152
builds stadium for Dempsey-Carpentier fight, 112
contracts with Tunney for one more fight beyond Dempsey rematch, 320, 377
creates American light heavyweight title, 116, 178
death of, 396
decides on Tunney as opponent for Dempsey, 251
Dempsey-Tunney rematch questions, 300, 333, 334, 368–69
envisions third Dempsey-Tunney bout, 373
full name, 150
gate and attendance at Dempsey-Tunney rematch, 368–69

Rickard, Tex (*cont'd*)
  heroes and villains strategy, 228, 257, 273, 380
  licensing issues for first Dempsey-Tunney fight, 251–54, 259, 260
  payoffs to sportswriters and editors for coverage, 28, 226
  persuades women to attend fights, 154–55, 168, 243–44, 282
  photo, *143*
  picks Leo Flynn to be Dempsey's manager, 329
  promotes Dempsey-Firpo fight, 204, 216–17
  promotes Dempsey-Sharkey fight, 329, 333–34
  promotes Dempsey-Tunney rematch, 336–37, 340, 341, 350, 351
  promotes Dempsey-Willard fight, 86
  promotes first Dempsey-Tunney fight, 256–57, 273, 277, 285, 289, 292
  promotes Nelson-Gans fight in Goldfield, Nevada, 152–56
  promotes Tunney-Greb fights, 120, 133, 228, 229
  promotes Tunney-Heeney fight after Dempsey rematch, 377, 378, 379, 380
  promotes Tunney-Levinsky fight, 108, 117–18
  promotes Tunney-Wills fight, 252–53
  promotes Willard-Firpo fight, 204, 209
  promotes Willard-Moran fight, 73
  refuses to consider Dempsey-Wills fight, 149, 180, 219
  sexual abuse scandal, 237–42
  stages his first Madison Square Garden fight, 73
  riding the rods, 24, 33
Righeimer, John, 351, 372
The Ring (magazine), 27, 161
The Ring Record Book, 83n, 93
Ringling, John, 349
Risko, Johnny, 246
Roberts, Al, 62–63, 68, 133
Robinson, Sugar Ray, 170, 171, 313, 347
Robinson, Wilbur, 280
Roche, Billy, 57, 58, 60, 63, 173
Rockefeller, Faith, 319, 386

Rockefeller, John D. Jr., 319
Rockefeller family, 350
Rogers, Will, 376, 389
Roman Circus Maximus, 277–78
Roosevelt, Alice, 280
Roosevelt, Archie, 280
Roosevelt, Franklin Delano, 79, 190, 191, 251, 280, 393
Roosevelt, Kermit, 240, 280
Roosevelt, Theodore Jr., 240, 280
Root, Jack, 131
Rosenbaum, Seymour, 100
Rosenbloom, Maxie, 97
Rosoff, Nat, 364
Rosoff, Subway Sam, 364
Ross, Burney, 31n, 97
Ross, Leonard, 14
Rothstein, Arnold, 102, 289, 341, 342
Rowe, Billy, 18
Rudolph, Al, 93
Runyon, Damon
  bestows Manassa Mauler nickname on Dempsey, 57
  comparison with Elmer Davis, 191
  covers Dempsey-Gibbons fight, 187, 196
  covers Dempsey-Sharkey fight, 333
  covers Dempsey-Tunney rematch, 361, 364
  covers Dempsey's European trip, 145, 146–47
  covers first Dempsey-Tunney fight, 257, 267, 275, 293, 309
  covers Tunney-Greb fights, 135, 137
  early coverage of Dempsey, 27, 28, 30
  and Gallico-Dempsey sparring session, 206, 207–8
  interest in Greb, 124–25
  as one of best sportswriters of his time, 309
  photo, *109*
  questionable ethics, 114, 115–16
  types of writing, 115, 257
Ruppert, Jacob, 280, 349
Russell, Bill, 260, 278
Russell, Don, 404
Ruth, Babe, 124, 215, 216, 280, 363
Ryan, Paddy, 72

S

Sailor Jack Dempsey, 401
Saint-Gaudens, Augustus, 70
Sampson, Lyman, 182
Sampson-Korner, Paul, 68
Sandburg, Carl, 336
Schaaf, Ernie, 66
Scheer, Vincent Morris, 102
Schenck, Joseph, 349
Schmeling, Max, 66, 103, 248, 333, 381
Schoenfeld, Sarah, 240–41
Schulberg, Budd, 67, 99, 102, 248, 402
Schwab, Charles, 281
Seabury, Samuel, 79
Seamon, Manny, 102
See, Leon, 64
Sells-Floto Circus, 116
Sesquicentennial Exhibition, Philadel-
    phia, as site of first Dempsey-
    Tunney fight, 253, 254, 260, 283, 290,
    369
Shade, Dave, 340
shadowboxing, 167
Shakespeare, William, Tunney's interest
    in, 10, 40–41, 265, 269, 326, 375
Sharkey, Jack
    fights Carnera, 65, 105n, 333
    fights Dempsey, 329–34, 337, 353
    fights Kingfish Levinsky, 105n
    fights Loughran, 168
    fights Maloney, 328–29
    fights Schmeling, 333
    fights Wills, 327–28, 329
    as heavyweight challenger, 313–14,
        381
    scheduled to fight Young Stribling,
        396
    Tunney description, 376
Sharkey Athletic Club, 16
Shaw, George Bernard, 248, 256, 265,
    323–24, 385, 387, 388
Shea, Robert, 138, 140–41
Shelby, Montana, as site of Dempsey-
    Gibbons fight, 178, 179–202
Shibe family, 281
Siki, Battling, 179, 242n
Siler, George, 155
Silver Slipper (nightclub), 227

Sinatra, Frank, 267
Sinclair, Harry, 281
Singer, Al, 103
Skelton, L. Q., 200
Slade, Herbert, 72
Sloan, Alfred, 349
The Slugging Blacksmith (play), 248
Smith, Al, 74–76, 77, 251, 281
Smith, Bill, 356
Smith, Ed "Gunboat," 31, 84, 93, 117,
    127, 163
Smith, Harry, 86
Smith, Jeff, 11
Smith, Mysterious Billy, 83
Smith, Ralph, 249–50
Smith, Red, 402
smokers, 4, 6, 12–13, 14, 15–16, 17, 18
Soldier Field, Chicago
    agreed-upon site of Dempsey-Tunney
        rematch, 336–37
    background and description, 350–51
soldier's dive, 9
Solodky, Harriet, 119, 120
The Southerner (movie), 339
sparring (George Bernard Shaw's phrase),
    387
sparring partners
    background, 135
    Benny Leonard as, 274
    for Dempsey before Shelby, Montana
        fight, 186–87
    Dempsey's treatment of, 207, 208, 268,
        272, 339–40
    exhibitions as part of vaudeville rou-
        tine, 324
    Gallico's experience with Dempsey,
        206–8
    professionals for Dempsey-Tunney
        fight training, 267–68, 276
    ranking fighters for Dempsey-Tunney
        fight training, 271–72
    Tunney and Corbett, 246, 246–47
Sparring with Hemingway (Schulberg),
    67
speakeasies, 227
Spencer, Herbert, 376
Sportlight (movie segments), 246
Sports Illustrated, 399

sportswriters
   attitude toward Dempsey, 293
   coverage of Dempsey-Tunney bout,
      274–75, 293
   and newspaper decisions, 28–29, 32
   payoffs to, 114, 115–16, 226
   press accounts of Dempsey-Tunney
      fight, 305–11
   Tunney's relationship with, 315,
      402–4
   see also Gallico, Paul; Lardner, Ring;
      McGeehan, W. O.; *New York Times;*
      Rice, Grantland; Runyon, Damon
St. Veronica's, New York City, *3,* 7–8, 9,
      10, 40, 268
Stack, Bill, 391
A Stag at Sharkey's (lithograph), 17
Stanton, George, 187–88, 190, 199–200
Stanwyck, Barbara, 221
Star Meadow Farm, 390, 392, 404, 405
Stars and Stripes (newspaper), 45
Staten Island Advance (newspaper), 176
Steiger, Rod, 67
Stern, Bill, 293n
Steuer, Max, 238, 240, 241, 242
Stillman's Gym, Manhattan, 263–64, 266
Stokowski, Leopold, 280
Sugar, Bert Randolph, 31n, 402
Sullivan, Ed, as New York *Daily News*
      reporter, 333, 342
Sullivan, John L.
   background, 71–73
   fights first match under Marquess of
      Queensberry rules, 247
   idolized by Tunney's father, 3
   introduced before Johnson-Jeffries
      fight, 160
   Irish pride in, 6
   loses heavyweight title to Jim Corbett,
      247
   nicknamed Boston Strong Boy, 6
   spars with Tunney friend Anthony
      Biddle, 76
   as stage actor, 248
   wins last bare-knuckle heavyweight
      title fight, 196
Sullivan, K.O., 47
Swanson, Gloria, 349
Swope, Gerald, 349

T
taking a dive, 63, 81, 161, 203, 249, 307,
      341, 344
   see also fixed fights
Talmadge, Norma, 281, 349
Tammen, Harry, 116
Tate, John, 93
Taylor, Estelle
   and Dempsey-Tunney rematch, 339,
      342, 348
   divorces Dempsey, 398
   and first Dempsey-Tunney fight, 302–3
   meets and marries Dempsey, 221–22
   movie career, 223–24, 250–51, 323
   relationship with Kearns, 222–23, 252
   stars with Dempsey in play *The Big
      Fight,* 225, 249–50, 288–89
   still making movies at time of 1929
      stock market crash, 396
The Ten Commandments (movie), 339
Tendler, Lew, 127
Terkel, Studs, 363–64
Texas Guinan's (nightclub), 227
Thaw, Harry, 238n
Thayer, Mary Dixon, 277
Thomas, Lowell, 390
Thompson, Bill, 338, 371
Thompson, Maurice, 83n
Thorpe, Jim, 124
three-knockdown rule, 210
Tilden, Bill, 124
The Times of London, 146, 147
Tom Jones (book), 385
Trant, Mike, 194, 268, 276, 287
Troilus and Cressida (play), 143, 265, 375,
      376
Tunney, Agnes (sister), 5, 49
Tunney, Gene
   agrees to payoffs to sportswriters and
      editors, 114, 226
   birth of, 7
   as businessman, 392–95
   characteristics, 5, 9, 109–10, 169, 226,
      269–70, 275, 302, 304, 315–16, 353,
      387, 402
   as child, 5, 6–7
   childhood interests, 9–11
   children of, 389–90
   comparison with Carpentier, 232

comparison with Corbett, 257

comparison with Dempsey, 26–27, 33–34, 256–59, 263, 268, 273, 276, 290, 293, 296, 304, 315–16, 394, 400–401

consideration of boxing as a career, 35, 39, 49, 51, 53, 54, 55, 61–62

crowd response after his win over Dempsey, 300

death of, 400, 401, 402–3, 405

desire to fight Dempsey, 169, 175, 228, 236, 245

desire to fight Dempsey again, 373

directs physical fitness program for Navy during World War II, 393

early professional fights, 16–19, 34–35

education, 10, 14

efforts toward enlisting in Marines, 37–38

as employee of Ocean Steamship Company, 10, 11, 12, 14–15, 33, 34, 36, 37, 39, 59

enters and wins AEF light heavyweight title, 49

epiphanies over early boxing success, 14

favorite training site, 134–35

fights Carpentier, 226, 232–36, 258

fights Dempsey, see Dempsey-Tunney fight; Dempsey-Tunney rematch

fights Gibbons, 236, 242, 243, 244–45, 258

fights Greb, 132–44, 134, 228, 229–31, 236

fights Heeney after Dempsey rematch, 377–80

fights in New Jersey, 61, 62–63, 68

fights Kaiser, 165–66

fights Levinsky, 116, 117–19, 236

fights Risko, 246

fights Soldier Jones, 111, 112, 113

films serial movie called The Fighting Marine, 260

first develops boxing skills, 6–7

first fight at Madison Square Garden, 113

first meets Jack Dempsey on Hudson River ferry ride, 56–59

full name, 5

given childhood gift of boxing gloves, 5, 6–7

graduates from St. Veronica's, 3, 10

initial curiosity about Dempsey, 51–52

injuries, 36–37, 38, 47, 68, 110–11

as intellectual, 228, 304, 323–24

lack of contenders after Dempsey, 380–81

later appreciation for, 401–2

learns from studying Dempsey fights with Carpentier, Brennan, and Firpo, 112, 258–59, 295

life after boxing, 390–95

loses American light heavyweight title to Greb, 132–42

as Marine, 36, 39–53

marries Polly Lauder, 386–87

meets and romances Polly Lauder, 317–20, 327, 337–38, 344, 371, 374–75, 376, 377, 381–82

moves his family from Greenwich Village to the Bronx, 301

moves to heavyweight division, 179, 237

origin of nickname "Gene," 5

as part-time athletic director at P.S. 41, 16, 17, 19, 34, 35, 38

photos, 36, 134, 226, 246, 256, 279, 317, 335, 370

post-retirement relationship with Dempsey, 395

as reader, 9, 10, 40–41, 268–70, 327, 391–92

receives heavyweight championship belt, 321

referees series of amateur fights at Yankee Stadium, 401

relationships with women, 226–28, 233, 243–44, 260, 267, 316, 347

retires as undefeated champion, 106, 381, 382

signs contract for one more fight beyond Dempsey rematch, 320, 377

spars with James J. Corbett, 246, 246–47

as "the fighting Marine," 56

treatment of Dempsey outside ring, 293, 300–301, 311–12

on vaudeville circuit, 324–26

view of black fighters, 229, 313

watches other fighters, 91, 112, 136, 333, 403

Tunney, Gene Lauder (son), 389, 390
Tunney, John (brother), 5, 49–50
Tunney, John (father)
  brags about son, 54
  death of, 177
  does not see son fight, 137, 144
  emigrates to U.S. from Ireland, 4
  family circumstances, 7–8
  family lives close to waterfront, 8–9
  interest in boxing, 3–4, 6
Tunney, John Varick (son), 389, 391, 395
Tunney, Jonathan (son), 389, 390
Tunney, Margaret (sister), 49
Tunney, Mary Jean Lydon (mother)
  described, 109
  desire for son to become priest, 5, 15,
    19, 61
  meets Lauder family, 377
  view of her son's boxing, 61, 144
Tunney, Maude (sister), 49
Tunney, Polly Lauder (wife)
  background, 318–19
  burgeoning romance with Gene Tun-
    ney, 318–20, 327, 337–38, 344, 371,
    374–75, 376, 377, 381–82
  children of, 389–90
  desire to marry Tunney if he will give
    up fighting, 320, 381
  full name, 317
  marries Tunney, 386–87
  meets Gene Tunney, 317–18
  meets Tunney's family, 377
  photos, 317, 370
Tunney, Rose (sister), 49
Tunney, Tom (brother), 5, 278, 284, 305
Two Minutes to Midnight (book), 191
Tyson, Mike, 169–70

U
Uncle Tom's Cabin (play), 248
Underwood, George, 127
Union League Club, Manhattan, 391
Universal Pictures, 219
Universum Box Promotion, 83n

V
Van Every, Edward, 180, 275, 306
Van Vliet, Fred, 9
Vanderbilt, Consuelo, 350

Vanderbilt, Cornelius J., Jr., 266–67, 282
Vanderbilt, William, 70–71
Vanderbilt family, 280, 350
Vauclain, Samuel, 281
vaudeville circuit, 199, 218, 324–26
Velez, Lupe, 224
Velodrome, Brooklyn, 100
Verch, Harry, 239
Villagers Athletic Club, Greenwich Vil-
  lage, 11–12, 15
Von Elm, George, 282

W
Wagner, Honus, 126
Walcott, Jersey Joe (heavyweight), 153n
Walcott, Joe (welterweight), 153n, 157
Wales, Prince of, 385
Walker, Frank, 189–90
Walker, George, 280
Walker, James J. "Jimmy," 53, 73–80, 141,
  254, 280, 314, 349, 389
Walker, Mickey, 106, 125, 223, 273
Walker, Sidney, starts out in Battle Roy-
  als, 242n
Walker, William, 141
Walker Law, 77, 80, 175, 254, 345
Walsh, Davis, 273
Ward, Jem, 327
Ward, William, 242n
  see also Norfolk, Kid
Ward, Willie, 14
Waterbury Auditorium, Connecticut, 93
Waterbury Republican, 94
Waterman, Frank, 77
Watson, Viola, 339
The Way of All Flesh (book), 264–65, 268
Weiner, Herman, 119
Weinert, Charley, 131, 172, 243
Wells, Bombardier Billy, 163, 186
Wells, H. G., 385, 391
Welsh, Regis, 176
West, Mae, 281
White, Andrew, 363
White, George, 280
White, J. Andrew, 293, 293n, 299
White, Stanford, 69, 71, 238n
Whitney, Harry Payne, 280
Widener, George D., 280
Wiener, Frank, 286, 290–92

Wiggins, Chuck, 129
Wilder, Thornton, 385, 386, 390
Wilkie, Wendell, 393
Wilkinson, Joan Tunney (daughter), 389, 394–95
Wilkinson, Lynn Carter (son-in-law), 394
Willard, Jess
    fights Dempsey, 52, 56, 56, 58–59, 86, 203, 310, 331, 399
    fights Ed "Gunboat" Smith, 127
    fights Firpo, 203–5
    fights Jack Johnson, 73, 203, 204, 310
    fights Moran, 73, 181
    number of fights, 93
Williams, Barney, 92, 104, 105
    see also Levinsky, Battling
Williams, David "Carbine," 390
Williams, Gypsy, 381
Williams, Hannah, 398
Williams, Joe, 81, 235, 333
Wills, Harry
    comparison with Jack Johnson, 219
    disinclination of Jack Johnson to fight, 162
    fights Firpo, 243
    fights Langford, 31n
    fights Sharkey, 327–28, 329
    question of possible fight against Dempsey, 148–49, 180, 219, 229, 250, 251–53, 254, 256, 270, 271, 276, 313, 325–26
Wilson, Gus, 234, 268, 273, 286, 299, 328
Wilson, Joe "Tug," 71–72

Wilson, Johnny, 127, 179n
Wilson, Woodrow, 36
Windsor, Fred "Windy," 82
Witherspoon, Tim, 93
women
    attracted to boxing by Tunney's good looks, 227, 233, 243–44, 267, 316
    as boxers, 148
    encouraged by Rickard to attend prize-fights, 154–55, 168, 243–44, 282
Woodlawn Cemetery, the Bronx, 396
World Series of 1919, 289, 344
Worthington, Reggie, 275
worthy opponent, defined, 60
Wrigley, William, Jr., 281, 349

X
Xenia, Princess, 350

Y
Yale University, 50, 51, 318, 375–76, 389, 391
Yankee Stadium, 329, 336, 379, 401
Young Ambrose, 111
Young Hector, 34
Young Jack Dempsey, 401
Young Stribling, 396

Z
Ziegfeld, Florenz, 280
Zukauskas, Joseph Paul, 314
    see also Sharkey, Jack
Zukor, Adolph, 349
Zulu Kid, 127

JACK CAVANAUGH is a veteran sportswriter who has covered scores of major boxing bouts, along with the Olympics, the World Series, Super Bowl games, the Masters golf tournament, and both the U.S. golf and tennis opens. His work has appeared most notably on the sports pages of the *New York Times,* for which he has covered hundreds of varied sports assignments. In addition, he has been a frequent contributor to *Sports Illustrated* and has written for *Reader's Digest, Tennis* and *Golf* magazines, and other national publications. He is also a former reporter for both ABC and CBS News. Cavanaugh currently is an adjunct writing professor at Fairfield University. He and his wife, Marge, live in Wilton, Connecticut.